Drugs, Behavior, and Modern Society

THIRD EDITION

Charles F. Levinthal
Hofstra University

Allyn and Bacon
BOSTON LONDON TORONTO SYDNEY TOKYO SINGAPORE

Executive Editor: *Carolyn Merrill*
Senior Editorial Production Administrator: *Michael Granger*
Composition Buyer: *Linda Cox*
Manufacturing Buyer: *Julie McNeill*
Cover Administrator: *Linda Knowles*
Editorial Production Service: *Andrea Cava*
Photo Researcher: *Laurie Frankenthaler*
Text Designer: *Carol Somberg*
Electronic Composition: *Omegatype Typography, Inc.*
Illustrations: *Seventeenth Street Studios*

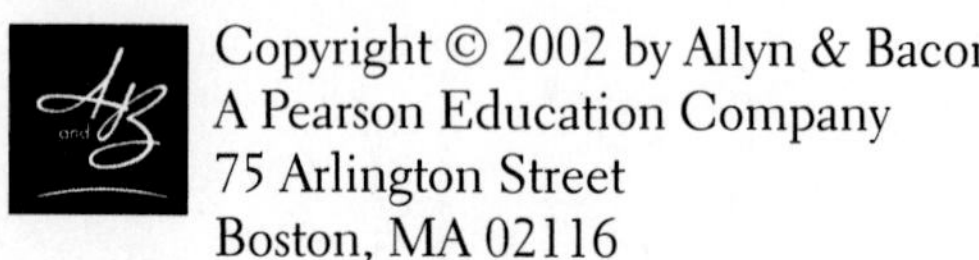

A Pearson Education Company
75 Arlington Street
Boston, MA 02116

Internet: www.ablongman.com

Between the time Web site information is gathered and published, it is not unusual for some sites to have closed. Also, the transcription of URLs can result in unintended typographical errors. The publisher would appreciate being notified of any problems with URLs so that they may be corrected in subsequent editions. Thank you.

Library of Congress Cataloging-in-Publication Data

Levinthal, Charles F., 1945–
Drugs, behavior, and modern society / Charles F. Levinthal.—3rd ed.
p. cm.
Includes bibliographical references and index.
ISBN 0-205-32366-9 (alk. paper)
1. Drugs. 2. Drug abuse. 3. Drugs—Physiological effect.
4. Psychotropic drugs. 5. Psychopharmacology. I. Title.
HV5801.L49 2002
362.29'0973—dc21 2001022686

Printed in the United States of America

10 9 8 7 6 5 4 3 2 1 VHP 05 04 03 02 01

Photo Credits: Photo credits appear on page 389, which should be considered an extension of the copyright page.

For
Beth, David and Brian,
Milt and Selma

Brief Contents

Contents

PART 2 LEGALLY RESTRICTED DRUGS IN OUR SOCIETY 77

6 LSD and Other Hallucinogens 124

7 Marijuana 147

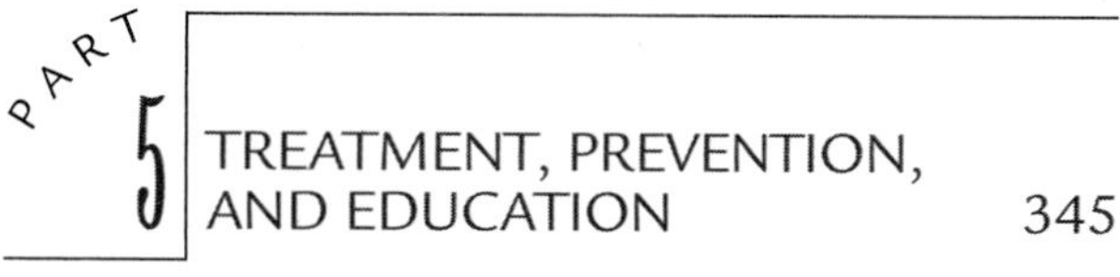

Preface

In today's world, drugs and their use present a social paradox, combining the potential for good and for bad. As a society and as individuals, we can be the beneficiaries of drugs or their victims. This is the message of *Drugs, Behavior, and Modern Society*. You will be introduced to the basic facts and the major issues concerning drug-taking behavior in a straightforward, comprehensive, and reader-friendly manner. A background in biology, sociology, psychology, or chemistry is not necessary. The only requirement is a sense of curiosity about the range of chemical substances that affect our minds and our bodies and an interest in the challenges these substances bring to our daily lives.

You are about to embark on a journey that began thousands of years ago. Drugs and drug-taking behavior have been around for a very long time, and you will find that the issues that we tend to associate with the present time are really issues that society has had to confront for quite a while. In an important way, drugs and drug-taking behavior reflect an important aspect of being human—we are an intensely curious species. This particular trait has led us to discover substances that make us feel stronger, more alert, calmer, more distant and dissociated from our surroundings, or simply good. It is the misuse and abuse of these substances that have resulted in massive problems in the United States and around the world.

To understand the complex issues surrounding drugs in our society, we need to recognize the enormous diversity that exists among drugs that affect the mind and the body. We must educate ourselves not only about illicit street drugs such as cocaine, amphetamines, heroin, and marijuana but also about legally available drugs such as alcohol, nicotine, and caffeine. *Drugs, Behavior, and Modern Society* has been designed to be the most comprehensive review of psychoactive drugs of any undergraduate college textbook available today. It is particularly notable for the attention given to two aspects of drug-taking behavior that have been underreported in other texts: steroid abuse and inhalant abuse. These topics are covered in chapters of their own, Chapters 8 and 13 respectively. Also highlighted is the recent growth of dietary supplements, whether herb-based or not, on the current drug scene, as well as the impact of "club drugs" on contemporary drug-taking behavior.

We need to recognize that the problems surrounding drug misuse and abuse are not someone else's concern but rather everyone's concern. Like it or not, the decision to use drugs today is one of life's choices, regardless of our racial, ethnic, or religious background, how much money we have, where we live, how much education we have acquired, whether we are male or female, or whether we are young or old. The potential for misuse and abuse is a problem facing all of us.

Features of the Third Edition

The third edition of *Drugs, Behavior, and Modern Society* is built upon the strengths of earlier editions. Like the second edition, the chapters are presented in five sections:

- Part 1 (Chapters 1–3): Drugs in Society/Drugs in Our Lives
- Part 2 (Chapters 4–8): Legally Restricted Drugs in Our Society
- Part 3 (Chapters 9–13): Legal Drugs in Our Society
- Part 4 (Chapters 14–16): Medicinal Drugs
- Part 5 (Chapters 17–18): Treatment, Prevention, and Education

As you will see, discussions of particular drugs have been grouped not in terms of their pharmacological or chemical characteristics but rather in terms of their access to the general public and societal attitudes toward their use. The last section of the book concerns itself with treatment, prevention, and education. In addition, several special features throughout the book will enhance your experience as a reader and serve as learning aids.

Quick Concept Checks

Sometimes, when the material gets complicated, you want to have a quick way of finding out if you understand the basic concepts being explained. I have included from time to time a Quick Concept Check, where you can see in a minute or two where you stand. Some of the Checks will be in a matching format; others will be an interpretation of a graph or diagram. In some cases you will be asked to apply the principles you have learned to a real-world situation.

Portraits

The Portrait feature in each chapter takes you into the lives of individuals who have either influenced our thinking about drugs in our society or have been impacted by drug use or abuse. Some of them are known to the public at large, but many are not. In any case, the Portraits add a human touch to the discussion of drugs and behavior. They remind us that throughout this book we are dealing with issues that affect real people in all walks of life, now and in the past.

Drugs . . . in Focus

There are many fascinating stories to tell about the role of drugs in our history and our present-day culture, along with the important facts and serious issues surrounding drug use. While some of the Drugs . . . in Focus features will summarize information that you can refer to at a later time when the need arises, several of them represent an interesting sidelight look on a question that you might have wondered about. Some examples of the latter type are the following:

- What Happened to the Coca in Coca-Cola? (Chapter 4)
- Crack Babies Revisited: Has There Been an Adverse Effect? (Chapter 4)
- Strange Days in Salem: Witchcraft or Hallucinogens? (Chapter 6)
- Can You Control a Marijuana High? (Chapter 7)
- Is Controlled Drinking Possible for Alcoholics? (Chapter 10)
- Why There are No (Live) Flies in Your Coffee (Chapter 12)
- Is There Any Truth Regarding "Truth Serum"? (Chapter 15)
- Penalties for Crack versus Penalties for Cocaine: A Racial Disparity? (Chapter 17)

Health Line

Helpful information regarding the effectiveness and safety aspects of particular drugs, specific aspects of drug-taking behavior, and new medical applications can be found in Health Line features throughout the book. Here are some examples of Health Line features:

- Effects of Psychoactive Drugs on Pregnant Women and Newborns (Chapter 2)
- Ibogaine: A Treatment Option for Drug Dependence? (Chapter 6)
- A Self-Administered Short Michigan Alcoholism Screening Test (SMAST) (Chapter 10)
- Ten Tips on How to Succeed When Trying to Quit Smoking (Chapter 11)
- Rohypnol as a Date-Rape Drug (Chapter 15)
- Hallucinations, Schizophrenia, Drugs, and the Brain (Chapter 16)

Health Alert

Information of a more urgent nature is provided in the Health Alert features. You will find important facts that you can use to recognize the signs of drug misuse or abuse and ways you can respond to emergency drug-taking situations, as well as warnings about risk situations. Examples of some Health Alert features are the following:

- Emergency Guidelines for a Bad Trip on LSD (Chapter 6)
- MDMA Toxicity: The Other Side of Ecstasy (Chapter 6)
- The Symptoms of Steroid Abuse (Chapter 8)
- Emergency Signs and Procedures in Acute Alcohol Intoxication (Chapter 9)
- Side Effects of Common Medications (Chapter 14)
- GHB and Date-Rape: Ways to Avoid Trouble (Chapter 15)

Point/Counterpoint Debates

Drug issues are seldom black or white, right or wrong. Some of the most hotly debated questions of our day involve the use, misuse, and abuse of drugs. These issues deserve a good deal of critical thought. This is the reason I have written a

Point/Counterpoint debate at the end of each of the five sections of the book. I have taken five important controversies concerning drugs, collected the primary viewpoints pro and con, and simulated a debate that two hypothetical people might have on that question. I invite you to read these debates carefully and try to come to your own position, as an exercise in critical thinking. Along with a consideration of the discussion questions that follow each feature, you may wish to continue the debate in your class.

New to This Edition

The third edition has been enhanced by an increased attention to major theoretical perspectives in the field of drug abuse and an expanded coverage of contemporary issues and concerns. Here are some examples:

- Increased emphasis on the Biopsychosocial Model throughout the book, conceptualizing drug-taking behavior as an interaction of biological, psychological, and social factors.
- Expanded coverage of important theoretical perspectives in drug abuse: The Family Systems Model (Chapters 1, 17, and 18), Public Health Model (Chapters 1 and 18), Harm Reduction Model (Chapter 2), and positions opposing the Disease Model in alcoholism and other forms of drug abuse (Chapter 10).
- New and expanded sections on important contemporary issues of public concern: Ecstasy and the growing popularity of so-called club drugs (Chapters 1, 4, 6, and 15), dietary supplements as alternative medicines (Chapters 1, 14, and 16) and as athletic performance enhancers (Chapter 8), methamphetamine abuse (Chapter 4), anabolic steroid abuse and body-image problems in young men (Chapter 8), caffeine consumption among young people (Chapter 12), risks in ordering prescription medications through web-based pharmacies over the Internet (Chapter 14), and date-rape risks when inadvertently ingesting certain depressant drugs (Chapter 15).

The Levinthal Web Site

The companion Web site for the book can be accessed at www.ablongman.com/levinthal. This Web site contains learning objectives, Web links to relevant sites of interest, and online practice tests. These multiple-choice and true-false questions allow you to practice your mastery of the course content before you take an actual test.

Other Features

Additional aids to your learning experience are a running glossary positioned on the page where new terminology is first introduced and, when necessary, a pronunciation guide for often difficult-to-pronounce drug names and terms. At the end of each chapter, a summary presented in a bulleted list allows an easy review of the chapter's main points. An alphabetized list of key terms that have previously been presented in the running glossary is provided, along with the page number where each of the terms first appeared.

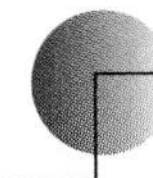

An Invitation to Readers

I welcome your reactions to *Drugs, Behavior, and Modern Society*, Third Edition. Please send any comments or questions to the following address: Dr. Charles F. Levinthal, Department of Psychology, Hofstra University, Hempstead, NY 11549. You can also fax them to me at (516) 463-6052 or e-mail them to me at PSYCFL@hofstra.edu. I hope to be hearing from you.

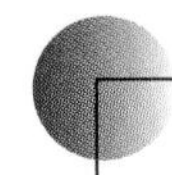

Acknowledgments

In the course of writing this edition of the book, as well as the previous editions, I have received much encouragement, assistance, and expert advice from a number of people. I have benefited from their generous sharing of materials, knowledge, and insights. The research librarians at the Axinn Library of Hofstra University were immensely helpful in gathering information for this book. Meredith Poulten, director of the Walk-In Center in Medway, Massachusetts, became the subject of the Portrait feature in Chapter 18 and provided me with a unique and personal insight into the real-world challenges that face professionals who are working with young people today. In addition, I am indebted to three Hofstra undergraduate students, Dana Liebling, Vita Greco, and Daniela Mignone for their help.

I am very fortunate to have worked with a superb team at Allyn and Bacon. I am especially indebted to my editor, Carolyn Merrill; her editorial assistant, Lara Zeises; and my production editor, Michael Granger. Their professionalism and friendship are greatly appreciated. I also want to acknowledge the efforts of those individuals whose talents and expertise contributed so much to the production quality of this book: Andrea Cava, Peggy Middendorf, Laurie Frankenthaler, Seventeenth Street Studios, and Carol Somberg.

A number of manuscript reviewers, whose identities had been kept secret from me up to now, made invaluable suggestions as I worked on the third edition. Now I know their names, and I thank each of them for their help: J. Douglas Bricker, Duquesne University; Denise C. Denton, Iowa State University; Sheila Garos, Texas Tech University; Roland Lamarine, California State University, Chico; Peter Manoleas, University of California, Berkeley; Linda Synovitz, Southeastern Louisiana University; and Harry A. Tiemann, Mesa State College.

On a more personal note, there are others who have given me their support over the years and to whom my appreciation goes beyond words. As always, I thank my mother, Mildred Levinthal, and my parents-in-law, Milton and Selma Kuby, for their encouragement and love.

Above all, my family has been a continuing source of strength. I will always be grateful to my wonderful sons, David and Brian, for their love and understanding. I am especially grateful to my wife, Beth, for her abiding love, support, and complete faith in my abilities.

Charles F. Levinthal

CHAPTER 1 Drugs and Behavior Today

After you have completed this chapter, you will understand

- Basic terminology concerning drugs and drug-taking behavior
- The origins and history of drugs and drug-taking behavior
- Present-day statistics of drug use in the United States
- Possible reasons why people take or do not take drugs
- Current trends in drug-taking behavior

He was seventeen, a high school junior. He looked at me with amazement, telling me by his expression that either my question was ridiculous or the answer was obvious. Why do kids do drugs? Because it's cool, he said, that's why. Kids do drugs to fit in with the cool people. It's a way of acting older. If it weren't cool, kids wouldn't do it.

PART 1 DRUGS IN SOCIETY/DRUGS IN OUR LIVES

Today, more than ever, drugs affect our daily lives. It is difficult to pick up a newspaper or to watch television without finding a report or program that concerns drug use or some issue associated with it. In your personal life, you have had to confront the reality of drugs around you. In school, you have probably been taught the risks involved in drug use, and very likely you have had to contend with pressure to share a drug experience with your friends or the possibility of drugs being sold to you. High school students on a Monday morning may boast about how much beer they consumed at a keg party over the weekend. For some students, alcohol consumption begins in junior high school or earlier. Experimentation with marijuana and mind-altering pills of all sorts seems commonplace. Tobacco consumption among young people, despite the fact that it is illegal for those under eighteen years old to purchase tobacco products, remains a major societal problem. Whether we like it or not, the decision to use drugs of all types and forms has become one of life's choices in American society and in communities around the world.

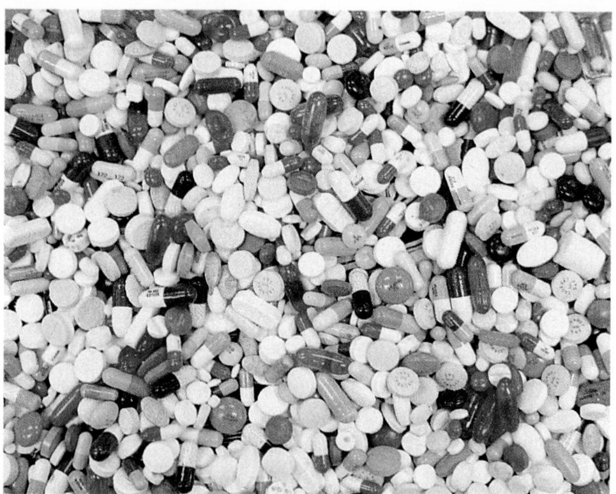

The problems associated with drug abuse and misuse in our society extend beyond the use of illegal drugs. We must also be concerned with the abuse and misuse of legally available substances such as alcohol, nicotine, and caffeine as well as prescription and over-the-counter medications.

At the same time, we live in a social environment of mixed messages. You probably can recall the images of Joe Camel, the Marlboro Man, and the Virginia Slims Woman in print advertisements, all of which conveyed the desirability of smoking to the public. Today, warning labels on cigarette packs and public service announcements serve to caution us about the serious health hazards of smoking. Television commercials may associate the drinking of beer with a sex life beyond your fondest dreams and then imply that you should "know when to say when." Prominent political figures, including a former U.S. president (Bill Clinton) and a former U.S. vice-president (Al Gore), have admitted their experiences with marijuana earlier in their lives. Yet marijuana remains an illegal substance, officially classified since 1970 in the same category as heroin, as will be noted in Chapter 2.[1] Antidrug campaigns in the media attempt to discourage young people from becoming involved with drugs, yet we observe a continual stream of sports figures, entertainers, and other high-profile individuals engaging in drug-taking behavior. Even though careers are frequently jeopardized and, in some cases, lives are lost as a result, powerful pro-drug-use messages continue to influence our lives.

These facts, as contradictory as some of them are, represent the present-day drug scene. In the chapters that follow, you will see that it is not just a "young person's problem" but one that encompasses every segment of our society. The availability of drugs and the potential for drug abuse present a challenge for people of all ages, from the young to the elderly. The personal and social problems associated with drugs extend in one way or another to both men and women and to people of all ethnic groups and socioeconomic levels. No group should believe themselves exempt.

Nonetheless, our concerns about the dangers of drug use should not prevent us from recognizing another important side to the topic of drugs today. You may know someone whose depression nearly led to suicide but who is now living a normal life after taking antidepressant drugs. You may know someone else who has been helped by a drug that controls anxiety. Millions of individuals in the United States and around the world who suffer from the torment of mental illness have benefited from drug treatment. With new therapeutic drugs continually being developed, you can be certain that in the near future even more effective drugs will be available to treat psychiatric disorders. There is tremendous excitement, and a good deal of hope, among those currently involved in drug research.

The purpose of this book is to answer your questions and address your concerns about drugs and behavior, to sort out the facts from the myths. A glance at the contents will show you the wide range of drugs that will be covered. As you will discover, our society has had as many problems contending with legal as with illegal drugs.

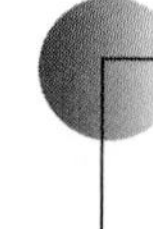

Looking at Drugs and Behavior

There are two basic ways in which we can look at the subject of drugs and behavior. First, we can speak of specific drugs that alter our feelings, our thoughts, our perceptions of the world, and our behavior. We call these **psychoactive drugs** because they influence the functioning of the brain and hence our behavior. The most dramatic examples are **illicit** (illegal) **drugs,** such as heroin, cocaine, marijuana, and LSD (lysergic acid diethylamide). Other psychoactive substances are **licit** (legal) **drugs,** such as alcohol, nicotine, and caffeine.

Second, we can speak of the circumstances that lead to drug-taking behavior. The use of psychoactive drugs can be, at least in part, a consequence of how we feel about ourselves in relationship to our parents, our friends and acquaintances, and the community in which we live. An exploration into the reasons why individuals engage in drug-taking behavior will be a primary topic in the chapters ahead.

Understanding the interplay between drugs and behavior is essential when we consider the dangerous potential of drug-taking behavior to become **drug dependence.** As many of us know all too well, a vicious circle can develop in which drug-taking behavior fosters more drug-taking behavior, in a spiraling pattern that is often extremely difficult to break. Individuals showing signs of drug dependence display intense cravings for the drug and, in many cases, require increasingly greater quantities in order to get the same, desired effect. They become preoccupied with their drug-taking behavior and eventually may feel that their lives have gotten out of control.

Drug dependence also can be analyzed on both a biological level and a social level. First, the use of psychoactive drugs modifies the functioning of the brain, both at the time during which the drug is present in the body and later when the drug-taking behavior stops. Drug dependence, therefore, produces long-lasting brain changes. As one expert has put it, a "switch" in the brain seems to be thrown following prolonged drug use. It starts as a voluntary behavior, but once that switch is thrown, a pattern of drug dependence takes over. Second, drug dependence is a result of a complex interaction of the individual and his or her environment. We cannot fully understand the problem of drug dependence without being aware of the social context in which drug-taking behavior occurs. As you will see in Chapter 17, the recognition that drug dependence can be defined in terms of biological and social components has important implications for treatment.[2]

Which drugs have the greatest potential for creating drug dependence? How can someone escape drug dependence once it is established? What factors increase or decrease the likelihood of drug-taking behavior in the first place? These are some of the important questions to be considered as we examine the impact of drugs and drug-taking behavior on our lives.

A Matter of Definition

Considering the ease with which we speak of drugs and drug use, it seems as if it should be relatively easy to define what we mean by the word **drug.** Unfortunately, there are significant problems in arriving at a clear definition. The standard approach is to characterize a drug as *a chemical substance that, when taken into the body, alters the structure or functioning of the body in some way.* In doing so, we are accounting for examples such as medications used for the treatment of physical disorders and mental illnesses, as well as for alcohol, nicotine, and the typical street drugs. Unfortunately, this broad definition could also refer to ordinary food and water. Because it does not make much sense for nutrients to be considered drugs, we need to refine our definition, adding the phrase, *excluding those nutrients considered to be related to normal functioning.*

Bear in mind, however, that we may still be on slippery ground. We can now effectively eliminate the cheese in your next pizza from consideration as a drug, but what about some exotic ingredient in the sauce? Sugar is safely excluded, even though it has significant energizing and therefore behavioral effects on us, but what about the cayenne pepper that burns your tongue? Is it fair to make this distinction?

We can learn two major lessons from this seemingly easy task of defining a drug. First of all, there is probably no perfect definition that would distinguish drugs from nondrugs without leaving a number of cases that fall within some kind of gray area. The best we can do is to set up a definition, as we have, that handles most of the substances we are likely to encounter.

The second lesson is more subtle. We often make the distinction between drugs and nondrugs not in terms of their physical characteristics but rather in terms of

psychoactive drugs: Drugs that affect feelings, thoughts, perceptions, or behavior.

illicit drugs: Drugs whose manufacture, sale, or possession is illegal.

licit drugs: Drugs whose manufacture, sale, or possession is legal.

drug dependence: A condition in which an individual feels a compulsive need to continue taking a drug. In the process, the drug assumes an increasingly central role in the individual's life.

drug: A chemical substance that, when taken into the body, alters the structure or functioning of the body in some way, excluding those nutrients considered to be related to normal functioning.

whether the substance in question has been *intended to be used primarily as a way of inducing a bodily or psychological change.*[3] By this reasoning, if the pizza maker intended to put that spice in the pizza to make it taste better, the spice would not be considered a drug. It would simply be another ingredient in the recipe. If the pizza maker intended the spice to intoxicate you or quicken your heart rate, then it would be considered a drug.

Ultimately, the problem is that we are trying to create a definition that fits our intuitive sense of what constitutes a drug. We may find it difficult to define pornography, but (as has been said) we know it when we see it. So it may be with drugs. Whether we realize it or not, when we discuss the topic of drugs, we are operating within a context of social and cultural values, a group of shared feelings about what kind of behavior (that is, what kind of drug-taking behavior) is right and what kind is wrong.

The judgments we make about drug-taking behavior even influence the terminology we use when referring to that behavior. When we say "drug misuse" and "drug abuse," for example, we are implying that something wrong is happening, that a drug is producing some harm to the physical health or psychological well-being of the drug user or to society in general.

But what criteria do we use to decide whether a drug is being misused or abused? We cannot judge on the basis of whether the drug is legal or illegal, since the legality of a psychoactive drug may depend not only on the drug's chemical properties but also on historical and cultural circumstances. Tobacco, for example, has deeply rooted associations in American history, dating to the earliest colonial days. Although it is objectionable to many individuals and harmful to the health of the smoker and others, tobacco is nonetheless legally available to adults. Alcohol is another substance that is legal, within the bounds of the law, even though it can be harmful to individuals who drink and potentially harmful to others who may be affected by the drinker's behavior. The difficulty of using a criterion based on legality is further complicated by cultural differences around the world. In Muslim countries, such as Iran and Saudi Arabia, alcohol is illegal; in Nepal and parts of India, marijuana is legal.

Instrumental and Recreational Use of Drugs

Given the differences in attitudes toward specific drugs across cultures and societies, it is useful to look closely at the relationship between drugs and behavior in terms of the intent or motivation on the part of the user. Depending on the intent of the individual, drug use can be categorized as either instrumental or recreational.[4]

By **instrumental use,** we mean that a person is taking a drug with a specific socially approved goal in mind. The user may want to stay awake longer, fall asleep more quickly, or recover from an illness. If you are a medical professional on call over a long period of time, taking a drug with the goal of staying alert is considered acceptable by most people. Recovery from an illness or achieving some reduction in pain are goals that are unquestioned. In these cases, drug-taking behavior occurs as a means toward an end that has been defined by our society as legitimate.

The legal status of the drug itself is not the issue here. The instrumental use of drugs can involve prescription and nonprescription (over-the-counter) drugs that are licitly obtained and taken for a particular medical purpose. Examples include an antidepressant prescribed for depression, a cold remedy for a cold, an anticonvulsant drug to control epileptic seizures, or insulin to maintain the health of a person with diabetes. The instrumental use of drugs can also involve drugs that are illicitly obtained, such as an amphetamine that has been procured through illegal means to help a person stay awake and alert after hours without sleep.

In contrast, **recreational use** means that a person is taking the drug not as a means to a socially approved goal but for the purposes of acquiring the effect of the drug itself. The motivation is to enjoy a pleasurable feeling or positive state of mind. Whatever happens as a consequence of the drug-taking behavior is viewed not as a means to an end, but as an end unto itself. Drinking alcohol and smoking tobacco are two examples of licit recreational drug-taking behavior. Involvement with street drugs, in the sense that one's goal is to alter one's mood or state of consciousness, falls into the category of illicit recreational drug-taking behavior (Figure 1.1).

Although this four-group classification scheme is helpful in understanding the complex relationship between drugs and behavior, there will be instances in which the category might be debated. Drinking an alcoholic beverage, for example, is considered as recreational drug-taking

instrumental use: Referring to the motivation of a drug user who takes the drug for a specific purpose other than getting "high."

recreational use: Referring to the motivation of the drug user who takes the drug only in order to get "high" or achieve some pleasurable effect.

Goal \ Legal Status	Legal (licit)	Illegal (illicit)
Instrumental	Taking Valium with a prescription to relieve anxiety Taking No Doz to stay awake on a long trip	Taking amphetamines without a prescription to stay awake the night before a test Taking morphine without a prescription to relieve pain
Recreational	Having an alcoholic drink to relax before dinner Smoking a cigarette or a cigar for enjoyment	Smoking marijuana to get high Taking LSD for the hallucinogenic effects

FIGURE 1.1

Categories of drug-taking behavior.
Source: Expanded from Goode, Erich (1999). *Drugs in American Society* (5th ed.). New York: McGraw-Hill, p. 121.

behavior under most circumstances. If it is recommended by a physician for a specified therapeutic or preventative purpose (see Chapter 9), however, the drinking might be considered instrumental in nature. You can see that whether drug use is judged to be recreational or instrumental is determined in no small part by the attitudes of the society in which the behavior takes place.

Misuse and Abuse of Drugs

How do misuse and abuse fit into this scheme? **Drug misuse** typically applies to cases in which a prescription or nonprescription drug is used inappropriately. Many instances of drug misuse involve instrumental goals. For example, drug doses may be increased beyond the level of the prescription in the mistaken idea that if a little is good, more is even better. Or doses may be decreased from the level of the prescription to make the drug supply last longer. Drugs may be continued past the time during which they were originally needed; they may be combined with some other drug; or a prescription drug might be shared by family members or lent to a friend even though the medical conditions may differ among them.

Drug misuse can be dangerous and potentially lethal, particularly when alcohol is combined with drugs that depress the nervous system. Drugs that have this particular feature include antihistamines, antianxiety drugs, and sleeping medications. Even if alcohol is not involved, however, drug combinations can still represent serious health risks, particularly for the elderly, who often take a large number of separate medications. This population is especially vulnerable to the hazards of drug misuse.

In contrast, **drug abuse** is typically applied to cases in which a licit or illicit drug is used in ways that produce some form of physical, mental, or social impairment. The primary motivation for individuals involved in drug abuse is recreational. We should remember that drugs with abuse potential include not only the common street drugs but also legally available psychoactive substances such as caffeine and nicotine (stimulants) and alcohol (a depressant), as well as a number of prescription drugs used for medical purposes. In this book, when there is no intent to make a value judgment as to the motivation or consequences of a particular type of drug-taking behavior, that behavior will simply be referred to as drug use.

Before examining the major role that drugs and drug-taking behavior play in our society today, it is worthwhile

drug misuse: Drug-taking behavior in which a prescription or nonprescription drug is used inappropriately.
drug abuse: Drug-taking behavior resulting in some form of physical, mental, or social impairment.

Drug Abuse and the College Student: An Assessment Tool

In a recent study conducted at Rutgers University, a cutoff score of five or more "yes" responses to the following twenty-five questions in the Rutgers Collegiate Substance Abuse Screening Test (RCSAST) was found to distinguish problem alcohol and other drug users from nonproblem users in a college student population. More research, however, must be done to determine if a score of 5 represents the best cutoff. It is important to remember that the RCSAST does not by itself determine the presence of substance dependence or abuse (see Chapter 2). Rather, the RCSAST is designed to be used as one part of a larger assessment battery aimed at identifying which young adults experience problems due to substance use and specifically what types of problems a particular individual is experiencing.

1. Have you gotten into financial trouble as a result of drinking or other drug use?
2. Is alcohol or other drug use making your college life unhappy?
3. Do you use alcohol or other drugs because you are shy with other people?
4. Has drinking alcohol or using other drugs ever caused conflicts with close friends of the opposite sex?
5. Has drinking alcohol or using other drugs ever caused conflicts with close friends of the same sex?
6. Has drinking alcohol or using other drugs ever damaged other friendships?
7. Has drinking alcohol or using other drugs ever been behind your losing a job (or the direct reason for it)?
8. Do you lose time from school due to drinking and/or other drug use?
9. Has drinking alcohol or using other drugs ever interfered with your preparations for exams?
10. Has your efficiency decreased since drinking and/or using other drugs?
11. Do you drink alcohol or use other drugs to escape from worries or troubles?
12. Is your drinking and/or using other drugs jeopardizing your academic performance?
13. Do you drink or use other drugs to build up your self-confidence?
14. Has your ambition decreased since drinking and/or drug using?
15. Does drinking or using other drugs cause you to have difficulty sleeping?
16. Have you ever felt remorse after drinking and/or using other drugs?
17. Do you drink or use drugs alone?
18. Do you crave a drink or other drug at a definite time daily?
19. Do you want a drink or other drug the next morning?
20. Have you ever had a complete or partial loss of memory as a result of drinking or using other drugs?
21. Is drinking or using other drugs affecting your reputation?
22. Does your drinking and/or using other drugs make you careless of your family's welfare?
23. Do you seek out drinking/drugging companions and drinking/drugging environments?
24. Has your physician ever treated you for drinking and/or other drug use?
25. Have you ever been to a hospital or institution on account of drinking or other drug use?

Source: Bennett, Melanie E.; McCrady, Barbara S.; Frankenstein, William; Laitman, Lisa A.; Van Horn, Deborah H. A.; and Keller, Daniel S. (1992). The Rutgers Collegiate Substance Abuse Screening Test: Identifying young adult substance abusers. Presentation at the meeting of the American Psychological Association, August, Washington DC. Reprinted with permission of the authors of the RCSAST.

to look at the ways in which they have been viewed in the past. Have drugs always been around? Have our attitudes toward drugs changed over time, and if so, in what ways? How did people feel about drugs and drug-taking behavior one hundred years ago, fifty years ago, twenty years ago, or even ten years ago? These are questions which we will now address.

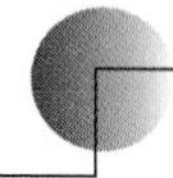

Drugs in Early Times

Try to imagine the circumstances under which a psychoactive drug might have been accidentally discovered. Thousands of years ago, perhaps hundreds of thousands of years ago, the process of discovery would have been as natural as eating, and the motivation as basic as simple curiosity. In cool climates, next to a cave dwelling may have grown a profusion of blue morning glories or brightly colored mushrooms, plants that produce hallucinogens similar to LSD. In desert regions, yellow-orange fruits grew on certain cacti, the source of the hallucinogenic drug peyote. Elsewhere, poppy plants, the source of opium, covered acres of open fields. Coca leaves, from which cocaine is made, grew on shrubs along the mountain valleys throughout Central and South America. The hardy cannabis plant, the source of mari-

In a wide range of world cultures throughout history, hallucinogens have been regarded as having deeply spiritual powers. Under the influence of drugs, this modern-day shaman communicates with the spirit world.

juana, grew practically everywhere.[5] It is entirely possible that some of this curiosity was inspired by observing the unusual behavior of animals as they fed on these plants. Within their own experience people made the connection, somewhere along the line, between the chewing of willow bark (the source of modern-day aspirin) and the relief of a headache, or the eating of the senna plant (a natural laxative) and the relief of constipation.

Of course, some of these plants made people sick, and many were sufficiently poisonous to cause death. Probably, however, the plants that had the strangest impact on humans were the ones that produced hallucinations. Having a sudden vision of something totally alien to everyday living must have been overwhelming, like a visit to another world. Individuals with prior knowledge about such plants, as well as about plants with therapeutic powers, would eventually acquire great power over others in the community. This knowledge was the beginning of **shamanism,** a practice among primitive societies in which an individual called a **shaman** acted as a healer through a combination of trances and plant-based medicines, usually in the context of a local religion. Shamans still function today in South America and Africa, alongside practitioners of modern medicine. As we will see in Chapter 6, hallucination-producing plants of various kinds play a major role in present-day shamanic healing.[6]

With the development of centralized religions in Egyptian and Babylonian societies, the influence of shamanism gradually declined. The power to heal through a knowledge of drugs passed into the hands of the priesthood, which placed a greater emphasis on formal rituals and rules than on hallucinations and trances. For a society based on strict and rigidly controlled religious principles, a man or woman having trance-like visions, whether induced by a hallucinogenic drug or self-hypnosis, would not be considered trustworthy. Who knew what vision might contradict some aspect of official religious doctrine?

Probably the most dramatic testament to the development of priestly healing during this period is a sixty-five-foot-long Egyptian scroll known as the **Ebers Papyrus,** named after the British Egyptologist who acquired it in 1872.[7] This mammoth document, dating from 1500 B.C., contains more than eight hundred prescriptions for practically every ailment imaginable, including simple wasp stings and crocodile bites, baldness, constipation, headaches, enlarged prostate glands, sweaty feet, arthritis, inflammations of all types, heart disease, and cancer. More than a hundred of the preparations contained castor oil as a natural laxative; some contained "the berry of the poppy," which is now recognized as referring to opium. Other ingredients were quite bizarre: lizard's blood, the teeth of swine, the oil of worms, the hoof of an ass, putrid meat with fly specks, and crocodile dung (excrement of all types being highly favored for its ability to frighten off the evil spirits of disease).[8]

How successful were these strange remedies? It is impossible to know because no records were kept on what happened to the patients. Although some of the ingredients, such as opium and castor oil, had true medicinal value, it may be that much of the improvement from these concoctions was psychological rather than physiological. In other words, improvements in the patient's condition resulted from the *belief* on the patient's part that he or she would be helped, a phenomenon known as the **placebo effect.** Psychological factors

---

shamanism: The philosophy and practice of healing in which the diagnosis or treatment is based on trancelike states, either on the part of the healer (shaman) or the patient.

shaman (SHAH-men): A healer whose diagnosis or treatment of patients is based at least in part on trances. These trances are frequently induced by hallucinogenic drugs.

Ebers Papyrus: An Egyptian document, dated approximately 1500 B.C., containing more than 800 prescriptions for common ailments and diseases.

placebo (pla-CEE-bo) effect: Any change in a person's condition after taking a drug based solely on that person's beliefs about the drug rather than on any physical effects of the drug.

---

have played a critical role throughout the history of drugs. Chapter 3 will examine in more detail the importance of the placebo effect as an explanation of some drug effects.

Along with substances that had genuine healing properties, other psychoactive drugs were put to other uses. In the early Middle Ages, Viking warriors ate the mushroom *Amanita muscaria*, known as fly agaric, and experienced increased energy, which resulted in wild behavior in battle. They were called Berserkers because of the bear skins they wore, and reckless, violent behavior has come to be called berserk. Later, witches operating on the periphery of Christian society created "witch's brews." They were said to induce hallucinations and a sensation of flying by consuming mixtures made of various plants such as mandrake, henbane, and belladonna. The toads that they included in their recipes did not hurt either: We know now that the sweat glands of toads contain a chemical related to DMT, a powerful hallucinogenic drug, as well as bufotenine, a drug that raises blood pressure and heart rate.[9]

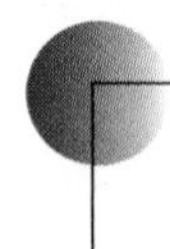

Drugs in the Nineteenth Century

Near the end of the nineteenth century, the medical profession could look back on a number of significant accomplishments with regard to drugs. Morphine was identified as the active ingredient in opium, a drug that had been in use for at least three thousand years and had become the physician's most reliable prescription to control the pain of disease and injury. The invention of the syringe made it possible to deliver the morphine directly and speedily into the bloodstream. Cocaine, having been extracted from coca leaves, was used as a stimulant and antidepressant. Sedative powers to calm the mind or induce sleep had been discovered in bromides and chloral hydrate.[10]

The nineteenth century also saw the development of drugs that were used for specific purposes or particular diseases. Anesthetic drugs had been discovered that made surgery painless for the first time in history. A few diseases could actually be prevented through the administration of vaccines, such as the vaccine against smallpox that had been introduced by Edward Jenner in 1796 and the vaccine against rabies introduced by Louis Pasteur in 1885. With the discovery of new pharmaceutical products, the modern era in the history of the healing arts was beginning.[11]

The social picture of drug-taking behavior during this time, however, was more complicated. By the 1890s, prominent leaders in the medical profession had begun to call attention to social problems resulting from the widespread and uncontrolled access to psychoactive drugs. Remedies called **patent medicines,** sold through advertisements, peddlers, or general stores, contained opium, alcohol, and cocaine and were promoted as answers to every common medical or nonmedical complaint.

Opium itself was cheap, easily available, and completely legal. Most people, from newborn infants to the elderly, in the United States and England "took opium" during their lives. The way in which they took it, however, was a critical social factor. The respectable way was to drink it, usually in a liquid form called *laudanum.* By contrast, the smoking of opium, as introduced by Chinese immigrants imported for manual labor in the American West, was considered degrading and immoral. Laws prohibiting opium smoking began to be enacted in 1875. In light of the tolerant attitude toward opium drinking, the strong emotional opposition to opium smoking may be viewed as more anti-Chinese than antiopium.[12]

Like opium, cocaine was also a drug in widespread use in Europe and North America and was taken quite casually in the form of beverages. The original formula for Coca-Cola, as the name suggests, contained cocaine until 1903, as did Dr. Agnew's Catarrh Powder, a popular remedy for chest colds. In the mid-1880s, Parke, Davis, and Company was selling cocaine and its botanical

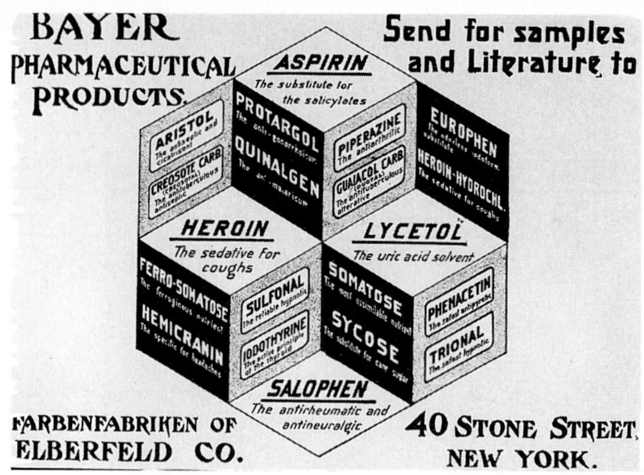

Around 1900, heroin was advertised as a completely safe remedy for common ailments, along with aspirin. No one knows the number of individuals who became dependent on heroin as a result.

patent medicine: A drug or combination of drugs sold through peddlers, shops, or mail-order advertisements.

source, coca, in more than a dozen forms, including coca-leaf cigarettes and cigars, cocaine inhalants, a coca cordial, and an injectable cocaine solution.[13] A Viennese doctor named Sigmund Freud, who was later to gain a greater reputation for his psychoanalytic theories than for his ideas concerning psychoactive drugs, called cocaine a "magical drug." In an influential paper published in 1884, Freud recommended cocaine as a safe and effective treatment for morphine addiction. When a friend and colleague became heavily addicted to cocaine, Freud quickly reversed his position, regretting for the rest of his life that he had been initially so enthusiastic in recommending its use.[14]

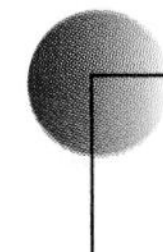

Drugs and Behavior in the Twentieth Century

By 1900, the promise of medical advances in the area of drugs was beginning to be matched by concern about the dependence that some of these drugs could produce. For a short while after its introduction in 1898, heroin (a drug derived from morphine) was completely legal and considered safe. In fact, it was even recommended by many physicians as a treatment for morphine addiction. Its powerful addictive properties, however, were soon evident. The enactment of laws restricting access to heroin and certain other psychoactive drugs, including marijuana, would eventually follow in later years, a topic discussed further in Chapter 2.

At the beginning of the twentieth century, neither the general public nor the government considered alcohol to be a drug. Nonetheless, the temperance movement dedicated to the prohibition of alcohol consumption, led by the Woman's Christian Temperance Union and the Anti-Saloon League, was a formidable political force. In 1920 the Eighteenth Amendment to the U.S. Constitution took effect, ushering in the era of Prohibition, which lasted for thirteen years.

Although successful in substantially reducing the rates of alcohol consumption in most states as well as the number of deaths attributed to alcohol-related diseases, Prohibition also succeeded in establishing a nationwide alcohol distribution network dominated by sophisticated criminal organizations.[15] Violent gang wars arose in major cities as one group battled another for control of the liquor trade. By the early 1930s, whatever desirable health-related effects Prohibition may have brought were perceived to be overshadowed by the undesirable social changes that had come along with it. Since its end in 1933, the social problems associated with the era of Prohibition have often been cited as an argument against the continuing restriction of psychoactive drugs in general.

Drugs and Behavior from 1945 to 1960

In the years following World War II, a medical revolution was underway. For the first time, physicians were able to control bacteria-borne infectious diseases through the administration of antibiotic drugs. Although penicillin had been discovered in a particular species of mold by Alexander Fleming in 1928, techniques for extracting large amounts from the mold were not perfected until the 1940s. Also during that time, Selman Waksman found that a species of fungus had powerful antibacterial effects, later to be the source of the drug streptomycin.[16] This era marked the birth of present-day chemotherapy.

In the field of psychiatry, advances in therapeutic drugs did not occur until the early 1950s, when quite accidentally a group of psychoactive drugs were discovered that relieved schizophrenic symptoms without producing heavy sedation. The first of these was **chlorpromazine** (brand name: Thorazine). Originally used as a drug to facilitate presurgical anesthesia, by 1954 chlorpromazine was identified as a drug that could reduce the hallucinations, agitation, and disordered thinking common to schizophrenia. Soon after, a torrent of new drugs were introduced not only for schizophrenia but for the whole range of mental illnesses. It was a revolution in psychiatric care, equivalent to the impact of antibiotics in medical care a decade earlier.

In the recreational drug scene in the post–World War II United States, a few features stand out. Smoking was considered romantic and sexy, as one could observe by going to the movies and seeing the hero and heroine lighting up their cigarettes or even sharing the same one. It was the era of the two-martini lunch, when social drinking was at its height of popularity and acceptance. Cocktail parties dominated the social scene. There was little or no public awareness that alcohol or nicotine consumption was drug-taking behavior.

However, the general perception of certain drugs such as heroin, marijuana, and cocaine was simple and negative: They were considered bad, illegal, and no one you knew had anything to do with them. Illicit drugs were seen as the province of criminals, the urban poor, and

chlorpromazine (chlor-PRO-mah-zeen): An antipsychotic (antischizophrenia) drug. Brand name is Thorazine (THOR-a-zeen).

James Dean was one of many Hollywood actors and actresses in the 1950s whose smoking was part of their glamorous screen image.

nonwhites.[17] The point is that a whole class of drugs were, during this period, outside the mainstream of American life. Furthermore, an atmosphere of fear and suspicion surrounded people who took such drugs. For the vast majority of Americans at this time, drugs were not considered an issue in their lives.

Drugs and Behavior since 1960

During the 1960s, basic premises of American life—the beliefs that working hard and living a good life would bring happiness and that society was stable and calm—were being undermined by disturbing events. We watched President John F. Kennedy assassinated in 1963 and Reverend Martin Luther King, Jr., and Senator Robert Kennedy gunned down in 1968. We worried about the continuing cold war and nuclear annihilation.

College students, in particular, found it difficult to be as optimistic about the future as their parents had been. The reality of the Vietnam War represented to many of them all that had gone wrong with the previous generation. A prominent historian describes the disillusion this way:

> *To the young the Vietnam War represented the return of all the rotten and useless in history, all the tyranny and horror that had diverted men from satisfying their best hopes and deepest faith. The war was viewed as the return of the dragon, the resuscitation of the old order.*[18]

They were searching for new answers to old problems, and their search led to experimentation with drugs that their parents had been taught to fear. The principal symbol of this era of defiance against the established order, or indeed against anyone over thirty years old, was marijuana. No longer was marijuana something foreign to middle America.

Marijuana, as well as other drugs such as LSD, "uppers," and "downers," became associated with sons and daughters in our own families and in our own neighborhoods. Along with the turbulence of this period came a disturbing increase in heroin abuse across the country. The issues surrounding drug abuse, once a problem associated with minority populations, inner cities, and the poor, were now too close to our personal lives for us to ignore.

One of the governmental responses to these events, particularly the increase in heroin addiction, was to finance basic research related to the effects of drugs on the brain. The timing could not have been better. During the early 1970s, a new branch of science, called **neuroscience,** was being established. Its intent was to bring researchers from formerly separate scientific fields

The famous Woodstock Festival concert drew an estimated 500,000 people to a farm in upstate New York in the summer of 1969. According to historian David Musto, ". . . it was said that the [use of marijuana] at the gigantic Woodstock gathering kept peace—as opposed to what might have happened if alcohol had been the drug of choice."

together in a new collaborative effort to understand the relationship between brain functioning and human behavior. In the area of drug research, pharmacologists (those who specialize in the study of drugs) were joined by biochemists, psychologists, and psychiatrists, among others.

One of the important discoveries that emerged from this era was the identification of receptors in the brain that are tailored specifically for drugs taken into the body. The findings of neuroscience research will be discussed in Chapter 3 and several of the chapters that follow.

With the decade of the 1980s came significant changes in the mood of the country in the form of a social and political reaction to earlier decades. If the media symbol had formerly been the "hippie," now it was the "yuppie," a young, upwardly mobile professional. The political climate grew more conservative, in all age groups. In the area of drugs, the concern about heroin addiction was being overshadowed by a new fixation: cocaine. At first, cocaine took on an aura of glamor and (because it was so expensive) became a symbol of material success. The media spotlight shone on a steady stream of celebrities in entertainment and sports who used cocaine. Not long after, however, the harsh realities of cocaine dependence were recognized. The very same celebrities who had accepted cocaine into their lives were now experiencing the consequences; many were in rehabilitation programs, and some had died from cocaine overdoses.

To make matters worse, in 1985, a new form of cocaine called crack, smokable and cheap, succeeded in extending the problems of cocaine dependence to the inner cities of the United States, to segments of American society that did not have the financial resources to afford cocaine itself. In the glare of intense media attention, crack dependence soon took on all the aspects of a national nightmare. Fortunately, by the end of the 1990s, the extent of crack abuse had greatly diminished, and the urban violence and social upheaval associated with it had declined. Nonetheless, the legacy of this era continues to be felt to the present day.[19] We will examine in Chapter 17, for example, the controversy over criminal penalties for crack possession and sale that are widely seen as disproportionately harsh, compared to penalties for other forms of drug-taking behavior.

QUICK CONCEPT  1.1

Understanding the History of Drugs and Behavior

Check your understanding of the changes in drug-taking behavior over history by matching the statement (on the left) with the appropriate historical period (on the right).

1. Opium and castor oil are first documented as therapeutic drugs.
2. Marijuana use symbolizes a generation's defiance against establishment values.
3. Waksman discovers antibacterial effects of streptomycin.
4. Opium use extends to all levels of Western society.
5. Cocaine use is at its peak as a symbol of glamor and material success.
6. Heroin is first introduced as a treatment for morphine addiction.
7. Antischizophrenic drugs begin widespread use in mental hospitals.
8. Vaccines against smallpox and rabies are introduced.

A. approximately 1500 B.C.
B. late 1700s to late 1880s
C. late 1800s
D. late 1940s
E. mid-1950s
F. late 1960s to early 1970s
G. early 1980s

Answers: 1. A 2. F 3. D 4. B 5. G 6. C 7. E 8. B

Drugs and Behavior in the New Millennium

Attitudes toward drug-taking behavior at the beginning of the twenty-first century are quite different from those that prevailed even as recently as twenty years ago. First of all, there is a far greater awareness today that a wide range of psychoactive drugs, whether they are licit or illicit, qualify as substances with varying levels of potential for misuse and abuse. The "war on drugs," declared officially in 1971 and still ongoing today in the United States, is no longer a war on a particular drug, such as heroin in the 1970s or cocaine in the 1980s. As a society, we need to be concerned with so-called "designer drugs," substances that do not fit the traditional categories of commonly abused drugs. We also need to address the widespread personal and social difficulties created by the abuse of alcohol,

neuroscience: A collaborative effort among researchers in many scientific disciplines to understand the human brain and its relationship to behavior.

steroids, inhalants, and nicotine, as well as the misuse of prescription drugs. In short, the battles being waged today are against a wide range of drug misuse and abuse, involving licit as well as illicit substances.

A second difference in attitude toward drug-taking behavior is related to the history of such behavior in our society since the late 1960s. It is important to recognize that, in 1980, about two-thirds of high school seniors had reported illicit drug use (principally marijuana smoking) at some time in their lives. They were the first generation to have grown up during the explosion of drug experimentation. Now, as the parents of teenagers at the beginning of the twenty-first century, they face the difficult challenge of dealing with the present-day drug-taking behaviors of their children. How can parents discourage such behavior in their sons or daughters without appearing hypocritical, since they themselves were part of the drug scene at an earlier time in their lives?[20]

Patterns of Drug Use in the United States

In arriving at some statistical picture of drug-taking behavior today, we first have to ask a fundamental question: How can we ever succeed in obtaining such information? Assuming that we cannot conduct large-scale random drug testing, the only alternative we have is simply to ask people about their drug-taking behavior through self-reports. We encourage honesty and arrange the data-collection procedure so as to convince the respondents that their answers are confidential, but the fact remains that any questionnaire is inherently imperfect because there is no way to verify the truthfulness of what people say about themselves. Nevertheless, questionnaires are all we have, and the statistics on drug use are based on such survey measures.

One of the best-known surveys, tapping into the drug-taking patterns of young people, has been conducted every year since 1975 by the University of Michigan. Typically, more than forty-five thousand American students in the eighth, tenth, and twelfth grades participate in the survey each year, as well as more than seven thousand college students and young adults between the ages of nineteen and thirty-two.[21]

The advantage of repeating the survey with a new sample year after year is that it enables us to look at trends in drug-taking behavior over time and compare the use of one drug relative to another. We can assume that the degree of overreporting and underreporting stays relatively constant over the years and does not affect the interpretation of the general trends. A major disadvantage of this survey, however, is the fact that high school dropouts are not included. Therefore, results may not fully represent drug use for these age groups.

Survey questions concerning drug use are phrased in four basic ways:

- Whether an individual has ever used a certain drug in his or her lifetime
- Whether an individual has used a certain drug over the previous year
- Whether an individual has used a certain drug within the previous thirty days
- Whether an individual has used a certain drug on a *daily* basis during the previous thirty days

You can see that these questions distinguish three important degrees of involvement with a given drug. The first question focuses on the extent of experimentation, including individuals who may have taken a drug only once or twice in their lives and who have stayed away from it ever since. The second and third questions focus on the extent of current but moderate drug use, while the fourth question focuses on the extent of heavy drug use. What do the numbers tell us? Consider first the data regarding high school seniors.

Illicit Drug Use among High School Seniors

We are naturally concerned with any level of drug-taking behavior among U.S. high school seniors, but it is at least encouraging to realize that levels of drug use are not as high as they were at the end of the 1970s. In 2000, for example, 41 percent of high school seniors reported use of an illicit drug over the previous year, less than the 54 percent reporting such use in the peak year of 1979 (Figure 1.2). If we look specifically at marijuana use over the previous year, the senior sample reported 37 percent, a reduction from a level of 51 percent in 1979. Cocaine use over the previous year for seniors was 5 percent, less than one-half of the number reporting such behavior in the peak year of 1985.

Nonetheless, the absolute percentages in 2000 were still substantial. They indicate that about four out of every ten high school seniors had used some form of illicit drug over the last twelve months, more than one out of three had smoked marijuana, and about one out of twenty had used cocaine. As will be shown shortly, the prevalence rates of many forms of illicit drug use rose significantly during the 1990s, not only among high school seniors but among younger students in the eighth and tenth grades

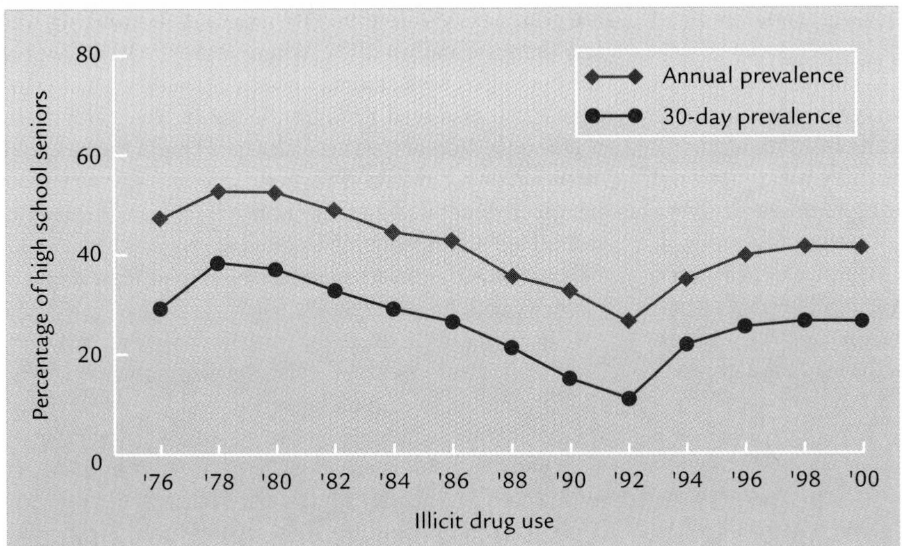

FIGURE 1.2

Trends in prevalence of illicit drug use among high school seniors.

Source: Johnston, Lloyd D. (2000, December 14). "Ecstasy" use rises sharply among teens in 2000; use of many other drugs stays steady, but significant declines are reported for some. News release from the University of Michigan, Ann Arbor, Table 2.

as well. Only recently has this dangerous upward trend started to reverse itself.[22]

Drugs among Youth in a Diverse Society

When we look at racial and ethnic differences in both illicit and licit drug use among adolescents, certain consistent patterns emerge from the University of Michigan survey. For seven major categories of drugs (marijuana, inhalants, hallucinogens, cocaine, crack cocaine, heroin, and alcohol), drug use among African Americans in the eighth grade is consistently lower than among white students in all categories except for marijuana smoking. By the senior year, levels of daily cigarette smoking and binge drinking among African Americans are substantially below those of white students of comparable age. A comparison of African American, Hispanic/Latino, and white seniors shows that white students generally have the highest annual prevalence rates in most categories, though Hispanic/Latino seniors show the highest prevalence rates for MDMA (Ecstasy), injectable heroin, cocaine, crack cocaine, and steroids (Table 1.1).[23]

Drug Use among College Students and Young Adults

The University of Michigan survey also allows a look at drug use among young people beyond high school. Compared to high school seniors, in 1999 college students reported lower prevalence rates in all major drug categories other than alcohol (see "Patterns of Alcohol Use"). Drug use among young adults one to ten years after high school was either higher or lower than college students, depending on the drug in question. In 1999, for example, young adults over the last twelve months were less inclined to use illicit drugs in general, as well as marijuana and

TABLE 1.1

Percentages of white, African American, and Hispanic/Latino high school seniors who answered "yes" to the question: Have you used a particular drug in the past year?

	WHITE	AFRICAN AMERICAN	HISPANIC/ LATINO
Marijuana	39.1	30.4	37.8
Inhalants	7.0	1.4	5.5
Hallucinogens	10.7	1.2	7.9
MDMA (Ecstasy)	5.1	0.5	6.0
Cocaine	6.7	0.9	7.5
Crack cocaine	2.8	0.4	3.5
Heroin (needle)	0.4	0.2	0.6
Heroin (no needle)	1.1	0.1	0.6
Alcohol	77.5	60.0	74.7
Steroids	1.7	0.7	2.9

Source: Johnston, Lloyd D., O'Malley, Patrick M., and Bachman, Jerald G. (2000). Data from 1998 and 1999 surveys combined. *Monitoring the Future: National survey results on drug use, 1975–1999. Volume 1: Secondary school students.* Rockville MD: National Institute on Drug Abuse, Table 4-9.

hallucinogens in particular, but they were more inclined to use heroin and cocaine.[24]

When you examine the drug-taking behavior of young adults, tracking them at two-year intervals for as long as fourteen years after graduating from high school, an interesting pattern emerges. As they make personal commitments, marrying and starting families, drug use drops substantially from levels reported in high school. Personal setbacks such as divorces, however, produce an increase in drug use, often to the same levels as when they were single. Evidently, previous drug use in high school makes it more likely that an individual will revert to old patterns of behavior in hard times.[25]

Patterns of Alcohol Use

Not surprisingly, the prevalence percentages related to the use of alcohol are much higher than for illicit drugs. While 25 percent of high school seniors in 2000 reported use of illicit drugs in the previous month, about half (51 percent) drank an alcoholic beverage, with 30 percent reporting at least one instance of binge drinking, defined as five or more drinks in a row, in the previous two weeks. These figures are down from nearly two decades earlier, when 72 percent reported in 1980 that they had consumed alcohol over the previous month and 41 percent reported binge drinking.

A partial explanation for the decline from 1980 to the present lies in the reduced accessibility to alcohol for this age group, with all U.S. states now having adopted a twenty-one-year-or-older requirement. Despite the decline, however, the present level of alcohol consumption among high school seniors is a matter of great concern. Alcohol consumption on a regular basis is widespread for individuals in this age group, despite the fact that it is officially illegal for any of them to purchase alcoholic beverages.

In contrast to high school seniors, the drinking habits of college students have shown less change over the past years. In 1999, 70 percent of college students surveyed drank at least once in the previous month, and 40 percent reported an instance of binge drinking. Evidently, the "know when to say when" message, as promoted by major beer companies, has not gotten through.[26]

Patterns of Nicotine Use

Roughly 21 percent of high school seniors in 2000 had established a regular habit of nicotine intake by smoking at least one cigarette every day. In fact, nicotine remains the drug most frequently used on a daily basis by high school students. The prevalence trends over the years, however, are complex. While the 2000 rate of daily smoking was less than the rate in 1977, when approximately 29 percent of high school seniors smoked cigarettes, a steady increase was observed through the 1990s. By 2000, there was a suggestion of a reversal, due perhaps to the national attention directed toward cigarette smoking among young people in general. Whether or not a long-term downward trend has begun remains to be seen. In 2000, about 11 percent of all seniors reported smoking at least a half a pack of cigarettes per day.

For students in the eighth and tenth grades, daily cigarette smoking rates also climbed through the 1990s, though the beginning of a reversal could be observed at the end of the decade. Nonetheless, in 2000 about 6 percent of tenth-graders and 3 percent of eighth-graders reported smoking at least a half a pack of cigarettes per day, a strikingly high level for these age groups considering the legal obstacles to buying cigarettes.

In general, fewer college students smoke cigarettes than high school seniors. The reason is a matter of differences in the populations studied here, rather than an actual change in smoking behavior from high school to college. Among high school seniors, noncollege-bound students are more than twice as likely to smoke cigarettes than college-bound students and more than twice as likely to smoke at least a half a pack per day. Therefore, the drop-off in smoking rates from seniors to college students is a result of excluding the heavier smokers in the college survey as they progress from secondary to postsecondary education. Nonetheless, the incidence of cigarette smoking among college students has increased steadily in the 1990s. In fact, this is one form of drug-taking behavior among college students for which the upward trend has not yet shown any signs of reversal.[27]

Trends in Drug Use in the 1990s

Until 1991, the rates of drug use among high school and college students in almost all categories showed a steady decline from peak levels in the late 1970s and early 1980s. However, beginning in 1992 and 1993, the University of Michigan surveys showed a significant reversal, sparking widespread concern that we might once again be in the throes of a drug epidemic. The increased level of drug-taking behavior was seen most dramatically in the annual incidence of marijuana smoking in 1998 among high school seniors, which was roughly 73 percent higher than in 1991. The overall incidence of illicit drug use increased roughly 41 percent from 1991 levels (see Figure 1.2).[28] Fortunately, by the end of the 1990s, prevalence rates began to level off and there were preliminary signs of a reversal.

Drug Use among Younger Students and across the Life Span

Beginning in 1991, we have also had extensive survey information about licit and illicit drug use among students as early as the eighth grade. Some of their responses are shown in Table 1.2. The percentages of drug use at this age and the upward trend in these percentages from 1991 to 1996 reflected a level of drug experimentation that was particularly disturbing. We were left to speculate as to the negative effect on still younger children, as they observed the drug-taking behavior of their older brothers and sisters.

By 1997, the upward trend among eighth-graders had leveled off somewhat and began to turn downward. Whether this signals a continuing reversal in this age group or represents just a momentary pause remains an open question. A comprehensive look at drug use among several age groups in the United States is given in Table 1.3.[29]

Patterns of Drug Awareness among Young People

Until it began to reverse itself in 1997, another troubling trend reflected in the University of Michigan surveys for much of the 1990s was the steady decline in the percentages of high school students, college students, and young adults who regarded regular drug use as potentially dangerous. These responses contrasted with reports beginning in 1978 that had showed a steady increase in such percentages. A spokesperson for the 1996 Michigan survey offered one possible reason for this reversal:

> *This most recent crop of youngsters grew up in a period in which drug use rates were down substantially from what they had been 10 to 15 years earlier. This gave youngsters less opportunity to learn from others' mistakes and resulted in what I call "generational forgetting" of the hazards of drugs.*[30]

Also troubling during much of the 1990s were changes in the way our society dealt with the potential risks of

TABLE 1.2

Percentage of drug use among eighth graders, 2000

	2000	PERCENT INCREASE SINCE 1991
Use of cigarettes in previous 30 days	14.6%	2%
Daily use of cigarettes	7.4	3
Use of marijuana in past year	15.6	151
Use of cocaine in past year	2.6	136
Use of inhalants in past year	9.4	4
Being drunk in past year	18.5	6

Source: Johnston, Lloyd D. (2000, December 14). "Ecstasy" use rises sharply among teens in 2000; use of other drugs stays steady, but significant declines are reported for some. News release from the University of Michigan, Ann Arbor, Tables 2 and 3.

TABLE 1.3

Drug use in the United States across the lifespan

	PERCENTAGE BY AGE GROUP FOR USE IN PAST YEAR/PAST MONTH				ESTIMATED TOTAL NUMBER OF USERS
	12–17	18–25	26 AND OLDER	TOTAL SAMPLE	PAST YEAR/PAST MONTH
Any illicit drug	20/11	30/17	8/4	12/7	26,220,000/14,820,000
Marijuana	14/8	25/15	5/3	9/5	19,573,000/11,177,000
Cocaine	2/0.5	5/2	1/0.5	2/0.7	3,691,000/1,501,000
Crack cocaine	0.4/0.1	1/0.4	0.4/0.2	0.5/0.2	1,035,000/413,000
Heroin	0.3/0.2	0.5/0.2	0.1/0.1	0.2/0.1	403,000/208,000
Hallucinogens	4/1	7/2	0.2/0.1	1/0.4	3,169,000/907,000
Alcohol	35/19	75/58	64/49	63/47	138,346,000/104,603,000
Nicotine (any tobacco use)	27/17	54/45	34/30	36/30	79,778,000/66,766,000

Source: Substance Abuse and Mental Health Services Administration (2000). *Summary of findings from the 1999 National Household Survey on drug abuse.* Rockville MD: Office of Applied Studies, Substance Abuse and Mental Health Services Administration, Tables G.5–G.9, G.21–G.25.

drug use. Drug abuse prevention programs in schools were scaled back or eliminated because of a lack of federal funding, parents were communicating less with their children about drug use, antidrug public service messages were less prominent in the media than they were in the 1980s, and media coverage in this area declined. At the same time, the cultural influences of the music and entertainment industry were, at best, ambivalent on the question of drug-taking behavior, particularly with respect to marijuana smoking (see Chapter 7). All of these elements can now be seen as contributing to the upward trend in drug use and the downward trend in negative attitudes toward it.

The reciprocal relationship between drug attitudes and drug use can be clearly understood by examining the respective trends over time. In Figure 1.3, across a span of nearly 25 years, the percentages who consider marijuana smoking as presenting a great risk form an almost perfect mirror image with the percentages smoking marijuana at least once in the previous month. Notice that the availability of marijuana has stayed relatively constant during this period.[31]

QUICK CONCEPT CHECK 1.2

Understanding Present Drug Use in the United States

Check your understanding of present drug use in the United States by marking the following statements true or false.

1. The University of Michigan survey included a sampling of all seventeen-to-eighteen-year-old individuals in the United States.
2. With the exception of alcohol and nicotine, the trend in drug use from the early 1980s to the present has been a steady decline.
3. A prominent reason students give for using drugs is that they are rebelling against authority figures, specifically their parents.
4. Marijuana is more available and its use is more prevalent now than it was in 1980.

Answers: 1. false 2. false 3. false 4. false

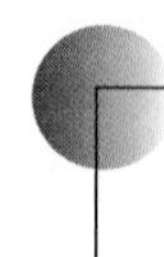

Why Some Individuals Use Drugs and Others Don't

Why do students and other young people take drugs? What factors influence the drug-taking behavior that we see in all these statistics? One study asked high school seniors to report their personal reasons for taking drugs.[32] The most frequently occurring responses among the classes of 1983 and 1984 included "to have a good time with my friends" (65 percent), "to experiment or see

FIGURE 1.3

Trends in perceived availability, perceived risk of marijuana use, and prevalence of marijuana use in the past month for high school seniors.
Source: Johnston, Lloyd D. (2000, December 14). "Ecstasy" use rises sharply among teens in 2000; use of many other drugs stays steady, but significant declines are reported for some. News release from the University of Michigan, Ann Arbor, Tables 2, 9, and 12.

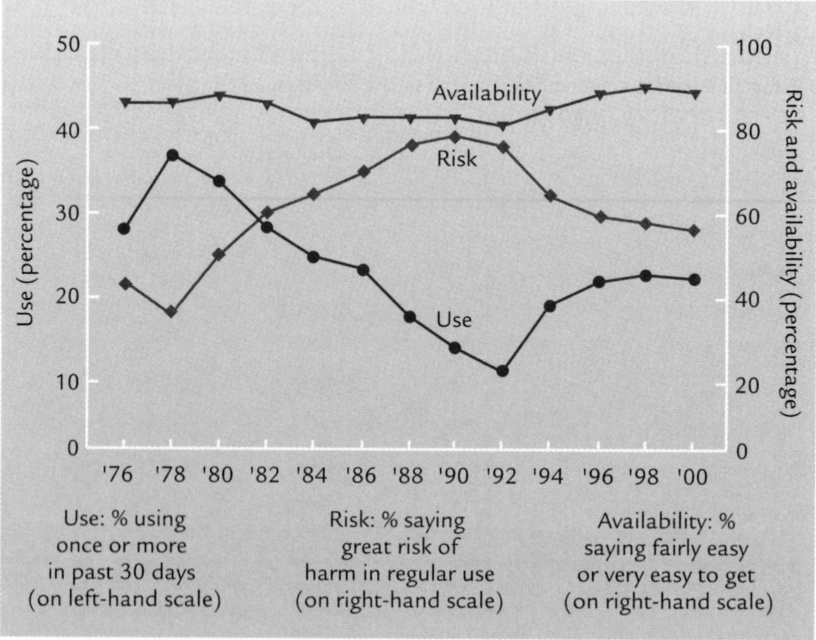

Peer influence is a major factor in predicting the extent of drug-taking behavior during adolescence. It can represent either a risk factor or a protective factor for drug abuse.

what it's like" (54 percent), "to feel good or get high" (49 percent), and "to relax or relieve tension" (41 percent). These responses were similar to reasons given by the class of 1976 in earlier surveys, and there is no reason to suspect significant differences today.

Is there any way of predicting which individuals may be inclined to take drugs and which individuals are likely to stay drug-free? One way of thinking about predicting drug use is to consider any given person as having a certain degree of vulnerability toward drug-taking behavior. This vulnerability seems to be shaped by two separate groups of factors in a person's life. The first are **risk factors,** which make it *more likely* that a person might be involved with drugs; the second are **protective factors,** which make it *less likely* that a person might be involved with drugs.

Together, risk factors and protective factors combine to give us some idea about the likelihood that drug-taking behavior will occur. The emphasis, however, should be on the phrase "some idea." We still would not know for certain which individuals would use drugs and which ones would not. An understanding of risk factors and protective factors in general and knowledge about which factors apply to a given individual are useful pieces of information in the development of effective drug abuse prevention programs (see Chapters 17 and 18).

Certain factors that may appear to be strong risk factors for drug-taking behavior in general (socioeconomic status, for example) turn out to have an association that is far from simple and may depend on the particular drug under discussion.[33] The most reliable set of risk factors consists of psychosocial characteristics that reflect a tendency toward nonconformity within society. Young people who take drugs are more inclined to attend school irregularly, have poor relationships with their parents, or get into trouble in general. Sociologists refer to such individuals as members of a deviant subculture.

The greater the number of risk factors for becoming part of a deviant subculture, the higher the probability that an individual will display some level of drug-taking behavior. Some of the risk factors that have been found to be important are the following: easy availability of drugs in one's environment, feelings of depression, an early history of alcohol intoxication beginning at age twelve or under, the number of adults you know who have a drug problem, the degree to which your friends would approve of your getting high on drugs, absence from school for reasons other than illness, and generally low educational aspirations.[34]

In general, as the number of risk factors increases, so does the likelihood of drug use and drug involvement. If we had to single out the most influential risk factor, it would be peer influence, as measured by the reported number of friends who use drugs.[35] The importance of peer influence evidently is found across cultural groups; white, African American, and Latino youngsters react in very similar ways.[36] By contrast, economic hardship and parental abuse do not appear to correlate with the inclination to use drugs.[37]

On the other hand, protective factors provide the basis for someone to have a stronger resistance against the temptations of drugs, despite the presence of risk factors in that person's life.[38] It is important that we not see these protective factors as simply the inverted image, or the negation of, opposing risk factors. Rather, each group of factors operates independently of the other. One way of thinking about protective factors is to view them as a kind of insurance policy against the occurrence of some future

risk factors: Factors in an individual's life that increase the likelihood of involvement with drugs.
protective factors: Factors in an individual's life that decrease the likelihood of involvement with drugs and reduce the impact that any risk factor might have.

event that you hope to avoid. The major protective factors are listed in Table 1.4.

Protective factors can serve as a buffering element among even high-risk adolescents, allowing them to have a greater degree of resilience against drug-taking behavior and a higher resistance to drug use than they would have had otherwise. In one study, protective factors were examined in one thousand high-risk male and female adolescents in the seventh and eighth grades, and information was collected on their drug use later in high school. As the number of protective factors increased, the resistance of these students to drug use increased as well. With six or more such factors in their lives, as many as 56 percent of the high-risk adolescents showed a resistance to drug use three years later. In contrast, with three or fewer factors, only 20 percent of the youths were drug-free.[39]

Recently, the concept of protective factors has been taken a step further. In research by the Search Institute in Minneapolis, as many as forty protective factors have been identified, referred to collectively as *developmental assets*.[40] Similar to the protective factors listed in Table 1.4, these developmental assets have been found to increase resistance not only to drug-taking behavior (such as problem alcohol use and illicit drug use) but to other high-risk behaviors (such as sexual activity and violence) as well (Figure 1.4).

TABLE 1.4

Major protective factors for drug-taking behavior among adolescents
An intact and positive home environment
Mother and father living together
Close parental involvement and supervision in child's activities
Strong parent–child attachment
Parent's educational level at high school or greater
A positive educational experience
High reading and math achievement levels
A close attachment to teachers
Aspirations/expectations to go to college
Parent's aspirations/expectations for child to go to college
Exposure to school-based prevention education
Conventional peer relationships
Socially conforming attitudes among child's peers
Parents with positive evaluations of child's peers
Positive attitudes and beliefs
High self-esteem
Involvement in religious activities and prosocial activities
Closeness to an adult outside the family

Source: Adapted from Smith, Carolyn; Lizotte, Alan J.; Thornberry, Terence P.; and Krohn, Marvin D. (1995). Resilient youth: Identifying factors that prevent high-risk youth from engaging in delinquency and drug use. *Current Perspectives on Aging and the Life Cycle, 4,* 217–247.

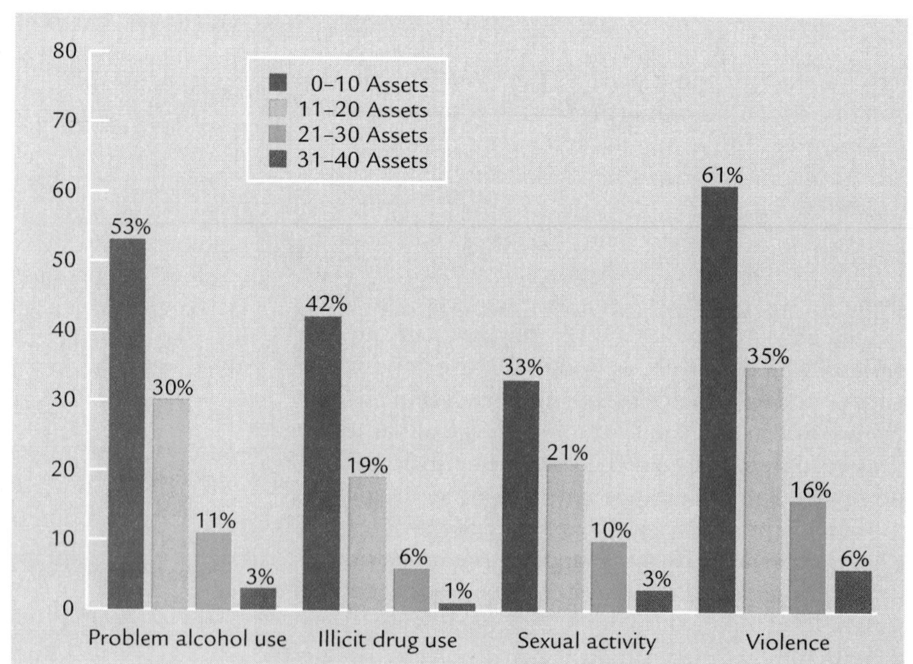

FIGURE 1.4

The percentages of four high-risk behaviors as a function of the number of developmental assets, based on responses of sixth- to twelfth-grade youth.
Source: Information courtesy of Search Institute, Minneapolis, Minnesota, 2000.

Looking to the Future and Learning from the Past

What does the future hold with respect to psychoactive drugs? Where should we direct our concerns? Predictions are always tricky to make, but with regard to drug-taking behavior there are historical patterns that can serve as guides.

Old Drugs, New Drugs

One certainty is that specific drugs will continue to come into and out of favor. New drugs will appear on the scene, and others may reappear like ghosts from the past, sometimes in new forms and involving new faces in the drug underground. Since 1991, for example, with cocaine declining in popularity in the United States, heroin has been on the upswing once more. Heroin is distributed in potent blends that can be snorted like cocaine or smoked like crack. On the one hand, these new forms circumvent the traditional need for hypodermic syringes and the associated dangers of being infected with the virus responsible for acquired immunodeficiency syndrome (AIDS). On the other hand, new populations of people formerly turned off to heroin because of their fear of needles are being introduced to it for the first time. As mentioned earlier, LSD and other hallucinogens, once the darlings of the psychedelic generation in the 1960s, have staged a comeback as well.[41]

A serious concern in today's drug scene is the popularity of "club drugs," a term referring to substances ingested by young adults at all-night dance parties such as "raves" or "trances," dance clubs, and bars. Examples of club drugs include MDMA (Ecstasy), GHB, Rohypnol, ketamine, methamphetamine, and LSD. When used in combination with alcohol, as they often are, these drugs carry considerably increased health risks, beyond their own individual toxicities. Since many club drugs are colorless, tasteless, and odorless, they can be slipped unobtrusively into drinks by individuals who want to intoxicate or sedate others. The potential danger of sexual assault, therefore, is a major problem.[42] Drugs . . . in Focus examines the major features of these six club drugs. A more detailed discussion will follow in Chapter 4 (methamphetamine), Chapter 6 (LSD, MDMA, and ketamine), and Chapter 15 (GHB and Rohypnol).

Another phenomenon that has attracted considerable attention, as we begin the twenty-first century, is the increasing prominence of herbal and nonherbal products, packaged and marketed as **dietary supplements,** that purport to enhance mood, energize the mind, or relieve feelings of anxiety. While clearly not as problematic as the reemergence of illicit drugs such as heroin and hallucinogens or the appearance of club drugs, the fact remains that these products need to be closely examined for their potential to create as well as resolve health problems. It is estimated that dietary supplements are used for medicinal purposes on a regular basis by 20 percent to 30 percent of the U.S. population. In the vast majority of cases, people are taking supplement preparations without any communication with a physician or other health professional.[43]

Since dietary supplements are not officially classified as drugs, governmental regulations for them are different

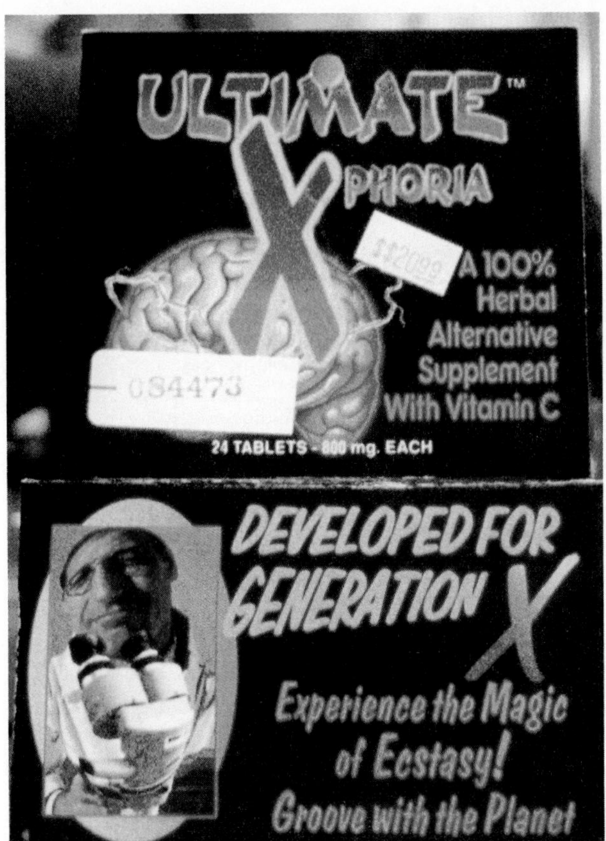

Ephedrine products offer a tempting prospect of increased energy and euphoria but also carry potential risks, sometimes deadly.

dietary supplements: Commercial preparations derived from vitamins, amino acids, or herbal extracts. Dietary supplement manufacturers are permitted to claim that these products can help with certain physical conditions associated with different stages of life, but they cannot be used to diagnose, treat, cure, or prevent physical disease.

DRUGS . . . IN FOCUS

Facts about Club Drugs

MDMA (methylenedioxymethamphetamine)

- Street names: Ecstasy, XTC, X, E, Adam, Clarity, Lover's Speed, Hug Drug, Euphoria, M&M
- Variations: MDA (methylenedioxyamphetamine), MDEA (methylenedioxyethylamphetamine)
- Forms: Tablet or capsule
- Drug type: Stimulant and hallucinogen
- Behavioral effects: Appetite suppression, excitation, perceptual distortions
- Physiological effects: increased heart rate and blood pressure, dehydration
- Length of effect: 3 to 6 hours
- Toxicity: Marked increase in body temperature; possible heart attack, stroke, or seizure; brain damage from chronic use (see Chapter 6)

GHB (gamma-hydroxybutyrate)

- Street names: Grievous Bodily Harm, G, Liquid X, Liquid Ecstasy, Georgia Home Boy
- Variations: Gamma-butyrolactone (GBL)
- Forms: Clear liquid, tablet, capsule, or white powder
- Drug type: Depressant
- Behavioral effects: Intoxication, euphoria, sedation, anxiety reduction
- Physiological effects: Central nervous system depressant, stimulation of growth-hormone release
- Length of effect: Up to 4 hours
- Toxicity: Overdoses produce drowsiness, loss of consciousness, impaired breathing, coma, potential death. GHB greatly potentiates the sedative action of alcohol (see Chapter 15).

Ketamine

- Street names: K, Special K, Vitamin K, Cat Valiums
- Variations: None
- Forms: Liquid, white powder snorted or smoked with marijuana or tobacco, intramuscular injection
- Drug type: Hallucinogen
- Behavioral effects: Dream-like state of consciousness, hallucinations
- Physiological effects: Increased blood pressure, potential seizures and coma
- Length of effect: 1 hour
- Toxicity: Impaired attention and memory, impaired motor coordination, disorientation (see Chapter 6)

Rohypnol (flunitrazepam)

- Street names: Roofies, Rophies, Roche, Rope, Forget-me pill
- Variations: None
- Forms: Tablet dissolvable in carbonated beverages
- Drug type: Antianxiety drug
- Behavioral effects: Sedation
- Physiological effects: Decreased blood pressure, visual disturbances, gastrointestinal disturbances
- Length of effect: 8 to 12 hours
- Toxicity: Anterograde amnesia (loss of memory for events experienced under its influence). Rohypnol effects are greatly potentiated by alcohol (see Chapter 15).

Methamphetamine

- Street names: Speed, Ice, Meth, Crystal, Crystal Meth, Crank, Fire, Glass, Ice, Rock Candy
- Variations: Amphetamines, with varying degrees of similarity
- Forms: Many forms; methamphetamine can be smoked, snorted, injected, or orally ingested
- Drug type: Stimulant
- Behavioral effects: Increased alertness and energy
- Physiological effects: Increased heart rate and blood pressure, decreased appetite
- Length of effect: Several hours
- Toxicity: Possible heart attack or cardiovascular collapse, seizures, cerebral hemorrhage, and coma (see Chapter 4)

LSD (lysergic acid diethylamide)

- Street names: Acid, Boomers, Yellow Sunshines, Barrels, Blotters, Cubes, Domes, Lids, Wedges
- Variations: Hallucinogens, with varying degrees of similarity
- Forms: Crystalline material soluble in water
- Drug type: Hallucinogen
- Behavioral effects: Distortions of visual perceptions, time periods, and space
- Physiological effects: Increased heart rate and blood pressure, sweating, tremors
- Length of effect: 30 to 90 minutes, though effects might last several hours
- Toxicity: Numbness, nausea (see Chapter 6)

Sources: Brands, Bruna; Sproule, Beth; and Marshman, Joan (1998). *Drugs and drug abuse: A reference text.* Toronto: Addiction Research Foundation. National Institute on Drug Abuse (1999, December). *Community Drug Alert Bulletin: Club Drugs.* Bethesda MD: National Institute on Drug Abuse.

from those that apply to prescription and over-the-counter medications. The Dietary Supplement Health and Education Act of 1994 required that supplement labels contain the statement that any claims made by the manufacturer "have not been evaluated by the U.S. Food and Drug Administration." In effect, this disclaimer allows these products to be marketed and sold in the United States without the rigorous process of review and evaluation that assures the consumer that they are safe to take and effective for medicinal purposes. Some examples of such dietary supplements are androstenedione, creatine, gingko biloba, ginseng, and St. John's wort. We will examine the safety and effectiveness of these dietary supplements in Chapters 8, 14, and 16, in the context of presently available drugs and medications.

What medical claims can be made for these preparations? On the one hand, the 1994 law clearly prohibits manufacturers from making any claim that refers to a form of disease. On the other hand, a federal ruling in 2000 stipulated that certain common physical conditions associated with different stages of life such as aging, adolescence, pregnancy, and menopause are not diseases, and therefore dietary supplement claims for helping these conditions are allowed. Uncommon or more serious conditions associated with these life stages would still be considered diseases, and supplement labels will be required to indicate that the products are not intended to "diagnose, treat, cure, or prevent" these particular conditions.

Unfortunately, the distinction between disease and non-disease can be difficult to make. For example, manufacturers can now claim that certain supplements may be able to treat muscle pain but are prohibited from mentioning joint pain, because the latter is a symptom of arthritis. They can claim to treat "mild memory loss associated with aging" but not more severe memory problems associated with Alzheimer's disease. Federal officials admit that, at best, it is a difficult line to draw. At worst, there are serious concerns that consumer protections are being compromised. As one critic has expressed it, the new regulations mean that "consumers at the beginning of the twenty-first century are about at the same place as consumers at the end of the nineteenth century."[44]

Beyond the potential risks associated with the instrumental use of dietary supplements, however, are the risks associated with the use of these products (particularly the herbal varieties) for recreational purposes by those individuals seeking a so-called natural "herbal high." For example, a product that claims to increase alertness may also produce extreme euphoria and disorientation. The medical risks of one of these substances, a stimulant derived from the Chinese herb *ma huang*, is highlighted in this chapter's Portrait.

Portrait: Peter Schlendorf and the Risks of an "Herbal High"

The last time Peter Schlendorf's friends saw him, the twenty-year-old college junior was sweating profusely, had a terrible headache, and complained that his skin tingled. They had bought a box of the herbal supplement Ultimate Xphoria from a local souvenir shop in Panama City Beach, Florida, where they were enjoying a typical college Spring Break in 1996. "We had heard that it was pretty good stuff. Because it was all natural herbs and it was supposed to be a little bit of a stimulant," one of his friends recalled. The recommended dose was four tablets, but the woman behind the counter in the shop assured them that she always took a dozen or more. His friends took eleven; Peter, wanting to be careful, took eight. Two hours later, Peter was dead, an apparent victim of cardiac arrest. An autopsy revealed no other drugs in his system, not even alcohol levels equivalent to one beer, except for the active ingredients in Ultimate Xphoria: ephedrine, pseudoephedrine, and caffeine.

Peter Schlendorf

The principal culprit was ephedrine, derived from a Chinese herb called *ma huang*, known for thousands of years to expand bronchial tubes, increase blood pressure and heart rate, and increase alertness. The original amphetamines in the 1920s were synthetic forms of ephedrine (see Chapter 4). At the time of Schlendorf's death, ephedrine was sold with little or no restriction as a dietary supplement in health food and convenience stores. Products similar to Ultimate Xphoria have been marketed under such names as Herbal Ecstacy, Cloud 9, Herbal XTC, Formula One, and Rave Energy, to name a few, some of them promising "sexual euphoria" as a result of the "ultimate brain food."

Since the 1994 passage of a federal law, the U.S. Food and Drug Administration (FDA) has been limited in its power to regulate herbal remedies and other dietary supplements. In the case of ephedrine, however, an FDA safety review conducted in 1997 concluded that there was sufficient evidence of significant health risks to establish a limit on the recommended dosage and its use for more than seven days, a prohibition of its sale in combination with other stimulants such as caffeine, and a warning label that "taking more than the recommended serving may result in heart attack, stroke, seizure, or death."

Sources: Burros, Marian (1997, June 3). F.D.A. plans to control herbal stimulant tied to deaths. *New York Times*, p. A14. Cowley, Geoffrey (1996, May 6). Herbal warning. *Newsweek*, pp. 60–68. Duffy, Mary (1999, October 12). Side effects raise flag on dangers of ephedra. *New York Times*, p. F7.

Why Drugs?

If the history of drugs teaches us anything, it is that there will always be an attraction to the drug experience. This certainty arises directly from the character of psychoactive drugs themselves, namely their ability to cause an alteration in consciousness. For a time, they can make us feel euphoric, light-headed, relaxed, or powerful, and there is little doubt that all this feels good. There may be other nonpharmacological ways of arriving at this state of mind, but drugs are easy and quick. They also seem to increase awareness of the environment and give the impression of a feeling that we are seeing or hearing things in a more intense way. No matter whether we are young or old, rich or poor, drugs can allow us to retreat from an uncomfortable environment, to feel no pain.

Unfortunately, in every generation there will be young people who are alienated from their families and the community of adults around them, who seek some form of temporary release from an unhappy existence. There will be a younger generation seeking some form of rebellion against traditional values. There will be adolescents testing the limits of their parents' love and tolerance. Despite our best efforts to prevent it from happening, there will be young people who are simply willing to try anything new, including drugs. Their curiosity, to find out "what it's like," brings us full circle to the earliest times in human history, when we nibbled on the plants in the field just to find out how they tasted. In the modern era, drug experimentation is neither a new nor a singular phenomenon; it can involve an alcoholic drink, an inhaled solvent from some household product, a cigarette, or an illicit drug. Whether this experimentation leads to a more intense level of drug use or drug abuse is another question. The personal and social dangers of drug-taking behavior are examined in the next chapter.

SUMMARY

A Matter of Definition

- Psychoactive drugs are those drugs that affect our feelings, perceptions, and behavior. Depending on the intent of the individual, drug use can be considered either instrumental or recreational.
- Drug abuse refers to cases in which a licit or illicit drug is used in ways that produce some form of impairment. Drug misuse refers to cases in which a prescription or nonprescription drug is used inappropriately.

Drugs in Early Times

- Probably the earliest experiences with psychoactive drugs came from tasting naturally growing plants. Individuals with knowledge about such plants were able to attain great power within their cultures.
- Ancient Egyptians and Babylonians in particular had extensive knowledge of both psychoactive and nonpsychoactive drugs. Some of these drugs had genuine beneficial effects.

Drugs in the Nineteenth Century

- Medical advances in the 1800s had succeeded in the isolation of active ingredients within many psychoactive substances. For example, morphine was identified as the major active ingredient in opium.
- Psychoactive drugs were in widespread use, principally in the form of patent medicines. Only by the end of the century were the risks of drug dependence beginning to be recognized.

Drugs and Behavior in the Twentieth Century

- Increased concern about the social effects of drug dependence led to restrictive legislation regarding the use of morphine, heroin, cocaine, and marijuana.
- Social pressure from the temperance movement resulted in the national prohibition of alcohol consumption in the United States from 1920 to 1933.
- After 1945, important strides were made in the development of antibiotics and psychiatric drugs.
- By the 1940s and 1950s, illicit drugs such as heroin, cocaine, and marijuana were outside the mainstream of American life.
- In the 1960s and 1970s, the use of marijuana and hallucinogenic drugs spread across the nation, along with an increase in problems related to heroin.
- A decline in heroin abuse in the 1980s was matched with an increase in cocaine abuse and the emergence of crack as a cheap, smokable form of cocaine.
- It is now recognized that a wide range of psychoactive drugs, licit or illicit, qualify as potential sources of misuse and abuse.

Patterns of Drug Use in the United States

- Surveys of illicit drug use among high school seniors in 2000 have shown that four in every ten seniors used an illicit drug over the last twelve months, more than one in three smoked marijuana, and one in twenty used cocaine.
- Since 1991, marijuana use among high school seniors has risen significantly, as has the use of other illicit drugs.
- Drug use in general and the use of individual psychoactive drugs vary greatly along racial and ethnic lines.

Why Some Individuals Use Drugs and Others Don't

- Risk factors for drug-taking behavior in adolescence include a tendency toward nonconformity within society and the influence of drug-using peers.
- Protective factors for drug-taking behavior include an intact home environment, a positive educational experience, and conventional peer relationships.

Looking to the Future and Learning from the Past

- Predictions regarding future drugs and drug-taking behaviors are largely founded on patterns from the past. New drugs will undoubtedly come on the scene; old drugs that are out of favor might regain popularity.
- It is unlikely that young people will stop experimenting with drugs, as they tend to experiment with a great many other things at this time in their lives.

KEY TERMS

chlorpromazine, p. 9
dietary supplements, p. 19
drug, p. 3
drug abuse, p. 5
drug dependence, p. 3
drug misuse, p. 5
Ebers Papyrus, p. 7
illicit drugs, p. 3
instrumental use, p. 4
licit drugs, p. 3
neuroscience, pp. 10–11
patent medicine, p. 8
placebo effect, p. 7
protective factors, p. 17
psychoactive drugs, p. 3
recreational use, p. 4
risk factors, p. 17
shaman, p. 7
shamanism, p. 7

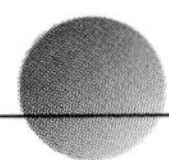

ENDNOTES

1. Grube, Joel W. (1995). Television alcohol portrayals, alcohol advertising, and alcohol expectancies among children and adolescents. In Susan E. Martin (Ed.), *The effects of the mass media on the use and abuse of alcohol* (NIAAA Research Monograph 28). Bethesda MD: National Institute on Alcohol Abuse and Alcoholism, pp. 105–121. Ifill, Gwen (1992, March 30). Clinton admits experiment with marijuana in 1960's. *New York Times*, p. A13. Slater, Michael D.; Rouner, Donna; Murphy, Kevin; Beauvais, Frederick; Van Leuven, James; and Rodríguez, Melanie Domenech (1996). Male adolescents' reactions to TV beer advertisements: The effects of sports content and programming context. *Journal of Studies in Alcohol, 57*, 425–433.
2. Leshner, Alan I. (1998, October). Addiction is a brain disease—and it matters. *National Institute of Justice Journal*, 2–6.
3. Jacobs, Michael R., and Fehr, Kevin O'B. (1987). *Drugs and drug abuse: A reference text.* Toronto: Addiction Research Foundation, pp. 3–5.
4. Goode, Erich (1999). *Drugs in American society* (5th ed.). New York: McGraw-Hill College, pp. 119–125.
5. Caldwell, A. E. (1970). *Origins of psychopharmacology: From CPZ to LSD.* Springfield IL: C. C. Thomas, p. 3.
6. Metzner, Ralph (1998). Hallucinogenic drugs and plants in psychotherapy and shamanism. *Journal of Psychoactive Drugs, 30*, 333–341.
7. Inglis, Brian (1975). *The forbidden game: A social history of drugs.* New York: Scribners, pp. 11–36.
8. Bryan, Cyril P. (1930). *Ancient Egyptian medicine: The Papyrus Ebers.* Chicago: Ares Publishers.
9. Grilly, David (1998). *Drugs and human behavior.* (3rd ed.). Boston: Allyn and Bacon, p. 2.

10. Sneader, Walter (1985). *Drug discovery: The evolution of modern medicines.* New York: Wiley, pp. 15–47.
11. Ibid.
12. Levinthal, Charles F. (1988). *Messengers of paradise: Opiates and the brain.* New York: Anchor Press/Doubleday, pp. 3–25.
13. Bugliosi, Vincent (1991). *Drugs in America: The case for victory.* New York: Knightsbridge Publishers, p. 215.
14. Freud, Sigmund (1884). Über Coca (On Coca). *Centralblatt feur die gesammte Therapie.* Translated by S. Pollak (1884). *St. Louis Medical and Surgical Journal, 47.*
15. Aaron, Paul, and Musto, David (1981). Temperance and prohibition in America: A historical overview. In Mark H. Moore and Dean R. Gerstein (Eds.), *Alcohol and public policy.* Washington DC: National Academy Press, pp. 127–181.
16. Sneader, *Drug discovery,* p. 296.
17. Helmer, John (1975). *Drugs and minority oppression.* New York: Seabury Press.
18. Cantor, Norman F. (1969). *Western civilization: Its genesis and destiny.* Vol. 2. New York: Scott, Foresman, pp. 845–846.
19. Egan, Timothy (1999, February 28). War on crack retreats, still taking prisoners. *New York Times,* pp. 1, 22–23.
20. Astin, Alexander W.; Parrott, Sarah A.; Korn, William S.; and Sax, Linda J. (1997). *The American freshman: Thirty year trends.* Los Angeles: Higher Education Research Institute, UCLA. *Back to school 1999—National survey of American attitudes on substance abuse V: Teens and their parents.* New York: The National Center on Addiction and Substance Abuse at Columbia University, August, 1999.
21. Johnston, Lloyd D. (2000, December 14). "Ecstasy" use rises sharply among teens in 2000; use of many other drugs stays steady, but significant declines are reported for some. News release from the University of Michigan, Ann Arbor. Johnston, Lloyd D., O'Malley, Patrick M., and Bachman, Jerald G. (2000a). *Monitoring the Future: National survey results on drug abuse, 1975–1999. Volume I: Secondary school students.* Rockville MD: National Institute on Drug Abuse.
22. Johnston, "Ecstasy" use, Table 2. Johnston, O'Malley, and Bachman, *Monitoring the Future, Volume I,* Tables 5–2 and 5–3.
23. Johnston, O'Malley, and Bachman, *Monitoring the Future, Volume I,* Table 4–9.
24. Johnston, O'Malley, and Bachman, *Monitoring the Future, Volume I,* Table 2–2. Johnston, Lloyd D.; O'Malley, Patrick M.; and Bachman, Jerald G. (2000b). *Monitoring the Future: National survey results on drug use, 1975–1999. Volume II: College students and young adults.* Rockville MD: National Institute on Drug Abuse, Table 2–2.
25. Bachman, Jerald G.; Wadsworth, Katherine N.; O'Malley, Patrick M.; and Johnston, Lloyd D. (1997). *Smoking, drinking, and drug use in young adulthood: The impacts of new freedoms and new responsibilities.* Mahwah NJ: Lawrence Erlbaum Associates.
26. Johnston, "Ecstasy" use, Tables 2 and 3. Johnston, O'Malley, and Bachman, *Monitoring the Future, Volume I,* Tables 2–2 and 2–3.
27. Johnston, Lloyd D. (2000, December 14). Cigarette use and smokeless tobacco use decline substantially among teens. News release from the University of Michigan, Ann Arbor. Johnston, O'Malley, and Bachman, *Monitoring the Future, Volume I,* Tables 2–3 and D–49, p. 25. Wechsler, Henry; Rigotti, Nancy A.; Gledhill-Hoyt, Jeana; and Lee, Hang (1998). Increased levels of cigarette use among college students. *Journal of the American Medical Association, 260,* 1673–1678.
28. Johnston, Drug trends, Table 2. Johnston, O'Malley, and Bachman, *Monitoring the Future, Volume I,* Table 2–2.
29. Johnston, "Ecstasy" use, Table 2. Johnston, O'Malley, and Bachman, *Monitoring the Future, Volume I,* Tables 2–1, 2–2, and 2–3. Substance Abuse and Mental Health Services Administration (2000). *Summary of findings from the 1999 National Household Survey on drug abuse.* Rockville MD: Office of Applied Studies, Substance Abuse and Mental Health Services Administration, Tables G.5 through G.9, G.21 through G.25.
30. Johnston, Lloyd D. (1996, December 19). The rise in drug use among American teens continues in 1996. News release from the University of Michigan, Ann Arbor, pp. 6–7.
31. Bachman, Jerald G.; Johnston, Lloyd D.; and O'Malley, Patrick M. (1998). Explaining recent increases in students' marijuana use: Impacts of perceived risks and disapproval, 1976 through 1996. *American Journal of Public Health, 88,* 887–891. Johnston, "Ecstasy" use, Figure 2.
32. Johnston, Lloyd, and O'Malley, Patrick M. (1986). Why do the nation's students use drugs and alcohol? Self-reported reasons from nine national surveys. *The Journal of Drug Issues, 16,* 29–66.
33. Goode, *Drugs,* pp. 91–118.
34. Jessor, Richard (1992). *Risk behavior in adolescence: A psychosocial framework for understanding action.* Boulder CO: Westview Press. Newcomb, Michael D.; Maddahian, Ebrahim; Skager, Rodney; and Bentler, P. M. (1987). Substance abuse and psychosocial risk factors among teenagers: Associations with sex, age, ethnicity, and type of school. *American Journal of Drug and Alcohol Abuse, 13,* 413–433.
35. Kandel, Denise B. (1980). Drug and drinking behavior among youth. *Annual Review of Sociology, 6,* 235–285.
36. Perez, R.; Padilla, A. M.; Ramirez, A.; and Rodríguez, M. (1980). Correlates and changes over time in drug and alcohol use within a barrio population. *American Journal of Community Psychology, 8,* 621–636. Watts, W. David, and Wright, Loyd S. (1990). The drug use-violent delinquency link among adolescent Mexican-Americans. In Mario De la Rosa, Elizabeth Y. Lambert, and Bernard Gropper (Eds.), *Drugs and violence: Causes, correlates, and consequences* (NIDA Research Monograph 103). Rockville MD: National Institute on Drug Abuse.

37. Fawzy, F. L.; Coombs, R. H.; Simon, J. M.; and Bowman-Terrell, M. (1987). Family composition, socioeconomic status, and adolescent substance use. *Addictive Behaviors, 12,* 79–83.
38. Scheier, Lawrence M., Botvin, Gilbert J., and Baker, Eli (1997). Risk and protective factors as predictors of adolescent alcohol involvement and transitions in alcohol use: A prospective analysis. *Journal of Studies in Alcohol,* 58, 652–667. Scheier, Lawrence M., Newcomb, Michael D., and Skager, Rodney (1994). Risk, protection, and vulnerability to adolescent drug use: Latent-variable models of three age groups. *Journal of Drug Education, 24,* 49–82.
39. Smith, Carolyn; Lizotte, Alan J.; Thornberry, Terence P.; and Krohn, Marvin D. (1995). Resilient youth: Identifying factors that prevent high-risk youth from engaging in delinquency and drug use. In J. Hagan (Ed.), *Delinquency and disrepute in the life course.* Greenwich CT: JAI Press, pp. 217–247.
40. Scales, Peter C., and Leffert, Nancy (1999). *Developmental assets: A synthesis of the scientific research on adolescent development.* Minneapolis: Search Institute. The power of assets, from the Search Institute web site, 2000.
41. Johnston, "Ecstasy" use, Table 6. Office of National Drug Control Policy (1998, Winter). *Pulse check: Trends in drug abuse, January–June 1998,* Washington DC: Office of National Drug Control Policy. Sabbag, Robert (1994, May 5). The cartels would like a second chance. *Rolling Stone,* pp. 35–37, 43. Wilkinson, Peter (1994, May 5). The young and the reckless. *Rolling Stone,* pp. 29, 32.
42. National Institute on Drug Abuse (1999, December). *Community drug alert bulletin: Club drugs.* Bethesda MD: National Institute on Drug Abuse. Office of National Drug Control Policy, *Pulse check.*
43. Lane, Earl (1999, May 9). FDA's message on a bottle. *Newsday,* pp. A7, A40–A41. The rise of alternative medicine (1997). *Pharmaceutical Practice, 13,* 50. Wong, Albert H. C., Smith, Michael, and Boon, Heather S. (1998). Herbal remedies in psychiatric practice. *Archives of General Psychiatry* , 55, 1033–1044.
44. Dietary supplement claims: FDA eases restrictions; consumer advocates wary of harmful effects (2000, January 6). *Newsday,* p. A22. Quotation by Bruce Silverglade.

Drug-Taking Behavior: The Personal and Social Concerns

After you have completed this chapter, you will understand

- The personal and social dangers of drug abuse
- Effective and lethal dose-response curves as indices of drug toxicity
- The DAWN statistics as measures of drug-related medical emergencies
- Drug tolerance and its problems for drug abusers
- The distinction between physical and psychological dependence
- The impact of drug abuse on pregnancy and AIDS
- The relationship between drug abuse and violent crime
- U.S. drug enforcement policy as an attempt to regulate drug-taking behavior

"It doesn't seem to matter whether you're on or off crack . . . you're crazy both times. If you're high, you think someone's goin' ta do something to you, or try an' take your stuff. If you're comin' down or are waiting to make a buy or just get off, you seem to get upset easy. . . . A lot of people been cut just because somebody looked at them funny or said somethin' stupid."[1]

—*A seventeen-year-old crack cocaine abuser*

Ask someone whether drugs present a major problem in the United States today, and you will get a loud, clear, affirmative answer. This is probably the only aspect of drug-taking behavior on which our opinions are unanimous. On a consistent basis, Americans rank drug abuse among the most important problems facing the nation, as reported by the Gallup Poll and other major surveys.[2] Yet, just because people agree that we have a problem does not necessarily mean that we are on the way to resolving it. A better question might focus on a more tangible issue. What are the specific problems that drugs present to us as individuals and to society?

This is more than an academic question. If we are to expend our energies as well as our public funds on ways to reduce "the drug problem," it is important to know or at least reach some degree of consensus as to where the problems are and which problems are most deserving of our efforts. Here is where people disagree and controversy exists. This chapter will concern itself with the various aspects of drugs that are known to present significant problems for individuals and for society in general. It will then explore the response our society has made to these problems, in the form of governmental policy.

At the outset we should recognize that the real culprits are not the drugs per se but rather certain forms of drug-taking behavior. If a drug, for example, were totally without any redeeming value (let us say it was extremely poisonous), most people would simply avoid it. It would have no street value (other than perhaps to a terrorist), and no one would seriously object to measures that restricted access to it. It would be a totally "bad" drug, but few people would care about it at all. When we characterize cocaine and heroin, for example, as "bad drugs" we are essentially saying that society has balanced the perceived risks of heroin or cocaine *use* against any potential benefits. Heroin as well as other opiates such as opium and morphine are excellent painkillers and have been used medically in many countries of the world. Cocaine is an excellent local anesthetic and has been used in a large number of medical procedures in the United States. Society has decided, however, that these positive applications in medicine are outweighed by the negative consequences for the general public, on both a personal and a social level.

The importance of focusing on drug-taking behavior rather than simply on drugs can be highlighted by a bizarre but true story from the mid-1970s. At that time, a number of male patients were being treated for alcoholism in a Veterans Administration hospital in California. In one ward, a patient was observed moving his bed into the men's room. Shortly afterward, several of his fellow patients, one by one, did the same.

What was behind this curious behavior? Evidently, these men, deprived of alcohol after years of alcohol abuse, had discovered that drinking enormous amounts of water, more than seven gallons a day, produced a "high" by altering the acid-to-base balance of their blood. They had found a medically dangerous but psychologically effective way of getting drunk. The fact that they were also urinating approximately the same amount of water each day accounted for their decision to move into the men's room.[3] The point of the story is that, in this case, water had become a psychoactive substance without technically being a drug (recall the definition from Chapter 1). Once again, the focus should be placed on the particular behavior and its consequences rather than on the substance itself.

In this chapter, our examination of the personal and social problems associated with drug-taking behavior will focus on three broad categories: the potential for toxicity, the potential for behavioral and physiological dependence, and finally the connection between drug-taking behavior and violence and crime. Subsequent chapters will address other issues of concern with regard to specific types of drugs.

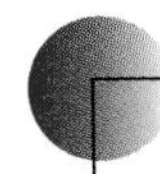

Drug Toxicity

When we say that a drug is toxic, we are referring to the fact that it may be dangerous, poisonous, or in some way interfering with a person's normal functioning. Technically, any substance, no matter how benign, has the potential for **toxicity** if the **dose,** the amount in which the substance is taken, is high enough. The question of a drug's safety, or its relative safety when compared to other drugs, centers on the possibility that it may be toxic at relatively low doses. We certainly do not want people to harm themselves accidentally when taking the drug in the course of their daily lives. When there is a possibility that the *short-term* effects of a particular drug will trigger a toxic reaction, then this drug is identified as having some level of **acute toxicity.**

toxicity (tox-IHS-ih-tee): The physical or psychological harm that a drug might present to the user.
dose: The quantity of drug that is taken into the body, typically measured in terms of milligrams (mg) or micrograms (μg).
acute toxicity: The physical or psychological harm a drug might present to the user immediately or soon after the drug is ingested into the body.

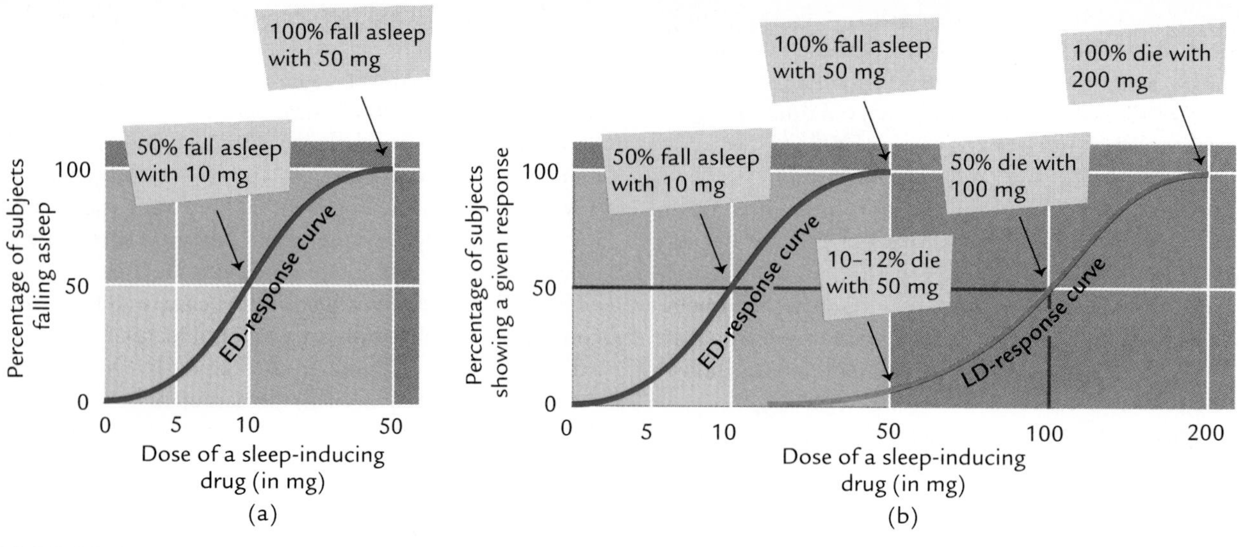

FIGURE 2.1

(a) An effective dose-response curve, and (b) an effective dose-response curve (left) alongside a lethal dose-response curve (right).

To understand the principle of toxicity in general, we need to examine an S-shaped graph called the **dose-response curve** (Figure 2.1a). Let us assume we have the results of data collected from laboratory tests of a hypothetical sleep-inducing drug. Increases in the dose level of the drug are producing the desired sleep-inducing effect in an increasingly large percentage of a test population of mice. At 10 milligrams (mg), 50 percent of the population has fallen asleep; at 50 mg, 100 percent has done so. There is always some variability in individual reactions to any drug; some mice may be internally resistant to the drug's effect while others may be quite susceptible. Any one animal may fall asleep with an extremely low dose or a dose of 50 mg, so we have to think of the **effective dose** (ED) of a drug on a test population in terms of probabilities, from 0 percent to 100 percent.

For example, the ED50 of a drug refers to the effective dose for 50 percent of the population; ED99 refers to the effective dose for 99 percent of the population. In this case, the ED numbers refer to the drug's effect of producing sleep. The same drug may be producing other effects (muscular relaxation, for instance) at lower doses; these drug effects would have their own separate dose-response curves. It is a good idea to remember that we are looking at the properties of a drug *effect* here, not the properties of the drug itself.

Now we can look at Figure 2.1b, where the effective dose-response curve is represented along with another S-shaped dose-response curve, also gathered from laboratory testing, in which the "response" is death. It makes sense that the second curve should be shifted to the right since the **lethal dose** (LD) generally involves greater amounts of a drug than the amounts necessary to produce an effect.

Emphasis should be placed on the word "generally" because the lethal dose-response curve overlaps with the effective dose-response curve in this example. While a 100 mg dose has to be taken in order to kill 50 percent of the test population, it can be seen that a dose of as little as 50 mg (or less) is lethal for at least a few of them. The LD50 of a drug refers to the lethal dose for 50 percent of the population; LD1 refers to a relatively lower dose that is lethal for 1 percent of the population.

It is useful to combine the effective and lethal doses of a drug in a ratio to arrive at some idea of that drug's

dose-response curve: An S-shaped graph showing the increasing probability of a certain drug effect as the dose level rises.

effective dose: The minimal dose of a particular drug necessary to produce the intended drug effect in a given percentage of the population.

lethal dose: The minimal dose of a particular drug capable of producing death in a given percentage of the population.

QUICK CONCEPT  2.1

Understanding Dose-Response Curves

Check your understanding of dose-response curves and the toxicity of drugs by answering the following question.

The following three sets of dose-response curves show the effective and lethal responses to three drugs A, B, and C.

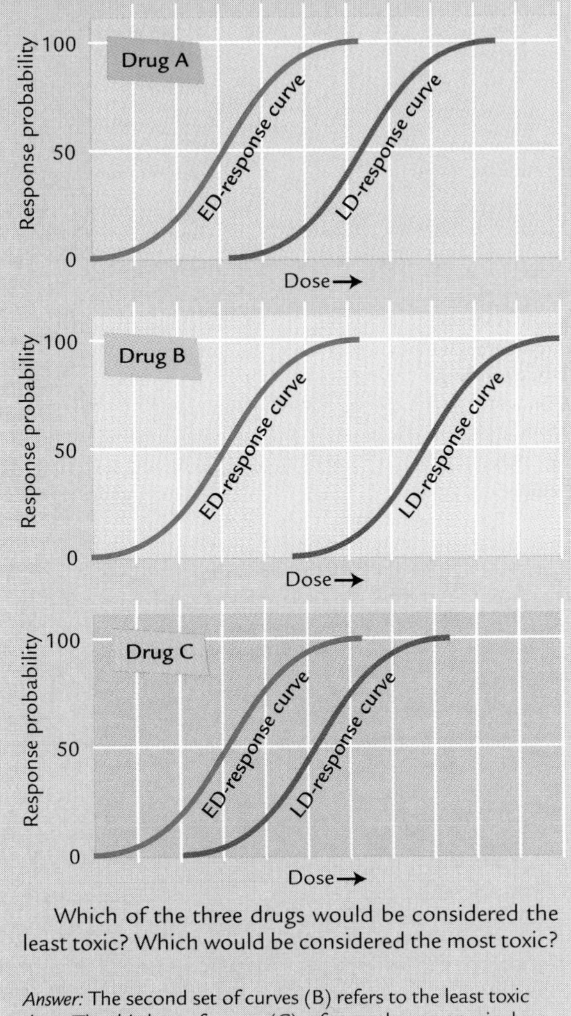

Which of the three drugs would be considered the least toxic? Which would be considered the most toxic?

Answer: The second set of curves (B) refers to the least toxic drug. The third set of curves (C) refers to the most toxic drug.

toxicity. The ratio of LD50/ED50 is called the **therapeutic index.** If the LD50 for a drug is 450 mg and the ED50 is 50 mg, then the therapeutic index is 9. In other words, you would have to take nine times the dose that would be effective for half of the population in order to incur a 50 percent chance of dying.

It can be argued, however, that a 50 percent probability of dying represents an unacceptably high risk even for a drug that has genuine benefits. To be more conservative in the direction of safety, the ratio of LD1/ED99 is often calculated. Here we are calculating the ratio between the dose that produces death in 1 percent of the population and the dose that would be effective in 99 percent. This second ratio, called the **margin of safety,** should be as high as possible. The higher the ratio, the safer, or less toxic, the drug. It can be seen that the margin of safety for the hypothetical drug examined in Figure 2.1 would present serious toxicity problems.

The therapeutic index or the margin of safety is very helpful when considering the toxicity of drugs that are manufactured by recognized pharmaceutical companies and regulated by the FDA, keeping in mind the possibility that a person might intentionally or unintentionally take a higher-than-recommended dose of the drug. But what about the toxicity risks in consuming illicit drugs? The reality of street drugs is that the buyer has no way of knowing what he or she has bought until the drug has been used, and then it is frequently too late.

Few if any illicit drug sellers make a pretense of being ethical businesspeople; their only objective is to make money and avoid prosecution by the law. Frequently, the drugs they sell are diluted with either inert or highly dangerous ingredients. Adulterated heroin, for example, may contain a high proportion of milk sugar as a harmless filler and a dash of quinine to simulate the bitter taste of real heroin, when the actual amount of heroin that is being sold is far less than the "standard" street dosage. At the other extreme, the content of heroin may be unexpectedly high and may lead to a lethal overdose, or else it may contain animal tranquilizers, arsenic, strychnine, insecticides, or other highly toxic substances.[4] Cocaine, LSD, marijuana, and all the other illicit drugs that are available to the drug abuser, as well as look-alike drugs that are unauthorized copies of popular prescription medications, present hidden and unpredictable risks of toxicity. Even if drugs are procured from a friend or someone you know, these risks remain. Neither of you is likely to

therapeutic index: A measure of a drug's relative safety for use, computed by the ratio of the lethal dose for 50 percent of the population over the effective dose for 50 percent of the population.

margin of safety: The ratio of a lethal dose for 1 percent of the population to the effective dose for 99 percent of the population.

Drugs . . . in Focus

Acute Toxicity in the News: Drug-Related Deaths

The following famous people have died either as a direct consequence or as an indirect consequence of drug misuse or abuse.

NAME	YEAR OF DEATH	AGE	REASONS GIVEN FOR DEATH
Marilyn Monroe actress	1962	36	overdose of Nembutal (a sedative-hypnotic medication); circumstances unknown
Lenny Bruce comedian	1966	40	accidental overdose of morphine
Judy Garland singer, actress	1969	47	accidental overdose of sleeping pills
Janis Joplin singer	1970	27	accidental overdose of heroin and alcohol
Jimi Hendrix singer, guitarist	1970	27	accidental overdose of sleeping pills
Elvis Presley singer, actor	1977	42	cardiac arrhythmia suspected to be due to an interaction of antihistamine, codeine, and Demerol (a painkiller), as well as Valium and several other tranquilizers
John Belushi comedian, actor	1982	33	accidental overdose of heroin combined with cocaine
David A. Kennedy, son of Robert F. Kennedy, U.S. senator	1984	28	accidental interaction of cocaine, Demerol, and Mellaril (an antipsychotic medication)
Len Bias college basketball player	1986	22	cardiac-respiratory arrest from accidental overdose of cocaine
Don Rogers professional football player	1986	23	cardiac-respiratory arrest from accidental overdose of cocaine
Abbie Hoffman antiwar and political activist	1989	52	suicide using phenobarbital combined with alcohol
River Phoenix actor	1993	23	cardiac-respiratory arrest from accidental combination of heroin and cocaine
Jonathan Melvoin keyboardist for the Smashing Pumpkins rock group	1996	34	accidental overdose of heroin
Chris Farley comedian, actor	1998	33	accidental overdose of heroin and cocaine

Note: Celebrities whose drug-related deaths have been attributed to the toxicity of alcohol alone or nicotine, tars, or carbon monoxide in tobacco products are not included in this listing.

Sources: Various media reports.

know the exact ingredients. The dangers of acute toxicity are always present.

Given the uncertainty that exists about the contents of many abused drugs, what measure or index of acute toxicity can we use to evaluate their effects on individuals in society? The natural tendency is to look first to the news headlines; think of all the well-known public individuals who have died as a direct consequence of drug misuse or abuse (Drugs . . . in Focus). Such examples, however, can be misleading. Celebrities are not necessarily representative of the drug-using population in general, and the drugs prevalent among celebrities, because of their expense, may not represent the drugs most frequently encountered by the rest of society. In order to have some idea of the toxic effects of psychoactive drugs in a broader context, we have to turn to the institutions that contend with drug toxicity on a daily basis: the emergency departments of hospitals around the country.

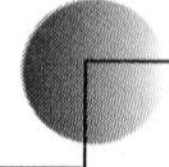

The DAWN Reports

Since 1980, the U.S. government has gathered data concerning drug-related medical emergencies in major metropolitan hospitals, through a program called the **Drug Abuse Warning Network (DAWN).** Two basic pieces of information are reported. The first concerns the

TABLE 2.1

Most frequent emergency department (ED) and medical examiner (ME) mentions

ED MENTIONS	1998 NUMBER OF MENTIONS	1998 PERCENTAGE OF TOTAL EPISODES	ME MENTIONS	1998 NUMBER OF MENTIONS	1998 PERCENTAGE OF TOTAL EPISODES
1. Alcohol-in-combination	185,002	34.1%	1. Cocaine	4,587	45.3%
2. Cocaine	172,014	31.7	2. Heroin/morphine	4,330	42.8
3. Heroin/morphine	77,645	14.3	3. Alcohol-in-combination	3,723	36.8
4. Marijuana/hashish	76,870	14.2	4. Codeine	1,240	12.3
5. Acetaminophen (Tylenol)	32,257	6.0	5. Diazepam (Valium)	781	7.7
6. Unspecified benzodiazepine	25,927	4.8	6. Marijuana/hashish	598	5.9
7. Alprazolam (Xanax)	17,833	3.3	7. Methadone	560	5.5
8. Clonazepam (Klonopin)	17,450	3.2	8. Diphenhydramine (Benadryl)	504	5.0
9. Ibuprofen (Advil)	17,146	3.2	9. Methamphetamine/speed	501	4.9
10. Aspirin	15,457	2.9	10. D-propoxyphene (Darvon)	423	4.2
11. Diazepam (Valium)	12,758	2.4	11. Amitriptyline (Elavil)	407	4.0
12. Hydrocodone	12,568	2.3	12. Nortripyline (Parmelor)	402	4.0
			13. Acetaminophen (Tylenol)	401	4.0

Note: Percentages add up to more than 100 because multiple drugs are often mentioned in each case. Some representative brand names are included in parentheses. Benzodiazepine is a category of antianxiety medications.

Sources: Substance Abuse and Mental Health Services Administration (2000). *Drug Abuse Warning Network annual emergency department data 1998.* Rockville MD: Office of Applied Studies, Substance Abuse and Mental Health Services Administration, Table 2.06a. Substance Abuse and Mental Health Services Administration (2000). *Drug Abuse Warning Network annual medical examiner data 1998.* Rockville MD: Office of Applied Studies, Substance Abuse and Mental Health Services Administration, p. 39.

number of cases in which a patient comes to an emergency department (ED) and mentions that the emergency was related to a particular drug or combination of drugs. These statistics are referred to literally as *ED mentions* and can refer to a range of emergency-department situations, from a relatively minor panic attack to a nearly successful suicide attempt. The second piece of information concerns the number of cases in which the patient actually dies and the coroner or medical examiner (ME) reports the death to be drug related. These latter cases are referred to as *ME mentions.*

The DAWN reports for 1998 are shown in Table 2.1, but before we look closely at the numbers, it is important to understand some basic problems we face in trying to interpret the data. The first is that the ED counts are based only on the drugs that are actually mentioned by the patient at the time of the emergency; what the patient says may or may not accurately reflect what is actually inside the patient's body. In the midst of a medical crisis, it is natural that a patient may be either extremely confused and disoriented, in considerable pain, or consciously concealing the reason for coming to the hospital. Consequently, statistical errors can be expected. In one study, laboratory tests showing the presence of drugs in the patient's body were compared with the DAWN ED-mention reports. The test results and the DAWN reports were identical in only 20 percent of the cases examined. Ten percent showed totally different drugs to be involved; in 70 percent the laboratory tests showed a greater number of drugs to be in the patient's body than the drug the patient had mentioned.[5] The DAWN reporting forms allow for the reporting of multiple drugs, up to four in the case of ED mentions and up to six in the case of ME mentions, and therefore give us some idea of medical problems associated with drug combinations. Even so, it turns out that much of this information is incomplete.

A second problem is that the information we are getting in the DAWN statistics is only from a group of urban hospitals. While approximately one-third of the U.S. population is served by these hospitals, we are not examining a random sample of the nation as a whole. Therefore, the absolute numbers may underestimate or overestimate

Drug Abuse Warning Network (DAWN): A federal program in which metropolitan hospitals report the incidence of drug-related lethal and nonlethal emergencies.

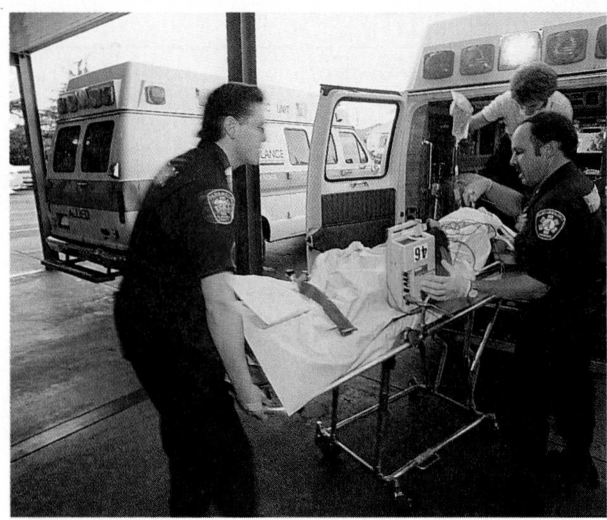

Emergency medical crews frequently have to deal with drug-related cases.

the actual extent of medical emergencies associated with a particular drug. Furthermore, medical examiners in urban hospitals reporting DAWN statistics perform only 60 percent of all autopsies in the United States. As a result, the ME-mention statistics may not necessarily reflect the actual extent of fatalities associated with a particular drug.[6]

A third problem centers around the absence of ED or ME mentions concerning alcohol alone. There is a very good reason for this omission. If emergencies related to alcohol alone were reported, the numbers would far exceed those related to any other drug, particularly when we consider the high percentage of car accidents and deaths resulting from drunk drivers. We would be reporting many hundreds of thousands of ED and ME mentions (see Chapter 9), more than all the other categories combined.

What is reported, instead, is the number of emergencies that result from cases in which alcohol is mentioned in conjunction with some other drug. These are referred to as *alcohol-in-combination mentions.* The high incidence of alcohol-in-combination cases, 34 percent of all ED mentions and 37 percent of all ME mentions, is an indication of the substantial percentage of emergencies arising not from one drug alone but rather from drug mixing, or **polydrug use.** About 75 percent of ED and ME mentions referred to combinations of two or more drugs.[7]

Clearly, as Table 2.1 shows, cocaine and opiates such as heroin or morphine account for a large portion of lethal drug-related emergencies, 45 percent and 43 percent, respectively. These statistics are quite dramatic, considering that there are relatively few cocaine and opiate users in the total population in the first place. In other words, a large percentage of drug-related deaths, as defined by the DAWN reports, is associated with a relatively small segment of society.

In contrast, a considerably larger number of people who smoke marijuana are involved in relatively fewer nonlethal emergencies (largely owing to panic attacks that bring them to the hospital). In 1998, the DAWN statistics showed that only two of the reported 598 ME mentions regarding marijuana were attributed to the direct effects of marijuana alone. The rest were the result of a combination of marijuana and some other drug or some other factor present at the time.

The comparison of ED and ME mentions regarding marijuana versus those regarding heroin and cocaine illustrates the need for caution in assessing the relative toxicity levels of various drugs from the DAWN statistics alone. It is important to examine the information in terms of a ratio, the number of drug-related emergencies in relation to the total number of drug users. For example, if one drug produced twice the number of ED and ME mentions as a second one but the number of users of the first drug was twice that of the second, then the toxicity levels of the two drugs would actually be equivalent.[8]

There is another feature of Table 2.1 that deserves attention. A considerable portion of the ED and ME mentions highlights the consequences of ingesting commonly prescribed or widely available over-the-counter medications. They include pain relievers such as acetaminophen (Tylenol), ibuprofen (Advil), d-propoxyphene (Darvon), and codeine. Others include antianxiety medications such as clonazepam (Klonopin), alprazolam (Xanax), and diazepam (Valium), as well as the antidepressant medication amitriptyline (Elavil).

There is no question that these medications have the potential for acute toxicity. However, the fact that licit medications appear as ED and ME mentions in the "most frequent" lists should be tempered by two observations. First, the quantities of these medications ingested in these circumstances had either far exceeded the recommended levels of dosage, or they had been combined with one or more other drugs, some licit and some illicit. Second, the total number of mentions regarding licit medications still does not come close to the number of mentions regarding specific illicit drugs or the alcohol-in-

polydrug use: Drug-taking behavior involving two or more drugs simultaneously.

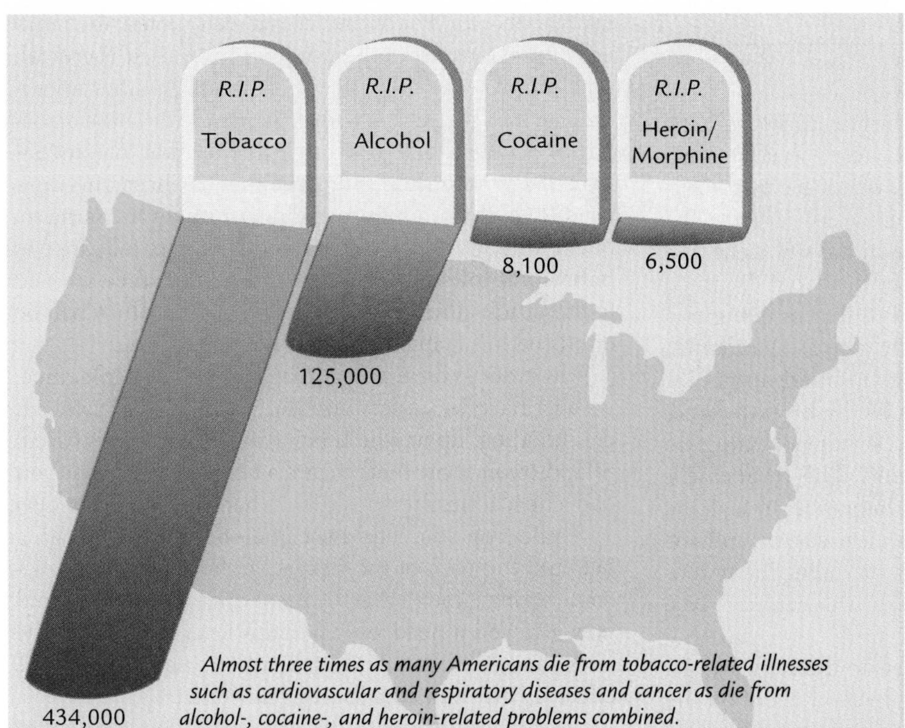
R.I.P.
Tobacco
R.I.P.
Alcohol
R.I.P.
Cocaine
R.I.P.
Heroin/
Morphine
8,100
6,500
125,000
434,000
Almost three times as many Americans die from tobacco-related illnesses such as cardiovascular and respiratory diseases and cancer as die from alcohol-, cocaine-, and heroin-related problems combined.

FIGURE 2.2

U.S. deaths per year from tobacco use as well as alcohol and other drug use, ca. 1990.
Source: National Institute on Drug Abuse (1994, September/October). *NIDA Notes,* p. 5.

combination category. The bottom line is that problems of acute toxicity can certainly occur as a result of the misuse of licit medications, but the primary culprits remain heroin and morphine, cocaine, and the use of alcohol in combination with other drugs.

DAWN statistics show that men and women appear in approximately equal numbers among ED mentions, but men outnumber woman by roughly three to one in the ME mentions. In other words, the lethal drug-related emergencies are more likely to involve male drug users.[9]

Since DAWN reports have been issued for more than a decade, we can get some idea of the changes that have taken place in the frequency of medical emergencies related to specific drugs in recent years. There has been a steady increase in heroin-related emergencies, almost certainly because the purity of available heroin is currently far higher than ever before. There has also been a dramatic increase in the number of cocaine-related emergencies, a result of the greater numbers of individuals using cocaine and changes in the way the drug is consumed. Smoking or injecting cocaine, more common practices since the mid-1980s, is more potentially lethal than snorting it. A recent increase in reported deaths due to the ingestion of methamphetamine (speed) has been attributed to a rise in that drug's popularity (and abuse), particularly in the western United States.

Through the DAWN reports we can appreciate the extent of acute toxicity involved with the ingestion of a particular drug, but we are unable to understand anything about the negative consequences of using a particular drug over a long period of time, the drug's **chronic toxicity.** Examples of chronic toxicity can be found in a wide range of psychoactive drugs, both legally and illegally obtained. Ironically, it is the chronic use of alcohol and tobacco that causes by far the greatest adverse health effects in our society. As we will see in Chapters 10 and 11, the number of people who die each year as a result of the drinking of alcohol or smoking of tobacco far outstrips the number of fatalities from the abuse of illicit drugs (Figure 2.2). What exactly are the problems associated with chronic drug-taking behavior? What is the best way to look at drug dependence in general? These are some of the questions to be examined in the next section.

chronic toxicity: The physical or psychological harm a drug might cause over a long period of time.

Drug Tolerance

Legend has it that in the first century B.C., King Mithridates VI of Pontus, a region near the Black Sea, grew despondent following a series of defeats by the Romans and decided to commit suicide by poison. The problem was that no amount of poison was sufficient, and the grim task had to be completed by the sword. It turned out that Mithridates, having lived in fear of being poisoned by rivals, had taken gradually increasing amounts of poison over the course of his life to build immunity. By the time he wanted to end his life by his own hand, he could tolerate such large doses that poisoning no longer presented any lethal possibility. This royal case is the first recorded example of drug tolerance. In fact, the phenomenon originally was called *mithridatism*, and several celebrated poisoners of history, including the notorious Lucretia Borgia in the early sixteenth century, were later to use the same technique.[10]

The concept of **tolerance** refers to the capacity of a drug dose to have a gradually diminished effect on the user as the drug is taken repeatedly. Another way of viewing tolerance is to say that over repeated administrations a drug dose needs to be increased in order to maintain an equivalent effect. A common illustration is the effect of caffeine in coffee. When you are first introduced to caffeine, the stimulant effect is usually quite pronounced; you might feel noticeably "wired" after a 5-ounce cup of coffee, containing approximately 100 mg of caffeine. After several days or perhaps a few weeks of coffee drinking, the effect is greatly diminished; you may be on the second or third cup by that time, consuming 200 to 300 mg of caffeine, in order to duplicate the earlier reaction. Some individuals who drink coffee regularly have developed such high levels of tolerance to caffeine that they are able to sleep comfortably even after several cups of coffee, while individuals with more infrequent ingestions of caffeine end up awake through the night after a single cup.

The danger that the tolerance effect presents is the possibility of death by drug overdose, frequently the cause of lethal emergencies (ME mentions) listed in the DAWN reports. Individuals involved in drug abuse are often taking drug doses that are precariously close to the LD-response curve amounts, as described earlier. These dosage levels may be sustainable by a drug abuser who has grown tolerant to the drug over repeated administrations but quite lethal to an individual being introduced to the drug for the first time.

Tolerance effects, in general, illustrate the need for us to look at the *interaction* between the actual amount of the drug taken and other factors involved in the drug-taking behavior. For example, as already noted, the number of previous times the drug has been used is crucial; repetition is what tolerance is all about. Another important factor is the setting within which the drug-taking behavior occurs. There is strong evidence that tolerance is maximized when the drug-taking behavior occurs consistently in the same surroundings or under the same set of circumstances.[11] We speak of this form of tolerance as **behavioral tolerance.** Other forms of tolerance are tied to the purely physiological effects of a drug; they will be discussed in Chapter 3.

In order to have a clear idea of behavioral tolerance, we first have to understand the processes of Pavlovian conditioning, upon which behavioral tolerance is based. Suppose you consistently heard a bell ring every time you had a headache. Previously, bells had never had any negative effect on you. The association between the ringing bell and the pain of the headache, however, would become strong enough that the mere ringing of a bell would now give you a headache, perhaps less painful than the ones you had originally but a headache nonetheless; this effect is Pavlovian conditioning at work.

A pioneering study by the psychologist Shepard Siegel showed a similar phenomenon occurring with drug-taking behavior. In his experiment, one group of rats was injected with doses of morphine in a particular room over a series of days and later tested for tolerance to that dose in the same room. Predictably, they displayed a lessened analgesic effect as a sign of morphine tolerance. A second group was tested in a room other than the one in which the injections had been given. No tolerance developed at all. They reacted as if they had never been given morphine before, even though they had received the same number of repeated injections as the first group.

Siegel explained the results by assuming that environmental cues in the room had elicited physiological effects *opposite* to the effect of the drug, in this case a heightened sensitivity to pain, or hyperalgesia. This compensatory effect produced by the environment would par-

tolerance: The capacity of a drug to produce a gradually diminished physical or psychological effect upon repeated administrations of the drug at the same dose level.

behavioral tolerance: The process of drug tolerance that is linked to drug-taking behavior occurring consistently in the same surroundings or under the same circumstances. Also known as *conditioned tolerance.*

QUICK CONCEPT  2.2

Understanding Behavioral Tolerance through Conditioning

Check your understanding of behavioral tolerance as proposed by Shepard Siegel by answering the following questions.

Suppose you have a rat that has been placed in an environment where it had been repeatedly injected with morphine. You now inject that rat with a saline solution (a substance that has no physiological effect). Assuming that morphine will make a person less sensitive to pain, how will this animal react to the saline injection? Will the rat be less sensitive to pain, more sensitive to pain, or will there be no effect? Explain your answer.

Answer: The rat will now be more sensitive to pain. The exposure to an environment associated with morphine injections will have induced a conditioned compensatory effect: a heightened sensitivity to pain. The saline injection produces no physiological effect of its own; however, because it is given in that same environment where the morphine was administered, the conditioned effect will remain and the rat's reaction will be hyperalgesia. (The experiment has been performed, by the way, and this predicted outcome does occur.)

tially counteract the analgesic effect of the drug, and the combination of the two effects would end up as a diminished response. Rats in the first group would be less affected by the morphine over time because there had been a consistent relationship between the environment in which the injections occurred and the injections themselves.[12]

This behavioral account of drug tolerance, also known as *conditioned tolerance*, explains why a heroin addict may easily suffer the consequences of an overdose when the drug has been taken in a different environment from the one more frequently encountered or in a manner different from his or her ordinary routine.[13] The range of tolerated doses of heroin can be enormous; amounts in the 200 to 500 mg range may be lethal for a first-time heroin user while amounts as high as 1800 mg may not even be sufficient to make a long-term heroin user sick.[14] You can imagine how dangerous it would be then if the conditioned compensatory responses a heroin addict had built up over time were suddenly absent.

Behavioral tolerance also helps to explain why a formerly drug-dependent individual is strongly advised to avoid the surroundings associated with his or her past drug-taking behavior. If these surroundings provoked a physiological effect opposite to the effect of the drug through their association with prior drug-taking behavior, then a return to this environment might create internal changes that only drugs could reverse. In effect, environmentally induced withdrawal symptoms would increase the chances of a relapse. The fact that conditioning effects have been demonstrated not only with respect to heroin but with alcohol, cocaine, nicotine, and other dependence-producing drugs as well makes it imperative that these phenomena be considered during the course of drug abuse treatment and rehabilitation.[15]

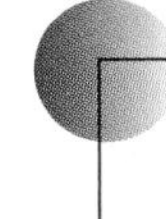

Physical and Psychological Dependence

When we refer to the idea of dependence in drug abuse, we are dealing with the fact that a person has a strong compulsion to continue taking a particular drug. Two possible models or explanations for why drug dependence occurs can be considered. The first is referred to as physical dependence, and the second is referred to as psychological dependence. The two models are not mutually exclusive; the abuse of some drugs can be a result of both physical and psychological dependence while the abuse of others can be a result of psychological dependence alone.

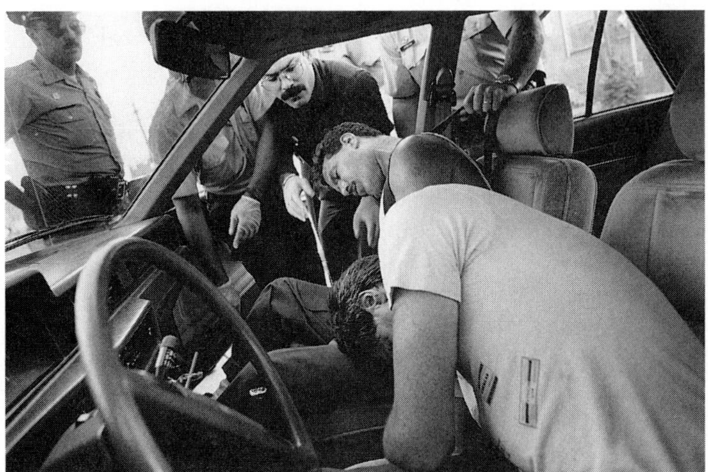

Having overdosed on pure heroin, the driver in the car has already died and the passenger would die soon afterward. The police found a needle injected through the driver's pants leg. The two men had just cashed their paychecks and bought the drugs.

Physical Dependence

The concept of **physical dependence** originates from observations of heroin addicts, as well as of those who abuse other opiate drugs, who developed strong physical symptoms following heroin withdrawal: a runny nose, chills and fever, inability to sleep, and hypersensitivity to pain. For barbiturate addicts in a comparable situation, symptoms include anxiety, inability to sleep, and sometimes lethal convulsions.[16] For chronic alcoholics, abstention can produce tremors, nausea, weakness, and tachycardia (a fast heart rate). If severe, symptoms may include delirium, seizures, and hallucinations.[17]

While the actual symptoms vary according to the drug being withdrawn, the fact that we observe physical symptoms at all suggests very strongly that some kind of physical need, perhaps as far down as the cellular level, has developed over the course of drug abuse. It is as if the drug, previously a foreign chemical, has become a normal part of the nervous system, and its removal and absence become abnormal. From this point of view, it is predictable that the withdrawal symptoms would involve symptoms that are opposite to effects the drug originally had on the body. For example, heroin can be extremely constipating, but eventually the body compensates for heroin's intestinal effects. Abrupt abstinence from heroin releases the processes that have been counteracting the constipation and the result of withdrawal is diarrhea. You may have noticed a strong resemblance between the action-counteraction phenomena of withdrawal and the processes Siegel has hypothesized as the basis for behavioral tolerance.

Psychological Dependence

The most important implication of the model of physical dependence, as distinct from psychological dependence, is that individuals involved in drug abuse continue the drug-taking behavior, at least in part, *in order to avoid the feared consequences of withdrawal.* This idea can form the basis for a general model of drug dependence only if physical withdrawal symptoms appear consistently for every drug considered as a drug of abuse. It turns out, however, that a number of abused drugs (cocaine, hallucinogens, and marijuana, for example) do not produce physical withdrawal symptoms, and the effects of heroin withdrawal are more variable than we would expect if physical dependence alone were at work. It is possible that drug abusers continue to take the drug not because they want to avoid the symptoms of withdrawal but because they crave the pleasurable effects of the drug itself. They may even feel that they need the drug in order to function at all. This is the way one heroin addict has expressed it:

> *I'm just trying to get high as much as possible. I would have to spend $25 a day on heroin to avoid withdrawal, but I actually use about $59 worth. If I could get more money, I would spend it all on drugs. All I want is to get loaded. I just really like shooting dope. I don't have any use for sex; I'd rather shoot dope. I like to shoot dope better than anything else in the world. I have to steal something every day to get my dope.*[18]

Many heroin addicts (between 56 percent to 77 percent in one major study) who complete the withdrawal process after abstaining from the drug become readdicted.[19] If physical dependence were the whole story, these phenomena would not exist. The withdrawal symptoms would have been gone by that time, and any physical need that may have been evident before would no longer be present.

When we speak of **psychological dependence,** we are offering an explanation of drug abuse based not upon the attempt of abusers to avoid unpleasant withdrawal symptoms but upon their desire to obtain pleasurable effects from the drug. Unfortunately, we are faced here with a major conceptual problem: The explanation by itself is circular and tells us basically nothing. If I were to say, for example, that I was taking cocaine because I was psychologically dependent on it, then I could as easily say I was psychologically dependent upon cocaine because I was abusing it. Without some *independent* justification, the only explanation for the concept of psychological dependence would be the behavior that the concept was supposed to explain!

Fortunately, there is independent evidence for the concept of psychological dependence, founded chiefly upon studies showing that animals are as capable of self-administering drugs of abuse as humans are. Using techniques developed in the late 1950s, researchers have been able to insert a **catheter** into the vein of a freely moving laboratory animal and arrange the equipment so that the animal can self-administer a drug intravenously whenever

physical dependence: A model of drug dependence based on the idea that the drug abuser continues the drug-taking behavior in order to avoid the consequences of physical withdrawal symptoms.
psychological dependence: A model of drug dependence based on the idea that the drug abuser is motivated by a craving for the pleasurable effects of the drug.
catheter (CATH-eh-ter): A device to deliver intravenous injections of a drug in a free-moving human or animal.

it presses a lever (Figure 2.3). It had been well known that animals would engage in specific behaviors in order to secure rewards such as food, water, or even electrical stimulation of certain regions of the brain. These objectives were defined as positive reinforcers because animals would learn to work in order to secure them. The question at the time was whether animals would self-administer drugs in a similar way. Could drugs be positive reinforcers as well?

The experiments showed clearly that animals would self-administer drugs such as cocaine and other stimulants, despite the fact that these drugs would not ordinarily produce physical symptoms during withdrawal. In one study, rats pressed the lever as many as 6,400 times for one administration of cocaine; others were nearly as eager for administrations of amphetamines.[20] Interestingly, a number of other drugs were aversive, judging from the reluctance of animals to work for them. Hallucinogens such as LSD, antipsychotic drugs, and antidepressant drugs were examples of drugs that animals clearly did not like.[21]

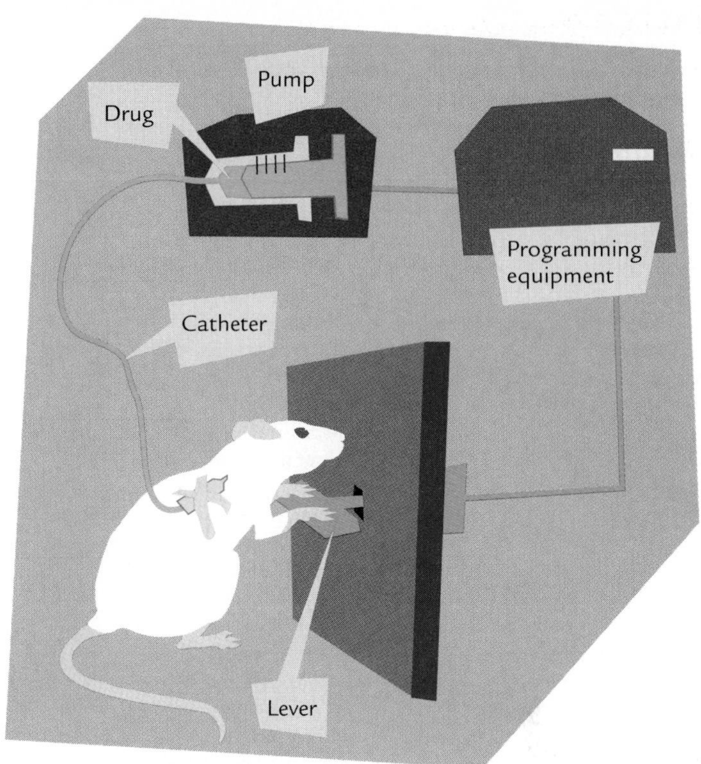

FIGURE 2.3

A simplified rendition of how drugs are self-administered in rats. The rat's pressure on a lever causes the pump to inject a drug through a catheter implanted into its vein.

By connecting the concept of psychological dependence to general principles of reinforcement, it is possible for us to appreciate the powerful effects of abused drugs. When presented with a choice of pressing levers for food or for cocaine, cocaine wins hands down even to the point of an animal starving to death.[22] When comparing the effects of heroin with cocaine, the differences are dramatic:

> *Those rats that self-administer heroin developed a stable pattern of use, maintained their pretest weight, continued good grooming behavior, and tended to be in good health. Their mortality rate was 36 percent after thirty days. Those self-administering cocaine . . . exhibited an extremely erratic pattern of use, with "binges" of heavy use alternating with brief periods of abstinence. They lost 47 percent of their body weight, ceased grooming behavior, and maintained extremely poor physical health. After thirty days, 90 percent were dead.*[23]

In the final analysis, from the standpoint of treating individuals who abuse drugs, it might not matter if there is physical dependence or psychological dependence going on. According to many experts in the field, the distinction between physical and psychological dependence has outgrown its usefulness in understanding the motivation behind drug abuse. Whether the discontinuation of an abused drug does induce major physical withdrawal symptoms (as in the case of heroin, alcohol, and barbiturates) or does not (as in the case of cocaine, amphetamines, and nicotine), the pattern of compulsive drug-taking behavior in all instances is remarkably similar. If the pattern of behavior is same, then there can be common strategies for treatment. Chapter 3 will examine the current understanding that most, if not all, drugs of abuse are linked together by virtue of common physiological processes in the brain.[24]

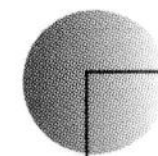

Psychiatric Definitions

Most health professionals use guidelines published by the American Psychiatric Association as a kind of official standard for defining problems associated with drug-taking behavior. In 1994 the fourth edition of the association's Diagnostic and Statistical Manual (DSM-IV) identified two specific behavioral

TABLE 2.2

Criteria for substance dependence and substance abuse according to the DSM-IV
Substance Dependence At least three out of the following must apply within a 12-month period: 1. Tolerance. The person has to take increasingly large doses of the drug to get the desired effect. Or else the person experiences a diminished effect from the same amount of the drug. 2. Withdrawal. When the drug is stopped, there are psychological or physiological withdrawal symptoms. Or else the substance is taken to relieve or avoid these symptoms. 3. Unintentional overuse. The person repeatedly takes more of the drug or takes it over a longer period of time than he or she intended. 4. Persistent desire or efforts to control drug use. The person tries to quit and repeatedly relapses into further drug use. 5. Preoccupation with the drug. The person spends a great deal of time in activities necessary to obtain the substance, use it, or recover from its effects. 6. The reduction or abandonment of important social, occupational, or recreational activities in order to engage in drug use. A person quits a job, neglects a child, or gives up other important activities. 7. Continued drug use despite major drug-related problems. A person repeatedly arrested for drug possession still maintains the drug habit, or a person with serious lung disease continues to smoke cigarettes, for example. Symptoms of the disturbance must have persisted for more than a month or occurred repeatedly over a longer period of time.
Substance Abuse At least one on the following must apply within a 12-month period: 1. Recurrent substance use resulting in a failure to fulfill major role obligations at work, school, or home. Examples include repeated absences from work, suspensions or expulsions from school, or neglect of children or one's household. 2. Recurrent drug use in situations in which use is physically hazardous. 3. Recurrent substance-related legal problems, such as an arrest for disorderly conduct or drug-related behavior. Symptoms of the disturbance must have persisted for more than a month or occurred over a longer period of time. 4. Continued drug use despite the knowledge of persistent social, occupational, psychological, or physical problems that would be caused or made more difficult by the use of the drug. *Important:* The person must have never met the criteria for substance dependence for this particular drug.

Source: Adapted from the *American Psychiatric Association: Diagnostic and statistical manual of mental disorders,* Fourth Edition. Washington, DC: American Psychiatric Association, 1994. Reprinted with permission from the *Diagnostic and statistical manual of mental disorders,* Fourth Edition. Copyright 1994 American Psychiatric Association.

conditions: **substance dependence** and **substance abuse** (Table 2.2).

Two features of the DSM-IV guidelines are worth noting. First, the guidelines consist of a listing of behavioral criteria to be used for the diagnosis (identification) of substance dependence or substance abuse. There is no discussion of why these problems have arisen or what circumstances produced them, only their behavioral features. The position of the American Psychiatric Association is that a judgment of whether a person has a problem of dependence or abuse should depend upon the behavior of that person, not the chemical that is being consumed. Second, the broader term "substance" has been substituted for the word "drug" in the guidelines, primarily because there is often confusion in the public mind in deciding what is defined as a drug and what is not, particularly in the instance of alcohol or nicotine use.[25]

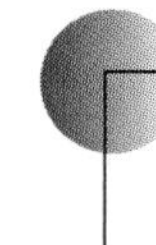

Special Problems in Drug Abuse

The discussion so far has dealt with drug-abuse problems, specifically the problems of acute and chronic toxicity, that affect only the drug user. Unfortunately, other people are frequently involved as well. Consider two special circumstances related to drug abuse that require discussions of their own: the problems of drug abuse in pregnancy and in association with AIDS.

Drug Abuse in Pregnancy

Prior to the 1960s, doctors and scientists regarded the placenta joining the bloodstream of a pregnant woman with that of the developing fetus as a natural barrier protecting the fetus from toxic substances in the mother. We now know that the idea of a "placental barrier" is clearly

substance dependence: A diagnostic term used in clinical psychology and psychiatry that identifies an individual with significant signs of a dependent relationship upon a psychoactive drug.

substance abuse: A diagnostic term used in clinical psychology and psychiatry that identifies an individual who continues to take a psychoactive drug despite the fact that the drug-taking behavior creates specific problems for that individual.

Effects of Psychoactive Drugs on Pregnant Women and Newborns

In addition to the adverse effect of psychoactive drugs on fetal development and pregnancy in general, a number of such drugs carry very specific risks. Here is a review of these effects.

Alcohol

- Fetal effects: Impairment in the supply of fetal oxygen and stimulation of excess prostaglandins possibly causing fetal malformations.
- Pregnancy effects: Risk of miscarriage during the second trimester of pregnancy if the mother consumed only one or two drinks a day.
- Newborn effects: Signs of alcohol withdrawal upon birth if the mother drank heavily. Fetal alcohol syndrome involving retardation of postnatal growth and nervous system, abnormal craniofacial features, numerous organ abnormalities. Increased risk of infant leukemia.

Tobacco

- Fetal effects: Reduced oxygen supply compounded by carbon monoxide that interferes with the blood's ability to carry oxygen throughout the body.
- Pregnancy effects: Increased frequency of spontaneous abortions and fetal death.
- Newborn effects: Increased risk of physical defects, lower birth weight. Also a higher risk that infants born to mothers who smoke will die before their first birthday.

Marijuana

- Fetal effects: Increased carbon monoxide levels in mother's blood, particularly in the last trimester, resulting in reduced oxygen in fetal blood.
- Pregnancy effects: Inconsistent findings, although there is a tendency for more males to be conceived than females if either parent is a heavy marijuana smoker.
- Newborn effects: Some evidence for abnormal sleep and arousal patterns if mothers have used marijuana.

Cocaine or Crack

- Fetal effects: Constriction of blood vessels, which reduces normal fetal blood flow and causes urogenital malformations.
- Pregnancy effects: High rates of spontaneous abortion and early separation of the placenta from the uterine wall, resulting in increased numbers of stillbirths. Increased risks of early onset of labor and preterm delivery.
- Newborn effects: Increased risk of intrauterine growth retardation: lower birth weight and smaller length and head circumference. Tendency to be jittery and easily startled. Fewer discernible withdrawal symptoms than in newborns exposed to heroin or other narcotics in utero. Increased incidence of sudden infant death syndrome (SIDS).

Heroin or Morphine

- Fetal effects: Reduced oxygen supply to the fetus, as well as reduced pancreatic, liver, and intestinal functioning.
- Pregnancy effects: In 10 to 15 percent of pregnant women using heroin, development of toxemia, a poisoning of the blood between the mother and the fetus.
- Newborn effects: Retardation of intrauterine growth. Likelihood of lung problems, brain hemorrhages, and respiratory distress. Risk for perinatally transmitted HIV infection and the development of AIDS. Dramatic withdrawal symptoms usually beginning forty-eight to seventy-two hours after delivery.

Prescription Drugs

- Accutane (isoretinoin): Major birth defects associated with this antiacne medication and Vitamin A derivative.
- Tetracycline antibiotics: Possibility of permanent discoloration of a child's teeth.
- Salicylates (aspirin products): Possibility of bleeding in the mother or fetus and of delay in delivery if taken close to term or prior to delivery.
- Dilantin (phenytoin): Increased risk of heart malformations, cleft lip, and mental retardation associated with this and other anticonvulsants.
- Hormones in birth control pills: Increased risk of congenital abnormalities, including heart and limb defects.
- Antianxiety drugs: Possible depression of respiration in newborn when taken during labor. Fourfold increase in cleft palates and malformations of the heart and limbs when taken during early pregnancy.
- Barbiturates: Birth defects resembling fetal alcohol syndrome associated with long-acting barbiturates such as phenobarbital. Withdrawal symptoms in the newborn four to seven days after delivery.

Sources: Cook, Paddy S., Peterson, Robert C., and Moore, Dorothy T. (1990). *Alcohol, tobacco, and other drugs may harm the unborn.* Rockville MD: Office of Substance Abuse Prevention. Shu, Xiao-Ou; Ross, Julie A.; Pendergrass, Thomas W.; Reaman, Gregory H.; Lampkin, Beatrice; and Robison, Leslie L. (1996). Parental alcohol consumption, cigarette smoking, and risk of infant leukemia: A children's cancer group study. *Journal of the National Cancer Institute, 88,* 24–31.

wrong. During gestation, almost all drugs cross the placenta and affect the unborn child.

It has been estimated that at some time during pregnancy about 19 percent of women in the United States have used alcohol, about 20 percent have smoked cigarettes, and about 6 percent have used some form of illicit drugs.[26] These women are at increased risk for obstetrical complications and for premature labor and delivery.

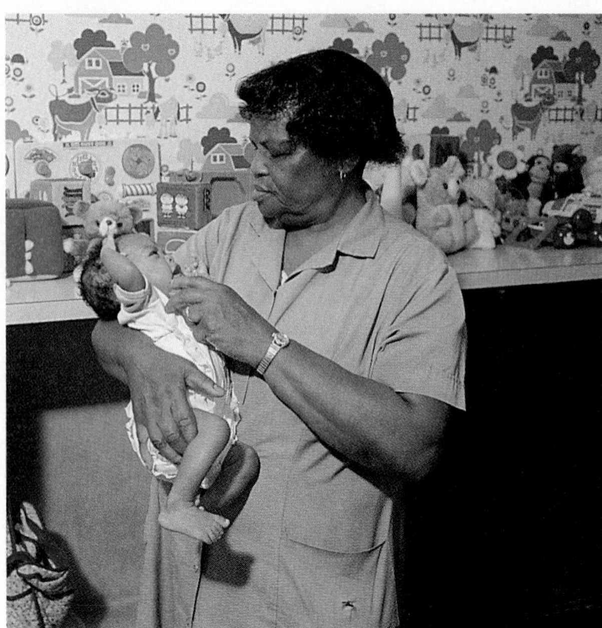

Babies born to women who have abused drugs during their pregnancy require special health care during their early months of development.

They are also more likely to suffer loss of the fetus through spontaneous abortions (miscarriages) and stillbirths than are women who abstain from drugs. The greater the extent of drug-taking behavior, the more likely there will be adverse consequences.

The timing of drug use during a pregnancy has a great deal to do with the specific risks to the fetus. Drug use during the early weeks of pregnancy, from the fourth to the eighth week following conception, is more likely to increase the risks of spontaneous abortions and physical malformations in the newborn than drug use later in the pregnancy. Drug use after the eighth month of pregnancy is frequently associated with growth retardation, prematurity and low birth weight, and neurological damage to the infant.[27] These warnings are generalizations, however, cutting across many categories of psychoactive substances. Health Line examines the specific risks associated with specific categories of drugs.

Drug Abuse and AIDS

One of the hazards associated with drug use by injection is the spread of disease when needles are shared. In the past, the contamination has primarily involved infectious hepatitis, a serious liver disease. Since the late 1970s, however, attention has turned to the potential spread of the human immunodeficiency virus (HIV) responsible for acquired immunodeficiency syndrome (AIDS). Since HIV-infected individuals may not show discernible AIDS symptoms for a considerable period of time (the median interval being ten years), there is unfortunately ample opportunity for contaminating others, either through sexual contact or some direct exchange of bodily fluids. Almost 60 percent of intravenous drug users in New York have tested HIV-positive, and the prevalence among similar populations in regions of the world as disparate as Europe and Asia is only slightly less.[28] Viewed in a different way, approximately one-third of all new AIDS cases in 1998 in the United States were found to be related directly or indirectly to drug use involving needles. A direct relationship refers to AIDS cases who were self-injecting drugs; an indirect relationship refers to AIDS cases who had either heterosexual or homosexual contact with an injecting drug user.[29]

In an effort to reduce the risk of HIV infection among injecting drug users, needle-exchange programs, in which addicts have the opportunity to trade in their used needles for sterile ones, have been operating successfully in several countries, including England, Canada, Australia, Sweden, and the Netherlands. In the United States, however, the idea of providing sterile needles to heroin users has met with considerable political and social resistance. Nonetheless, such programs do exist in dozens of U.S. communities, either officially sanctioned or operating underground. It has been estimated that needle-exchange programs can reduce new cases of HIV infection by one-third. In 1997, the National Institutes of Health officially endorsed the safety and efficacy of needle-exchange programs for reducing HIV infections, though, as we enter the new millennium such programs in many regions of the United States are still officially illegal.[30]

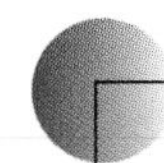

Drugs, Violence, and Crime

Important questions often end up being the most complicated ones to answer. Consider the question of whether drugs cause violence and crime. We can look at the news headlines reporting acts of social violence linked to the world of illicit drugs and the impact of those acts on our society: innocent children killed in the cross fire of rival drug gangs, thousands of crimes against individuals and property to pay for the addict's drug habit, terrorization of whole communities by drug dealers. Illicit drugs and crime are bound together in a web of greed and callous disregard for human life.

The association clearly exists. Figure 2.4 shows the results of a continuing survey conducted by the U.S.

	Percentage Testing Positive for Any Drug (0–100)	Methamphetamine	Cocaine	Opiates	Marijuana	Multiple Drugs
Birmingham, AL	64	0	37	4	39	15
Cleveland, OH	71	0	40	4	43	25
Denver, CO	67	3	41	3	44	22
Los Angeles, CA	62	9	36	6	32	20
New York, NY	75	0	44	15	41	24
Phoenix, AZ	64	17	32	8	36	24
Portland, OR	64	20	23	13	35	23
San Diego, CA	64	26	17	9	36	22
San Jose, CA	55	24	14	4	34	19
Washington, D.C.	69	0.9	38	16	35	25

(Percentage Testing Positive: Methamphetamine, Cocaine, Opiates, Marijuana, Multiple Drugs)

FIGURE 2.4

Prevalence of drug use (alcohol and nicotine excluded) among male adult arrestees in ten U.S. cities in 1999. Percentages for cocaine, opiates, multiple drugs, and any drug are generally much higher among adults than juveniles; percentages for marijuana are generally higher among juveniles than adults.
Source: National Institute of Justice (2000). 1999 annual report on drug use among adult and juvenile arrestees. Washington DC: Arrestee Drug Abuse Monitoring Program, Department of Justice.

Department of Justice in which individuals arrested for a serious offense (most commonly burglary, assault, grand larceny, and drug possession) are tested for various drugs through a urinanalysis. In 1999, the percentage of male arrestees testing positive for any illicit drugs ranged from 50 to 77 percent, and the percentage for cocaine ranged from 14 to 51 percent. Methamphetamine showed the greatest variation by geographical region, from 0 percent in the eastern U.S. cities to 28 percent in some areas of the West.[31]

Undoubtedly, a wide range of violent acts and crimes can be connected to some form of alcohol or illicit drug use (Figure 2.5).[32] But we have to be extremely careful in the conclusion we draw from the statistics. Do drugs actually *cause* violent behavior and crime? If they do, which drugs have a greater responsibility than others? As we will see, the question of the relationship between drugs and societal problems such as violence and crime has to be broken down into three specific issues, and we need to examine them one at a time.

Pharmacological Violence

First of all, we should address the issue of whether a drug causes violent or criminal behavior while the drug is actually present in the individual's system. Although the statistics show that a large proportion of people have some illicit drug in their system at the time of arrest, it is difficult to say whether the offense was committed as a result of the influence of that drug. This possibility is often

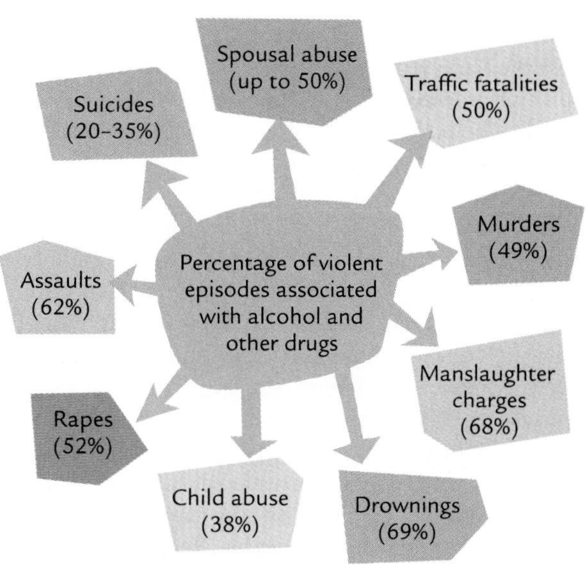

FIGURE 2.5

The strong association between alcohol and other drug use and episodes of violence and death.

referred to as **pharmacological violence.** The uncertainty that pharmacological violence has indeed occurred stems from the fact that the detection period in standard urinalysis drug tests can range from approximately 2 to 4 days in the cases of cocaine, methamphetamine, and opiates and up to 30 days in the case of marijuana (see Chapter 8). Therefore, testing positive for a drug at the time of arrest for a violent crime indicates only that the individual *might* have become violent while under the influence of the drug.

In some instances, the physiological nature of the drug itself makes the possibility of pharmacological violence quite unlikely. Marijuana by itself, for example, makes the user more lethargic than active, in effect quite mellow in circumstances in which there may be some interpersonal conflict. Heroin produces a passive state of mind that reduces the inclination toward violent behavior. In fact, as rates of heroin abuse rise, the incidence of crimes against individuals (as opposed to crimes against property) declines.[33]

Psychoactive stimulants such as amphetamines and cocaine or the hallucinogenic PCP (known as angel dust), however, produce an on-edge manner and a social paranoia that can lead to violent behavior, although there is no current evidence that these drugs specifically stimulate violent behavior. We need to be careful in the interpretation of studies reporting violent behavior in unselected populations. For example, in a study conducted at an Atlanta medical center, more than half of all patients being treated for acute cocaine intoxication were reported to be aggressive, agitated, and paranoid just prior to and at the time of hospital admission. It is impossible to determine whether these patients were mentally unstable to begin with, prior to their taking cocaine. People who have long-standing psychological problems may be overrepresented in any population of cocaine abusers.[34]

Crack cocaine has the dubious reputation of making the crack smoker irritable, suspicious, and inclined to lash out at another person at the slightest provocation.[35] Whether or not these effects are due to being under the influence of the drug, however, is unclear. Tendencies toward violence are observed during times of *crack withdrawal* as well as crack intoxication.

Of all the psychoactive drugs we could consider, the one with the most definitive and widely reported links to violent behavior is alcohol. In this case, the violence is clearly pharmacological, since the effects of being drunk from the ingestion of alcohol are apparent almost immediately. On a domestic level, males involved in spouse abuse commonly report having been drinking or having been drunk during many of the times that abuse has occurred. Moreover, violent crime outside the home is strongly related to alcohol intoxication. The more violent the crime, the greater the probability that the perpetrator of the crime was drunk while committing it. Studies show at least a majority of all homicides and almost a majority of all sexually aggressive acts (rapes and attempted rapes) are committed while the offender is drunk.[36]

Does the chronic use of drugs cause individuals to engage in criminal behavior in general? There is little evidence that drugs *cause* an increase in one's general inclination toward antisocial behavior. In other words, it is not true that drugs alone are capable of changing the personality of the user, turning him or her from being some kind of upstanding pillar of the community into a social menace. As discussed in the last chapter, social risk factors can be identified that lead toward deviant behavior, as defined by the societal norms, and that deviant behavior includes both drug abuse and criminal behavior. One aspect of that deviant behavior cannot be considered the cause of the other. Frequently, individuals with the greatest chance of abusing drugs have socioeconomic backgrounds that also produce the greatest chance of criminal behavior: a low level of education, a broken family, little or no social supervision, and low social status.[37] As one researcher has put it,

> *Teenagers who begin illegal drug use are also likely to have committed other criminal acts beforehand, whether or not they have been caught. It is likely that this relationship may be sufficient to explain the higher crime rate of marijuana users. It is not so much that marijuana use causes crime (except, of course, the crime of using the drug), but that those who use marijuana are also the type of people more likely to commit criminal acts.*[38]

Economically Compulsive Violence

To what extent are criminal acts being committed for the expressed purpose of obtaining the money to support a drug habit? We can speak of the possibility of **economically compulsive violence,** if the violent act stems from the costliness of the drug-taking behavior.

pharmacological violence: Violent acts committed while under the influence of a particular psychoactive drug, with the implication that the drug caused the violence to occur.
economically compulsive violence: Violent acts that are committed by a drug abuser in order to secure money to buy drugs.

A 1990 survey of a sample of 361 adolescent crack users in the Miami area showed that 59 percent participated in 6,669 robberies over a twelve-month period, averaging 31 robberies per individual, or roughly one every twelve days. Yet, while the majority of these robberies were carried out in order to buy drugs, we cannot assume that they all involved the classic picture of break-ins and holdups. Approximately 25 percent of the sample had robbed drugs from drug dealers or other users, while 40 percent had been themselves victims of a drug robbery.[39] Nonetheless, a large proportion of the crimes committed in order to obtain drug money involved violent acts directed toward individuals within the community. Particular targets included storekeepers, children, and the elderly.

When robbery is the means for financing drug abuse, the extent of this crime has been shown to be closely related to the market conditions at the time. When heroin prices are high, for example, the level of property crime goes up; when heroin prices are low, the crime level goes down as well. In other words, heroin abusers steal more in order to maintain a stable consumption of heroin if the drug becomes more expensive to obtain. Therefore, deliberate elevation of drug prices when accomplished by reducing the supply not only fails to reduce the incidence of abuse but also tends to increase the incidence of criminal behavior among drug abusers.[40] Economically compulsive violence, therefore, appears to be a major component of the link between drugs and crime.

Pharmacological violence

Ingestion of drug causing individuals to become excitable, irrational, or inclined to exhibit violent behavior

Economically compulsive violence

Need for money to buy drugs as the primary motivation for violence

The Drug-Violence Connection

Systemic violence

- Disputes over territory between rival drug dealers
- Violent acts committed to enforce discipline
- Elimination of police informants
- Punishment for selling adulterated drugs
- Punishment for defrauding the drug dealer

FIGURE 2.6

The three aspects of drugs and violence.

Systemic Violence

A third important source of social violence and criminal behavior is inherent within the drug world itself. Researchers use the term **systemic violence** to refer to the violence that arises from characteristic features of drug dealing (Figure 2.6). Systemic violence can result from such situations as territorial disputes, the consequences of selling inferior grades of the illicit drug, or fraudulent handling of funds from drug sales (referred to as "messing up the money"). The prominence of systemic violence in crack cocaine abuse since the mid-1980s is particularly striking. Studies show that as the involvement of a youth in crack distribution increases, the more likely that person is to become a criminal offender. The probability also increases that major felonies will be committed.[41]

The question of which factor causes the other cannot be easily answered. It is quite possible that a combination of modeling behavior and self-selection is occurring here. Inherently violent individuals may be useful in maintaining tight discipline in groups that focus upon drug taking and drug selling; they may be useful as combatants in territorial disputes in general. As a result, the participation of highly violent individuals in the selling and distribution of crack adds an extremely dangerous dimension to the violence and social upheaval already associated with illicit drugs.[42]

In addition, the most violent drug users may be the most respected role models for young people. Sociologists have observed that in many communities, adolescents feel the need to prove that they can be brutal in order to avoid being harassed by their peers. The pressure to be an accepted member of such a community may be more responsible for a drug abuser's committing frequent violent acts than the effects of the drugs themselves, or even the need for money to buy drugs.

systemic violence: Violence that arises from the traditionally aggressive patterns of behavior within a network of illicit drug trafficking and distribution.

Given the link between the distribution of crack cocaine and systemic violence, it should not be surprising that a decline in the prevalence of crack abuse, first observed in the latter 1990s, has been accompanied by a decline in homicide rates and violent crime in the areas where crack abuse had been dominant. In addition, community-based policing procedures have focused on breaking up drug gangs and large street-level drug markets, thus changing the pattern of drug buying and selling. An expert in the area of criminal justice has put it this way:

> *The reconfiguration of drug markets in the mid-1990s appreciably reduced the level of neighborhood violence. As distribution retired indoors, turf battles were eliminated, and because organizers of drug businesses hired a few trusted friends rather than easily replaceable workers, there was less conflict between them. Distributors were robbed by users less frequently because they were more protected selling indoors to known customers.*[43]

In addressing the connections between drug-taking behavior and crime, it is important to include patterns of criminal behavior that are associated with affluent populations as well as impoverished ones. The spread of illicit drug dependence to higher socioeconomic levels of society, since the 1970s, has led to an increase in white-collar crimes of fraud and embezzlement that are motivated by the need for drug money. In such cases, we are speaking of economically compulsive acts. While generally nonviolent in nature, these criminal acts involve substantially greater amounts of lost revenue than the burglaries and robberies common to poorer neighborhoods.

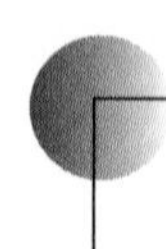

Governmental Policy, Regulation, and Laws

How should we as a society respond to the social problems of drug-taking behavior? We are faced with an overwhelming flood of illicit drugs entering the United States from around the world, only a small fraction of which is ever identified, much less confiscated, despite the well-publicized drug seizures.[44] We can express our moral outrage that the situation has become so bad, that drug abuse is costing society such an enormous amount of money and wasting so many lives. Social despair is so well entrenched in some portions of society that solutions seem to be nonexistent. The official responses U.S. society has made through its history, in terms of regulatory controls over drugs, can be understood more clearly in terms of its attitudes toward drug-taking behavior and drug users than in terms of the drugs themselves.

Efforts to Regulate Drugs, 1900–1970

Until about 1900 in the United States, the governmental attitude toward addictive behavior was one of **laissez-faire,** roughly translated as "allow [people] to do as they please," which meant there was little regulation or control. It was a well-ingrained philosophy, going back to our early days as a nation, that government should stay out of the lives of its citizens. Nonmedical use of opiates was not considered respectable and in some circles was seen as immoral, but it was no more disreputable than heavy drinking.

> *Employees were not fired for addiction. Wives did not divorce their addicted husbands, or husbands their addicted wives. Children were not taken from their homes and lodged in foster homes or institutions because one or both parents were addicted. Addicts continued to participate fully in the life of the community. Addicted children and young people continued to go to school, Sunday school, and college.*[45]

Prior to the twentieth century, there were movements to ban alcoholic consumption but none to ban the wholesale use of opium, morphine, heroin, or cocaine. The only exception was the strong opposition to the smoking of opium, an attitude directed principally toward Chinese immigrants in the western states, as noted in Chapter 1.

By the turn of the century, however, a wave of reform sentiment began to sweep the country. In 1905 the popular magazine *Collier's* criticized the fradulant claims and improper labeling of patent medicines that contained large amounts of alcohol, opiates, and cocaine. Large-scale abuses in the meatpacking industry, publicized in 1906 in Upton Sinclair's novel *The Jungle,* turned the stomach of the American public and quickly pressured President Theodore Roosevelt and Congress to take action.

The result was the enactment of the Pure Food and Drug Act. The 1906 law required that food and drug manufacturers list the amounts of alcohol or "habit-forming" drugs, specified as any opiate or cocaine, on the label of the product, but the sale or use of any of these substances

laissez-faire (LAY-say FAIR) (Fr.): The philosophy of exerting as little control and regulation as possible.

Portrait Harry J. Anslinger—America's First Drug Czar

By the time Harry J. Anslinger became the first commissioner of the Federal Bureau of Narcotics (FBN) in 1930, the nation's drug-law-enforcement policy had been established. Anslinger had been a rising young star in the Prohibition Unit at the Treasury Department during the twenties, convinced that drug addiction was absolutely immoral and that its cure was a matter of preventing the addict from getting hold of the drug.

The end of Prohibition, however, had placed pressure on Congress to reduce the Treasury's enforcement budget, and the Great Depression put strains on federal expenditures in general. Anslinger and the FBN faced hard times. The savior, ironically enough, was marijuana. Beginning in the early 1930s, rumors of "degenerate Spanish-speaking residents" in the Southwest going on criminal rampages while smoking marijuana were being spread in newspapers and popular magazines. Anslinger seized upon these unsubstantiated reports, calling marijuana the "assassin of youth." In his view, a new menace at our shores deserved new legislation, not to mention continued financial support for the agency dedicated to fighting it. The Marijuana Tax Act of 1937 was Anslinger's creation.

U.S. Commissioner of Narcotics, Harry J. Anslinger

Anslinger's thirty-two-year tenure at the FBN and his stature as the defender of the purity of American youth, or at least the purity of their circulatory systems, could not have been possible without strong support from several important conservative U.S. legislators in the House and Senate. During the late 1940s and into the 1950s, Anslinger began to emphasize the link between drug addiction in the United States with the threat of international Communism from abroad. The target was Communist China, which Anslinger repeatedly claimed was the primary source of domestic heroin in the United States, even though the evidence clearly pointed to politically friendlier nations of Southeast Asia as the real culprits. Only after Anslinger's resignation in 1962, following considerable pressure from President John Kennedy, would the focus of attention be turned to the problem of heroin trafficking in Burma, Laos, and Thailand.

Given the anti-Communist stance of the FBN, it is not surprising that one of Anslinger's staunchest supporters during the late 1940s and early 1950s was Senator Joseph R. McCarthy, whose congressional subcommittee was then engaged in a ruthless crusade against "known Communists" inside the government. What was not known at the time, however, was that Anslinger during this period was secretly allowing McCarthy, a morphine addict as well as an alcoholic, to buy unrestricted supplies of morphine without FBN interference. When McCarthy died in 1957 of "acute hepatitis, cause unknown," Anslinger wrote in a memoir, "I thanked God for relieving me of my burden."

Source: McWilliams, John C. (1990). *The Protectors: Harry J. Anslinger and the Federal Bureau of Narcotics, 1930–1962.* Cranbury NJ: Associated University Press.

was left unrestricted. The law was the first of a series of legislative controls over food, drinks, drugs, and eventually cosmetics. As Chapter 14 will describe, this legislation eventually evolved into the present-day Food and Drug Administration.

The second major piece of legislation of the early part of the century was the Harrison Act of 1914. This new law concerned itself with opiate drugs (defined as narcotics) and cocaine. Cocaine was not defined as a narcotic under the law, but it became lumped together with opiates and often was referred to as a narcotic as well. Although the application of the term to cocaine was incorrect (narcotic literally means "stupor-inducing" and cocaine is anything but that), the association has unfortunately stuck. In the years after the enactment of the Harrison Act, several restricted drugs, including marijuana and the hallucinogenic peyote, were also officially classified as narcotics without regard to their pharmacological characteristics. Today, many people still think of any illegal drug as a narcotic, and for many years the bureau at the Treasury Department charged with drug-enforcement responsibilities was called the Federal Bureau of Narcotics (FBN) and their agents known on the street as "narks."

By 1933, as the Prohibition Era ended, the attention of drug-enforcement policymakers, led by Harry Anslinger, the newly installed FBN director, turned from the control of alcohol consumption to the identification of marijuana as a major public menace (Portrait). Congressional committees heard testimony from police claiming that marijuana, now called the "killer weed," aroused sexual excitement and led to violent crimes. The movie *Reefer Madness,* now a cult classic on many university campuses, depicted the moral slide of supposedly innocent young people introduced to marijuana. The result was the Marijuana Tax Act of 1937, after which growers, sellers, and buyers of marijuana were subject to tax. State laws made possession of marijuana illegal.

The 1960s saw a number of amendments to the enforcement laws then in effect, as new drugs of abuse came

TABLE 2.3

The five schedules of controlled substances in the Comprehensive Drug Abuse Prevention and Control Act

Schedule I
High potential for abuse, No accepted medical use. Research use only; separate records must be maintained, and the drugs must be stored in secure vaults.

Examples: heroin, LSD, mescaline, marijuana

Schedule II
High potential for abuse. Some accepted medical use, though use may lead to severe physical or psychological dependence. Prescriptions must be written in ink, or typewritten, and signed by a medical practitioner. Verbal prescriptions must be confirmed in writing within 72 hours and may be given only in a genuine emergency. No prescription renewals are permitted. Separate records must be maintained, and the drugs must be stored in secure vaults.

Examples: codeine, morphine, cocaine, methadone, amphetamines, short-acting barbiturates

Schedule III
Some potential for abuse. Accepted medical use, though use may lead to low-to-moderate physical dependence or high psychological dependence. Prescriptions may be oral or written. Up to five prescription renewals are permitted within 6 months.

Examples: long-acting barbiturates, narcotic solutions (for example, paregoric or tincture of opium in alcohol) or mixtures (for example, 1.8% codeine)

Schedule IV
Low potential for abuse. Accepted medical use. Prescriptions may be oral or written. Up to five prescription renewals are permitted within 6 months.

Examples: antianxiety drugs and sedative-hypnotics (for example, Valium and Miltown)

Schedule V
Minimal abuse potential. Widespread medical use. Minimal controls for selling and dispensing.

Examples: prescription cough medicines not containing codeine, laxatives

Source: Physicians' desk reference (48th ed.). (1994). Montvale NJ: Medical Economics Data, p. 2665.

onto the scene. The Federal Bureau of Narcotics became the Federal Bureau of Narcotics and Dangerous Drugs, and Anslinger, whose tenure as director rivaled that of FBI Director J. Edgar Hoover in longevity and power, retired in 1962.

Rethinking the Approach toward Drug Regulation

The Comprehensive Drug Abuse Prevention and Control Act of 1970 was an attempt to organize the control of drugs under five classifications called *schedules of controlled substances,* based upon their potential for abuse (see Table 2.3). These categories have defined the extent to which various drugs are authorized to be available to the general public in the United States. Schedules I and II refer to drugs presenting the highest level of abuse potential, and Schedule V refers to drugs presenting the least. All drugs, except those included under Schedule I, are legally available on either a prescription or nonprescription basis.

Under the system establishing schedules of controlled substances, drugs that are considered more dangerous and more easily abused are subject to progressively more stringent restrictions on their possession, the number of prescriptions that can be made, or the manner in which they can be dispensed. In the case of Schedule I drugs (heroin, LSD, mescaline, marijuana, for example), no acceptable medical use has been authorized by the U.S. government and availability of these drugs is limited to research purposes only. The federal penalties for possession and sale of Schedule I drugs, as well as those for violating the restrictions set for other controlled substances, will be examined in Chapter 17.

The 1970 law moved the administration of drug enforcement from the Treasury Department to the Justice Department, ending the long era of attempts to regulate drug-taking behavior through taxation. As prevention and treatment programs for drug abuse were set up and funds were allocated for educational material, the emphasis started to shift from penalties on the drug user to penalties on drug dealing. In 1988 the Omnibus Drug Act imposed, among its features, penalties for money laundering when associated with drug smuggling and sales. Under this act, a new cabinet-level position, a "drug czar," was established to coordinate the efforts of the many federal agencies and departments that were by now involved in drug regulation and drug-law enforcement.

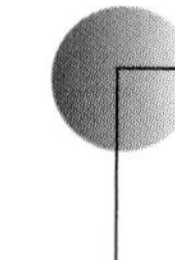

Enforcement of Drug Laws on a Local and International Scale

The enforcement picture today is far more complex than it was fifty years ago, when the consideration was chiefly the "supply" side (the availability of drugs) of the problem, without much consideration of the "demand" side (the dependence of individuals on drugs capable of being abused). Society is putting more emphasis on drug-abuse treatment and prevention than ever before. Nonetheless, treatment and prevention programs in the Reagan and Bush administrations represented only 30 percent of the federal budget to control drug abuse. During the Clinton administration, the amount allotted to treatment and prevention programs increased, but most of the funds in the $18 billion drug-control budget were still directed toward efforts to reduce the supply of illicit drugs.[46]

Obviously, an enormous amount of federal funds are expended specifically to hold back the continuing influx of illicit drugs entering the country. The Drug Enforcement Administration (DEA) has agents in more than forty foreign countries, working with the Departments of Defense and State, Central Intelligence Agency (CIA), U.S. Coast Guard and other branches of the military, and Immigration and Naturalization Service (INS).

Our attempts to stem the flood of illicit drugs into this country, however, are complicated by a number of economic and political factors on a global scale. Despite American pressure to spray herbicides on more than 135,000 acres of coca fields in Colombia, for example, cocaine production in 1998 set an all-time record. Colombia has now passed Peru and Bolivia as the largest grower and processor of coca in the world, establishing itself as the supplier of 80 percent of the world's cocaine and 65 percent of the heroin sold on U.S. streets. Despite its status as a principal U.S. trading partner, the country of Mexico, immediately to our south, remains a major drug trafficking route not only of cocaine and heroin from South America but also of marijuana, methamphetamine, and illegal prescription medications (Figure 2.7).[47]

Where has nearly a century of drug regulation taken us? We are now at the end of the third decade of the U.S. "war on drugs," declared officially by President Nixon in 1971; the price tag for this war has exceeded $200 billion. Each year more money is requested to carry on the fight, but the struggle continues to be frustrating in the extreme and the nation grows increasingly battle-weary (see Point/Counterpoint, pages 75–76). In 1987, the U.S. Office of Technology Assessment issued a comprehensive

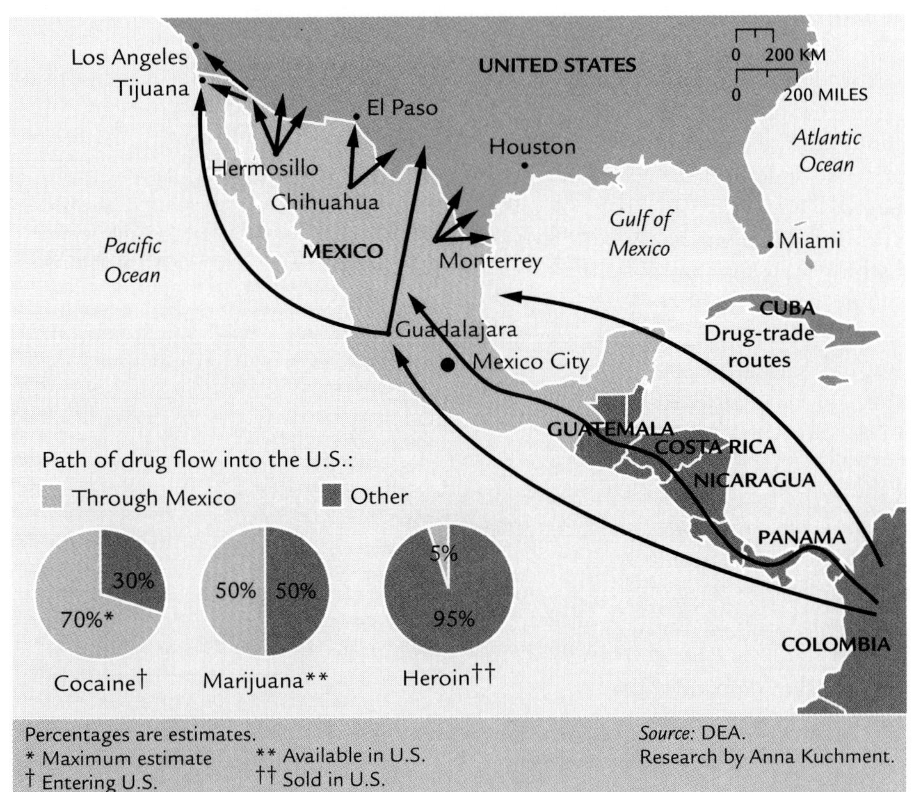

FIGURE 2.7

Principal trade routes for three types of illicit drugs in the 1990s, with a major hub in Mexico.
Source: Newsweek-Stanford Kay. © 1997, Newsweek, Inc. All rights reserved. Reprinted by permission.

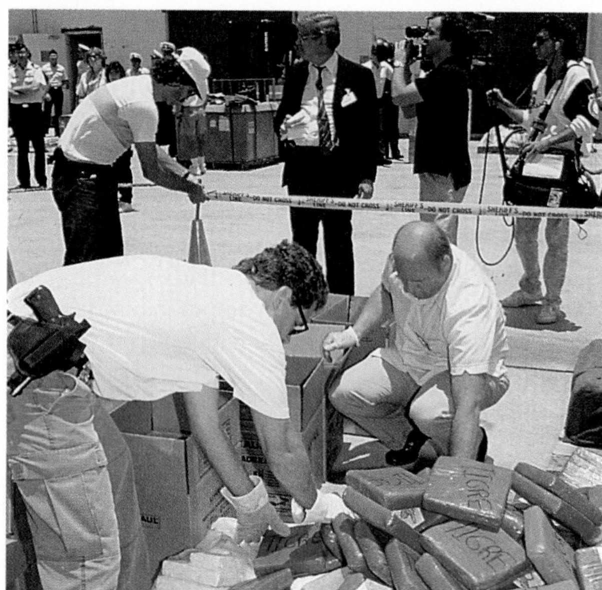

The large quantities of confiscated illicit drugs are only a small fraction of the actual amount that successfully enters the United States.

report on the efforts to intercept and block the entrance of illicit drugs into the country. It concluded that despite a *doubling* of the money devoted to drug interdiction from 1982 to 1987, the amount of smuggled drugs had continued to increase. While the expenditures have increased by 1400 percent since 1981, there is no clear-cut correlation between budget allocations from year to year and the availability of illicit drugs.[48] As a federal drug-law-enforcement official has commented, "It reminds me of that cartoon. This king is slamming his fist on the table, saying 'If all my horses and all my men can't put Humpty Dumpty together again, then what I need is *more* horses and *more* men!'"[49]

Many experts in the field of drug abuse view the solution not to be in faraway countries, at U.S. borders, or in U.S. prisons, but in the communities of the United States.[50] One political scientist has put it this way: "If the 'war' is to be won, it will be won in the hearts and minds of people who might be inclined to consume drugs." A recommendation gaining increasing support would shift the emphasis from "use reduction" to "harm reduction," acknowledging that drugs may never be absent from our society (Health Line).[51]

The public policy issues surrounding the "demand" side of the drug abuse equation, particularly as it pertains to drug-abuse prevention, will be considered in greater detail in Chapters 17 and 18.

Health Line

Harm Reduction as a Drug-Abuse Policy

Given the difficulties in reducing the problems of drug abuse, it is natural that some have questioned the present policy objective of "zero tolerance" with regard to illicit drug-taking behavior, that is, an eventual eradication of illicit drug use in the United States. Opponents of this policy have argued that governmental efforts should focus instead on minimizing the various medical, psychological, and social costs associated with drug-taking behavior rather than on eliminating such behavior entirely. This latter approach has been called the Harm Reduction approach.

Examples of the Harm Reduction approach include needle-exchange programs, discussed in this chapter, to lower the incidence of HIV infection among intravenous drug abusers, methadone maintenance programs for the treatment of heroin abusers (see Chapter 5), efforts to reduce the incidence of driving while under the influence of alcohol (see Chapter 10), and the use of nicotine patches to avoid the effects of cigarette smoking such as emphysema and lung cancer (see Chapter 11). A more controversial application of the Harm Reduction approach is the suggestion that we should attempt to reduce the level of heavy drug use down to a level of occasional use, rather than no use at all.

With regard to cigarette smoking and marijuana use, a recent study indicates that some teenagers may already be "harm reducing." In the University of Michigan survey, high school seniors engaging in occasional marijuana smoking and occasional cigarette smoking indicated a higher perceived risk of "regular substance use" than did high school seniors engaging in heavy use, even though there was no difference in the perceived risk of "occasional substance use." In other words, occasional users may have been moderating their behavior to minimize the harmful effects they associated with heavy drug-taking behavior. Whether prevention programs that emphasize the risks of heavy drug use, as opposed to emphasizing the risks of any level of use, can be successful in reducing significant levels of drug-taking behavior is a question that advocates of the Harm Reduction approach will be investigating in the future with great interest.

Sources: Drucker, Ernest (1995). Harm reduction: A public health strategy. *Current Issues in Public Health, 1,* 64–70. Goldstein, Avram (1994). *Addiction: From biology to drug policy.* New York: Freeman. Resnicow, Ken; Smith, Matt; Harrison, Lana; and Drucker, Ernest (1999). Correlates of occasional cigarette and marijuana use: Are teens harm reducing? *Addictive Behaviors, 24,* 251–266.

SUMMARY

Toxicity

- A drug's harmful effects are referred to as its toxicity. Acute toxicity can be measured in terms of a drug's therapeutic index or its margin of safety, each of which can be computed from its effective and lethal dose-response curves.

The DAWN Reports

- Drug Abuse Warning Network (DAWN) statistics, which reflect drug-related lethal and nonlethal emergencies in major metropolitan hospitals in the United States, offer another measure of acute drug toxicity. In general, DAWN statistics show that cocaine and narcotic drugs are both highly toxic and that many emergencies involve drugs being taken in combination with alcohol.

Drug Tolerance

- A tolerance effect refers to the capacity of a drug to have a gradually diminished effect over repeated administrations; in effect, a greater dose has to be taken to maintain the original effect of the drug. Tolerance effects can be quite dangerous, since experienced drug users often end up taking potentially lethal dose levels.

Physical and Psychological Dependence

- Drugs can be viewed in terms of a physical dependence model, in which the compulsive drug-taking behavior is tied to an avoidance of withdrawal symptoms, or a psychological dependence model, in which the drug-taking behavior is tied to a genuine craving for the drug and highly reinforcing effects of the drug on the user's body and mind.

Psychiatric Definitions

- The American Psychiatric Association currently recognizes two major conditions associated with drug-taking behavior: substance abuse and substance dependence. The broader term "substance" is used instead of "drug," because there is often confusion in the public mind in deciding what is defined as a drug and what is not.

Special Problems in Drug Abuse

- Increasing attention has been directed toward the harmful effects that drug abuse has on pregnant women, in terms of problems with the pregnancy itself and with the neural development of the fetus.
- There is also concern with the increased risk of HIV infection (and the spread of AIDS) among intravenous drug users when needles are shared.

Drugs, Violence, and Crime

- While there is an overall association between the taking of illicit drugs and crime, a careful analysis indicates that the drug with the closest connection to social violence is alcohol, and that heroin and marijuana cause the user to be less inclined toward violence rather than more so.
- It is clear that drug abuse forces many drug users to commit criminal acts (generally property theft) to support the drug habit. It is also clear that there is a high level of social violence and criminal behavior inherent in the trafficking and distribution of illicit drugs.

Governmental Policy, Regulation, and Laws

- Since the beginning of the twentieth century, U.S. society's philosophy toward drug-taking behavior has been that we should restrict it by reducing the availability of illicit drugs and making it as difficult as possible for the potential drug user to engage in drug-taking behavior.
- The Harrison Act of 1914 was the first of several legislative efforts to impose criminal penalties on the use of opiates and cocaine and later marijuana, hallucinogens, and several other types of drugs.
- The Comprehensive Drug Act of 1970 organized the federal control of drugs under five classifications called schedules.

Enforcement of Drug Laws on a Local and International Scale

- Today's drug-law-enforcement program in the United States places considerable emphasis upon the interdiction of drugs entering the country, with less emphasis upon treatment and prevention of drug abuse.

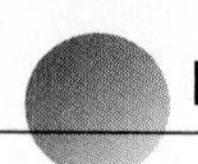

KEY TERMS

acute toxicity, p. 27
behavioral tolerance, p. 34
catheter, p. 36
chronic toxicity, p. 33
dose, p. 27
dose-response curve, p. 28
Drug Abuse Warning Network (DAWN), p. 30
economically compulsive violence, p. 42
effective dose, p. 28
laissez-faire, p. 44
lethal dose, p. 28
margin of safety, p. 29
pharmacological violence, p. 42
physical dependence, p. 36
polydrug use, p. 32
psychological dependence, p. 36
substance abuse, p. 38
substance dependence, p. 38
systemic violence, p. 43
therapeutic index, p. 29
tolerance, p. 34
toxicity, p. 27

ENDNOTES

1. Inciardi, James A. (1990). The crack-violence connection within a population of hard-core adolescent offenders. In Mario De La Rosa, Elizabeth Y. Lambert, and Bernard Gropper (Eds.), *Drugs and violence: Causes, correlates, and consequences* (NIDA Research Monograph 103). Rockville MD: National Institute on Drug Abuse, pp. 92–111. Quotation on pp. 98–99.
2. Gallup, George (1999). *The Gallup Poll: Public Opinion 1998*. Wilmington DE: Scholarly Resources, Inc, p. 60.
3. Cummings, Nicholas A. (1979). Turning bread into stone: Our modern antimiracle. *American Psychologist, 34*, 1119–1129.
4. Treaster, Joseph B., and Holloway, Lynette (1994, September 4). Potent new blend of heroin ends 8 very different lives. *New York Times*, pp. 1, 37.
5. Ungerleider, J. Thomas; Lundberg, George D.; Sunshine, Irving; and Walberg, Clifford B. (1980). The Drug Abuse Warning Network (DAWN) Program. *Archives of General Psychiatry, 37*, 106–109.
6. Karch, Steven B. (1996). *The pathology of drug abuse* (2nd ed.). Boca Raton FL: CRC Press, p. 9.
7. Substance Abuse and Mental Health Services Administration (2000). *Drug Abuse Warning Network annual emergency department data 1998*. Rockville MD: Office of Applied Studies, Substance Abuse and Mental Health Services Administration, Tables 2.06a, 2.19. Substance Abuse and Mental Health Services Administration (2000). *Drug Abuse Warning Network annual medical examiner data 1998*. Rockville MD: Office of Applied Studies, Substance Abuse and Mental Health Services Administration, pp. 34, 39.
8. Substance Abuse. Annual medical examiner data, pp. 38, 39, 47.
9. Substance Abuse. Annual emergency department data, Tables 2.02, 2.06a. Substance Abuse. Annual medical examiner data, pp. 34, 44.
10. Lankester, E. Ray (1889). Mithridatism. *Nature, 40*, 149.
11. Siegel, Shepard (1990). Drug anticipation and the treatment of dependence. In Barbara A. Ray (Ed.), *Learning factors in substance abuse* (NIDA Research Monograph 84). Rockville MD: National Institute on Drug Abuse, pp. 1–24.
12. Siegel, Shepard (1975). Evidence from rats that morphine tolerance is a learned response. *Journal of Comparative and Physiological Psychology, 89*, 489–506.
13. Siegel, Shepard; Hinson, Riley E.; Krank, Marvin D.; and McCully, Jane. (1982). Heroin "overdose" death: Contribution of drug-associated environmental cues. *Science, 216*, 436–437.
14. Brecher, Edward M., and the editors of *Consumer Reports*. (1972). *Licit and illicit drugs*. Mount Vernon NY: Consumers Union.
15. Siegel, Shepard (1999). Drug anticipation and drug addiction. The 1998 H. David Archibald Lecture. *Addiction, 94*, 1113–1124.
16. Jaffe, Jerome H. (1985). Drug addiction and drug abuse. In Alfred G. Gilman, Louis S. Goodman, Theordore W. Rall, and Ferid Murad (Eds.), *The pharmacological basis of therapeutics*. New York: Macmillan, pp. 532–581.
17. Blum, Kenneth. (1991). *Alcohol and the addictive brain*. New York, Free Press, p. 17.
18. Pinel, John P. J. (1990). *Biopsychology*. Boston: Allyn and Bacon, p. 483.
19. Simpson, D. Dwayne, and Marsh, Kerry L. (1986). Relapse and recovery among opioid addicts 12 years after treatment. In Frank M. Tims and Carl G. Leukefeld (Eds.), *Relapse and recovery in drug abuse* (NIDA Research Monograph 72). Rockville MD: National Institute on Drug Abuse, pp. 86–103. Simpson, D. Dwayne, and Sells, Saul B. (1982). Effectiveness of treatment for drug abuse: An overview of the DARP research program. *Advances in Alcohol and Substance Abuse, 2*, 7–29.
20. Halikas, James A. (1997). Craving. In Joyce H. Lowinson, Pedro Ruiz, Robert B. Millman, and John G. Langrod (Eds.), *Substance abuse: A comprehensive textbook*. Baltimore: Williams and Wilkins, pp. 85–90. Pickens, Roy, and Thompson, Travis (1968). Cocaine-reinforced behavior in rats: Effects of reinforcement magnitude and fixed-ratio size. *Journal of Pharmacology and Experimental Therapeutics, 161*, 122–129.
21. Hoffmeister, F. H., and Wuttke, W. (1975). Psychotropic drugs as negative reinforcers. *Pharmacological Reviews, 27*, 419–428. Yokel, R. A. (1987). Intravenous self-administration: Response rates, the effect of pharmacological challenges and drug preferences. In Michael A. Bozarth (Ed.), *Methods of assessing the reinforcing properties of abused drugs*. New York: Springer-Verlag, pp. 1–34.
22. Johanson, Chris E. (1984). Assessment of the abuse potential of cocaine in animals. In John Grabowski (Ed.), *Cocaine:*

Pharmacology, effects, and treatment of abuse. Rockville MD: National Institute on Drug Abuse, pp. 54–71.

23. Quotation from Goode, Erich. (1989). *Drugs in American society* (3rd ed.). New York: McGraw-Hill, p. 49. Data from Bozarth, Michael A., and Wise, Roy A. (1985). Toxicity associated with long-term intravenous heroin and cocaine self-administration in the rat. *Journal of the American Medical Association, 254*, 81–83.
24. Goode, Erich (1999). *Drugs in American society* (5th ed.). New York: McGraw-Hill College, pp. 44–52. Stewart, Jane, De Wit, Harriet, and Eikelboom, Roelof (1984). Role of unconditioned and conditioned drug effects in the self-administration of opiates and stimulants. *Psychological Review, 91*, 251–268.
25. American Psychiatric Association (1994). *Diagnostic and statistical manual* (4th ed.). Washington DC: American Psychiatric Association, pp. 180–183.
26. National Institute on Drug Abuse (1996). *National pregnancy and health survey. Drug use among women delivering livebirths: 1992.* Rockville MD: National Institute on Drug Abuse, pp. 8–11. Young, Nancy K. (1997). Effects of alcohol and other drugs on children. *Journal of Psychoactive Drugs, 29*, 23–42.
27. Cook, Paddy S., Petersen, Robert C., and Moore, Dorothy T. (1990). *Alcohol, tobacco, and other drugs may harm the unborn.* Washington DC: Office of Substance Abuse Prevention.
28. Stimson, Gerry V. (1991, May). The prevention of HIV infection in injecting drug users: Recent advances and remaining obstacles. *Newsletter of the International Working Group on AIDS and Drug Use, 5*, 14–19.
29. Infectious diseases and drug abuse (1999, August). *NIDA Notes, 14* (2), 15.
30. Garrett, Laurie (1997, February 19). Needle exchange debate. *Newsday*, p. A19. National Institute on Drug Abuse (1995). *Cooperative agreement for AIDS community-based outreach/intervention research program, 1990–Present.* Rockville MD: National Institute on Drug Abuse.
31. National Institute of Justice (2000). 1999 annual report on drug use among adult and juvenile arrestees. Washington DC: Arrestee Drug Abuse Monitoring Program, Department of Justice, pp. 1–4.
32. National Clearinghouse for Alcohol and Drug Information (1989). *Prevention Plus II: Tools for creating and sustaining drug-free communities.* Rockville MD: Office of Substance Abuse, p. 3. Rivara, Frederick P.; Mueller, Beth A.; Somes, Grant; Mendoza, Carmen T.; Rushforth, Norman B.; and Kellermann, Arthur L. (1997). Alcohol and illicit drug abuse and the risk of violent death in the home. *Journal of the American Medical Association, 278*, 569–575.
33. De La Rosa, Mario, Lambert, Elizabeth Y., and Gropper, Bernard (1990). Introduction: Exploring the substance abuse-violence connection. In *Drugs and violence: Causes, correlates, and consequences* (NIDA Research Monograph 103). Rockville MD: National Institute on Drug Abuse, pp. 1–7.
34. Roth, Jeffrey A. (1994, February). Psychoactive substances and violence: Research brief. Washington DC: National Institute of Justice.
35. Gold, Mark S. (1991). *The good news about drugs and alcohol: Curing, treating and preventing substance abuse in the new age of biopsychiatry.* New York: Villard Books.
36. Bushman, Brad J. (1993, October). Human aggression while under the influence of alcohol and other drugs: An integrative research review. *Current Directions in Psychological Science*, 148–152. Goode, *Drugs* (5th ed.), pp. 153–158. Roth, *Psychoactive substances.*
37. Harris, Jonathan (1991). *Drugged America.* New York: Four Winds Press, p. 112.
38. White, Jason M. (1991). *Drug dependence.* Englewood Cliffs NJ: Prentice Hall, p. 200.
39. Inciardi, The crack-violence connection.
40. Silverman, Lester P., and Spruill, Nancy L. (1977). Urban crime and the price of heroin. *Journal of Urban Economics, 4*, 80–103.
41. Inciardi, The crack-violence connection.
42. Fagan, Jeffry, and Chin, Ko-lin (1990). Violence as regulation and social control in the distribution of crack. In Mario De La Rosa, Elizabeth Y. Lambert, and Bernard Gropper (Eds.), *Drugs and violence: Causes, correlates, and consequences* (NIDA Research Monograph 103). Rockville MD: National Institute on Drug Abuse, pp. 8–43. Office of Juvenile Justice and Delinquency Prevention (1999, July). *1996 national youth gang survey. Summary.* Washington DC: U.S. Department of Justice, pp. 38–39.
43. Berger, Gilda (1989). *Violence and drugs.* New York: Franklin Watts, p. 16. Blumstein, Alfred, and Rosenfeld, Richard (1998, October). Assessing the recent ups and downs in U.S. homicide rates. *National Institute of Justice Journal*, 9–11. Curtis, Richard (1998, October). The improbable transformation of inner-city neighborhoods: Crime, violence, drugs, and youths in the 1990s. *National Institute of Justice Journal*, 16–17. Quotation on p. 17. Harris, *Drugged America*, p. 117.
44. Bugliosi, Vincent T. (1991). *Drugs in America: A citizen's call to action.* New York: Knightsbridge Publishing, p. 25.
45. Brecher. *Licit and illicit drugs*, pp. 6–7.
46. Office of National Drug Control Policy (1999). National drug control strategy 1999. Washington DC: White House Office of National Drug Control Policy.
47. Golden, Tim (1998, December 23). U.S. help for Mexican military has not curtailed drug traffic. *New York Times*, pp. A1, A12. Rohter, Larry (1999, November 20). Colombia tries, yet cocaine thrives. *New York Times*, p. A6.
48. National drug control strategy.
49. Herbert Kleber, quoted in Joseph B. Treaster. (1992, June 14). Twenty years of war on drugs, and no victory yet. *New York Times*, p. E7.
50. Alter, Jonathan (1999, September 9). The buzz on drugs. *Newsweek*, pp. 24–28. Egan, Timothy (1999, March 7). Hard time: Less crime, more criminals. *New York Times*, Section 4, pp. 1, 16. Massing, Michael (1998). *The fix.* New York: Simon and Schuster.
51. F. LaMond Tullis, quoted in Treaster, Joseph B. (1992, June 14). Twenty years of war on drugs. *New York Times*, p. E7. Marlatt, G. Alan (1996). Harm reduction: Come as you are. *Addictive Behaviors, 21*, 779–788.

CHAPTER 3

How Drugs Work in the Body and on the Mind

After you have completed this chapter, you will understand

- The ways drugs enter and exit the body
- Factors determining the physiological impact of drugs
- The sympathetic and parasympathetic branches of the autonomic nervous system
- The basic organization of the brain
- How neurons work and how they communicate with each other
- Explanations of drug actions on neurotransmitters
- Tolerance effects and psychological dependence
- The placebo effect in drug-taking behavior

"His brain could have been held in one hand, easily in two. It would have looked like a grayish-colored wrinkled blob, barely three pounds in weight. It wouldn't have pulsated with life like his heart. Not terribly impressive, you might say. Yet here was this person's entire life, all the years of memories, his talents and aspirations, his virtues and his shortcomings. And here, at one time, were all the chemicals that made it work. If you believe that this person had a soul, this is where it might have been."

—*A neuroscientist reflecting on the human brain and the human mind*

Some of you might have heard of this classic public-service announcement, which aired frequently on television in the late 1980s.

This is your brain (view of egg held in hand).

This is drugs (view of sizzling frying pan).

This is your brain on drugs (view of egg frying in pan).

Any questions?[1]

Giving the viewer considerable "food for thought," its message was immediate and compelling: Don't do drugs because they fry your brain. Doctors were speaking metaphorically, of course. In effect, they were saying that there are certain classes of drugs that have a devastating impact on the human brain. Therefore, stay away from them.

At the same time, an equally important message is that there are other classes of drugs that have enormously beneficial effects on the brain. Drugs are used to treat major mental illnesses such as schizophrenia and depression (see Chapter 16) and play a major role in reducing pain and relieving feelings of anxiety (see Chapters 5 and 15). Whether drugs in general have a positive or negative effect on us depends upon how they interact with physiological processes in the body.

As noted in Chapter 1, psychoactive drugs affect our behavior and experience through their effects on the functioning of the brain. Therefore, our knowledge about drugs and their effects is closely connected with the progress we have made in our understanding of the ways drugs work in the brain. This chapter will describe the basic functions of the nervous system and the ways in which drugs alter these functions. It will serve as a foundation for understanding specific classes of drugs covered in the chapters that follow.

A reasonable place to start is to answer the question: How do drugs get into the body in the first place?

How Drugs Enter the Body

There are four principal routes through which drugs can be delivered into the body: *oral administration, injection, inhalation,* and *absorption through the skin or membranes.* In all four delivery methods, the goal is for the drug to be absorbed into the bloodstream. In the case of psychoactive drugs, a drug effect depends not only on reaching the bloodstream but on reaching the brain as well.

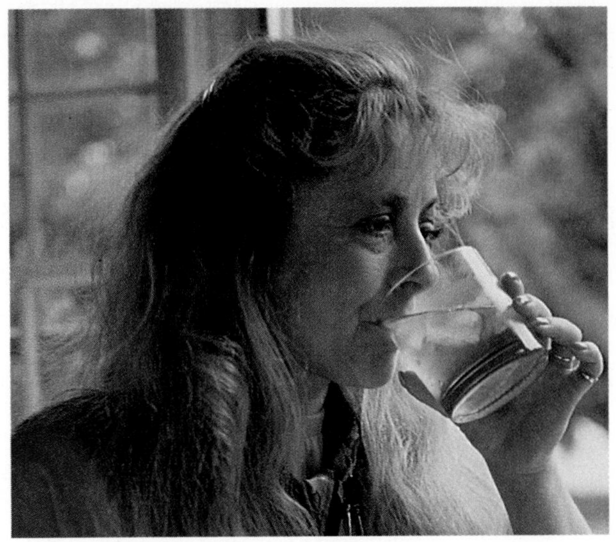

Orally consumed drugs are absorbed into the brain relatively slowly, though for a liquid beverage containing alcohol, the opposite applies: it is easily absorbed.

Oral Administration

Ingesting a drug by mouth, digesting it, and absorbing it into the bloodstream through the gastrointestinal tract is the oldest and easiest way of taking a drug. On the one hand, oral administration and reliance upon the digestive process for delivering a drug into the bloodstream provides a degree of safety. Many naturally growing poisons taste so vile that we normally spit them out before swallowing; others will cause us to be nauseous and the drug will be expelled through vomiting.

In the case of hazardous substances that are not spontaneously rejected, we can benefit from the relatively long absorption time for orally administered drugs. Most of the absorption process is accomplished between five and thirty minutes after ingestion, but absorption is not usually complete for as long as six to eight hours. Therefore, there is at least a little time after accidental overdoses or suicide attempts to induce vomiting or pump the stomach.

On the other hand, the gastrointestinal tract contains a number of natural barriers that may prevent certain drugs that we *want* absorbed into the bloodstream from doing so. We first have to consider the degree of alkalinity or acidity in a drug, defined as its pH value. The interior of the stomach is highly acidic and the fate of a particular drug depends upon how it reacts with that environment. Weakly acidic drugs such as aspirin are absorbed better in the stomach than highly alkaline drugs such as morphine, heroin, or cocaine. Insulin is destroyed by stomach acid so it cannot be administered orally, whereas a neutral substance like alcohol is readily absorbed at all points in the gastrointestinal tract.

If it survives the stomach, the drug needs to proceed from the small intestine into the bloodstream. The membrane separating the intestinal wall from blood capillaries is made up of two layers of fat molecules, making it necessary for substances to be *lipid-soluble* or soluble in fats, in order to pass through. Even after successful absorption into blood capillaries, however, substances must still pass through the liver for another "screening" before being released into the general circulation. There are enzymes in the liver that destroy a drug by metabolizing (breaking down) its molecular structure, prior to its excretion from the body. There is a further barrier separating the circulatory system from brain tissue, which will be discussed in a later section.

As a result of all these natural barriers, orally administered drugs must be ingested at deliberately elevated dose levels, in order to allow for the fact that some proportion of the drug will not make it through to the bloodstream. We can try to compensate for the loss of the drug during digestion, but even then we may be only making a good guess. The state of the gastrointestinal tract changes constantly over time, making it more or less likely that a drug will reach the circulatory system. The presence or absence of undigested food or whether the undigested food interacts with the chemical nature of the drug are examples of factors that make it difficult to make exact predictions about the strength of the drug when it finally enters the bloodstream.

Injection

A solution to the problems of oral administration is to bypass the digestive process entirely and deliver the drug more directly into the bloodstream. One option is to inject the drug through a hypodermic syringe and needle.

The fastest means of injection is an **intravenous** (i.v.) injection, since the drug is delivered into a vein without any intermediary tissue. An intravenous injection of heroin in the forearm, for example, arrives at the brain in less than fifteen seconds. The effects of abused drugs delivered in this way, often called *mainlining*, are not only rapid but extremely intense. In a medical setting, intravenous injections provide an extreme amount of control over dosage and the opportunity to administer multiple drugs at the same time. The principal disadvantage, however, is that the effects of intravenous drugs are irreversible. In the event of a mistake or unexpected reaction, there is no turning back unless some other drug is available that can counteract the first one. In addition, repeated injections through a particular vein may cause the vein to collapse or develop a blood clot.

With **intramuscular** (i.m.) injections, the drug is delivered into a large muscle (usually in the upper arm, thigh, or buttock) and is absorbed into the bloodstream through the capillaries serving the muscle. Intramuscular injections have slower absorption times than intravenous injections, but they can be administered more rapidly in emergency situations. Our exposure to intramuscular injections comes early in our lives when we receive the standard schedule of inoculations against diseases such as measles, diphtheria, and typhoid fever. Tetanus and flu shots are also administered in this way.

A third injection technique is the **subcutaneous** (s.c. or sub-Q) delivery, in which a needle is inserted into the tissue just underneath the skin. Because the skin has a less abundant blood supply relative to a muscle, a subcutaneous injection has the slowest absorption time of all the injection techniques. It is best suited for situations in which it is desirable to have a precise control over the dosage and a steady absorption into the bloodstream. The skin, however, may be easily irritated by this procedure. As a result, only relatively small amounts of a drug can be injected under the skin, compared to the quantity that can be injected into a muscle or vein. When involved in drug abuse, subcutaneous injections are often referred to as *skin-popping*.

All injections require a needle to pierce the skin, so there is an inherent risk of bacterial or viral infection if the needle is not sterile. The practice of injecting heroin or cocaine with shared needles, for example, promotes the spread of infectious hepatitis and AIDS (see Chapter 2). If administered orally, drugs do not have to be any more sterile than the foods we eat or the water we drink.

Inhalation

Next to ingesting a drug, the simplest way of receiving its effects is to inhale it in some form of gaseous or vaporous state. The alveoli within the lungs can be imagined as a huge surface area with blood vessels lying immediately behind it. Our bodies are so dependent upon the oxygen in the air we breathe that we have evolved an extremely efficient system for getting oxygen to its destinations. As a consequence of this highly developed system, the psychoactive effect of an inhaled drug is even faster than a drug

intravenous (i.v.): Into a vein.
intramuscular (i.m.): Into a muscle.
subcutaneous (s.c. or sub-Q): Underneath the skin.

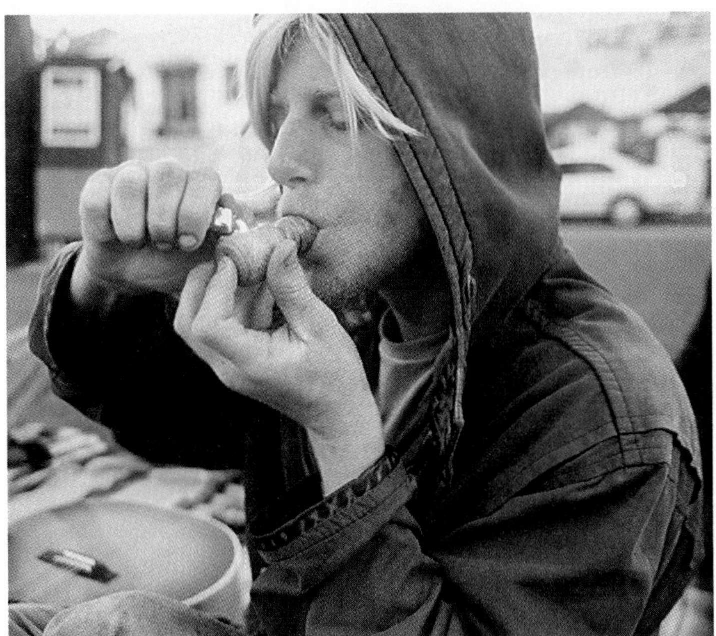

Drugs consumed by inhalation are absorbed extremely quickly, aided by a very efficient delivery system from lungs to brain.

delivered through intravenous injection. Traveling from the lungs to the brain takes only five to eight seconds.

One way of delivering a drug through inhalation is to burn it and breathe in the smoke-borne particles in the air. Drugs administered through smoking include nicotine from cigarettes, opium, tetrahydrocannabinol (THC) from marijuana, free-base cocaine, crack cocaine, and crystallized forms of methamphetamine. Drugs such as paint thinners, gasoline, and glues can also be inhaled because they evaporate easily and the vapors travel freely through the air. In medical settings, general anesthetics are administered through inhalation, since the concentration of the drug can be precisely controlled.

The principal disadvantage of inhaling smoked drugs, as you probably expect, arises from the long-term hazards of breathing particles in the air that contain not only the active drug but also tars and other substances produced by the burning process. Emphysema, asthma, and lung cancer can result from smoking in general (see Chapter 11). There is also the possibility in any form of drug inhalation that the linings leading from the throat to the lungs will be severely irritated over time.

Absorption through the Skin or Membranes

Drug users over the ages have been quite creative in finding other routes through which drugs can be administered. One way is to sniff or snort a drug in dust or powder form into the nose. Once inside the nose, it adheres to thin mucous membranes and dissolves through the membranes into the bloodstream. This technique, referred to as an **intranasal** administration, is commonly used in taking snuff tobacco or cocaine. Snuff tobacco, chewing tobacco, and cocaine-containing coca leaves can also be chewed without swallowing over a period of time or simply placed in the cheek so that they are slowly absorbed through the membranes of the mouth. Nitroglycerin tablets for heart-disease patients are typically administered **sublingually,** with the drug placed underneath the tongue and absorbed into the bloodstream.

At the opposite end of the body, medicines can be placed as a suppository into the rectum, where the suppository gradually melts and the medicine is absorbed through thin rectal membranes. This method is less reliable than an oral administration, but it may be necessary if the individual is vomiting or unconscious. The newest technique involves a **transdermal patch,** which allows a drug to slowly diffuse through the skin without breaking the skin surface. Transdermal patches have been used for long-term administration of nitroglycerin, estrogen, and motion-sickness medication, and more recently nicotine. Newly developed procedures to enhance the process of skin penetration include the promising technique of administering low-frequency ultrasound, which allows large molecules such as insulin to pass through the skin. Insulin administration is an especially interesting application because, until now, the only effective way of getting it into the bloodstream has been through injection.[2]

Drugs . . . in Focus on page 56 summarizes the various ways drugs can be administered into the body.

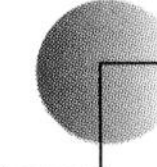

How Drugs Exit the Body

Having observed how a drug is absorbed into the bloodstream and, in the case of a psychoactive drug, into

intranasal: Applied to the mucous membranes of the nose.
sublingual: Applied under the tongue.
transdermal patch: A device attached to the skin that slowly delivers the drug through skin absorption.

Drugs . . . in Focus

Ways to Take Drugs: Routes of Administration

Oral Administration (by Mouth)

- Method: By swallowing or consuming in eating or drinking
- Advantages: Slow absorption time; possibility of rejecting poisons and overdoses
- Disadvantages: Slow absorption time; no immediate effect
- Examples: Medications in pill form, marijuana (baked in food), amphetamine and methamphetamine, barbiturates, LSD (swallowed or licked off paper), PCP, opium, methadone, codeine, caffeine, alcohol

Injection (by Hypodermic Syringe)

INTRAVENOUS INJECTION

- Method: By needle positioned into a vein
- Advantages: Very fast absorption time; immediate effects
- Disadvantages: Cannot be undone; risks of allergic reactions
- Examples: PCP, methamphetamine, heroin, methadone, morphine

INTRAMUSCULAR INJECTION

- Method: By needle positioned into a large muscle
- Advantages: Quicker to administer than an intravenous injection
- Disadvantages: Somewhat slower absorption time than an intravenous injection; risk of piercing a vein by accident
- Examples: Many inoculations

SUBCUTANEOUS INJECTION

- Method: By needle positioned underneath the skin
- Advantages: Easiest administration of all injection techniques
- Disadvantages: Slower absorption time than an intramuscular injection; risk of skin irritation and deterioration
- Examples: Heroin and other narcotics

Inhalation (by Breathing)

SMOKING

- Method: By burning drug and breathing smoke-borne particles into the lungs
- Advantages: Extremely fast absorption time
- Disadvantages: Effect limited to time during which drug is being inhaled; risk of emphysema, asthma, and lung cancer from inhaling tars and hydrocarbons in the smoke; lung and throat irritation over chronic use
- Examples: Nicotine (from tobacco), marijuana, hashish, methamphetamine, ice, free-base cocaine, crack cocaine, PCP, heroin, and opium

VAPOROUS INHALATION

- Method: By breathing in vapors from drug
- Advantages: Extremely fast absorption time
- Disadvantages: Effect limited to time during which drug is being inhaled; lung and throat irritation over chronic use
- Examples: Surgical and dental anesthetics, paint thinners, gasoline, cleaning fluid

Absorption (through Skin or Membranes)

- Method: By positioning drug against skin, inserting it against rectal membrane, snorting it against mucous membranes of the nose, or placing it under the tongue or against the cheek so it diffuses across into bloodstream
- Advantages: Quick absorption time
- Disadvantages: Irritation of skin or membranes
- Examples: Cocaine, amphetamine, methamphetamine, nicotine, snuff tobacco, coca leaves

the brain, we now will consider the ways in which the body eliminates it. The most common means of elimination is through excretion in the urine after a series of actions in the liver and kidneys. In some cases, elimination occurs through excretion in exhaled breath, feces, sweat, saliva, or (in the case of nursing mothers) breast milk.

The sequence of metabolic events leading to urinary excretion begins with a process called **biotransformation,** chiefly through the action of specific enzymes in the liver. The products of biotransformation, referred to as **metabolites,** are structurally modified forms of the original drug. Generally speaking, if these metabolites are water-soluble, they are passed along to the kidneys and eventually excreted in the urine. If they are less water-soluble, then they are reabsorbed into the intestines and excreted through defecation. On rare occasions, a drug may pass through the liver without any biotransformation at all and be excreted intact. The hallucinogenic

biotransformation: The process of changing the molecular structure of a drug into forms that make it easier to be excreted from the body.

metabolite (me-TAB-oh-lite): A by-product resulting from the biotransformation process.

drug *Amanita muscaria* is an example of this kind of drug (see Chapter 6).

A number of factors influence the process of biotransformation and urinary excretion and, in turn, the rate of elimination from the body. For most drugs, biotransformation rates will increase as a function of the drug's concentration in the bloodstream. In effect, the larger the quantity of a drug, the faster the body tries to get rid of it. An exception, however, is alcohol, for which the rate of biotransformation is constant no matter how much alcohol has been ingested (see Chapter 9). The activity of enzymes required for biotransformation may be increased or decreased by the presence of other drugs in the body. As a result, the effect of one drug may interact with the effect of another, creating a potentially dangerous combination. An individual's age can also be a factor. Because enzyme activity in the liver declines after the age of forty, older people eliminate drugs at a slower pace than do younger people. We will look at the consequences of drug interactions and individual differences in the next section of this chapter.

Finally, it is important to point out that drugs are gradually eliminated from the body at different rates simply on the basis of their chemical properties. In general, if a drug is fat-soluble, the rate will be slower than if a drug is water-soluble. On average, we can look at the rate of elimination of a particular drug through an index called its **elimination half-life**, the amount of time it takes for the drug in the bloodstream to decline to 50 percent of its original equilibrium level. Many drugs such as cocaine and nicotine have half-lives of only a few hours; marijuana and some prescription medications are examples of drugs with much longer half-lives.[3] Understanding the variation in rates of elimination is extremely important if we are to develop drug-testing procedures to detect the presence of abused drugs, a topic to be examined in Chapter 8.

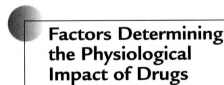

Factors Determining the Physiological Impact of Drugs

The type of delivery route into the bloodstream, as has been discussed, places specific constraints upon the effect a drug may produce. Some drug effects are optimized, for example, by an oral administration, whereas others require more direct access to the bloodstream. Other factors must be considered as well. If a drug is administered repeatedly, the timing of the administrations plays an important role in determining the final result. If two drugs are administered close together in time, we must also consider how these drugs interact with each other. Finally, it is possible that two identical drugs taken by two individuals may have different effects by virtue of the characteristics of the drug user at the time of administration. These three factors will now be considered.

Timing

All drugs, no matter how they are delivered, share some common features when we consider their effects over time. There is initially an interval (the **latency period**) during which the concentration of the drug is increasing in the blood but is not yet high enough for a drug effect to be detected. How long this latency period will last is related generally to the absorption time of the drug. As the concentration of the drug continues to rise, the effect will become stronger. A stage will be eventually reached when the effect attains a maximum strength, even though the concentration in the blood continues to rise. This point is unfortunately the point at which the drug may produce undesirable side effects. One solution to this problem is to administer the drug in a time-release form. In this approach, a large dose is given initially in order to enable the drug effect to be felt; then smaller doses are programmed to be released at specific intervals afterward to postpone, up to twelve hours or so, the decline in the drug's concentration in the blood. The intention is to keep the concentration of the drug in the blood within a "therapeutic window" high enough for the drug to be effective while low enough to avoid any toxic effects. When drugs are administered repeatedly, there is a risk that the second dose will boost the concentration of the drug in the blood too high before the effect of the first dose has a chance to decline (Figure 3.1).

Drug Interactions

Two basic types of interactions may occur when two drugs are mixed together. In the first type, two drugs in combination may produce an effect that is greater than the effect of either drug administered separately. In some cases, the combination effect is purely *additive*. For example, if the effect of one drug alone is equivalent to a 4 and the effect of another drug is a 6, then the combined

elimination half-life: The length of time it takes for a drug to be reduced to 50 percent of its equilibrium level in the bloodstream.

latency period: An interval of time during which the blood levels of a drug are not yet sufficient for a drug effect to be observed.

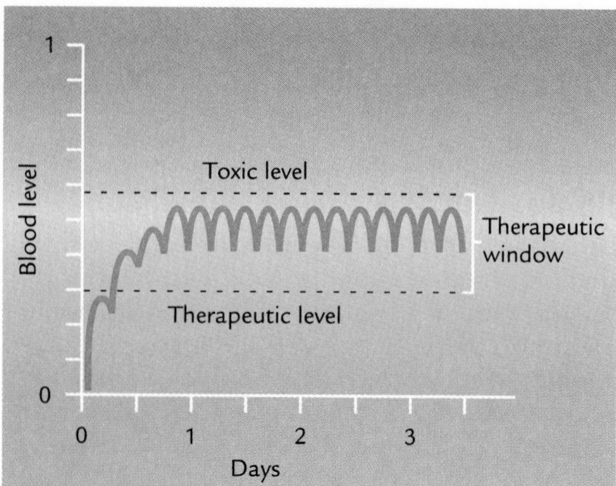

FIGURE 3.1

The therapeutic window. Time-release drugs administer the drug in small amounts over time in order to stay between the therapeutic level and the toxic level.

additive effect is equivalent to a value of 10. In other cases, however, the combination effect is *hyperadditive*, with the combined effect exceeding the sum of the individual drugs administered alone, as in the two drugs in the first example combining to a value of 13 or more. Any hyperadditive effect produced by a combination of two or more drugs is referred to as **synergism.** In some synergistic combinations, one drug may even double or triple the effect of another. It is also possible that one drug might have no effect at all unless it is taken simultaneously with another. This special form of synergism is called **potentiation;** it is as though a drug with no effect at all by itself, when combined with a drug having an effect of 6, produces a result equivalent to a 10. The danger of such interactions is that the combined effect of the drugs is so powerful as to become toxic. In extreme cases, the toxicity can be lethal.

In the second type of interaction, two drugs can be *antagonistic* if the effect of one drug is diminished to some degree when administered with another, a situation comparable to a drug with the effect of 6 and a drug with the effect of 4 combining to produce an effect of 3. Later chapters will discuss drugs that are totally antagonistic to each other, in that the second exactly cancels out, or neutralizes, the effect of the first. Health Alert warns that dangerous interactions can result not only from drug–drug combinations but from food–drug combinations as well. Another Health Alert in Chapter 16 will review the potentially dangerous consequences of combining drugs with herb-derived dietary supplements.

QUICK CONCEPT  3.1

Understanding Drug Interactions

Check your understanding of drug interactions by assuming the following values to represent the effects of Drugs A, B, and C, when taken individually:

- Drug A 0
- Drug B 20
- Drug C 35

Identify the type of drug interaction when the following values represent the effect of two drugs in combination.

1. Drug A combined with Drug B 30

____

2. Drug B combined with Drug C 55

____

3. Drug A combined with Drug C 15

____

4. Drug B combined with Drug C 85

____

5. Drug B combined with Drug C 0

____

6. Drug A combined with Drug B 20

____

Answers: 1. potentiation 2. additive 3. antagonistic 4. synergistic (hyperadditive) 5. antagonistic 6. additive

Individual Differences

Some variations in drug effects may be related to an interaction between the drug itself and specific characteristics of the person taking the drug. One characteristic is an individual's weight. In general, a heavier person will

synergism (SIN-er-jih-zum): The property of a drug interaction in which the combination effect of two drugs exceeds the effect of either drug administered alone.
potentiation: The property of a drug interaction in which one drug combined with another drug produces an effect when one of the drugs alone would have had no effect.

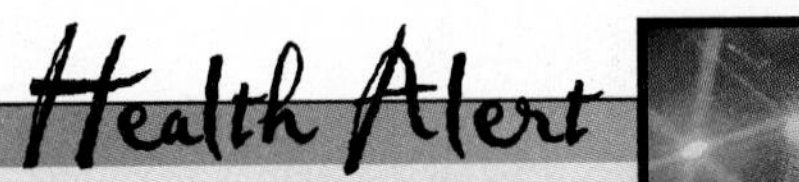

Combinations That Do More Harm Than Good

It would be impossible to list every known drug-drug interaction or food-drug interaction. However, here are some examples. Any adverse reaction to a combination of drugs or a combination of a drug with something eaten should be reported to a physician immediately.

Hyperadditive Effects

Alcohol with barbiturate-related sleep medications, cardiovascular medications, insulin, anti-inflammatory medications, antihistamines, painkillers, antianxiety medications

Septra, Bactrim, or related types of antibiotics with Coumadin (an anticoagulant)

Tagamet (a heartburn and ulcer treatment medication) with Coumadin

Aspirin, Aleve, Advil, or related painkillers with Coumadin

Plendil (a blood pressure medication) or Procardia (an angina treatment) with grapefruit juice

Lanoxin (a medication for heart problems) with licorice

Lanoxin with bran, oatmeal, or other high-fiber foods

Antagonistic Effects

Morphine/heroin with naloxone or naltrexone

Norpramin or related antidepressants with bran, oatmeal, or other high-fiber foods

Possible Toxic Reactions

Internal bleeding by a combination of Parnate and Anafranil (two types of antidepressants)

Elevated body temperature by a combination of Nardil (an antidepressant) with Demerol (a painkiller)

Excessive blood pressure or stroke by a combination of Parnate, Nardil, or related antidepressants with cheddar cheese, pickled herring, or other foods high in tyramine

Agitation or elevated body temperature by a combination of Paxil, Prozac, Zoloft, or related antidepressants with Parnate, Nardil, or related antidepressants

Irregular heartbeat, cardiac arrest, and sudden death by a combination of Hismanal or Seldane (two antihistamines) with Nizoral (an antifungal drug)

Source: Graedon, Joe, and Graedon, Teresa (1995). *The people's guide to deadly interactions.* New York: St. Martin's Press.

require a greater amount of a drug than a lighter person to receive an equivalent drug effect, all other things being equal. It is for this reason that drug dosages are expressed as a ratio of drug amount to body weight. This ratio is typically expressed in metric terms, as milligrams-per-kilogram (mg/kg).

Another characteristic is gender. Even if a man and a woman are exactly the same weight, differences in drug effects can still result on the basis of gender differences in body composition and sex hormones. Women have, on average, a higher proportion of fat, due to a greater fat-to-muscle ratio, and a lower proportion of water than men. When we look at the effects of alcohol consumption in terms of gender, we find that the lower water content (a factor that tends to dilute the alcohol in the body) in women makes them feel more intoxicated than men, even if the same amount of alcohol is consumed.

Relative to men, women also have reduced levels of enzymes that break down alcohol in the liver, resulting in higher alcohol levels in the blood and a higher level of intoxication.[4] We suspect that the lower level of alcohol biotransformation may be related to an increased level of estrogen and progesterone in women. Whether gender differences exist with regard to drugs other than alcohol is presently unknown.

Still another individual characteristic that influences the ways certain drugs affect the body is ethnic background. About 50 percent of all people of Asian descent, for example, show low levels of one of the enzymes that normally breaks down alcohol in the liver shortly before it is excreted. With this particular deficiency, alcohol metabolites tend to build up in the blood, producing a faster heart rate, facial flushing, and nausea.[5] As a result, many Asians find drinking to be quite unpleasant.

Ethnic variability can be seen in terms of other drug effects as well. It has been found that Caucasians have a faster rate of biotransformation of antipsychotic and antianxiety medications than Asians and, as a result, end up with relatively lower concentrations of drugs in the blood. One consequence of this difference is in the area of psychiatric treatment. Asian schizophrenic patients require significantly lower doses of antipsychotic medication in order for their symptoms to improve, and they experience medication side effects at much lower doses than do Caucasian patients. Since other possible factors such as diet, life-style, and environment do not account for these differences, we can speculate that these differences have a genetic basis.[6]

In some cases, differences in the physiological response to a particular drug can explain differential patterns of drug-taking behavior. For example, researchers have recently found that African Americans have a slower rate of nicotine metabolism following the smoking of cigarettes, relative to whites. This finding might be the reason why African Americans, on average, report smoking fewer cigarettes per day than whites. If we assume that an equivalent level of nicotine needs to be maintained in both populations, fewer cigarettes smoked but a higher level of nicotine absorbed per cigarette will produce the same effect as a greater number of cigarettes smoked but a lower nicotine level absorbed per cigarette. African American smokers may be taking in and retaining relatively more nicotine per cigarette, and as a result not having to smoke as many cigarettes per day.[7]

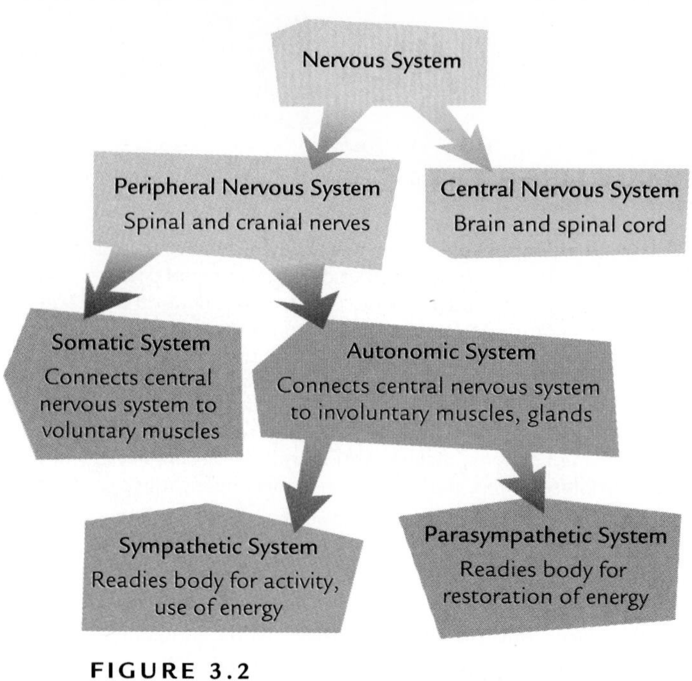

FIGURE 3.2

Organizational chart of the nervous system.

Introducing the Nervous System

Before we can begin to deal with the specific impact of drugs on the brain, we need first to understand some basic facts about the overall organization of the nervous system, of which the brain is a part.

In simplest terms, the nervous system is designed to do two basic things: to take in information from the environment around us and to control our bodily responses so that we can live effectively in that environment. But, of course, we do a lot more than that. We interpret the information coming in, try to make sense of it, remember some of it for a later time, and more than occasionally generate some information on our own in a process called thinking.

We can understand these different functions in terms of divisions within the nervous system. In general, the nervous system is divided into the **central nervous system (CNS)**, consisting of the brain and the spinal cord, and the **peripheral nervous system,** consisting of all the nerves and nerve fibers that connect the CNS to the environment and to our muscles and glands (Figure 3.2).

The Peripheral Nervous System

The peripheral nervous system is essentially the system that brings information in and later, after processing in the CNS, executes our behavioral response. On the input side, it includes the visual pathway, the auditory pathway, and other channels of sensory information about the world around us. On the output side, motor pathways in the peripheral nervous system that control our reactions to that world produce two basic acts.

The first type, called a *somatic* response, is a voluntary reaction, executed by skeletal muscles that are attached to bone. When you lift your arm, for example, you have executed a series of motor commands that ultimately results in contractions of flexor and extensor muscles. In this case, the movement is deliberate, conscious, and controlled.

A second type of reaction, called an *autonomic* response, is usually involuntary and executed by smooth muscles that form the walls of arteries, veins, capillaries, and internal organs as well as cardiac muscles that form the walls of the heart. When you blush, for example, the capillaries are dilating, or enlarging, underneath the surface of your skin, an effect that produces a reddening color and a feeling of warmth. As most of us know from

central nervous system (CNS): The portion of the nervous system that consists of the spinal cord and the brain.
peripheral nervous system: The portion of the nervous system consisting of nerves and nerve fibers that carry information to the central nervous system and outward to muscles and glands.

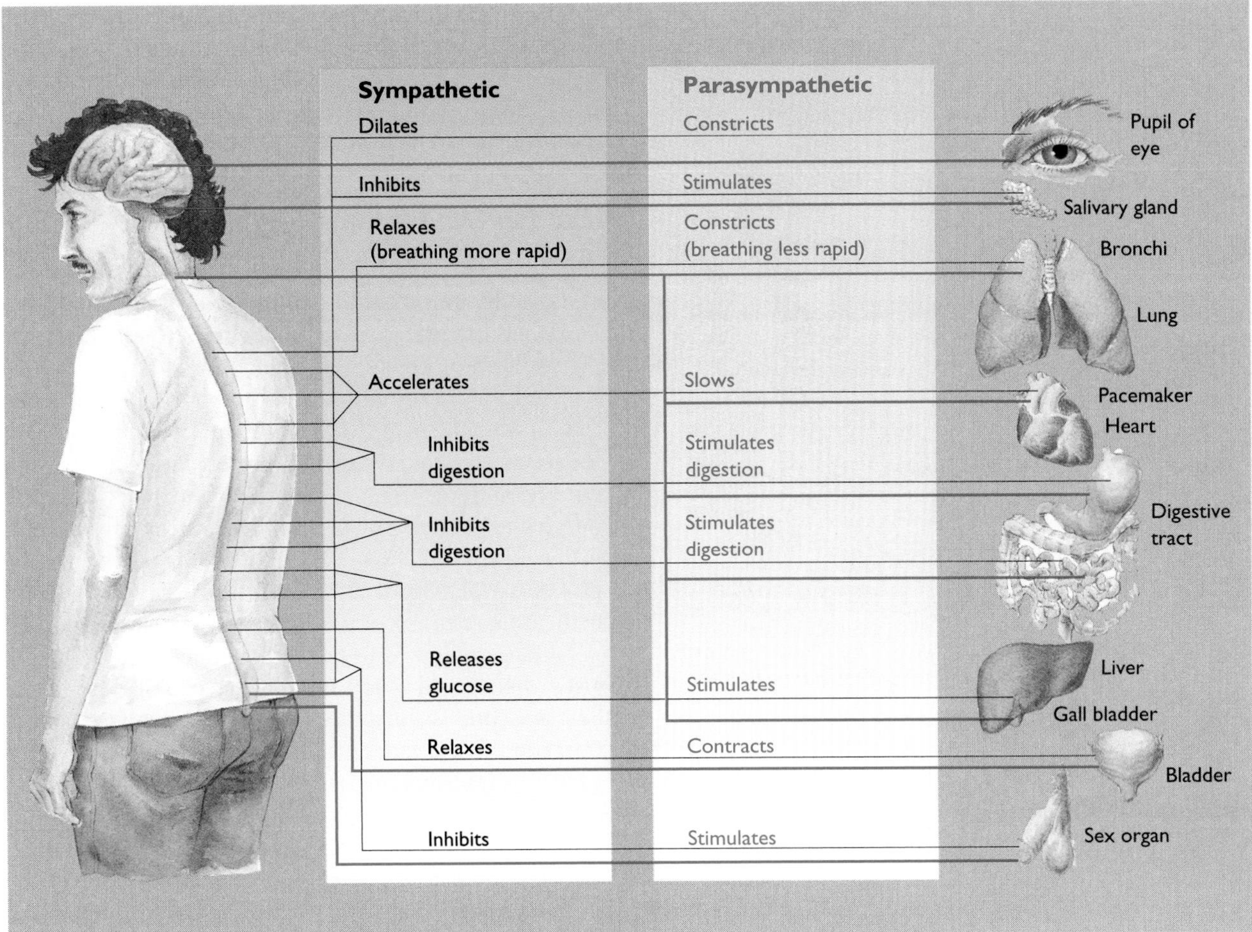

FIGURE 3.3

Functions of the sympathetic and parasympathetic branches of the autonomic nervous system.

personal experience, blushing often occurs when we do not necessarily want it to, and it is difficult to make it go away. And yet it is a reaction to a situation that has been processed through our sensory pathways and interpreted within the brain; in this case, some emotional content has triggered this autonomic response.

We should not think of autonomic responses, however, as merely an annoyance. Indeed, we need them to survive. If we were to take the time to execute deliberate commands to breathe regularly, to have our hearts beat at an appropriate rate, or to carry out the thousands of changes that our internal organs make, we certainly would not last very long. The autonomic control that we have evolved is a product of the interplay of two subsystems, each delivered to smooth and cardiac muscles and to glands through its own set of nerve fibers. These subsystems are referred to as the **sympathetic** and **parasympathetic branches of the autonomic nervous system.**

Sympathetic and Parasympathetic Responses

Autonomic responses are divided into two general categories (Figure 3.3). The first is oriented toward dealing with some kind of emergency or stress. If we are in a

sympathetic branch of the autonomic nervous system: The portion of the autonomic nervous system controlling bodily changes that deal with stressful or emergency situations.

parasympathetic branch of the autonomic nervous system: The portion of the autonomic nervous system controlling the bodily changes that lead to increased nurturance, rest, and maintenance.

During emergency situations, specific bodily changes are produced through stimulation of the sympathetic branch of the autonomic nervous system.

situation that is perceived as a threat to our internal well-being or to our survival, the sympathetic system is in charge. During times of *sympathetic activation,* the heart rate goes up, blood pressure goes up, the bronchi in the lungs dilate to accommodate a greater amount of oxygen, the pupil dilates to allow more light into the eye, and other bodily systems alter their level of functioning, so we are in a better position to fight, to flee, or simply to feel frightened. Not all systems, however, increase their activity during sympathetic activation. The gastrointestinal tract is inhibited; we obviously do not want to be digesting our lunch when we are battling for our lives.

The second category of response is totally opposite to the first. We cannot be "on alert" all our lives; we need some time to regroup our forces, to orient ourselves toward a state of calm and rest necessary for nurturance and internal maintenance. Heart rate and blood pressure now go down, bronchi and pupils constrict, and the gastrointestinal tract is now excited rather than inhibited. These and other changes constitute *parasympathetic activation* and are an important counterpoint to the activation of the sympathetic system.

We can swing back and forth between sympathetic and parasympathetic activation as the need arises and the situation presents itself, and in many instances the momentary state of the autonomic nervous system is somewhere in between the two extremes. Some psychoactive drugs, however, produce autonomic changes, in addition to their direct effects on the brain. They may produce a swing toward sympathetic activation or a swing toward parasympathetic activation.

The Central Nervous System

The central nervous system, located along the central axis of the body, consists of the spinal cord and the brain. It is here that interpretations of our sensory input occur and the intricate processing of information is accomplished. Some of our sensory nerves, such as those originating at locations from the neck down, enter the CNS at the level of the spinal cord; others, such as those nerves coming from our eyes and ears, enter at the level of the brain. Complex information entering at the spinal cord is carried by neural pathways upward into the brain for further processing; the processing of simpler information may not involve the brain at all, resulting instead in merely reflexive responses.

Consider how your body might react, in terms of the systems discussed so far. Imagine, as you read this page, that someone is sneaking up behind you and grabbing your shoulder. A sudden start and jerking of your body is a result of information that has little to do with the brain; the reaction is accomplished at a spinal level. You may then decide to look around and see who it is, in which case you are now dealing with visual and possibly some auditory information, and the brain will be interpreting the input either as a practical joke or a real threat. In the latter case, the sympathetic nervous system will begin to be activated after a few seconds, orienting your body toward dealing with this situation through changes in your smooth and cardiac muscles.

The most important part of the CNS, at least for advanced species such as ourselves, is the brain. It is nearly impossible to overestimate its role in our everyday lives. Every gesture we make, every feeling, every experience we have of our surroundings, every insight or memory, is a result of a complex, beautifully modulated pattern of activity among approximately 100 billion specialized cells called **neurons.** We owe our entire cognitive universe, all of what we are or think we are, to the functioning of these cells. It is here that psychoactive drugs are doing their work, for good or for bad.

---

neuron: The specialized cell in the nervous system designed to receive and transmit information.

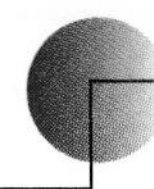

Understanding the Brain

Proceeding upward from the spinal cord, starting at the point where the CNS enlarges into the brain, neuroanatomists have classified brain tissue into three major sections: the *hindbrain*, the *midbrain*, and finally the *forebrain* (Figure 3.4). The older and more primitive systems of the brain tend to be underneath the newer and more sophisticated ones, so as we travel upward from hindbrain to midbrain to forebrain on our quick tour, we are dealing with structures that have evolved ever more recently and have greater involvement in complex behaviors. You can think of this arrangement in brain anatomy as similar to an archaeological dig, where the strata of previous civilizations extend downward into greater and greater antiquity. Understanding the brain in terms of the orderliness of its development over the span of evolutionary history helps to make sense of its complexity.

The Hindbrain

At the top of the spinal cord, neural tissue suddenly widens and enlarges into the hindbrain. The *medulla* lies at the point of the hindbrain where this enlargement has just begun. It is essentially the coordinator of the basic life-support systems in our body. Blood pressure is controlled here, as are the rhythms of breathing, heart rate, digestion, and even vomiting. Death would be seconds away, were it not for the normal functioning of the medulla. Unfortunately, it is highly sensitive to opiates, alcohol, barbiturates, and other depressants. When levels of any of these drugs are excessive in overdose cases, the respiratory controls in the medulla are inhibited and death can result from asphyxiation (lack of breathing). Even if a person survives, the lack of oxygen in the blood while he or she is not breathing can result in severe brain damage. On a more positive note, the vomiting center in the medulla is sensitive to the presence of poisons in the blood and is able to initiate vomiting to get rid of unwanted and potentially harmful substances.

Another hindbrain structure, situated just above the medulla, is the *pons*. We can view the pons in terms of our ability to maintain the necessary level of alertness to survive. Within the pons are structures that determine when we sleep and when we wake up, as well as the main portion of a structure called the *reticular formation* that energizes the rest of the brain to be alert to incoming information. Drugs that affect the patterns of our sleep influence the sleep centers in the pons.

Behind the medulla and the pons in the hindbrain is the *cerebellum*, an important structure for the maintenance

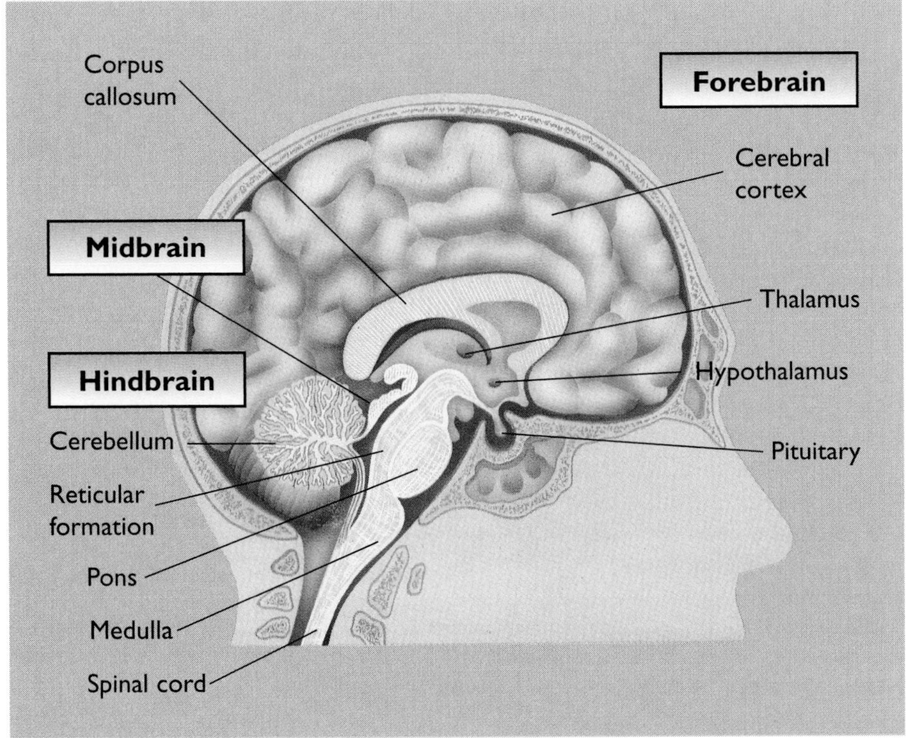

FIGURE 3.4

Basic structures of the human brain.

of balance and for the execution of smooth movements of the body. The dizziness and lack of coordination we experience after consuming alcohol is related in large part to alcohol's depressive effect on the cerebellum.

The Midbrain

The midbrain, located just above the hindbrain, is a center for the control of important sensory and motor reflexes as well as the processing of pain information.

Without a specific region of the midbrain called the *substantia nigra,* we would not be able to control the movements of our bodies effectively. Parkinson's disease, a disorder characterized by muscular tremors and other motor difficulties, is a result of a degeneration of the substantia nigra. Unfortunately, symptoms that resemble Parkinson's disease are frequently observed in patients taking antipsychotic medication, an issue that will be explored further in Chapter 16.

The Forebrain

In the uppermost section of the brain are two important areas to consider. The first area, lying immediately above the midbrain, includes the *hypothalamus* and the *limbic system.* It is through these structures that we are able to carry out the appropriate motivational and emotional acts that ensure our survival as a species. Feeding behavior, drinking behavior, and sexual behavior are controlled by the hypothalamus.

The limbic system surrounds the hypothalamus and plays a central role in organizing emotional behavior during times of stress. Experimental lesions in points within the limbic system can turn a tame animal into a raging monster or a wild animal into a docile one. Not surprisingly, theories about the basis for psychological dependence have focused on the limbic system. Some of these ideas will be explored later in the chapter. Drugs that deal with symptoms of anxiety, depression, and schizophrenia affect regions within the limbic system.

The second forebrain area of concern, and the most important from the standpoint of understanding human behavior, is a two-sided, wrinkled sheet of neural tissue, with a thickness approximately equivalent to the height of a capital letter on this page and overhanging almost all of the brain: the hemispheres of the **cerebral cortex.** Its appearance resembles that of a giant walnut, an association that prompted early physicians in the Middle Ages to prescribe walnuts as medicine for diseases of the brain (obviously, a nutty idea).[8]

When we arrive at the cerebral cortex (or cortex, for short), we have arrived at the pinnacle of the brain both functionally and spatially. Specific regions of the cerebral cortex are concerned with processing visual, auditory, and somatosensory (touch) information, while other regions control the organization of complex and precise movements. A large percentage of cortical tissue is devoted to the task of associating one piece of information with another. In the human brain, more than 80 percent of the cortex, called the association cortex, concerns itself with the integration of ideas. Of all the areas within the association cortex, the most recently evolved is a region closest to the front of the brain called the *prefrontal cortex.* Our higher-order, intellectual abilities as well as our personality characteristics emerge from activity in this region.

QUICK CONCEPT  3.2

Understanding Drugs and Brain Functioning

Check your understanding of the relationship between certain psychoactive drugs and functions of the brain by matching the most likely part of the brain to be affected by a given drug, given the description of its behavioral effects.

DRUGS	PARTS OF THE BRAIN MOST LIKELY TO BE AFFECTED
1. Drug X changes the pattern of your sleep.	cerebral cortex
2. Drug Y interferes with your long-term memory.	medulla
3. Drug Z raises your general arousal level.	cerebellum
4. Drug U interferes with your ability to control food intake.	pons
5. Drug V interferes with your ability to breathe.	hypothalamus
6. Drug W makes you very dizzy.	reticular formation

Answers: 1. pons 2. cerebral cortex 3. reticular formation 4. hypothalamus 5. medulla 6. cerebellum

cerebral cortex: The portion of the forebrain devoted to a high level of information processing.

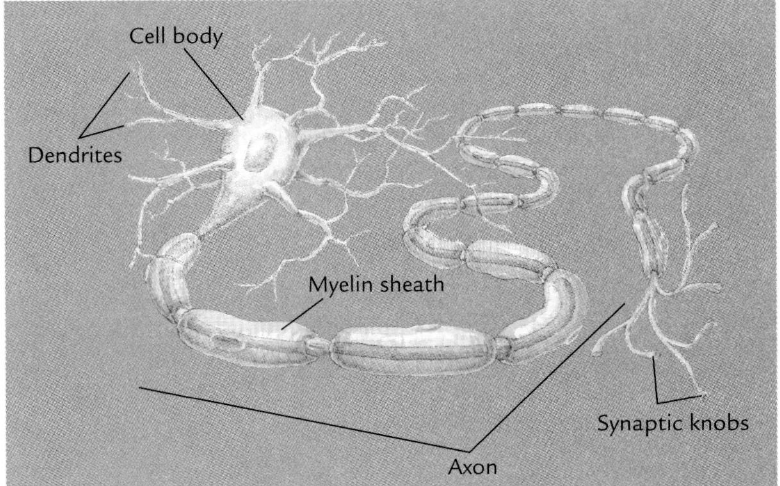

FIGURE 3.5

Basic structure of a neuron. The axon is shown surrounded by the myelin sheath, which increases the transmission of nerve impulses.

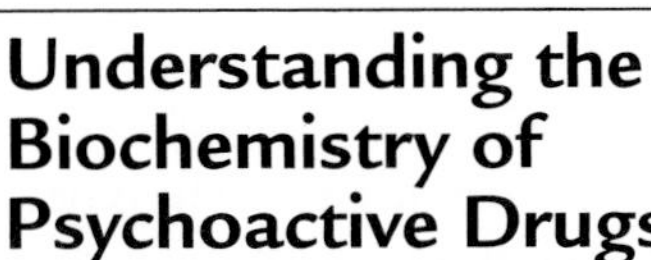

Understanding the Biochemistry of Psychoactive Drugs

Gaining some perspective about brain anatomy lays the foundation for our understanding of *where* certain psychoactive drugs are active, but it does not help us to understand *how* they work. In order to answer this second question, we need to know something about neurons themselves, the specialized cells designed to communicate information within the nervous system.

Introducing Neurons

Here is a scary thought. There are an estimated 100 billion neurons in the brain, and the number of possible interconnections that exist among them all has been estimated to be greater than the total number of atomic particles in the known universe.[9] Therefore, you might call it an understatement that the brain is the most complex organ of the body. How can we possibly begin to understand the brain amidst such complexity? Or rather, are our own brains sophisticated enough to understand how our brains work?

Fortunately, the task is not as insurmountable as it appears. The neuron itself, as the basic unit of the nervous system, can be understood in relatively simple terms. Imagine the neuron at any moment in time as a tiny device that is either on or off, like a light switch. There is no intermediate state. In this respect, the nervous system is digital like a computer, since a computer consists simply of electrical circuits that are permitted only two states, open or closed. In terms of the neuron, the "on" state is accomplished by the generation of an electrical change in its membrane, referred to as a *nerve impulse.* Just as the neuron is the basic unit that forms the structure of the nervous system, the nerve impulse is the basic unit that forms the language of the nervous system.

The role of the neuron is to receive information and to transmit information, carrying out this mission through its three principal components: the *cell body,* the *dendrites,* and the *axon* (Figure 3.5). The cell body comprises the bulk of the neuron and contains the nucleus and other elements that relate it to other types of cells in the body, such as muscle cells, skin cells, and blood cells. What makes the neuron unique is its appendages, extending out from the cell body, some rather short and one quite long. The short ones are called dendrites and represent the part of the neuron that receives information from the outside. The long appendage, called the axon, is the part that transmits information outward. The axon is essentially the carrier of the messages of the neuron.

When a nerve impulse is generated, the impulse travels down the length of the axon at speeds up to 120 meters per second (roughly 270 miles per hour) until it reaches the axon's end point. If we followed the axon along its length, starting from the cell body (and sometimes that distance may be as long as a meter in length), we would see that toward its end the axon diverges like the branches of a tree. At the terminal point of each of these branches are small button-like structures called *synaptic knobs.* We have arrived at the crucial point of the story: the gap between neurons known as the **synapse.**

synapse (SIN-apse): The juncture between neurons. It consists of a synaptic knob, the intervening gap, and receptor sites on a receiving neuron.

Synaptic Communication

The basic scenario is as follows: Located inside each synaptic knob are *synaptic vesicles* which produce and store millions of chemical molecules called **neurotransmitters.** Without neurotransmitters, the nerve impulse, upon arrival at the terminal points of the axon, would sputter out like a wet fuse, and the neuron would have no function at all. Instead, the nerve impulse causes the release of neurotransmitter molecules out of the vesicle and into special receptor sites in the membranes of dendrites on the other side of the synapse. These receptors have internal shapes that are designed to match the external shape of the neurotransmitter, which allows the neurotransmitter and receptor to fit together closely, like a key fitting into a lock (Figure 3.6). When the neurotransmitter has successfully locked into the receptor site, an electrical change (technically, a change in the electrical potential) occurs in the membrane of the receiving neuron. Neuron A has now communicated with neuron B.

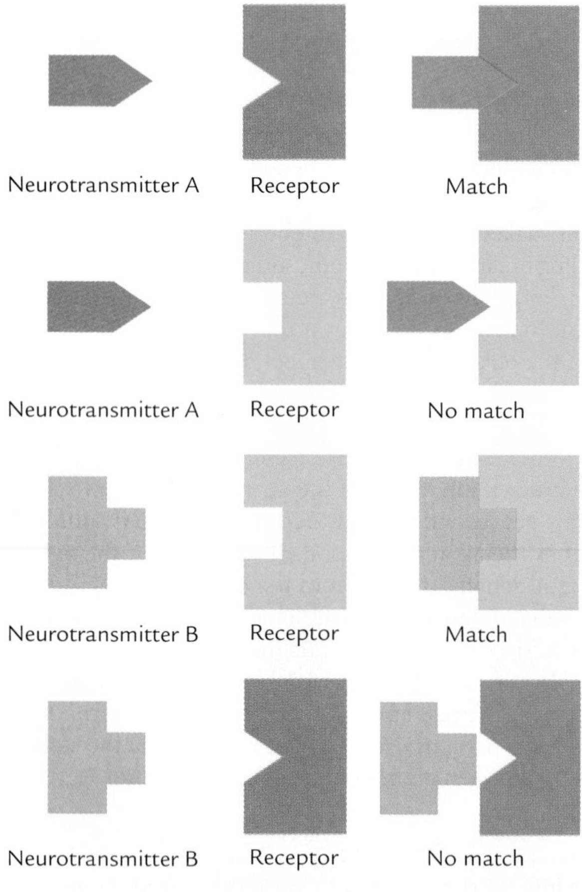

FIGURE 3.6

Communication between neurons depends on a match between neurotransmitter and receptor.

But what exactly is the message? It takes one of two forms: it is either a message to excite or a message to inhibit. The receiving neuron, like all neurons in the nervous system, is continually "firing"—that is, it is continually creating nerve impulses. Basically, there are two alternatives for change: either an increase in activity (excitation) or a decrease (inhibition). Excitation, therefore, makes the neuron emit a greater number of nerve impulses per second's time; inhibition makes the neuron emit a lesser number of nerve impulses per second's time. Whether the effect will be excitatory or inhibitory depends on the specific neurotransmitter that is present at the synapse.

It should be understood that synaptic communication is happening hundreds of times every second. In fact, in order to allow neurons to fire in very quick succession, the neurotransmitter molecules cannot remain in the receptor sites for more than a millisecond or two. Once the neurotransmitter binds itself to the receptor, it is expelled and returns back to the synaptic knob. The process of "returning back," called **reuptake,** is essentially a way of getting the neurotransmitter back to the knob where it can be released again (Figure 3.7).

Successful reuptake, however, is not a certainty. In the vicinity of the synapse are enzymes that are capable of deactivating the neurotransmitter molecule. These enzymes control the amounts of neurotransmitter in the region of the synapse so as to prevent too many molecules from "clogging" the receptor sites and interfering with the normal process of one neuron communicating with another. As a result of these enzymes, some of the neurotransmitter molecules do not make it back. Under normal circumstances the neurons then synthesize more to make up for any deficiency.

Although the principle of synaptic communication rests upon the possibility of conveying only two messages, either excitation or inhibition, it turns out that not just two neurotransmitters do all the work. In fact, more than fifty have been studied. In the next section, we will focus on the six most prominent neurotransmitters in relation to psychoactive drugs.

neurotransmitter: A chemical substance that a neuron uses to communicate information at the synapse.

reuptake: The process by which a neurotransmitter returns from the receptor site back to the synaptic knob.

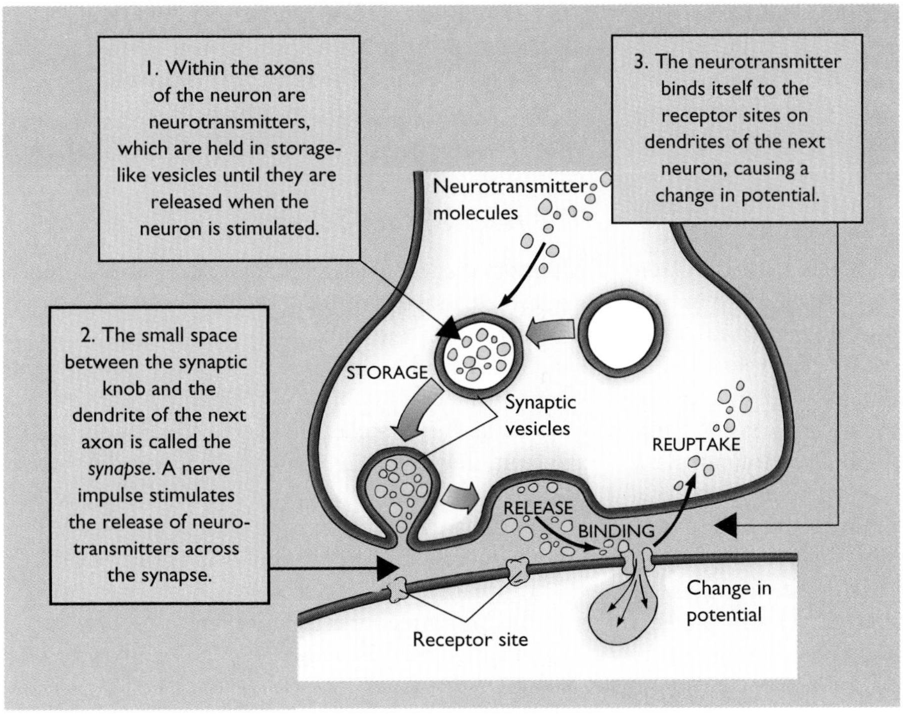

FIGURE 3.7

Sequence of events in synaptic communication.

1. Within the axons of the neuron are neurotransmitters, which are held in storage-like vesicles until they are released when the neuron is stimulated.
Neurotransmitter molecules
3. The neurotransmitter binds itself to the receptor sites on dendrites of the next neuron, causing a change in potential.
2. The small space between the synaptic knob and the dendrite of the next axon is called the *synapse*. A nerve impulse stimulates the release of neuro-transmitters across the synapse.
STORAGE
Synaptic vesicles
REUPTAKE
RELEASE
BINDING
Change in potential
Receptor site

The Major Neurotransmitters in Brief: The Big Six

Acetylcholine was the first molecule to have been firmly established as a neurotransmitter. There are two types of receptor sites that are sensitive to acetylcholine.

The first type, *muscarinic receptors*, so named because they are responsive to the drug muscarine, are located in the parasympathetic autonomic nervous system. If a drug is antimuscarinic, that means that it interferes with the role of acetylcholine in stimulating parasympathetic reactions of the body. Examples are atropine and scopolamine (see Chapter 6). Atropine, when applied to the eyes, for example, causes the pupils to dilate by inhibiting the parasympathetic tendency for the pupils to constrict. This is useful in eye examinations where the retina needs to be inspected for possible problems.

The second type, *nicotinic receptors*, so named because they are responsive to nicotine (see Chapter 11), are found near the end points of motor neurons, where skeletal muscles are innervated, as well as throughout the cerebral cortex. Some antinicotinic drugs, such as the poison curare, affect these motor neurons so dramatically that the body can become paralyzed within seconds. Deficiencies in acetylcholine, in nicotinic receptors, or in both, have been tied to Alzheimer's disease, a degenerative condition resulting in memory loss and mental confusion.

Norepinephrine, the second major neurotransmitter, is concentrated in the hypothalamus and limbic system but also found throughout the brain. In the peripheral nervous system, it is the principal neurotransmitter for sympathetic autonomic activation, but its role here is independent of its effects in the brain. Norepinephrine helps to regulate our mood states; Chapter 16 will discuss how drugs that boost the levels of norepinephrine also help relieve symptoms of depression.

The role of **dopamine**, the third major neurotransmitter, affects three important aspects of our behavior. The first aspect is motor control: the ability to start a movement when we want to, to stop it when we want to, and to execute the movement in a smooth, precisely determined manner. A deficiency in motor control, as mentioned

acetylcholine (a-SEE-til-KOH-leen): A neurotransmitter active in the parasympathetic autonomic nervous system, cerebral cortex, and peripheral somatic nerves.

norepinephrine (NOR-ep-ih-NEH-frin): A neurotransmitter active in the sympathetic autonomic nervous system and in many regions of the brain.

dopamine (DOPE-ah-meen): A neurotransmitter in the brain whose activity is related to emotionality and motor control.

earlier, is dramatically seen in symptoms of Parkinson's disease, a disorder arising from a degeneration of dopamine-releasing neurons in the substantia nigra of the midbrain. The second aspect is emotionality. Problems in dopamine-releasing neurons in the cortex and limbic system are strongly suspected to be at the root of schizophrenia. The role of dopamine in schizophrenia and efforts to develop drugs that relieve schizophrenic symptoms will be discussed in Chapter 16. Third, as we will see shortly, dopamine in the brain plays a major role in producing the craving feelings that encourage a continuing pattern of drug-taking behavior.

Serotonin, the fourth neurotransmitter, is concentrated in the pons and medulla, in the limbic system, and in the cortex. At the level of the hindbrain, serotonin plays an important role in regulating patterns of sleep. At the level of the limbic system, it shares with norepinephrine responsibility for establishing appropriate mood levels, avoiding wild swings upward that result in mania or downward that result in depression. As you can predict, many drugs that relieve mania and depression act upon serotonin-releasing neurons. Several hallucinogenic drugs, such as LSD, stimulate serotonin-releasing neurons in the cortex, a topic that will be explored further in Chapter 6.

Gamma aminobutyric acid (GABA), the fifth neurotransmitter, is an important inhibitory neurotransmitter throughout the brain. Antianxiety medications, often referred to as tranquilizers, stimulate GABA-releasing neurons, providing a reduction in feelings of stress and fear, as will be discussed in Chapter 15. Since this neurotransmitter is a major source of inhibitory control, it should not be surprising that GABA deficiencies are associated with an increased tendency to suffer epileptic seizures.

The sixth major neurotransmitter is actually a grouping of neurotransmitters collectively known as **endorphins.** They are natural painkillers produced by the brain and bear a remarkable resemblance to morphine. Chapter 5 will discuss how the discovery of endorphins has helped us understand more clearly not only the nature of pain but also the nature of opiate addiction.

Drugs . . . in Focus shows the ways that various psychoactive drugs work in the brain, in terms of how they alter the activity of a specific neurotransmitter. Some drugs, such as amphetamines, work at the synapse in multiple ways.

Physiological Aspects of Drug-Taking Behavior

There are three important concepts related to drug-taking behavior that arise from the physiology of the nervous system. The first is the blood-brain barrier; the second is the physiological basis for drug tolerance; and the third is the current theory that psychological dependence may be related to activity in a specific area of the brain.

The Blood-Brain Barrier

Mentioned earlier in the chapter was a barrier that restricts the passage of drugs and other molecules from the bloodstream to the brain. This exclusionary system is called the **blood-brain barrier.** Because it is important to maintain a level of stability in the brain, we are quite fortunate that this "gatekeeper" keeps the environment of the brain free from the biochemical ups and downs that are a fact of life in the bloodstream. The key factor in determining whether or not a drug passes through the blood-brain barrier is the degree to which that drug is fat-soluble.

Despite the obstacles, many types of drugs easily pass into the brain: nicotine, alcohol, cocaine, barbiturates, and caffeine, to name a few. Among the opiates, heroin, which is highly fat-soluble, crosses the blood-brain barrier faster and more completely than morphine. Penicillin, by contrast, hardly enters the brain at all.[10]

The presence of a blood-brain barrier is an issue not only for the study of psychoactive drugs but for certain medical treatments as well. For example, one of the effective treatments for Parkinson's disease is the administration of the drug L-Dopa, a shortened name for levodopa. The reason for using this drug stems from the root cause of Parkinson's disease: a dopamine deficiency in the substantia nigra. Taking dopamine itself is of no help, since its lack of fat-solubility excludes it from ever getting into the brain. Fortunately, L-Dopa, a metabolic precursor to dopamine, is fat-soluble. Therefore, L-Dopa can enter the brain and then change into dopamine. As

serotonin (SER-ah-TOH-nin): A neurotransmitter in the brain whose activity is related to emotionality and sleep patterns.
gamma aminobutyric acid (GABA) (GAM-ma a-MEEN-o-byoo-TEER-ik ASS-id): An inhibitory neurotransmitter in the brain. Antianxiety drugs tend to facilitate the activity level of GABA in the brain.
endorphins (en-DOR-fins): A class of chemical substances, produced in the brain and elsewhere in the body, that mimic the effects of morphine and other opiate drugs.
blood-brain barrier: A system whereby substances in the bloodstream are excluded from entering the nervous system.

DRUGS . . . IN FOCUS

Drug Effects and Synaptic Communication in the Nervous System

DRUG	RESULT	MECHANISM
amphetamines	CNS stimulation	Mimicking of norepinephrine at the receptor site; inducement of norepinephrine release at synapses without the presence of an action potential
antianxiety drugs in general	Reduction in anxiety and stress	Stimulation of GABA receptors in the brain
antidepressant drugs, MAO-inhibitor type	Reduction in depressive symptoms	Inhibition of enzymes that metabolize norepinephrine and serotonin
antidepressant drugs, tricyclic type	Reduction in depressive symptoms	Slowing down of reuptake of norepinephrine and serotonin at their receptor sites
antipsychotic drugs, typical type	Reduction in schizophrenic symptoms	Dopamine blocked from entering receptor sites in the brain
atropine	Stimulation of the sympathetic autonomic system	Inhibition of acetylcholine at muscarinic receptor sites
botulinus toxin	Paralysis of skeletal muscles (known as botulism)	Acetylcholine prevented from being released at synapses stimulating muscle cells
caffeine	CNS stimulation	Adenosine (an inhibitory neurotransmitter) blocked from entering its receptor sites
cocaine	CNS stimulation and local anesthesia	Blocking the reuptake of norepinephrine and dopamine at their receptor sites
curare	Paralysis of skeletal muscles	Acetylcholine blocked from entering receptor sites in muscle cells
LSD	Visual hallucinations and disordered thinking	Stimulation of receptor sites sensitive to serotonin
morphine, heroin, and codeine	Pain relief and euphoria	Stimulation of endorphins at receptors in the spinal cord and brain
strychnine sulphate	Generalized convulsions; possible death by asphyxiation	Glycine (an inhibitory neurotransmitter) blocked from entering receptor sites in the spinal cord
tetanus toxin	Generalized convulsions; possible death by asphyxiation	Glycine and GABA prevented from being released at synapses stimulating muscle cells

a result, dopamine levels in the brain rise, and the symptoms of Parkinson's disease are relieved.[11]

It has recently become possible to create fat-soluble molecules in the laboratory rather than finding them in nature. Pharmacologists have succeeded in combining protein-based drugs that are presently excluded by the blood-brain barrier with a fatty acid, enabling the drug to slip through into the brain. It may be possible in the future to design special molecules that not only ferry protein drugs across the barrier but also regulate the release of the drugs once they are in the brain.[12]

Biochemical Processes Underlying Drug Tolerance

The last chapter covered the phenomenon of drug tolerance as a behavioral effect, accomplished through Pavlovian conditioning. Tolerance can also be a result of two types of physiological processes, one in the liver and the other in the neuron itself.

In the first type, called *metabolic (dispositional) tolerance*, a drug may facilitate over repeated administrations the processes that produce the drug's biotransformation in the liver. The rate of alcohol elimination, for example, increases over time if alcohol is ingested repeatedly over an extended period. When the liver breaks down the drug faster than it had initially, a smaller amount is left available for absorption into the blood. In the case of alcohol, the habitual drinker feels less of an alcoholic effect and compensates by increasing the amount consumed.

In the second type, called *cellular (pharmacodynamic) tolerance*, changes occur in the synapses of neurons themselves. Receptors that have been stimulated by

Portrait Solomon H. Snyder—On the Cutting Edge of Discovery

If you look at the real breakthroughs in any specific field, you will find the work of people who simply have had a new way of thinking about a problem and the courage to take some risks with new ideas.

Consider the career of Solomon H. Snyder, distinguished pharmacologist and director of neuroscience research at Johns Hopkins University in Baltimore. Early in the 1970s, at the very beginning of the neuroscience revolution (see Chapter 1), Snyder turned to the study of morphine. At that time, scientists knew that morphine had to act upon neurons in the brain, but no one understood how this happened. They knew that morphine was highly addictive, but no one knew why.

Snyder saw the advantage of looking at the receptors on the surface of neurons as the key elements in linking morphine to the functions of the brain. By 1973, together with a graduate student in his laboratory, Candace Pert, he succeeded in identifying the opiate receptor. It was the first time a specific receptor had been found to be sensitive to a particular psychoactive drug. Then the pieces started to fall into place.

Solomon H. Snyder

If these receptors existed, could they be sensitive to something we produce ourselves, a morphine-like substance that helps us to kill pain and gives us a natural euphoria similar to what we get from opiate drugs? That substance was soon identified by Snyder and scientists in other laboratories as a family of chemicals called endorphins.

Success with the opiate receptor led Snyder to study the possibility that other receptors could be identified that were sensitive to brain neurotransmitters. By 1978, Snyder and his students found the receptors for dopamine and argued that it was these receptors that held the key for understanding schizophrenia.

Snyder's laboratory team has since identified receptors for serotonin, GABA, and even caffeine. More recently, his studies have shown that carbon monoxide, normally a highly toxic molecule, acts in very small quantities as an important neurotransmitter in the brain, responsible for setting down memories. Largely through Snyder's efforts, the investigation of receptors has become the fundamental basis for understanding the brain itself.

Sources: Kanigel, Robert (1986). *Apprentice to genius: The making of a scientific dynasty.* New York: Macmillan Publishing Co. Levinthal, Charles F. (1988). *Messengers of Paradise: Opiates and the brain.* New York: Anchor Press/Doubleday. Radetsky, Peter (1991, April). The brainiest cells alive. *Discover*, pp. 82–90.

the drug over time may become less sensitive, and the effect on the receiving neuron at a synapse may be diminished. Repeated blocking of receptor sites by a drug over time may cause a compensatory reaction through an increase in the number of receptor sites or an increased amount of neurotransmitter that is released.[13]

A Physiological Basis for Psychological Dependence

Amphetamines, cocaine, heroin, alcohol, and nicotine may be very different from a pharmacological standpoint, but they are remarkably similar in the way people and animals react to them. There is a tremendous feeling of satisfaction as these drugs enter the bloodstream and the brain, and an intense craving for repeating the experience. The parallels are numerous enough to entertain the idea that there might exist a common physiological process in the brain that links them all together. It may not be a coincidence that there is a system of neurons near the hypothalamus and limbic system that animals will work hard to stimulate electrically. We cannot say how they are feeling at the time, but their behavior indicates that they want to "turn on" this region of their brains. Could there be a connection to the craving and intense "rush" of heroin, cocaine, or amphetamine?

Two of the key elements in the rewarding effect of these psychoactive drugs are dopamine and a grouping of neurons lying in a region of the limbic system called the **nucleus accumbens.** When laboratory animals are injected with amphetamines, heroin, cocaine, alcohol, or nicotine, for example, there is a release of dopamine in the nucleus accumbens, and since dopamine acts as an inhibitory neurotransmitter, the activity level of neurons in the nucleus accumbens goes down. Administration of any substance that interferes with the action of dopamine in this region eliminates the desire of animals to work for the self-administration of these abused drugs. While we cannot say, of course, that these animals no longer experience feelings of craving as a result, you will recall that

nucleus accumbens (NEW-clee-us ac-CUM-buns): A region in the limbic system of the brain considered to be responsible for the rewarding effects of several drugs of abuse.

self-administration behavior in animals closely parallels the pattern of human behavior that characterizes psychological dependence. Therefore, these studies can be used to understand the neural changes caused by drug abuse. Considering the evidence now in hand, a persuasive argument can be made that dopamine-related processes in the nucleus accumbens underlie the pleasurable effects of many abused drugs.[14]

It is not hard to see the applications to the real-world treatment of drug dependence. Drugs that affect activity in the nucleus accumbens are currently being developed to reduce the feelings of craving that cause drug-dependent individuals to relapse. One such drug, ibogaine (an extract from a plant that grows in West Africa), has offered promise in this regard, but questions have arisen concerning its toxic effects on the brain. Variations of ibogaine and alternative drug formulations that have less toxic properties are presently under active investigation (see Chapter 6). The future looks quite hopeful that the right neurochemical combination will eventually be found.[15]

Continued research on the influence of dopamine in drug dependence also has the potential to allow us to understand why some individuals may be more susceptible than others toward drug-taking behavior. As an example, in a recent study, twenty-three drug-free men with no history of drug abuse were given doses of methylphenidate (brand name: Ritalin), a psychoactive stimulant when ingested by adults. Twelve of the men experienced a pleasant feeling, nine felt annoyed or distrustful, and two felt nothing at all. Measurements of a subclass of dopamine receptors in the brains of these subjects showed a consistent pattern. The men with the least concentration of dopamine receptors were the ones experiencing pleasant effects. It is reasonable to hypothesize that those individuals with the fewest dopamine receptors might be the most vulnerable to drug abuse. Their drug-taking behavior might, in part, be compensation for an inadequate number of dopamine receptors necessary to experience pleasurable feelings without drugs.[16]

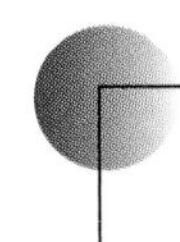

Psychological Factors in Drug-Taking Behavior

This chapter has considered the physiological effects of psychoactive drugs, down to the level of a single neuron in the brain. It has also pointed out that certain physiological factors such as weight and gender must be taken into account in order to predict particular drug effects. Yet, even if we controlled these factors completely, we would still frequently find a drug effect in an individual person to be different from time to time, place to place, and situation to situation. Predictions about how a person might react would be far from perfectly accurate.

Therefore, a good way of thinking about an individual's response to a particular drug is to consider the drug effect to be a three-way interaction of the drug's pharmacological properties (the biochemical nature of the substance), the individual taking the drug (set), and the immediate environment within which drug-taking behavior is occurring (setting). Whether one or more of these factors dominate in the final analysis seems to depend upon the dosage level. Generally speaking, the higher the drug dose, the greater the contribution made by the pharmacology of the drug itself; the lower the dose, the greater the contribution of individual characteristics of the drug-taker or environmental conditions.[17]

Expectation Effects

One of the most uncontrollable factors in drug-taking behavior is the set of expectations a person may have about what the drug will do. If you believe that a beer will make you drunk or feel sexy, the chances are increased that it will do so; if you believe that a marijuana cigarette will make you high, the chances are increased that it will. You can consider the impact of negative expectations in the same way; when the feelings are strong that a drug will have no effect on you, the chances are lessened that you will react to it. In the most extreme case, you might experience a drug effect even when the substance you ingested was completely inert, that is, pharmacologically ineffective. Such inert substances are called **placebos** (from the Latin, "I will please"), and the reaction to them is referred to as the *placebo effect.*

The concept of a placebo goes back to the earliest days of pharmacology. The bizarre ingredients prescribed in the Ebers Papyrus (see Chapter 1) were effective to the extent that people *believed* that they were effective, not from any known factor in these ingredients. No doubt, the placebo effect was strong enough for

placebo (pla-CEE-bo): Latin term translated "I will please." Any inert substance that produces a psychological or physiological reaction.

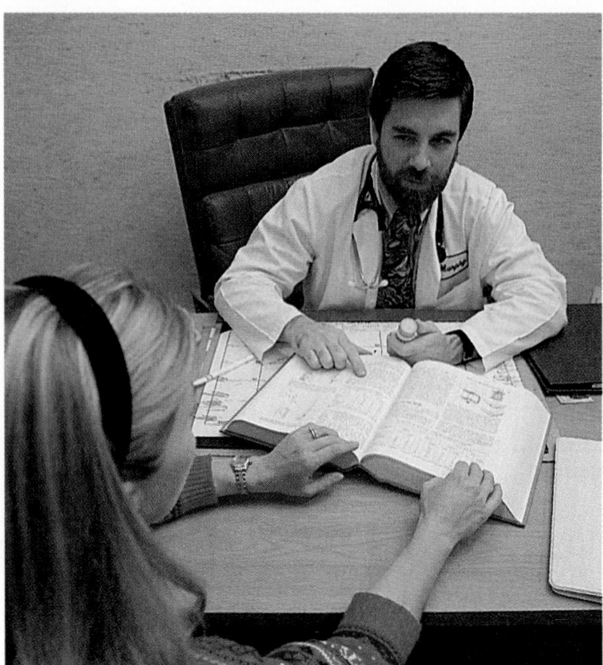

The likelihood of a placebo effect is maximized when the patient highly regards the expertise of the physician prescribing a drug.

medical symptoms to diminish. During the Middle Ages, in one of the more extreme cases of the placebo effect, Pope Boniface VIII reportedly was cured of kidney pains when his personal physician hung a gold seal bearing the image of a lion around the pope's thigh.[18]

It would be a mistake to think of the placebo effect as involving totally imaginary symptoms or totally imaginary reactions. Physical symptoms, involving specific bodily changes, can occur on the basis of placebo effects alone. How likely is it that a person will react to a placebo? The probability will vary from drug to drug, but in the case of morphine, the data are very clear. In 1959 a review of studies in which morphine or a placebo was administered in clinical studies of pain concluded that a placebo-induced reduction in pain occurred 35 percent of the time. Considering that morphine itself had a positive result in only 75 percent of the cases, the placebo effect is a very strong one.[19] Unfortunately, it is not clear how we can predict whether a person will react strongly or weakly to a placebo. We do know, however, that the enthusiasm or lack of enthusiasm of the prescribing physician can play a major role. In one study that varied the attitude of the physician toward a particular medication, negative attitudes toward the medication resulted in the least benefits, whereas positive attitudes resulted in the most.[20]

It is not at all clear how the placebo effect is accomplished. In the case of pain relief, there is evidence that we have the natural ability to increase the levels of endorphins in the bloodstream and the brain from one moment to the next, but the nature of our ability to alter other important substances in our bodies is virtually unknown. Recent studies have documented a 33 percent increase in lung capacity among asthmatic children who inhaled a bronchodilator containing a placebo instead of medication and the development of skin rashes in people who have been exposed to fake poison ivy, to name a few examples of placebo-induced physiological reactions. Placebo research forces us to acknowledge the potential for psychological control over physiological processes in our bodies.[21]

Given the power of the placebo effect in drug-taking behavior, it is necessary to be very careful when carrying out drug research. For a drug to be deemed truly effective, it must be proved to be better not only in comparison to a no-treatment condition (a difference that could conceivably be due to a placebo effect) but also in comparison to an identical-looking drug that lacks the active ingredients of the drug being evaluated. For example, if the drug under study is in the shape of a round red pill, another round red pill without the active ingredients of the drug (called the *active placebo*) must also be administered for comparison.

The procedures of these studies also have to be carefully executed. Neither the individual administering the drug or placebo nor the individual receiving the drug or placebo should know which substance is which. Such precautions, referred to as **double-blind** procedures, represent the minimal standards for separating the pharmacological effects of a drug from the effects that arise from one's expectations and beliefs.[22] We will return to the issue of interactions between drug effects and expectations when we consider alcohol intoxication in Chapter 9.

double-blind: A procedure in drug research in which neither the individual administering nor the individual receiving a chemical substance knows whether the substance is the drug being evaluated or an active placebo.

SUMMARY

How Drugs Enter the Body

- There are four basic ways to administer drugs into the body: oral administration, injection, inhalation, and absorption through the skin or membranes. Each of these presents constraints on which kinds of drugs will be effectively delivered into the bloodstream.

How Drugs Exit the Body

- Most drugs are eliminated from the body through urinary excretion. Drugs are broken down for elimination by the action of enzymes in the liver. An index of how long this process takes is called the elimination half-life.

Factors Determining the Physiological Impact of Drugs

- The physiological effect of a drug can vary as a factor of the time elapsed since its administration, the possible combination of its administration with other drugs, and finally the personal characteristics of the individual consuming the drug.
- Some characteristics that can play a definite role in the effect of a drug include the individual's weight, gender, and ethnic background.

Introducing the Nervous System

- Understanding the organization of the nervous system helps us to understand where psychoactive drugs are working in our bodies.
- The nervous system consists of the peripheral nervous system and the central nervous system, with the latter divided into the brain and spinal cord. Within the peripheral nervous system are autonomic nerves that control our cardiac and smooth muscles to respond either to stress (sympathetic activation) or to demands for nurturance and renewal (parasympathetic activation).

Understanding the Brain

- Within the brain are three major divisions: the hindbrain, midbrain, and forebrain. The forebrain is the most recently evolved region of the brain and controls the most complex behaviors and processes the most complex information.
- Many drugs affect all levels of the brain, in one way or another.

Understanding the Biochemistry of Psychoactive Drugs

- Understanding the functioning of neurons and their interaction through synaptic communication helps us to understand how psychoactive drugs work in our bodies.
- In general, drugs work at the neuronal level by altering the way in which neurotransmitters are released and bind to receptor sites.
- While the mechanisms behind the effects might vary, psychoactive drugs cause neurotransmitters to be either more or less active at the synapse.

Physiological Aspects of Drug-Taking Behavior

- Three important issues need to be understood in looking at the physiological effect of drugs: the extent to which drugs pass from the bloodstream to the brain, the extent to which tolerance effects occur, and the extent to which a drug influences neuronal activity in the region of the nucleus accumbens in the brain.

Psychological Factors in Drug-Taking Behavior

- Although the physiological actions of psychoactive drugs are becoming increasingly well understood, great variability in the effect of these drugs still remains, largely because of psychological factors.
- The most prominent psychological factor is the influence of personal expectations on the part of the individual consuming the drug. The impact of expectations on one's reaction to a drug, a phenomenon called the placebo effect, is an important consideration in drug evaluation and research.

KEY TERMS

acetylcholine, p. 67
biotransformation, p. 56
blood-brain barrier, p. 68
central nervous system (CNS), p. 60
cerebral cortex, p. 64
dopamine, p. 67
double-blind, p. 72
elimination half-life, p. 57
endorphins, p. 68
gamma aminobutyric acid (GABA), p. 68
intramuscular, p. 54
intranasal, p. 55
intravenous, p. 54
latency period, p. 57
metabolite, p. 56
neuron, p. 62
neurotransmitter, p. 66
norepinephrine, p. 67
nucleus accumbens, p. 70
parasympathetic branch of the autonomic nervous system, p. 61
peripheral nervous system, p. 60
placebo, p. 71
potentiation, p. 58
reuptake, p. 66
serotonin, p. 68
subcutaneous, p. 54
sublingual, p. 55
sympathetic branch of the autonomic nervous system, p. 61
synapse, p. 65
synergism, p. 58
transdermal patch, p. 55

ENDNOTES

1. Public-service message, "Frying Pan." Partners for a Drug-free America, New York, 1987.
2. Mitragotri, Samir, Blankschtein, Daniel, and Langer, Robert (1995). Ultrasound-mediated transdermal protein delivery. *Science, 269,* 850–853.
3. Hawks, Richard L., and Chiang, C. Nora (1986). Examples of specific drug assays. In Richard L. Hawks and C. Nora Chiang (Eds.), *Urine testing for drugs of abuse* (NIDA Research Monograph 73). Rockville MD: National Institute on Drug Abuse, pp. 84–112. Julien, Robert M. (2001). *A primer of drug action* (9th ed.). New York: Worth, pp. 27–31.
4. Frezza, Mario; DiPadova, Carlo; Pozzato, Gabrielle; Terpin, Maddalena; Baraona, Enrique; and Lieber, Charles S. (1990). High blood alcohol levels in women: The role of decreased gastric alcohol dehydrogenase activity and first-pass metabolism. *New England Journal of Medicine, 322,* 95–99.
5. Nakawatase, Tomoko V., Yamamoto, Joe, and Sasao, Toshiaki (1993). The association between fast-flushing response and alcohol use among Japanese Americans. *Journal of Studies on Alcohol, 54,* 48–53.
6. Goodman, Deborah (1992, January–February). NIMH grantee finds drug responses differ among ethnic groups. *ADAMHA News,* pp. 5, 15.
7. Perez-Stable, Eliseo J.; Herrera, Brenda; Jacob III, Peyton; and Benowita, Neal L. (1998). Nicotine metabolism and intake in black and white smokers. *Journal of the American Medical Association, 280,* 152–156.
8. Levinthal, Charles F. (1990). *Introduction to physiological psychology* (3rd ed.). Englewood Cliffs NJ: Prentice Hall, p. 63.
9. Thompson, Richard F. (1993). *The brain: A neuroscience primer* (2nd ed.). New York: Freeman, p. 3.
10. Julien, *A primer of drug action,* pp. 18–19.
11. Levinthal, *Introduction to physiological psychology,* p. 155.
12. Goldstein, Gary W., and Betz, A. Lorris (1986). The blood-brain barrier. *Scientific American, 255* (3), 74–83.
13. Martin, William R. (1987). Tolerance and physical dependence. In George Adelman (Ed.), *Encyclopedia of neuroscience.* Boston: Birkhauser, pp. 1223–1225.
14. Di Chiara, Gaetano (1999). Drug addiction as dopamine-dependent associative learning disorder. *European Journal of Pharmacology, 375,* 13–30. Self, David W. (1998). Neural substrates of drug craving and relapse in drug addiction. *Annals of Medicine, 30,* 379–389.
15. Lick, Stanley D., and Maisonneuve, Isabelle M. (1998). Mechanisms of antiaddictive actions of ibogaine. *Annals of the New York Academy of Sciences, 844,* 214–226. O'Hearn, Elizabeth, and Molliver, Mark E. (1997). The olivocerebellar projection mediates ibogaine-induced degeneration of Purkinje cells: A model of indirect, trans-synaptic excitotoxicity. *Journal of Neuroscience, 17,* 8828–8841.
16. Volkow, Nora D.; Wang, Gene-Jack; Fowler, Joanna S.; Logan, Jean; Gatley, Samuel J.; Gifford, Andrew; Hitzemann, Robert; Ding, Yu-Shin; and Pappas, Naomi (1999). Prediction of reinforcing responses to psychostimulants in humans by brain dopamine D_2 receptor levels. *American Journal of Psychiatry, 156,* 1440–1443.
17. Goode, Erich (1999). *Drugs in American society* (5th ed.). New York: McGraw-Hill College, p. 9.
18. Kornetsky, Conan (1976). *Pharmacology: Drugs affecting behavior.* New York, Wiley, p. 23. Shapiro, Arthur K., and Shapiro, Elaine (1997). *The powerful placebo: From ancient priest to modern physician.* Baltimore: Johns Hopkins University Press.
19. Beecher, H. K. (1959). *Measurement of subjective responses: Quantitative effects of drugs.* New York: Oxford University Press.
20. Schindel, L. E. (1962). Placebo in theory and practice. *Antibiotica et Chemotherapia, Advances, 10,* 398–430. Cited in Kornetsky, *Pharmacology,* p. 36.
21. Blakeslee, Sandra (1998, October 13). Placebos prove so powerful even experts are surprised. *New York Times,*

pp. F1, F4. Flaten, Magne Arve, Simonsen, Terje, and Olsen, Harald (1999). Drug-related information generates placebo and nocebo responses that modify the drug response. *Psychosomatic Medicine, 61,* 250–255. Levinthal, Charles F. (1988). *Messengers of paradise: Opiates and the brain.* Anchor Press/Doubleday. Talbot, Margaret (2000, January 9). The placebo prescription. *New York Times Magazine,* pp. 34–39, 44, 58–60.

22. Quitkin, Frederic M. (1999). Placebos, drug effects, and study design: A clinician's guide. *American Journal of Psychiatry, 156,* 829–836.

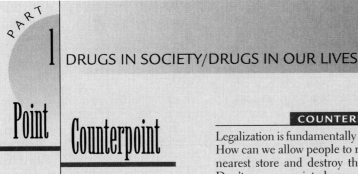

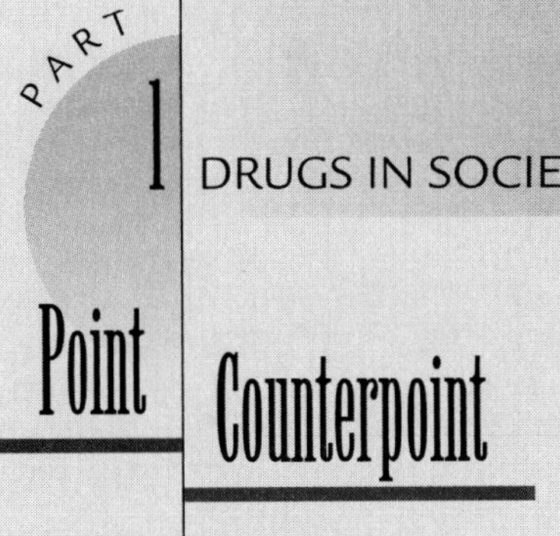

PART
1
DRUGS IN SOCIETY/DRUGS IN OUR LIVES
Point
Counterpoint

Should We Legalize Drugs?

The following discussion of viewpoints represents the opinions of people on both sides of the controversial issue of the legalization of drugs. Read them with an open mind. Don't think you have to come up with the final answer, nor should you necessarily agree with the argument you heard last. Many of the ideas in this discussion come from the sources listed.

POINT

Legalization would get the problem under some degree of control. The "war on drugs" does nothing but increase the price of illicit drugs to what the market will bear, and it subsidizes the drug dealers and drug barons around the world. If we legalize drugs, we can take the profit out of the drug business because legalization would bring the price down dramatically. We could regulate drug sales, as we do now with nicotine and alcohol, by setting up centers that would be licensed to sell cocaine and heroin, as well as sterile syringes, while any drug sales to minors would remain a criminal offense. Regulations would also ensure that drugs maintained standards of purity; the health risks of drug contamination would be avoided.

COUNTERPOINT

Legalization is fundamentally immoral. How can we allow people to run to the nearest store and destroy their lives? Don't we as a society have a responsibility for the health and welfare of people in general? If the drugs (pure or impure) were available, the only effect would be to increase the number of drug abusers. When Britain allowed physicians to prescribe heroin to "registered" addicts, the number of heroin addicts rose five-fold (or more according to some informal estimates), and there were then cases of medical abuse as well as drug abuse. A few unscrupulous doctors were prescribing heroin in enormous amounts, and a new drug culture was created.

POINT

How moral is the situation now? We have whole communities living at the mercy of drug dealers. Any increase in drug users would be more than compensated for by the gains of freedom from such people. Even if the sale of crack were kept illegal, conceding that this drug is highly dangerous to society, we would have an 80 percent reduction in the black market for drugs, a substantial gain for the welfare of society. We can't guarantee that our inner cities would no longer be places of hopelessness and despair, but at least we would not have the systemic violence associated with the drug world. Besides, with all the money saved from programs set up to prevent people from getting hold of illicit drugs, we could increase the funding for drug treatment programs for all the drug abusers who want them and for research into ways of understanding the nature of drug dependence.

COUNTERPOINT

No doubt, many drug abusers seek out treatment and want to break their drug dependence. Perhaps there may be some individuals who seek treatment under legalization because there would no longer be a social stigma associated with drug abuse, but many drug abusers have little or no long-term commitment toward drug treatment. In the present situation, the illegality of their behavior allows us to compel them to seek and stay in treatment, as well as monitor their abstinence by periodic drug testing. How could we do this when the drug was legal? Besides, how would we approach the education of young people if drugs were legal? We could not tell them that cocaine would give them cancer or emphysema, as we warn them of the dangers of nicotine, only that it would prevent them from being a productive member of society and would have long-term effects on their brains. If the adults around them were allowed to take cocaine, what would be the message to the young? Simply wait until you're twenty-one?

POINT

We already have educational programs about alcohol abuse; the message for heroin and cocaine abuse would be similar. The loss of productivity due to any increased availability of drugs would not be as significant as the present loss of productivity we have with alcohol and cigarettes. With the tax revenues obtained from selling drugs legally, we could have money for more extensive antidrug advertising. We could send a comprehensive message to our youth that there are alternatives to their lives that do not include psychoactive substances. In the meantime, we would be removing the "forbidden fruit" factor in drug-taking behavior. Drugs wouldn't be a big deal.

COUNTERPOINT

Arguing that people take drugs because they are forbidden or hard to get ignores the basic psychological allure of drugs. If you lowered the price of a very expensive sports car, would you have fewer people wanting to buy one? Of course not. People would want a fast car because they like fast cars, just as people will still want to get high on drugs. Legalizing present drugs would only encourage the development of more dangerous drugs in the future. Look at what happened with crack. Cocaine was bad enough but crack appeared on the scene, making the situation far worse.

POINT

It can be argued that crack was marketed because standard cocaine powder was too expensive for people in the inner cities. If cocaine had been legally available, crack might not ever have been created because the market would not have been there. Even with crack remaining illegal under a legalization plan, there is at least the possibility that the appeal of crack would decline. The trend has been lately that illegal drugs are getting stronger, while legal drugs (alcoholic beverages and cigarettes) are getting weaker as people become more health-conscious. Legalization might make presently illicit drugs weaker in strength, as public opinion turns against them. The main problem we face is that spending 60 percent of a multibillion-dollar drug-law-enforcement program on the "supply" side of the question, and only 40 percent on reducing the demand for drugs is not working. If one source of drugs is controlled, another source takes its place. The link between drugs and crime is a direct result of the illegality of drugs. It's not the drug addicts that are destroying the country; it's the drug dealers. Right now, the criminals are in charge. We have to change that. Only legalization would take away their profits, and refocus our law-enforcement efforts on other crimes that continue to undermine our society.

COUNTERPOINT

The frustration is understandable, but let's not jump into something merely because we're frustrated. We can allocate more funds for treatment without making drugs legal. We can increase funds for scientific research without making drugs legal. We need a more balanced program, not an entirely new one. Polls do not indicate general support for drug legalization. Between 60 percent and 80 percent of the U.S. public supports continued prohibition of drugs. Most citizens appear to recognize that legalization would make a bad situation worse, not better.

Critical Thinking Questions for Further Debate

1. Is it valid in this debate to make a distinction between "hard drugs" such as heroin and cocaine and "soft drugs" such as marijuana and hallucinogens?
2. What is your prediction of what would happen if all our drug-abuse-prevention efforts were focused exclusively on the Harm Reduction approach?

Sources: Dennis, Richard J. (1990, November). The economics of legalizing drugs. *The Atlantic,* pp. 126–132. Hamill, Pete. (1988, August 15). Facing up to drugs: Is legalization the solution? *New York,* pp. 20–27. Inciardi, James. (1991). *The drug legalization debate.* Newbury Park CA: Sage Publications. Jarvik, Murray E. (1990). The drug dilemma: Manipulating the demand. *Science, 250,* 387–392. Miller, Richard L. (1991). *The case for legalizing drugs.* New York: Praeger. Trebach, Arnold S., and Inciardi, James A. (1993). *Legalize it: Debating American drug policy.* Washington DC: American University Press. Wilson, James Q. (1990, February). Against the legalization of drugs. *Commentary,* 21–28.

CHAPTER 4 The Major Stimulants: Cocaine and Amphetamines

After you have completed this chapter, you will understand

- The history of cocaine
- How cocaine works in the brain
- Patterns of cocaine abuse
- Treatment programs for cocaine abuse
- The history of amphetamines
- How amphetamines work in the brain
- Patterns of methamphetamine abuse

S. F. is a brilliant, young physician attending a case conference at a metropolitan medical center where he is a resident. He has been on call for thirty-six hours and cannot concentrate on the presentation. S. F. is lonely, depressed, and overworked. All he can think about is his fiancée, who is several hundred miles away. He knows that her father will not permit her to marry until he is able to support her, and with his loans and meager salary, that could take years. He excuses himself from the conference, takes a needle syringe from the nurses' station, and locks himself in a bathroom stall. He fills the syringe with cocaine and plunges the needle into his arm. Within seconds, the young doctor feels a rush of euphoria. His tears dry up; he regains his composure and quickly rejoins the conference.

The date is 1884, the place is Vienna, and the doctor is Sigmund Freud.

The time, place, and identity of S. F. in this fictionalized clinical vignette, based upon the facts of Freud's life, may have surprised you, but unfortunately the overall picture of cocaine abuse is all too familiar.[1] The year could have been 1984 instead of 1884, and the individual involved could have been anyone twenty-eight years old, as Freud was at the time, or some other age. Freud was extremely lucky; he never became dependent upon cocaine, though a close friend did and millions of people have since Freud's time. The story of cocaine is both ancient and modern. While its origins stretch back more than four thousand years, cocaine abuse continues to represent a major portion of the present-day drug crisis. For this reason, it is important to understand its history, the properties of the drug itself, and the ways in which it has the ability to destroy a person's life.

This chapter will focus not only on cocaine but also on another group of stimulant drugs, referred to collectively as amphetamines. Although cocaine and amphetamines are distinct in terms of their pharmacology (their characteristics as biochemical substances), there are enough similarities in their behavioral and physiological effects and patterns of abuse to warrant their being discussed together. In general, cocaine and amphetamines represent the two major classes of psychoactive stimulants, drugs that energize the body and create feelings of euphoria. Other less powerful stimulants, such as nicotine, caffeine, and clinical antidepressants, will be discussed in later chapters.

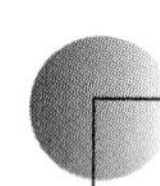

The History of Cocaine

Cocaine is derived from small leaves of the coca shrub *(Erythroxylon coca)*, grown in the high-altitude rain forests and fields that run along the slopes of the Peruvian and Bolivian Andes in South America. Like many other psychoactive drugs, cocaine use has a long history. We can trace the practice of chewing coca leaves, which contain about 2 percent cocaine, back to the Inca civilization, which flourished from the thirteenth century until its conquest by the Spaniards in 1532, as well as to other Andean cultures dating back five thousand years.

Ancient Inca records indicate that coca chewing was appreciated for giving increased strength and stamina to workers who labored in this harsh mountainous environment. Coca was even used to measure time and distance: A journey would commonly be described in terms of the mouthfuls of coca leaves that a person would chew in making the trip. Coca was considered a gift from the god Inti to the Incas, allowing them to endure life in the Andes without suffering.[2]

To this day, coca chewing is part of the culture of this region. It is estimated that about 2 million Peruvian men who live in the Andean highlands, representing 90 percent of the male population in that area, chew coca leaves.[3] These people, called *acullicadores*, mix their own blend of coca, chalk, lime, and ash to achieve the desired effects, whether it is to fight fatigue or socialize with friends.[4]

This pattern of cocaine use among these people, however, produces few instances of toxicity or abuse. The reason lies in the very low doses of cocaine that chewed coca leaves provide; in this form, absorption from the digestive system is slow, and relatively little cocaine is distributed to the brain. A much more serious problem has been the introduction of an addictive mixture of coca paste containing a much higher percentage of cocaine combined with tobacco, called a *bazuco*, which is then smoked as a cigarette. Making matters worse, dangerously high levels of kerosene, gasoline, and ether are involved in the coca-refining process and end up in the cigarettes themselves.[5]

Cocaine in Nineteenth-Century Life

Coca leaves were brought back to Europe from the Spanish colonies soon after the conquest of the Incas, but their potency was nearly gone after the long sea voyage. Perhaps, it was said at the time, the reported effects of coca were merely exaggerations after all. Coca leaves were ignored for nearly three hundred years. By the late 1850s, however, the active ingredient of the coca plant had been chemically isolated. In 1859, Alfred Niemann, a German chemist, observed its anesthetic effect on his tongue and its bitter taste, and named it "cocaine." Interest in the drug was renewed, and by the 1860s the patent medicine industry in the United States and Europe lost no time in taking advantage of cocaine's appeal.

Commercial Uses of Cocaine

By far the most successful commercial use of cocaine in the nineteenth century was a mixture of coca and wine invented in 1863 by a Corsican chemist and businessman, Angelo Mariani. We know now that the combination of alcohol and cocaine produces a metabolite with an elimination half-life several times longer than cocaine

cocaine: An extremely potent and dependence-producing stimulant drug, derived from the coca leaf.

alone, so the mixture tends to be quite intoxicating (see Health Alert on page 82). No wonder "Vin Mariani" became an instant sensation. A long list of endorsements by celebrities accumulated over the next few decades from satisfied customers such as U.S. President William McKinley, Thomas Edison, the surgeon general of the U.S. Army, General Ulysses S. Grant, Sarah Bernhardt, Jules Verne, the Prince of Wales, the czar of Russia, and Popes Pius X and Leo XII. In a letter to Mariani, Frederic Bartholdi, the sculptor of the Statue of Liberty, wrote that if he had been drinking Vin Mariani while designing the statue, it would have been more than three times taller.[6] We can only assume that this comment was intended to be complimentary.

Meanwhile in the United States, Atlanta pharmacist John Pemberton promoted an imitation form of Vin Mariani that he called French Wine Cola. Shortly after, in 1885, he took out the alcohol, added soda water, and reformulated the basic mixture to combine coca with the syrup of the African kola nut containing about 2 percent caffeine: Coca-Cola was born. Early advertisements for Coca-Cola emphasized the drink as a brain tonic that made you feel more productive and as a remedy for such assorted nervous ailments as sick headaches and melancholia (a word used at the time to mean depression).[7] The medicinal slant to the early promotion of Coca-Cola is probably the reason why soda fountains began to appear in drugstores.[8]

A number of competing brands with similar formulations sprang up with names such as Care-Cola, Dope Cola, Kola Ade, and Wiseola, and the Parke-Davis Company began to sell several products containing cocaine.[9] Eventually, public pressure brought about official restrictions on the patent medicine industry, which, by the beginning of the twentieth century, was marketing more than fifty thousand unregulated products.[10] The Pure Food and Drug Act of 1906 specified that all active ingredients had to be listed on patent medicine labels. In Canada, the Proprietary and Patent Medicine Act of 1908 banned cocaine from patent medicines entirely, but in the United States no further restrictions on cocaine sales or use were imposed until the Harrison Act of 1914 (see Chapter 2).

The Coca-Cola Company, aware of the growing tide of sentiment against cocaine, changed the formula in 1903 from regular coca leaves to decocainized coca leaves, which retained the coca flavoring that remains to this day (Drugs . . . in Focus). The "pause that refreshed" America was now due only to the presence of sugar and caffeine.

The use of cocaine was also becoming a major factor in the practice of medicine. In the United States, William

In the late nineteenth century, the Coca-Cola Co. advertised its beverage in medicinal terms. A company letterhead of this period spoke of Coca-Cola as containing "the tonic properties of the wonderful coca plant."

Halstead, one of the most distinguished surgeons of the time and one of the founders of Johns Hopkins Medical School, studied the effect of cocaine on anesthetizing nerves and whole limbs. In the process, he acquired a cocaine habit of his own (which was replaced several years later by a dependence on morphine). It was in Europe, however, that the psychological implications of cocaine were most extensively explored, ironically through the triumphs and tragedies of Sigmund Freud.

Freud and Cocaine

In 1884 Freud was a struggling young neurologist, given to bouts of depression and self-doubt but nonetheless determined to make his mark in the medical world. He had read a report by a German army physician that supplies of pure cocaine could help soldiers endure fatigue and feel better in general. Freud secured some cocaine for himself and found the experience exhilarating; his depression lifted, and he felt a new sense of boundless energy. His friend and colleague Dr. Ernst von Fleischl-Marxow, addicted to morphine and enduring a painful

DRUGS . . . IN FOCUS

What Happened to the Coca in Coca-Cola?

Every day, in a drab factory building in a New Jersey suburb of Maywood, a select team of employees of the Stepan Company carries out a chemical procedure that has been one of the primary responsibilities of the company since 1903. They remove cocaine from high-grade coca leaves. The remainder, technically called "decocainized flavor essence" is then sent to the Coca-Cola Company as part of the secret recipe for the world's favorite soft drink.

Each year, the Stepan Company is legally sanctioned by the U.S. government (and carefully monitored by the DEA) to receive shipments of about 175,000 kilograms of coca leaves from South American coca farms, separate the cocaine chemically, and produce about 1,750 kilograms of high-quality cocaine. Its annual output is equivalent to approximately 20 million hits of crack, worth about $200 million if it were to make it to the illicit drug market. Fortunately, the Stepan Company has an impeccable security record.

In case you are wondering what happens to the cocaine after it is removed from the coca leaves, it turns out that Stepan finds a legitimate market in the world of medicine. Tincture of cocaine is regularly used as a local anesthetic to numb the skin prior to minor surgical procedures such as stitching up a wound. Surgeons frequently use cocaine as a topical ointment when working on the nose or throat. As a result, the Stepan Company essentially has it both ways. It is the exclusive U.S. supplier of cocaine for use in medical settings as well as decocainized coca for your next can of Coke. As a recent article in the *Wall Street Journal* has put it, "The two markets end up sending Stepan's products into virtually every bloodstream in America."

Source: Miller, Michael W. (1994, October 17). Quality stuff: Firm is peddling cocaine, and deals are legit. *Wall Street Journal,* pp. A1, A14.

illness, borrowed some cocaine from Freud and found favorable results as well. Freud immediately saw the prospects of fame and fortune. In a letter to his fiancée, Martha, he wrote: "If it goes well I will write an essay on it and I expect it will win its place in therapeutics by the side of morphium [morphine] and superior to it."[11]

Before long, Freud was distributing cocaine to his friends and his sisters and even sent a supply to Martha. In the words of Freud's biographer Ernest Jones, "From the vantage point of our present knowledge, he was rapidly becoming a public menace."[12] We can gain some perspective on the effect cocaine was having on Freud's life at this time through an excerpt from a personal letter to Martha:

> *Woe to you, my Princess, when I come. I will kiss you quite red and feed you till you are plump. And if you are forward you shall see who is the stronger, a gentle little girl who doesn't eat enough or a big wild man* who has cocaine in his body [underlined in the original]. *In my last severe depression I took coca again and a small dose lifted me to the heights in a wonderful fashion. I am just now busy collecting the literature for a song of praise to this magical substance.*[13]

Within four months, his "song of praise" essay, *Über Coca* (Concerning coca), was written and published.

Unfortunately, the sweetness of Freud's romance with cocaine turned sour. Freud himself escaped becoming dependent upon cocaine, though later in his life he clearly became dependent on nicotine (see Chapter 11). His friend, Fleischl, however, was not so lucky. Within a year, Fleischl had increased his cocaine dose to twenty times the amount Freud had taken and had developed a severe cocaine-induced psychosis in which he experienced hallucinations that snakes were crawling over his skin (a phenomenon now referred to as **formication**). Fleischl suffered six years of painful agony and anguish until his death.

The story of Freud's infatuation with cocaine and his later disillusionment with it can be seen as a miniature version of the modern history of cocaine itself.[14] Between 1880 and 1910, the public reaction to cocaine went from wild enthuasiasm to widespread disapproval. As this chapter will later describe, a similar cycle of attitudes swept the country and the world between 1970 and 1985.

formication: Hallucinatory behavior, produced by chronic cocaine or amphetamine abuse, in which the individual feels insects or snakes crawling either over or under the skin.

QUICK CONCEPT CHECK 4.1

Understanding the History of Cocaine

Check your understanding of the history of cocaine by matching the names on the left with the identifications on the right. Be careful; some identifications may not match up with any of the names.

1. Angelo Mariani
2. John Pemberton
3. William Halstead
4. Sigmund Freud
5. Ernst von Fleischl-Marxow

a. Friend of Sigmund Freud; first documented case of cocaine psychosis
b. Developer of Coca-Cola, originally containing cocaine
c. Early advocate of restricting cocaine use in the United States
d. Cofounder of Johns Hopkins Medical School; early developer of cocaine to anesthetize nerves and whole limbs
e. A popular figure in present-day Peru
f. Early advocate of cocaine use; originator of psychoanalysis
g. Promoter of a popular coca-laced wine

Answers: 1. g 2. b 3. d 4. f 5. a

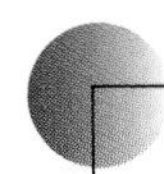

Acute Effects of Cocaine

While the effects of cocaine on the user vary in degree with the route of administration, the purity of the dose, and the user's expectations about the experience, certain features remain the same. The most characteristic reaction is a powerful burst of energy. If the cocaine is injected intravenously, the effect is virtually instantaneous and extremely intense (often referred to as a "rush"), peaking in three to five minutes and wearing off in thirty to forty minutes. If snorted through the nose, the effect begins in about three minutes, peaking after fifteen to twenty minutes, and wearing off in sixty to ninety minutes.

Users also experience a general sense of well-being, although in some instances cocaine may precipitate a panic attack.[15] When cocaine levels diminish, the mood changes dramatically. The user becomes irritable, despondent, and depressed (Figure 4.1). These aftereffects are uncomfortable enough to produce a powerful craving for another dose.

The depression induced in the aftermath of a cocaine high can lead to suicide. In 1985, during one of the peak years of cocaine abuse in the United States, as many as one out of five suicide victims in New York City showed evidence of cocaine in their blood at autopsy. The prevalence of cocaine use was greatest among victims who were in their twenties and thirties, and for African Americans and Latinos.[16] In a 1989 survey of teenage callers to the 800–COCAINE hotline, one out of seven reported a previous suicide attempt.[17] On the basis of these studies, cocaine use has become recognized as a significant risk factor for suicide attempts.

Cocaine's effect on sexual arousal is often cited as having been the basis for calling it "the aphrodisiac of the 1980s." On the one hand, interviews of cocaine users frequently include reports of spontaneous and prolonged erections in males and multiple orgasms in females during initial doses of the drug. On the other hand, cocaine's reputation for increasing sexual performance (recall Freud's reference in his letter to Martha) may bias users toward a strong expectation that there will be a sexually stimulating reaction, when in reality the effect is a much weaker one. As one cocaine abuser expressed it, "Everybody says that it's an aphrodisiac. Again, I think some people say it because it's supposed to be. I think that it's just peer group identification. . . . I never felt that way. I was more content to sit there and enjoy it."[18] The fact is that

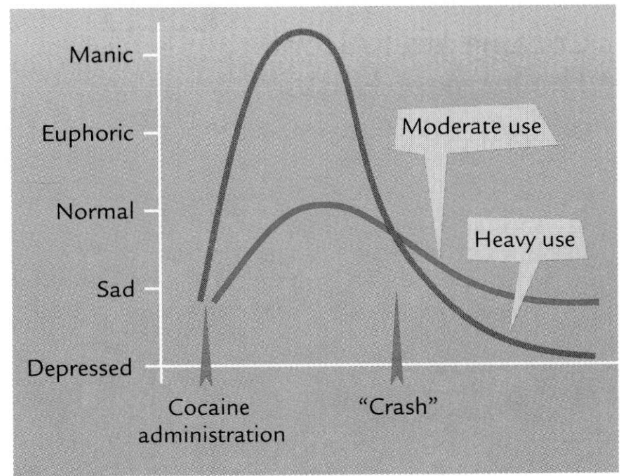

FIGURE 4.1

Ups and downs of a typical dose of cocaine.

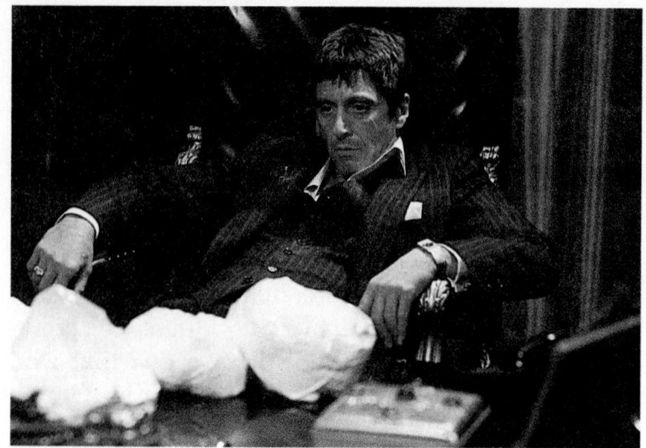

The depiction of actor Al Pacino as a cocaine kingpin. Scarface *is an example of Hollywood's glamorization of cocaine during the early 1980s.*

chronic cocaine use results in decreased sexual performance and a loss of sexual desire, as the drug essentially takes the place of sex.

Cocaine produces a sudden elevation in the sympathetic branch of the autonomic nervous system. Heart rate and respiration are increased, while appetite is diminished. Blood vessels constrict, pupils in the eyes dilate, and blood pressure rises. The cocaine user may start to sweat and appear suddenly pale. The powerful sympathetic changes can lead to a cerebral hemorrhage or congestive heart failure. Cardiac arrhythmia results from cocaine's tendency to bind to heart tissue itself. As you may recall from Chapter 2, more than four thousand cocaine-related deaths were reported in the 1998 DAWN survey, making cocaine the drug mentioned most frequently by medical examiners in hospital emergency rooms.[19]

The extreme effects of cocaine on bodily organs, particularly the heart, stem from its ability not only to excite the sympathetic system but to inhibit the parasympathetic system as well (Health Alert). Given the high level of sympathetic arousal, it is not surprising that behavioral skills will be adversely affected. In a study of drivers showing reckless behavior on the road, those found to have been under the influence of cocaine were wildly overconfident in their abilities, taking turns too fast or weaving through traffic. One highway patrol officer called this behavior "diagonal driving. They were just as involved in changing lanes as in going forward." Yet they passed the standard sobriety tests designed to detect alcohol intoxication.[20]

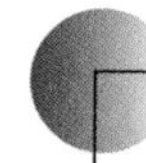

Chronic Effects of Cocaine

Repeated and continued use of cocaine produces undesirable mood changes that can only be alleviated when the person is under the acute effects of the drug. Chronic cocaine abusers are often irritable, depressed, and paranoid. As was true in Fleischl's experience with cocaine, long-term abuse can produce the disturbing hallucinatory experience of formication. The

Health Alert

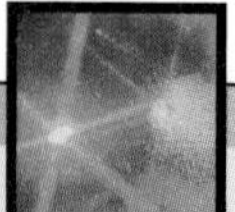

Cocaine after Alcohol: The Increased Risks of Cocaethylene Toxicity

The risks of dying from cocaine arise from the drug's powerful excitatory effects on the body. Abnormal heart rhythms can lead to labored breathing and cardiac arrest, increased blood pressure can produce a cerebral hemorrhage, and increased body temperature can trigger epileptic seizures.

The potential for any of these toxic reactions is, unfortunately, increased when alcohol is already in the bloodstream. The biotransformation of cocaine and alcohol (ethanol), when ingested in combination, produces a metabolite called *cocaethylene.* One effect of cocaethylene is a three- to five-fold increase in the elimination half-life of cocaine. As a result, cocaine remains in the bloodstream for a much longer time. More important, cocaethylene has a specific excitatory effect on blood pressure and heart rate that is greater than that produced by cocaine alone.

While the combination of alcohol and cocaine is associated with a prolonged and enhanced euphoria, it also brings an eighteen- to twenty-five-fold increased risk of immediate death. The fact that 62–90 percent of cocaine abusers are also abusers of alcohol makes the dangers of cocaethylene toxicity a significant health concern.

Sources: Andrews, Paul (1997). Cocaethylene toxicity. *Journal of Addictive Diseases, 16,* 75–84. Pirwitz, M.; Willard J.; Landau, C.; Lange, R.; Glamann, B.; Kessler, D.; Foerster, E.; Todd, E.; and Hillis, D. (1995). Influence of cocaine, ethanol, or their combinations on epicardial coronary arterial dimensions in humans. *Archives of Internal Medicine, 155,* 1186–1191.

sensation of "cocaine bugs" crawling on or under the skin can become so severe that abusers may scratch the skin into open sores or even pierce themselves with a knife to cut out the imaginary creatures. These hallucinations, together with feelings of anxiety and paranoia, make up a serious mental disorder referred to as **cocaine psychosis.**

When snorted, cocaine causes bronchial muscles to relax and nasal blood vessels to constrict; the opposite effects occur when the drug wears off. As the bronchial muscles contract and nasal blood vessels relax, chronic abusers endure continuously stuffy or runny noses and bleeding of nasal membranes. In advanced cases of this problem, the septum of the nose can develop lesions or become perforated with small holes, both of which present serious problems for breathing.

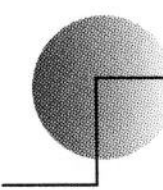

Medical Uses of Cocaine

When applied topically on the skin, cocaine has the ability to block the transmission of nerve impulses, deadening all sensations from the area. This local anesthetic effect of cocaine remains its only legitimate medical application. In procedures in which tubes are passed through the nose or throat, cocaine is applied on the membranes to ease the discomfort.

There are, however, potential problems in the use of cocaine even for these specific, beneficial circumstances. One danger is that cocaine may be inadvertently absorbed into the bloodstream. There is also the possibility for abuse. Finally, the local anesthetic effects are brief because cocaine breaks down so rapidly. Synthetic drugs such as lidocaine (brand name: Xylocaine) have the advantage of acting as local anesthetics over a longer period of time, and because they do not have the euphoriant effects of cocaine, the abuse potential is reduced. Consequently, lidocaine and other similar drugs, by injection into the gums, are widely used as local anesthetics during dental procedures.

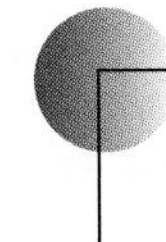

How Cocaine Works in the Brain

Cocaine greatly enhances the activity of dopamine, and to a lesser extent, norepinephrine in the brain. In the case of both neurotransmitters, the actual effect is to block the reuptake process at the synapse, so the neurotransmitters stimulate the postsynaptic receptors longer and to a greater degree.[21] Unlike the amphetamines (discussed later in this chapter), the structure of cocaine does not appear to resemble the structure of either norepinephrine or dopamine, so why cocaine should block their reuptake so effectively is not at all clear. What has been determined, however, is that the euphoria experienced through cocaine is directly related to the effect of dopamine in the region of the brain that controls pleasure and reinforcement in general: the nucleus accumbens (see Chapter 3).

One feature of cocaine is quite unlike that of other psychoactive drugs. While many cocaine abusers develop a pattern of drug tolerance, requiring increased doses to duplicate the initial cocaine effect, others sometimes experience the opposite: a hypersensitization to the drug. In other words, long-term cocaine abusers may become *more* sensitive to the drug over repeated administrations. This phenomenon, referred to as the **kindling effect,** makes cocaine particularly dangerous, since cocaine has the potential for setting off brain seizures. Repeated exposure to cocaine can lower the threshold for seizures, through a sensitization of neurons in the limbic system over time. As a result of the kindling effect, deaths from cocaine overdose may occur from relatively low dose levels.[22]

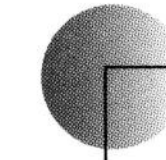

Present-Day Cocaine Abuse

The difficult problems of cocaine abuse in the United States and around the world mushroomed during the early 1970s and continue to the present day, though the incidence of abuse is down from peak levels reached around 1986. In ways that resembled the brief period of enthusiasm for cocaine in 1884, attitudes during the early period of this "second epidemic" were incredibly naive. Fueled by media reports of use among the rich and famous, touted as the "champagne of drugs," cocaine became synonymous with the glamorous life.

The medical profession at this time was equally nonchalant about cocaine. The widely respected *Comprehensive textbook of psychiatry* (1980) stated the following: "If it is used no more than two or three times a week, cocaine creates no serious problem. . . . At present chronic cocaine use does not usually present a medical problem."[23]

cocaine psychosis: A set of symptoms, including hallucinations, paranoia, and disordered thinking, produced from chronic use of cocaine.

kindling effect: A phenomenon in the brain that produces a heightened sensitivity to repeated administrations of a drug. This heightened sensitivity is the opposite of the phenomenon of tolerance.

These attitudes began to change as the 1980s unfolded. The death of actor-comedian John Belushi in 1982, followed by the drug-related deaths of other entertainers and sport figures (see Drugs . . . in Focus, page 30) produced a slow but steady reversal of opinion about the safety and desirability of cocaine. The greatest influence, however, was the arrival of crack cocaine on the drug scene in 1985, which will be examined in the next sections.

From Coca to Cocaine

In order to understand the ways in which cocaine is abused, we should look at the various steps that the raw coca goes through to become reasonably pure cocaine (Figure 4.2). During the initial extraction process, coca leaves are soaked in various chemical solvents so that cocaine can be drawn out of the plant material itself. Leaves are then crushed, and alcohol is percolated through them to remove extraneous matter. After sequential washings and a treatment with kerosene, the yield is cocaine that is approximately 60 percent pure. This is the coca paste, which, as mentioned earlier, is combined with tobacco and smoked in many South American countries.

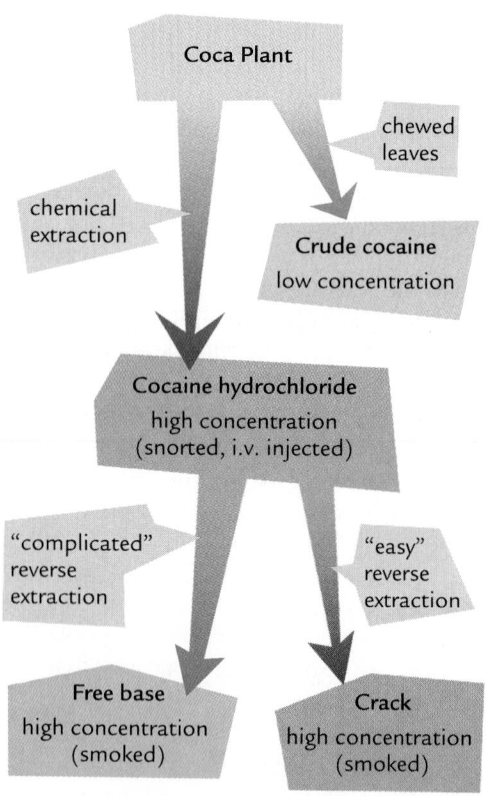

FIGURE 4.2

Steps in producing various forms of cocaine from raw coca.

Cocaine in this form, however, is not water-soluble and therefore cannot be injected into the bloodstream. An additional step of treatment with oxidizing agents and acids is required to produce a water-soluble drug. The result is a white crystalline powder called **cocaine hydrochloride,** about 99 percent pure cocaine and classified chemically as a salt.

When in the form of cocaine hydrochloride, the drug can be injected intravenously or snorted. The amount injected at one time is about 16 mg. Intravenous cocaine can also be combined with heroin in a highly dangerous mixture called a *speedball.*

If cocaine is snorted, the user generally has the option of two methods. In one method, a tiny spoonful of cocaine is carried to one nostril while the other nostril is shut, and the drug is taken with a rapid inhalation. In the other method, cocaine is spread out on a highly polished surface (often a mirror) and arranged with a razor blade in several lines each containing from 20 to 30 mg. The cocaine is then inhaled into one nostril by means of a straw or rolled piece of paper. During the early 1980s, a $100 bill was a fashionable alternative, emphasizing the level of income necessary to be taking cocaine in the first place.[24]

From Cocaine to Crack

Options beyond the intake of cocaine hydrochloride widened with the development of **free-base cocaine** during the 1970s and **crack cocaine** (or simply **crack**) during the mid-1980s. In free-base cocaine, the hydrochloride is removed from the salt form of cocaine, thus liberating it as a free base. The aim is to obtain a smokable form of cocaine, which by entering the brain more quickly, produces a more intense effect. The technique for producing free-base cocaine, however, is extremely hazardous, since it is necessary to treat cocaine powder with highly flammable agents such as ether. If the free base still contains some ether residue, igniting the drug will cause it to explode into flames.

Crack cocaine is the result of a cheaper and safer chemical method, but the result is essentially the same: a smokable form of cocaine. Treatment with baking soda yields small rocks, which can then be smoked in a small pipe.[25] When they are smoked, a cracking noise accompanies the burning, hence the origin of the name "crack."

cocaine hydrochloride: The form of cocaine that is inhaled (snorted) or injected into the bloodstream.
free-base cocaine: A smokable form of cocaine.
crack cocaine or **crack:** A smokable form of cocaine.

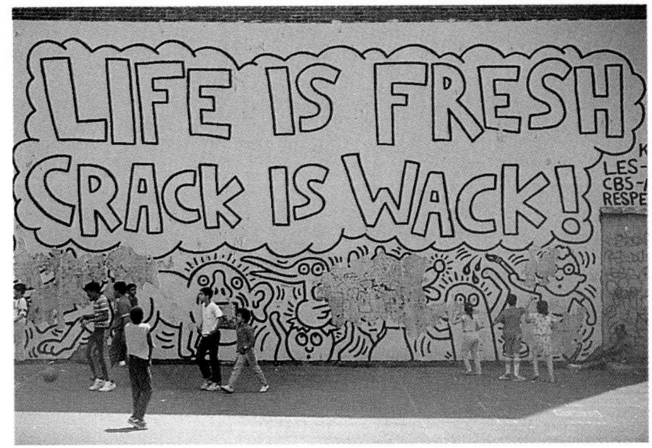

A message of prevention is a community's response to the desolation and misery resulting from crack cocaine abuse.

How dangerous is crack? There is no question that the effect of cocaine when smoked exceeds the effect of cocaine when snorted; for some users, it even exceeds the effect of cocaine when injected. Inhaling high-potency cocaine (the purity of cocaine in crack averages about 75 percent) into the lungs, and almost immediately into the brain, sets the stage for uncontrollable psychological dependence. And at a price of $3 to $20 per dose, cocaine is no longer out of financial reach (Table 4.1). The answer is that crack is very dangerous indeed. Beyond its effect on the user, however, is the effect on the society where crack is prevalent. Women who are crack abusers find that their drug cravings overwhelm their maternal instincts, resulting in the neglect of the basic needs of their children, either in postnatal or prenatal stages of life. In New York, for example, the number of reported cases of child abuse and neglect increased from 36,000 in 1985 to 59,000 in 1989, a change largely attributed to the introduction of crack. As discussed in Chapter 2, the enormous monetary profits from the selling of crack caused inner-city crime and violence to skyrocket (Figure 4.3 on page 86).[26]

While crack abuse remains a problem as we begin the new millennium, the number of new crack abusers is down substantially, particularly in the inner-city communities of the United States. While 36 percent of all males over 36 years old who were arrested in New York in 1998 had used crack, little more than 4 percent of those 15 to 20 years old had done so. A principal reason for this change in prevalence rates is the present-day stigmatized image of the "crack head," considered by one's peers to be a social loser in his or her community.[27]

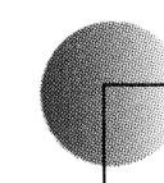

Patterns of Cocaine Abuse

In 1999, the National Household Survey on Drug Abuse estimated that approximately 11 million Americans had used cocaine at some time in their lives, 1.7 million had used it during the past year, and 700,000 had used it during the past month. Of these totals, approximately 2.7 million Americans had used crack at some time in their lives, 500,000 had used it during the past year, and 200,000 had used it during the past month (Health Alert).[28]

TABLE 4.1

Street names for cocaine

TYPE OF COCAINE	STREET NAME
Cocaine	blow, C, coke, big C, lady, nose candy, snowbirds, snow, stardust, toot, white girl, happydust, cola, flake, pearl, Peruvian lady, freeze, geeze, doing the line
Free-base cocaine	freebase, base
Crack cocaine	crack, rock, kibbles and bits, crell
Crack cocaine combined with PCP (see Chapter 6)	beam me up Scottie, space cadet, tragic magic
Cocaine combined with heroin	speedball
Cocaine combined with heroin and LSD	Frisco special, Frisco speedball

Source: Bureau of Justice Statistics Clearinghouse (1992). *Drugs, behavior and crime.* Washington DC: Department of Justice, pp. 24–25.

Health Alert

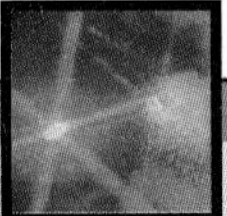

The Physical Signs of Possible Cocaine Abuse

- Dilated (enlarged) pupils
- Increased heart rate
- Increased irritability
- Paranoia
- Sneezing and irritability in the nose (if cocaine has been snorted)
- Feelings of depression
- Insomnia
- Decreased appetite and significant weight loss

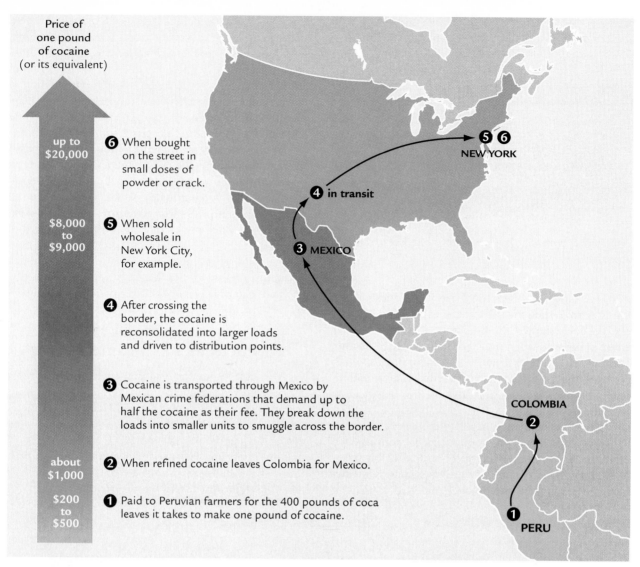

Price of one pound of cocaine (or its equivalent)

up to $20,000 — 6 When bought on the street in small doses of powder or crack.

$8,000 to $9,000 — 5 When sold wholesale in New York City, for example.

4 After crossing the border, the cocaine is reconsolidated into larger loads and driven to distribution points.

3 Cocaine is transported through Mexico by Mexican crime federations that demand up to half the cocaine as their fee. They break down the loads into smaller units to smuggle across the border.

about $1,000 — 2 When refined cocaine leaves Colombia for Mexico.

$200 to $500 — 1 Paid to Peruvian farmers for the 400 pounds of coca leaves it takes to make one pound of cocaine.

5 6 NEW YORK

4 in transit

3 MEXICO

COLOMBIA 2

1 PERU

FIGURE 4.3

From farm prices in Peru to street prices as crack, the value of cocaine escalates from as little as $200 for the 400 pounds of coca necessary to produce one pound of cocaine to $20,000 for the crack doses made from that pound of cocaine.

Source: New York Times, March 4, 1997, p. A20. Copyright © 1997 by The New York Times Company. Reprinted by permission.

Although the incidence of cocaine abuse in the United States was lower in the 1990s than it had been during the 1980s, medical emergencies associated with cocaine use, as measured through the DAWN statistics, have increased dramatically. In 1998, there were approximately 172,000 cocaine-related emergencies reported by metropolitan hospitals, more than twice the number reported in 1990. It is evident that emergency departments have borne a great burden in the acute care of cocaine abusers.[29] What options are there for the long-term treatment of individuals with cocaine dependence?

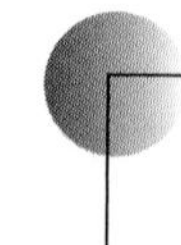

Treatment Programs for Cocaine Abuse

One way of grasping the extent of the cocaine-abuse problem is to look at the number of people who have wanted to get help. In 1983 a nationwide toll-free hotline, 1–800–COCAINE was established as a twenty-four-hour service for emergency and treatment information. From 1983 to 1990, more than 3 million callers responded, averaging more than 1,000 a day.[30]

We have also seen, through the statistics gathered from the hotline over the years, the changing face of cocaine abuse. In 1983 the typical cocaine abuser was college educated (50 percent), employed (83 percent), earning more than $25,000 a year (52 percent), and taking cocaine powder intranasally (61 percent). By 1988, however, the typical cocaine abuser had not gone to college (83 percent) and was earning less than $25,000 a year (80 percent). From 1983 to 1988, the percentage of individuals reporting an abuse of a free-base form of cocaine had more than doubled to 56 percent. In 1986 alone, one year after the introduction of crack, half of all calls to the hotline referred to problems of crack abuse. These demographic changes present new challenges in treatment. New programs must be sensitive not only to the ethnic diversity of present-day cocaine abusers but also to the diversity in the pattern of cocaine abuse.[31]

Treating cocaine abuse presents difficulties that are peculiar to the power of cocaine itself. This is the way one treatment expert has put it:

> *Coming off cocaine is one of the most anguished, depressing experiences. I've watched people talk about coming off freebase and one of the things I noticed was the nonverbal maneuvers they use to describe it. It looks like they're describing a heart attack. They have fists clenched to the chest. You can see that it hurts. They can recreate that hurt for you because it's a devastating event. They'll do almost anything to keep from crashing on cocaine. And on top of that they'll do just about anything to keep their supply coming. Postcocaine anguish is a strong inducement to use again—to keep the pain away.*[32]

Seven Rules for Cocaine Abusers Who Want to Quit

- **The time to stop using cocaine is now.** If you say, "I'll quit tomorrow," then you are saying, "I have no intention of quitting."
- **Stop all at once, not gradually.** Each time you use cocaine, you are fueling the desire for more and postponing the process of recovery.
- **Stop using all other drugs of abuse, including alcohol and marijuana.** Cocaine abusers often think that the problem is with cocaine alone. Use of alcohol and marijuana can be the initial step to a relapse back to cocaine.
- **Change your life-style.** If you encounter conditions that are associated with cocaine, your craving will increase. This problem is particularly difficult in the early stages of cocaine withdrawal.
- **Whenever possible, avoid situations, people, and places that cause drug urges.** Yesterday's abstinences doesn't guarantee the same result today. It's a matter of "one day at a time." Trying to test yourself by approaching drug situations and monitoring your reaction is a big mistake, according to drug-treatment experts.
- **Find other rewards.** Learn to enjoy life without cocaine. Learn how to reconnect with a drug-free world. You may have even forgotten how to talk about anything except cocaine.
- **Take good care of your body. Eat right and exercise.** Normal eating habits are wrecked while you are abusing cocaine. Chances are good that your physical condition has deteriorated, and you may be suffering from significiant vitamin deficiencies. A healthy diet and a program of regular exercise are two major factors in your long-term recovery prospects.

Source: Weiss, Roger D., and Mirin, Steven, M. (1987). *Cocaine.* Washington DC: American Psychiatric Press, pp. 136–139.

The varieties of treatment for cocaine abuse all have certain features in common. The initial phase is detoxification and total abstinence: The cocaine abuser aims to achieve total withdrawal with the least possibility of physical injury and minimal psychological discomfort. During the first twenty-four to forty-eight hours, the chances are high that there will be profound depression, severe headaches, irritability, and disturbances in sleep.[33]

In severe cases involving a pattern of compulsive use that cannot be easily broken, the cocaine abuser needs to be admitted for inpatient treatment in a hospital facility. The most intensive interventions, medical supervision, and psychological counseling can be made in this kind of environment. The early stages of withdrawal are clearly the most difficult, and the recovering abuser can benefit from around-the-clock attention that only a hospital staff can give.

The alternative approach is an outpatient program, under which the individual remains at home but travels regularly to a facility for treatment. An outpatient program is clearly a less expensive route to take, but it may work only for those who recognize the destructive impact of cocaine dependence on their lives and enter treatment with a sincere desire to do whatever is needed to stop.[34]

For cocaine abusers who have failed in previous attempts in outpatient treatment or for those who are in denial of their cocaine dependence, an inpatient approach may be the only answer (Health Line). For some,

Portrait Doc Gooden—Triumphs and Tribulations

The parade of athletes who struggle against drug abuse is seemingly endless. Over the years, we have witnessed their personal wins and losses, much like the games they have played. There have been the casualties of college basketball player Len Bias and professional football player Dan Rodgers. In 1986, their untimely deaths from cocaine overdoses galvanized the nation to take a serious look at the power of this drug to take the lives of healthy, talented young men. In the 1980s, there were other victims who escaped death but whose athletic careers were demolished: Stanley Wilson, Cincinnati Bengals running back, for example, whose suspension from football after testing positive for cocaine took place on the eve of Super Bowl XXIII in 1989. In the life of baseball pitcher Dwight (Doc) Gooden, we have watched an emotional roller coaster of a baseball career studded with triumphs and defeats, and we simply have had to hold our breath as the seasons continue on.

By the mid-1990s, Doc Gooden had gone from a pitcher with legend potential (the youngest Cy Young Award winner) in 1985 to an outcast who could not stop his drug tests from coming up positive for cocaine. In 1987, he had entered a twenty-eight-day program at a drug treatment center in New York after being suspended from the New York Mets for failing a drug test during spring training. Health professionals who understand the complexity of cocaine dependence would refer to such a program as the kind of casual approach that represents "the standard cosmetic treatment that so often fails." After a comeback in the early 1990s, Gooden was suspended again in 1994 after repeated drug-test failures.

Dwight "Doc" Gooden

This time as a New York Yankee, however, a supporting cast was on hand for him. Former Yankee Steve Howe, himself suspended seven times in his career for drug-abuse violations, would travel with Gooden as his friend and mentor. In addition, Gooden could lean on his sponsor at Narcotics Anonymous, Ron Dock, a recovering addict who would be less impressed with someone playing pro baseball than with a person staying clean for a day.

A payoff of sorts took place in May 1996. Free of cocaine since late 1994, Gooden succeeded in pitching a stunning no-hitter. Howe remarked at the time, "It's more than an athletic achievement; it's a life achievement." Dock agreed: "For the first time he is spiritually grounded."

How will his story end? As they say, we just have to stay tuned. In recent years, still active as a major-league pitcher, Gooden could look back on a life blessed with second chances:

> *If my career were to end today, I have plenty to be thankful for—especially during my second time around. I appreciate the game in a way I never could have in the eighties, having learned that my gifts were indeed that, gifts to be treasured and nourished and protected.*

Postscript: Gooden announced his retirement as a baseball pitcher in March 2001.

Sources: Curry, Jack (1997, August 21). Strong start by Gooden revives rotation. *New York Times*, pp. B7, B9. Gooden, Dwight (1999). *Heat: My life on and off the diamond.* New York: Morrow, p. 233. Heyman, Jon (1996, May 21). Operation Doc. *Newsday*, pp. A70–71.

it is important to stay away from an environment where cocaine and other drugs are prevalent and peer pressure to resume drug-taking behavior is intense. This factor is particularly crucial among adolescents:

> *Peer acceptance is of utmost importance to adolescents. In order to interrupt the addiction cycle, youth are cautioned to avoid drug-using friends. Since many addicted adolescents are alienated from the mainstream and what few friends they have are users, this challenge can appear overwhelming. Recovering adolescents often comment that they can't find friends who don't at least drink.*[35]

A third alternative is a combined approach in which a shortened inpatient program, seven to fourteen days in length, is followed by an intensive outpatient program that continues for several months (Portrait).

Whether on an inpatient or outpatient basis, there are several approaches for treatment. For cocaine abusers specifically, there is the self-help support group Cocaine Anonymous, modeled after the famous Alcoholics Anonymous program (see Chapter 10). In these group sessions, recovering cocaine abusers feel less isolated, learn from the life experiences of other members, and attain a sense of accomplishment from remaining drug free. In many cases, an intensive relearning process has to go on, since cocaine abusers often cannot remember a life without cocaine. Formal psychotherapy sessions can also be provided on an individual, group, or family basis.

The newest strategy in developing treatment programs for cocaine abusers is to identify specific chemical compounds that can reduce or prevent cocaine dependence. One promising candidate is selegiline (brand name: Eldepryl), a drug commonly used to treat Parkinson's disease. Preliminary research has shown that selegiline reduces the euphoric feelings provided by cocaine and may also reduce feelings of cocaine craving. Chemical compounds are also being developed that allow the immune system to split cocaine molecules into harmless fragments whenever cocaine enters the body. In doing so, it is possible to prevent cocaine dependence as well as the consequences of a cocaine overdose. Currently, pharmacological approaches toward cocaine-abuse treatment, as well as the combination of pharmacological and behavioral approaches, are being vigorously pursued.[36]

Success rates for cocaine-abuse treatment depend on a host of factors: the severity of the cocaine abuse, the strength of the motivation to give it up, and the extent to which the program matches up with the abuser's personal needs. In one study of 127 abusers who took part in an outpatient treatment program, 65 percent completed the program after six to twelve months and more than 75 percent were still drug free after a one-to-two-year follow-up.[37] Nonetheless, relapse is always a significant concern among recovering cocaine abusers. A specialist in cocaine-abuse rehabilitation tells this story: "A woman was doing very well in treatment. Then one day she was changing her baby's diaper. She used baby powder and the sight of the white powder induced a tremendous craving for cocaine."[38] You might recognize this phenomenon as an instance of behavioral conditioning, discussed in Chapter 2 (Drugs . . . in Focus).

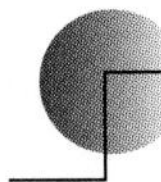

Amphetamines

One of humanity's fondest dreams is to have the power of unlimited endurance, to be able to banish fatigue from our lives, to be capable of endless energy as if we had discovered some internal perpetual-motion machine. We all have wanted, at some time in our lives, to be a superhero. Cocaine, as we know, gives us that illusion. The remainder of this chapter will examine another powerful drug source for these feelings of invincibility: amphetamines. As we will see, the attractions and problems of abuse associated with cocaine and amphetamines are very similar.

The History of Amphetamines

The origin of modern amphetamines dates back almost five thousand years to a Chinese medicinal herb called

DRUGS . . . IN FOCUS

Crack Babies Revisited: Has There Been an Adverse Effect?

In the late 1980s, at the height of the crack abuse explosion, one particularly alarming possibility concerned the children of women who had been crack abusers during their pregnancies (frequently referred to as "crack babies"). Might these innocents incur long-term mental and physical deficits later in life as a result of *in utero* exposure to cocaine? The early signs were not promising. These newborns had lower birth weights and smaller head circumferences, and they displayed tremors, excessive crying, disturbed sleep patterns, and diminished responsiveness, all of which were abnormalities typical of cocaine exposure. The question remained, however, whether there would be deficits in social skills and mental ability when these infants grew older.

One of the difficulties in arriving at an answer is the fact that the mothers who are cocaine abusers during their pregnancies are more accurately polydrug abusers, in that they typically abuse alcohol, marijuana, and tobacco as well as cocaine. It is impossible to tease out the individual effect of cocaine itself. In addition, studies have to be very carefully controlled to ensure that any comparisons between drug-exposed and non-drug-exposed children are not confused with differences in the age of the child, ethnicity, gender, or socioeconomic status. A recent study looked at two groups of preschoolers, matched on these variables. Both groups were found to be below-average in social skills and mental abilities related to language, but they were not different from each other. These findings, by the way, are consistent with the findings of several studies that have examined this issue. The consensus among health professionals, therefore, is that developmental difficulties of children can be a result of many risk factors (see Chapter 1), including inadequate prenatal care and poor maternal nutrition, but that cocaine exposure itself prior to their birth does not play a major role. Nonetheless, ongoing studies are investigating whether more subtle differences in cognitive ability may exist and whether *in utero* cocaine exposure might have a delayed influence as children advance into adolescence.

Sources: Phelps, LeAdelle, Wallace, Nancy V., and Bontrager, Annie (1997). Risk factors in early child development: Is prenatal cocaine/polydrug exposure a key variable? *Psychology in the Schools, 34,* 245–252. Zickler, Patrick (1999, September). NIDA studies clarify developmental effects of prenatal cocaine exposure. *NIDA Notes, 14* (3), 5–6.

ma huang (Ephedra vulgaris) that was used to clear bronchial passageways during bouts of asthma and other forms of respiratory distress. According to Chinese legend, this herb was first identified by the Emperor Shen Nung, who also is credited with the discovery of tea and marijuana.

German chemists isolated the active ingredient of *ma huang* in 1887, naming it ephedrine. It was soon obvious that ephedrine stimulated the sympathetic nervous system in general (see Portrait in Chapter 1). In 1927, Gordon Alles, a research chemist from Los Angeles, developed a synthetic form of ephedrine and named the new drug **amphetamine.** The pharmaceutical company Smith, Kline and French Laboratories marketed the Alles formula under the brand name Benzedrine in 1932 as a nonprescription inhalant for asthma sufferers. By the beginning of World War II, amphetamine had gained the reputation of being a CNS stimulant appetite suppressant and bronchial dilator.

Wartime conditions, however, provided an additional application for amphetamine: to keep soldiers "pepped up" during long hours of battle. During the war, both U.S. and German troops were being given amphetamine to keep them awake and alert. Japanese kamikazi pilots were on amphetamine during their suicide missions. The advantages over cocaine, the other stimulant drug available at the time, were two-fold: amphetamine was easily absorbed into the nervous system from the gastrointestinal tract so it could be taken orally, and its effects were much longer lasting, generally about seven hours.

After the war, amphetamine use was adapted for peacetime purposes. Amphetamine, often referred to as bennies, was a way for college students to stay awake to study for exams and for long-distance truck drivers to fight fatigue on the road. Truckers would take a "St. Louis" if they had to go from New York to Missouri and back or a "Pacific turnabout" if they needed to travel completely across country and back, without stopping to sleep.[39]

In the meantime, the word got around that amphetamine produced euphoria as well. As you might expect, this news created a flourishing black market, as amphetamine began to be sought for recreational purposes. People found ways of opening up the nonprescription amphetamine inhalers, withdrawing the contents, and getting high by drinking it or injecting it intravenously. Since each inhaler contained 250 mg of amphetamine, there was enough for several powerful doses. During the early 1960s, injectable amphetamines could be bought with forged prescriptions or even by telephoning a pharmacy and posing as a physician. By 1965, amendments to federal drug laws tightened the supply of prescription amphetamines, requiring manufacturers, wholesalers, and pharmacies to keep careful records of amphetamine transactions, but amphetamines soon became available from illegal laboratories.[40]

Amphetamine abuse in the United States reached a peak about 1967, declining slowly over the 1970s as other drugs of abuse, notably cocaine, grew in popularity. By 1970, 10 percent of the U.S. population over fourteen years of age had used amphetamine, and more than 8 percent of all drug prescriptions were for amphetamine in some form.[41] For about two decades afterward, amphetamine abuse steadily faded from prominence in the drug scene. Cocaine and later crack cocaine became the dominant illicit stimulant of abuse. Only since the mid-1990s has amphetamine abuse resurfaced as a significant social concern.

The Different Forms of Amphetamine

In order to understand amphetamine abuse, both past and present, it is necessary to know something about the molecular structure of amphetamines themselves and their relationship to important neurotransmitters in the brain. As you can see at the top of Figure 4.4, amphetamine can be represented in terms of carbon (C), hydrogen (H), and nitrogen (N) atoms, in a prescribed arrangement. What you are seeing, however, is only one version of amphetamine, the "right-handed" form, since amphetamine contains a "left-handed" version as well (imagine a mirror image of Figure 4.4). The more potent version is the right-handed form, called dextroamphetamine or **d-amphetamine** (brand name: Dexedrine). It is stronger than the left-handed form, called levoamphetamine or l-amphetamine, which is not commonly available. A modified form of d-amphetamine, formulated by substituting CH_3 (called a methyl group) instead of H at one end, is called **methamphetamine.** This slight change in the formula allows for a quicker passage across the blood-brain barrier. It is methamphetamine, often called *meth* or *speed,* that has been the primary form of amphetamine abuse in recent years.

amphetamine (am-FEH-ta-meen): A family of ephedrine-based stimulant drugs.

d-amphetamine: Shortened name for dextroamphetamine, a potent form of amphetamine, marketed under the brand name Dexedrine.

```
                      C = C                          H
                     /     \        H   CH3         /
Dextroamphetamine   C       C - C  -  C  -  N
                     \\     //      H    H          \
                      C - C                          H

                      C = C                          H
                     /     \        H   CH3         /
Methamphetamine     C       C - C  -  C  -  N
                     \\     //      H    H          \
                      C - C                          CH3

                  HO
                     \
                      C = C                          H
                     /     \        H    H          /
Dopamine       HO - C       C - C  -  C  -  N
                     \\     //      H    H          \
                      C - C                          H

                  HO
                     \
                      C = C                          H
                     /     \        OH   H          /
Norepinephrine HO - C       C - C  -  C  -  N
                     \\     //      H    H          \
                      C - C                          H
```

FIGURE 4.4

The molecular structure of dextroamphetamine, methamphetamine, dopamine, and norepinephrine.

How Amphetamines Work in the Brain

We can get a good idea of how amphetamines work in the brain by looking carefully at the molecular structures of dopamine and norepinephrine alongside d-amphetamine and methamphetamine in Figure 4.4. Notice how similar they all are, with only slight differences among them. Because of the close resemblance to dopamine and norepinephrine, it is not hard to imagine amphetamines increasing the activity level of these two neurotransmitters. Specifically, amphetamines cause increased amounts of dopamine and norepinephrine to be released from synaptic knobs and also slow down their reuptake from receptor sites. As described in Chapter 3, dopamine figures prominently in regions of the brain associated with positive reinforcement. The euphoric effects of amphetamines, and the craving for them during abstinence, are considered to result from a stimulation of these regions.

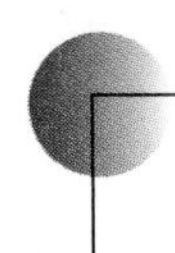

Acute and Chronic Effects of Amphetamines

The acute effects of amphetamine, in either d-amphetamine or methamphetamine form, closely resemble those of cocaine. However, amphetamine effects extend over a longer period of time. For intervals of eight to twenty-four hours, there are signs of increased sympathetic autonomic activity, such as faster breathing and heart rate as well as hyperthermia (increased body temperature) and elevated blood pressure. Users experience feelings of euphoria and invincibility, decreased appetite, and an extraordinary boost in alertness and energy. Adverse and potentially lethal bodily changes include convulsions, chest pains, or stroke. These serious health risks have, unfortunately, been reflected in the DAWN statistics, in which methamphetamine-related hospital emergencies doubled from 1990 to 1999.[42]

Chronic effects of amphetamine abuse are both bizarre and unpleasant, particularly in the case of methamphetamine. Heavy methamphetamine abusers may experience formication hallucinations similar to those endured by cocaine abusers. They may become obsessed with the delusion that parasites or insects have lodged in their skin and so attempt to scratch, cut, or burn their skin in an effort to remove them. It is also likely that they will engage in compulsive or repetitive behaviors that are fixated upon ordinarily trivial aspects of life; an entire night might be spent, for example, counting the corn flakes in a cereal box.[43]

The most serious societal consequence of methamphetamine abuse is the appearance of paranoia, wildly bizarre delusions, hallucinations, tendencies toward violence, and intense mood swings. In the words of one health professional, "It's about the ugliest drug there is."[44] Because the symptoms have been observed with the chronic abuse of amphetamines of any type, they are referred to collectively as **amphetamine psychosis.** These "psychotic" effects, often persisting for weeks or even months after the drug has been withdrawn, so closely resemble the symptoms of paranoid schizophrenia that it has been speculated that the two conditions have the same underlying chemical basis in the brain: an overstimulation of dopamine-releasing neurons in those regions that control emotional reactivity.[45] Recently, a study of heavy methamphetamine users showed changes in chemical metabolites in those regions of the brain that are associated with Parkinson's disease, suggesting that this group

methamphetamine: An often abused type of amphetamine, once marketed under the brand name Methedrine. Methamphetamine abusers refer to it as speed or meth.

amphetamine psychosis: A set of symptoms, including hallucinations, paranoia, and disordered thinking, resulting from high doses of amphetamines.

Methamphetamine abuse produces an enormous increase in alertness and energy, but frightening hallucinations and compulsive behaviors also can occur.

may be predisposed to acquiring Parkinson symptoms later in life, due to their methamphetamine exposure.[46]

Patterns of Methamphetamine Abuse and Treatment

In the United States, the emergence of widespread methampetamine abuse was intermingled with the marijuana and LSD scene during San Francisco's "Summer of Love and Peace" in 1967. Almost from the beginning, however, speed freaks—as methamphetamine abusers were called—whose behaviors were anything but loving or peaceful, became the outcasts of that society:

> *A subculture of drug users who used speed almost exclusively—popping it or shooting it—developed, and began to evince all the symptoms we now associate with classic amphetamine abuse. These wild-eyed, manic burnout cases would blither on endlessly, rip off anything not welded in place, then go into fits of erratic and violent behavior. . . . They were shunned by other sorts of drug users, and ended up congregating with the only segment of the population who could stomach their company—other speed freaks.*[47]

In the meantime, prescription amphetamines, widely administered during the 1960s for weight control and as a way to combat drowsiness, resulted in large numbers of abusers from practically every segment of society. Even though d-amphetamine was classified as a Schedule II drug in 1970 and the number of d-amphetamine prescriptions decreased by 90 percent from 1971 and 1986, the pills were still out there, and people found ways to continue an abusive pattern of drug-taking behavior.

Present-Day Patterns of Methamphetamine Abuse

The popularity of one drug of abuse or another can often change rapidly, and the present picture with respect to stimulants is no exception. As crack cocaine became increasingly associated with the urban poor and powder cocaine with upscale affluence in the 1980s, amphetamine abuse declined dramatically. In the 1990s, however, as crack cocaine and powder cocaine abuse began to diminish, amphetamines reemerged on the drug scene. Methamphetamine, once dominant in the countercultural 1960s, now reestablished itself as the stimulant of abuse in the central and western regions of the United States. Initially, it attracted the working class rather than the poor or the affluent (Table 4.2).

> *Methamphetamine . . . made inroads among many blue-collar people because it did not carry the stigma of being a hard drug. . . . It's what people used to get them through a shift at the factory or keep up on a construction site.*[48]

Administered by snorting, injecting, or smoking, methamphetamine has become one of the few drugs reported as equally or more prevalent than other illicit drugs in areas outside America's inner cities. Once dispersed so that only small quantities of methamphetamine were produced in rural areas, distribution is now in the grips of organized groups operating out of southern California and Mexico, and trafficking routes extend through several U.S. states, including Arizona, Colorado, Iowa, Missouri, Nebraska, North Dakota, and Texas. Methamphetamine laboratories are typically situated in remote rural or desert areas, frequently inside mobile homes, campers, and vans, making their detection by law enforcement agencies extremely difficult. By the late 1990s, pharmacies were being encouraged to restrict the quantity of cold remedies containing pseudoephedrine being sold on an "over-the-counter" basis, since it could be used in the process of manufacturing methamphetamine. Whether methamphetamine will become a nationwide abuse problem in the United States, rather than a regional one,

TABLE 4.2

Street names for amphetamines

TYPE OF AMPHETAMINE	STREET NAME
amphetamines in general	bennies, uppers, ups, A, pep pills, white crowns, whites
dextroamphetamine	dexies, cadillacs, black beauties
methamphetamine	meth, speed, crank, little whites, white crosstops, crystal meth, quill, yellow bam, zip, go fast, chalk, shabu, spoosh
smokable methamphetamine*	ice, crystal, crystal meth, L.A., L.A. glass, quartz, cristy, hanyak
methcathinone (a synthetic analog of methamphetamine)	khat, cat, goob

*Slang terms often confuse smokable and nonsmokable forms of methamphetamine, so some street names may overlap the two categories.

Source: Drug Enforcement Agency, Office of National Drug Control Policy.

remains a question that cannot be answered at the present time.[49]

As with smokable crack cocaine, a smokable form of methamphetamine called **ice** (its name originating from its quartz-like, chunky crystallized appearance) presents special problems and concerns. Ice appeared on the drug scene in Hawaii in the late 1980s, but its abuse did not expand to the mainland to a significant degree until the latter 1990s. The combination of a very high-potency methamphetamine, from 98 to 100 percent pure, and a highly efficient delivery route through the lungs makes this drug particularly well suited for abuse. In addition, the fact that methamphetamine can be smoked (and needles can be avoided) somehow allows the abuser to rationalize that he or she is not engaging in "heavy drugs." Percentage levels of high-school seniors having used ice at least once in their lives have hovered around 4 percent from 1995 to 2000.[50] Health Line examines another type of stimulant abuse that is a potential problem.

The course of methamphetamine withdrawal, and amphetamine withdrawal in general, is very similar to the course of events described earlier for cocaine. First there is the "crash" when the abuser feels intense depression, hunger, agitation, and anxiety within one to four hours after the drug-taking behavior has stopped. Withdrawal from amphetamines, during total abstinence from the drug, takes between six and eighteen weeks, during which the intense craving for amphetamine slowly subsides. As in cocaine-abuse treatment, there are inpatient and outpatient programs, depending on the circumstances and motivation of the abuser. Self-help groups such as Cocaine Anonymous are useful as well, since the symptoms of amphetamine withdrawal and cocaine withdrawal are nearly identical. Unfortunately, relatively few methamphetamine abusers attempt treatment because they perceive themselves as in control over their drug use. As a recent report has expressed it:

> *This perception is particularly dangerous because the crossover from initial use to loss of control is rapid for meth users, and generally they have lost control long before they can acknowledge it. . . . This attitude of denial makes it difficult to convince meth abusers to enter and stay in treatment.*[51]

Methcathinone Abuse: A New Breed of Cat

Methcathinone is a type of "designer drug," in that it can be completely synthesized in the laboratory, its chemical structure engineered to closely resemble methamphetamine. Because it is a near-relative of an alkaloid called *cathinone,* commonly found in the leaves of the khat bush in East Africa and southern regions of Arabia, methcathinone is frequently referred to as "cat."

During the late 1970s and early 1980s, methcathinone was a widely abused drug in the former Soviet Union and Baltic nations. It was estimated that more than half of all drug abusers in that region had used it at least once and that it specifically constituted more than 20 percent of all illicit drug abuse in the Soviet Union. In 1989, samples of methcathinone were brought to Michigan, where laboratories were set up for production and distribution. Since then, an increasing number of cases of methcathinone-related emergencies have appeared in the Upper Peninsula portion of Michigan, as well as in Indiana, Minnesota, and Wisconsin. The drug produces roughly the same general effects as does methamphetamine, with one exception: the effects reportedly last much longer, up to six days. Methcathinone is now classified as a Schedule I controlled substance.

Sources: Calkins, Richard F., Aktan, Georgia B., and Hussain, Kathryn L. (1995). Methcathinone: The next stimulant epidemic? *Journal of Psychoactive Drugs, 27,* 277–285. Gygi, Melanie P., Gibb, James W., and Hanson, Glen R. (1996). Methcathinone: An initial study of its effects on monoaminergic systems. *Journal of Pharmacology and Experimental Therapeutics, 276,* 1066–1072.

ice: A smokable form of methamphetamine.

QUICK CONCEPT  4.2

Understanding Patterns of Stimulant Abuse

Check your understanding of the changing patterns of psychostimulant abuse from 1975 to the present by identifying the following statements with an (a) event prior to 1986 or (b) event subsequent to 1986.

1. Cocaine use is very expensive and restricted primarily to the wealthy. ______
2. Crack cocaine presents serious societal problems in the inner cities. ______
3. Typical cocaine abuser has not gone to college and earns less than $25,000 a year. ______
4. The nationwide toll-free hotline 1-800-COCAINE is established. ______
5. A smokable form of methamphetamine called ice appears on the drug scene. ______
6. The number of d-amphetamine prescriptions declines by 90 percent. ______

Answers: 1. prior 2. subsequent 3. subsequent 4. prior 5. subsequent 6. prior

Medical Uses for Amphetamines and Similar Stimulant Drugs

While amphetamines in general continue to present potential problems of abuse, there are approved medical applications for amphetamines and amphetamine-like stimulant drugs in specific circumstances. Dextroamphetamine (brand name: Dexedrine), a combination of dextroamphetamine and amphetamine (brand name: Adderall), and an amphetamine-like drug, methylphenidate (brand name: Ritalin), are widely prescribed for elementary-school-age children diagnosed as hyperactive and unable to maintain sufficient attention levels in school, technically referred to as **attention deficit/hyperactivity disorder (ADHD).** These children, more than three times as many boys as girls, are of average to above average intelligence but are underperforming academically.

About 70 percent of the approximately one million children in the United States who take stimulants for ADHD each year respond successfully to the treatment. In 1999, a major study examining the effects of medication over a fourteen-month period found that medication was more effective in reducing ADHD symptoms than behavioral treatment and nearly as effective as a combined approach of medication and behavioral treatment. The major side effect of stimulant medications, however, is a suppression of height and weight gains during these formative years, reducing growth to about 80 to 90 percent of normal levels. Fortunately, growth spurts during the summer, when children are typically no longer taking the medication, usually compensate for this problem.[52]

Why a stimulant drug would successfully *reduce* hyperactivity, rather than increase it, has been a great mystery among professionals in this field, and several theories have been advanced in an attempt to explain this apparent paradox. First, the therapeutic effects cannot be attributed to the fact that we are dealing with children rather than adults; in fact, ADHD has been increasingly diagnosed in adults as well, and the medicinal benefits for these adults are comparable to those for children. One possible explanation is that ADHD individuals in general are overly tired as a result of an unusually low CNS arousal level. By this reasoning, a stimulant would set the arousal level higher, making them more alert and attentive. Another explanation holds that the primary advantage of stimulants in treating ADHD is that they bolster the brain's ability to allocate attention during complex problem solving. For those children who have difficulty in maintaining attention in the classroom, a stimulant may allow them to perform better and reduce the frustration and agitation that stem from their failures.[53]

In 1996, the Swiss pharmaceutical company Ciba-Geigy sent letters to hundreds of thousands of pharmacies and physicians in the United States, warning them to exert greater control over Ritalin tablets and prescriptions to obtain them. The alert came in response to reports that Ritalin was becoming a drug of abuse among young people, who were crushing the tablets and snorting the powder as a new way of getting a stimulant high. Frequently, high school students have bought Ritalin from classmates who were prescribed the drug for an ADHD condition. Some college students are allegedly using Ritalin to study late into the night, while others are taking Ritalin on a purely recreational basis.[54]

attention-deficit/hyperactivity disorder (ADHD): A behavioral disorder characterized by increased motor activity and reduced attention span.

Narcolepsy (an unpredictable and uncontrollable urge to fall asleep during the day) and obesity are two other conditions for which stimulant drugs have been applied in treatment. In 1999, modafinil (brand name: Provigil) was approved for treating narcolepsy. The advantage of Provigil over traditional stimulant treatments like dextroamphetamine is that it does not present problems of abuse and produces fewer adverse side effects. Until it was withdrawn from the market in 2000, phenylpropanolamine (the active ingredient in Acutrim and Dexatrim), an amphetamine-like appetite suppressant available on a nonprescription basis, had been used as a treatment for obesity (see Chapter 14). The potential for abuse is the primary reason that physicians have generally steered away from amphetamines for this purpose (Table 4.3).[55]

There is also a wide range of amphetamine-like drugs available to the public, many of them on a nonprescription basis, for use as nasal decongestants. In most cases, their effectiveness stems from their primary action on the peripheral nervous system rather than on the CNS. Even so, the potential for misuse exists: some continue to take these drugs over a long period of time because stopping their use may result in unpleasant rebound effects such as nasal stuffiness. This reaction, by the way, is similar to the stuffy nose that is experienced in the chronic administration of cocaine.[56]

TABLE 4.3

Common amphetamine-like drugs for weight control and nasal congestion relief

GENERIC NAME	BRAND NAME
FOR APPETITE SUPPRESSION IN WEIGHT CONTROL	
phendimetrazine	Bontril, Prelu-2
phentermine	Adipex, Fastin, Ionamin
FOR RELIEF OF NASAL CONGESTION	
ephedrine	Primatene
naphazoline	Privine, 4-way Fast-Acting Nasal Spray
oxymetazoline	Afrin, Dristan
phenylephrine	Neo-Synephrine, Vicks Sinex
pseudoephedrine	Sudafed, Comtrex, many others

Note: Fenfluramine (brand name: Pondimin) and dexfenfluramine (brand name: Redux) are two other prescription drugs for weight control, but they differ from traditional amphetamine-like medications in that (1) they are not stimulants and (2) they excite serotonin rather than dopamine systems in the brain. The current status of these drugs will be discussed in Chapter 14.

Source: Physicians' desk reference (54th ed.). (2000). Montvale NJ: Medical Economics Data. *Physicians' desk reference for nonprescription drugs* (17th ed.). (1996). Montvale NJ: Medical Economics Data.

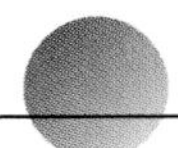

SUMMARY

The History of Cocaine

- Cocaine, one of the two major psychoactive stimulants, is derived from coca leaves grown in the mountainous regions of South America. Coca chewing is still prevalent among certain groups of South American Indians.
- During the last half of the nineteenth century, several patent medicines and beverages were sold that contained cocaine, including the original formulation for Coca-Cola.
- Sigmund Freud was an early enthusiast of cocaine as an important medicinal drug, promoting cocaine as a cure for morphine dependence and depression. Soon afterward, Freud realized the strong dependence that cocaine could bring about.

Acute Effects of Cocaine

- Cocaine produces a powerful burst of energy and sense of well-being. In general, cocaine causes an elevation in the sympathetic autonomic nervous system.

Chronic Effects of Cocaine

- Long-term cocaine use can produce hallucinations and deep depression, as well as physical deterioration of the nasal membranes if cocaine is administered intranasally.

Medical Uses of Cocaine

- The only accepted medical application for cocaine is its use as a local anesthetic.

How Cocaine Works in the Brain

- Within the CNS, cocaine blocks the reuptake of receptors sensitive to dopamine and norepinephrine. As a result, the activity level of these two neurotransmitters in the brain is enhanced.

Present-Day Cocaine Abuse

- Despite a permissive attitude toward cocaine use during the 1970s and early 1980s, attitudes toward cocaine use since the second half of the 1980s have changed dramatically.
- The emergence in 1986 of relatively inexpensive, smokable crack cocaine expanded the cocaine-abuse problem to new segments of the U.S. population and made cocaine abuse one of the major social issues of our time.

Treatment Programs for Cocaine Abuse

- Cocaine abusers can receive treatment through inpatient programs, outpatient programs, or a combination of the two. Relapse is a continual concern for recovering cocaine abusers.

Amphetamines

- Amphetamines, the second of the two major psychoactive stimulants, have their origin in a Chinese medicinal herb, used for thousands of years as a bronchial dilator; its active ingredient, ephedrine, was isolated in 1887.
- The drug amphetamine (brand name: Benzedrine) was developed in 1927 as a synthetic form of ephedrine. By the 1930s, various forms of amphetamines, specifically d-amphetamine and methamphetamine, became available around the world.

Acute and Chronic Effects of Amphetamines

- Amphetamine is effective as a general arousing agent, as an antidepressant, and as an appetite suppressant, in addition to its ability to keep people awake for long periods of time.
- While the acute effects of amphetamines resemble those of cocaine, amphetamines have the particular feature of producing (when taken in large doses) symptoms of paranoia, delusions, hallucinations, and violent behaviors, referred to as amphetamine psychosis. The bizarre behaviors of the "speed freak," the name given to a chronic abuser of methamphetamine, illustrate the dangers of amphetamine abuse.

Patterns of Methamphetamine Abuse and Treatment

- With the emphasis on cocaine abuse during the 1980s, amphetamine abuse was less prominent in the public mind. Recently, however, there has been a resurgence of amphetamine-abuse cases involving methamphetamine.
- Treatment for amphetamine abuse generally follows along the same lines as treatment for cocaine abuse.

Medical Uses for Amphetamines and Similar Stimulant Drugs

- Amphetamine-like stimulant drugs have been developed for approved medical purposes. They present fewer problems than amphetamines themselves, which have a potential for abuse.
- Methylphenidate (brand name: Ritalin), pemoline (brand name: Cylert), and dextroamphetamine (brand name: Adderall) are three drugs prescribed for children diagnosed with attention-deficit/hyperactivity disorder (ADHD).
- Other medical applications for amphetamine-like drugs include their use as a treatment for narcolepsy, as an appetite suppressant for weight control, and as a means for temporary relief of nasal congestion.

KEY TERMS

amphetamine, p. 90
amphetamine psychosis, p. 91
attention-deficit/hyperactivity disorder (ADHD), p. 94
cocaine, p. 78
cocaine hydrochloride, p. 84
cocaine psychosis, p. 83
crack cocaine or crack, p. 84
d-amphetamine, p. 90
formication, p. 80
free-base cocaine, p. 84
ice, p. 93
kindling effect, p. 83
methamphetamine, p. 91

ENDNOTES

1. Rosencan, Jeffrey S., and Spitz, Henry I. (1987). Cocaine reconceptualized: Historical overview. In Henry I. Spitz and Jeffrey S. Rosencan (Eds.), *Cocaine abuse: New directions in treatment and research.* New York: Brunner/Mazel, p. 5.
2. Inglis, Brian (1975). *The forbidden game: A social history of drugs.* New York: Scribner's, pp. 49–50. Montoya, Ivan D., and Chilcoat, Howard D. (1996). Epidemiology of coca derivatives use in the Andean region: A tale of five countries. *Substance Use and Misuse, 31,* 1227–1240.
3. Jaffe, Jerome (1985). Drug addiction and drug abuse. In Louis S. Goodman and Alfred Gilman (Eds.), *The pharmacological basis of therapeutics* (7th ed.). New York: Macmillan, p. 552.
4. Nahas, Gabriel G. (1989). *Cocaine: The great white plague.* Middlebury VT: Paul S. Eriksson, pp. 154–162.
5. Kusinitz, Marc (1988). *Drug use around the world.* New York: Chelsea House Publishers, pp. 91–95.
6. Karch, Steven B. (1996). *The pathology of drug abuse* (2nd ed.). Boca Raton FL: CRC Press, pp. 2–3. Nuckols, Caldwell C. (1989). *Cocaine: From dependency to recovery* (2nd ed.). Blue Ridge Summit PA: Tab Books, p. *x*.
7. Brecher, Edward M., and the editors of *Consumer Reports* (1972). *Licit and illicit drugs.* Boston: Little, Brown, p. 270. Weiss, Roger D., and Mirin, Steven M. (1987). *Cocaine.* Washington DC: American Psychiatric Press, p. 6.
8. McKim, William A. (2000). *Drugs and behavior* (4th ed.). Upper Saddle River NJ: Prentice Hall, p. 203.
9. Erickson, Patricia G.; Adlaf, Edward M.; Murray, Glenn F.; and Smart, Reginald G. (1987). *The steel drug: Cocaine in perspective.* Lexington MA: D. C. Heath, p. 9.
10. Musto, David (1973). *The American disease: Origins of narcotic control.* New Haven CT: Yale University Press.
11. Cole, John R. (1998). Freud's dream of the botanical monograph and cocaine the wonder drug. *Dreaming, 8,* 187–204. Quotation from Jones, Ernest (1953). *The life and work of Sigmund Freud.* Vol. 1. New York: Basic Books, p. 81.
12. Jones, *The life and work of Sigmund Freud,* p. 81.
13. Ibid., p. 84.
14. Brecher, *Licit and illicit drugs,* pp. 272–280.
15. Aronson, T. A., and Craig, T. J. (1986). Cocaine precipitation of panic disorder. *American Journal of Psychiatry, 143,* 643–645.
16. Marsuk, Peter M.; Tardiff, Kenneth; Leon, Andrew C.; Stajic, Marina; Morgan, Edward B.; and Mann, J. John (1992). Prevalence of cocaine use among residents of New York City who commited suicide during a one-year period. *American Journal of Psychiatry, 149,* 371–375.
17. Office of Substance Abuse Prevention (1989). *What you can do about drug use in America* (DHHS publication No. ADM 88–1572). Rockville MD: National Clearinghouse for Alcohol and Drug Information.
18. Philips, J. L., and Wynne, R. D. (1974). *A cocaine bibliography—nonannotated.* Rockville MD: National Institute on Drug Abuse, 1974. Cited in Ernest L. Abel. (1985). *Psychoactive drugs and sex.* New York: Plenum Press, p. 100.
19. Kaufman, Marc J.; Levin, Jonathan M.; Ross, Marjorie H.; Lange, Nicholas; Rose, Stephanie L.; Kukes, Thellea J.; Mendelson, Jack H.; Lukas, Scott E.; Cohen, Bruce M., and Renshaw, Perry F. (1998). Cocaine-induced cerebral vasoconstriction detected in humans with magnetic resonance angiography. *Journal of the American Medical Association, 279,* 376–380. Substance Abuse and Mental Health Services Administration (2000). *Drug Abuse Warning Network annual medical examiner data 1998.* Bethesda MD: Substance Abuse and Mental Health Services Administration, Office of Applied Studies, p. 39. Volkow, Nora D.; Fowler, Joanna S.; Wolf, Alfred P.; et al. (1990). Effects of chronic cocaine abuse on postsynaptic dopamine receptors. *American Journal of Psychiatry, 147,* 719–724.
20. Experiment in Memphis suggests many drive after using drugs (1994, August 28). *New York Times,* p. 30.
21. Clouet, D., Asqhar, K., and Brown, R. (Eds.) (1988). *Mechanisms of cocaine abuse and toxicity* (NIDA Research Monograph 88). Rockville MD: National Institute on Drug Abuse. Koob, George T.; Vaccarino, Franco J.; Amalric, Marianne; and Swerdlow, Neal R. (1987). In Seymour Fisher, Allen Raskin, and E. H. Uhlenhuth (Eds.), *Cocaine: Clinical and biobehavioral aspects.* New York: Oxford University Press, pp. 80–108. Wise, Roy A. (1984). Neural mechanisms of the reinforcing action of cocaine. In J. Grabowski (Ed.), *Cocaine: Pharmacology, effects, and treatment of abuse* (NIDA Research Monograph 50). Rockville MD: National Institute on Drug Abuse, pp. 15–33.
22. Post, Robert M.; Weiss, Susan R. B.; Pert, Agu; and Uhde, Thomas W. (1987). Chronic cocaine administration: Sensitization and kindling effects. In Seymour Fisher, Allen Raskin, and E. H. Uhlenhuth (Eds.), *Cocaine: Clinical and biobehavioral aspects.* New York, Oxford University Press, pp. 109–173. Weiss and Mirin, *Cocaine,* pp. 48–49.
23. Kaplan, Harold I., Freedman, Arnold M., and Sadock, Benjamin J. (1980). *Comprehensive textbook of psychiatry.* Vol. 3. Baltimore MD: Williams and Wilkins, p. 1621.
24. Flynn, John C. (1991). *Cocaine: An in-depth look at the facts, science, history, and future of the world's most addictive drug.* New York: Birch Lane/Carol Publishing, pp. 38–46.
25. Ibid., p. 44.
26. Humphries, Drew (1998). Crack mothers at 6: Prime-time news, crack/cocaine, and women. *Violence against Women, 4,* 45–61. Massing, Michael (1998). *The fix.* New York: Simon and Schuster, p. 41.
27. Egan, Timothy (1999, September 19). A drug ran its course, then hid with its users. *New York Times,* pp. 1, 46. Furst, R. Terry; Johnson, Bruce D.; Dunlap, Eloise; and

Curtis, Richard (1999). The stigmatized image of the "crack head": A sociocultural exploration of a barrier to cocaine smoking among a cohort of youth in New York City. *Deviant Behavior, 20,* 153–181.

28. Substance Abuse and Mental Health Services Administration (2000). *Summary of findings from the 1999 National Household Survey on Drug Abuse.* Rockville MD: Substance Abuse and Mental Health Services Administration, Office of Applied Studies, Table G.6.
29. Substance Abuse and Mental Health Services Administrations (2000). *Drug Abuse Warning Network annual emergency department data 1998.* Rockville MD: Substance Abuse and Mental Health Services Administration, Office of Applied Studies, Table 2.06a.
30. Gold, Mark S. (1990). *800–COCAINE.* New York: Bantam Books.
31. Nuckols, *Cocaine,* pp. 144–146. Lee, Felicia R. (1994, September 10). A drug dealer's rapid rise and ugly fall. *New York Times,* pp. 1, 22.
32. Nuckols, *Cocaine,* p. 42.
33. Ibid., pp. 71–72.
34. Weiss and Mirin, *Cocaine,* p. 125.
35. Fox, C. Lynn, and Forbing, Shirley E. (1992). *Creating drug-free schools and communities: A comprehensive approach.* New York: HarperCollins, p. 165.
36. Bartzokis, G.; Beckson, M.; Newton, T.; Mandelkern, M.; Mintz, J.; Foster, J. A.; Ling, W.; and Bridge, T. P. (1999). Selegiline effects on cocaine-induced changes in medial temporal lobe metabolism and subjective ratings of euphoria. *Neuropsychopharmacology, 20,* 582–590. Landry, Donald W. (1997, February). Immunotherapy for cocaine addiction. *Scientific American,* 42–45. Martellotta, M. Cristina; Balducci, Claudia; Fattore, Liana; Cossu, Gregorio; Gessa, Gian Luigi; Pulvirenti, Luigi; and Fratta, Walter. (1998). Gamma-hydroxybutyric acid decreases intravenous cocaine self-administration in rats. *Pharmacology, Biochemistry, and Behavior, 59,* 697–702.
37. Washton, Arnold M., Gold, Mark S., and Pottash, A. C. (1986). Treatment outcome in cocaine abusers. In L. S. Harris (Ed.), *Problems of drug dependence, 1985* (NIDA Research Monograph 67). Rockville MD: National Institute on Drug Abuse, pp. 381–384.
38. Barnes, Deborah M. (1988). Breaking the cycle of addiction. *Science, 241,* p. 1029.
39. McKim, *Drugs and behavior,* p. 205.
40. Brecher, *Licit and illicit drugs,* pp. 282–283.
41. Greaves, George B. (1980). Psychosocial aspects of amphetamine and related substance abuse. In John Caldwell (Ed.), *Amphetamines and related stimulants: Chemical, biological, clinical, and sociological aspects.* Boca Raton FL: CRC Press, pp. 175–192. Peluso, Emanuel, and Peluso, Lucy S. (1988). *Women and drugs.* Minneapolis: CompCare Publishing.
42. Facts about methamphetamine (1996, November/December). *NIDA Notes,* p. 19. Substance Abuse and Mental Health Services Administration (1999). *Year-end 1999 emergency department data from the Drug Abuse Warning Network.* Bethesda MD: Substance Abuse and Mental Health Services Administration, Office of Applied Statistics, Table 2.
43. Goode, Erich (1998). *Drugs in American society* (5th ed.). New York, McGraw-Hill College, p. 274.
44. Bai, Matt (1997, March 31). White storm warning: In Fargo and the prairie states, speed kills. *Newsweek,* pp. 66–67. Quotation by Mark A. R. Kleiman, p. 67.
45. Goode, *Drugs in American Society,* p. 274.
46. Ernst, Thomas; Chang, Linda; Leonido-Yee, Maria; and Speck, Oliver (2000). Evidence for long-term neurotoxicity associated with methamphetamine abuse: A 1H MRS study. *Neurology, 54,* 1344–1349.
47. Young, Stanley (1989, July). Zing! Speed: The choice of a new generation. *Spin magazine,* pp. 83, 124–125. Reprinted in Erich Goode (Ed.) (1992), *Drugs, society, and behavior 92/93.* Guilford CT: Dushkin Publishing, p. 116.
48. Johnson, Dirk (1996, February 22). Good people go bad in Iowa, and a drug is being blamed. *New York Times,* pp. A1, A19. Quotation on p. A19.
49. National Institute of Justice (2000, April). *Drugs in the heartland: Methamphetamine use in rural Nebraska.* Washington DC: National Institute of Justice, U.S. Department of Justice. Snyder, Karen (1997, May 5). Action call; industry groups stepping up methamphetamine control push. *Drug Topics,* p. 70. Swan, Neil (1996, November/December). Response to escalating methamphetamine abuse builds on NIDA-funded research. *NIDA Notes,* pp. 1, 5–6, 18.
50. Community Epidemiology Work Group (1996). *Epidemiologic trends in drug abuse,* Vol. 1: Highlights and executive summary. Rockville MD: National Institute on Drug Abuse, pp. 7–8. Johnston, Lloyd D. (2000, December 14). "Ecstasy" use rises sharply among teens in 2000; use of many other drugs stays steady, but significant declines are reported for some. News release from the University of Michigan, Ann Arbor, Table 1.
51. Gawin, Frank H., and Ellinwood, Everett H. (1988). Cocaine and other stimulants: Action, abuse, and treatment. *New England Journal of Medicine, 318,* 1173–1182. King, George R., and Ellinwood, Everett H. (1997). Amphetamines and other stimulants. In Joyce H. Lowinson, Pedro Ruiz, Robert B. Millman, and John G. Langrod (Eds.), *Substance abuse: A comprehensive textbook.* Baltimore MD: Williams and Wilkins, pp. 207–223. National Institute of Justice (1999, May). *Meth matters: Report on methamphetamine users in five western cities.* Washington DC: National Institute of Justice, U.S. Department of Justice. Quotation on p. xii.
52. Jacobvitz, D.; Sroufe, A.; Stewart, M.; and Leffert, N. (1990). Treatment of attentional and hyperactivity problems in children with sympathomimetic drugs: A comprehensive review. *Journal of the American Academy of Child and Adolescent Psychiatry, 29,* 677–688. Taylor, Eric (1999). Commentary: Development of clinical services

for attention-deficit/hyperactivity disorder. *Archives of General Psychiatry, 56,* 1088–1096. The MTA Cooperative Group (1999). A 14-month randomized clinical trial of treatment strategies for attention-deficit/hyperactivity disorder. *Archives of General Psychiatry, 56,* 1073–1086.

53. Mattay, Venkata S.; Berman, Karen F.; Ostrem, Jill L.; Esposito, Guiseppe; Van Horn, John D.; Bigelow, Llewellyn B.; and Weinberger, Daniel R. (1996). Dextroamphetamine enhances "neural network-specific" physiological signals: A positron-emission tomography rCBF study. *Journal of Neuroscience, 16,* 4816–4822.
54. Crossette, Barbara (1996, February 29). Agency sees risk in drug to temper child behavior. *New York Times,* p. A14.
55. Green, P. M. and Stillman, M. J. (1998). Narcolepsy. Signs, symptoms, differential diagnosis, and management. *Archives of Family Medicine, 7,* 472–478. Narcoleptic's dream? New drug deemed safer than stimulants (1998, December 29). *Newsday,* p. A21.
56. Julien, Robert M. (1998). *A primer of drug action* (8th ed.). New York: Freeman, pp. 141–143.

CHAPTER 5

The Major Narcotics: Opium, Morphine, and Heroin

After you have completed this chapter, you will understand

- The history of opium and opium-derived drugs
- The effects of narcotic drugs on the mind and body
- The neurochemical basis for opiate effects
- Patterns of heroin abuse
- The potential lethality of heroin abuse
- The issue of controlled heroin intake
- Treatment strategies for heroin dependence

Billie Holiday died in 1959 at the age of forty-four, her illustrious singing career having ended in the depths of heroin addiction. The bittersweet rendition she could give to a popular song, the sorrowful phrasing she could bring to the blues are today a standard for any contemporary jazz vocalist. Her advice to others in her autobiography was to the point: "All dope can do for you is kill you—and kill you the long slow hard way. And it can kill people you love right along with you. And that's the truth, the whole truth, and nothing but."

There is no escaping the ambivalence we feel about opium and the opiates that are derived from it. Here is a family of drugs that has the power to banish pain from our lives and at the same time the power to enslave our minds.

This chapter will concern itself with the medical uses and recreational abuses of opiate-derived and opiate-related drugs. Together, these drugs are referred to as **narcotics** (from the Greek word for "stupor"), in that they produce a dreamlike effect on the user and at higher doses induce a state of sleep. The most important characteristic of narcotic drugs, however, is that they have powerful analgesic properties; they greatly reduce feelings of pain.

As noted in Chapter 2, the term "narcotic" has often been used inappropriately to mean *any* illicit psychoactive drug or at least any drug that causes some degree of dependence, including such unlikely examples as cocaine and amphetamine. Even today, the term can be misleading, because other drugs having no relationship to opium are far more effective in inducing sleep (see Chapter 15). Nonetheless, we are stuck with this inexact terminology; it is not likely to disappear anytime soon.

Narcotic drugs, in general, are divided into three main categories. The first includes **opium** and three natural components that can be extracted from it: morphine, codeine, and thebaine (Figure 5.1). The second category includes opium derivatives that are created by making slight changes in the chemical composition of morphine. The best example of this type is heroin. Although technically an opiate derivative, heroin is commonly included with morphine, codeine, and thebaine, and collectively all four chemicals, along with opium itself, are referred to simply as **opiates.** The third category includes synthetic drugs that are not chemically related to morphine or any of its derivatives but nonetheless produce opiate-like effects that are behaviorally indistinguishable from the effects of opiates themselves. Drugs of this type are commonly referred to as **synthetic opiates** or *synthetic opiate-like drugs.* This last category is a result of a continuing effort to discover a drug that achieves the same degree of analgesia as the opiates but without the potential for abuse.

narcotics: A general term technically referring to opiate-related or opiate-derived drugs. It is often mistakenly used to include several other illicit drug categories as well.
opium: An analgesic and euphoriant drug acquired from the dried juice of the opium poppy.
opiates: Any ingredients of opium or chemical derivatives of these ingredients. Opiates generally refer to opium, morphine, codeine, thebaine, and heroin.
synthetic opiates: Synthetic drugs unrelated to morphine that produce opiate-like effects.

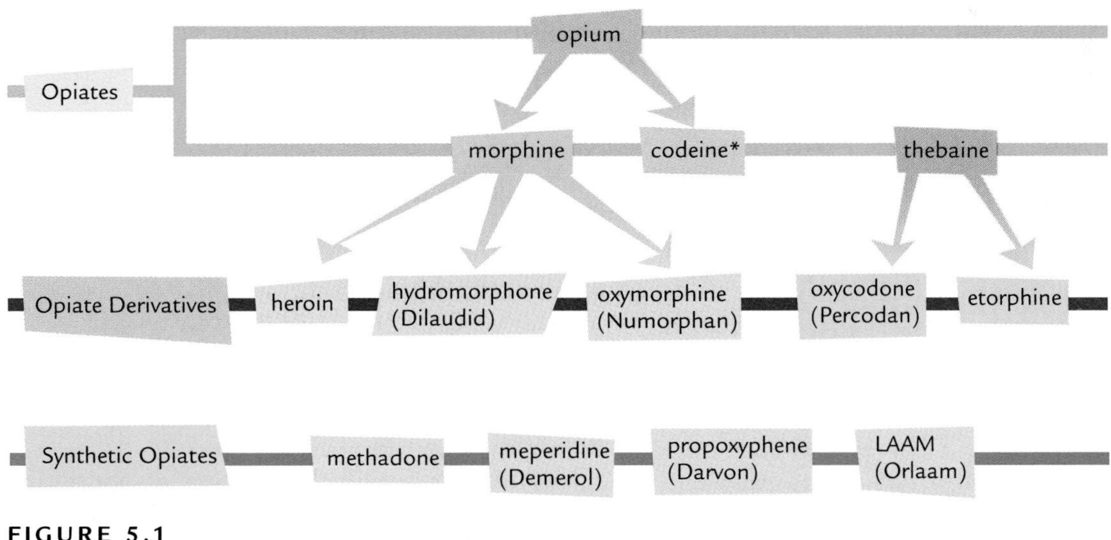

FIGURE 5.1

Major opiates, opiate derivatives, and synthetic opiates.
**Morphine is the present-day source for codeine.*
(Note: Brand names are shown in parentheses.)

Opium in History

Like cocaine, the origins of heroin and other opiates go back to the fields of faraway times and places. This particular story begins with the harvesting of raw opium in remote villages of Myanmar (formerly Burma), Laos, Thailand, Afghanistan, Mexico, Colombia, and other countries where the weather is hot and labor is cheap. The source is the opium poppy, known by its botanical name as *Papaver somniferum* (literally "the poppy that brings sleep"), an annual plant growing three to four feet high. Its large flowers are typically about four or five inches in diameter and can be white, pink, red, or purple. This variety is the only type of poppy that produces opium; common garden plants such as the red Oriental poppy or the yellow California poppy look similar but do not yield psychoactive ingredients.

The present-day method of opium harvesting has not essentially changed for more than three thousand years. When the petals of the opium poppy have fallen but the seed capsule of the plant underneath the petals is not yet completely ripe, laborers make small, shallow incisions in the capsules, allowing a milky white juice to ooze out. The next day, this substance will have oxidized and hardened by contact with the air. At this point, now reddish brown and having a consistency of heavy syrup, it is collected, plant by plant, onto large poppy leaves. Later, it will darken further and form small gumlike balls that look like tar, taste bitter, and smell like new-mown hay.[1]

Opium was first described in specific detail in the early third century B.C., but we can be fairly sure that it was used for at least a thousand years before that. A ceramic opium pipe has been excavated in Cyprus, dating from the Late Bronze Age, about 1200 B.C. Cypriot vases from that era depict incised poppy capsules. From evidence contained in the Ebers Papyrus writings (see Chapter 1), Egyptians were knowledgeable about the medicinal value of opium.[2]

In the second century A.D., Claudius Galen, the famous Greek physician and surgeon to Roman gladiators, recommended opium for practically everything. He wrote that it

> *. . . resists poison and venomous bites, cures chronic headache, vertigo, deafness, apoplexy, dimness of sight, loss of voice, asthma, coughs of all kinds, spitting of blood, tightness of breath, colic, . . . jaundice, hardness of the spleen, . . . urinary complaints, fever, . . . leprosies, the troubles to which women are subject, melancholy, and all pestilences.*[3]

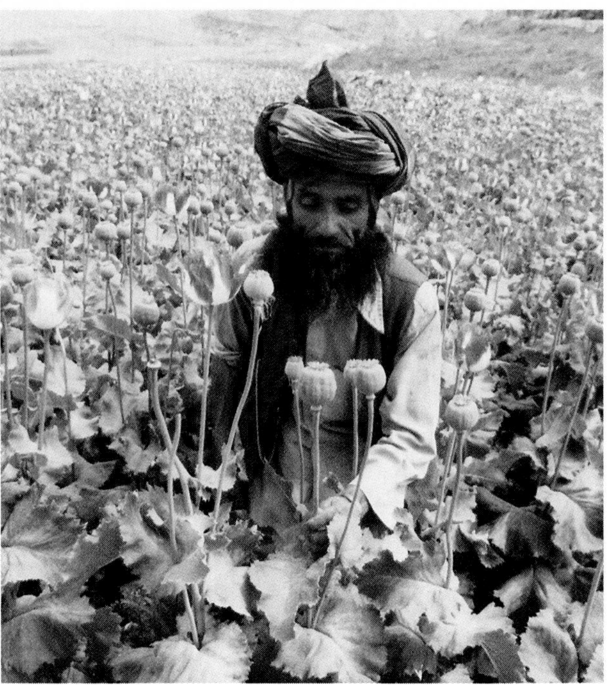

A farmer harvests raw opium in an Afghan field of opium poppies.

Galen's enthusiasm for the instrumental use of opium is an early example of "over-prescribing." Interestingly, however, there are no records in ancient times that refer to the recreational use of opium, nor with any problems of opium dependence.[4]

Western Europe was introduced to opium in the eleventh and twelfth centuries from returning crusaders who had learned of it from the Arabs. At first, opium was used only by sorcerers as an ingredient in their potions. Later, during the first stirrings of modern medicine in Europe, opium began to be regarded as a therapeutic drug. In 1520, a physician named Paracelsus, promoting himself as the foremost medical authority of his day, introduced a medicinal drink combining opium, wine, and an assortment of spices. He called the mixture *laudanum* (derived from the Latin phrase meaning "something to be praised"), and before long the formula of Paracelsus was being called the stone of immortality. Even though Paracelsus himself denounced many of the doctrines of earlier physicians in history, he continued the time-honored tradition of recommending opium for practically every known disease.

In 1680, the English physician Thomas Sydenham, considered the father of clinical medicine, introduced a highly popular version of opium drink similar to that of Paracelsus, called Sydenham's Laudanum. For the next two hundred years or so, the acceptable form of taking opium among Europeans and later Americans would be in the form of a drink, either Sydenham's recipe or a host of variations. Sydenham's enthusiasm for the drug was no less than that of his predecessors. "Among the remedies," he wrote, "which it has pleased Almighty God to give man to relieve his sufferings, none is so universal and so efficacious as opium."[5] The popularity of opium drinking for purposes that had nothing to do with a particular ailment, however, fostered the emergence of opium as a recreational drug.

Opium in China

Sometime in the eighteenth century, China invented a novel form of opium use, opium smoking, which eventually became synonymous in the Western mind with China itself. However, for at least eight hundred years before that, the Chinese used opium only in a very limited way. They took it almost exclusively on a medicinal basis, consuming it orally in its raw state as a painkiller and treatment for diarrhea.

The picture changed dramatically in the eighteenth century for the basic reason that the British people had fallen in love with Chinese tea. British merchants wanted to buy tea and send it home, but what could they sell to China in exchange? The problem was that there were few, if any, commodities that China really wanted from the outside. In their eyes, the rest of the world was populated by "barbarians" with inferior cultures, offering little or nothing the Chinese people needed.

The answer was opium. In 1773, British forces had conquered Bengal Province in India and suddenly had a monopoly on raw opium. It was now easy to introduce opium to China as a major item of trade. Opium was successfully smuggled into China through local British and Portuguese merchants, allowing the British government and its official trade representative, the East India Company, to present a public image of not being directly involved in the opium trade. Opium, flooding into China from its southern port of Canton, found a ready market as a recreational drug, and not surprisingly opium dependence soon became a major social problem. Despite repeated edicts by the Chinese emperor to reduce the use of opium within China or cut the supply line from India, the monster flourished.[6]

By 1839, the tension had reached a peak. In a historic act of defiance against the European powers, including Britain, an imperial commissioner appointed by the Chinese emperor to deal with the opium problem once and for all confiscated a huge quantity of opium and burned it publicly in Canton. Events escalated shortly after until open fighting between Chinese and British soldiers broke out. The Opium War had begun.

By 1842, British artillery and warships had overwhelmed a nation unprepared to deal with European firepower. In a humiliating treaty, China was forced to sign over to Britain the island of Hong Kong and its harbor (until the distant year of 1997), grant to British merchants exclusive trading rights in major Chinese ports, and pay a large amount of money to reimburse Britain for losses during the war. Despite these agreements, fighting broke out again between 1858 and 1860; this time the British soldiers and sailors were joined by French and American men-at-arms. Finally, in a treaty signed in 1860, China was required to legalize opium within its borders. The Opium War had succeeded in opening up the gates of China, much against its will, to the rest of the world.[7]

Opium in Britain

To the average Briton in the mid-1800s, the Opium War in China was purely a trade issue, with little or no direct impact upon his daily life. Nonetheless, opium itself was everywhere. The important difference between China and Britain with respect to opium, as noted in Chapter 1, was not in the extent of its consumption but in the way it was consumed. The acceptable form of opium use in Victorian England was opium drinking in the form of laudanum, whereas the Oriental practice of opium smoking was linked to a perceived lifestyle of vice and degradation and associated with the very lowest fringes of society. The contrast was strikingly ironic. Opium dens, with all the evil connotations that the phrase has carried with it into modern times, were the places where opium was *smoked*; the respectable parlors of middle-class British families were the places where opium was *drunk*.

In a sense, opium was the aspirin of its day. Supplies were unlimited and cheaper than gin or beer; medical opinion was at most divided on the question of any potential harm; there was no negative public opinion and seldom any trouble with the police. An opium addict, as long as there were no signs of opium smoking, was considered no worse than a drunkard. Nearly all infants and young children in Britain during this period were given opium, often from the day they were born. Dozens of laudanum-based patent medicines, with appealing names like Godfrey's Cordial, A Pennysworth of Peace, and Mrs. Winslow's Soothing Syrup were used to dull teething pain or colic, or merely to keep the children quiet. The administration of opium to babies was particularly attractive in the new, industrial-age life-style of female workers, who had to leave their infants in the care of elderly women or young children when they went off to work in the factories.[8]

A nineteenth-century advertising card for a popular opium remedy was directed toward young mothers and their children.

Out of this atmosphere of acceptance sprang a new cultural phenomenon: the opium-addict writer. Just as LSD was to be promoted in the 1960s as an avenue toward a greatly expanded level of creativity and imagination (see Chapter 6), a similar belief was spreading during this period with respect to opium. The leader of the movement was Thomas DeQuincey, and his book *Confessions of an English Opium Eater*, published in 1821, became the movement's bible. It is impossible to say how many people started to use opium recreationally as a direct result of reading DeQuincey's *Confessions*, but there is no doubt that the book made the practice fashionable.

Opium in the United States

In many ways, opium consumption in the United States paralleled its widespread use in Britain. In one survey of thirty-five Boston drugstores in 1888, 78 percent of the prescriptions that had been refilled three or more times contained opium. Opium poppies were cultivated in Vermont and New Hampshire, in Florida and Louisiana, and later in California and Arizona. It was not until 1942 that the growing of opium poppies was outlawed in the United States.

Women outnumbered men in opium use during the nineteenth century by as much as three to one. The principal reason for this gender difference lay in the social attitudes toward women at the time. Men could engage in the recreational use of alcohol in the time-honored macho tradition, but such use among women was not considered respectable. Only opium use, in the form of laudanum and similar products, was open to American women. As one researcher has expressed it, the consequence was that "husbands drank alcohol in the saloon; wives took opium at home."[9]

Throughout the 1800s, opium coexisted alongside alcohol, nicotine (in tobacco products), and cocaine as dominant recreational drugs. As late as 1897, the Sears, Roebuck catalog was advertising laudanum for sale for about six cents an ounce, while other opium products were addressed specifically to the alcoholic. For example, Sears' "White Star Secret Liquor Cure" was advertised as designed to be added to the gentleman's after-dinner coffee so that he would be less inclined to join his friends at the local saloon. In effect, he would probably nearly fall asleep at the table, since the "cure" was opium. If the customer were to become dependent on opium, perhaps as a result of the "liquor cure," fortunately he could order "A Cure for the Opium Habit," promoted on another page of the same catalog. Chances were good that the ingredients in this one included alcohol.[10] Opium habits were often replaced by cocaine habits (see Chapter 4) and vice versa.

Given the openness of opium drinking in the nineteenth-century United States, we can only surmise that the fanatical reaction against opium smoking was based on anti-Chinese prejudice. It is clear that intense hostility existed toward the thousands of Chinese men and boys brought to the West in the 1850s and 1860s to build the railroads. Since most of the Chinese workers were recruited from the Canton area, where opium traffic was particularly intense, the practice of opium smoking was well known to them and it served as a safety valve for an obviously oppressed society of men. In 1875 San Francisco outlawed opium smoking for fear, to quote a newspaper of the time, that "many women and young girls, as well as young men of respectable family, were being induced to visit the dens, where they were ruined morally and otherwise."[11] No mention was ever made of any moral ruin coming out of drinking opium at home.

A federal law forbidding opium smoking soon followed, while the regulation of opium use by any other means failed to receive legislative attention at that time. By the beginning of the twentieth century, however, the desire for social control of opium dens became overshadowed by the emergence of opium-related drugs that presented a greater threat than smoked opium.[12]

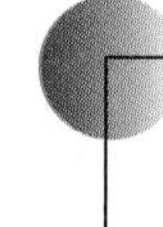

Morphine and the Advent of Heroin

In 1803, a German drug clerk named Friedrich Wilhelm Adam Sertürner first isolated a yellowish-white substance in raw opium that turned out to be its primary active ingredient. He called it morphium, later changed to **morphine,** in honor of Morpheus, the Greek god of dreams. For the first time, more than three-fourths of the total weight of opium (containing inactive resins, oils, and sugars) could be separated out and discarded. Morphine represented roughly 10 percent of the total weight of opium, but it was found to be roughly ten times stronger than raw opium. All the twenty-five or so opiate products that were eventually isolated from opium were found to be weaker than morphine and formed a far smaller proportion of opium. Besides morphine, other major opiate products were **codeine** (0.5 percent of raw opium) and **thebaine** (0.2 percent of raw opium), both of which were found to have a considerably weaker opiate effect.

In the scientific community, Sertürner's discovery was recognized as a major achievement of its time. It was not until 1856, however, with the invention of the hypodermic syringe, that morphine became a widely accepted medical drug. With the syringe it could be injected into the bloodstream rather than administered orally, bypassing the gastrointestinal tract and thus speeding the delivery of effects. The new potential of a morphine injection coincided with the traumas of the Civil War in the United States (1861–1865) and later the Franco-Prussian War in Europe (1870–1871).

Information about the syringe came too late for morphine injections to be widespread during the American conflict, but millions of opium pills and oral doses of morphine were distributed to soldiers injured in battle. It is not surprising that large numbers of soldiers became dependent on opiates and maintained the condition in the years that followed. After the Civil War, opiate dependence in general was so widespread among returning veterans that the condition was often called "the soldier's disease."[13]

Against the backdrop of increasing worry about opiate dependence, a new painkilling morphine derivative called **heroin** was introduced into the market in 1898 by the Bayer Company in Germany, the same company that had been highly successful in developing acetylsalicylic acid as an analgesic drug and marketing it as "Bayer's Aspirin" (see Chapter 14). About three times stronger than morphine, and strangely enough believed initially to be free of morphine's dependence-producing properties, heroin (from the German *heroisch*, meaning "powerful") was hailed as an entirely safe cough suppressant preferable to codeine. It is incredible that from 1898 to 1905, no fewer than forty medical studies concerning injections of heroin failed to pick up on its potential for dependence! The abuse potential of heroin, which we now know exceeds that of morphine, was not fully recognized until as late as 1910.[14]

Why is heroin more potent than morphine? The answer lies in the fact that heroin consists of two acetyl groups joined to a basic morphine molecule. These attachments make heroin more fat-soluble and hence more rapidly absorbed into the brain. Once inside the brain, however, the two acetyl groups break off, making the effects of heroin chemically identical to that of morphine. One way of understanding the relationship between the two drugs is to imagine morphine as the contents inside a plain cardboard box and the heroin as the box with gift wrapping. The contents remain the same, but the wrapping increases the chances the box will be opened.

Heroin and Opiate Dependence in American Society

The end of the nineteenth century marked a turning point in the history of opium and its derivatives. Opiate dependence would never again be treated casually. By 1900, there were, by one conservative estimate, 250,000 opiate-dependent people in the United States, and the actual number could have been closer to 750,000 or more. If we rely upon the upper estimate, then we would be speaking of roughly one out of every hundred Americans, young or old, living at that time. Compare this figure with the current estimate of 600,000 opiate (chiefly heroin) abusers in the United States, with a current population nearly four times the population in 1900, and you can appreciate the impact opiate abuse was having on society in the early twentieth century.

The size of the opiate-abusing population alone at that time would probably have been sufficient grounds for social reformers to seek some way of controlling these drugs, but there was also the growing fear that the problems of opiate abuse were becoming closely associated with criminal elements or the underworld. There was a gnawing anxiety that opiates were creating a

morphine: The major active ingredient in opium.
codeine (COH-deen): One of the three active ingredients in opium, used primarily to treat coughing.
thebaine (THEE-bayn): One of three active ingredients in opium.
heroin: A chemical derivative of morphine. It is approximately three times as potent as morphine and a major drug of abuse.

significant disruption in American society. A movement began to build toward instituting some system of governmental regulation.

Opiate Use after 1914

The Harrison Act of 1914 (see Chapter 2) radically changed the face of opiate use and abuse in the United States. It ushered in an era in which the addict was

> *. . . no longer seen as a victim of drugs, an unfortunate with no place to turn and deserving of society's sympathy and help. He became instead a base, vile, degenerate who was weak and self-indulgent, who contaminated all he came in contact with and who deserved nothing short of condemnation and society's moral outrage and legal sanction.*[15]

The situation, however, did not change overnight. Most important, the 1914 legislation did not actually ban opiate use. It simply required that doctors register with the Internal Revenue Service the opiate drugs (as well as cocaine and other coca products) that were being prescribed to their patients and pay a small fee for the right to prescribe such drugs. The real impact of the new law came later, in the early 1920s, as a result of several landmark decisions sent down from the U.S. Supreme Court. In effect, the decisions interpreted the Harrison Act more broadly. Under the Court's interpretation of the Harrison Act, no physician was permitted to prescribe opiate drugs for "nonmedical" use. In other words, it was now illegal for addicted individuals to obtain drugs merely to maintain their habit, even from a physician.

Without a legal source for their drugs, opiate abusers were forced to abandon opiates altogther or to turn to illegal means, and the drug dealer suddenly provided the only place where opiate drugs could be obtained. In 1924 a new law outlawed the importation of opium into the United States, if the opium was to be made into heroin. Since there was ordinarily no way of telling what the destination of imported opium might be, the presumption was always that its purpose was illegal. As a result, legitimate opium sources were cut off, and the importation of any opiate-related drug was now in the hands of the smuggler.

Heroin became the perfect black market drug. It was easier and more profitable to refine it from raw opium overseas and ship it into the country in small bags of odorless heroin powder than it was to transport raw opium with its characteristic odor. In addition, because it had to be obtained illegally, heroin's price tag skyrocketed to thirty to fifty times what it had cost when it was available from legitimate sources.[16]

With the emergence of restrictive legislation, the demographic picture also changed dramatically. No longer were the typical takers of narcotic drugs characterized as female, predominantly white, middle-aged, and middle-class, as likely to be living on a Nebraskan farm as in a Chicago townhouse. In their place were young, predominantly white, urban adult males, whose opiate drug of choice was intravenous heroin and whose drug supply was controlled by organized crime.[17]

Heroin Addiction in the 1960s and 1970s

Three major social developments in the 1960s brought the heroin story back into the consciousness of the United States. The first began in late 1961, when a crackdown on heroin smuggling resulted in a significant shortage of heroin on the street. The price of heroin suddenly increased, and heroin dosages became more adulterated than ever before. Predictably, the high costs of maintaining heroin dependence encouraged new levels of criminal behavior, particularly in urban ghettos. Heroin abuse soon imposed a cultural stranglehold on many African American and Latino communities in the major cities.

A second development, beginning in the 1960s, affected the white majority more directly. Fanned by extensive media attention, a youthful counterculture of hippies, flower children, and the sexually liberated swept the country.

> *It was a time of unconventional fashions and anti-establishment attitudes. In unprecedented numbers, middle- and upper-class people experimented with illegal drugs to get high. They smoked marijuana; tried the new synthetic properties of amphetamines and barbiturates; rediscovered the almost forgotten product of the coca plant, cocaine; and, for the first time, people from the mainstream of American life began to experiment with derivatives of the opium poppy. Thus, heroin addiction made its insidious way back to the forefront of national concern.*[18]

Finally, disturbing news about heroin addiction began to appear that focused not only on Americans at home but also on American armed forces personnel stationed in Southeast Asia in connection with the Vietnam War. Faced with a combination of despair and boredom, a lack of definable military mission or objective, opposition at home to the conflict itself, and the unusual stresses of fighting a guerrilla war, many of these soldiers turned to psychoactive drugs as a way of coping. Reports beginning in the late 1960s indicated an increasingly widespread recreational abuse of heroin, along with alcohol,

Military involvement in Vietnam brought U.S. soldiers in contact with unusually potent doses of heroin and other psychoactive drugs.

marijuana, and other drugs, among U.S. soldiers. One returning Vietnam veteran related the atmosphere of polydrug abuse at the time:

> *The last few months over there were unbelievable. My first tour there in '67, a few of our guys smoked grass, you know. Now the guys walk right in the hootch with a jar of heroin or cocaine. Almost pure stuff. Getting smack [heroin] is like getting a bottle of beer. Everybody sells it. Half my company is on the stuff.*[19]

With respect to heroin, the problem was exacerbated by the fact that Vietnamese heroin was 90 to 98 percent pure, compared to 2 to 10 percent pure in the United States at the time, and incredibly cheap to buy. A 250-mg dose of heroin, for example, could be purchased for $10, while the standard intravenous dose on the streets of a major U.S. city would amount to only 10 mg. A comparable 250 mg of highly diluted U.S. heroin would have cost about $500. With the purity of heroin supplies so high, most U.S. soldiers smoked or sniffed it to get an effect; some drank it mixed with alcohol, even though most of the drug was lost as it was filtered through the liver en route to the bloodstream.[20]

Beyond the concern about the soldiers overseas, there was also the worry that up to 100,000 Vietnam veterans would be returning home hopelessly addicted to heroin. It has been estimated from survey data that about 11 percent of Army returnees in 1971 were regular users of heroin and about 22 percent had tried it at least once. Urine tests (appropriately named Operation Golden Flow), conducted near the end of a soldier's tour of duty, revealed a percentage of about one half of that level, but there were strong indications that users in uniform had voluntarily given up heroin prior to their being shipped home.

Fortunately, the worst fears were not borne out. A comprehensive investigation in 1974 showed that only 1 to 2 percent of Vietnam veterans were regular heroin abusers one year following their return from overseas, approximately the same percentage as those entering the military from the general population.[21] Why were we so lucky? Evidently, the use of heroin was situationally specific to involvement in Vietnam. Once home in the states, in the vast majority of cases, the environmental cues and motivational factors for drug abuse were no longer present. Does that mean that it is possible to abuse heroin without becoming dependent upon it? This question will be addressed later in the chapter.

Heroin and Synthetic Opiates since the 1980s

At one time, the major source of white powder heroin smuggled into the United States was Turkey, where the opium was grown, and the center of heroin manufacture and distribution was Marseilles in southern France (the infamous French Connection, as popularized in the 1970 movie of the same name). International control over the growing of Turkish opium in 1973 brought this route of heroin distribution to an end, but it succeeded only in encouraging other parts of the world to fill the vacuum. The "Golden Triangle" region of Laos, Myanmar (formerly Burma), and Thailand became the principal players in providing the United States with heroin. Joining southeast Asian heroin suppliers were southwest Asian nations such as Afghanistan, Pakistan, and Iran, as well as the central Asian nations of Kazakhstan, Kyrgystan, Tajikistan, Turkmenistan, and Uzbekistan that had been, until 1991, regions of the Soviet Union. As a consequence of these new sources, the purity of imported heroin increased from around 5 percent to over 18 percent.[22]

Although the growth of crack-cocaine abuse in the 1980s pushed the issue of heroin abuse temporarily off the front page, heroin abuse itself continued in new forms and variations. One significant development was the appearance around 1985 of a relatively pure and inexpensive form of Mexican heroin called **black tar.** In addition, new synthetic forms of heroin were appearing on the street, created in illegal drug laboratories within the United States. One such synthetic drug was derived from **fentanyl,** a prescription narcotic drug. Chemical modifications of fentanyl, anywhere from ten to a thousand times stronger than heroin, were sold under the common name "China White." The risks of overdose death increased dramatically. From a technical point of view, however, this and other similar "designer drugs" were not illegal, due to a loophole in the drug laws; because they were not chemically identical to heroin, no specific law applied to them. In 1986, however, the Controlled Substance Analogue Act closed this unfortunate loophole. The laws now state that any drug with a chemical structure or pharmacological effect similar to that of a controlled substance is as illegal as the genuine article. Nonetheless, such look-alike opiates are still available as illicit drugs of abuse.

The mid-1990s witnessed still another shift in the pattern of heroin trafficking. The dominant supply of white powder heroin in the United States, judged from the analysis of drug seizures, no longer originated in Asia but rather South America, principally Colombia (see Drugs . . . in Focus).

Street heroin from South American sources was now both cheaper and purer. Heroin purities exceeded 60 percent, at least ten times more powerful than the typical street heroin in the 1970s. In 1994, a 90-percent-pure brand of heroin circulating in New York City took heroin abusers by surprise; several overdose deaths occurred within a period of five days. Street prices for a milligram of heroin in New York fell from $1.81 in 1988 to as little as 37 cents in 1994. By government estimates, heroin consumption nationwide in 1996 had doubled from a decade earlier. As one writer put it, "If the U.S. auto industry cut the price of its sedans by half and redesigned them to go 180 mph, no one would wonder why sales hit the roof."[23]

Since the mid-1990s, there has also been a shift in the perception of heroin abuse itself. As the popularity of cocaine abuse declined and the incidence of crack abuse began to ebb, the spotlight once more turned toward the allure of heroin. For a brief time, popular movies and fashion photography provided provocative images that glamorized heroin abuse, referred to as "heroin chic." The pharmacological nature of present-day heroin, however, has had a more long-lasting effect. Due to the availability of increasingly pure heroin, the drug no longer needs to be injected. Instead, it can be snorted (inhaled through the nose) or smoked. New heroin abusers are frequently smoking mixtures of heroin and crack cocaine or heating heroin and inhaling its vapors. These methods of heroin abuse may avoid potential HIV infections or hepatitis through contaminated needles, but they do not prevent the dependence that heroin can produce or the risk of heroin overdose. Unfortunately, heroin snorting or smoking has also opened the door to new populations of potential heroin abusers who had previously stayed away from the drug because of their aversion to hypodermic needles. University of Michigan surveys from 1997 to 2000 have indicated that about 2 percent of all high school seniors report heroin use at some time in their lives, approximately twice the prevalence rate that was reported in 1980.[24]

DRUGS . . . IN FOCUS

Colombian Heroin Now Dominant in the United States

In 1990, all but 4 percent of the heroin seized by U.S. federal agents came from Asian sources and none from Columbia or any other region in South America. As recently as 1994, Asian suppliers accounted for more than 60 percent of the total entering the United States. A dramatic reversal in less than a year's time, however, has now made Colombia the main supplier, generating nearly two-thirds of the heroin market.

In a shrewd marketing strategy, Colombian drug producers have in the late 1990s complemented their cocaine trafficking with heroin, as demand for cocaine declines and demand for heroin increases. These suppliers typically make a profit on heroin that is several times greater than the profit on cocaine, using distribution networks already in place and requiring only a marginal increase in supplier costs. As a result, Colombians have been able to afford to provide purer heroin at cheaper prices than was previously available from Asia, thus capturing the heroin market.

Sources: National Institute on Drug Abuse (1996). *Epidemiologic trends in drug abuse.* Vol. 1: *Highlights and executive summary.* Bethesda MD: National Institute on Drug Abuse, pp. 40–42. Wren, Christopher (1996, February 11). Colombians taking over heroin trade. *New York Times,* p. 51.

black tar: A potent form of heroin, generally brownish in color, originating in Mexico.

fentanyl (FEN-teh-nil): A chemical derivative of thebaine, used as a prescription painkiller. The street name for fentanyl and related compounds is China White.

"Heroin chic" in fashion photography during the mid-1990s featured models with an emaciated look and, at times, poses that suggested the experience of heroin abuse.

QUICK CONCEPT **CHECK** 5.1

Understanding the History of Drugs

Check your understanding of the historical background for opiates and other psychoactive drugs discussed in earlier chapters by answering the following question. Imagine yourself to be living as a male adult in the year 1900. Check yes or no to indicate whether or not the following psychoactive drugs would be available to you.

1. heroin	❑ yes	❑ no
2. cocaine	❑ yes	❑ no
3. crack cocaine	❑ yes	❑ no
4. d-amphetamine	❑ yes	❑ no
5. morphine	❑ yes	❑ no

Answers: 1. yes 2. yes 3. no 4. no 5. yes

Effects on the Mind and the Body

Approximately 95 percent of all recreational narcotic use in the United States comes from heroin abuse; therefore, we will concentrate on the effects of narcotic drugs from the perspective of the heroin abuser. We have to be careful, however, to recognize that the specific effects can be quite variable. The intensity of a response to heroin can change as a factor of (1) the quantity and purity of the heroin taken, (2) the route through which heroin is administered, (3) the interval since the previous dose of heroin, and (4) the degree of tolerance of the user to heroin itself. In addition, there are psychological factors related to the setting, circumstances, and expectations of the user that make an important difference in what an individual feels after taking heroin.[25] Nonetheless, there are several major effects that occur often enough to qualify as typical of the experience.

If heroin is injected intravenously, there is an almost immediate tingling sensation and sudden feeling of warmth in the lower abdomen, resembling a sexual orgasm, for the first minute or two. There is a feeling of intense euphoria, variously described as a "rush" or a "flash," followed later by a state of tranquil drowsiness that heroin abusers often call being "on the nod." During this period, lasting from three to four hours, any interest in sex is greatly diminished. In the case of male heroin abusers, the decline in sexual desire is due, at least in part, to the fact that narcotics reduce the levels of testosterone, the major male sex hormone.[26]

An individual's first-time experience with heroin, however, may be considerably less pleasant. Opiates in general cause nausea and vomiting, as the reflex centers in the medulla are suddenly stimulated. Some first-time abusers find the vomiting so aversive that they never try the drug again; others consider the discomfort largely irrelevant because the euphoria is so powerful.

There are a number of additional physiological changes in the body. A sudden release of histamine in the bloodstream produces an often intense itching over the entire body and a reddening of the eyes. Heroin will also cause pupillary constriction, resulting in the characteristic "pinpoint pupils" that are used as an important diagnostic sign for narcotic abuse in general. As with sedative-hypnotic drugs (see Chapter 15), heroin also reduces the sensitivity of respiratory centers in the medulla to levels of carbon dioxide, resulting in a depression in breathing. At high doses, respiratory depression is a major risk factor that can result in death. Blood pressure is also depressed from heroin intake. Finally, a distressing, though nonlethal, effect of heroin is the slowing down of the gastrointestinal tract, causing a labored defecation and long-term constipation.[27]

Medical Uses of Narcotic Drugs

We have focused upon the acute effects of narcotic drugs in the context of heroin abuse, but it is also important to look at the beneficial effects that narcotic drugs can have in a medical setting (Table 5.1).

Beneficial Effects

Excluding heroin, which is a Schedule I drug in the United States and therefore unavailable even for medical use, narcotic drugs are administered with three primary therapeutic goals in mind: the relief of pain, the treatment of acute diarrhea, and the suppression of coughing. These applications are not at all new; they have been employed throughout the long history of opiate drugs.

The first and foremost medical use of narcotic drugs today is for the treatment of pain. For a patient suffering severe pain following surgical procedures or from burns or incurable cancer, morphine is the drug of choice. The actual impact on pain, however, is not a simple one. Patients report that morphine has indeed reduced their suffering caused by pain but not their perception of pain itself. They say that the pain can now be ignored because it does not bother them anymore, but if their attention is drawn to the pain, they will acknowledge that it is still there. Strangely enough, they are aware of the pain, but the pain no longer distresses them.

The second application capitalizes on the effect of opiates in slowing down peristaltic contractions in the intestines that occur as part of the digestive process. As noted earlier, one problem associated with the chronic abuse of heroin, as well as of other opiates, is constipation. However, for individuals with dysentery, a bacterial infection of the lower intestinal tract causing pain and severe diarrhea, this negative side effect becomes desirable. In fact, the control of diarrhea by morphine is literally life-saving, since acute dehydration (loss of water) from diarrhea can frequently be fatal. An added benefit is that it takes much less morphine to affect gastrointestinal activity than to produce analgesia, so dose levels can be smaller. A traditional treatment is the administration of a camphorated form of opium called **paregoric.**

The third application focuses on the effect of narcotic drugs to suppress the cough reflex center in the medulla. In cases in which an **antitussive** (cough-suppressing) drug is necessary, codeine is frequently prescribed, either by itself or combined with other medications such as aspirin or acetaminophen (brand names: Tylenol among others). As an alternative treatment for coughing, a nonaddictive, nonopiate drug, **dextromethorphan,** is available in over-the-counter syrups and lozenges as well as in combination with antihistamines (see Chapter 14). The "DM" designation in these cough-control preparations refers to dextromethorphan.

TABLE 5.1

Major narcotic drugs in medical use

GENERIC NAME	BRAND NAME*	RECOMMENDED DOSE FOR ADULTS
morphine	Duramorph	5–10 mg (i.v.)
	Roxanol	10–30 mg (oral)
	Oramorph	15–100 mg (oral)
codeine		30–60 mg (oral, i.m., or s.c.)
hydromorphone	Dilaudid	1–4 mg (i.m. or s.c.)
oxymorphone	Numorphan	1–1.5 mg (i.m. or s.c.)
oxycodone	Percodan	4.5 mg (oral) with aspirin
	Percocet	5 mg (oral) with acetaminophen
hydrocodone	Hycodan	5 mg (oral)
	Vicodin	5 mg (oral) with acetaminophen
methadone	Dolorphine	5–10 mg (oral, i.v., or s.c.)
meperidine	Demerol	50–100 mg (oral or i.m.)
propoxyphene	Darvon	65 mg (oral)
	Darvocet-N	50 mg (oral) with acetaminophen
pentazocine	Talwin	12.5 mg (oral) with aspirin
fentanyl	Duragesic	2.5–10 mg (time release by transdermal patch)
LAAM	Orlaam	10 mg (oral)

*Only a portion of the brands are listed here. Some narcotic drugs are available only under their generic names or under either their generic or brand names.

Note: i.v. = intravenous; i.m. = intramuscular; s.c. = subcutaneous.

Source: Physicians' desk reference (52nd ed.) (1998). Montvale NJ: Medical Economics Data.

paregoric (PAIR-a-GORE-ik): A form of opium used medically for the control of gastrointestinal difficulties.

antitussive: Having an effect that controls coughing.

dextromethorphan (DEX-troh-meh-THOR-fan): A popular nonnarcotic ingredient used in over-the-counter cough remedies.

Possible Complications

Given the many simultaneous effects of opiates on the body, it is natural that some concerns should be attached to their medical use, even though the overall effect is beneficial. For example, respiration will be depressed for four to five hours even following a therapeutic dose of morphine, so caution is advised when the patient suffers from asthma, emphysema, or pulmonary heart disease. Nausea and vomiting can also be a problem for patients receiving morphine, especially if they walk around immediately afterward. As a result, patients are advised to remain still, either sitting or lying down, for a short period following their medication. In addition, opiate medications decrease the secretion of hydrochloric acid in the stomach and reduce the pushing of food through the intestines, a condition that can lead to intestinal spasms. Finally, although opiates will have a sleep-inducing effect in high doses, it is not recommended that they be used as a general sedative-hypnotic treatment, unless sleep is being prevented by pain or coughing.[28]

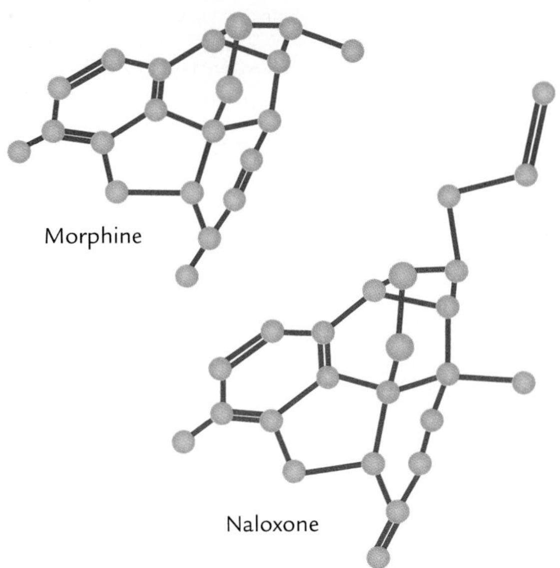

FIGURE 5.2

Only minor differences exist between a morphine molecule and a naloxone molecule.

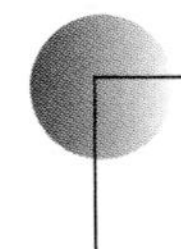

How Opiates Work in the Brain

It is useful to view the neurochemical basis for a number of psychoactive drugs in terms of their influence upon various neurotransmitters in the brain. For example, the stimulant effects of cocaine and amphetamine are related to changes in norepinephrine and dopamine (see Chapter 4). In the case of opiate drugs, however, as a result of major discoveries in the 1970s, it is clear that we are dealing with a more direct effect: the activation of receptors in the brain that are specifically sensitive to morphine.

During the 1960s, suspicions grew that a morphine-sensitive receptor, or a family of them, exists in the brain. One major clue came from the discovery that small chemical alterations in the morphine molecule would result in a group of new drugs with strange and intriguing properties. Not only would these drugs produce little or no *agonistic* effects, that is they would not act like morphine, but instead they would act as *opiate antagonists*, that is they would reverse or block the effects of morphine (Figure 5.2).

The most complete opiate antagonist to be identified, **naloxone** (brand name: Narcan), turned out to have enormous therapeutic benefits in the emergency treatment of narcotic-overdose situations. In such cases, intramuscular or intravenous injections of naloxone reverse the depressed breathing and blood pressure in a matter of a minute or so, an effect so fast that emergency-room specialists view the reaction as "miraculous." The effect lasts for one to four hours. Higher doses of naloxone bring on symptoms that are very similar to those observed following an abrupt withdrawal of narcotic drugs. Interestingly, in normal undrugged people, naloxone produces only negligible changes, either on a physiological or a psychological level. Only if morphine or other narcotic drugs are already in the body does naloxone have an effect.[29]

Beyond its practical application, the discovery of naloxone had theoretical implications as well. The argument went as follows: If such small molecular changes could so dramatically transform an agonist into an antagonist, then some receptor in the brain must exist in such a way that it can be easily excited or inhibited. The concept of a special morphine-sensitive receptor fits these requirements.

The actual receptors themselves were discovered in 1973, precisely where you would have expected them to be, in the spinal cord and brain, where pain signals are known to be processed, and in the limbic system of the brain, where emotional behaviors are coordinated. In other words, it was clear that the analgesic and euphoric

naloxone (nah-LOX-ohn): A pure antagonist for morphine and other opiate drugs. Brand name is Narcan.

Drugs . . . in Focus

What Do Endorphins Tell Us about Ourselves?

Here is a sampling of research findings about endorphins:

- Under stressful circumstances, people can become temporarily analgesic (insensible to pain) without any external drugs. There are well-documented cases of soldiers who have been oblivious to their injuries during the heat of battle, athletes who are unaware of their pain until the game is over, and individuals in primitive societies who endure painful religious rituals or initiation rites without complaint. Increased levels of endorphins are considered to provide this analgesia.
- Electrical stimulation of a midbrain region in experimental animals results in a profound analgesia. This effect is reversible, at least in part, by naloxone. As a consequence, it is believed that the analgesia results from an increased level of endorphins.
- The analgesia that is accomplished by acupuncture, the Chinese technique of inserting needles into the skin at precisely defined points in the body, is completely reversible by naloxone. It is reasonable to conclude that acupuncture produces increased levels of endorphins.
- Endorphin levels measured in the placental bloodstream of pregnant women near to the time of childbirth are greatly elevated from levels normally present in nonpregnant women, reaching a peak during labor itself. It is believed that as a result, women in labor are enduring less pain than they would have if endorphin levels were unchanged. Endorphins may protect them against an even greater amount of discomfort.
- Some studies have shown increased levels of endorphins among compulsive runners and other athletes. This increase could explain the euphoria, and in some instances analgesia, felt during strenuous physical exercise. Nonetheless, there are also increased levels of adrenalin at the same time, which cannot be ruled out as contributing to this effect.
- Emaciated anorexic women have been found to have higher endorphin levels than control patients without anorexic symptoms. When body weights return to normal, the endorphin levels decline. Anorexic women often report feeling high and often engage compulsively in physical exercise. These feelings and this behavior might be tied to endorphin disturbances in the body.
- Laboratory rats like chocolate, seemingly as much as humans do. In tasks in which they are trained to work for chocolate rewards, injections of naloxone will make them less eager to perform the tasks. It is possible that at least a portion of the pleasure of eating chocolate may be linked to the release of endorphins.

Sources: Dum, J., and Herz, A. (1984). Endorphinergic modulation of neural reward systems indicated by behavioral changes. *Pharmacology, Biochemistry, and Behavior, 21,* 259–266. Levinthal, Charles F. (1988). *Messengers of paradise: Opiates and the brain.* New York: Anchor Press/Doubleday.

properties of morphine were due to the stimulation of these receptors.

Why would these receptors exist in the first place? No one seriously considers the possibility that receptors in the brain have been patiently waiting millions of years in evolutionary history for the day that the juice of the opium poppy could finally slip inside them! The only logical answer is that we must be producing our own morphine-like chemicals that activate these receptors.

As a result of a series of important discoveries from 1975 to the early 1980s, three groups of natural morphine-like molecules have been identified: enkephalins, beta-endorphin, and dynorphins. Together, they are known as **endogenous opioid peptides,** inasmuch as they are (1) all peptide molecules (amino acids strung together like a necklace), (2) opiate-like in function, and (3) produced within the central nervous system. Unfortunately, this is such an unwieldy name that more frequently they are simply referred to as *endorphins.* Since their discovery, endorphins have been studied with regard to a wide range of human behaviors. Drugs . . . in Focus lists some of the findings of these studies.

What can we then conclude about the effect of opiates on the brain? The answer, as we now understand it, is that the brain has the ability to produce its own "opiate-like" substances, called endorphins, and contains a special set of receptor sites to receive them. By an amazing quirk of fate, the opium poppy yields a similarly shaped chemical that fits into these receptor sites, thus producing equivalent psychological and physiological effects.

endogenous opioid peptides (en-DODGE-eh-nus OH-pee-oid PEP-teyeds) also known as *endorphins:* A class of chemicals produced inside the body that mimic the effects of opiate drugs.

Naloxone acts as an opiate antagonist because its structural features enable it to fit into these receptor sites, replacing the drug molecules that have gotten in. This is why naloxone can "undo" the acute effects of an opiate drug like heroin. Since 1993, the exact structure of the morphine receptor has been identified, advancing hope that new classes of drugs will eventually be available to control pain as effectively as morphine but without the undesirable side effects. In the meantime, research is also being directed toward understanding the functioning of the nucleus accumbens in the brain (see Chapter 3), in an effort to reduce the powerful effects of heroin craving and heroin-seeking behavior.[30]

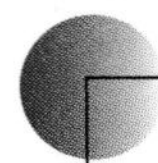

Patterns of Heroin Abuse

The dominant route of administration in heroin abuse is intravenous injection, usually referred to as either *mainlining* or *shooting*. Heroin can also be administered by a variety of other routes. Heroin smoking is popular in Middle Eastern countries and in Asia, but until very recently it has seldom been observed in the United States. Newcomers to heroin may begin their abuse either by snorting the drug through the nose or injecting it subcutaneously (skin-popping). Experienced heroin abusers may snort heroin in order to avoid using a needle or choose the subcutaneous route when they can no longer find veins in good enough condition to handle an intravenous injection. An oral administration for heroin or any other narcotic (except for methadone) is virtually worthless because absorption is extremely poor. American soldiers in Vietnam who were abusing heroin often took the drug orally. However, because of the extremely high purity of the heroin they were consuming, their dose levels far exceeded levels found on American streets.

Tolerance and Withdrawal Symptoms

A prime feature of chronic heroin abuse is the tolerance that develops, but the tolerance effects themselves are not across the board with regard to all of the responses commonly associated with heroin. Gastrointestinal effects of constipation and spasms do not show much tolerance at all, while distinctive pupillary responses (the pinpoint feature of the eyes) eventually subside over chronic use. The greatest signs of tolerance are seen in the degree of analgesia, euphoria, and respiratory depression. The intense thrill of the intravenous injection will be noticeably lessened. The overall decline in heroin reactions, however, is dose-dependent. If the dose level is high, then tolerance effects will be more dramatic than if the dose level is low.

The first sign of heroin withdrawal, a marked craving for another fix, generally begins about four to six hours after the previous dose and gradually intensifies to a peak over the next thirty-six to seventy-two hours, with other symptoms beginning from a few hours later (Table 5.2). The abuser is essentially over the withdrawal period in five to ten days, though mild physiological disturbances, chiefly elevations in blood pressure and heart rate, are observed as long as six months later. Generally, these long-term effects are associated with a gradual withdrawal from heroin rather than an abrupt one.

The overall severity of heroin-withdrawal symptoms is a function of the dosage levels of heroin that have been sustained. When dosage levels were in the "single digits" (under 10 percent), the withdrawal symptoms were comparable to a moderate to intense case of the flu. In more severe cases, the withdrawal process can result in a significant loss of weight and body fluids. With recent increases in the purities of street heroin in the 1990s, the symptoms of withdrawal are greater. Only rarely, however, is the process of heroin withdrawal life threatening, unlike the withdrawal from barbiturate drugs (see Chapter 15).

TABLE 5.2

Symptoms of administering heroin and of withdrawing heroin

ADMINISTERING	WITHDRAWING
Lowered body temperature	Elevated body temperature
Decreased blood pressure	Increased blood pressure
Skin flushed and warm	Piloerection (gooseflesh)
Pupillary constriction	Tearing, runny nose
Constipation	Diarrhea
Respiratory depression	Yawning, panting, sneezing
Decreased sex drive	Spontaneous ejaculations and orgasms
Muscular relaxation	Restlessness, involuntary twitching and kicking movements*
Nodding, stupor	Insomnia
Analgesia	Pain and irritability
Euphoria and calm	Depression and anxiety

*Probably the source of the expression "kicking the habit."

Source: Adapted from Grilly, David M. (1998). *Drugs and human behavior* (3rd ed.). Boston: Allyn and Bacon, p. 222.

It should not be surprising that withdrawal symptoms are essentially the mirror image of symptoms observed when a person is under the influence of heroin. If we are dealing with a group of endorphin-sensitive receptors that are, in the case of the heroin abuser, being stimulated by the opiates coming in from the outside, then it is reasonable to assume that over time, the production of endorphins would decline. Why produce stuff on your own when you are getting it from an external source? By that argument, withdrawal from heroin would then be a matter of cutting off those receptors from that external source, resulting in a reaction opposite to the one that would have occurred, had the receptors been satisfied in the first place. Over a period of time, coinciding with the withdrawal period for a heroin abuser, we would expect that the normal production of endorphins would reestablish itself and there would be little or no need for the external supply of heroin.

The receptor explanation for heroin dependence sounds reasonable and does account for the presence of withdrawal symptoms, but unfortunately it is an oversimplification for heroin abuse in general. We would expect that once the endorphin-sensitive receptors regain their natural supply of endorphins, heroin abuse will end, but we know that it does not.

In the case of heroin abusers, their tendency to continue taking heroin is propelled by a number of factors. There is, first of all, the combination of fear and distress associated with the prospect of experiencing withdrawal symptoms, along with a genuine craving for the effects themselves, as a result of the physical and psychological dependence that heroin brings.

In addition, long-term heroin abuse frequently produces such a powerful conditioned-learning effect that the social setting in which the drug-taking behavior has occurred takes on reinforcing properties of its own. Even the act of inserting a needle can become pleasurable. Some heroin abusers (called needle freaks) continue to insert needles into their skin and experience heroin-like effects even when there is no heroin in the syringe. In effect, the heroin abuser is responding to a placebo. Any long-term treatment for heroin abuse, as will be discussed in a later section, must address itself to a range of physical, psychological, and social factors in order to be successful.

The Lethality of Heroin Abuse

Considering the statistics of deaths resulting from heroin abuse (see Chapter 2), you might be surprised to learn that heroin itself is considered a relatively nontoxic drug. As one expert has put it:

> *Unlike alcohol, the amphetamines, and the barbiturates, which are toxic to the body over the long run with relatively heavy use, the narcotics are relatively safe. The organs are not damaged, destroyed, or even threatened by even a lifetime of narcotic addiction. There are no major malformations of the body, no tissue damage, no physical deterioration directly traceable to the use of any narcotic, including heroin.*[31]

A notable exception, however, is found in the case of heroin administered through inhalation. Smoked heroin has been linked to the development of leukoencephalopathy, an incurable neurological disease in which a progressive loss of muscle coordination can lead to paralysis and death.[32]

Even though chronic heroin abuse through administrations other than inhalation may not present specific medical problems, it is abundantly clear that the practice of heroin abuse in general is highly dangerous and potentially lethal. The reasons have to do with the problems related to the acute effects of the drug. First, heroin has a relatively small ratio of LD (lethal dose) to ED (effective dose). Increase a dose that produces a high in a heroin abuser by ten or fifteen times and you will be in the dosage range that is potentially fatal. As a result, death by overdose is an ever-present risk. If we now take into account the virtually unknown potency of street heroin in any given fix, we can begin to appreciate the hazards involved. The "bag" sold to a heroin abuser may look like the same amount each time, but the actual heroin content may be anywhere from none at all to 90 percent. Therefore, it is easy to underestimate the amount of heroin being taken in. In addition, the user risks possible adverse effects from any toxic substance that has been "cut" with the heroin. Adding to the complexity, deaths from heroin overdose are frequently consequences of synergistic combinations of heroin with other abused drugs such as stimulants like cocaine or depressants like alcohol, Valium, or barbiturates. In some cases, individuals have smoked crack as their primary drug of abuse and snorted heroin to ease the agitation associated with crack. In other cases, lines of cocaine and heroin are alternately inhaled in a single session, a practice referred to as "criss-crossing." In the DAWN reports (see Chapter 2), the combinations of heroin with cocaine or heroin with alcohol were the first and second most frequently observed causes of heroin-related deaths. Relatively few heroin-related fatalities were due to the abuse of heroin alone. A listing of street names for heroin and heroin combinations is given in Table 5.3.

As noted in Chapter 3, it is also possible that some heroin abusers develop unstable levels of tolerance that are tied to the environmental setting in which the heroin

TABLE 5.3

Street names for narcotic drugs

TYPE OF NARCOTIC	STREET NAME
morphine	Big M, Miss Emma, white stuff, M, dope, hocus, unkie, stuff, morpho
white heroin	Junk, smack, horse, scag, H, stuff, hard stuff, dope, boy, boot, blow, jolt, spike, slam
Mexican heroin	Black tar, tootsie roll, chapapote (Spanish for "tar"), Mexican mud, peanut butter, poison, gummy balls, black jack
heroin combined with amphetamines	Bombitas
heroin combined with cocaine	Dynamite, speedball, whizbang, goofball
heroin combined with marijuana	Atom bomb, A-bomb
heroin combined with cocaine and marijuana	Frisco special, Frisco speedball
heroin combined with cocaine and morphine	Cotton brothers
codeine combined with Doriden (a nonbarbiturate sedative-hypnotic)	Loads, four doors, hits

Sources: U.S. Department of Justice, Drug Enforcement Administration. (1986). *Special Report: Black tar heroin in the United States,* p. 4. U.S. Department of Justice, Bureau of Justice Statistics Clearinghouse. (1992). *Drugs, crime, and the justice system,* pp. 24–25.

QUICK CONCEPT  5.2

Understanding Effects of Administering and Withdrawing Heroin

Without peeking at Table 5.2, check your understanding of the effects of heroin, relative to withdrawal symptoms, by noting whether the following symptoms are associated with administering heroin or withdrawing it.

SYMPTOM	ADMINISTERING	WITHDRAWING
1. coughing and sneezing		
2. skin flushed and warm		
3. decreased sex drive		
4. yawning and panting		
5. pain and irritability		
6. pupillary constriction		
7. increased blood pressure		
8. diarrhea		
9. analgesia		

Answers: 1. withdrawing 2. administering 3. administering 4. withdrawing 5. withdrawing 6. administering 7. withdrawing 8. withdrawing 9. administering

is administered. A heroin dose experienced in an environment that has not been previously associated with drug taking may have a significantly greater effect on the abuser than the same dose taken in more familiar surroundings. As a result of all these factors, the specific effect on the abuser is highly unpredictable.

While the overriding danger of excessive amounts of heroin is the potentially lethal effects of respiratory depression, abusers can die from other physiological reactions. In some instances, death can come so quickly that the victims are found with a needle still in their veins, possibly due to a massive release of histamine or an allergic reaction to some filler in the heroin to which the abuser was hypersensitive. Intravenous injections of heroin increase the risks of hepatitis or HIV infections, while unsterile water used in the mixing of heroin for these injections can be contaminated with bacteria.

An extra risk began to appear during the mid-1980s. In some forms of synthetic heroin illicitly produced in clandestine laboratories in the United States, manufacturers failed to remove an impurity called MPTP that destroys dopamine-sensitive neurons in the substantia nigra of the midbrain. As a result, young people exposed to this type of heroin have acquired full-blown symptoms of Parkinson's disease (see Chapter 3) that are virtually identical in character to the symptoms observed in elderly patients suffering from a progressive loss of dopamine-sensitive neurons in their brains.

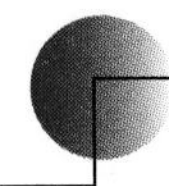

Heroin Abuse and Society

While society over the years has had to deal with the reality of drug abuse in many forms, many people still

DRUGS . . . IN FOCUS

The Secret and Dangerous Life of a Chipper

The man lives in a condo on the fashionable Upper East Side of Manhattan, drives an expensive car, takes vacations with his wife to Europe and the Caribbean, pulls down a six-figure salary as a company executive, and has been taking heroin for the last twenty years. Outwardly, he seems to have his life in firm control, and upon casual inspection he appears to be the model of the successful chipper. A closer look, however, reveals the elements of a struggle with forces he has yet to subdue.

His life has been an alternating cycle in which he would take heroin for a week or two, then stop for three weeks and begin again. "For the first two weeks after I've stopped," he has said, "it does not occupy my thoughts in an overwhelming sense. But by the third week it is creeping in there and it just gets to the point when I want it. I say: 'It's time. I've been good enough. I want my reward.' . . . The drug is an enhancement of my life. I see it as similar to a guy coming home and having a drink of alcohol."

Despite the facade of security, his life as a chipper is full of dangers. After an overdose 11 years ago, he no longer injects his heroin, preferring to snort it from the corner of a credit card or the clip of a ballpoint pen. He buys his heroin from a friend who has been his supplier for years, but he runs the continual risk of being detected and losing his job. Sampling as potentially dependence-inducing a drug as heroin or cocaine has to be an extremely risky business. One drug abuse expert has commented that it is a little like playing Russian roulette: "Not everyone will become addicted, but you can't predict who will and who won't."

Source: Treaster, Joseph B. (1992, July 22). Executive's secret struggle with heroin's powerful grip. *New York Times*, pp. A1, B4.

see heroin abuse as the ultimate drug addiction and the heroin abuser as the ultimate "dope addict." It is true that many heroin abusers fit this image: people driven to stay high on a four- to eight-hour schedule, committing a continuing series of predatory crimes. Yet the actual picture of the present-day heroin abuser is more complex. A major study has shown that while robbery, burglary, and shoplifting accounted for 44 percent of an abuser's income and nearly two-thirds of that abuser's criminal income, a substantial amount of income came from either victimless crimes (such as pimping or prostitution) or noncriminal activity. Often a heroin abuser would work in some capacity in the underground drug industry and be paid in heroin instead of dollars.[33]

A related question with regard to our image of the heroin abuser is whether or not controlled heroin abuse is possible. Is heroin abuse a situation that is, by definition, out of control? For thousands of heroin abusers, the answer is yes. Yet for other individuals, heroin is not a compulsion. It has been estimated that for every regular heroin abuser in the United States, there are three or four occasional abusers who do not appear to be physically dependent on the drug. The practice of controlled or paced heroin intake is referred to as **chipping**, and the occasional heroin abuser is known as a *chipper*.

An important study conducted by Norman E. Zinberg in 1984 analyzed a group of people who had been using heroin on a controlled basis for more than four years.[34] Over the course of one year, 23 percent reported taking heroin less than once a month, 36 percent reported taking it one to three times a month, and 41 percent reported taking it twice a week. Four years of exposure to heroin would seem to have been sufficient time to develop a compulsive dependence, but that did not happen. The observation that most compulsive heroin-dependent individuals never had any period of controlled use implies that controlled heroin abuse is not merely an early transitional stage that will eventually turn into uncontrolled heroin dependence. The chipper and the classic heroin abuser seem to belong to two separate populations. What factors differentiate them?

Zinberg's study showed that, unlike compulsive heroin abusers, occasional abusers tend to avoid heroin use in the presence of known addicts, rarely use heroin on a binge basis, and most often know the heroin dealer personally. Their motivations are different as well. Occasional abusers tend to use heroin for relaxation and recreation rather than to escape from difficulties in their lives or to reduce depression (see Drugs . . . in Focus).

From a behavioral standpoint the chipper appears to be avoiding the environmental influences (the social setting) that reinforce drug dependence; in addition, there may be a physiological distinction. Suppose for a moment

chipping: The taking of heroin on an occasional basis.

that one group of people had more endorphin-sensitive receptors in their brains than another group, or else had some deficiency in the ability to produce endorphins for those receptors. It is possible that the first group would not have the capacity for these receptors to be properly filled, resulting in a natural tendency to seek out external agents to do the job. This group would be inclined toward greater psychological and physical dependence than a group with a more normal internal endorphin system.

Although this account is highly speculative, it may explain differences between occasional and compulsive heroin abuse. It may, in part, help to explain why the vast majority of Vietnam veterans who had been exposed to heroin overseas discontinued its abuse upon their return to their homes and why patients exposed to morphine for the relief of postsurgical pain, or pain from any physical disorder, seldom if ever develop dependence. Naturally, we cannot ignore the role of sociocultural differences in the development of chronic heroin abuse. Nonetheless, it is entirely possible that differences within the chemical makeup of the brain are a contributing factor.[35]

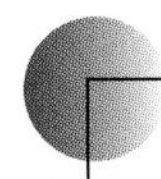

Treatment for Heroin Abuse

For the heroin abuser seeking out treatment for heroin dependence, the two primary difficulties are the short-term effects of heroin withdrawal and the long-term effects of heroin craving. Any successful treatment, therefore, must produce both a short-term and long-term solution.

Opiate Detoxification

Traditionally, it has been possible to make the process of withdrawal from heroin, called **detoxification** ("detox"), less distressing to the abuser by reducing the level of heroin in a gradual fashion under medical supervision rather than by stopping "cold turkey" (a term probably inspired by the gooseflesh appearance of the abuser's skin during abrupt withdrawal). In medical settings, synthetic opiates such as **propoxyphene** (brand name: Darvon) or **methadone** have been administered to replace the heroin initially; then doses of these so-called transitional drugs are decreased over a period of two weeks or so.[36]

Since around 1995, a much faster process of withdrawal called **ultra-rapid opioid detoxification** has been developed, owing in large part to an increased understanding of how the brain reacts to heroin itself and its withdrawal. The procedure is to administer, while the patient is under general anesthesia or heavy sedation, dosage levels of naloxone sufficient to completely block the morphine-sensitive receptors, in combination with an administration of **clonidine** (brand name: Catapres), a drug traditionally prescribed for the control of high blood pressure. Clonidine has proved helpful because it inhibits norepinephrine in a small region of the pons called the **locus coeruleus,** which contains a high concentration of neurons that are sensitive to both norepinephrine and opiate drugs.

Through animal studies, researchers know that stimulation of the locus coeruleus produces behavioral signs of fear and anxiety that are virtually identical to symptoms produced by withdrawal from opiate drugs. Because opiates inhibit norepinephrine-sensitive neurons, the locus coeruleus remains in a relatively calm state while the individual is taking heroin. When heroin is withdrawn, however, the norepinephrine-sensitive neurons become hyperactive. Clonidine inhibits these hyperactive neurons and, as a result, reduces the intensity of withdrawal symptoms. The combination of clonidine with naloxone treatment achieves complete heroin withdrawal in as little as six hours.[37]

Methadone Maintenance

For the heroin abuser seeking out medical treatment for heroin dependence, the most immediate problem is getting the drug out of the abuser's system during detoxification with a minimum of discomfort and distress. As mentioned earlier, the naloxone and clonidine combination has been particularly important in speeding up withdrawal and reducing the severity of physiological symptoms.

After detoxification, however, the long-term problem of drug dependence remains. The craving for heroin

detoxification: The process of drug withdrawal in which the body is allowed to rid itself of the chemical effects of the drug in the bloodstream.

propoxyphene (pro-POX-ee-feen): A synthetic opiate useful in treating heroin abuse. Brand name is Darvon.

methadone: A synthetic opiate useful in treating heroin abuse.

ultra-rapid opioid detoxification: A procedure involving the administration of naloxone and clonidine to heroin abusers while anesthetized or under heavy sedation, in order to achieve complete heroin withdrawal in a matter of hours.

clonidine (CLAHN-eh-deyen): A drug, ordinarily used for treating high blood pressure, that reduces the distress of narcotic withdrawal. Brand name is Catapres.

locus coeruleus (LOH-cus ser-ROOL-ee-us): A region of the pons in the brain, having a high concentration of receptors sensitive to norepinephrine and endorphins.

persists, and the abuser most often has little choice but to return to a drug-oriented environment where the temptations to satisfy the craving still exist. Since the mid-1960s, one strategy has been to have a detoxified heroin abuser participate in a program in which oral administrations of the synthetic opiate methadone are essentially substituted for the injected heroin. This treatment approach, called **methadone maintenance,** was initiated in New York City through the joint efforts of Vincent Dole, a specialist in metabolic disorders, and Marie Nyswander, a psychiatrist whose interest has focused on narcotic dependence. Their idea was that if a legally and carefully controlled narcotic drug was available to heroin abusers on a regular basis, the craving for heroin would be eliminated, their drug-taking life-style would no longer be needed, and they could now turn to more appropriate social behaviors such as steady employment and a more stable family life.

For the Dole–Nyswander treatment program, now serving more than 100,000 former heroin abusers in the United States, methadone has definite advantages. First of all, since it is a legal, inexpensive narcotic drug (when dispensed through authorized drug-treatment centers), criminal activity involved in the purchase of heroin on the street can be avoided. Methadone is slower acting and more slowly metabolized, so that, unlike heroin, its effects last approximately twenty-four hours and can be easily absorbed through an oral administration. Since it is a narcotic drug, methadone binds to the endorphin-sensitive receptors in the brain and prevents feelings of heroin craving, yet its slow action avoids the rush of a heroin high.

Typically, clients in the program come to the treatment center daily for an oral dose of methadone, dispensed in orange juice, and the dose is gradually increased to a maintenance level over a period of four to six weeks. The chances of an abuser turning away from illicit drug use are increased if the higher doses of methadone are made conditional upon a "clean" (drug-free) urinanalysis.[38]

Successful maintenance has also been improved by the introduction of a new synthetic opiate **LAAM** (levo-alpha-acetylmethadol), marketed under the brand name Orlaam. The advantage of LAAM is a longer duration so that treatment clients need to receive the drug only three times a week instead of every day.[39] Another drug showing promise for use in maintenance programs is the synthetic opiate **buprenorphine** (brand name: Buprenex). Though it must be taken daily, buprenorphine does not induce physical signs of dependence and effectively suppresses the craving for heroin among abusers. Safety and effectiveness studies of buprenorphine have been very positive, but the FDA has not yet approved its use in treatment of opiate dependence.[40]

The general philosophy behind maintenance programs is that heroin abuse is a metabolic disorder requiring a maintenance drug for the body, just as a diabetic patient needs a maintenance supply of insulin. In other words, the maintenance drug "normalizes" the drug abuser.

As a social experiment, methadone-maintenance programs have met with a mixture of success and failure. On the one hand, evaluations of this program have found that 71 percent of former heroin abusers who have stayed in methadone maintenance for a year or more have stopped intravenous drug taking, thus lessening the risk of AIDS. In a major study, drug-associated problems declined from about 80 percent to between 17 and 28 percent, criminal behavior was reduced from over 20 percent to less than 10 percent, and there was a slight increase in permanent employment.[41] While never attracting more than 20 percent of the heroin-dependent community, methadone maintenance does attract those who perceive themselves as having a negligible chance of becoming abstinent on their own. It is reasonable to assume that we are looking at the potential rehabilitation of a hard-core subpopulation within heroin abusers.[42]

On the other hand, maintenance programs are not without problems. The first has to do with the moral question of opiate maintenance itself. Some critics have seen these treatments as a cop-out that perpetuates rather than discourages the sense of low self-esteem among heroin abusers, a system that serves the needs of society over the needs of the individual. Methadone programs, they argue, simply substitute one type of dependence with another, and the goal should eventually be abstinence from all drugs.[43]

Although maintenance programs do help many heroin abusers, particularly those who stay in the program over an extended period of time, there are strong indications that the programs do not help the overall vulnerability toward drug abuse in general. In other words, methadone blocks the yearning for heroin but it is less effective in blocking the simple craving to get high. Alcohol abuse among methadone-maintenance clients, for ex-

methadone maintenance: A treatment program for heroin abusers in which heroin is replaced by the long-term intake of methadone.

LAAM: The synthetic narcotic drug levo-alpha-acetyl-methadol used in the treatment of heroin abuse. Brand name is Orlaam.

buprenorphine (BYOO-preh-NOR-feen): A presently experimental synthetic opiate heroin abuse treatment. Brand name is Buprenex.

Portrait Mother Hale and Her Thousand Babies

It began in 1969, when Clara Hale of Harlem took into her home her first drug-addicted baby. Hale's daughter had seen a woman sitting on a wooden crate, nodding off from heroin, with a two-month-old baby slipping out of her arms, and she told the woman to go to her mother's house. Hale was sixty-four at the time, looking forward to retirement as a foster mother, but she could see that the baby had acquired the effects of the heroin from the mother, and she quickly accepted the baby's need for care. She had no medical or nursing education or experience with drug rehabilitation, but word soon began to spread of her special brand of caring and love. "It wasn't their fault they were born addicted," she would say. Over the next three months, twenty-two cribs filled her house.

When Hale's babies eventually overwhelmed the facilities of her home, she moved to a five-story brownstone that became known as Hale House. Many of her little patients arrived still trembling from the withdrawal of heroin and alcohol. When crack cocaine joined heroin as the prominent drugs of abuse, Hale accepted crack babies as well, helping them recover from fetal toxins with hugging and rocking. At least one baby, often the neediest one, would sleep in her room at night, next to her bed.

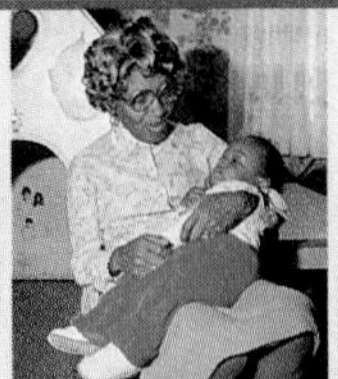
Clara Hale

The policy of Hale House was to reunite the children with their families when the parents recovered from drug abuse. They were able to do so with about 90 percent of the children, and a large number of them remained extremely close to Hale over the years. Hale House now provides not only housing for about seventeen babies but also education programs for mothers coming out of detoxification and apprenticeship training programs for young people. Recently, babies infected with HIV through their mothers have presented special challenges for Hale House, but they have not been turned away.

Mother Hale, as she was known, died in 1992 at the age of eighty-seven. She had received presidential tribute as "an American hero," the woman who founded a haven for nearly a thousand babies over the years. She herself disagreed. "I'm not an American hero," she said recently before her death. "I'm simply a person who loves children."

Sources: Lambert, Bruce (1992, December 20). Clara Hale, 87, who aided addicts' babies, dies. *New York Times*, p. 50. Rist, Curtis (1992, December 19). "Mother" Hale dies. *Newsday*, p. 6.

ample, ranges from 10 percent to 40 percent, suggesting that alcohol may be substituting for narcotics during the course of treatment, and one study found that as many as 43 percent of those who had successfully given up heroin had become dependent on alcohol. Cocaine and methamphetamine abuse can also be problems as well. Unfortunately, urinanalysis tests may be scheduled too infrequently to allow identification of other patterns of drug abuse among clients in these programs.[44] Furthermore, methadone is sometimes diverted away from the clinics and onto the streets for illicit use. As a result of the growth in methadone-maintenance clinics, the availability of street methadone has increased dramatically, adding to the already long list of abusable drugs.[45] Nonetheless, the shortcomings of the methadone-maintenance approach and its variations do not detract from their value as an important option in present-day heroin abuse treatment.

Behavioral and Social-Community Programs

In order to help deal with the tremendous social stresses that reinforce a continuation of heroin abuse, programs called **therapeutic communities** (Daytop Village, Samaritan Village, and Phoenix House are examples) have been developed, in which the abuser establishes temporary residence in a drug-free group setting and receives intensive counseling, typically from former heroin abusers or former abusers of other drugs, who have successfully given up drugs. Other approaches have been developed that combine detoxification, treatment with a long-term form of naloxone called **naltrexone** (brand name: ReVia, previously marketed as Trexan), psychotherapy, and vocational rehabilitation, under one comprehensive plan of action. These programs, called **multimodality programs,**

therapeutic communities: Living environment for individuals in treatment for heroin and other drug abuse, where they learn social and psychological skills needed to lead a drug-free life.

naltrexone (nal-TREX-ohn): A long-lasting form of naloxone. Brand name prior to 1994 was Trexan; brand name has since been changed to ReVia.

multimodality programs: Treatment programs in which a combination of detoxification, psychotherapy, and group support is implemented.

are designed to focus simultaneously on the multitude of needs facing the heroin abuser, with the goal being a successful reintegration into society. As a continuing effort to help the recovering heroin abuser, there are also twelve-step group support programs such as Narcotics Anonymous, modeled after similar programs for those recovering from alcohol or cocaine dependence.[46]

SUMMARY

Opium in History

- A drug with a very long history, opium's medicinal and recreational use stretch back approximately 5,000 years.
- During the nineteenth century, opium even figured in global politics as the instigating factor for the Opium War fought between China and Britain. At the time, opium use was widespread in Britain and the United States at all levels of society.

Morphine and the Advent of Heroin

- The discovery of morphine in 1803 as the principal active ingredient in opium revolutionized medical treatment of pain and chronic diseases.
- At the end of the nineteenth century, heroin was introduced by the Bayer Company in Germany. Initially, it was believed that heroin lacked the dependence-producing properties of morphine.

Heroin and Opiate Dependence in American Society

- The abuse potential of morphine and especially heroin was not fully realized until the beginning of the twentieth century. Social and political developments in the United States after the passage of the Harrison Act in 1914 drove heroin underground, where it acquired a growing association with criminal life.
- Heroin abuse became associated with African American and other minority communities in urban ghettos after World War II; later, the drug revolution and the military involvement in Vietnam during the 1960s and 1970s brought the issues of heroin abuse to a wider population.

Effects on the Mind and the Body

- The effects of narcotic drugs such as heroin include euphoria, analgesia, gastrointestinal slowing, and respiratory depression.
- Respiratory depression is the major risk factor for heroin intake.

Medical Uses of Narcotic Drugs

- In medical settings, narcotic drugs have been extremely helpful in the treatment of pain, in the treatment of dysentery, and in the suppression of coughing.
- Side effects of narcotic medication include respiratory depression, nausea, intestinal spasms, and sedation. There is also concern that narcotic drugs may be misused and diverted to nonmedical purposes.

How Opiates Work in the Brain

- Since the 1970s, we know that the effects of morphine and similar drugs are the result of the activation of morphine-sensitive receptors in the brain.
- Three families of chemical substances produced by the brain bind to these receptors. These chemicals are collectively known as endorphins.

Patterns of Heroin Abuse

- Chronic heroin abuse is subject to tolerance effects over time. Withdrawal effects include intense craving for heroin and physical symptoms such as diarrhea and dehydration.
- One of the major problems surrounding heroin abuse is the unpredictability in the content of a heroin dose.

Treatment for Heroin Abuse

- Treatment for heroin abuse includes short-term detoxification and long-term interventions addressing the continuing craving for the drug and physical dependence factors in the body.
- Methadone-maintenance programs focus on the physiological needs, whereas therapeutic communities and support groups focus on a long-term reintegration into society.

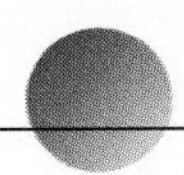

KEY TERMS

antitussive, p. 110
black tar, p. 108
buprenorphine, p. 118
chipping, p. 116
clonidine, p. 117
codeine, p. 105
detoxification, p. 117
dextromethorphan, p. 110
endogenous opioid peptides, p. 112
fentanyl, p. 108
heroin, p. 105
LAAM, p. 118
locus coeruleus, p. 117
methadone, p. 117
methadone maintenance, p. 118
morphine, p. 105
multimodality programs, p. 119
naloxone, p. 111
naltrexone, p. 119
narcotics, p. 101
opiates, p. 101
opium, p. 101
paregoric, p. 110
propoxyphene, p. 117
synthetic opiates, p. 101
thebaine, p. 105
therapeutic communities, p. 119
ultra-rapid opioid detoxification, p. 117

ENDNOTES

1. Levinthal, Charles F. (1988). *Messengers of paradise: Opiates and the brain.* New York: Anchor Press/Doubleday, p. 4.
2. Merlin, M. D. (1984). *On the trail of the ancient opium poppy.* Cranbury NJ: Associated University Press.
3. Scott, James M. (1969). *The white poppy: A history of opium.* New York: Funk and Wagnalls, p. 111.
4. Nencini, Paolo (1997). The rules of drug-taking: Wine and poppy derivatives in the ancient world. VIII. Lack of evidence of opium addiction. *Substance Use and Misuse,* 32, 1581–1586.
5. Levinthal, *Messengers of paradise,* pp. 3–25. Snyder, Solomon H. (1977). Opiate receptors and internal opiates. *Scientific American,* 236 (3), 44.
6. Beeching, Jack (1975). *The Chinese opium wars.* New York: Harcourt Brace Jovanovich, p. 23.
7. Owen, David E. (1934). *British opium policy in China and India.* New Haven CT: Yale University Press. Waley, Arthur (1958). *The opium war through Chinese eyes.* London: Allen and Unwin.
8. Fay, Peter W. (1975). *The opium war 1840–1842.* Chapel Hill: University of North Carolina Press, p. 11.
9. Brecher, Edward M., and the editors of *Consumer Reports* (1972). *Licit and illicit drugs.* Boston: Little, Brown, p. 17.
10. Kaplan, Eugene H., and Wieder, Herbert. (1974). *Drugs don't take people; People take drugs.* Secaucus NJ: Lyle Stuart.
11. Brecher, *Licit and illicit drugs,* pp. 42–43.
12. Levinthal, *Messengers of paradise,* pp. 16–17.
13. Courtright, David T. (1982). *Dark paradise: Opiate addiction in America before 1940.* Cambridge MA: Harvard University Press, p. 47.
14. Scott, Ian (1998, June). A hundred-year habit. *History Today,* pp. 6–8. Terry, Charles E., and Pellens, Mildred. (1928/1970). *The opium problem.* Montclair NJ: Patterson Smith.
15. Smith, Roger (1966). Status politics and the image of the addict. *Issues in Criminology,* 2 (2), 172–173.
16. Zackon, Fred (1986). *Heroin: The street narcotic.* New York: Chelsea House Publishers, p. 44.
17. McCoy, Alfred W., with Read, Cathleen B., and Adams, Leonard P. (1972). *The politics of heroin in southeast Asia.* New York: Harper and Row, pp. 5–6.
18. Zackon, *Heroin,* p. 45.
19. Bentel, David J., Crim, D., and Smith, David E. (1972). Drug abuse in combat: The crisis of drugs and addiction among American troops in Vietnam. In David E. Smith and George R. Gay (Eds.), *It's so good, don't even try it once: Heroin in perspective.* Englewood Cliffs NJ: Prentice Hall, p. 58.
20. McCoy, *The politics of heroin,* pp. 220–221. Karch, Steven B. (1996). *The pathology of drug abuse* (2nd ed.). Boca Raton FL: CRC Press, p. 288.
21. Robins, Lee N., David, Darlene H., and Goodwin, Donald W. (1974). Drug use by U.S. Army enlisted men in Vietnam: A follow-up on their return home. *American Journal of Epidemiology,* 99 (4), 235–249.
22. Greenhouse, Steven (1995, February 12). Heroin from Burmese surges as U.S. debates strategy. *New York Times,* p. 3.
23. Holloway, Lynette (1994, August 31). 13 heroin deaths spark wide police investigation. *New York Times,* pp. A1, B2. Leland, John (1996, August 26). The fear of heroin is shooting up. *Newsweek,* pp. 55–56. Quotation on p. 56.
24. Johnston, Lloyd D. (2000, December 14). "Ecstasy" use rises sharply among teens in 2000; use of many other drugs stays steady, but significant declines are reported for some. News release from the University of Michigan, Ann Arbor, Table 2. Sabbag, Robert (1994, May 5). The cartels would like a second chance. *Rolling Stone,* pp. 35–57. Schoemer, Karen (1996, August 26). Rockers, models, and the new allure of heroin. *Newsweek,* pp. 50–54.
25. Winger, Gail, Hofmann, Frederick G., and Woods, James H. (1992). *A handbook on drug and alcohol abuse: The biomedical aspects.* New York: Oxford University Press, 1992, pp. 44–46.
26. Abel, Ernest L. (1985). *Psychoactive drugs and sex.* New York: Plenum Press, pp. 175–204.
27. Winger, Hofmann and Woods, *Handbook on drug and alcohol abuse,* pp. 46–50.

28. Jaffe, Jerome H., and Martin, William M. (1985). Opioid analgesics and antagonists. In Alfred G. Gilman, Louis S. Goodman, Theodore W. Rall, and Ferid Murad (Eds.), *The pharmacological basis of therapeutics* (7th ed.). New York: Macmillan, pp. 491–531.
29. Ibid., pp. 525–527.
30. Randall, Teri (1993). Morphine receptor cloned—improved analgesics, addiction therapy expected. *Journal of the American Medical Association, 270,* 1165–1166. Self, David W. (1998). Neural substrates of drug craving and relapse in drug addiction. *Annals of Medicine, 30,* 379–389.
31. Goode, Erich (1999). *Drugs in American society* (5th ed.). New York: McGraw-Hill, p. 328.
32. Karch, *The pathology of drug abuse,* p. 291.
33. Johnson, Bruce D.; Goldstein, Paul J.; Preble, Edward; Schmeidler, James; Lipton, Douglas S.; Spunt, Barry; and Miller, Thomas (1985). *Taking care of business: The economics of crime by heroin abusers.* Lexington MA: Lexington Books.
34. Zinberg, Norman E. (1984). *Drug, set, and setting: The basis for controlled intoxicant use.* New Haven CT: Yale University Press, pp. 46–81.
35. Melzack, Ronald (1990). The tragedy of needless pain. *Scientific American, 262* (2), 27–33.
36. Schuckit, Marc A. (1995). *Drug and alcohol abuse: A clinical guide to diagnosis and treatment* (4th ed.). New York: Plenum Press, pp. 155–162.
37. Koob, George F., Maldonado, Rafael, and Stinus, Luis (1992). Neural substrates of opiate withdrawal. *Trends in Neuroscience, 15,* 186–191. O'Connor, Patrick G., and Kosten, Thomas R. (1998). Rapid and ultrarapid opioid detoxification techniques. *Journal of the American Medical Association, 279,* 229–234. San, Luis, and Arranz, Belen (1999, August). Pros and cons of ultrarapid opiate detoxification. *Addiction,* p. 1280. Simon, David L. (1997). Rapid opioid detoxification using opioid antagonists: History, theory, and the state of the art. *Journal of Addictive Diseases, 16,* 103–121.
38. Stitzer, Maxine L.; Bickel, Warren K.; Bigelow, George E.; and Liebson, Ira A. (1986). Effect of methadone dose contingencies on urinalysis test results of polydrug-abusing methadone-maintenance patients. *Drug and Alcohol Dependence, 18,* 341–348.
39. Eissenberg, Thomas; Bigelow, George F.; Strain, Eric C.; Walsh, Sharon L.; Brooner, Robert K.; Stitzer, Maxine L.; and Johnson, Rolley E. (1997). Dose-related efficacy of levomethadryl acetate for treatment of opioid dependence: A randomized clinical trial. *Journal of the American Medical Association, 277,* 1945–1951.
40. Mendelson, Jack H., and Mello, Nancy K. (1992). Human laboratory studies of buprenorphine. In Jack D. Blaine (Ed.), *Buprenorphine: An alternative treatment for opioid dependence* (NIDA Research Monograph 121). Rockville MD: National Institute on Drug Abuse, pp. 38–60. Mumford, Geoff (2000, September/October). Washington agonizes over a partial-agonist. *Psychological Science Agenda.* Washington DC: American Psychological Association, pp. 12–13. National Institute on Drug Abuse (1999, October 19). *Buprenorphine update: Questions and answers.* Rockville MD: National Institute on Drug Abuse. O'Connor, Patrick G.; Oliveto, Alison, H.; Shi, Julia M.; Triffleman, Elisa G.; Carroll, Kathleen M.; Kosten, Thomas R.; Rousaville, Bruce J.; Pakes, Juliana A.; and Schottenfeld, Richard S. (1998). A randomized trial of buprenorphine maintenance for heroin dependence in a primary care clinic for substance users versus a methadone clinic. *American Journal of Medicine, 105,* 100–105.
41. Ball, John C.; Lange, W. Robert; Myers, C. Patrick; and Friedman, Samuel R. (1988). Reducing the risk of AIDS through methadone maintenance treatment. *Journal of Health and Social Behavior, 29,* 214–226. Maddux, James F., and Desmond, David P. (1997). Outcomes of methadone maintenance 1 year after admission. *Journal of Drug Issues, 27,* 225–238. Rhoades, Howard M.; Creson, Dan; Elk, Ronith; Schmitz, Joy; and Grabowski, John (1998). Retention, HIV risk, and illicit drug use during treatment: Methadone dose and visit frequency. *American Journal of Public Health, 88,* 34–39. Sees, Karen L.; Delucchi, Kevin L.; Masson, Carmen; Rosen, Amy; Clark, H. Westley; Robillard, Helen; Banys, Peter; and Hall, Sharon M. (2000). Methadone maintenance vs 180-day psychosocially enriched detoxification for treatment of opioid dependence. *Journal of the American Medical Association, 283,* 1303–1310.
42. Hargreaves, William A. (1983). Methadone dose and duration for maintenance. In James R. Cooper, Fred Altman, Barry S. Brown, and Dorynne Czechowicz (Eds.), *Research on the treatment of narcotic addiction,* pp. 19–79. Kreek, Mary Jeanne (1991). Using methadone effectively: Achieving goals by application of laboratory, clinical, and evaluation research and by development of innovative programs. In Roy W. Pickens, Carl G. Leukefeld, and Charles R. Schuster (Eds.), *Improving drug abuse treatment* (NIDA Research Monograph 106), pp. 245–266.
43. Myerson, D. J. (1969). Methadone treatment of addicts. *New England Journal of Medicine, 281,* 380. Prendergast, Michael L., and Podus, Deborah (1999, May 10). Methadone debate reflects deep-rooted conflicts in field. *Alcoholism and Drug Abuse Weekly,* p. 5.
44. Kosten, Thomas R., Rounsaville, Bruce J., and Kleber, Herbert D. (1986). A 2.5 year follow-up of treatment retention and reentry among opioid addicts. *Journal of Substance Abuse Treatment, 3,* 181–189. Maddux, James F., and Desmond, David P. (1986). Relapse and recovery in substance abuse careers. In Frank M. Tims and Carl G. Leukefeld (Eds.), *Relapse and recovery in drug abuse* (NIDA Research Monograph 72). Rockville MD: National Institute on Drug Abuse, pp. 49–71. Wasserman, David A.; Korcha, Rachel; Havassy, Barbara E.; and Hall, Sharon M. (1999). Detection of illicit opioid and cocaine use in methadone maintenance treatment. *American Journal of Drug and Alcohol Abuse, 25,* 561–571.

45. Faupel, Charles E. (1991). *Shooting dope: Career patterns of hard-core heroin users.* Gainesville: University of Florida Press, pp. 170–173. Gollnisch, Gernot (1997). Multiple predictors of illicit drug use in methadone maintenance clients. *Addictive Behaviors, 22,* 353–366.
46. Greenstein, Robert A., Fudala, Paul J., and O'Brien, Charles P. (1997). Alternative pharmacotherapies for opiate addiction. In Joyce H. Lowinson, Pedro Ruiz, Robert B. Millman, and John G. Langrod (Eds.), *Substance abuse: A comprehensive texbook.* Baltimore MD: Williams and Wilkins, pp. 415–425. Simon, Rapid opioid detoxification.

CHAPTER 6

LSD and Other Hallucinogens

After you have completed this chapter, you will understand

- The classification of hallucinogenic drugs
- The history of LSD
- Facts and fictions about LSD effects
- Prominent hallucinogens other than LSD
- The special dangers of phencyclidine (PCP), ketamine, and MDMA (Ecstasy)

I was forced to interrupt my work in the laboratory in the middle of the afternoon and proceed home, being affected by a remarkable restlessness combined with a slight dizziness. At home I lay down and sank into a not unpleasant intoxicated-like condition, characterized by an extremely stimulated imagination. In a dreamlike state with eyes closed . . . I perceived an uninterrupted stream of fantastic pictures, extraordinary shapes with intense, kaleidoscopic play of colors.

—*Albert Hofmann,* LSD: My problem child *(1980)*

On an April afternoon in 1943, Albert Hofmann, a research chemist at Sandoz Pharmaceuticals in Basel, Switzerland, went home early from work, unaware that his fingertips had made contact with an extremely minute trace of a new chemical he had been testing that day. The chemical was **lysergic acid diethylamide (LSD)**, and as the opening passage indicates, Hofmann unknowingly experienced history's first "acid trip." Three days later, having pieced together the origin of his strange experience, he decided to try a more deliberate experiment. He chose a dose of 0.25 mg, a concentration that could not, so he thought, possibly be effective. His plan was to start with this dose and gradually increase it to see what would happen.

The dose Hofmann had considered inadequate was actually about five times greater than an average dose for LSD. As he later recalled his experience,

> *My condition began to assume threatening forms. Everything in my field of vision wavered and was distorted as if seen in a curved mirror. I also had the sensation of being unable to move from the spot.*[1]

A little while later, his experience worsened:

> *The dizziness and sensation of fainting became so strong at times that I could no longer hold myself erect, and had to lie down on a sofa. My surroundings had now transformed themselves in more terrifying ways. Everything in the room spun around, and the familiar objects and pieces of furniture assumed grotesque, threatening forms. . . . I was seized by the dreadful fear of going insane. I was taken to another place, another time.*[2]

His experience then became pleasant:

> *Kaleidoscopic, fantastic images surged in on me, alternating, variegated, opening and then closing themselves in circles and spirals. . . . It was particularly remarkable how every acoustic perception, such as the sound of a door handle or a passing automobile, became transformed into optical perceptions. Every sound generated a vividly changing image, with its own consistent form and color.*[3]

Hofmann's vivid remembrances are presented here at length because they succinctly convey some of the major facets of a hallucinogenic drug experience: the distortions of visual images and body sense, the frightening reaction that often occurs when ordinary reality is so dramatically changed, and the strange intermingling of visual and auditory sensations. These effects will be considered later as this chapter explores the bizarre world of hallucinogenic drugs.

Like many of the drugs that have been examined in the preceding chapters, hallucinogenic drugs such as LSD and several others have a story that belongs both in the twentieth century and in the distant past. Hofmann worked in the modern facilities of an international pharmaceutical company, but the basic material on his laboratory bench was derived from a fungus that has been around for millions of years. It has been estimated that as many as six thousand plant species around the world have some psychoactive properties.[4] This chapter will focus on a collection of special chemicals called *hallucinogenic drugs* or simply **hallucinogens,** often pharmacologically dissimilar to one another but with the common ability to distort perceptions and alter the user's sense of reality.

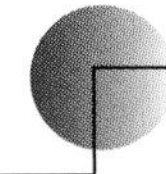

A Matter of Definition

Definitions are frequently reflections of the definer's attitude toward the thing that is being defined, and the terminology used to describe hallucinogens is no exception. For those viewing these drugs with a "positive spin," particularly for those who took LSD in the 1960s, hallucinogens have been described as *psychedelic,* meaning "mind-expanding" or "making the mind manifest." For others viewing these drugs with more alarm than acceptance, the popular descriptive adjectives have been *psychotomimetic,* meaning "having the appearance of a psychosis," *psychodysleptic,* meaning "mind-disrupting," or even worse, *psycholytic,* meaning "mind-dissolving." You can see that the description one chooses to use carries with it a strong attitude, pro or con, toward the drug's effects.

As a result of all this emotional baggage, the description of these drugs as hallucinogenic, meaning "hallucination-producing," is probably the most even-handed way of defining their effects; that is the way they will be referred to in this chapter. Some problems, however, still need to be considered. Technically, a

lysergic acid diethylamide (LSD) (leye-SER-jik ASS-id di-ETH-il-la-meyed): A synthetic, serotonin-related hallucinogenic drug.
hallucinogens (ha-LOO-sin-oh-jens): A class of drugs producing distortions in perception and body image at moderate doses.

hallucination is the reported perception of something that does not physically exist. For example, a schizophrenic might hear voices that no one else hears, and therefore we must conclude (at least the nonschizophrenic world must conclude) that such voices are not real. In the case of hallucinogens, the effect is more complicated because we are dealing with a perceived alteration in the existing physical environment. Drug experts have used the term *illusionogenic*, as a more accurate way of describing drugs that produce these kinds of experiences.

We should also be aware of another qualification when we use the term "hallucinogen." Many drugs that produce distinctive effects when taken at low to moderate dose levels turn out to produce hallucinations when the dose levels are extremely high. Examples of this phenomenon appeared in Chapter 4 with cocaine and amphetamines and will appear in Chapter 13 with inhalants. Here the category of hallucinogens will be limited to only those drugs that produce marked changes in perceived reality at relatively low dosages.

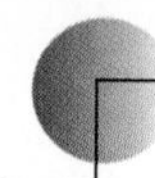

Classifying Hallucinogens

Most hallucinogens can be classified in terms of the particular neurotransmitter in the brain that bears a close resemblance to the molecular features of the drug. As shown in Table 6.1, hallucinogens fall into three principal categories: (1) those that are chemically similar to serotonin (LSD, psilocybin, morning glory seeds, DMT, and harmine), (2) those that are chemically similar to norepinephrine (mescaline, DOM, MDMA, and MDA), and (3) those that are chemically similar to acetylcholine (atropine, scopolamine, hyoscyamine, and ibotenic acid). The implication is that any drug that resembles a neurotransmitter has the potential either to stimulate or to inhibit the receptors sensitive to that neurotransmitter. In addition, a fourth category comprises a few hallucinogens (PCP and ketamine are examples) that are chemically unlike any known neurotransmitter; these drugs will be called miscellaneous hallucinogens.

TABLE 6.1

Major categories of hallucinogens

CATEGORY	SOURCE
Hallucinogens related to serotonin	
lysergic acid diethylamide (LSD)	A synthetic derivative of lysergic acid, which is in turn a component of ergot
psilocybin	Various species of North American mushrooms
lysergic acid amide or morning glory seeds	Morning glory seeds
dimethyltryptamine (DMT)	The bark resin of several varieties of trees and some nuts native to Central and South America
harmine	The bark of a South American vine
Hallucinogens related to norepinephrine	
mescaline	The peyote cactus in Mexico and the U.S. Southwest
2,5,-dimethoxy-4-methylamphetamine (DOM or more commonly STP)	A synthetic mescaline-like hallucinogen
MDMA (Ecstasy) and MDA	Two synthetic hallucinogens
Hallucinogens related to acetylcholine	
atropine	*Atropa belladonna* plant, known as deadly nightshade, and the datura plant
scopolamine (hyoscine)	Roots of the mandrake plant, henbane herb, and the datura plant
hyoscyamine	Roots of the mandrake plant, henbane herb, and the datura plant
ibotenic acid	*Amanita muscaria* mushrooms
Miscellaneous hallucinogens	
phencyclidine (PCP)	A synthetic preparation, developed in 1963, referred to as angel dust
ketamine	A PCP-like hallucinogen

Source: Schultes, Richard E., and Hofmann, Albert (1979). *Plants of the gods: Origins of hallucinogenic use.* New York: McGraw-Hill.

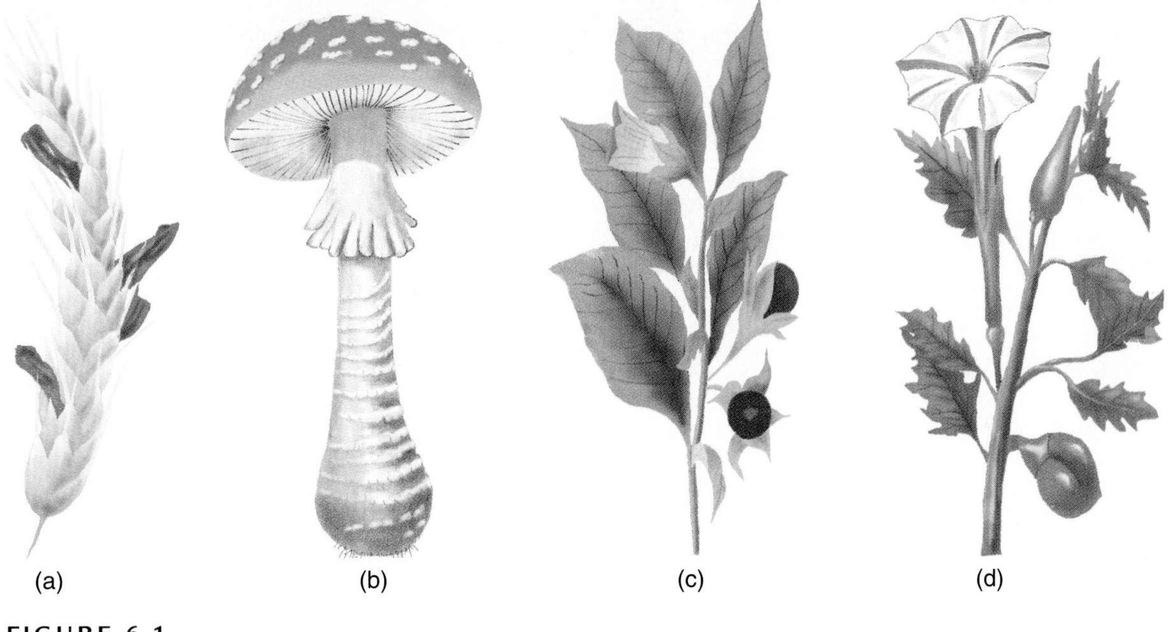

FIGURE 6.1

Botanical sources for four hallucinogenic drugs: (a) Claviceps tulasne *(ergot), (b)* Amanita muscaria *(ibotenic acid), (c)* Atropa belladonna *(atropine), (d)* Datura stramonium *(atropine, scopolamine, and hyoscyamine). They are shown the same size, when in actuality they are not.*

As Figure 6.1 indicates, several of these drugs have natural botanical origins.

Lysergic Acid Diethylamide (LSD)

The most widely known hallucinogen is LSD, which does not exist in nature but is synthetically derived from **ergot**, a fungus present in moldy rye and other grains. One of the compounds in ergot, lysergic acid, is highly toxic, inducing a condition called **ergotism.** Historians have surmised that widespread epidemics of ergotism (called St. Anthony's fire) occurred periodically in Europe during the Middle Ages, when extreme famine forced people to bake bread from infected grain. In one particularly deadly episode in 944, an outbreak of ergotism claimed as many as forty thousand lives.[5]

The features of this calamity were two-fold. One form of ergotism produced a reduction in blood flow toward the extremities, leading to gangrene, burning pain, and the eventual loss of limbs. The other form produced a tingling sensation on the skin, convulsions, disordered thinking, and hallucinations.

Even though the scientific link between this strange affliction and lysergic acid has been known since the 1700s, outbreaks of ergotism have occurred in recent times. A major one took place in a small French community in 1951. Hundreds of townspeople went totally mad on a single night:

> *Many of the most highly regarded citizens leaped from windows or jumped into the Rhône, screaming that their heads were made of copper, their bodies wrapped in snakes, their limbs swollen to gigantic size or shrunken to tiny appendages.... Animals went berserk. Dogs ripped bark from trees until their teeth fell out.*[6]

Albert Hofmann's professional interest in lysergic acid centered on its ability to reduce bleeding and increase contractions in smooth muscle, particularly the uterus. He was trying to find a nontoxic chemical version that would be useful in treating problems associated with childbirth. The

ergot (ER-got): A fungus infecting rye and other grains.
ergotism: A physical and/or psychological disorder acquired by ingesting ergot-infected grains. One form of ergotism involves gangrene and eventual loss of limbs; the other form is associated with hallucinations, convulsions, and disordered thinking.

DRUGS . . . IN FOCUS

Strange Days in Salem: Witchcraft or Hallucinogens?

In the early months of 1692, in Salem, Massachusetts, eight young girls suddenly developed a combination of bizarre symptoms: disordered speech, odd body postures, and convulsive fits. They also began to accuse various townspeople of witchcraft. During the summer, in a series of trials, more than 150 people were convicted of being witches and 20 were executed. Accusations were also made in neighboring villages in the county and in Connecticut. Nothing approaching the magnitude of the Salem witch trials has since occurred in American history.

Over the years, a number of theories have attempted to account for these strange events: a case of adolescent pranks, general hysteria, or some kind of political scapegoating. An interesting and controversial speculation has been advanced that these girls were showing the hallucinogenic and convulsive symptoms of ergotism, acquired from fungus-infected rye grain. Arguments that support this theory include the following:

- Rye grain, once harvested, was stored in barns for months, and the unusually moist weather in the area that year could have promoted the growth of ergot fungus during storage. Of twenty-two Salem households with some afflicted member, sixteen were located close to riverbanks or swamps.
- Children and teenagers would have been particularly vulnerable to ergotism because they ingest more food, and hence more poison, per body weight than do adults.
- The Salem girls as well as the accused "witches" frequently displayed hallucinatory behavior and physical symptoms common to convulsive ergotism.

The role of ergotism in the Salem witch trials of 1692 has been vigorously debated by both historians and pharmacologists. The readings listed below provide more information on this intriguing possibility.

Sources: In favor: Caporael, Linnda R. (1976). Ergotism: The Satan loosed in Salem? *Science, 192,* 21–26. Matossian, Mary K. (1982). Ergot and the Salem witchcraft affair. *American Scientist, 70,* 355–357. Matossian, Mary K. (1989). *Poisons of the past: Molds, epidemics, and history*. New Haven CT: Yale University Press, pp. 113–122. Against: Spanos, Nicholas P., and Gottlieb, Jack (1976). Ergotism and the Salem village witch trials. *Science, 194,* 1390–1394.

LSD molecule was number twenty-five in a series of variations that Hofmann studied in 1938, and his creation was officially named LSD-25 for that reason. He thought at the time that the compound had possibilities for medical use but went on to other pursuits, returning to it five years later in 1943, the year of his famous LSD experience.

The Beginning of the Psychedelic Era

Sandoz Pharmaceuticals applied for FDA approval of LSD in 1953, and as was a common practice at the time, the company sent out samples of LSD to laboratories around the world for scientific study. The idea was that LSD might be helpful in the treatment of schizophrenia by allowing psychiatrists to gain insight into subconscious processes, which this drug apparently unlocked. One of the researchers intrigued by the potential psychotherapeutic applications of LSD was the psychiatrist Humphrey Osmond of the University of Saskatchewan in Canada, who coined the word "psychedelic" to describe its effects and whose interest also extended to other hallucinogens such as mescaline.

In 1953, Osmond introduced the British writer Aldous Huxley to mescaline, and Huxley later reported his experiences, under Osmond's supervision, in his essay *The Doors of Experience.* Prior to 1960, LSD was being administered to humans under fairly limited circumstances, chiefly as part of research studies in psychiatric hospitals and psychotherapy sessions on the West Coast. As would be later revealed in court testimony in the 1970s, there were also top-secret experiments conducted by governmental agencies such as the CIA that were interested in LSD for possible application in espionage work. Word of its extraordinary effects, however, gradually spread to regions outside laboratories or hospitals. One of those who picked up on these events was a young clinical psychologist and lecturer at Harvard University named Timothy Leary.

Leary's first hallucinatory experience (in fact his first psychoactive drug experience of any kind) was in Mexico in 1960, when he ate some mushrooms containing the hallucinogen psilocybin. This is his recollection of the effect on him:

> *During the next five hours, I was whirled through an experience which could be described in many extravagant metaphors but which was above all and without question the deepest religious experience of my life.*[7]

Back at Harvard, his revelations sparked the interest of a colleague, Richard Alpert. The two men were soon holding psilocybin sessions with university students and whoever else was interested, on and off campus. At first these studies retained some semblance of scientific control. For example, a physician was on hand, and objective observers of behavior reported the reactions of the subjects. Later, these procedures were altered. Physicians were no longer invited to the sessions, and Leary himself began taking the drug at the same time. His argument was that he could communicate better with the subject during the drug experience, but his participation seriously undermined the scientific nature of the studies.

In 1961, Leary, Alpert, and other associates turned to LSD as the focus of their investigations, in their homes and other locations off the Harvard campus. Though these experiments were technically separate from the university itself, public relations concerns on the part of the academic community were mounting. Leary further aggravated the situation through his writings. In a 1962 article published in the *Bulletin of the Atomic Scientists*, he suggested that the Soviets could conceivably dump LSD into the water supply and, in order to prepare for such an attack, Americans should dump LSD into their own water supply so that citizens would then know what to expect. The U.S. government was not amused.

In 1963, after a Harvard investigation, Leary and Alpert were dismissed from their academic positions, making it the first time in the twentieth century that a Harvard faculty member had been fired. As you can imagine, such events brought enormous media exposure. Leary was now "Mr. LSD" (see Portrait), and suddenly the public was acquainted with a class of drugs that had been previously unknown to them.[8]

For the rest of the 1960s, LSD became not only a drug but also one of the symbols for the cultural revolt of a generation of youth against the perceived inadequacies of the established, older generation. Leary himself told his followers that they were "the wisest and holiest generation that the human race has ever seen" and advised them to "turn on, tune in, and drop out."[9] The era has been described in this way:

> *There were psychedelic churches, ashrams, rock festivals, light shows, posters, comic books and newspapers, psychedelic jargon and slang. Every middle-sized city*

Portrait Timothy Leary—Whatever Happened to Him?

For the average college student, the question regarding Timothy Leary might not be "Whatever happened to him?" but rather, "Who was this guy anyway?" So for those of you who ask the latter question, here is a capsule rendition of Leary's impact on the drug scene in the 1960s, along with an update.

Until 1960, Leary's career was conventional. As a clinical psychologist, he had written a widely acclaimed textbook and devised a respected personality test (called the Leary). An experience with psilocybin in Mexico in 1960, however, turned his life around. The more extensive his exposure to hallucinogenic drugs became, the more he took on the self-appointed role of Pied Piper for what was referred to then as the "acid generation."

By the middle of the 1970s, Leary had been sentenced to twenty years for marijuana possession (the longest sentence ever imposed for such an offense), had gone to federal prison, escaped, evaded the authorities in Algeria and Switzerland for a few years, been recaptured, and finally released. LSD advocacy was no longer on his agenda by this time, and in fact LSD had lost its mystique years earlier. Leary hit the college lecture circuit, talking about space migration and life extension and calling himself a "stand-up philosopher."

Timothy Leary in the early 1990s

In the late 1980s, Leary discovered computers. He formed a software company, marketed a number of successful video games, and viewed interactive computer programming and virtual reality in particular as the consciousness expansion of the 1990s, the newest route to cerebral stimulation.

Leary never stopped being a social activist. In 1994 he was detained by the police in an Austin, Texas, airport for smoking—a cigarette, this time. Leary said that he wanted to draw attention to people being "demonized" by no-smoking restrictions on their lives.

A year after his death in 1996, Leary's friends arranged to have his cremated remains delivered by rocket into space. It was estimated that he would orbit the earth every ninety minutes for approximately two years, perhaps as many as ten, before burning up during reentry. You might say it would be the ultimate trip.

Sources: Brozan, Nadine (1994, May 12). Chronicle: Timothy Leary lights up. *New York Times*, p. D26. Timothy Leary: Getting high on high tech (1986, December 22). *Newsweek*, p. 48. Lee, Martin A., and Shlain, Bruce (1985). *Acid dreams: The complete social history of LSD.* New York: Grove Weidenfeld. Simons, Marlise (1997, April 22). A final turn-on lifts Timothy Leary off. *New York Times*, pp. A1, A4.

The multicolored images that epitomized the psychedelic era of the 1960s.

> *had its enclaves, and there was a drug culture touring circuit. . . . Everyone had his own idea of what was meant by turning on, tuning in, and dropping out—his own set and setting—and the drug culture provided almost as many variations in doctrine, attitude, and way of life, from rational and sedate to lewd and violent, as the rest of society.*[10]

To paraphrase the words of songwriter and singer Bob Dylan, "the times were a-changin'," but not always for the better. LSD became a battleground unto itself. In congressional hearings on LSD use by the nation's youth, scientists, health officials, and law-enforcement experts testified to a growing panic over the drug. Newspaper stories emphasized the dangers with alarmist headlines: "A monster in our midst—a drug called LSD" and "Thrill drug warps mind, kills," among them. Sandoz quietly allowed its LSD patent lapse in 1966 and did everything it could to distance itself from the controversy. Hofmann himself called LSD his "problem child."

In 1966, LSD was made illegal, later becoming a Schedule I drug, with possession originally set as a misdemeanor and later upgraded to a felony. By the 1970s, LSD had become entrenched as a street drug, and taking LSD had become a component of the already dangerous world of illicit drugs. The story of LSD will be updated in a later section, but first it is important to understand the range of effects LSD typically produces.

Acute Effects of LSD

LSD is considered one of the most, if not *the* most, powerful psychoactive drugs known. Its potency is so great that effective dose levels have to be expressed in terms of micrograms, one millionths of a gram, often called *mikes*. The typical street dose ranges from 50 to 150 micrograms, though sellers often claim that their product contains more. The effective dose can be as small as 10 micrograms, with only one-hundredth of a percent being absorbed into the brain. Compare these figures to the fact that a single pain-relief tablet contains 325,000 micrograms of aspirin, and you can appreciate the enormous potency of LSD.[11]

Taken orally, LSD is rapidly absorbed into the bloodstream and the brain, with effects beginning within thirty to sixty minutes. Once its concentration has peaked (in about ninety minutes), the elimination half-life, or the time it takes for 50 percent of the drug to diminish in the bloodstream (see Chapter 3), is approximately three hours. Within five to twelve hours, LSD effects are over.[12]

Surprisingly, given its extreme potency, the toxicity of LSD is relatively low. Generalizing from studies of animals given varying doses of LSD, we can estimate that a lethal dose of LSD for humans would have to be roughly three hundred to six hundred times the effective dose, a fairly comfortable margin of safety. In 1998, the DAWN statistics listing the frequency of admissions to hospital emergency rooms showed that less than 1 percent were related to ingestion of LSD, and to this day there has never been a single definitive case in which a death has been attributed to an LSD overdose.[13]

Street forms of LSD may contain color additives or adulterants with specific flavors, but the drug itself is odorless, tasteless, and colorless. LSD is sold on the street in single-dose "hits." It is typically swallowed in the form of powder pellets (microdots) or gelatin chips (windowpanes) or else licked off small squares of absorbent paper

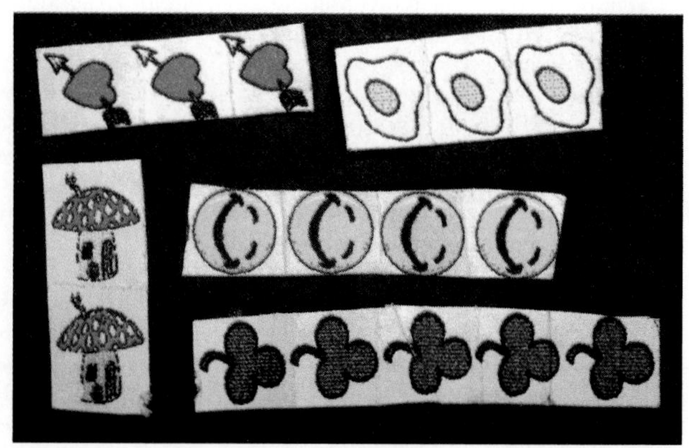

Acid blotters with various designs.

that have been soaked in liquid LSD (blotters). In the past, blotters soaked with LSD have been decorated with pictures of mystical symbols and signs, rocket ships, or representations of Mickey Mouse, Snoopy, Bart Simpson, or other popular characters.

LSD initially produces an excitation of the sympathetic autonomic activity: increased heart rate, elevated blood pressure, dilated pupils, and a slightly raised body temperature. There is an accompanying feeling of restlessness, euphoria, and a sensation that inner tension has been released. There may be laughing or crying, depending on the expectations and setting.[14]

Between thirty minutes and two hours later, a "psychedelic trip" begins, characterized by four distinctive features. The best way to describe these effects is in the words of individuals who have experienced them:[15]

- Images seen with the eyes closed.

  Closing my eyes, I saw millions of color droplets, like rain, like a shower of stars, all different colors.

- An intermingling of senses called **synesthesia**, which often involves sounds appearing as hallucinatory visions.

  I clapped my hands and saw sound waves passing before my eyes.

- Perception of a multilevel reality.

  I was sitting on a chair and I could see the molecules. I could see right through things to the molecules.

- Strange and exaggerated appearances of common objects or experiences.

  A towel falling off the edge of my tub looked like a giant lizard crawling down.

  When my girlfriend was peeling an orange for me, it was like she was ripping a small animal apart.

During the third and final phase, approximately three to five hours after first taking LSD, the following features begin to appear:

- Great swings in emotions or panic.

  It started off beautifully. I looked into a garden . . . and suddenly, it got terrible . . . and I started to cry. . . . And then, my attention wandered, and something else was happening, beautiful music was turned on. . . . Then suddenly I felt happy.

- A feeling of timelessness.

  Has an hour gone by since I last looked at the clock? Maybe it was a lifetime. Maybe it was no time at all.

- A feeling of ego disintegration, or a separation of one's mind from one's body.

  Boundaries between self and nonself evaporate, giving rise to a serene sense of being at one with the universe. I recall muttering to myself again and again, "All is one, all is one."

Whether these strong reactions result in a "good trip" or a "bad trip" depends heavily on the set or expectations for the drug, the setting or environment in which the LSD is experienced, and the overall psychological health of the individual.

Effects of LSD on the Brain

LSD closely resembles the molecular structure of serotonin; therefore, it is not surprising that LSD should have effects on receptors in the brain that are sensitive to serotonin. As a result of research in the 1980s, it turns out that the critical factor behind LSD's hallucinogenic effects lies in its ability to stimulate a special subtype of serotonin-sensitive receptors, commonly called S_2 receptors. In fact, all hallucinogens, even those drugs whose structures do not resemble serotonin, are linked together by the common ability to excite S_2 receptor sites. Drugs that specifically block S_2 receptors, leaving all other subtypes unchanged, will block the behavioral effects of hallucinogens. In addition, the ability of a particular drug to produce hallucinogenic effects is directly proportional to its ability to bind to S_2 receptors.[16]

Patterns of LSD Use

The enormous publicity surrounding Timothy Leary and his followers in the 1960s made LSD a household word. As many as fifty popular articles about LSD were published in major U.S. newspapers and magazines between March 1966 and February 1967 alone. By 1970, however, the media had lost interest, and hardly anything was appearing about LSD. Even so, while media attention was diminishing, the incidence of LSD abuse was steadily rising. In four Gallup Poll surveys conducted between 1967 and 1971, the percentage of college students reported to have taken LSD at least once in their lives rose dramatically from 1 to 18 percent.[17]

synesthesia: A subjective sensation (as of vision) other than the one (as of sound) being stimulated.

From the middle 1970s to the early 1990s, the numbers showed a steady decline. By 1986, the University of Michigan survey indicated that the lifetime incidence of LSD taking among high school seniors was 7 percent, down from 11 percent in 1975. By the end of the 1990s, however, prevalence rates were reaching levels that exceeded those of a quarter-century earlier. About 11 percent of high school seniors in 2000 reported taking LSD at some time in their lives.

It should be noted that today's LSD users are different from those of a previous generation in a number of ways. Typical LSD users now take the drug less frequently and, because the dosage of street LSD is presently about one-fourth the level common to the 1960s and 1970s, they remain high for a briefer period of time. They also report using LSD simply to get high, rather than to explore alternative states of consciousness or gain a greater insight into life. For current users, LSD no longer has the symbolic significance that it had in an earlier time. Fortunately, increased LSD use has not been reflected in an increase in hospital emergency cases (according to the DAWN reports), probably because of the lower dosage levels available.[18]

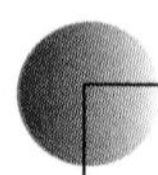

Facts and Fictions about LSD

Given the history of LSD use and the publicity about it, it is all the more important to look carefully at the facts about LSD and to unmask the myths. Six basic questions that are often asked about this drug are examined in the following sections.

Will LSD Produce a Dependence?

There are three major reasons why LSD is not likely to result in a drug dependence, despite the fact that the experience at times is quite pleasant.[19] First, LSD and other hallucinogens cause the body to build up a tolerance to their effects faster than any other drug category. As a result, one cannot remain on an LSD-induced high day after day, for an extended period of time. Second, LSD is not the drug for someone seeking an easy way to get high. As one drug expert has put it,

> *The LSD experience requires a monumental effort. To go through eight hours of an LSD high—sensory bombardment, psychic turmoil, emotional insecurity, alternations of despair and bliss, one exploding insight upon the heels of another, images hurtling through the mind as fast as the spinning fruit of a slot machine—is draining and exhausting in the extreme.*[20]

Third, the LSD experience seems to control the user rather than the other way around. It is virtually impossible to "come down" from LSD at will. Besides, the unpredictability of the LSD experience is an unpopular feature for those who would want a specific and reliable drug effect every time the drug is taken.

Will LSD Produce a Panic or a Psychosis?

One of the most notorious features of LSD is the possibility of a bad trip. Examples abound of sweet, dreamlike states rapidly turning into nightmares. Perhaps the greatest risks are taken when a person is slipped a dose of LSD and begins to experience its effect without knowing that he or she has taken a drug. Panic reactions do occur, however, even when a person is fully aware of having taken LSD. Although the probability of having a bad trip is difficult to estimate, there are very few regular LSD abusers who have not experienced a bad trip or had a disturbing experience as part of an LSD trip. The best treatment for adverse effects is the companionship and reassurance of others throughout the period when LSD is active. Health Alert includes some specific procedures for dealing with LSD panic episodes.

Despite the possibility of an LSD panic, there is no strong evidence that the panic will lead to a more permanent psychiatric breakdown. Long-term psychiatric problems are relatively uncommon, with one study conducted in 1960 showing that there was no greater probability of a person's attempting suicide or developing a psychosis after taking LSD than when undergoing ordinary forms of psychotherapy.[21] The incidents that do occur typically involve people who were unaware that they were taking LSD, showed unstable personality characteristics prior to taking LSD, or were experiencing LSD under hostile or threatening circumstances.

The possible link between the character of LSD effects and symptoms of schizophrenia has also been examined closely. It is true that on a superficial level, the two behaviors show some similarities, but there are important differences. LSD hallucinations are primarily visual, best seen in the dark, and, as mentioned earlier, more accurately characterized as illusions or pseudohallucinations; schizophrenic hallucinations are primarily auditory, seen with open eyes, and qualify as true hallucinations. Individuals taking LSD are highly susceptible to suggestion and will usually try to communicate the experience to others; the schizophrenic individual is typically resistant to suggestion and withdrawn from his or her surroundings. Therefore, it is unlikely that LSD is

Health Alert

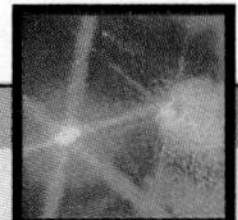

Emergency Guidelines for a Bad Trip on LSD

- Stay calm with the individual. Do not move around quickly, shout, cry, or become hysterical. Any sense of panic on your part will make an LSD panic worse. Speak in a relaxed, controlled manner.
- Reassure the individual that the situation is temporary and that you will not leave until he or she returns to a normal state. Encourage the individual to breathe deeply and calmly. Advise him or her to view the trip as though watching a movie or TV program.
- Reduce any loud noises or bright lights but do not let the individual go into the dark. Darkness tends to encourage hallucinations in a person under LSD.
- Allow the individual to move around without undue restrictions. He or she can sit, stand, walk, or lie down if this helps the situation. You can divert attention from the panic by encouraging the individual to beat time to music or by dancing.
- If your assistance does not produce a reduction in the panic, seek out medical attention immediately. Under medical supervision, LSD panics can be treated with benzodiazepines such as chlordiazepoxide (Librium) or diazepam (Valium), or if the symptoms are severe, by antipsychotic medication such as haloperidol (Haldol).

Sources: Palfai, Tibor, and Jankiewicz, Henry (1991). *Drugs and human behavior.* Dubuque IA: W. C. Brown, p. 445. Robbins, Paul R. (1996). *Hallucinogens.* Springfield NJ: Enslow Publishers, pp. 83–85. Trulson, Michael E. (1985). *LSD: Visions or nightmares.* New York: Chelsea House, p. 101.

mimicking the experience of a schizophrenic psychosis (see Chapter 16).

Will LSD Increase Creativity?

The unusual visual effects of an LSD experience may lead you to assume that your creativity is enhanced, but the evidence indicates otherwise. Professional artists and musicians creating new works of art or songs while under the influence of LSD typically think that their creations are better than anything they have yet produced, but when the LSD has worn off, they are far less impressed. Controlled studies generally show that individuals under LSD *feel* that they are creative, but objective ratings do not show a significant difference from levels prior to the LSD.[22]

Will LSD Damage Chromosomes?

In March 1967, a study published in the prestigious scientific journal *Science* described a marked increase in chromosomal abnormalities in human white blood cells that had been treated with LSD in vitro (that is, the cells were outside the body at the time).[23] Shortly after, three other studies were reported in which chromosomal abnormalities in the white blood cells of LSD abusers were higher than those of people who did not use drugs, while three additional studies reported no chromosomal effect at all.

By the end of that year, a second study was published by the people whose report had started the controversy in the first place. They wrote that eighteen LSD abusers had two to four times the number of chromosomal abnormalities in their white blood cells, when compared with fourteen control subjects. Interestingly, the subjects in this study were not exactly model citizens. Everyone of them had taken either one or more of amphetamines, barbiturates, cocaine, hallucinogens, opiates, or antipsychotic medication. How the authors got away with describing their study as "chromosomal damage induced by LSD-25" is anyone's guess.

The picture was confused, to say the least. Not only were many of these studies unreplicable, but many were methodologically flawed as well. Most important, when studies actually looked at the chromosomes of *reproductive cells themselves* for signs of breakage from exposure to LSD, the results were either ambiguous or entirely negative. By 1971, after nearly a hundred studies had been carried out, the conclusion was that LSD did not cause chromosomal damage in human beings at normal doses, and that there was no evidence of a high rate of birth defects in the children of LSD users.[24] Yet, in the highly politicized climate of the late 1960s, the media tended to emphasize the negative findings without any scrutiny into their validity or relevance. The public image of LSD causing genetic damage still persists, despite the lack of scientific evidence. This is not to say, however, that there is no basis for exercising some degree of caution. Women should avoid LSD, as well as other psychoactive drugs, during pregnancy, especially in the first three months.[25]

Will LSD Have a Residual Effect?

One of the most disturbing aspects of taking LSD is the possibility of reexperiencing the effects of the drug long after the drug has worn off, sometimes as long as several years later. These experiences are referred to as Hallucinogen Persisting Perception Disorder, or simply "flashbacks." The likelihood of LSD flashbacks is not precisely known. Some studies estimate its rate of incidence as only 5 percent, whereas others estimate it as high as 33 percent. It is reasonable to assume that the range of estimates is related to differences in the dosage levels ingested.

Flashback effects can sometimes be frightening and other times be quite pleasant; they can occur among LSD novices or "once-only" drug takers as well as among experienced LSD abusers. While they appear without warning, there is a higher probability that they will occur when the individual is beginning to go to sleep or has just entered a dark environment.[26]

Because they are not common to any other psychoactive drug, the reason why LSD flashbacks might occur is not well understood. It is possible that LSD has a peculiar ability to produce some biochemical changes that remain dormant for a period of time and then suddenly reappear or that some remnant of the drug has the ability to persist over extended periods of time. It is also possible that individuals who ingest LSD are highly suggestible to social reminders about the original exposure to LSD.

Whether or not LSD produces major long-term deficits in the behavior of the user remains largely unknown. Memory problems and visuospatial impairments have been reported in some studies but not confirmed in others. Unfortunately, several problems persist in research studies examining long-term effects of LSD. Often, they have included either individuals with a history of psychiatric disorders prior to LSD ingestion or regular users of other illicit drugs and alcohol. As a result, it has been impossible to tease apart the long-term effects of LSD alone.[27]

Will LSD Increase Criminal or Violent Behavior?

As noted in Chapter 2, it is very difficult to establish a clear cause-and-effect relationship between a drug and criminal or violent behavior. Once again, in the highly charged era of the 1960s, stories related to this question were publicized and conclusions were drawn without any careful examination of the actual facts. Take for example, the 1964 case of a woman undergoing LSD therapy treatment who murdered her lover three days after her last LSD session.[28] The details of the case, overlooked by most subsequent media reports, reveal that the woman had been physically abused by the man, he had caused her to have an abortion, and the woman already had a serious mental disorder before going into treatment. The fact that the homicide took place well after the LSD had left her body indicates that the murder was not an instance of pharmacological violence. Other cases in which violent behavior appeared to be associated with an LSD experience turned out in fact to be associated with the use of other hallucinogenic drugs.

It is possible, however, that an individual can "freak out" on LSD. The effects of a euphoriant drug such as LSD can lead to a feeling of invulnerability. This feeling, in turn, can lead to dangerous and possibly life-threatening behavior. While we cannot reliably estimate the likelihood of these effects or pinpoint the circumstances under which they might occur, we should recognize that psychological reactions to LSD are inherently unpredictable, and caution is advised.

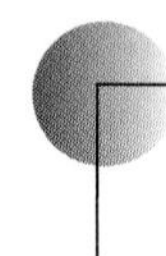

Psilocybin and Other Hallucinogens Related to Serotonin

The source of the drug **psilocybin** is a family of mushrooms native to southern Mexico and Central America. Spanish chroniclers in the sixteenth century wrote of "sacred mushrooms" revered by the Aztecs as *teonanacatl* (roughly translated as "God's flesh") and capable of providing extraordinary visions when eaten. Their psychoactive properties had been known for a long time, judging from stone-carved representations of these mushrooms discovered in El Salvador and dating back to as early as 500 B.C. Today, shamans in remote villages in Mexico and Central America (see Chapter 1) continue the use of psilocybin mushrooms, among other hallucinogenic plants, to provide healing on both physical and spiritual levels.[29]

Native use of these mushrooms disappeared from historical accounts until the late 1930s, when several varieties were identified. In 1955, a group of Western observers documented the hallucinogenic effects of the *Psilocybe mexicana* in a native Indian group living in a remote mountainous region of southern Mexico. Three years later, samples worked their way to Switzerland, where Albert Hofmann, already known for his work on LSD, identified the active ingredient and named it psilocybin. As was his habit, Hofmann sampled some of the mushrooms himself and wrote later of his reactions:

> *Thirty minutes after my taking the mushrooms, the exterior world began to undergo a Mexican character. . . . I saw only Mexican motifs and colors. When*

psilocybin (SIL-oh-SEYE-bin): A serotonin-related hallucinogenic drug originating from a species of mushrooms.

the doctor supervising the experiment bent over me to check my blood pressure, he was transformed into an Aztec priest.[30]

We can never know whether the Aztec character of these hallucinogenic effects was a result of suggestion or that Aztec designs may have been inspired over the centuries by the effects of psilocybin.

Once ingested, psilocybin loses a portion of its molecule, making it more fat-soluble and more easily absorbed into the brain. This new version, called **psilocin,** is the actual agent that works on the brain. Since LSD and psilocin are chemically similar, the biochemical effects are also similar. In fact, if you have developed a tolerance to LSD, you have become tolerant to psilocybin effects as well.[31]

Far less potent than LSD, psilocybin is effective at dose levels measured in the more traditional units of milligrams rather than micrograms. At doses of 4 to 5 mg, psilocybin causes a pleasant, relaxing feeling; at doses of 15 mg and more, hallucinations, time distortions, and changes in body perception appear. A psilocybin trip generally lasts from two to five hours, considerably shorter than an LSD trip.

Individuals who have experienced both kinds of hallucinogens report that, relative to LSD, psilocybin produces effects that are more strongly visual, less emotionally intense, and more euphoric, with fewer panic reactions and less chance of paranoia. On the other hand, experimental studies of volunteers taking high doses of psilocybin have established that the drug produces drastic enough changes in mood, sensory perception, and thought processes to qualify as a psychotic syndrome.

As with LSD, psilocybin (often called simply "shrooms") has become increasingly available as a drug of abuse. In 2000, about 35 percent of high school seniors reported that non-LSD hallucinogens were either "fairly easy" or "very easy" to get, while about 47 percent felt the same way about LSD itself.[32]

Lysergic Acid Amide (LAA)

In addition to their reverence for psilocybin mushrooms, the Aztecs also ingested locally grown morning glory seeds, calling them *ololuiqui,* and used their hallucinogenic effects in religious rites and healing. Like many Native American practices, the recreational use of morning glory seeds has survived in remote areas of southern Mexico. In 1961 Albert Hofmann (once again) identified the active ingredient in these seeds as **lysergic acid amide (LAA),** after having sampled its hallucinogenic properties. As the chemical name suggests, this drug is a close relative to LSD.

The LAA experience, judging from Hofmann's report, is similar to that of LSD, though LAA is only one-tenth to one-thirtieth as potent and the hallucinations tend to be dominated by auditory rather than visual images. Commercial varieties of morning glory seeds are available to the public, but suppliers have taken the precaution of coating them with an additive that causes nausea and vomiting, if eaten, to minimize their abuse.[33]

Dimethyltryptamine (DMT)

The drug **dimethyltryptamine (DMT)** is obtained chiefly from the resin of the bark of trees and nuts native to the West Indies as well as to Central and South America, where it is generally inhaled as a snuff. An oral administration does not produce psychoactive effects. The similarity of this drug's effects to those of LSD and its very short duration gave DMT the reputation during the psychedelic years of the 1960s of being "the businessman's LSD." Presumably, someone could take a DMT trip during lunch and be back at the office in time for work in the afternoon.

An inhaled 30 mg dose of DMT produces physiological changes within ten seconds, with hallucinogenic effects peaking around ten to fifteen minutes later. Paranoia, anxiety, and panic can also result at this time, but most symptoms are over in about an hour.[34] A chemical found in *Bufo* toads is similar to DMT (see Drugs... in Focus).

Harmine

Among native tribes in the western Amazon region of South America, the bark of the *Banisteriopsis* vine yields the powerful drug **harmine.** A drink containing harmine, called *ayahuasca,* is frequently used by local shamans for healing rites. It is chemically similar to serotonin, like LSD and the other hallucinogens examined

psilocin (SIL-oh-sin): A brain chemical related to serotonin, resulting from the ingestion of psilocybin.
lysergic acid amide (LAA) (leye-SER-jik ASS-id A-meyed): A hallucinogenic drug found in morning glory seeds, producing effects similar to those of LSD.
dimethyltryptamine (DMT) (dye-METH-il-TRIP-ta-meen): A short-acting hallucinogenic drug.
harmine (HAR-meen): A serotonin-related hallucinogenic drug frequently used by South American shamans in healing rituals.

DRUGS . . . IN FOCUS

Bufotenine and the *Bufo* Toad

Bufotenine is a drug with a strange past. Found in a family of beans native to Central and South America, bufotenine is better known as a chemical that can be isolated from the skin and glands of the *Bufo* toad, from which it gets its name. As noted in Chapter 1, *Bufo* toads figured prominently in the magical potions of European witches. Evidence also exists that *Bufo* toads were incorporated into the ceremonial rituals of ancient Aztec and Mayan cultures. Largely as a result of these historical references, it has been widely assumed that bufotenine was the primary contributor to the psychoactive effects of these concoctions and that bufotenine itself is a powerful hallucinogen.

It turns out that these conclusions are wrong. The few studies in which human volunteers were administered bufotenine indicate that the substance induces strong excitatory effects on blood pressure and heart rate but no hallucinatory experiences. Some subjects report distorted images with high dosages of the drug, but this might well occur as oxygen is cut off from parts of the body, particularly the optic nerve carrying visual information to the brain. It is likely that whatever hallucinogenic effects *Bufo* toads may produce are brought on by another chemical also found in these toads that functions similarly to the hallucinogen DMT.

Despite the confusion as to which substance is responsible for its psychoactive properties, *Bufo* toads continue to fascinate the public. Widely exaggerated and frequently unsubstantiated reports of "toad licking" and "toad smoking" periodically circulate in the media. The bottom line, however, is that the dangers of consuming toad tissue are substantial. Besides the extreme cardiovascular reactions, toxic effects also include a skin condition called **cyanosis** (literally, "turning blue"). Actually, the description may be an understatement. Skin color has been observed to be closer to an eggplant purple.

Sources: Horgan, J. (1990, August). Bufo abuse. *Scientific American,* pp. 26–27. Lyttle, Thomas, Goldstein, David, and Gartz, Jochen (1996). Bufo toads and bufotenine: Fact and fiction surrounding an alleged psychedelic. *Journal of Psychoactive Drugs, 28,* 267–290.

so far. Its behavioral effects, however, are somewhat different. Unlike LSD, harmine makes the individual withdraw into a trance, and the hallucinatory images (often visions of animals and supernatural beings) are experienced within the context of a dreamlike state. Reports among shamans refer to a sense of suspension in space or flying, falling into one's body, or experiencing one's own death.[35]

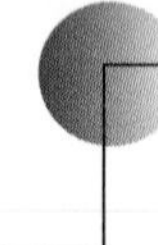

Hallucinogens Related to Norepinephrine

Several types of hallucinogens have a chemical composition similar to norepinephrine. As you may recall from Chapter 4, amphetamines are also chemically similar to norepinephrine. Consequently, sometimes norepinephrine-related hallucinogens produce amphetamine-like stimulant effects. As we will see, this is the case with MDMA but not with mescaline or DOM.

Mescaline

The hallucinogen **mescaline** is derived from the **peyote** plant, a spineless cactus with a small greenish crown that grows above ground and a long carrotlike root. This cactus is found over a wide area, from the southwestern United States to northern regions of South America, and many communities in these regions have discovered its psychoactive properties. Given the large distances between these groups, it is remarkable that they prepare and ingest mescaline in a highly similar manner. The crowns of the cactus are cut off, sliced in small disks called buttons, dried in the sun, and then consumed. An effective dose of mescaline from peyote is 200 mg, equivalent to about five buttons. Peak response to the drug takes place thirty minutes to two hours after consumption. As Drugs . . . in Focus describes, mescaline is still used

bufotenine (byoo-FOT-eh-neen): A serotonin-related drug obtained either from a bean plant in Central and South America or the skin of a particular type of toad.
cyanosis (seye-ah-NOH-sis): A tendency for the skin to turn bluish purple. It can be a side effect of the drug bufotenine.
mescaline (MES-kul-leen): A norepinephrine-related hallucinogenic drug. Its source is the peyote cactus.
peyote (pay-YO-tay): A species of cactus and the source for the hallucinogenic drug mescaline.

DRUGS . . . IN FOCUS

Present-Day Peyotism and the Native American Church

Among Native Americans within the United States, the ritual use of peyote buttons, called peyotism, can be traced to the eighteenth century when the Mescalero Apaches (from whom the word *mescaline* was derived) adopted the custom from Mexican Indians who had been using peyote for more than three thousand years. By the late 1800s, peyotism had become widely popular among tribes from Wisconsin and Minnesota to the West Coast. It was not until the early twentieth century, however, that peyote use became incorporated into an official religious organization, the Native American Church of North America, chartered in 1918.

The beliefs of the Native American Church membership, estimated to include anywhere from 50,000 to 250,000 Native Americans in the United States and Canada, combine traditional tribal customs and practices with Christian morality. To them, life is a choice between two roads that meet at a junction. The Profane Road is paved and wide, surrounded by worldly passions and temptations. The Peyote Road is a narrow and winding path, surrounded by natural, unspoiled beauty; it is also a path of sobriety (since alcohol poisons the goodness of the body), hard work, caring for one's family, and brotherly love. Only the Peyote Road leads to salvation. In their weekly ceremonies, lasting from Saturday night until Sunday afternoon, church members swallow small peyote buttons as a sacrament, similar to the ritual of taking communion, or drink peyote tea. It is considered sacrilegious to take peyote outside the ceremonies in the church.

While peyote remains classified as a Schedule I drug and therefore banned, federal law and the laws of twenty-three U.S. states have exempted the sacramental use of peyote from criminal penalties. The American Indian Religious Freedom Act of 1978 affirmed the sentiment of the U.S. Congress that peyote was sacred to Native American Church members and that peyote use should be constitutionally protected. Nonetheless, in 1990, the Supreme Court ruled that a state had the constitutional right to ban all peyote use regardless of the circumstances, if it chose to do so. As a response to this decision, the Religious Freedom Restoration Act of 1993 was enacted, reestablishing an exemption from federal and state controlled substance laws when peyote is used for religious purposes in traditional Native American ceremonies.

Sources: Calabrese, Joseph D. (1997). Spiritual healing and human development in the Native American Church: Toward a cultural psychiatry of peyote. *Psychoanalytic Review, 84,* 237–255. Indian religion must say no (1990, October 6). *The Economist,* pp. 25–26. Morgan, George (1983). Recollections of the peyote road. In Lester Grinspoon and James B. Bakalar (Eds.), *Psychelic reflections.* New York: Human Sciences Press, pp. 91–99. Oregon peyote law leaves 1983 defendant unvindicated (1991, July 9). *New York Times,* p. A14. Schultes, Richard E., and Hofmann, Albert (1979). *Plants of the gods: Origins of hallucinogenic use.* New York: McGraw-Hill, pp. 132–143.

today as part of religious worship among many Native Americans in the United States and Canada.

The psychological and physiological effects of mescaline are highly similar to those of LSD, though some have reported that mescaline hallucinations are more sensual, with fewer changes in mood and the sense of self. Nonetheless, double-blind studies comparing the reactions to LSD and mescaline show that subjects cannot distinguish between the two when dose levels are equivalent. While the reactions may be the same, the mescaline trip comes at a greater price, as far as physiological reactions are concerned. Peyote buttons taste extremely bitter and can cause vomiting, headaches, and unless the stomach is empty, distressing levels of nausea.[36]

Today mescaline can be synthesized as well as obtained from the peyote cactus. The mescaline molecule resembles the chemical structure of norepinephrine but stimulates the same S_2 receptors as LSD and other hallucinogens that resemble serotonin. As a result, mescaline and LSD share a common brain mechanism.[37]

DOM

A group of synthetic hallucinogens has been developed that shares mescaline's resemblance to amphetamine but does not produce the strong stimulant effects of amphetamine. One example of these synthetic drugs, **DOM,** appeared in the 1960s and 1970s, when it was frequently combined with LSD and carried the street name of STP. The nickname supposedly was a reference to the well-known engine oil additive, while others took it to mean a "super terrific psychedelic." It is roughly eighty times more potent than mescaline, though still far weaker than

DOM: A synthetic norepinephrine-related hallucinogenic drug, derived from amphetamine. DOM or a combination of DOM and LSD is often referred to by the street name STP.

LSD. At low doses of about 3 to 5 mg, DOM produces euphoria; with higher doses of 10 mg or more, severe hallucinations result, often lasting from sixteen to twenty-five hours. Though similar to LSD in many respects, DOM has the reputation of producing a far higher incidence of panic attacks, acute psychoses, and other symptoms of a very bad trip. Cases have been reported of STP being added as an adulterant to marijuana.[38]

MDMA (Ecstasy)

Another synthetic amphetamine-related hallucinogen, abbreviated **MDMA,** first appeared on the scene in the 1980s. While subject to abuse as a new designer drug, it also became known to a number of psychiatrists who used the drug as part of their therapy, believing that MDMA had a special ability to enhance empathy among their patients. In fact, some therapists at the time suggested the name *empathogens* (meaning "generating a state of empathy") to describe MDMA and related drugs. Eventually, after several years of hesitations and reversals, the Drug Enforcement Administration put MDMA permanently on the Schedule I list of controlled substances, meaning that there was no accepted medical application for the drug.[39]

Since the early 1990s, MDMA has become prominent among the new club drugs (see Chapter 1), especially popular at dance clubs and all-night "rave" parties. Widely available under names such as Ecstasy (not to be confused with the stimulant Herbal Ecstasy), E, XTC, X, Essence, Clarity, and Adam, MDMA has the reputation of having the stimulant qualities of amphetamines and the hallucinogenic qualities of mescaline. In 2000, approximately one out of nine high school seniors reported having taken Ecstasy at some point in their lives, and other surveys of college students have indicated that the prevalence rate may be as high as one out of four. Presently, an additional concern among public health and law enforcement officials is that the popularity of Ecstasy is increasing not only among young people but older populations as well.[40]

Unfortunately, Ecstasy has serious problems of short-term and long-term toxicity. The major acute effect is severe hyperthermia (and heatstroke), which can be potentially lethal when experienced in the already overheated environments where Ecstasy is ingested. There is also evidence of long-term degeneration of serotonin-using neurons in areas of the brain concerned with learning and memory. The specific memory deficits in Ecstasy abusers have been tied to alterations in serotonin activity. The Health Alert feature highlights the major areas of MDMA toxicity. Compounding the potential problems, patterns of abuse have included the highly risky practice of "Ecstasy stacking," in which young people take three or more tablets at once or combine Ecstasy with LSD, alcohol, marijuana, or other drugs.[41]

Health Alert

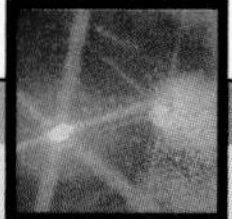

MDMA Toxicity: The Other Side of Ecstasy

- *Possible physical effects:*
  hyperthermia and heatstroke
  dehydration and electrolyte depletion
  irregular heartbeat or increased heart rate
  kidney and liver failure
  jaw-clenching and other forms of muscle spasms
  neuronal damage
- *Possible psychological effects:*
  agitation and confusion
  depression and anxiety
  long-term impairments in memory recall

Note: As with other illicit drugs, adulterated versions raise significant concerns. In the case of MDMA, adulterants include dextromethorphan (a common cough suppressant) at approximately thirteen times the dose found in over-the-counter cough medications. At this dosage, dextromethorphan itself functions as a hallucinogen and inhibits sweating, further risking hyperthermia and heatstroke. More powerful hallucinogens and hyperthermic drugs have also been identified as adulterants in MDMA batches.

Sources: Boils, Karen I. (1999). Memory impairment in abstinent MDMA ("Ecstasy") users. *Journal of the American Medical Association, 281,* 494. Cloud, John (2000, June 5). The lure of ecstasy. *Time,* pp. 62–68. Rella, J. G., Nelson, L. S., and Hoffman, L. S. (1999). 5 years of 3,4-methylenedioxymethamphetamine (MDMA) toxicity. *Journal of Toxicology: Clinical Toxicology, 37,* 648. Schwartz, Richard H., and Miller, Norman S. (1997). MDMA (Ecstasy) and the rave: A review. *Pediatrics, 100,* 705–708.

MDMA (Ecstasy): A synthetic norepinephrine-related hallucinogenic drug. Once considered useful for psychotherapeutic purposes, this drug is now known to produce significant adverse side-effects, including neuronal damage.

Hallucinogens Related to Acetylcholine

Of the acetylcholine-related hallucinogens, some enhance the neurotransmitter and some inhibit it. Some examples include *Amanita muscaria* mushrooms, atropine, scopolamine, and hyoscyamine.

Amanita muscaria

The ***Amanita muscaria*** mushroom, also called the fly agaric mushroom because of its ability to lure and sedate flies and other insects, grows in the upper latitudes of the Northern Hemisphere, usually among the roots of birch trees. The mushroom has a bright red cap speckled with white dots; the dancing mushrooms in Walt Disney's film *Fantasia* were inspired by the appearance (if not the hallucinogenic effects) of this fungus.

Amanita mushrooms are one of the world's oldest intoxicants. Many historians hypothesize that this mushroom was the basis for the mysterious and divine substance called soma that is celebrated in the *Rig-Veda*, one of Hinduism's oldest holy books, dating from 1000 B.C. It is strongly suspected that amanita mushrooms were used in Greek mystery cults and were probably the basis for the legendary nectar of the Gods.[42]

The effects of amanita mushrooms can be lethal if dose levels are not watched very carefully. They produce muscular twitching and spasms, vivid hallucinations, dizziness, and heightened aggressive behavior. It was briefly mentioned in Chapter 1 that Viking warriors were reputed to have ingested amanita mushrooms before sailing off to battle. The drug-induced strength and savagery of these "berserk" invaders were so widely feared that a medieval prayer was written especially for protection from their attacks: "From the intolerable fury of the Norseman, O Lord, deliver us."

Until the 1960s it was believed that the active ingredient in *Amanita muscaria* was, as the name suggests, muscarine, and that this was the drug that excited receptors sensitive to acetylcholine in the parasympathetic autonomic nervous system. Our present knowledge, however, is that the principal psychoactive agent in these mushrooms that accomplishes this effect is a chemical called *ibotenic acid.*

A hallucinogenic drug related to ibotenic acid, called **ibogaine,** is found in the iboga root in the western coastal region of central Africa. While higher doses of ibogaine are potentially lethal, powdered forms of the iboga root in small amounts have been used in ceremonies of the Bwiti cult among several tribal groups in Gabon and the Congo, in an effort to communicate with the spirit world and seek advice from the ancestors. Among these people, iboga root is slowly chewed and the intoxication from ibotenic acid, often lasting for as long as thirty hours, is believed to allow an individual to travel down a road through a visionary landscape to the dwellings of the spirits of the dead. It is interesting that the imagery of progressing through a "trip" pervades so many experiences with hallucinogenic drugs, in both primitive and modern settings. Recently, attention has focused on the role that ibogaine may play in drug abuse treatment, specifically in cases of cocaine, opiate, alcohol, and nicotine dependence (Health Line).[43]

The Hexing Drugs and Witchcraft

A number of natural plants contain chemicals that share a common feature: the ability to block the parasympathetic effects of acetylcholine in the body. The drugs with this ability, called *anticholinergic drugs,* produce specific physiological effects. The production of mucus in the nose and throat, as well as saliva in the mouth, is reduced. Body temperature is elevated, sometimes to very high fever levels. Heart rate and blood pressure go up, and the pupils dilate considerably. Psychological effects include a feeling of delirium, confusion, and generally a loss of memory for events occurring during the drugged state.[44] The amnesic property is one of the primary reasons for the minimal street appeal of these drugs.

The principal anticholinergic drugs are **atropine, scopolamine** (also called hyoscine), and **hyoscyamine.** They are found in various combinations and relative amounts in a large number of psychoactive plants. Four of the better known ones are examined here.

***Amanita muscaria* (a-ma-NEE-ta mus-CAR-ee-ah)**: A species of mushroom containing the hallucinogenic drug ibotenic acid.

ibogaine (IH-bo-gayn): A hallucinogenic drug originating from the West African iboga root.

atropine (At-tro-peen): An anticholinergic hallucinogenic drug derived from the *Atropa belladonna* plant.

scopolamine (scoh-POL-ah-meen): An anticholinergic hallucinogenic drug. Also called hyoscine.

hyoscyamine (HEYE-oh-SEYE-eh-meen): An anticholinergic hallucinogenic drug found in mandrake and henbane plants.

Health Line

Ibogaine: A Treatment Option for Drug Dependence?

There has been recent interest in the possibility that ibogaine is more than just a hallucinogen; it could also be useful in the treatment of drug-dependent individuals. The biochemistry of the drug and behavioral studies in animals are certainly intriguing. Ibogaine is an antagonist of receptors in the nucleus accumbens, an area of the brain known to be critical in establishing the reinforcing properties of many drugs of abuse (see Chapter 3). Ibogaine reduces the level of cocaine self-administration in rats by up to 60–80 percent and of morphine, alcohol, and nicotine self-administration to a lesser but significant degree. There has also been a reduction in opiate-withdrawal symptoms in animals after treatment with ibogaine.

Anecdotal reports with human subjects indicate that ibogaine can be useful in reducing feelings of craving for a range of drugs of abuse, possibly tied to the influence of ibogaine in the nucleus accumbens. However, research showing brain degeneration in the cerebellum of animals, as well as severe motor tremors, after ibogaine administration has caused the FDA to delay clinical trials with humans until further studies have been conducted. The fact that ibogaine is a powerful hallucinogen has also led to a reluctance among government officials to pursue its use in drug-abuse treatment. An ibogaine metabolite, noribogaine (pronounced nor-IH-bo-gayn), shows promise in avoiding some of the side effects of ibogaine itself, and it appears that the anti-craving effects of ibogaine in the brain are essentially due to this metabolite. Whether noribogaine produces the same effects on the cerebellum as ibogaine remains to be determined.

Sources: Baumann, Michael (1999, November). Comparative neurobiology of ibogaine and noribogaine. First International Conference on Ibogaine, New York University School of Medicine, New York. O'Hearn, Elizabeth, and Molliver, Mark E. (1997). The olivocerebellar projection mediates ibogaine-induced degeneration of Purkinje cells: A model of indirect, trans-synaptic excitotoxicity. *Journal of Neuroscience, 17,* 8828–8841. Popik, Piotr, and Glick, Stanley D. (1996). Ibogaine: A putatively anti-addictive alkaloid. *Drugs of the Future, 21,* 1109–1115.

- Atropine is principally derived from the ***Atropa belladonna*** plant, also called deadly nightshade. Its lethal reputation is quite justified, since it is estimated that ingesting only a dozen or so berries is sufficient for death to occur. Many recipes for poisons through history have been based on this plant. At lower, more benign dose levels, plant extracts can be applied to the eyes, causing the pupils to dilate. Egyptian and Roman women used this technique to enhance their beauty or at least improve their appearance. The term *belladonna* ("beautiful lady") originates from this application. The psychological effects of atropine are generally associated with the anticholinergic effects of heart-rate acceleration and general arousal.
- The **mandrake** plant is an oddly shaped potato-like plant with a long forked root that has traditionally been imagined to resemble a human body. In ancient times, mandrake was considered to have aphrodisiac properties. According to medieval folklore, mandrake plants supposedly shrieked when they were uprooted, understandably driving people mad.

  Mandrake contains a combination of atropine, scopolamine, and hyoscyamine. Because low doses act as a depressant, mandrake has been used as a sedative-hypnotic drug to relieve anxiety and induce sleep. At higher doses, it produces bizarre hallucinations and muscular paralysis.
- **Henbane** is a strong-smelling herb, native to widespread areas of the Northern Hemisphere, with purple-veined, yellowish flowers and hairy leaves. Its English name, meaning "harmful to hens," originates from the observation that henbane seeds were toxic to chickens and other birds. The lethal possibilities for henbane potions have been described by writers since the days of the Roman Empire. Hamlet's father in Shakespeare's play was supposedly murdered with henbane poison. Lower doses of henbane, however, have been used in a more benign way, as an anesthetic and

***Atropa belladonna* (a-TROH-pah BEL-ah-DON-ah):** A plant species, also called deadly nightshade, whose berries can be highly toxic. It is the principal source of atropine.
mandrake: A potato-like plant containing anticholinergic hallucinogenic drugs.
henbane: An herb containing anticholinergic hallucinogenic drugs.

QUICK CONCEPT  6.1

Understanding Variations in Hallucinogens

Check your understanding of the psychological differences among major hallucinogens by matching the hallucinatory experience (in the left column) with the hallucinogenic drug most apt to produce such effects (in the right column).

PSYCHOLOGICAL EXPERIENCE	HALLUCINOGEN
1. "The images I saw were Mexican designs as if they were created by an Aztec artist."	DMT LSD *Atropa belladonna*
2. "As I heard the bells, I also saw the vibrations move through the air."	ibogaine psilocybin
3. "The hallucinations were gone sixty minutes after they had started."	mescaline *Amanita muscaria*
4. "As I ate the red-topped mushrooms, I felt my muscles twitch. I could see vivid hallucinations."	
5. "I felt as if I were flying through the air."	

Answers: 1. psilocybin 2. LSD, principally 3. DMT 4. *Amanita muscaria* 5. *Atropa belladonna*

painkiller. We now know that the predominant drugs in henbane are scopolamine and hyoscyamine.

- Various species of the datura plant, containing a combination of atropine, scopolamine, and hyoscyamine, grow wild in locations throughout the world. In the United States, one particular species, ***Datura stramonium***, is called jimsonweed, a contraction of "Jamestown weed" (the name given to it by early American colonists). Consumption of the seeds or berries of jimsonweed produces hypnotic and hallucinogenic effects, together with disorientation, confusion, and amnesia. At high doses, jimsonweed is quite toxic. In recent years, there have been occasional reports of hospitalizations and even deaths among teenagers who have eaten jimsonweed seeds as an inexpensive way to get high.[45]

During medieval times, mixtures of deadly nightshade, mandrake, and henbane were major factors in the psychoactive effects of witches' potions, producing a disastrous combination of physiological and psychological effects. Satanic celebrations of the Black Mass centered on the ingestion of such brews. The atropine, in particular, produced a substantial elevation in arousal, probably leading to the feeling that the person was flying (or at least capable of it), while the hallucinogenic effects enabled the person to imagine communing with the Devil.[46] Witches were reputed to have prepared these mixtures as ointments and rubbed them on their bodies and on broomsticks, which they straddled. The chemicals would have been easily absorbed through the skin and the membranes of the vagina. The Halloween image of a witch flying on a broomstick has been with us ever since.

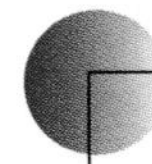

Phencyclidine (PCP)

Perhaps the most notorious of all the hallucinogens is **phencyclidine (PCP)**, often referred to as *angel dust.* The appearance of this drug from the miscellaneous group as an illicit drug in the late 1960s brought special problems to the already dangerous drug scene.

The weird combination of stimulant, depressant, and hallucinogenic effects makes PCP difficult to classify. Some textbooks treat the discussion of PCP in a chapter on hallucinogens, as is done here, whereas others include it in a chapter on stimulants because some features of PCP intoxication resemble the effect of cocaine, though its medical use has always been as a depressant. A growing consensus of opinion has it that PCP, because it produces a feeling of being dissociated or cut off from oneself and the environment, should be described as a *dissociative anesthetic hallucinogen.*[47]

History and Abuse of PCP

Technically PCP is a synthetic depressant, and it was originally introduced in 1963 as a depressant drug by the Parke-Davis pharmaceutical company, under the brand name of Sernyl. It was marketed as a promising new surgical anesthetic that had the advantage of not depressing

***Datura stramonium* (duh-TOOR-ah strah-MOH-nee-um)**: A species of the datura family of plants with hallucinogenic properties. In the United States, the plant is called jimsonweed.
phencyclidine (PCP) (fen-SEYE-klih-deen): A dissociative anesthetic hallucinogen that produces disorientation, agitation, aggressive behavior, analgesia, and amnesia. It has various street names, including angel dust.

respiration or blood pressure or causing heart-beat irregularities like other anesthetics. In addition, PCP had a higher therapeutic ratio than many other anesthetics available at that time. By 1965, however, it was withdrawn from human applications after reports that nearly half of all patients receiving PCP showed signs of delirium, disorientation, hallucinations, intense anxiety, or agitation. For a time, PCP was used for animal anesthesia, but this application ended by the late 1970s. In 1979, PCP was classified as a Schedule I drug.

PCP can be taken orally, intravenously, or by inhalation, but commonly it is smoked either alone or in combination with other drugs. Whatever its mode of administration, the results are extremely dangerous, with an unpredictability that far exceeds that of LSD or other hallucinogens. The symptoms may include manic excitement, depression, severe anxiety, sudden mood changes, disordered and confused thought, paranoid thoughts, and unpredictable aggression. Because PCP has analgesic properties as well, individuals taking the drug often feel invulnerable to threats against them and may be willing and able to withstand considerable pain.

Hallucinations also occur, but they are quite different from the hallucinations experienced under the influence of LSD. There are no colorful images, no intermingling of sight and sound, no mystical sense of being "one with the world." Instead, a prominent feature of PCP-induced hallucinations is the change in one's body image. As one PCP abuser has expressed it,

> *The most frequent hallucination is that parts of your body are extremely large or extremely small. You can imagine yourself small enough to walk through a key hole, or you can be lying there and all of a sudden you just hallucinate that your arm is twice the length of your body.*[48]

Individuals under the influence of PCP may also stagger, speak in a slurred way, and feel depersonalized or detached from people around them. A prominent feature is a prolonged visual stare, often called "doll's eyes."

The effects of PCP last from as little as a few hours to as long as two weeks, and they are followed by partial or total amnesia and dissociation from the entire experience. Considering these bizarre reactions, it is not surprising that PCP deaths occur more frequently from the behavioral consequences of the PCP experience than from its physiological effects. Suicides, accidental or intentional mutilations, drownings (sometimes in very small amounts of water), falls, and threatening behavior leading to the individual's being shot are only some of the possible consequences.[49]

Patterns of PCP Abuse

It is strange that a drug with so many adverse effects would be subject to deliberate abuse, but such is the case with PCP. Reports of PCP abuse began surfacing in 1967 among the hippie community in San Francisco, where it became known as the PeaCe Pill. Word quickly spread that PCP did not live up to its name. Inexperienced PCP abusers were suffering the same bizarre effects as had the clinical patients earlier in the decade. By 1969, PCP had been written off as a garbage drug, and it dropped out of sight as a drug of abuse.

In the early 1970s, PCP returned under new street names and in new forms (Table 6.2). No longer a pill to be taken orally, PCP was now in powdered or liquid form. Powdered PCP could be added to parsley, mint, oregano, tobacco, or marijuana, rolled as a cigarette, and smoked.[50] Liquid PCP could be used to soak leaf mixtures of all types, including manufactured cigarettes, which could then be dried and smoked. Many new users have turned to PCP as a way to boost the effects of marijuana. Making matters worse, as many as 120 different designer-drug variations of PCP have been developed in illicit laboratories around the country and the world. The dangers of PCP abuse, therefore, are complicated by the difficulty in knowing whether or not a street drug has been adulterated with PCP and what version of PCP may be present.

The DAWN statistics have given us some idea of the demographic features of the PCP abuser who ends up receiving emergency treatment: predominantly male (64 percent), between eighteen and thirty-four years old

TABLE 6.2

Street names for phencyclidine (PCP) and PCP-like drugs

PCP	jet fuel
angel dust	sherms (derived from the reaction that it hits you like a Sherman tank)
monkey dust	superkools
peep	cyclones
supergrass	zombie dust
killer weed	ketamine
ozone	special K
embalming fluid	
rocket fuel	

Note: In the illicit drug market, PCP and ketamine are frequently misrepresented and sold as mescaline, LSD, marijuana, amphetamine, or cocaine.

Source: Milburn, H. Thomas (1991). Diagnosis and management of phencyclidine intoxication. *American Family Physician, 43,* 1293.

QUICK CONCEPT  6.2

Understanding PCP

Check your understanding of the effects of PCP by listing three major features of PCP intoxication that are significantly different from the effects of other hallucinogens.

Answer: Correct responses can include any of the following: analgesia, amnesia, prolonged stare, absence of synesthesia, absence of mysticism, unpredictable aggression, extreme disorientation, feelings of being cut off from oneself or the environment.

(61 percent), and a large proportion dependent on PCP (26 percent). Amazingly, some regular PCP abusers have managed to avoid medical-care facilities, even as they mix PCP with alcohol or marijuana, combinations that only add to the unpredictability of the final result.[51]

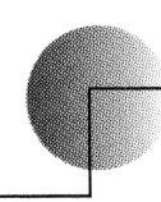

Ketamine

Ketamine, a drug chemically similar to PCP, is also classified as a dissociative anesthetic hallucinogen. Like PCP, ketamine has a mixture of stimulant and depressive properties, though its depressive effect is more extreme and does not last as long as that of PCP. Ketamine was used as an emergency surgical anesthetic on the battlefield in Vietnam as well as in standard hospital-based operations in which gaseous anesthetics could not be employed. It has also been used occasionally in short surgical procedures involving the head and neck or in the treatment of facial burns where it is not possible to use an anesthetic mask. Adverse side effects, however, have limited its therapeutic use. These problems include unpredictable and sometimes violent jerking and twitching of the body, as well as vivid and unpleasant dreams during and after surgery. During recovery, patients may experience hallucinations and feelings of disorientation. Delayed effects of ketamine, such as nightmares, have been reported to occur for weeks or longer after surgery.[52]

Ketamine abuse began to be reported in the 1980s. More recently, under the names "Special K" and "Vitamin K," it has been included among current club drugs on the scene (see Chapter 1). Its popularity has increased among college students and patrons of dance clubs and all-night rave parties. Like PCP, ketamine produces a dream-like intoxication, accompanied by an inability to move or feel pain. There are also experiences of dizziness, confusion, and slurred speech. As is the case with dissociative hallucinogens, ketamine produces amnesia, in that abusers frequently cannot later remember what has happened while under its influence. The primary hazard of acute ketamine ingestion is the depression of breathing. Little is known, however, of the chronic effects of extended ketamine abuse over time, except that experiences of "flashbacks" have been reported.[53]

As with other club drugs that produce depressive effects on the central nervous system, there is the dangerous potential for ketamine to be abused as a "date-rape" drug. Women who may unwittingly take the drug can be rendered incapacitated, without the ability to recall the experience. In 1999, ketamine became classified as a Schedule III controlled substance.[54]

ketamine (KET-ah-meen): A dissociative anesthetic hallucinogen related to phencyclidine (PCP).

SUMMARY

A Matter of Definition

- Hallucinogens are, by definition, drugs that produce distortions of perception and of the sense of reality. These drugs have also been called psychedelic ("mind-expanding") drugs. In some cases, users of hallucinogens feel that they have been transported to a new reality.
- Other classes of drugs may produce hallucinations at high dose levels, but hallucinogens produce these effects at low or moderate dose levels.

Classifying Hallucinogens

- Hallucinogens can be classified in four basic groups. The first three relate to the chemical similarity between the particular drug and one of three major neurotransmitters: serotonin, norepinephrine, or acetylcholine.
- The fourth, miscellaneous group includes synthetic hallucinogens, such as phencyclidine (PCP) and ketamine, which bear little resemblance to any known neurotransmitter.

Lysergic Acid Diethylamide (LSD)

- Lysergic acid diethylamide (LSD), the best-known hallucinogenic drug, belongs to the serotonin group. It is synthetically derived from ergot, a toxic rye fungus that has been documented as being responsible for thousands of deaths over the centuries.
- Albert Hofmann synthesized LSD in 1943, and Timothy Leary led the psychedelic movement in the 1960s that popularized LSD use.
- Though the LSD experience is often unpredictable, certain features are commonly observed: colorful hallucinations, synesthesia in which sounds often appear as visions, a distortion of perceptual reality, emotional swings, a feeling of timelessness, and an illusory separation of mind from body.
- It is now known that LSD affects a subtype of brain receptors sensitive to serotonin, referred to as S_2 receptors.
- Since the early 1990s, there has been a resurgence in LSD abuse, particularly among young individuals.

Facts and Fictions about LSD

- LSD does not produce psychological or physical dependence and has only a slight chance of inducing a panic or psychotic state (providing that there is a supportive setting for the taking of LSD).
- LSD does not elevate one's level of creativity, does not damage chromosomes (though there remains a chance of birth defects if LSD is ingested when pregnant), and a relationship between LSD abuse and violent behavior has not been established. Flashback experiences, however, are potential hazards.

Psilocybin and Other Hallucinogens Related to Serotonin

- Other hallucinogens related to serotonin are psilocybin, lysergic acid amide (LAA), dimethyltryptamine (DMT), and harmine.

Hallucinogens Related to Norepinephrine

- Mescaline is chemically related to norepinephrine, even though S_2 receptors are responsible for its hallucinogenic effects.
- Two synthetic hallucinogens, DOM and MDMA, are variations of the amphetamine molecule. MDMA (Ecstasy) is currently a popular club drug, but research studies indicate that it poses serious neurological risks to the user.

Hallucinogens Related to Acetylcholine

- A number of anticholinergic hallucinogens, so named because they diminish the effects of acetylcholine in the parasympathetic nervous system, have been involved in sorcery and witchcraft since the Middle Ages.
- These so-called hexing drugs contain a combination of atropine, scopolamine, and/or hyoscyamine. Sources for such drugs include the deadly nightshade plant, mandrake roots, henbane seeds, and the datura plant family.

Phencyclidine (PCP) and Ketamine

- A dangerous form of hallucinogen abuse involves phencyclidine (PCP). Originally a psychedelic street drug in the 1960s, PCP quickly developed a reputation for producing a number of adverse reactions.
- PCP reappeared in the early 1970s, in smokable forms either alone or in combination with marijuana. Extremely aggressive tendencies, as well as behaviors resembling acute schizophrenia, have been associated with PCP intoxication.
- Ketamine is popular as a club drug and produces a dream-like intoxication, accompanied by an inability to move or feel pain. Like PCP, ketamine also produces amnesia and potentially a depression in breathing.

KEY TERMS

Amanita muscaria, p. 139
Atropa belladonna, p. 140
atropine, p. 139
bufotenine, p. 136
cyanosis, p. 136
Datura stramonium, p. 141
dimethyltryptamine (DMT), p. 135
DOM, p. 137
ergot, p. 127
ergotism, p. 127
hallucinogens, p. 125
harmine, p. 128
henbane, p. 140
hyoscyamine, p. 139
ibogaine, p. 139
ketamine, p. 143
lysergic acid amide (LAA), p. 135
lysergic acid diethylamide (LSD), p. 125
mandrake, p. 140
MDMA (Ecstasy), p. 138
mescaline, p. 136
peyote, p. 136
phencyclidine (PCP), p. 141
psilocin, p. 135
psilocybin, p. 134
scopolamine, p. 139
synesthesia, p. 131

ENDNOTES

1. Hofmann, Albert (1980). *LSD: My problem child.* New York: McGraw-Hill, p. 17.
2. Ibid., pp. 17–18.
3. Ibid., p. 19.
4. Brophy, James J. (1985). Psychiatric disorders. In Marcus A. Krupp, Milton J. Chatton, and David Werdegar (Eds.), *Current medical diagnosis and treatment.* Los Altos CA: Lange Medical Publication, p. 674.
5. Mann, John (1992). *Murder, magic, and medicine.* New York: Oxford University Press, pp. 41–51.
6. Fuller, John G. (1968). *The day of St. Anthony's fire.* New York: Macmillan, preface.
7. Leary, Timothy (1973). The religious experience: Its production and interpretation. In Gunther Weil, Ralph Metzner, and Timothy Leary (Eds.), *The psychedelic reader.* Secaucus NJ: Citadel Press, p. 191.
8. Lee, Martin A., and Shlain, Bruce (1985). *Acid dreams: The complete social history of LSD.* New York: Grove Weidenfeld, pp. 71–118.
9. Leary, Timothy (1968). *High priest.* New York: New American Library, p. 46.
10. Grinspoon, Lester, and Bakalar, James B. (1979). *Psychedelic drugs reconsidered.* New York: Basic Books, p. 68.
11. Brown, F. Christine (1972). *Hallucinogenic drugs.* Springfield IL: C. C. Thomas, pp. 46–49. Goode, Erich (1999). *Drugs and American society* (5th ed.). New York: McGraw-Hill College, p. 224.
12. Schuckit, Marc A. (1995). *Drug and alcohol abuse: A clinical guide to diagnosis and treatment* (4th ed.). New York: Plenum, pp. 189–190.
13. Jacobs, Michael R., and Fehr, Kevin O'B. (1987). *Drugs and drug abuse: A reference text* (2nd ed.). Toronto: Addiction Research Foundation, p. 345. Substance Abuse and Mental Health Services Administration (2000). *Drug Abuse Warning Network annual emergency department data 1998.* Rockville MD: Substance Abuse and Mental Health Services Administration, Office of Applied Studies, p. 39.
14. Brophy, Psychiatric disorders. Jacobs and Fehr, *Drugs and drug abuse,* pp. 337–347.
15. Goode, *Drugs and American society,* pp. 245–249. Snyder, Solomon H. (1986). *Drugs and the brain.* New York: Freeman, pp. 180–181.
16. Aghajanian, G. K. and Marek, G. J. (1999). Serotonin and hallucinogens. *Neuropsychopharmacology, 21 (Suppl. 2),* 16S–23S. Jacobs, Barry J. (1987). How hallucinogenic drugs work. *American Scientist, 75,* 386–392. Snyder, *Drugs and the brain,* pp. 195–205.
17. Goode, *Drugs and American society,* pp. 254–255.
18. Brands, Bruna, Sproule, Beth, and Marshman, Joan (1998). *Drugs and drug abuse: A reference text.* Toronto, Canada: Addiction Research Foundation, p. 328. Henderson, Leigh A., and Glass, William J. (Eds.) (1994). *LSD: Still with us after all these years.* New York: Lexington Books. Johnston, Lloyd D. (2000, December 14). "Ecstasy" use rises sharply among teens in 2000; use of many other drugs stays steady, but significant declines are reported for some. News release from the University of Michigan, Ann Arbor, Table 1. Karch, Steven B. (1996). *The pathology of drug abuse* (2nd ed.). Boca Raton FL: CRC Press, p. 269.
19. Goode, *Drugs and American society,* p. 256.
20. Ibid., p. 256.
21. Cohen, Sidney (1960). Lysergic acid diethylamide: Side effects and complications. *Journal of Nervous and Mental Diseases, 130,* 30–40. Levine, Jerome, and Ludwig, Arnold M. (1964). The LSD controversy. *Comprehensive Psychiatry,* 5 (5), 314–321.
22. Wells, Brian (1974). *Psychedelic drugs: Psychological, medical, and social issues.* New York: Jason Aronson, pp. 170–188.
23. Cohen, M. M., and Marmillo, M. J. (1967). Chromosomal damage in human leukocytes induced by lysergic acid diethylamide. *Science, 155,* 1417–1419.
24. Dishotsky, Norman I.; Loughman, William D.; Mogar, Robert E.; and Lipscomb, Wendell R. (1971). LSD and genetic damage. *Science, 172,* 431–440. Grinspoon and Bakalar, *Psychedelic drugs reconsidered,* pp. 188–191.
25. Brown, *Hallucinogenic drugs,* pp. 61–64. Wells, *Psychedelic drugs,* pp. 104–109.
26. Abraham, Henry D. (1983). Visual phenomenology of the LSD flashback. *Archives of General Psychiatry, 40,* 884–889. Frosh, William A. (1969). Patterns of response to self-administration of LSD. In Roger E. Meyer (Ed.), *Adverse reactions to hallucinogenic drugs.* Washington DC: Public Health Service. Schlaadt, Richard G., and Shannon, Peter T. (1994). *Drugs: Use, misuse, and abuse.* Englewood Cliffs NJ: Prentice Hall, p. 273.
27. Halpern, John H., and Pope, Harrison G. (1999). Do hallucinogens cause residual neuropsychological toxicity? *Drugs and Alcohol Dependence,* 53, 247–256.
28. Knudsen, Knud (1964). Homicide after treatment with lysergic acid diethylamide. *Acta Psychiatrica Scandinavica, 40* (Supplement 180), 389–395.
29. Metzner, Ralph (1998). Hallucinogenic drugs and plants in psychotherapy and shamanism. *Journal of Psychoactive Drugs,* 30, 333–341.
30. Hofmann, *LSD,* p. 112.
31. Brown, *Hallucinogenic drugs,* pp. 81–88.
32. Johnston, "Ecstasy" use, Table 13. Vollenweider, Franz X.; Vollenweider-Scherpenhuyzen, Margaret F. I.; Babler, Andreas; Vogel, Helen; and Hell, Daniel (1998). Psilocybin induces schizophrenia-like psychosis in humans via a serotonin-2 agonist action. *Neuroreport,* 9, 3897–3902.
33. Hofmann, *LSD,* pp. 119–127. Schultes, Richard E., and Hofmann, Albert (1979). *Plants of the gods: Origins of hallucinogenic use.* New York: McGraw-Hill, pp. 158–163.
34. Brands, Sproule, and Marshman, *Drugs and drug abuse,* pp. 512–513.
35. Grinspoon and Bakalar, *Psychedelic drugs reconsidered,* pp. 14–15.

36. Ibid., pp. 20–21. Hollister, Leo E., and Sjoberg, Bernard M. (1964). Clinical syndromes and biochemical alterations following mescaline, lysergic acid diethylamide, psilocybin, and a combination of the three psychotomimetic drugs. *Comprehensive Psychiatry, 5,* 170–178.
37. Jacobs, *How hallucinogenic drugs work,* pp. 386–392.
38. Brecher, Edward, and the editors of *Consumer Reports* (1972). *Licit and illicit drugs.* Boston: Little, Brown, pp. 376–377.
39. Metzner, Hallucinogenic drugs and plants. Schmidt, C. J. (1987). Psychedelic amphetamine, methylendioxymethamphetamine. *Journal of Pharmacology and Experimental Therapeutics, 240,* 1–7.
40. Cloud, John (2000, June 5). The lure of ecstasy. *Time,* pp. 62–68. Feuer, Alan (2000, August 6). Distilling the truth in the ecstasy buzz. *New York Times,* pp. 25, 28. Johnston, "Ecstasy" use, Table 1. Schwartz, Richard H., and Miller, Norman S. (1997). MDMA (Ecstasy) and the rave: A review. *Pediatrics, 100,* 705–708.
41. Boils, Karen I. (1999). Memory impairment in abstinent MDMA ("Ecstasy") users. *Journal of the American Medical Association, 281,* 494. Kish, Stephen J.; Furukawa, Yoshiaki; Ang, Lee C.; Vorce, Shawn P.; and Kalasinsky, Kathryn S. (2000). Striatal serotonin is depleted in brain of a human MDMA (Ecstasy) user. *Neurology, 55,* 294–296. Morgan, Michael J. (1999). Memory deficits associated with recreational use of "ecstasy" (MDMA). *Psychopharmacology, 141,* 30–36. Rella, J. G., Nelson, L. S., and Hoffman, R. S. (1999). 5 years of 3,4-methylenedioxymethamphetamine (MDMA) toxicity. *Journal of Toxicology: Clinical Toxicology,* 37, 648. Study finds brain damage from use of Ecstasy (1999, June 28). *Alcoholism and Drug Abuse Weekly,* p. 7.
42. Wasson, R. Gordon (1968). *Soma: Divine mushroom of immortality.* New York: Harcourt, Brace and World.
43. Cohen, Sidney (1964). *The beyond within: The LSD story.* New York: Atheneum, p. 17. Popik, Piotr, and Glick, Stanley D. (1996). Ibogaine: A putatively anti-addictive alkaloid. *Drugs of the Future, 21,* 1109–1115.
44. Levinthal, Charles F. (1990). *Introduction to physiological psychology* (3rd ed.). Englewood Cliffs NJ: Prentice Hall, pp. 157–158.
45. Freedman, Mitchell (1994, October 15). One teen's tale of jimsonweed. *Newsday,* p. A14. Schultes and Hofmann, *Plants of the gods,* pp. 106–111.
46. Schultes and Hofmann, *Plants of the gods,* pp. 86–91.
47. Julien, Robert M. (2001). *A primer of drug action* (9th ed.). New York: Worth, pp. 353–359.
48. James, Jennifer, and Andresen, Elena (1979). Sea-Tac and PCP. In Harvey V. Feldman, Michael H. Agar, and George M. Beschner (Eds.), *Angel dust: An ethnographic study of PCP users.* Lexington MA: Lexington Books, p. 133.
49. Grinspoon and Bakalar, *Psychedelic drugs reconsidered,* pp. 32–33. Petersen, Robert C., and Stillman, Richard C. (1978). Phencyclidine: An overview. In Robert C. Petersen and Richard C. Stillman (Eds.), *Phencyclidine (PCP) abuse: An appraisal* (NIDA Research Monograph 21). Rockville MD: National Institute on Drug Abuse, pp. 1–17. Robbins, *Hallucinogens,* pp. 12–14.
50. Linder, Ronald L., Lerner, Steven E., and Burns, R. Stanley (1981). *PCP: The devil's dust.* Belmont CA: Wadsworth, pp. 2–19. Zukin, Stephen, Sloboda, Zili, and Javitt, Daniel C. (1997). Phencyclidine (PCP). In Joyce H. Lowinson, Pedro Ruiz, Robert B. Millman, and John G. Langrod (Eds.), *Substance abuse: A comprehensive textbook.* Baltimore MD: Williams and Wilkins, pp. 238–246.
51. Substance Abuse and Mental Health Services Administration (1999). *Drug Abuse Warning Network annual emergency department data 1997.* Rockville MD: Substance Abuse and Mental Health Services Administration, Office of Applied Studies, pp. 44–46.
52. Brands, Sproule, and Marshman, *Drugs and drug abuse,* pp. 523–525.
53. Ibid.
54. Feds classify ketamine as controlled substance (1999, August 2). *Alcoholism and Drug Abuse Weekly,* p. 7.

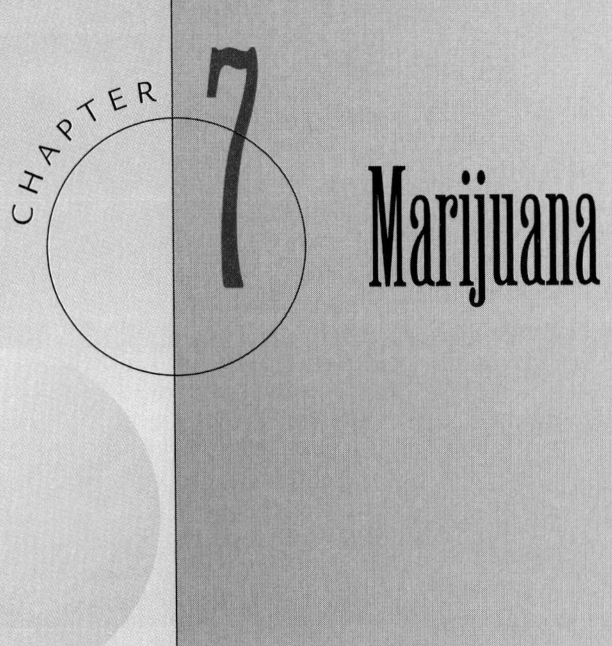

Marijuana

After you have completed this chapter, you will understand

- The history of marijuana and other cannabis products
- Acute effects of marijuana
- The neural basis for marijuana effects
- Long-term effects of marijuana
- The amotivational syndrome and the gateway theory
- Medical applications of marijuana
- Patterns of marijuana abuse
- The question of marijuana decriminalization

The cannabis plant is a scrawny thing, a fighter of a plant. “It needs little care to thrive . . . ,” researcher Ernest Abel has said. “It is ubiquitous. It flourishes under nearly every possible climatic condition. It sprouts from the earth not meekly . . . but defiantly, arrogantly, confident that whatever the conditions it has the stamina to survive.”

It might be fair to characterize *Cannabis sativa*, the source of marijuana, as a weed with an attitude. Whether it is hot or cold, wet or dry, cannabis will grow abundantly from seeds that are unbelievably hardy and prolific. A handful of cannabis seeds, tossed on the ground and pressed in with one's foot, will usually anchor and become plants. Its roots devour whatever nutrients there are in the soil, like a vampire sucking the life blood from the earth.[1]

It is not surprising that, as a result, marijuana has managed to grow in some unorthodox places. It can be found in median strips of interstate highways or in ditches alongside country roads. The top prize for most unusual location, assuming the story is accurate, has to go to a variety known as Manhattan Silver. Reportedly, it originated from cannabis seeds flushed down a New York sewer during a sudden police raid in the 1960s. Once the seeds hit the sewer, they produced a plant that, in the absence of light, grew silverish white leaves instead of green, hence its name.[2]

Considering its botanical source, it is fitting that the psychological and physiological effects of marijuana should show something of an independent nature as well. It is not easy to place marijuana within a classification of psychoactive drugs. When we consider a category for marijuana, we are faced with an odd assortment of unconnected properties. Marijuana produces some excitatory effects, but it is not generally regarded as a stimulant. It produces some sedative effects, but a person faces no risk of slipping into a coma or dying. It produces mild analgesic effects, but it is not related pharmacologically to opiates or opiate-like drugs. It produces hallucinations at high doses, but its structure does not resemble LSD or any other drug formally categorized as a hallucinogen. Marijuana is clearly a hybrid drug, in a league of its own.

Few other drugs have been so politicized in recent history as marijuana. It is frequently praised by one side or condemned by the other, on the basis of emotional issues rather than an objective view of research data. The pro-marijuana faction tends to dismiss reports of potential dangers and emphasize the benefits; the antimarijuana faction tends to do the opposite, pointing out that marijuana continues to be a Schedule I controlled substance, along with heroin and LSD. Marijuana has often been regarded, over the last thirty years or so, not only as simply a drug with psychoactive properties but also as a symbol of an individual's attitude toward the establishment. This makes it even more critical that we look at the effects of marijuana as dispassionately as possible.

A Mexican harvester gathers his crop of Cannabis sativa, *later to be processed into marijuana or hashish.*

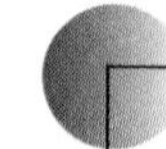

A Matter of Terminology

Marijuana (sometimes spelled *marihuana*) is frequently referred to as a synonym for cannabis, but technically the two terms are separate. Cannabis is the botanical term for the hemp plant ***Cannabis sativa***. With a potential height of about eighteen feet, cannabis has sturdy stalks, four-cornered in cross-section, that have been commercially valuable for thousands of years in the manufacture of rope, twine, shoes, sailcloth, and containers of all kinds. Pots made of hemp fiber discovered at archaeological sites in China date the origins of cannabis cultivation as far back as the Stone Age. It is arguably the oldest cultivated plant not used for food.[3]

Spaniards brought cannabis to the New World in 1545, and English settlers brought it to Jamestown, Virginia, in 1611, where it became a major commercial crop, along with tobacco. Like other eighteenth-century farmers in the region, George Washington grew cannabis in the fields of his estate at Mount Vernon. Entries in his

***Cannabis sativa* (CAN-uh-bus sah-TEE-vah)**: A plant species, commonly called hemp, from which marijuana and hashish are obtained.

diary indicate that he maintained a keen interest in cultivating better strains of cannabis, but there is no reason to believe he was interested in anything more than a better-quality rope.

Marijuana is obtained not from the stalks of the cannabis plant but from its serrated leaves. The key psychoactive factor is contained in a sticky substance, or resin, that accumulates on these leaves. Depending on the growing conditions, cannabis will produce either a greater amount of resin or a greater amount of fiber. In a hot, dry climate, such as North Africa, for example, the fiber content is weak, but so much resin is produced that the plant looks as if it is covered with dew. In a cooler, more humid climate, such as North America, less resin is produced, but the fiber is stronger and more durable.[4]

As many as eighty separate chemical compounds, called **cannabinoids,** can be extracted specifically from cannabis resin. Among these, the chief psychoactive compound and the active ingredient that produces the intoxicating effects is **delta-9-tetrahydrocannabinol (THC)**. The isolation and identification of THC in 1964 was a major step toward understanding the effects on the brain of marijuana and similar preparations obtained from *Cannabis sativa.*

Knowing these facts, we are now in a position to categorize various forms of cannabis products in terms of the origin within the cannabis plant and the relative THC concentration. The first and best-known of these products, **marijuana,** consists of leaves and occasionally flowers of the cannabis plant that are first dried and then shredded. During the 1960s and 1970s, the typical THC concentration of street marijuana imported from Mexico was about 1 to 2 percent; more recently, marijuana has been imported principally from Colombia and other South American countries and contains a THC concentration of about 4 percent. Marijuana, smoked as a cigarette, is the form of cannabis most familiar to North Americans.

A more potent form of marijuana, originating in California and Hawaii, is obtained by cultivating only the unpollinated, or seedless, portion of the cannabis plant. Without pollination, the cannabis plant grows bushier, the resin content is increased, and a greater THC concentration, as high as 6 percent, is achieved. This form is called **sinsemilla,** from the Spanish meaning "without seeds."

Still stronger is a form in which the resin itself is scraped from cannabis flowers, dried, and either smoked by itself or in combination with tobacco. This form, called **hashish,** has a THC concentration of 8 to 14 percent and is commonly available in Europe, Asia, and the Middle East. The most potent forms of cannabis are **hashish oil** and **hashish oil crystals,** produced by boiling hashish in alcohol or some other solvent, filtering out the alcohol, and leaving a residue with a THC concentration ranging from 15 to 60 percent.[5]

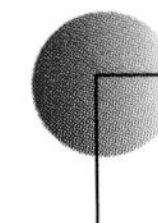

The History of Marijuana and Hashish

The first direct reference to a cannabis product as a psychoactive agent dates from 2737 B.C., in the writings of the mythical Chinese emperor Shen Nung. The focus was on its powers as a medication for rheumatism, gout, malaria, and, strangely enough, absent-mindedness.[6] Mention was made of its intoxicating properties, but the medicinal possibilities evidently were considered more important. In India, however, its use was clearly recreational. The most popular form, in ancient times as well as in the present day, can be found in a liquid made from cannabis leaves called **bhang,** with a potency usually equal to that of a marijuana cigarette in the United States.

The Muslim world also grew to appreciate the psychoactive potential of cannabis, encouraged by the fact that, in contrast to its stern prohibition of alcohol

cannabinoids (CAN-a-bih-noyds): Any of several dozen active substances in marijuana and other cannabis products.

delta-9-tetrahydrocannabinol (THC) (DEL-tah 9-TEH-trah-HEYE-dro-CAN-a-bih-nol): The active psychoactive ingredient in marijuana and hashish.

marijuana: The most commonly available psychoactive drug originating from the cannabis plant. The THC concentration ranges from approximately 1 to 4 percent. Also spelled marihuana.

sinsemilla: A form of marijuana obtained from the unpollinated or seedless portion of the cannabis plant. It has a higher THC concentration than regular marijuana, as high as 6 percent.

hashish (hah-SHEESH): A drug containing the resin of cannabis flowers. The THC concentration ranges from approximately 8 to 14 percent.

hashish oil: A drug produced by boiling hashish, leaving a potent psychoactive residue. The THC concentration ranges from approximately 15 to 60 percent.

hashish oil crystals: A solid form of hashish oil.

bhang: A liquid form of marijuana popular in India.

consumption, the Koran did not specifically ban its use. It was here in a hot, dry climate conducive to maximizing the resin content of cannabis that hashish was born, and its popularity spread quickly during the twelfth century from Persia (Iran) in the east to North Africa in the west.

Hashish in the Nineteenth Century

In Western Europe knowledge about hashish or any other cannabis product was limited until the beginning of the nineteenth century. Judging from the decree made by Pope Innocent VIII in 1484 condemning witchcraft and the use of hemp in the Black Mass, we can assume that the psychoactive potential of cannabis was known by some portions of the population. Nonetheless, there is no evidence of widespread use.

By about 1800, however, cannabis had become more widely known and the subject of a popular craze. One reason was that French soldiers who had served in Napoleon's military campaigns in Egypt brought hashish back with them to their homes in France. Another reason was a wave of romanticism that swept Europe, including an increased interest in exotic stories of the East, notably the *Arabian Nights* and the tales of Marco Polo, which contained references to hashish. In Paris during the 1840s, a small group of prominent French artists, writers, and intellectuals formed the Club des Hachichins ("Club of the Hashish-Eaters"), where they would gather, in the words of their leader, "to talk of literature, art, and love" while consuming large quantities of hashish. The mixture consisted of a concentrated hemp paste, mixed with butter, sweeteners, and flavorings such as vanilla and cinnamon. Members included Victor Hugo, Alexandre Dumas, Charles Baudelaire, and Honoré de Balzac.

Marijuana and Hashish in the Twentieth Century

Chances are that anyone living in the United States at the beginning of the twentieth century would not have heard of marijuana, much less hashish. By 1890, cotton had replaced hemp as a major cash crop in southern states, although cannabis plants continued to grow wild along roadsides and in the fields. Some patent medicines during this era contained marijuana, but it was a small percentage compared with the number containing opium or cocaine.[7]

It was not until the 1920s that marijuana began to be a noticeable phenomenon. Some historians have related the appearance of marijuana as a recreational drug to social changes brought on by Prohibition, when it was suddenly difficult to obtain good-quality liquor at affordable prices. Its recreational use was largely restricted to jazz musicians and people in show business. "Reefer songs" became the rage of the jazz world; even the mainstream clarinetist and bandleader Benny Goodman had his popular hit "Sweet Marihuana Brown." Marijuana clubs, called tea pads, sprang up in the major cities; more than five hundred were estimated in Harlem alone, outnumbering the speakeasies where illegal alcohol was dispensed. These marijuana establishments were largely tolerated by the authorities because at that time marijuana was not illegal and patrons showed no evidence of making a nuisance of themselves or disturbing the community. Marijuana was not considered a social threat.[8]

The Antimarijuana Crusade

This picture started to change by the end of the 1920s and early 1930s. Even though millions of people had never heard of the plant, much less smoked it, marijuana became widely publicized as a "killer weed." The antimarijuana campaign, encouraged by the Federal Bureau of Narcotics (see Chapter 2), was so intense that the American public soon came to view marijuana as a pestilence singlehandedly destroying a generation of American youth.

How did this transformation occur? In order to understand the way in which marijuana smoking went from a localized, negligible quirk to a national social issue, we have to look at some important changes in American society that were taking place at the time.

The practice of smoking marijuana and the cultivation of cannabis plants for that purpose had been filtering slowly into the United States since 1900 as a result of the migration of Mexican immigrants. They entered the country through towns along the Mexican border and along the Gulf Coast. In Mexican communities, marijuana was, in the words of one historian, "a casual adjunct to life . . . —a relaxant, a folk remedy for headaches, a mild euphoriant cheaply obtained for two cigarettes for the dollar."[9]

It is no exaggeration to say that these immigrant communities were met with hostility and prejudice, and the smoking of an alien and foreign-sounding substance did not smooth their reception. In effect, it was a social rerun of the Chinese-opium panic of the 1880s (see Chapter 5) but with the Mexicans on the receiving end. Rumors about the violent behavioral consequences of marijuana smoking among Mexicans began to spread, largely unchallenged by objective data. In addition, economic upheavals during the Depression made it particularly convenient to vent frustrations on immigrant communities that were perceived as competing for a dwindling number of American jobs and straining an already weak economy.

Considering the hysteria against marijuana smoking and cannabis use in general, it is not surprising that the Marijuana Tax Act of 1937 had little difficulty in gaining support in Congress. Like the Harrison Act of 1914, the regulation of marijuana was accomplished indirectly. The act did not ban marijuana; it merely required everyone connected with marijuana, from growers to buyers, to pay a tax. It was a deceptively simple procedure that, in effect, made it virtually impossible to comply with the law. In the absence of compliance, a person was in violation of the act and therefore subject to arrest. It was the state's responsibility to make possession of marijuana or any other product of *Cannabis sativa* illegal. Shortly after the tax act of 1937 was imposed, all of the states adopted a uniform law that did just that.

During the rest of the 1940s and 1950s, marijuana research was virtually at a standstill. The theory that marijuana was connected with violence slowly faded away, only to be replaced with a new concept, advanced by the FBN: the gateway theory. According to this idea, marijuana was purported to be dangerous because its abuse would lead to the abuse of heroin, cocaine, or other illicit drugs. This gateway hypothesis will be examined later in the chapter.

While marijuana research declined, penalties for involvement with it steadily increased. In certain states, the penalties were severe. Judges frequently had the option of sentencing a marijuana seller or user to life imprisonment. In Georgia, a second offense of selling marijuana to a minor could be punishable by death.

Ironically, in 1969, more than three decades after its passage, the U.S. Supreme Court ruled the 1937 Marijuana Tax Act to be unconstitutional precisely because marijuana possession was illegal. The argument was made that requiring a person to pay a tax (and that was all that the 1937 act concerned) in order to possess an illegal substance amounted to a form of self-incrimination, which would be a specific violation of the Fifth Amendment to the Constitution. It turns out that the case in question here was brought to the high court by none other than Timothy Leary (see Chapter 6), and the court's decision succeeded in overturning a marijuana conviction judged against him.[10]

The 1968 rally at Hyde Park in London was one of many held in support of the legalization of marijuana.

Challenging Old Ideas about Marijuana

Prior to 1960, arrests and seizures for possession of marijuana were relatively rare and attracted little or no public attention. The social consensus was that marijuana was a drug that could be comfortably associated with, and isolated to, ethnic and racial minorities. It was relatively easy for most Americans to avoid the drug entirely. In any event, until 1960, involvement with marijuana was a deviant act, during an era when there was little tolerance for personal deviance.

By the mid-1960s, this consensus began to dissolve. Marijuana smoking was suddenly an attraction on the campuses of U.S. colleges and universities, affecting a wide cross-section of the nation. At the same time, the experimental use of drugs, particularly marijuana, by young people set the stage for a wholesale questioning of what it meant to respect authority, on an individual as well as governmental level.

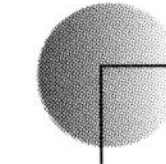

Acute Effects of Marijuana

In the United States, THC is usually ingested by smoking a hand-rolled marijuana cigarette referred to as a **reefer** or, more commonly, a **joint.** Exactly how much THC is administered depends on the specific THC concentration level in the marijuana (often referred to as its quality), how deeply the smoke is inhaled into the lungs, and how long it is held in the lungs before being exhaled. In general, an experienced smoker will ingest more THC than a novice smoker by virtue of being able to inhale more deeply and hold the marijuana smoke in his or her lungs longer, for twenty-five seconds or longer, thus maximizing THC absorption into the bloodstream.

The inhalation of any drug into the lungs produces extremely rapid absorption, as noted in earlier chapters, and marijuana is no exception. In the case of THC, effects are felt within seconds. Peak levels are reached in the blood within ten minutes and start to decline shortly afterward. Behavioral and psychological effects generally last from two to four hours. At this point, low levels of THC linger for several days because they are absorbed into fatty tissue and excretion from fatty tissue is notoriously slow.[11]

One implication arising from a slow elimination rate is that the residual THC, left over from a previous administration, can intensify the effect of marijuana on a subsequent occasion. In this way, regular marijuana smokers often report a quicker and more easily obtained high, achieved with a smaller quantity of drug, than more intermittent smokers.[12]

It is also important to see the implication of slow marijuana elimination with regard to drug testing. Urine tests for possible marijuana abuse typically measure levels of THC metabolites (broken down remnants of THC); because of the slow biotransformation of marijuana, these metabolites are detectable in the urine even when the smoker no longer feels high or shows any behavioral effects. Metabolites can remain in the body several days after smoking a single joint and several weeks later if there has been chronic marijuana smoking. Some tests are so sensitive that a positive level for marijuana can result from passive inhalation of marijuana smoke-filled air in a closed environment, even though the THC levels in these cases are substantially below levels that result from active smoking. The bottom line is that marijuana testing procedures are unable to indicate *when* marijuana has been smoked (if it has been smoked at all), only that exposure to marijuana has occurred (see Chapter 8).[13]

Acute Physiological Effects

Immediate physiological effects after smoking marijuana are relatively minor. It has been estimated that a human would need to ingest a dose of marijuana that was from twenty thousand to forty thousand times the effective dose before death would occur; in fact, there is no clearly documented case of a human death occurring from marijuana alone.[14] Nonetheless, there is a dose-related increase in heart rate during early stages of marijuana ingestion, up to 160 beats per minute when dose levels are high. Blood pressure either increases, decreases, or remains the same, depending primarily on whether the individual is standing, sitting, or lying down.[15] A dilation of blood vessels on the cornea resulting in bloodshot eyes peaks in about an hour after smoking a joint. Frequently there is a drying of the mouth and an urge to drink.

Other physiological reactions are inconsistent, and at least part of the inconsistency can be attributed to cultural and interpersonal influences. For example, the observation that marijuana smoking makes you feel extremely hungry and crave especially sweet things to eat (often referred to as "having the munchies") generally holds true in studies of North Americans but not for Jamaicans, who consider marijuana an appetite suppressant. Likewise, North Americans often report enhanced sexual responses following marijuana use, whereas in India marijuana is considered a sexual depressant. These reactions, being subjective in nature, can very well be slanted in one direction or the other by the mind-set (expectations) of the marijuana smoker going into the experience. A good example is the effect on sexual responses. If you believe that marijuana turns you on sexually, the chances are that it will.

Although expectations undoubtedly play a prominent role here, we should be aware of the possibility that varying effects may also be due to differences in the THC concentration of the marijuana being smoked. In the case of sexual reactivity, studies of male marijuana smokers have shown that low-dose marijuana tends to enhance sexual desire while high-dose marijuana tends to depress it, even to the point of impotence. It is quite possible that the enhancement is a result of a brief rise in the male sex hormone, testosterone, and the depression a result of a rebound effect that lowers testosterone below normal levels. Typically, the THC concentration in India is higher than that in North America. As a result, we would expect different effects on sexual reactivity. The same argument could be made with respect to the differences in marijuana's effect on appetite.[16]

reefer: A common name for a marijuana cigarette.
joint: A marijuana cigarette.

In 1998, about 14 percent of all emergency department (ED) mentions in the DAWN statistics (see Chapter 2) involved marijuana, making it the fourth highest category behind alcohol-in-combination, cocaine, and heroin. In only a small percentage of these cases, however, was marijuana the sole drug present in the patient's system at the time. In general, emergency department incidents have risen in the 1990s. Whether this increase is the result of more people smoking marijuana or higher THC concentration in the available marijuana remains uncertain.[17]

Acute Psychological and Behavioral Effects

Chapter 5 noted that a first-time heroin abuser frequently finds the experience more aversive than pleasurable. With marijuana, it is likely that a first-time smoker will feel no discernible effects at all. It takes some practice to be able to inhale deeply and keep the smoke in the lungs long enough for a minimal level of THC, particularly in low-quality marijuana, to take effect. Novices often have to be instructed to focus on some aspect of the intoxicated state in order to start to feel intoxicated. The psychological reactions, once they do occur, however, are fairly predictable.

The marijuana high, as the name implies, is a feeling of euphoria, well-being, and peacefulness. Marijuana smokers typically report an increased awareness of their surroundings, as well as a sharpened sense of sight and sound. Frequently they feel that everything is suddenly very funny, and even the most innocent comments or events can set off uproarious laughter. Usually mundane ideas can seem filled with profound implications, and the individual may feel that creativity has been increased. As with LSD, however, no objective evidence shows that creativity is enhanced by marijuana. Commonly, time seems to pass more slowly while a person is under the influence of marijuana, and events appear to be elongated in duration. Finally, marijuana smokers frequently report that they feel sleepy and sometimes dreamy. The usual THC concentrations of a marijuana joint are not sufficient to be particularly sleep-inducing, though stronger cannabis preparations with higher THC can have strong sleep-inducing effects, particularly when combined with alcohol.[18]

At the same time, marijuana produces significant deficits in behavior. The major deficit is a decline in the ability to carry out tasks that involve attention and memory. Speech will be increasingly fragmented and disjointed; individuals will often forget what they, or others, have just said. The problem is that marijuana typically causes such a rush of distracting ideas to come to mind that it is difficult to concentrate on new information coming in. By virtue of a diminished focus of concentration, the performance of both short-term and long-term memory tasks is impaired. All these difficulties increase in magnitude as a direct function of the level of THC in the marijuana (Drugs . . . in Focus).[19]

It should not be surprising that complex motor tasks, like driving a car, are also more poorly performed while a person is under the influence of marijuana. It is not necessarily a matter of reaction time; studies of marijuana smokers in automobile simulators indicate that they are as quick to respond as control subjects. The problem arises from a difficulty in attending to peripheral information and making an appropriate response while driving.[20] One researcher has put it this way:

> *Marijuana-intoxicated drivers might be able to stop a car as fast as they normally could, but they may not be as quick to notice things that they should*

DRUGS . . . IN FOCUS

Can You Control a Marijuana High?

Experienced marijuana smokers often report that they can turn off their high, if the motivation is sufficiently strong, and behave as if in a normal (undrugged) state. Is this really true?

Controlled laboratory studies, in which specific behaviors can be carefully measured, provide the only source for a scientific answer. In one such study, a group of marijuana smokers were instructed to minimize, as much as they could, the subjective effects of marijuana. When given a time estimation task, these subjects performed more accurately than subjects who were not given the instructions. When given a recall task, however, the two groups were not different in their performance. All the marijuana smokers showed an impairment, regardless of efforts by some of them to resist the drug's effects.

So it appears that only some behaviors are subject to manipulation. Marijuana smokers may *feel* normal, but other aspects of their behavior remain seriously impaired.

Source: Cappell, Howard, and Pliner, Patricia (1974). Cannabis intoxication: The role of pharmacological and psychological variables. In Loren L. Miller (Ed.), *Marijuana: Effects of human behavior.* Orlando FL: Academic Press, pp. 233–264.

stop for. This is probably because they are attending to internal events rather than what is happening on the road.[21]

In a survey of nearly six thousand teenage drivers conducted in 1982, results showed that those who had driven six or more times a month after smoking marijuana were approximately two-and-a-half times as likely to have an accident than those who did not. For those individuals who had driven fifteen or more times a month after smoking marijuana, the increased changes rose to three times as likely. A more recent study in 1994, conducted in Memphis, Tennessee, found that 33 percent of all reckless drivers tested positive for marijuana and 18 percent tested positive for both marijuana and cocaine. A trauma center in Maryland reported in 1995 that a positive test for marijuana was found for 32 percent of all injured automobile drivers and 39 percent of all injured motorcycle drivers. Given the slow elimination of marijuana, it is uncertain whether all of those testing positive were actually high while driving; nevertheless, the percentages are substantially higher than for the general population.[22]

An additional problem is quite serious. The decline in sensory–motor performance will persist well after the point at which the marijuana smoker no longer feels high, when there has been chronic heavy marijuana use. A recent study has shown significant impairments in attention and memory tasks among heavy marijuana users (daily smokers) twenty-four hours after they had last used the drug. Therefore, we have to recognize the possibility that some important aspects of behavior can be impaired following marijuana smoking, even when an individual is not aware of it. This effect may be due to the very slow rate with which marijuana is eliminated from the body.[23]

Emotional problems as a result of smoking marijuana are rare among Americans, who are typically exposed to relatively low THC concentrations, though some distortion of body image, paranoia, and anxiety may occur. It is possible that marijuana smoking among individuals predisposed toward or recovering from a psychosis may trigger psychotic behavior. Nonetheless, there is little or no support for the idea that low doses of marijuana will provoke such reactions in otherwise normal individuals.

In contrast, a substantially higher incidence of psychiatric problems arising from THC exposure has been reported in India and North Africa. In such cases, however, the THC concentrations being ingested, the frequency with which THC is ingested, and the duration of THC exposure over a lifetime are all far greater than would be encountered in the United States.[24]

QUICK CONCEPT  7.1

Understanding the Effects of Marijuana

Check your understanding of the effects of marijuana by checking off the response (on the right) that you think is appropriate to the circumstances related to marijuana or other cannabis products (on the left).

CIRCUMSTANCE	INCREASES THE EFFECT	DECREASES THE EFFECT
1. The resin content in the cannabis is low.	______	______
2. You have decided to inhale more deeply.	______	______
3. You are smoking hashish instead of marijuana.	______	______
4. This is the first time you have ever smoked marijuana.	______	______

Answers: 1. decreases the effect 2. increases the effect 3. increases the effect 4. decreases the effect.

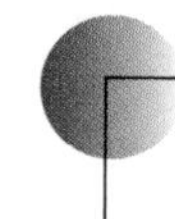

Effects of Marijuana on the Brain

Ever since THC was isolated in 1964 as the primary agent for the intoxicating properties of marijuana, the next step has been to find out specifically how THC affects the brain to produce these effects. In 1990, the mechanism was discovered. It turns out that, just as with morphine, special receptors in the brain are stimulated specifically by THC. They are concentrated in areas of the brain that are important for short-term memory and motor control. Unlike morphine-sensitive receptors, however, the THC-sensitive receptors are not found in the lower portions of the brain that control breathing. As a result, no matter how high the THC concentration in the brain, there is no danger of an accidental death by asphyxiation.

Once we have identified a specific receptor for a drug, the question inevitably becomes, Why is it there? As noted in Chapter 5, when the morphine-sensitive receptor was discovered, it made sense to speculate about a natural morphine-like substance that would fit into that receptor. The same speculation surrounded the discovery of the THC-sensitive receptor until 1992, when researchers isolated a natural substance, dubbed **anandamide,** that activates this receptor and appears to produce the same effects as THC in the brain.

The functions of anandamide and THC-sensitive receptors remain largely a mystery. One study has found that THC stimulates neurons in the nucleus accumbens in rats, the same area that is affected by a host of other psychoactive drugs, including heroin, cocaine, and nicotine. The effect, however, is much weaker than with drugs that produce strong signs of dependence. Animals will self-administer marijuana in laboratory studies and, in fact, are able to discriminate high-potency from low-potency marijuana, but their behavior is not as compulsive as that observed with heroin, cocaine, or nicotine.[25]

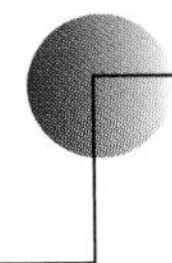

Chronic Effects of Marijuana

Is chronic marijuana smoking harmful over a period of time? What is the extent of tolerance and dependence? Are there long-term consequences for organ systems in the body? Will marijuana lessen one's potential as a productive human being in society? Will marijuana abuse lead to the abuse of other drugs? These are questions to be considered next.

Tolerance

It is frequently reported that experienced marijuana smokers tend to become intoxicated more quickly and to a greater extent than nonexperienced smokers, when exposed to marijuana joints with equivalent THC concentrations. For many years, this observation suggested that repeated administrations of marijuana was producing sensitization, or reverse tolerance (a greater sensitivity), rather than tolerance (a lesser sensitivity). If this were true, then we would have been faced with the troubling conclusion that marijuana operates in a totally opposite way to any other psychoactive drug considered so far. Fortunately, when animals or humans are studied in the laboratory, marijuana smoking shows tolerance effects that are consistent and clear-cut.

Why then the difference with the experience of humans outside the laboratory? One factor involves the way in which we measure the quantity of THC consumed. Reaching an effective high from marijuana requires some degree of practice. For example, novice marijuana smokers may not have mastered the breathing technique necessary to allow the minimal level of THC to enter the lungs. They may have to smoke a relatively large number of marijuana joints initially before they achieve a high. Later, when they have acquired the technique, they may need fewer joints to accomplish the same effect. In these circumstances, however, a calculation of the number of joints consumed does not reflect the amount of THC ingested. If you were to control the THC content entering the body, as is done in laboratory studies, you would find the predictable results of tolerance over repeated administrations.

Another factor involves the slow elimination rate of marijuana. Regular marijuana smokers are likely to have a residual amount of THC still in the system. This buildup of THC would elevate the total quantity of THC consumed with every joint and induce a quicker high. Once again, the impression of sensitization is false; we are actually observing the enhanced effects of an accumulation of THC in the body. As before, once dosage levels are controlled, the results indicate a consistent pattern of tolerance rather than sensitization. In general, tolerance effects following repeated administrations of THC are greater as the dosage level of THC increases.

Dependence

It is possible to observe signs of physical dependence (that is, withdrawal symptoms) following chronic administrations of marijuana, but the level of marijuana smoking has to be quite extreme. In one study, human volunteers were administered large doses of THC every four hours over a ten- to twenty-day period. Within twelve hours after the last administration, subjects reported irritability, restlessness, hot flashes, nausea, and vomiting.[26] In contrast, when another group was required to smoke one marijuana joint daily for twenty-eight days, a condition far closer to the typical exposure to marijuana, no withdrawal symptoms were observed.[27]

Thus physical dependence is not much of an issue with marijuana; however, there may be evidence of psychological dependence. The consensus among experts in the field is that while marijuana is generally reinforcing, there is nowhere near the degree of craving and compulsiveness in smoking marijuana that there is in taking alcohol, opiates, stimulants, or sedative-hypnotic drugs.

anandamide (a-NAN-duh-meyed): A naturally occurring chemical in the brain that fits into THC-sensitive receptor sites, producing many of the same effects as marijuana.

Cardiovascular Effects

THC produces significant increases in heart rate, but there is no conclusive evidence of adverse effects in the cardiovascular functioning in young, healthy people. The reason why the emphasis is on a specific age group is that most of the studies looking at possible long-term cardiovascular effects have involved marijuana smokers under the age of thirty-five; little or no information has been compiled about older populations. For those people with preexisting disorders such as heart disease, high blood pressure, or arteriosclerosis (hardening of the arteries), it is known that the acute effects of marijuana on heart rate and blood pressure can worsen their condition.

Respiratory Effects and the Risk of Cancer

The technique of marijuana smoking involves the deep and maintained inhalation into the lungs of unfiltered smoke on a repetitive basis, probably the worst scenario for incurring chronic pulmonary problems. In addition, a marijuana joint (when compared with a tobacco cigarette) typically contains about the same levels of tars, 50 percent more hydrocarbons, and an unknown amount of possible contaminants (Table 7.1). Joints are often smoked more completely because the smoker tries to waste as little marijuana as possible.

TABLE 7.1

A comparison of the components of marijuana and tobacco smoke

COMPONENT	MARIJUANA	TOBACCO
Carbon monoxide (mg)	17.6	20.2
Carbon dioxide (mg)	57.3	65.0
Ammonia (micrograms)	228.0	178.0
Acetaldehyde (micrograms)	1200.0	980.0
Acetone (micrograms)*	443.0	578.0
Benzene (micrograms)*	76.0	67.0
Toluene (micrograms)*	112.0	108.0
THC (tetrahydrocannabinol) (micrograms)	820.0	–
Nicotine (micrograms)	–	2850.0
Napthalene (nanograms)	3000.0	1200.0

*See Chapter 13 for information about the health risks of inhaling these chemicals.

Source: Julien, Robert M. (2001). *A primer of drug action* (9th ed.). New York: Worth, p. 317.

Given all these factors, marijuana smoking presents several risks. One of the immediate consequences affects the process of breathing. When marijuana is inhaled initially, the passageways for air entering and leaving the lungs widen, but after chronic exposure, an opposite reaction occurs. As a result, symptoms of asthma and other breathing difficulties are increased. Overall, while the effects of a single inhalation of marijuana smoke presents greater problems than a single inhalation of tobacco smoke, we need to remember that the patterns of consumption are far from comparable. All things considered, on a statistical basis, you can think of one joint as being equivalent to five cigarettes in terms of the amount of carbon monoxide intake, four cigarettes in terms of tar intake, and ten cigarettes in terms of the amount of microscopic damage to cells lining the airways. The use of a water pipe reduces the harm somewhat, but the risks are still present. In a recent study, molecular abnormalities in the respiratory tracts of heavy marijuana smokers have been identified that resemble the changes in the respiratory tracts of cigarette smokers.

Given these risks, does smoking marijuana produce a higher incidence of cancer? It may be too soon to answer that question. The marijuana smokers who were twenty years old in the late 1960s are only in their early fifties now, so they are just approaching the peak ages when cancers appear. We have to wait and see. Fortunately, there is the possibility, as is the case with cigarette smoking (see Chapter 11), that the risk of cancer might decline after a person has stopped smoking marijuana.[28]

Effects on the Immune System

When THC is administered to animals, the immune system is suppressed, resulting in a reduction in the body's defense reactions to infection and disease. In humans, the evidence is inconclusive. Some studies indicate that THC has a suppressive effect; others indicate that no immunological changes occur at all. Because marijuana smoking has not been found to be associated with a higher incidence of any major chronic disease, we can tentatively conclude that marijuana smoking does not have a major impact on the immune system. Yet long-term epidemiological studies, in which marijuana-exposed and control populations are compared with regard to the frequency of various diseases, have not been conducted on a large-scale basis.[29]

Effects on Sexual Functioning and Reproduction

The reproductive systems of both men and women are adversely affected by marijuana smoking. In men, marijuana reduces the level of testosterone, reduces sperm count in the semen, and increases the percentage of abnormally formed sperm. In women, marijuana results in a reduction in the level of luteinizing hormone (LH), a hormone necessary for the fertilized egg to be implanted in the uterus. As little as one marijuana joint smoked immediately following ovulation is evidently sufficient for this LH suppression to occur. Despite these hormonal changes in both males and females, however, little or no effect on fertility has been observed.[30]

The research is sparse on the question, but there does not appear to be evidence of birth defects in the offspring of women who have smoked marijuana during their pregnancy. Studies indicate, however, a lower birth weight and shorter length among newborns, as well as a reduction in the mother's milk. It may be unfair to associate these effects specifically with marijuana smoking, as other drugs including alcohol and nicotine are often being consumed during the same period. Even so, the best advice remains that women should avoid marijuana during pregnancy.[31]

Neural Effects and the Amotivational Syndrome

Though chronic exposure to marijuana has frequently been suspected of producing some form of brain damage or long-term impairment in neural functioning, there is little or no evidence in support of this idea.[32] It has also been suspected that marijuana may produce more subtle neurological changes that would affect one's personality, motivation to succeed, or outlook on life.

In 1968, William McGlothin, a psychologist, and Louis West, a psychiatrist, proposed that chronic marijuana smoking among young people was responsible for a generalized sense of apathy in their lives and an indifference to any long-term plans or conventional goals. These changes were called the **amotivational syndrome.** In their words,

> *Regular marijuana use may contribute to the development of more passive, inward-turning personality characteristics. For numerous middle-class students, the subtly progressive change from conforming, achievement-oriented behavior to a state of relaxed and careless drifting has followed their use of significant amounts of marijuana. . . . Such individuals exhibit greater introversion, become totally involved with the present at the expense of future goals, and demonstrate a strong tendency toward regressive, childlike magical thinking.*[33]

In effect, McGothlin and West, and probably a large number of other people in the late 1960s, were saying, "These people don't seem to care anymore and marijuana's to blame for it."

The issue of the amotivational syndrome revolves around two basic questions that need to be examined separately. The first question deals with whether such a syndrome exists in the first place, and the second deals with whether chronic abuse of marijuana is a causal factor. As to the existence of the syndrome, the evidence does suggest that students who smoke marijuana are at a disadvantage academically. Studies of high school students indicate that those who smoke marijuana earn lower grades in school, are less likely to continue on to college, are more likely to drop out, and miss more classes than those who do not smoke it.[34] In a survey of high school students graduating in 1980 and 1981, those who smoked marijuana on a daily basis reported several problems in their lives that are related to motivation: a loss of energy (43 percent), negative effects on relationships (39 percent), interference with work and the ability to think clearly (37 percent), less interest in other activities (37 percent), and inferior performance in school or on the job (34 percent).[35]

The involvement of marijuana smoking as a causal agent in these problems, however, is open to question. To understand the difficulties in analyzing data on this question, consider the results of a 1987 study comparing problems before and after the onset of marijuana abuse (Figure 7.1) and showing substantial increases in the incidence of poor grades, conflict with parents, feelings of depression, and suicide attempts.[36]

The changes are genuine, but we cannot easily establish a direct causal link between marijuana and such global problems, other than to acknowledge that the presence of THC in a student's system during school hours would be reflected later in a decline in overall academic performance. More broadly speaking, we cannot exclude the possibility that marijuana smoking may be, in the words of one expert in the field, "just one behavior in a constellation of related problem behaviors and personality and familial factors" that hamper an adolescent's ability to do well in school and in life.[37] We also cannot exclude the possibility that an involvement with marijuana may closely correlate with involvement in a deviant

amotivational syndrome: A state of listlessness and personality change involving a generalized apathy and indifference to long-range plans.

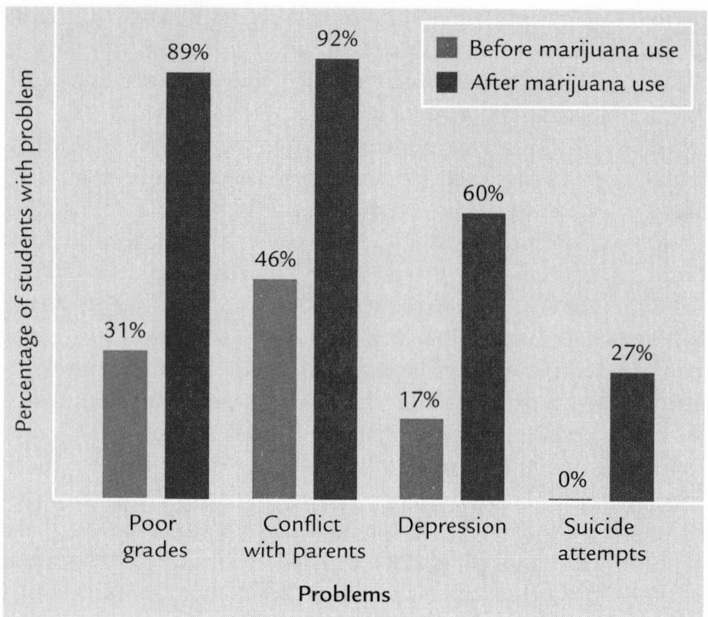

FIGURE 7.1

A deceptively simple comparison of adolescent problems before and after marijuana use.

subculture, a group of friends and associates who feel alienated from traditional values such as school achievement and a promising future. Either of these factors, in combination with the regular ingestion of a sedative drug such as marijuana, can account for the motivational changes that are observed. The point is that we cannot conclude that such changes are purely pharmacological.

With respect to long-term neural deterioration from marijuana smoking, the research is extremely sparse. There is recent evidence, however, that concern over this possibility may be unwarranted. In a study of approximately 1,300 volunteers under the age of 65, changes in the scores in a well-established test of mental ability administered in 1982 and again in 1994 showed, on average, a cognitive decline over the intervening twelve years. Nonetheless, no significant differences in cognitive decline were found among heavy marijuana users, light marijuana users, and nonusers. In other words, we can tentatively conclude that there is indeed a decline as we get older, but marijuana use does not appear to make it worse.[38]

The Gateway Hypothesis

The final concern regarding chronic effects of marijuana deals with the extent to which marijuana smoking leads to a greater incidence of drug abuse in general, a contention that is often referred to as the **gateway hypothesis.** As in consideration of the issues surrounding the amotivational syndrome earlier, the evidence must be studied very carefully.

From a statistical perspective, two major pieces of evidence are uncontroversial. On the one hand, an overwhelming proportion of young marijuana smokers do *not* go on to use other illicit drugs. As expressed in a 1999 newspaper editorial on this question, "The nation's . . . boom and economic expansion is being fueled today by millions of baby boomers who once did, indeed, inhale. They later went into business, not cocaine or heroin." On the other hand, marijuana smokers in general are many times more likely to consume illicit drugs, such as cocaine and heroin, during their lifetimes than are non-marijuana smokers. Not surprisingly, the greater the frequency of marijuana smoking and the earlier a person first engages in marijuana smoking, the greater the likelihood of his or her being involved in other illicit drugs.[39]

But is there a causal link between marijuana smoking and the use of other illicit drugs? Erich Goode, sociologist and drug-abuse researcher, distinguishes between two explanations, which he calls the intrinsic and the sociocultural schools of thought. The intrinsic argument is that there is some inherent property of marijuana exposure itself that leads to physical or psychological dependence on other illicit drugs. According to this viewpoint, the pleasurable sensations of marijuana create a biological urge to consume more potent substances, through a combination of drug tolerance and drug dependence. In contrast, the sociocultural argument holds that the relationship exists not because of the pharmacological effects of marijuana but because of the activities, friends, and acquaintances that are associated with marijuana smoking. In other words, the sociocultural explanation asserts that those who smoke marijuana tend to have friends who not only smoke marijuana themselves but also abuse other drugs. These friends are likely to have positive attitudes toward substance abuse in general and to provide opportunities for drug experimentation.

gateway hypothesis: The idea that the abuse of a specific drug will inherently lead to the abuse of other more harmful drugs.

QUICK CONCEPT  7.2

Understanding the Adverse Effects of Chronic Marijuana Abuse

Check your understanding of the possible adverse effects of either acute or chronic exposure to marijuana by checking off true or false next to each of the assertions.

ASSERTION	TRUE	FALSE
1. The immune system will be impaired.	______	______
2. The chances of getting cancer will be unaffected.	______	______
3. Driving ability will be significantly impaired.	______	______
4. Birth defects will be more frequent.	______	______
5. It is likely that academic performance will decline when a person smokes marijuana regularly.	______	______
6. Marijuana smoking will cause the smoker to experiment with harder drugs in the future.	______	______

Answers: 1. false 2. false 3. true 4. false 5. true 6. false

Professionals in the drug-abuse field have concluded that there is no support for the intrinsic explanation. It turns out that the relationship between marijuana and later drug abuse is not a unique phenomenon; a similar relationship exists with regard to exposure to alcohol and cigarettes. A major study of high school students graduating in 1985 showed that those who had smoked a pack or more of cigarettes each day had a ten times greater likelihood of using cocaine and a six times greater likelihood of smoking marijuana. Alcohol consumption also related positively to marijuana and cocaine abuse. Therefore, if any gateway drugs exist, they are the legally available substances of alcohol and tobacco, not marijuana, because alcohol and tobacco are typically available to young people at a very early age. But even in these cases, we are not speaking of a pharmacological property that causes people to engage in further drug experimentation.[40]

The consensus is that any early exposure to psychoactive substances in general, and illicit drugs such as marijuana in particular, represents a "deviance-prone pattern of behavior" that will be reflected in a higher incidence of exposure to psychoactive drugs of many types later in life. It is interesting to note that early adolescent marijuana use among males also increases the risk in late adolescence of delinquency, having multiple sexual partners, not always using condoms during sex, perceiving drugs as not harmful, and having problems with cigarettes and alcohol. Generally speaking, marijuana smokers show a greater inclination toward risk-taking behavior and a more permissive attitude with regard to social norms.[41]

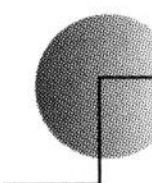

Medical Uses for Marijuana

Even though the medicinal benefits of marijuana have been noted for thousands of years, strong antimarijuana sentiment has made it difficult until the last twenty or so years to conduct an objective appraisal of possible clinical applications. Three principal medical uses have been explored: the treatment of glaucoma, the treatment of asthma, and the treatment of debilitating nausea.

Glaucoma

In 1971, it was found that smoked marijuana significantly reduced intraocular (within the eye) pressure in normal human subjects. This discovery led to an important potential application for individuals suffering from glaucoma, a disease in which intraocular pressure rises so high as to damage the optic nerve and eventually produce blindness. Since then, experimental studies have examined the effectiveness of marijuana (either smoked or ingested orally) or THC eye drops in reducing glaucoma symptoms. These approaches have been shown to be effective, but the medical consensus is that other nonmarijuana drugs are of equal or greater value.

Asthma

Marijuana produces an initial bronchodilation, followed by a subsequent bronchoconstriction. In the case of asthmatic conditions, in which the primary problem is a bronchoconstriction reducing the flow of air into and out of the lungs, it would appear that marijuana would not be advised at all. However, it turns out that orally administered THC results in bronchodilation without the expected constriction later on. Consequently, THC has a positive effect on asthmatic symptoms. As in its application for the treatment of glaucoma, however, other forms of treatment have been shown to be at least equally effective.

Portrait Kenny and Barbra Jenks vs. America's War on Drugs

In the late 1980s, Kenny Jenks, a hemophiliac, and his wife, Barbra, both developed AIDS. Neither of them had smoked marijuana in their lives before, but the nausea and weight loss that the disease brought on gave them little choice. Every antinausea medication their physician had prescribed failed to work; Kenny's weight dropped from 155 to 112 pounds in six weeks. For them, smoking two or three joints of marijuana, harvested from two ten-inch cannabis plants in their Panama City Beach, Florida, home, was the only way to keep their weight up and their nausea down. All went well until one day in March 1990, when twelve policemen bashed a battering ram through their door, seized the plants, and arrested the Jenkses on charges of growing marijuana and possessing more than one ounce of it.

Forbidden to grow their own, Kenny and Barbra then applied for and won approval to be two of approximately a dozen individuals in the United States with permission to smoke marijuana for medical purposes. The marijuana they receive comes from a special farm in Louisiana where the federal government harvests its own crop of cannabis. The Jenkses call their marijuana ditch weed, and it is conceded that the potency leaves much to be desired.

Even so, the Jenkses prefer smoking government-variety marijuana to taking Marisol pills, an FDA-approved antinausea medication containing pure THC. They speculate that there must be other components in the marijuana besides THC that are helping to relieve their symptoms. Besides, Marisol gets them too high; they don't want to be intoxicated, only to make their symptoms go away.

Kenny, Barbra, and a handful of others are the lucky ones to have received approval for their marijuana smoking before the program was canceled in 1992. Others who have been denied approval essentially operate outside the law (see Point/Counterpoint, page 184).

Sources: Baum, Dan (1993, August 5–11). Doctor's orders: The Clinton administration relaxes the ban on marijuana—for medical purposes only, of course. *Ithaca Times*, pp. 6–7, 9. Berger, Joseph (1993, October 11). Mother's homemade marijuana. *New York Times*, pp. B1, B5. Doblin, Richard E., and Kleiman, Mark A. R. (1991). Marijuana as medicine: A survey of oncologists. In Arnold S. Trebach and Kevin B. Zeese (Eds.), *New frontiers in drug policy*. Washington DC: Drug Policy Foundation, pp. 242–245. Nieves, Evelyn (2001, January/February). Half an ounce of healing. *Mother Jones*, pp. 49–53.

Nausea

Chemotherapy in the course of cancer treatment produces an extreme and debilitating nausea, lack of appetite, and loss of body weight, symptoms that are clearly counterproductive in helping an individual contend with an ongoing fight against cancer. AIDS patients suffer from similar symptoms, as do those diagnosed with the gastrointestinal ailment Crohn's disease. During these circumstances, standard antiemetic (antivomiting) drugs are frequently ineffective. The beneficial effect of marijuana, specifically THC, as an antiemetic drug is an important application of marijuana as a medical treatment. This chapter's Portrait examines the present-day dilemma of turning to an illegal drug for medicinal purposes.[42]

The Medical Marijuana Controversy

The use of marijuana per se as a therapeutic agent has distinct disadvantages. First of all, the typical administration through smoking presents, as described earlier, a significant health risk to the lungs. In addition, because marijuana is insoluble in water, suspensions in an injectable form cannot be prepared. Since 1985, however, two legal prescription drugs containing THC or variations of it have been made available in capsule form. **Dronabinol** (brand name: Marisol) is essentially THC in a sesame oil suspension; **nabilone** (brand name: Cesamet) is a synthetic variation of THC. Both drugs have been shown to be clinically effective as antinausea treatments, though the personal reactions of patients taking these drugs vary considerably.[43]

While these prescription drugs are presently in use, U.S. federal authorities, administering FDA guidelines, have until recently been reluctant to reclassify marijuana itself or any other cannabis product from a Schedule I category (defining drugs that are considered to have no medical applications) to a Schedule II category. Only a handful of compassionate-use applications have been

dronabinol (droh-NAB-ih-nol): A prescription drug containing delta-9-tetrahydrocannabinol (THC). Brand name is Marisol.

nabilone (NAB-ih-lone): A prescription drug containing a synthetic variation of delta-9-tetrahydrocannabinol (THC). Brand name is Cesamet.

approved, and the entire procedure for reviewing new compassionate-use requests was terminated in 1992.

Nonetheless, despite official opposition from federal authorities, advocacy for the medical application of marijuana has grown considerably. In 1999, the Institute of Medicine, a branch of the National Academy of Sciences, issued a major report concluding that, while not recommending marijuana for long-term use, short-term use appears to be suitable for treating certain physical conditions, when patients fail to respond well to traditional medications. By 2000, eight U.S. states (Alaska, Arizona, California, Colorado, Hawaii, Maine, Nevada, Oregon, and Washington) had voted by public referendum to allow marijuana smoking for medical purposes, when prescribed by a physician. Importantly, the federal government has eased restrictions on the availability of high-grade marijuana for studies on its effectiveness as a medical treatment. In the meantime, alternative approaches for administration are being actively investigated. One example is the ongoing development of a marijuana patch that could deliver THC into the bloodstream without the hazards of smoking. The Part 2 Point/Counterpoint (page 184) presents the arguments for and against the medical application of marijuana.[44]

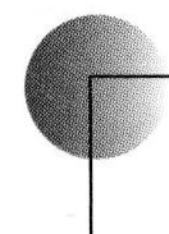

Patterns of Marijuana Smoking

From their days in elementary school on, most young Americans have had to come to terms with marijuana as a pervasive element in their lives. Just as nearly all adolescents have had to make the decision to drink or not to drink, to smoke cigarettes or not to smoke them, they have also had to decide whether or not to smoke marijuana.

Marijuana is undoubtedly the dominant illicit drug in U.S. society, used by 81 percent of current illicit drug users (Figure 7.2). For six out of every ten illicit drug users, marijuana is the *only* illicit drug being used. From the house-to-house survey conducted by the National Institute on Drug Abuse in 1999, it is estimated that an astounding 76 million Americans, more than one-third of the U.S. population over the age of twelve, have smoked marijuana at least once during their lives. About 11 million Americans, about one out of twenty, are estimated to have smoked marijuana within the last thirty days.[45]

Through the University of Michigan survey we can get an idea of the prevalence rates among young people, particularly the dramatic increases observed since 1992. Among high school seniors surveyed in 2000, approximately 36 percent reported having smoked marijuana in the past year, 22 percent reported having done so in the past month, and 6 percent smoked on a daily basis. Granted, these numbers are still below the peak levels reached in the late 1970s. However, they continue to be substantially higher than levels observed in 1990 and 1991. Among eighth graders, 16 percent reported smoking marijuana in the past year and 9 percent in the past month, also up substantially from 1990 and 1991. The current status of prevention programs, understandably under considerable pressure to reduce rates of marijuana smoking as well as involvement in other drugs among young people, will be examined in Chapter 18.[46]

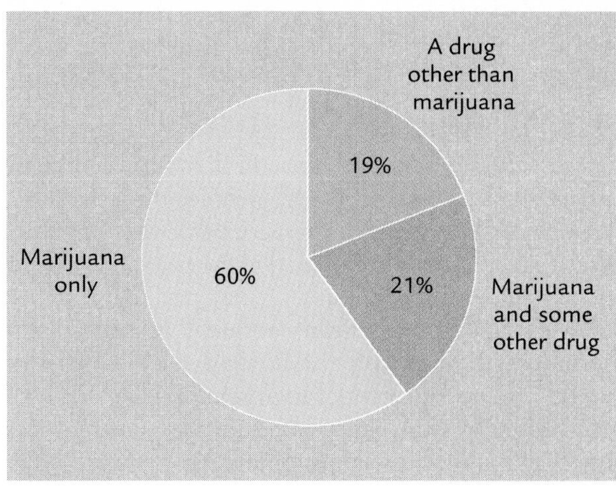

FIGURE 7.2

Types of drugs used by illicit drug users in the past month.

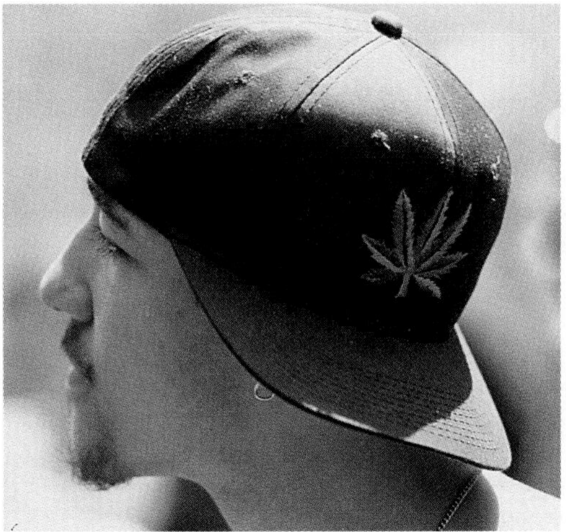

The image of Cannabis sativa *today.*

Current Trends as Causes for Concern

In addition to the rise in the number of marijuana smokers among young people, there is also a change in the way marijuana use is perceived. Chapter 1 noted that until 1991, the trend in the percentage of students who think that marijuana smoking and drug abuse in general carry significant personal risks had been steadily upward. Survey results showed a reversal after 1991. While 58 percent of high school seniors in 2000 considered "regular marijuana smoking" harmful, this figure was down substantially from 79 percent in 1991.[47]

We have also seen a growing popular culture that reinforces the behavior of marijuana smoking as a cool thing to do. The transformation since the beginning of the 1990s has been dramatic. In 1990, marijuana smoking was nearly invisible and considered uncool. According to one college student in 1993, "The image of the pot smoker was very much a hippie thing. Now it's completely different. There's a whole mode of dress, music and style that didn't exist three years ago."[48]

A further concern with regard to present-day marijuana use has to do with an increased potency in the cannabis products that are available. A typical marijuana joint in the psychedelic era contained approximately 1 to 2 percent THC; the average concentration now is 4 percent. The higher-potency form, sinsemilla, is more widely available than ever before, as is hashish. It is reasonable to assume that the adverse effects of chronic marijuana smoking, with THC concentrations approaching 15 percent in some strains of sinsemilla, will be more intense than the relatively mild symptoms we have encountered in the past (Drugs . . . in Focus).

A final concern applies to any illicit street drug: the possibility for adulteration. As emphasized in earlier chapters, what you buy is not always what you get. Each year brings with it a new cast of ingredients, some of them newly introduced drugs and others merely inventive creations from already available materials, ready to be combined with marijuana either to weaken its effects (and increase the profits of the seller) or to change the overall psychoactive result by some synergistic or other interactive effect.

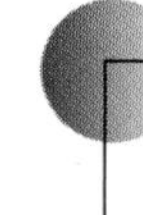

The Issue of Decriminalization

What then should public policy be toward marijuana smoking in the United States today? To deal with this question, we need first to review how public policy with respect to marijuana regulation has evolved since the 1970s. As described earlier, the dramatic emergence during the 1960s of marijuana as a major psychoactive drug initiated a slow but steady reassessment of myths that had been attached to it for decades. By 1972, the American Medical Association, the American Bar Association, and even the leading conservative commentator and author

DRUGS . . . IN FOCUS

Street Language for Marijuana

In the 1960s, when marijuana smoking first became widely popular, the street language was fairly simple. Marijuana was either grass or pot, and a marijuana cigarette was a joint. Here is a sampling of the street language of the 1990s, though the names (and prices) are constantly changing.

- marijuana: skunk, boom, doobie
- marijuana and alcohol: Herb and Al
- getting high on marijuana: getting lifted, booted, red, smoked out or choked out, hit the hay, poke, toke up, blast a stick, burn one, fly Mexican Airlines, mow the grass, boot the gong
- $3 bag of marijuana: a tray
- $5 "nickel" bag: a nick (usually just enough for one joint)
- $40 bag: a sandwich bag
- kinds of marijuana: chronic, chocolate tide, indigo, Hawaiian, Tropicana, Acapulco gold, Panama red
- water pipe similar to a bong: a shotgun
- joints: "blunts" (after the Phillies Blunt cigars that marijuana smokers cut open, hollow out, and fill with marijuana; other brands used, White Owls and Dutch Masters)

Sources: Bureau of Justice Statistics Clearinghouse (1992). *Drugs, crime, and the justice system,* Washington DC: Department of Justice, pp. 24–25. Henneberger, Melinda (1994, February 6). "Pot" surges back, but it's, like, a whole new world. *New York Times,* Sect. 4, p. 18.

A DEA officer confiscates and destroys a domestic crop of Cannabis sativa *in Kentucky.*

William F. Buckley were proposing a liberalization of laws regarding the possession of marijuana. During the same year, the National Commission on Marijuana and Drug Abuse, authorized by the Comprehensive Drug Abuse Prevention and Control Act of 1970, encouraged state legislators around the country to consider changes in their particular regulatory statutes related to marijuana.[49] Since that time, eleven states, including California, New York, Colorado, Minnesota, and North Carolina, have adopted some form of decriminalization laws with respect to the possession of marijuana in small amounts (usually less than one ounce or so). Essentially, **decriminalization** has meant that possession under these circumstances is considered a civil (noncriminal) offense, punishable by a small fine, rather than imprisonment.

The trend toward marijuana decriminalization on a state-by-state basis has largely stalled in recent years. No U.S. state has voted for decriminalization since the 1980s, and two states (Alaska and Oregon) that had previously decriminalized marijuana possession have since voted to recriminalize it. As discussed earlier, the focus of changes in legislation regarding marijuana use has been directed toward the question of its medical application rather than decriminalization per se. Clearly, however, the era of strenuous law enforcement against marijuana smoking at low levels of usage is over. As the sociologist Erich Goode has expressed it:

> *For all practical purposes, the possession of marijuana has become decriminalized in the United States. Since present trends are moving toward de facto legal acceptance of small-quantity marijuana possession, it will not make a great deal of difference whether this attitude is recognized by law or not. Consequently, the debate over marijuana criminalization borders on being obsolete.*[50]

You may find it surprising or not surprising (depending on your personal views) that official decriminalization has not been demonstrated to result in an upturn in the incidence of marijuana smoking. Statistics drawn from states that either have or have not decriminalized show little or no difference.[51] In addition, attitude surveys conducted in California before and after the enactment of such statutes indicate that the acceptance of marijuana among college students actually declined following decriminalization.[52]

decriminalization: The policy of making the possession of small amounts of a drug subject to a small fine but not criminal prosecution.

SUMMARY

A Matter of Terminology

- Marijuana is one of several products of the *Cannabis sativa*, or common hemp plant, grown abundantly throughout the world.
- Various cannabis products are distinguished in terms of the content of cannabis resin and, in turn, the concentration of THC, the active psychoactive agent.

The History of Marijuana and Hashish

- The earliest records of marijuana come from Chinese writings nearly five thousand years ago; hashish has its origins in North Africa and Persia in the ninth or tenth centuries A.D.
- In the United States, marijuana was available in patent medicines during the late 1800s, but its popularity did not become extensive until the 1920s.
- Federal and state regulation of marijuana began in the 1930s; penalties for possessing and selling marijuana escalated during the 1940s and 1950s.
- The emergence of marijuana on American college campuses and among American youth in general during the late 1960s, however, forced a reexamination of

public policy regarding this drug, leading to a more lenient approach in the 1970s.

Acute Effects of Marijuana

- Because marijuana is almost always consumed through smoking, the acute effects are rapid; but because it is absorbed into fatty tissue, its elimination is slow. It may require days or weeks in the case of extensive exposure to marijuana for THC to leave the body completely.
- Acute physiological effects include cardiac acceleration and a reddening of the eyes. Acute psychological effects, with typical dosages, include euphoria, giddiness, a perception of time elongation, and an increased hunger and sexual desire. There are impairments in attention and memory, which interfere with complex visual-motor skills such as driving an automobile.
- The acute effects of marijuana are now known to be due to the binding of THC at special receptors in the brain.

Chronic Effects of Marijuana

- Chronic marijuana use produces tolerance effects; there is no physical dependence when doses are moderate and only a mild psychological dependence.
- Carcinogenic effects are suspected because marijuana smoke contains many of the same harmful components that tobacco smoke does, and in the case of marijuana smoking inhalation is deeper and more prolonged.
- The hypothesis that there exists an amotivational syndrome attributed to the pharmacological effects of marijuana has been largely discredited, as has the idea that marijuana inherently sets the stage for future drug abuse.

Medical Uses for Marijuana

- While marijuana has been useful in the treatment of glaucoma and asthma, its most effective application to date has been in the treatment of symptoms of chemotherapy-induced nausea. The use of marijuana for medicinal purposes remains controversial.

Patterns of Marijuana Smoking

- The current incidence of marijuana smoking among adolescents and young adults is lower than in the late 1970s, but clearly a resurgence has occurred.
- Other areas of concern are the greater potency of marijuana that is now available and the continuing potential risk of marijuana adulteration.
- Present public policy toward marijuana smoking has evolved to the point of essentially decriminalizing the possession of marijuana in small amounts.

KEY TERMS

amotivational syndrome, p. 157
anandamide, p. 155
bhang, p. 149
cannabinoids, p. 149
Cannabis sativa, p. 148
decriminalization, p. 163
delta-9-tetrahydrocannabinol (THC), p. 149
dronabinol, p. 160
gateway hypothesis, p. 158
hashish, p. 149
hashish oil, p. 149
hashish oil crystals, p. 149
joint, p. 152
marijuana, p. 149
nabilone, p. 160
reefer, p. 152
sinsemilla, p. 149

ENDNOTES

1. Abel, Ernest L. (1980). *Marihuana, the first twelve thousand years.* New York: Plenum Press, p. ix.
2. Bloomquist, Edward R. (1968). *Marijuana.* Beverly Hills CA: Glencoe Press, pp. 4–5.
3. Abel, *Marihuana,* p. 4. Palfai, Tibor, and Jankiewicz, Henry (1991). *Drugs and human behavior.* Dubuque IA: W. C. Brown, p. 452.
4. Abel, *Marihuana,* pp. x–xi.
5. Goode, Erich (1999). *Drugs in American society* (5th ed.). New York: McGraw-Hill College, p. 210.
6. Abel, *Marihuana,* p. 12.
7. Bonnie, Richard J., and Whitebread, Charles H. (1974). *The marihuana conviction: A history of marihuana prohibition in the United States.* Charlottesville VA: University Press of Virginia, p. 3.
8. Abel, *Marihuana,* pp. 218–222.

9. Bonnie and Whitebread, *The marihuana conviction*, p. 33.
10. Lee, Martin A., and Shlain, Bruce (1985). *Acid dreams: The complete social history of LSD*. New York: Grove Weidenfeld.
11. Julien, Robert M. (1998). *A primer of drug action* (8th ed.). New York: Freeman, pp. 327–331.
12. Ibid., pp. 330–331.
13. *Allen and Hanbury's athletic drug reference* (1992). Research Triangle Park NC: Clean Data, p. 33. Wadler, Gary I., and Hainline, Brian (1989). *Drugs and the athlete*. Philadelphia: F. A. Davis, pp. 208–209.
14. Grinspoon, Lester, and Bakalar, James B. (1997). Marihuana. In Joyce H. Lowinson, Pedro Ruiz, Robert B. Millman, and John G. Langrod (Eds.), *Substance abuse: A comprehensive texbook*. Baltimore MD: Williams and Wilkins, pp. 199–206.
15. Jones, Reese T. (1980). Human effects: An overview. In Robert C. Petersen (Ed.), *Marijuana research findings: 1980* (NIDA Research Monograph 31). Rockville MD: National Institute on Drug Abuse, p. 65.
16. Grilly, David M. (1989). *Drugs and human behavior*. Boston: Allyn and Bacon, p. 245.
17. Substance Abuse and Mental Health Services Administration (2000). *Drug Abuse Warning Network annual emergency department data 1998*. Rockville MD: Substance Abuse and Mental Health Services Administration, Office of Applied Studies, Table 2, pp. 19–20.
18. Winger, Gail, Hofmann, Frederick G., and Woods, James H. (1992). *A handbook on drug and alcohol abuse* (3rd ed.). New York: Oxford University Press, pp. 123–125.
19. Hooker, William D., and Jones, Reese T. (1987). Increased susceptibility to memory intrusions and the Stroop interference effect during acute marijuana intoxication. *Psychopharmacology, 91*, 20–24.
20. Delong, Fonya L., and Levy, Bernard I. (1974). A model of attention describing the cognitive effects of marijuana. In Loren L. Miller (Ed.), *Marijuana: Effects on human behavior*. New York: Academic Press, pp. 103–117. Gieringer, Dale H. (1988). Marijuana, driving, and accident safety. *Journal of Psychoactive Drugs, 20*, 93–101.
21. McKim, William A. (2000). *Drugs and behavior* (4th ed.). Englewood Cliffs NJ: Prentice Hall, p. 309.
22. Brookoff, D.; Cook, C. S.; Williams, C.; and Mann, C. S. (1994). Testing reckless drivers for cocaine and marijuana. *New England Journal of Medicine, 331*, 518–522. Hingson, R.; Heeren, T.; Mangione, T.; Morelock, S.; and Mucatel, M. (1982). Teenage driving after using marijuana or drinking and traffic accident involvement. *Journal of Safety Research, 13*, 33–38. Kurzthaler, Ilse; Hummer, Martina; Miller, Carl; Sperner-Unterweger, Barbara; Gunther, Verena; Wechdorn, Heinrich; Battista, Hans-Juergen; and Fleischhacker, W. Wolfgang (1999). Effect of cannabis use on cognitive functions and driving ability. *Journal of Clinical Psychiatry, 60*, 395–399. Soderstrom, C. A.; Dischinger, P. D.; Kerns, T. J.; and Trifillis, A. L. (1995). Marijuana and other drug use among automobile and motorcycle drivers treated at a trauma center. *Accident Analysis and Prevention, 27*, 131–135.
23. Block, Robert I. (1997). Editorial: Does heavy marijuana use impair human cognition and brain function? *Journal of the American Medical Association, 275*, 560–561. Pope, Harrison G., Jr., and Yurgelun-Todd, Deborah (1996). The residual cognitive effects of heavy marijuana use in college students. *Journal of the American Medical Association, 275*, 521–527.
24. Winger, Hofmann, and Woods, *A handbook on drug and alcohol abuse*, pp. 118, 127–129.
25. Ameri, Angela (1999). The effects of cannabinoids on the brain. *Progress in Neurobiology, 58*, 315–348. Chait, L. D., and Burke, K. A. (1994). Preference for high- versus low-potency marijuana. *Pharmacology, Biochemistry, and Behavior, 49*, 643–647. Tanda, Gianluigi, Pontieri, Francesco E., and Di Chiara, Gaetano (1997). Cannabinoid and heroin activation of mesolimbic dopamine transmission by a common μ_1 opioid receptor mechanism. *Science, 276*; 2048–2049. Wickelgren, Ingrid (1997). Research news: Marijuana: Harder than thought? *Science, 276*, 1967–1968.
26. Jones, Reese T., and Benowitz, Neal (1976). The 30-day trip: Clinical studies of cannabis tolerance and dependence. In Monique C. Braude and Stephen Szara (Eds.), *Pharmacology of marijuana*. Vol. 2. Orlando FL: Academic Press, pp. 627–642.
27. Frank, Ira M.; Lessin, Phyllis J.; Tyrrell, Eleanore D.; Hahn, Pierre M.; and Szara, Stephen. (1976). Acute and cumulative effects of marijuana smoking on hospitalized subjects: A 36-day study. In Monique C. Braude and Stephen Szara (Eds.), *Pharmacology of marijuana*. Vol. 2. Orlando FL: Academic Press, pp. 673–680.
28. Julien, Robert M. (2001). *A primer of drug action* (9th ed.). New York: Worth, p. 318. Marijuana as medicine: How strong is the science? (1997, May). *Consumer Reports*, pp. 62–63. Study: Marijuana, cocaine have harmful effects on lungs (1998, September 7). *Alcoholism and Drug Abuse Weekly, 10*, p. 8. Sussman, Steve; Stacy, Alan W.; Dent, Clyde W.; Simon, Thomas R.; Johnson, C. Anderson (1995). Marijuana use: Current issues and new research directions. *Journal of Drug Issues, 26*, 695–733.
29. Committee on Substance Abuse, American Academy of Pediatrics (1999). Marijuana: A continuing concern for pediatricians. *Pediatrics, 104*, 982–985. Hollister, Leo E. (1988). Marijuana and immunity. *Journal of Psychoactive Drugs, 20*, 3–7. Petersen, Robert C. (1984). Marijuana overview. In Meyer D. Glantz (Ed.), *Correlates and consequences of marijuana use* (Research Issues 34). Rockville MD: National Institute on Drug Abuse, p. 10.
30. Brands, Bruna, Sproule, Beth, and Marshman, Joan (Eds.). *Drugs and drug abuse: A reference text* (3rd ed.). Toronto: Addiction Research Foundation. Committee on Substance Abuse, Marijuana. Grinspoon and Bakalar, Marihuana, pp. 203–204.
31. Grinspoon and Bakalar, Marihuana, p. 203.

32. Hollister, Leo E. (1986). Health aspects of cannabis. *Pharmacological Reviews, 38,* 1–20.
33. McGothlin, William H., and West, Louis J. (1968). The marijuana problem: An overview. *American Journal of Psychiatry, 125,* 372.
34. Goode, *Drugs in American society,* pp. 232–233.
35. Fox, C. Lynn, and Forbing, Shirley E. (1992). *Creating drug-free schools and communities: A comprehensive approach.* New York: HarperCollins, p. 60.
36. *Drug Abuse Update* (1987, September). Atlanta: National Families in Action, p. 4.
37. Goode, *Drugs in American society,* p. 233.
38. Lyketsos, Constantin G., Garrett, Elizabeth, and Anthony, James C. (1999). Cannabis use and cognitive decline in persons under 65 years of age. *American Journal of Epidemiology, 149,* 794–800.
39. Cited in Medical Marijuana: Editorials debate "gateway" effect (1999, April 12). *American Health Line,* URL: http://www.ahl.com.
40. Goode, *Drugs in American society,* pp. 227–231. Johnston, Lloyd D., O'Malley, Patrick M., and Bachman, J. G. (1987). *National trends on drug use and related factors among American high school students and young adults, 1975–1986.* Rockville MD: National Institute on Drug Abuse, pp. 133–153. Kandel, Denise B., Yamaguchi, K., and Chen, K. (1992). Stages of progression in drug involvement from adolescence to adulthood: Further evidence for the gateway theory. *Journal of Studies in Alcohol, 53,* 447–458. National Center on Addiction and Substance Abuse (1999). *Non-medical marijuana: Rite of passage or Russian roulette?* New York: National Center on Addiction and Substance Abuse at Columbia University. Petersen, Marijuana overview, p. 4.
41. Brook, Judith S., Balka, Elinor B., and Whiteman, Martin (1999). The risks for late adolescence of early adolescent marijuana use. *American Journal of Public Health, 89,* 1549–1554. Goode, Drugs in American society, pp. 226–227.
42. Cohen, Sidney (1980). Therapeutic aspects. In Robert C. Petersen (Ed.), *Marijuana Research findings: 1980* (NIDA Research Monograph 31). Rockville MD: National Institute on Drug Abuse, pp. 199–221. Julien, *A primer of drug action* (9th ed.), pp. 322–324.
43. Plasse, Terry F.; Gorter, Robert W.; Krasnow, Steven H.; Lane, Montague; Shepard, Kirk V.; and Wadleigh, Robert G. (1991). Recent clinical experience with dronabinol. International conference on cannabis and cannabinoids, Chania, Greece. *Pharmacology, Biochemistry, and Behavior, 40,* 695–700.
44. Ault, Alicia (1999). Institute of Medicine says marijuana has benefits. *The Lancet, 353,* 1077. Maine voters approve medical marijuana referendum (8 November, 1999). *Alcoholism and Drug Abuse Weekly,* p. 5. Researchers' access to marijuana eased (22 May, 1999). *Newsday,* p. A10.
45. Substance Abuse and Mental Health Services Administration (2000). *Summary of findings from the 1999 National Household Survey on Drug Abuse.* Rockville MD: Substance Abuse and Mental Health Services Administration, Office of Applied Studies, Tables G.5, G.6.
46. Johnston, Lloyd D. (2000, December 14). "Ecstasy" use rises sharply among teens in 2000; use of many other drugs stays steady, but significant declines are reported for some. News release from the University of Michigan, Ann Arbor, Tables 2 and 3.
47. Johnston, Table 9. Johnston, O'Malley, and Bachman, *National survey results,* Table 8–1.
48. Leland, John (1993, November 1). Just say maybe. *Newsweek,* pp. 50–54, quotation on p. 52.
49. National Commission on Marihuana and Drug Abuse (1972). *Marihuana: A signal of misunderstanding.* Washington DC: Government Printing Office, pp. 151–167.
50. Goode, *Drugs in American society,* p. 401.
51. Johnston, Lloyd D. (1980, January 16). Marijuana use and the effects of marijuana decriminalization. Unpublished testimony delivered at the hearings on the effects of marijuana held by the Subcommittee on Criminal Justice, Judiciary Committee, U.S. Senate, Washington DC, p. 5.
52. Sommer, Robert (1988). Two decades of marijuana attitudes: The more it changes, the more it is the same. *Journal of Psychoactive Drugs, 20,* 67–70.

Anabolic Steroids and Drug Abuse in Sports

After you have completed this chapter, you will understand

- The history of drug abuse in sports
- How anabolic steroids work
- The health risks of steroid abuse
- Patterns of steroid abuse
- Dietary supplements used as ergogenic aids
- Present-day drug testing in amateur and professional athletics

Charlie Francis, former coach of Canadian sprinter Ben Johnson, was once asked whether he felt that it was cheating to encourage Johnson to take anabolic steroids prior to the 1988 Olympic Games in Seoul, even though he knew the drugs had been banned by the International Olympic Committee. "I don't call it cheating," he said. "My definition of cheating is doing something nobody else is doing."

In a world where running a hundredth of a second faster can mean the difference between a gold medal or a silver, where throwing a javelin a few centimeters farther or lifting a kilogram or two more can make you either the champion or an also-ran, temptations abound. In this high-pressure world, athletes are continually on the lookout for a winning edge. The advantage formula may involve an unusual technique in training, a new attitude toward winning, or a special diet. Or it could involve the use of drugs. This chapter looks at the problem of drug abuse in the world of sports—in particular, the abuse of anabolic steroids.

The use of anabolic steroids to achieve that winning edge is a problem not only among athletes who are in the public eye but also among a growing number of young people who simply want to look better by developing the musculature of their bodies. The serious dangers in such drug-taking behavior, whether the motivation lies in competitive drive or in personal vanity, are major problems that need to be examined closely. It is instructive to look first at how drugs in general have affected competitive sports over the centuries.

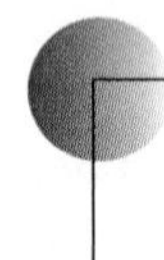

Drug-Taking Behavior in Sports

The first recorded athletic competition, the ancient Olympic Games in Greece, is also the place where we find the first recorded use of psychoactive drugs in sports. As early as 300 B.C., Greek athletes ate hallucinogenic mushrooms, either to improve their performance in the competition or to achieve some kind of mystical connection to the gods. Later, Roman gladiators and charioteers used stimulants to sustain themselves longer in competition, even when injured by their opponents.

In the modern era, drugs have continued to be a factor in athletic competitions. By the end of the nineteenth century, world-class athletes were experimenting with a variety of stimulant and depressant drugs, including cocaine, caffeine, alcohol, nitroglycerine, opiates, strychnine, and amphetamines. In 1886, while competing in a cross-country race, a Welsh cyclist died of a combination of opiates and cocaine (now referred to as a speedball), the first drug-related death ever recorded in sports. During the 1904 Olympics, U.S. marathoner Tom Hicks collapsed after winning the race and lost consciousness. When he was revived, doctors were told that he had taken a potentially lethal mixture of strychnine (a CNS stimulant when administered in low doses) and brandy.[1]

With the introduction of anabolic steroid drugs specifically patterned after the male sex hormone, testosterone, a new element entered the arena of competitive sports. Here was a class of drugs that did more than temporarily alter the behavior of the athlete; these drugs actually altered the athlete's physical body.

Anabolic steroid drugs had been studied since the 1930s as a treatment for anemia (low red-blood-cell count) and conditions that caused muscles to waste away. Following the end of World War II, steroid drugs were administered to people who were near death from starvation and weight loss. It quickly became apparent, however, that steroids could be useful when given to otherwise healthy individuals as well. As pharmaceutical companies began to introduce dozens of new body-building drugs based on the testosterone molecule, it was natural that information about anabolic steroids would come to the attention of athletes, as well as their coaches and trainers.[2]

What Are Anabolic Steroids?

To understand how testosterone-based steroids produce **ergogenic** (performance-enhancing) changes, we first have to recognize that testosterone itself has two primary effects on the human body. The first and most obvious effect is **androgenic** (literally, "man-producing"), in that the hormone promotes the development of male sex characteristics. As testosterone levels rise during puberty, boys acquire an enlarged larynx (resulting in a deeper voice), body hair, and an increase in body size, as well as genital changes that make them sexually mature adults. The second effect is **anabolic** (upward-changing), in that it promotes the development of protein and, as a result, an increase in muscle tissue. Muscles in men are inherently larger than muscles in women because of the anabolic action of testosterone in the male body.

Steroid drugs based on alterations in the testosterone molecule are therefore called **anabolic-androgenic steroids.** The goal, however, has been to develop drugs

ergogenic (ER-go-JEN-ik): Performance-enhancing.
androgenic (AN-droh-JEN-ik): Acting to promote masculinizing changes in the body.
anabolic (AN-ah-BALL-ik): Acting to promote protein growth and muscular development.
anabolic-androgenic steroids: Drugs that promote masculinizing changes in the body and increased muscular development.

TABLE 8.1

Anabolic steroids currently available in the United States

TYPE OF STEROID	GENERIC NAME	BRAND NAME
Oral	danazol	Danocrine capsules
	methyltestosterone	Android capsules, Testred capsules, Virilon capsules
	oxyandrolone	Oxandrin tablets
	oxymetholone	Android-50 tablets
	stanozolol	Winstrol tablets
Intramuscular injection	nandrolone decanoate	Deca-durabolin IM
	testosterone cyprionate	Virilon IM
	testosterone enantrate	Delatestryl IM
Transdermal patch	testosterone	Androderm transdermal system, Testoderm transdermal system

Note: Several brands of anabolic steroids, previously available through legitimate sources, are now only available as illicit drugs. Androstenedione (brand names: Andro, Androstene, and others) and creatine are two examples of nonprescription dietary supplements that are currently available for ergogenic purposes.

Source: Physician's desk reference (54th ed.) (2000). Montvale NJ: Medical Economics Company, Inc.

that emphasize the anabolic function while retaining as little of the androgenic function as possible. For that reason, they are most often called simply **anabolic steroids.** Unfortunately, as we will see, it has not been possible to develop a testosterone-derived drug without at least some androgenic effects (Table 8.1).

It is important that anabolic steroids not be confused with **adrenocortical steroids,** drugs that are patterned after glucocorticoid hormones secreted by the adrenal glands. The major drug of this latter type is cortisone (brand name, among others: Hydrocortone injection or tablets). The molecular structure of these drugs qualifies them to belong to the steroid family, but there is no relationship to testosterone or any testosterone-like effects. Adrenocorticoid steroids are useful in the medical treatment of tissue inflammation; in sports, they reduce the inflammation associated with muscular injuries. Their effect on muscular development can be viewed as *catabolic* (downward-changing), in that muscles tend to weaken as a result, so their long-term use is unlikely to be a desirable option for athletes.[3]

Anabolic Steroids at the Modern Olympic Games

By the time of the 1952 Olympic Games in Helsinki, athletes were well acquainted with ergogenic drugs. Legally available amphetamines (see Chapter 4), in particular, were commonplace, particularly in events that emphasized speed and endurance. Among events requiring strength and size, anabolic steroids were seen to be perfectly suited for gaining a competitive advantage.

It is debatable which country first used anabolic steroids. U.S. athletic officials have claimed that Soviet weight-lifting champions were using steroids in international competitions in 1954; British officials have claimed that a U.S. hammer thrower used steroids prior to 1954. Whoever has the dubious honor of being first, steroid use became the norm by the 1956 Olympic Games in Melbourne for both men and women athletes.

Steroid use was clearly out in the open during the 1968 Olympic Games in Mexico City. An estimated one-third of the entire U.S. track and field team, not merely the strength-event and field-event competitors but the sprinters and middle-distance runners as well, were using anabolic steroids. The controversy did not concern

anabolic steroids: Drugs patterned after the testosterone molecule that promote masculine changes in the body and increased muscular development. The full name is anabolic-androgenic steroids.
adrenocortical steroids: A group of hormones secreted by the adrenal glands. Their anti-inflammatory action makes them useful for treating arthritis and muscular injuries.

the appropriateness or morality of taking steroids, only which particular steroids worked best. Strength-event athletes were taking at least two to five times the therapeutic recommendations (based on the original intent of replacing body protein). The taking of multiple types of steroids, as well as the simultaneous use of injectable and oral forms, were becoming popular. The following year, an editor of *Track and Field News* dubbed anabolic steroids "the breakfast of champions." In 1971, one U.S. weight lifter commented in reference to his Soviet rival,

> *Last year the only difference between me and him was I couldn't afford his drug bill. Now I can. When I hit Munich [in 1972] I'll weigh in at about 340, or maybe 350. Then we'll see which is better, his steroids or mine.*[4]

In the meantime, the masculine features of many female athletes from eastern European countries in the 1960s and 1970s, not to mention the number of Olympic records that were suddenly broken, made it reasonable to ask whether they were either men disguised as women or genetic "mistakes." Questions about the unusually deep voices of East German women swimmers prompted their coach, at one point, to respond: "We came here to swim, not to sing." From information that has come to light since then, we now know that the effects were chiefly due to large doses of steroids. Until the late 1980s, the East German government was conducting a scientific program specifically to develop new steroid formulations that would benefit their national athletes and, at the same time, be undetectable by standard screening procedures. In 2000, the principal physician in the East German Swimming Federation at the time when these steroids were being administered was brought to trial and convicted on charges that the program caused bodily harm to more than four dozen young female swimmers from 1975 to 1985.

The 2000 Olympic Games in Sydney, Australia, instituted the strictest drug-testing procedures to date for all competing athletes, including a new screening for EPO, a drug that enhances endurance by increasing red blood cells. For the first time, a specific phrase was inserted into the Olympic Oath, recited by all athletes at the beginning of the games: ". . . committing ourselves to a sport without doping and without drugs." Unfortunately, accusations of ergogenic drug use and expulsions of athletes continued to plague the Sydney Olympic Games, as they had in previous ones since the 1950s.[5]

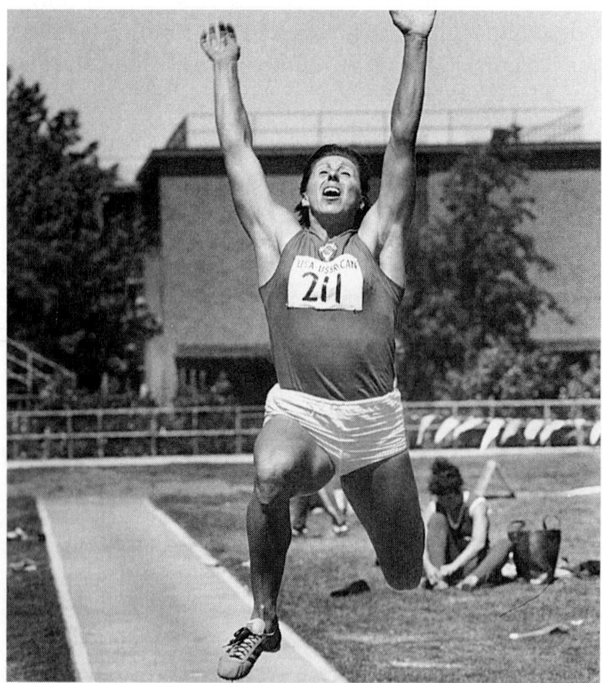

Russian pentathlon champion Nadezhda Tkachenko was one of several world-class female athletes in the 1970s who later tested positive for anabolic steroids.

Anabolic Steroids in Professional and Collegiate Sports

The wholesale use of anabolic steroids in international athletics soon filtered down to sports closer to home. Beginning in the early 1960s, trainers in the National Football League began to administer anabolic steroids to their players. By the 1970s and 1980s, virtually all of the NFL teams were familiar with these drugs. Estimates of how many players were on anabolic steroids varied from 50 percent to 90 percent. We will never know precisely the full extent of the practice, except to say that it was certainly substantial.

Several professional football players remarked at the time that their steroid use had begun while they were playing on collegiate teams, and indeed football players in several colleges and universities during the 1980s were implicated in steroid use. Football players were not alone in this regard. Use of anabolic steroids had found its way into other collegiate and high school sports, including track and field, baseball, basketball, gymnastics, lacrosse, swimming, volleyball, wrestling, and tennis. It is fair to say that until the late 1980s, when screening procedures became commonplace, there was no sport, professional or amateur, for which the use of anabolic steroids was not an accepted element in training.[6]

A Milestone Year in the History of Anabolic Steroids

Two events in 1988 made that year a turning point in the history of anabolic steroids in sports. Magazine articles and news accounts had been exposing the widespread use of steroids since 1969, but public interest was only briefly aroused and media coverage would quickly dwindle. In September 1988, however, in a dramatic and highly publicized moment in the Seoul Olympic Games, the Canadian sprinter Ben Johnson won the gold medal in the men's 100-meter dash in the world-record-breaking time of 9.79 seconds, only to be denied his achievement shortly afterward when it was determined that he had tested positive for anabolic steroids. Stunned, the world suddenly had to confront the pervasiveness of the practice as well as its consequences once and for all (Portrait).

About a month later, another dramatic development emerged when a major study published in the *Journal of the American Medical Association* reported the outcome of the first nationwide survey on use of anabolic steroids among adolescent boys in the United States. The survey found that approximately 7 percent of all high school seniors were using or had used anabolic steroids. More than 77 percent of the users were white and middle class; more than 52 percent had parents who were college graduates; nearly 50 percent had started using steroids before they were fifteen years old. More than 47 percent said that their motivation was to improve their athletic performance, but almost 27 percent said that the motivation was completely outside the realm of organized sports: they simply wanted to look better.[7]

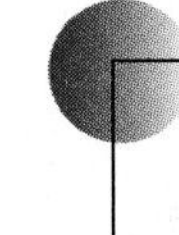

The Hazards of Anabolic Steroids

One of the problems that complicates any look at the adverse effects of steroid abuse is that the dosage levels vary over an enormous range. Further, it is virtually

Portrait: Ben Johnson and the Olympic Gold Medal

It would be an understatement to say that Ben Johnson returned home to Canada from the 1988 Olympic Games in disgrace. One column in the *Ottawa Citizen* carried the angry headline, "Thanks a lot, you bastard." Johnson's world record had been taken away in Seoul, and the first Canadian gold medalist in a 100-meter event since 1928 was now not only denied his achievement but also forbidden to participate in any competition for two years. Johnson's agent estimated that the total financial loss from the cancellation of major endorsement deals would approach $10 million for 1989 alone and probably $25 million over his career.

Charlie Francis, Johnson's Olympic coach, had been shocked when he first heard of the positive drug test but for a different reason from what you might suspect:

> *I felt spinning with confusion. I assumed that Ben had been nailed for an anabolic steroid, but it made no sense to me. For the past three years, some of my sprinters had been using an injectable form of the steroid furazabol, which we referred to as Estragol. I knew that it couldn't be detected, since the IOC's [International Olympic Committee's] lab equipment hadn't been programmed to identify furazabol's metabolites, the breakdown substances produced in the body. . . . Just what was going on here?*

The test, as Francis found out shortly afterward, was positive for stanozolol, a chemical cousin to furazabol:

> *I was floored. To my knowledge, Ben had never injected stanozolol. He occasionally used Winstrol, an oral version of the drug, but for no more than a few days at a time, since it tended to make him stiff. He'd always discontinued the tablets at least six weeks before a meet, well beyond the accepted "clearance time"—the number of days required for a given drug to clear an athlete's system and become undetectable.*

Ben Johnson

Interestingly, nowhere in his reaction was a denial that steroids had been a part of Johnson's training, as well as the training of others on the Canadian team, only that they had been caught.

In a special investigation into the scandal, conducted six months after the Seoul Olympics, Francis testified that international standards, and the majority of world records, were steroid-dependent. As he later wrote in his 1990 autobiography, of steroids in world-class athletics during the previous two decades or more, "The IOC and the IAAF [International Amateur Athletics Federation] refused to admit that most of the best athletes were already using the drugs."

Postscript: In 1993 Ben Johnson tested positive again for steroid use after a short-lived return to competitive running. He was banned from competitive track and field events for life.

Sources: Cohen, Roger (1993, March 6). Johnson is banned for life after testing positive for drugs. *New York Times,* p. 32. Francis, Charlie, with Coplon, Jeff (1990). *Speed trap: Inside the biggest scandal in Olympic history.* New York: St. Martin's Press. Quotations on pp. 2, 3, and 91.

Anabolic steroids produce massive development of musculature, a prized asset in competitive body building.

impossible to know the exact dosage levels or even the exact combinations of steroids a particular individual may be taking. It is estimated that a "typical" body builder on anabolic steroids may be taking in a minimum of three to ten times the therapeutic doses recommended for the medical use of these drugs, but in some cases, the estimates have gone as high as a hundred to a thousand times the recommended therapeutic dose.[8]

Effects on Hormonal Systems

At these huge dosages, anabolic steroids are literally flooding into the body, upsetting the delicate balance of hormones and other chemicals that are normally controlled by testosterone. The primary effect in men is for the testes gland to react to the newly increased testosterone levels in the blood by producing *less* testosterone on its own. In other words, the gland is getting the incorrect message that its services are no longer needed. As a result, the testicles shrink, and a lower sperm count leads to sterility, reversible for most men but irreversible in a small number of cases. Paradoxically, the male breasts enlarge (a condition called **gynecomastia**) because steroids break down eventually into estradiol, the female sex hormone. Other related consequences include frequent, sustained, and often painful penile erections (a condition called **priapism**) and an enlargement of the prostate gland. Severe acne, particularly on the shoulders and back, results from an increase in the secretions of the sebaceous glands in the skin. Other testosterone-related effects include two changes in hair growth patterns: increased facial hair growth and accelerated balding on the top of the head.

Some athletes attempt to counter these undesirable hormonal effects by combining anabolic steroids with human chorionic gonadotropin (HCG), a hormone that ordinarily stimulates the testes to secrete testosterone. In theory, this strategy can work, but the dosages have to be carefully controlled, something that self-medicating athletes are unlikely to do. Repeated HCG treatments can actually have the opposite effect from the one that is intended, making matters worse rather than better. In addition, HCG itself has its own adverse effects, including headaches, mood swings, depression, and retention of fluids.[9]

Among women taking anabolic steroids, the dramatically increased levels of testosterone in bodies that normally have only trace amounts produce major physiological changes, only some of which return to normal when steroids are withdrawn. Table 8.2 lists the major reversible and irreversible effects among women.

Effects on Other Systems of the Body

Given the fact that the liver is the primary means for clearing drugs from the body (see Chapter 3), it is not surprising that large doses of anabolic steroids should take their toll on this particular organ. The principal result is a greatly increased risk of developing liver tumors. The type of liver tumors frequently seen in these circumstances are benign (noncancerous) blood-filled cysts, with the potential for causing liver failure. In addition, a rupture in these cysts can produce abdominal bleeding, requiring life-saving emergency treatment. Fortunately, these liver abnormalities are reversible when steroids are withdrawn from use.[10]

There is evidence from animal studies that increased steroid levels in the body can produce high blood pressure and high cholesterol levels, as well as heart abnormalities. Whether cardiovascular effects present a problem for steroid abusers, however, is not well established, and some researchers consider the often publicized cardiovascular risks associated with anabolic steroids to be highly exaggerated. The one or two documented cases of heart-disease–related deaths among abusers have been tied to factors other than the chronic intake of steroid drugs.[11]

Psychological Problems

Stories abound of mood swings and increased aggressiveness, often referred to by athletes as "'roid rage," when taking anabolic steroids. The relationship between increased

gynecomastia (GEYE-neh-coh-MAST-ee-ah): An enlargement of the breasts.

priapism (PREYE-ah-pih-zem): A condition marked by persistent and frequently painful penile erections.

TABLE 8.2

Reported side effects of anabolic steroids in ten women

EFFECT	NUMBER REPORTING THE EFFECT	REVERSIBLE AFTER END OF USE
Lower voice	10	no
Increased facial hair	9	no
Enlarged clitoris	8	no
Increased aggressiveness	8	yes
Increased appetite	8	unknown
Decreased body fat	8	unknown
Diminished or stopped menstruation	7	yes
Increased sexual drive	6	yes
Increased acne	6	yes
Decreased breast size	5	unknown
Increased body hair	5	no
Increased loss of scalp hair	2	no

Note: The ten women were all weight-trained athletes.

Sources: Strauss, Richard H., and Yesalis, Charles E. (1993). Additional effects of anabolic steroids in women. In Charles E. Yesalis (Ed.), *Anabolic steroids in sport and exercise.* Champaign IL: Human Kinetics Publishers, pp. 151–160. Strauss, Richard H., Ligget, M. T., and Lanese R. R. (1985). Anabolic steroid use and perceived effects in ten weight-trained women athletes. *Journal of the American Medical Association, 253,* 2871–2873.

testosterone and emotionality is not well understood, but numerous anecdotal reports force us to consider the possibility that real psychological changes are going on.[12] As an example, this is how one sports writer recalled the unusual behavior of the professional football player Lyle Alzado:

> *I was covering the Los Angeles Raiders when Alzado, who had played previously with the Denver Broncos and Cleveland Browns, joined [the team] in 1982. In 1984, I was talking to one of his teammates across the Raiders' dressing room, when Alzado, with no provocation, picked up his gray metal stool and threw it in my direction, shouting something about "reporters in the locker room." Shaken, I asked several players who knew him best what was bugging him. They said Alzado probably just had a steroid injection and to stay out of his way. Good advice.*[13]

Conclusions from more rigorous investigations into this question are unfortunately not consistent. In one double-blind laboratory study, subjects who were given

QUICK CONCEPT  8.1

Understanding the Effects of Anabolic Steroids

Check your understanding of the effects of anabolic steroids by answering whether or not the following conditions can be attributed to steroid use.

1. severe acne on the lower extremities of the body
2. increased aggressiveness and mood swings
3. premature balding in men
4. increased development of the testicles
5. enlarged breasts (gynecomastia) among women
6. accelerated growth in adolescents around the time of puberty

Answers: 1. no 2. yes 3. yes 4. no 5. no 6. no

testosterone made a greater number of aggressive responses on average than control subjects who were given a placebo, but changes in behavior were not observed in all subjects. In fact, a large majority of subjects exhibited little change in personality after testosterone administration. In another equally controlled study, little change was observed in *any* subject. It is important to realize that research studies of this type may not be in a position to identify emotional changes due to steroid abuse. It is likely that the amount of anabolic steroids ingested by athletes engaging in this form of drug-taking behavior greatly exceeds those levels that can be safely studied in the laboratory.[14]

Special Problems for Adolescents

During puberty, a particularly crucial process among boys is the growth of the long bones of the body, which results in an increase in height. Anabolic steroids suppress growth hormones; as a result, muscular development is enhanced but overall body growth is stunted. Among girls, testosterone-related drugs delay the onset of puberty, making the body shorter, lighter, and more "girl-like" while enhancing the user's overall strength.[15]

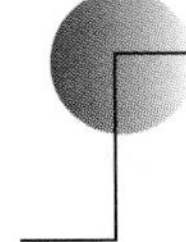

Patterns of Anabolic Steroid Abuse

In 1990, as a response to the increasing awareness of the abuse of anabolic steroids both in and out of competitive sports, Congress passed the Anabolic Steroids Control Act, reclassifying anabolic steroids as Schedule III controlled substances, on a par with codeine preparations and barbiturates. Jurisdiction was transferred from the Food and Drug Administration (FDA) to the Drug Enforcement Administration (DEA). As a result of this legislation, pharmacies are permitted to fill prescriptions up to a maximum of five times, but penalties can result in a five-year prison term and a $250,000 fine for illegal nonmedical sales and a one-year term and a $1,000 fine for nonmedical possession. Penalties are doubled for repeated offenses or for selling these drugs to minors (see Chapter 17).

Despite the new regulations in effect, as you might expect, steroid abuse today continues to be a problem. Its distribution has now become a black-market enterprise. Commonly referred to as 'roids, these drugs are channeled principally through people associated with body-building gyms and through mail-order companies that frequently change their locations and identities to stay one step ahead of the law. It is estimated that the illicit anabolic steroid market is valued at between $300 million to $400 million each year, with the drugs smuggled into the United States from Europe, Canada, and Mexico. In 2000, the University of Michigan survey reported that 3% of eighth-grade boys and 3.5% of tenth-grade boys and 2.5% of high school seniors had used anabolic steroids in their lifetime.[16]

The Potential for Steroid Dependence

Some anabolic steroids can be taken orally, others through intramuscular injections; abusers, however, often administer a combination of both types in a practice called *stacking*. Hard-core abusers may take a combination of three to five different pills and injectables simultaneously, or they may consume any steroid that is available ("shotgunning"), with the total exceeding a dozen. In addition to the complications that result from so many different types of steroids being taken at the same time, multiple injections into the buttocks or thighs, with 1.5 inch needles (called darts or points), are painful and inevitably leave scars. If these needles are shared, as they frequently are, the risk of hepatitis or HIV contamination is significant.

Steroid abusers often follow a pattern called *cycling*, in which steroids are taken for periods lasting from four to eighteen weeks, each separated by an "off" period of abstention. Unfortunately, when the drugs are withdrawn, the newly developed muscles tend to "shrink up," throwing the abuser into a panic that his or her body is losing the gains that have been achieved. In addition, abstention from steroids can lead to signs of depression, such as problems sleeping, lack of appetite, and general moodiness. All these effects encourage a return to steroids, frequently in even larger doses, and a craving for the euphoria that the person felt while on them.

A variation of the cycling pattern is the practice of *pyramiding*. An individual starts with low doses of steroids, gradually increases the doses over several weeks prior to an athletic competition, then tapers off entirely before the competition itself in an attempt to escape detection during drug testing. However, pyramiding leads to the same problems during withdrawal and abstention as cycling, except that the symptoms occur during the competition itself.

A major problem associated with steroid abuse is the potential for an individual to believe that his or her physique will forever be imperfect. In a kind of "reverse anorexia" that has been called **muscle dysmorphia,** some body builders continue to see their bodies as weak and small when they look at themselves in the mirror, despite their greatly enhanced physical development. Peer pressure at the gyms and clubs is a factor in never being satisfied with the size of one's muscles, but it is becoming apparent that societal pressures play a role as well. In the case of males, it is interesting to examine the evolution of the design of G.I. Joe action figures over the years, from the original toy introduced in 1964 to the most recent incarnation introduced in 1998 (Figure 8.1). Just as the Barbie doll has been criticized as setting an impossible ideal for the female body among girls, male-oriented action figures can be criticized on the same basis for boys.[17]

It has been estimated that between 13 and 18 percent of those who have taken steroids show signs of physical and psychological dependence, in that they are unable to control or cut down on them, take more steroids than they intended, develop a tolerance to them, or take them to relieve or avoid undesirable withdrawal symptoms (Health Alert). Unfortunately, few prevention programs have addressed themselves to the potential for steroid abuse.[18]

Counterfeit Steroids and the Placebo Effect

As with many illicit drugs, some products marketed to look like anabolic steroids are not the real thing. The

muscle dysmorphia (dis-MORF-ee-ah): The perception of one's own body as small and weak and one's musclature as inadequately developed, despite evidence to the contrary. Also known as megorexia, the condition of muscle dysmorphia is a form of body dysmorphic disorder.

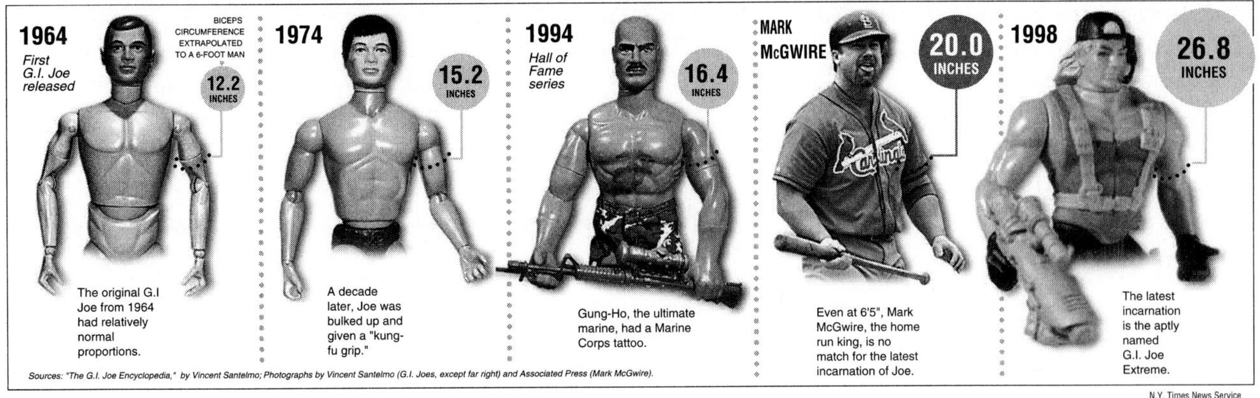

FIGURE 8.1

The muscular development of the G.I. Joe action figure has increased dramatically since its introduction in 1964. The estimated bicep circumference for a 6-foot man, based upon dimensions of the action figure, has more than doubled.

Source: As G.I. Joe bulks up, concern for the 98-pound weakling (1999, May 30). *New York Times,* p. D2.

problem here is that athletes are notoriously superstitious and easily leave themselves open to placebo effects. On the one hand, in the case of anabolic steroids, the effects on muscle development are usually so dramatic that it is difficult to mistake the response as simply a result of a placebo effect. On the other hand, several other forms of ergogenic drugs have far more subtle effects, and psychological factors can end up playing a greater role. Consider the clever strategy a baseball trainer claims to have used for the St. Louis Cardinals in the 1960s:

> *In 1964, I devised a yellow RBI pill, a red shutout pill, and a potent green hitting pill. Virtually every player on the team took them, and some wouldn't go out on the field until they took my pills. They worked so well that we won the pennant. We used*

Health Alert

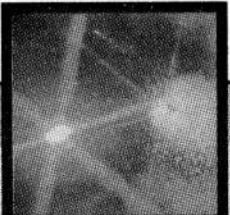

The Symptoms of Steroid Abuse

For Both Sexes

1. Rapid increases in strength and/or size beyond what you would expect in a relatively short time. Putting on ten to twenty pounds of solid muscle within a period of a few weeks or so should be a strong warning.
2. Involvement in activities in which steroid abuse is known to be condoned or encouraged
3. Sudden increases in appetite and preoccupation with changes in one's physical condition
4. Recent appearance of acne, particularly on the upper back, shoulders, and arms
5. Premature male-pattern baldness, including a rapidly receding hairline or loss of hair from the top rear of the head
6. A puffy appearance in the face as if the individual is retaining water
7. An increase in moodiness or unusual shifts in mood
8. A reddening of the face, neck, and upper chest, appearing as if one is constantly flushed
9. A yellowing of the skin or the whites of the eyes, stemming from a disturbance in liver function

For Men

1. An enlargement of the breasts, often accompanied by protruding nipples
2. An increase in sexual interest and a tendency to display that interest more aggressively

For Women

1. A lowering of the vocal range
2. Smaller or flatter breasts (see Table 8.2)

Source: Wright, James E., and Cowart, Virginia S. (1990). *Anabolic steroids: Altered states.* Carmel IN: Benchmark Press, pp. 71–91.

them again in 1967 and 1968 and also won the pennant. They worked because I never told them that the pills were placebos.[19]

Frequently, a bogus drug can achieve enormous popularity simply by word of mouth. A former steroid "customer" relates the following story:

> *Bolasterone. It swept the country. They made millions. Millions, those California guys. All it was, was vegetable oil, a little bit of testosterone, and liquid aspirin. And they called it Bolasterone. And they hyped it up so much. It was selling for $250 to $275 a bottle. You would do anything to get this stuff. [They said] "Mr. Olympia used it! Secretly." I tell you, Madison Avenue could not have come up with a better campaign to sell this stuff. . . . If you had a bottle of it, I mean you could sell it for anything. . . . [It was hyped] through the grapevine. Underground. The network was incredible. From gym to gym to gym. . . . They'll say, "Did you see M.? He put on 15 pounds in a week." "What the hell is he using?" "Don't say anything. He's using Bolasterone!" "Wow. What the hell is it? Can you get it?" "Yeah, I can."*[20]

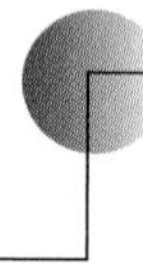

Nonsteroid Hormones and Ergogenic Supplements

Certainly anabolic steroids have dominated the ergogenic drug scene, but other illicit drugs continue to be available for performance-enhancing purposes.

Human Growth Hormone

One illicit alternative, **human growth hormone (hGH),** has become increasingly popular, according to experts in this field, because it is more widely available and cheaper than in previous years, in contrast to the ever more costly illicit steroids. Those who take this pituitary hormone, however, face the increased risk of developing a significant side effect called **acromegaly,** a condition resulting in a coarse and misshapen head, enlarged hands and feet, and damage to various internal organs.

Prior to 1985, hGH was obtained from the pituitary glands of human cadavers, but now genetically engineered hGH (brand names: Protropin and Humatrope) is available, approved by the FDA for the treatment of rare cases of stunted growth. While the distribution of these drugs is controlled by their manufacturers as carefully as possible, supplies manage to get diverted for illicit use. Because hGH has a very short half-life, no screening procedure has yet been developed to detect it, so long as the individual abstains from it immediately prior to the test.[21]

Some of the other ergogenic drugs and aids presently used for illicit athletic or body-building purposes are listed in Table 8.3.

Dietary Supplements as Ergogenic Aids

Specific products classified as dietary supplements are currently being consumed for their presumed ergogenic effects. Since these supplements are not classified by the FDA as drugs (see Chapter 1), they can be marketed and sold without a prescription. As a result, there is no regulatory limitation on the dosage levels that can be safely ingested or evaluation of effectiveness.

A prominent example of this type of dietary supplement is **androstenedione.** Technically speaking, androstenedione is not an anabolic steroid because it is not based upon the specific structure of testosterone itself. It is, however, testosterone-related because it is a naturally occurring metabolic precursor to testosterone. In other words, the body converts androstenedione to testosterone due to the action of specific enzymes in the liver. At the recommended daily dose of 300 mg, androstenedione has been found to increase testosterone levels by an average of 34 percent above normal.[22]

Androstenedione rose to prominence in the late 1990s when it became public that St. Louis Cardinals baseball player Mark McGwire had been taking the supplement during his phenomenal 1998 hitting season (70 home runs, far eclipsing the previous record). A storm of controversy ensued, with some commentators suggesting that McGwire's record be disallowed because of his androstenedione use. While banned by the National Football League and other professional and amateur sports organizations, androstenedione is not banned in Major League Baseball and, as such, McGwire's use was not illegal.

In 1999, McGwire discontinued taking the supplement, basing his decision largely on his concern about

---

human growth hormone (hGH): A naturally occurring hormone promoting growth, particularly in the long bones of the body.

acromegaly (A-kroh-MEG-ah-lee): A condition resulting in structural abnormalities of the head, hands, and feet, as well as damage to internal organs.

androstenedione (AN-dro-steen-DIE-own): A dietary supplement, acting as a metabolic precursor to testosterone, that is available for use as an ergogenic agent.

TABLE 8.3

Nonsteroid ergogenic drugs in sports and bodybuilding		
DRUG	LICIT USE OR NATURAL ORIGIN	ILLICIT APPLICATION
Zeranol	Drug to fatten cattle	Anabolic agent
Carnitine	Nonprotein amino acid	Anabolic agent
Clenbuterol	Drug to treat asthma in Europe; not approved for any purpose in the U.S.	Anabolic agent
Deprenyl	Drug to treat Parkinson's disease; inhibitor of monoamine oxidase (MAO)	Amphetamine-like stimulant for endurance events
erythropoietin (EPO)	Naturally occurring hormone, to treat anemia	Increases red blood cells; enhances oxygen-carrying capacity of the blood
beta blockers	To treat high blood pressure, cardiac arrhythmias, and social anxiety	Increases steadiness in archery and other shooting events

Sources: Dolan, Edward F. (1992). *Drugs and sports* (rev. ed.). New York: Franklin Watts, p. 17. Kammerer, R. Craig (1993). Drug testing and anabolic steroids. In Charles E. Yesalis (Ed.), *Anabolic steroids in exercise and sport.* Champaign IL: Human Kinetics Publishers, pp. 283–308. Wadler, Gary I., and Hainline, Brian (1989). *Drugs and the athlete.* Philadelphia: F. A. Davis, pp. 159–177.

his effect as a role model on young people. Interestingly, his 1999 hitting record diminished only slightly, still reaching the third-highest total home runs in professional baseball history. However, the publicity surrounding androstenedione use and its easy availability has been blamed for a 30 percent increase among eighth grade boys and a 75 percent increase among tenth grade boys in the use of anabolic steroids from 1998 to 2000.[23]

Another dietary supplement to have recently gained prominence as an ergogenic agent is the amino acid **creatine.** Ingestion of creatine has been found to enhance the increase in fat-free mass, physical performance, and muscle size as a response to heavy-resistance weight training. It has been theorized that these effects may be due to the retention of water by muscle cells, causing them to expand in size. The expansion of muscle cells then triggers the production of more protein and an increase in muscle mass. While short-term use of creatine has not been found to influence blood pressure or kidney function, long-term adverse effects have not been fully determined.[24]

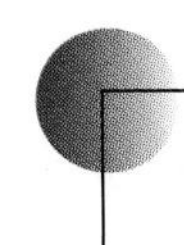

Current Drug-Testing Procedures and Policies

Since the mid-1960s, organizers of major athletic competitions have attempted to develop effective screening procedures to prevent the use of ergogenic drugs from resulting in one competitor having an unfair advantage over another. Needless to say, neither have these procedures proved perfect nor have they served as an effective deterrent for drug use among athletes. We are used to hearing about championship events accompanied by reports of an athlete disqualified from competing or denied the honor of winning because he or she tested positive for a particular banned substance. Ironically, the present status of drug testing as a fact of life in modern sports has brought with it a new form of contest, pitting the skill and ingenuity of the laboratory scientist whose job it is to detect the presence of ergogenic drugs against the skill and ingenuity of the athlete in devising ways to use them without detection.

This section looks at drug-testing techniques designed to detect not only performance-enhancing drugs that are relevant to sports but also a wider range of illicit drugs, such as heroin, cocaine, and marijuana. Within some sports organizations, such as the National Collegiate Athletic Association (NCAA), drug tests are conducted not only for the presence of ergogenic drugs but also for the presence of drugs that have no particular ergogenic benefits. In the case of marijuana, for example, the proper description for its effects with regard to athletic competitions might be *ergolytic* (performance-hampering). The policy is defended on the premise that athletes have the potential for exposure to illicit substances, and no collegiate

creatine (CREE-ah-teen): A dietary supplement available for ergogenic uses.

athlete should be permitted to compete while engaging in illegal activity. Related issues surrounding drug testing in the general population, particularly in the workplace, will be examined in Chapter 17.

Techniques for Drug Testing

Present-day drug-testing procedures begin with a urine sample from the individual in question. The advantages lie in the ease and noninvasiveness of collecting urine, the ease with which urine can be analyzed for specific factors, and the fact that drugs or their metabolites (by-products) are usually very stable in frozen urine. Therefore, it is possible to provide long-term storage of positive samples, in the event that the results are disputed. The disadvantages are that many perceive urine collection to be a humiliating experience, a dehydrated athlete immediately after competing may find it difficult to urinate, and there may be ways to tamper with the urine sample prior to testing. Despite these problems, however, this procedure is considered to be the most practical way of testing for drugs. Testing procedures based on saliva, blood, or hair samples are available but not widely used.

The two major urinanalysis methods are the **enzyme immunoassay (EIA)** technique and a procedure combining **gas chromatography and mass spectrometry (GC/MS).** In both methods, the collected urine is divided into two samples prior to being sent off to the laboratory, so that if the analysis of one sample yields a positive outcome the analysis can be repeated on the other sample. This reanalysis procedure is often required if an individual appeals the original test result.[25]

With the EIA method, a separate test must be run on each particular drug that is being screened. First, at an earlier time, the substance to be tested for (THC or cocaine, for example) has been injected into an animal, eliciting specific immunological antibodies to that substance. The antibodies are then purified into a testing substrate. The combination of the collected urine and the testing substrate will yield a specific reaction if the urine contains the banned substance. A popular commercial testing kit for screening major controlled substances (opiates, amphetamines, cocaine, benzodiazepines, and marijuana), called **EMIT (enzyme multiplied immunoassay technique)**, has been marketed by Syva Laboratories, a subsidiary of Syntex Corporation in Palo Alto, California, since the early 1970s. This kit is relatively inexpensive and can be used to screen large numbers of urine samples. It is so widely available that its trademark name, EMIT, is often used to mean any form of EIA method.

With the GC/MS method, the urine is first vaporized and combined with an inert gas, then passed over a number of chemically treated columns. Through the process of gas chromatography, technicians are able to identify the presence of a banned substance by the different colorations that are left on the columns. After this has been done, the gas is then ionized (converted into an electrically active form) and sent through an electric current and magnetic field that separates out each of the different ions (electrically charged particles) in the gas. Through the process of mass spectrometry, a particular "fingerprint," or "signature," of each chemical substance can be detected and measured. The GC/MS technique is considered more definitive than the EIA technique, but it is considerably more expensive and time-consuming. It is also the only testing procedure adequate to screen for anabolic steroids.[26]

Sensitivity and Specificity

As you might imagine, the two principal questions surrounding drug-testing methods are (1) how much of the banned substance needs to be in the urine before it is picked up as a positive test (the sensitivity of the test) and (2) whether it is possible to yield a false-positive result in which the test comes out positive but the urine is in actuality "clean" (the specificity of the test). In this regard, the GC/MS test is more sensitive and specific than the EIA test.

Frequently, the GC/MS analysis is performed as a confirmation of a positive EIA test. Nonetheless, false positives can occur even with the GC/MS test. Eating a poppy seed roll prior to drug testing, for example, has resulted in false-positive indications of opiate use; therapeutic levels of ibuprofen (brand names: Advil, Motrin, and Nuprin, among others) have resulted in false-positive indications of marijuana smoking. In addition, the passive inhalation of marijuana smoke can leave sufficient levels of THC metabolites to result in false-positive indications of marijuana smoking, though the density of smoke that needs to be present for this to happen makes it unlikely that individuals would be completely unaware that they were being exposed to marijuana.[27]

enzyme immunoassay (EIA): One of the two major drug-testing techniques for detecting banned substances or drugs.
gas chromatography/mass spectrometry (GC/MS): A drug-testing technique based on the combination of gas chromatography and mass spectrometry.
EMIT (enzyme multiplied immunoassay technique): A commercial testing kit for screening major controlled substances, based upon the enzyme immunoassay test.

National concern about drug abuse in all its forms has caused us to consider an increased level of drug testing in our society. Here is an editorial cartoonist's comment on the extent to which this policy might be applied.

Masking Drugs and Chemical Manipulations

Two specific ways have been attempted to disguise the prior use of anabolic steroids so that the outcome of a drug test is a false-negative; both are now relatively obsolete. The first was to take the antigout drug probenecid (brand name: Benemid). Available since 1987, it does mask the presence of anabolic steroids, but it is now on the list of banned substances for competitive athletes and is easily detected by GC/MS techniques. The second way was to increase the level of epitestosterone in the body. The standard procedure for determining the present or prior use of anabolic steroids is to calculate the ratio of testosterone against the level of epitestosterone, a naturally occurring hormone that is usually stable at relatively low levels in the body. International athletic organizations have agreed on a ratio of 6:1 or higher as the standard for indicating steroid use. If epitestosterone is artificially elevated, the ratio can be manipulated downward so as to indicate a false-negative result in drug testing. However, suspiciously high levels of epitestosterone can now be detected by GC/MS techniques, so this form of manipulation is no longer successful.[28]

Pinpointing the Time of Drug Use

It is important to remember that a positive result in a drug test indicates merely that the test has detected a minimal level of a drug or its metabolite. It has not determined when that drug was introduced into the body or the length of time drug-taking behavior was going on. The time it takes for the body to get rid of the metabolites of a particular drug varies considerably, from a few hours to a few weeks. Table 8.4 shows the range of detection periods for major drugs of abuse.

TABLE 8.4

Detection periods for various drugs

DRUG	DETECTION PERIOD	DRUG	DETECTION PERIOD
alcohol	1/2 to 1 day	opiates and opiate-like drugs	
amphetamines and derivatives	1–7 days	Dilaudid	2–4 days
barbiturates		Darvon	6–48 hours
amobarbital, pentobarbital	2–4 days	heroin or morphine	2–4 days
phenobarbital	Up to 30 days	methadone	2–3 days
secobarbital	2–4 days	phencyclidine (PCP)	
benzodiazepines	Up to 30 days	Casual use	2–7 days
cocaine		Chronic, heavy use	Several months
Occasional use	6–12 hours	Quaalude	2–4 days
Repeated use	Up to 48 hours	anabolic steroids	
marijuana (THC)		Fat-soluble injectables	6–8 months
Casual use up to 4 joints per week	5–7 days	Water-soluble oral types	3–6 weeks
Daily use	10–15 days	over-the-counter cold medications containing ephedrine derivatives as decongestants	48–72 hours
Chronic, heavy use	1–2 months		

Sources: Allen and Hanbury's Athletic drug reference (1994). Durham NC: Clean Data, p. 19. Inaba, Darryl S., and Cohen, William E. (1989). *Uppers, downers, all arounders.* Ashland OR: Cinemed, p. 206.

QUICK CONCEPT CHECK 8.2

Understanding Drug Testing

Check your understanding of present-day drug-testing results by indicating whether or not the following statements are true.

1. EMIT results are more sensitive than GC/MS results. ❑ yes ❑ no
2. Benemid is an effective way of achieving a false-negative result. ❑ yes ❑ no
3. The time of marijuana smoking is one conclusion that drug testing has great difficulty in determining. ❑ yes ❑ no
4. Athletes are generally very cooperative in achieving the least number of false-negative outcomes. ❑ yes ❑ no
5. Anabolic steroid screening is presently mandated by the International Olympic Committee for winners of Olympic events. ❑ yes ❑ no

Answers: 1. no 2. no 3. yes 4. no 5. yes

An additional point to remember is that the future possibility of a positive drug test cannot be an effective deterrent against the abuse of drugs. For example, an athlete can easily manipulate the result of a scheduled drug test by planning to be off the drug long enough prior to testing for the metabolites to be relatively low. Only through a random (unannounced) testing program can the test results adequately reflect the level of drug-taking behavior.

Unfortunately, random drug testing is costly. Relatively few colleges and considerably fewer high schools can afford a random schedule of drug testing; most high schools cannot afford drug testing at all. And it is worth considering the following fact: For all those individuals who are abusing anabolic steroids or other ergogenic drugs outside of organized athletic programs, no fear of a positive drug test exists because they will never be required to undergo any form of drug testing, random or otherwise.

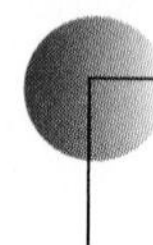

What Can Be Done about Anabolic Steroid Abuse?

Anabolic steroids and other ergogenic agents are quite different from many of the abused drugs covered in previous chapters in that they affect the way we look and how we compare to others rather than the way we feel. Charles E. Yesalis, one of the leading experts in steroid abuse, has put it this way:

> *If you were stranded on a desert island, you might use cocaine if it were available, but nobody would use steroids. On a desert island, nobody cares what you look like and there is nothing to win. We are the ones who have made the determination that appearance and winning are all important. We're telling kids in our society that sports is more than a game. Until we change those signals, for the most part, we might as well tell people to get used to drug use.*[29]

The future of the fight against anabolic steroid abuse is, in part, staked to whether we can change the winner-take-all mentality of our culture. Unfortunately, there seems to be little cause for optimism. Numerous surveys taken among young athletes and nonathletes alike indicate that the social signals are crystal clear and they are more than willing to take up the challenge, despite the risks. They have typically been asked variations on the following question: "If you had a magic drug that was so fantastic that if you took it once you would win every competition you would enter, from the Olympic decathlon to Mr. Universe, for the next five years, but it had one minor drawback—it would kill you five years after you took it—would you still take the drug?" More than half of those polled answered yes to this question.[30]

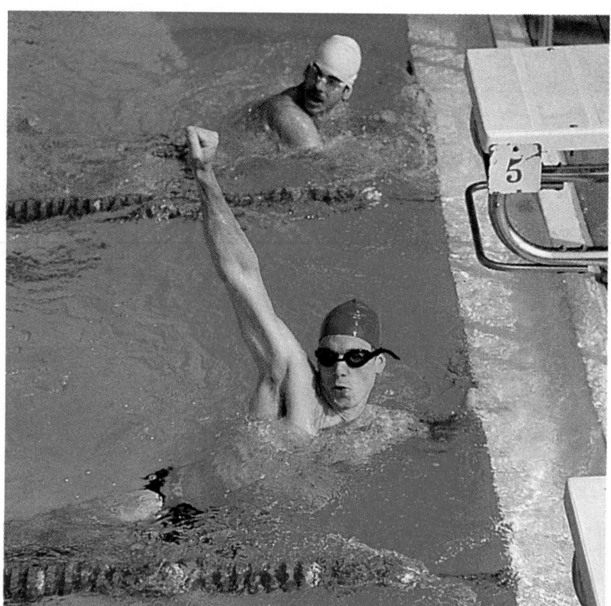

The pressure to be number one exists in all areas of athletic competition.

There seems to be a more general sense of competition that goes beyond dreams of athletic performance. It is apparent that an idealized body image is part of today's standard for a sense of sexuality and social acceptance. This standard might not be news at all to women, but it is a fairly recent development for men. In 2000, a study investigated young men in the United States, France, and Austria. They were asked to alter an image of a male body on a computer screen to reflect their perception of their own bodies, how they would like their bodies to look, and the body type they thought women found most attractive. The images created of their own bodies were roughly accurate; their idealized bodies had about twenty-eight pounds more muscle; they predicted that women would prefer about an additional two pounds of muscle. Interestingly, when women were given the chance to devise the ideal male body type from their perspective, they selected, as the authors expressed it, "a very ordinary looking male body."[31]

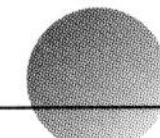

SUMMARY

Drug-Taking Behavior in Sports

- The use of ergogenic (performance-enhancing) drugs in athletic competition has a long history, dating from the original Olympic Games in ancient Greece.
- In the modern era, the principal type of ergogenic drugs has been anabolic steroids. These synthetic drugs are all based on variations of the testosterone molecule.
- Since the late 1980s, anabolic steroids have been popular with body builders as well as competitive athletes. This latter group typically takes steroids in enormous quantities and administers them in a largely unsupervised fashion.

The Hazards of Anabolic Steroids

- The hazards of steroid use include liver tumors, mood swings, and increased aggressiveness.
- For men, the effects include lower sperm count, enlargement of the breasts, atrophy of the testicles, baldness, and severe acne. For women, masculinizing changes occur, only some of which are reversible if steroids are withdrawn.

Patterns of Anabolic Steroid Abuse

- Since 1990, possession and sales of anabolic steroids have been illegal without specific medical prescriptions. These drugs are now distributed through illicit black-market channels.
- A proportion of individuals taking large doses of steroids develop both physical and psychological dependence.

Nonsteroid Hormones and Ergogenic Supplements

- Human growth hormone (hGH) is a nonsteroid hormone that has been used for ergogenic purposes.
- Two dietary supplements, androstenedione and creatine, have been prominent recently as ergogenic aids.

Current Drug-Testing Procedures and Policies

- Drug-testing procedures, chiefly for those in organized athletics, have become increasingly sophisticated in their ability to detect the presence of banned substances.
- Two major techniques, both based on urine samples, are enzyme immunoassay (EIA) and a combination of gas chromatography and mass spectrometry (GC/MS).
- The ultimate goal of drug-testing procedures is to make it impossible to yield either a false-negative or false-positive result.

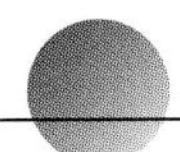

KEY TERMS

androstenedione, p. 176
creatine, p. 177
EMIT (enzyme multiplied immunoassay technique), p. 178
enzyme immunoassay (EIA), p. 178
ergogenic, p. 168
gas chromatography/mass spectrometry (GC/MS), p. 178
gynecomastia, p. 172
human growth hormone (hGH), p. 176
muscle dysmorphia, p. 174
priapism, p. 172

ENDNOTES

1. Dolan, Edward F. (1986). *Drugs in sports* (rev. ed.). New York: Franklin Watts, pp. 17–18. Meer, Jeff (1987). *Drugs and sports.* New York: Chelsea House, p. 21. Wadler, Gary I., and Hainline, Brian (1989). *Drugs and the athlete.* Philadelphia: F. A. Davis, pp. 3–17.
2. Meer, *Drugs and sports,* pp. 61–75. Taylor, William N. (1991). *Macho medicine: The history of the anabolic steroid epidemic.* Jefferson NC: McFarland and Co., pp. 3–16.
3. Bhasin, Shalender; Storer, Thomas W.; Berman, Nancy; Callegari, Carlos; Clevenger, Brenda; Phillips, Jeffrey; Bunnel, Thomas J.; Tricker, Ray; Shirazi, Aida; and Casaburi, Richard (1996). The effects of supraphysiologic doses of testosterone on muscle size and strength in normal men. *New England Journal of Medicine, 335,* 1–7. Lombardo, John (1993). The efficacy and mechanisms of action of anabolic steroids. In Charles E. Yesalis (Ed.), *Anabolic steroids in sport and exercise.* Champaign IL: Human Kinetics Publishers, p. 100.
4. Scott, Jack (1971, October 17). It's not how you play the game, but what pill you take. *New York Times Magazine,* p. 41.
5. Catlin, Don H., and Murray, Thomas H. (1996). Performance-enhancing drugs, fair competition, and Olympic sport. *Journal of the American Medical Association, 276,* 231–237. Dickman, Steven (1991). East Germany: Science in the disservice of the state. *Science, 254,* 26–27. Gold medal gymnast fails her drug test (2000, September 26). *New York Times,* p. S2. Longman, Jere (2000, September 26). A night full of magic, under the cast of a shadow. *New York Times,* pp. S1, S5. Maimon, Alan (2000, February 6). Doping's sad toll: One athlete's tale from East Germany. *New York Times,* pp. A1, A6. Yesalis, Charles E., Courson, Stephen P., and Wright, James (1993). History of anabolic steroid use in sport and exercise. In Charles E. Yesalis (Ed.), *Anabolic steroids in sport and exercise.* Champaign IL: Human Kinetics Publishers, pp. 1–33.
6. W.W.F.'s McMahon indicted (1993, November 19). *New York Times,* p. B12. Yesalis, Courson, and Wright, History of anabolic steroid use, pp. 40–42.
7. Buckley, William E.; Yesalis, Charles E.; Friedl, Karl E.; Anderson, William A.; Streit, Andrea L.; and Wright, James E. (1988). Estimated prevalence of anabolic steroid use among male high school seniors. *Journal of the American Medical Association, 260,* 3441–3445. Yesalis, Charles E. (1993). Introduction. In Charles E. Yesalis (Ed.), *Anabolic steroids in sport and exercise.* Champaign IL: Human Kinetics Publishers, pp. xxxi–xxxii.
8. Brower, Kirk J.; Catlin, Donald H.; Blow, Frederic C.; Eliopulos, George A.; and Bereford, T. P. (1991). Clinical assessment and urine testing for anabolic-androgenic steroid abuse and dependence. *American Journal of Drug and Alcohol Abuse, 17,* 161–172. Council on Scientific Affairs (1990). Medical and nonmedical uses of anabolic-androgenic steroids. *Journal of the American Medical Association, 264,* 2923–2927.
9. Friedl, Karl E. (1993). Effects of anabolic steroids on physical health. In Charles E. Yesalis (Ed.), *Anabolic steroids in sport and exercise.* Champaign IL: Human Kinetics Publishers, pp. 107–150. Galloway, Gantt P. (1997). Anabolic-androgenic steroids. In Joyce H. Lowinson; Pedro Ruiz; Robert B. Millman; and John G. Langrod (Eds.). *Substance abuse: A comprehensive textbook.* Baltimore: Williams and Wilkins, pp. 308–318.
10. Friedl, *Effects of anabolic steroids,* pp. 121–131.
11. Ibid., pp. 116–121. Karch, Steven B. (1996). *The pathology of drug abuse* (2nd ed.). Boca Raton FL: CRC Press, pp. 409–429.
12. Su, Tung-Ping; Pagliaro, Michael; Schmidt, Peter J.; Pickar, David; Wolkowitz, Owen; and Rubinow, David R. (1993). Neuropsychiatric effects of anabolic steroids in male normal volunteers. *Journal of the American Medical Association, 269,* 2760–2764.
13. Greenberg, Alan (1991, June 29). Alzado has a serious message to kids about steroids—Don't use them. *Hartford (CT) Courant,* cited in Jim Ferstle (1993), Evolution and politics of drug testing. In Charles E. Yesalis (Ed.), *Anabolic steroids,* p. 276.
14. Sharp, Martin, and Collins, David (1998). Exploring the "inevitability" of the relationship between anabolic-androgenic steroid use and aggression in human males. *Journal of Sport and Exercise Psychology, 20,* 379–394. Tricker, Ray; Casaburi, Richard; Storer, Thomas W.; Clevenger, Brenda; Berman, Nancy; Shirazi, Aida; and Bhasin, Shalender (1996). The effects of supraphysiological doses of testosterone on angry behavior in healthy eugonal men—A clinical research center study. *Journal of Clinical Endocrinology, 81,* 3754–3758.
15. Bahrke, Michael S. (1993). Psychological effects of endogenous testosterone and anabolic-androgenic steroids. In Charles E. Yesalis (Ed.), *Anabolic steroids in sport and exercise.* Champaign IL: Human Kinetics Publishers, pp. 161–192.
16. Johnston, Lloyd D. (2000, December 14). "Ecstasy" use rises sharply among teens in 2000; use of many other drugs

stays steady, but significant declines are reported for some. News release from the University of Michigan, Ann Arbor, Table 1.

17. Pope, Harrison G.; Gruber, Amanda J.; Choi, Priscilla; Olivardia, Roberto; and Phillips, Katherine A. (1997). Muscle dysmorphia: An underrecognized form of body dysmorphic disorder. *Psychosomatics*, 38, 548–557. Wroblewska, Anna-M. (1997). Androgenic-anabolic steroids and body dysmorphia in young men. *Journal of Psychosomatic Research*, 42, 225–234.
18. Bahrke, Michael S., Yesalis, Charles E., and Brower, Kirk J. (1998). Anabolic-androgenic steroid abuse and performance-enhancing drugs among adolescents. *Sport Psychiatry*, 7, 821–838. Beel, Andrea; Maycock, Bruce; and McLean, Neil (1998). Current perspectives on anabolic steroids. *Drug and Alcohol Review*, 17, 87–103. Karch, *The pathology of drug abuse.* Schrof, Joanne M. (1992, June 1). Pumped up. *U.S. News and World Report*, pp. 55–63.
19. Quotation by Bob Bauman (1992). In Bob Goldman and Ronald Klatz, *Death in the locker room II: Drugs and sports.* Chicago: Elite Sports Medicine Publications, pp. 10–11.
20. Goldstein, Paul J. (1990). Anabolic steroids: An ethnographic approach. In Geraline C. Lin and Lynda Erinoff (Eds.), *Anabolic steroid abuse* (NIDA Research Monograph 102). Rockville MD: National Institute on Drug Abuse, p. 84.
21. Catlin, Don; Wright, Jim; Pope, Harrison; and Liggett, Mariah (1993). Assessing the threat of anabolic steroids: Sportsmedicine update. *The physician and sportsmedicine*, 21, 37–44. Wadler and Hainline, *Drugs and the athlete*, pp. 70–74.
22. Leder, Benjamin Z.; Longcope, Christopher; Catlin, Don H.; Ahrens, Brian; and Schoenfeld, Joel S. (2000). Oral androstenedione administration and serum testosterone concentrations in young men. *Journal of the American Medical Association*, 283, 779–782.
23. Johnston, "Ecstasy" use, Table 1. Mravic, Mark (2000, February 21). Ban it, bud. *Sports Illustrated*, pp. 24, 26.
24. Gower, Timothy (1999, February 17). Safety and the search for muscle in a bottle. *New York Times*, p. 14. Mihic, Sasa; MacDonald, Jay R.; McKenzie, Scott; and Tarnopolsky, Mark A. (2000). Acute creatine loading increases fat-free mass, but does not affect blood pressure, plasma creatinine, or CK activity in men and women. *Medicine and Science in Sports and Exercise*, 32, 291–296.
25. Wadler and Hainline, *Drugs and the athlete*, pp. 201–202.
26. Meer, *Drugs and sports*, pp. 92–95.
27. *Allen and Hanbury's athletic drug reference* (1994). Durham NC: Clean Data, pp. 65–66. Struempler, Richard E. (1987, May/June). Excretion of codeine and morphine following ingestion of poppy seeds. *Journal of Analytical Toxicology*, 11, 97–99. Wadler and Hainline, *Drugs and the athlete*, pp. 208–209.
28. Catlin, Wright, Pope, and Liggett, Assessing the threat, p. 39.
29. Quotation of Charles E. Yesalis. In Wright and Cowart, *Anabolic steriods*, p. 196. Schwerin, Michael J.; Corcoran, Kevin J.; Fisher, Leslee; Patterson, David; Askew, Waide; Orlich, Tracy; and Shanks, Scott (1996). Social physique anxiety, body esteem, and social anxiety in bodybuilders and self-reported anabolic steroid users. *Addictive Behaviors*, 21, 1–8.
30. Elliot, Diane, and Goldberg, Linn (1996). Intervention and prevention of steroid use in adolescents. *American Journal of Sports Medicine*, 24, 546–546. Goldman, Bob, and Klatz, Ronald (1992). *Death in the locker room II: Drugs and sports.* Chicago: Elite Sports Medicine Publications, pp. 23–24.
31. Pope, Harrison G.; Gruber, Amanda J.; Mangweth, Barbara; Bureau, Benjamin; deCol, Christine; Jouvent, Roland; and Hudson, James I. (2000). Body image perception among men in three countries. *American Journal of Psychiatry*, 157, 1297–1301. Quotation on p. 1300.

Point Counterpoint

Should Marijuana Be Available for Medicinal Use?

The following discussion of viewpoints presents the opinions of people on both sides of the controversial issue of whether marijuana should be available for medicinal purposes. Read them with an open mind. Don't think you have to come up with the final answer, nor should you necessarily agree with the argument presented last. Many of the ideas in this feature come from sources listed.

POINT

Marijuana has been a Schedule I drug since the classification of controlled substances began in 1970. It is presently not considered worthy of any medical application. There is no question that marijuana carries a substantial potential for abuse. If we were to change its status to a Schedule II category, we would be authorizing an abusable drug for widespread use. Given the dramatic rise in marijuana smoking among young people since 1992, this move would make an already bad situation far worse.

COUNTERPOINT

The logic escapes me. Morphine and cocaine are presently Schedule II drugs. No one questions their abuse potential. In fact, one could argue that historically their abuse potential has exceeded that of marijuana. Yet morphine and cocaine are available for specific medical applications. Granted we should not change other drugs such as LSD and heroin from the Schedule I category, but why exclude marijuana from Schedule II when morphine and cocaine are already there? Besides, referendum voters in Arizona, California, and other U.S. states have approved medical use by licensed physicians since the mid-1990s.

POINT

The referendum in Arizona demonstrates how dangerous it is to decide these things by popular vote. Arizona voters approved not only marijuana but also LSD and heroin for medical use as long as the drug was prescribed by a physician. Can you imagine the problems if heroin and LSD were now available by a simple piece of prescription paper? Is there no end to it?

COUNTERPOINT

It can be argued that Arizona might have gone too far. We're talking marijuana here, and nothing else should be confusing the issue. Besides, the California referendum authorized the medical use of marijuana only. That's where the debate should be directed.

POINT

There are good arguments against this trend. At a time when drugs are being considered so casually by our society, medical applications for marijuana would be tantamount to our political leaders sending a message of permissiveness to young people.

COUNTERPOINT

We're debating a medical and scientific issue. We should not confuse it with politics or social concerns.

POINT

Forget about politics; social concerns, however, can never be ignored when public policy changes are being debated.

COUNTERPOINT

I agree, but let's not discuss a medical and scientific issue solely on the basis of its societal impact.

POINT

All right. What is the medical and scientific basis for medical marijuana? The answer is: merely the anecdotal evidence from a select group of people. Besides, Marisol (synthetic THC) is already available for medical uses. Isn't that enough? Where is the evidence that marijuana would be better?

COUNTERPOINT

Good question. There is ample anecdotal evidence that people suffering from nausea and glaucoma fail to find Marisol to be helpful, whereas they respond favorably to marijuana. Alternative drugs that are currently available for nausea and glaucoma are either very expensive (some cost as much as $1,000 per month) or have undesirable side effects. But do you know why we don't know much about the specific medical benefits of marijuana? Because the federal government has, prior to 1997, refused to approve specific research directed at finding out. What would happen if the results come out that the benefits outweigh the negative side effects?

POINT

Then the therapeutic advantages would still have to be weighed against the social problems that increased marijuana availability would cause.

COUNTERPOINT

Let's put it this way. Suppose you had a close relative dying from cancer and the chemotherapy was causing such nausea that body weight was declining at an alarming rate. If marijuana promoted a better quality of life in those last months, wouldn't the social concerns seem relatively unimportant. Wouldn't it be sad if politicians changed their minds only after someone close to them had died?

Critical Thinking Questions for Further Debate

1. How likely do you think it would be that increased availability of marijuana would lead to increased use of LSD and other presently illicit drugs?
2. If you were a physician faced with a patient who could be helped by marijuana but you knew that marijuana was officially designated as a Schedule I substance, what would you do?

Sources: Medical marijuana: Cross-eyed and painless (1991, July 6). *The Economist*, p. 89. Pollan, Michael (1997, July 20). Living with medical marijuana. *New York Times Magazine*, pp. 22–29, 40, 48, 54–56. Stimmel, B. (1995). Medical marijuana: To prescribe or not to prescribe, that is the question. *Journal of Addictive Diseases*, *14*, 1–3.

Alcohol: Social Beverage/ Social Drug

After you have completed this chapter, you will understand

- How alcoholic beverages are produced
- Alcohol use through history
- Patterns of alcohol consumption
- The pharmacology of alcohol
- Acute physiological and behavioral effects of alcohol
- Strategies for responsible alcohol consumption

I was invited to address a convention of high school teachers on the topic of drug abuse. When I arrived at the convention center to give my talk, I was escorted to a special suite, where I was encouraged to join the executive committee in a round of drug taking—the drug was a special high-proof single-malt whiskey. Later, the irony of the situation had its full impact. As I stepped to the podium under the influence of a psychoactive drug (i.e., the whiskey), I looked out through the haze of cigarette smoke at an audience concerned with the unhealthy impact of drugs on their students. The welcoming applause gradually gave way to the melodic tinkling of ice cubes in liquor glasses, and I began. They did not like what I had to say.

—John P. J. Pinel
Biopsychology *(1997)*

Pinel's observation in this opening vignette sums up the central problem plaguing American society in its dealings with alcohol use and abuse: the frequent failure to acknowledge that alcohol is indeed a psychoactive drug.[1] You may have heard someone remark, "He drinks a little too much, but at least he's not doing drugs." To many people, an alcoholic beverage is simply a social beverage; in actuality, it is a social drug.

We can see this problem reflected in a number of ways. College courses that cover drug abuse and its effect on society, perhaps the one you are taking right now, are often entitled "Drugs and Alcohol." Would you personally have expected to cover the effects of alcohol in a course simply entitled "Drugs" in your college catalog? If you answer no, then alcohol had better stay in the course title.

Even the U.S. federal government perpetuates the distinction, with separate agencies for alcohol abuse (the National Institute on Alcohol Abuse and Alcoholism, NIAAA) and the abuse of other drugs (the National Institute on Drug Abuse, NIDA). This bureaucratic partitioning admittedly has historic roots, and there may be valid reasons to continue the division from a management or budgetary point of view, but it has inadvertently reinforced an unfortunate and inaccurate notion that alcohol is somehow a substance that stands apart from other drugs of potential abuse. Fortunately, the phrase "alcohol and other drug abuse," often shortened to "AOD abuse," has become increasingly popular as a way of conveying the idea that problems of substance abuse can come from many sources (see Chapter 17). This chapter will consider alcohol as a drug with a unique history and tradition and its own set of acute risks. The next chapter will turn to its chronic effects, specifically the problems of alcohol abuse and alcoholism.

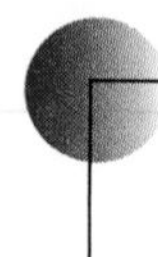

What Makes an Alcoholic Beverage?

Creating **ethyl alcohol**, through a process known as **fermentation**, is one of the easier things to do. Almost every culture in the world, at one time or another, has stumbled on the basic procedure. All you need is organic material with a sugar content (honey, grapes, berries, molasses, rye, apples, corn, sugar cane, rice, pumpkins, to name some examples) left undisturbed in a warm container for a time, and nature does the work. Microscopic yeast cells, floating through the air, land on this material and literally consume the sugar in it, so that, for every one sugar molecule consumed, two molecules of alcohol and two molecules of carbon dioxide are left behind as waste. The carbon dioxide bubbles out, and what remains is an alcoholic beverage, less sweet than the substance that began it all but with a new, noticeable kick. Basic fermentation results in an alcohol content of approximately 12 percent, best exemplified by standard grape wine.

The process of fermenting starchy grains such as barley to produce beer, called **brewing**, is somewhat more complicated. The barley first needs to be soaked in water until it sprouts, producing an enzyme that is capable of breaking down the starch into sugar. It is then slowly dried, the sprouts are removed, and the remainder (now called **barley malt**) is crushed into a powder. The barley malt is combined with water, corn, and rice to form a mixture called a **mash.** The water activates the enzyme so that the starches convert into sugars. The addition of yeast to the mash starts the fermentation process and produces an alcohol content of approximately 4.5 percent. The dried blossoms of the hop plant, called *hops*, are then added to the brew for the characteristic pungent flavoring and aroma.

Relying on fermentation alone gives a potentially maximal concentration of alcohol of about 15 percent. The reason for this limit is that an alcohol content above this level starts to kill the yeast and, in doing so, stops the fermentation process. In order to obtain a higher alcoholic content, another process, called **distillation,** must occur.

Distillation involves heating a container of some fermented mixture until it boils. Because alcohol has a lower boiling temperature than water, the vapor produced has a higher alcohol-to-water ratio than the original mixture. This alcohol-laden vapor is then drawn off into a special coiled apparatus (often referred to as a *still*), cooled until

ethyl alcohol: The product of fermentation of natural sugars. It is generally referred to simply as *alcohol*, though several types of nonethyl alcohol exist.
fermentation: The process of converting natural sugars into ethyl alcohol by the action of yeasts.
brewing: The process of producing beer from barley grain.
barley malt: Barley after it has been soaked in water, sprouts have grown, sprouts have been removed, and the mixture has been dried and crushed to a powder.
mash: Fermented barley malt, following liquification and combination with yeasts.
distillation: A process by which fermented liquid is boiled then cooled, so that the condensed product contains a higher alcoholic concentration than before.

TABLE 9.1

Prominent alcoholic beverages and their sources

BEVERAGE	SOURCE
Wines	
Red table wine	Fermented red grapes
White table wine	Fermented skinless grapes
Champagne	White wine bottled before yeast is gone, so that remaining carbon dioxide produces a carbonated effect
Sparkling wine	Red wine prepared like champagne or with carbonation added
Fortified wines	Wines whose alcohol content is raised or fortified to 20% by the addition of brandy (see below), for example, sherry, port, Marsala, and Madeira
Wine-like variations	
Hard cider	Fermented apples
Sake	Fermented rice
Beers	
Draft beer	Types of beer vary depending on brewing procedures. Draft and lager beers and ales contain 3–6% alcohol; malt liquor contains up to 8% alcohol
Lager beer	
Ale	
Malt liquor	
Distilled spirits	
Brandy	Distilled from grape wine, cherries, peaches, or other fruits
Liqueur or cordial	Brandy or gin, flavored with blackberry, cherry, chocolate, peppermint, licorice, etc. Alcohol content ranges from 20% to 55%
Rum	Distilled from the syrup of sugar cane or from molasses
Scotch whiskey	Distilled from fermented corn and barley malt
Rye whiskey	Distilled from rye and barley malt
Blended whiskey	A mixture of two or more types of whiskey
Bourbon whiskey	Distilled primarily from fermented corn
Gin	Distilled from either barley, potato, corn, wheat, or rye, and flavored with juniper berries
Vodka	Approximately 95% pure alcohol diluted by mixing with water
Tequila	Distilled from the fermented juice of the maguey plant
Aquavit or akvavit	Distilled from grains or potatoes, flavored with caraway seeds
Grain neutral spirits	Approximately 95% pure alcohol, used either for medicinal purposes or diluted and mixed in less-concentrated distilled spirits

Source: Adapted from Becker, Charles E., Roe, Robert L., and Scott, Robert A. (1979). *Alcohol as a drug: A curriculum on pharmacology, neurology, and toxicology.* Huntington NY: Robert Krieger Publishing, pp. 10–12.

it condenses back to a liquid, and poured drop by drop into a second container. This new liquid, referred to as **distilled spirits** or simply *liquor*, has an alcohol content considerably higher than 15 percent, generally in the neighborhood of 40 to 50 percent.

It is possible through further distillations to achieve an alcohol content of up to 95 percent. The alcohol content of distilled spirits is not, however, commonly described by percentage but rather by the designation "proof." Any proof is twice the percentage of alcohol: an 80-proof whiskey contains 40 percent alcohol, a 190-proof vodka contains 95 percent alcohol.

The three basic forms of alcoholic beverages are wine, beer, and distilled spirits. Table 9.1 shows the sources of some well-known examples.

Alcohol Use through History

Historians point out that fermented honey, called *mead*, was probably the original alcoholic beverage, dating from approximately 8000 B.C. Beer, requiring more effort than simple fermentation, came on the scene much later, with the Egyptians establishing the first official brewery about 3700 B.C. At that time, beer was quite

distilled spirits: The liquid product of distillation, also known as *liquor*.

different from the watery forms we know today. It was more similar to a bread than a beverage, and the process of producing it was closer to baking than to brewing.[2]

Evidence of the development of wine comes from references to its sale in the Code of Hammurabi, king of Babylonia, recorded about 1700 B.C. Wine-making itself, however, appears to have begun more than three thousand years before that. Excavations of an ancient village in modern-day Iran have revealed the remains of wine-stained pottery dating back to as early as 5400 B.C.[3]

The first documented distillation of alcohol was the conversion of wine into brandy during the Middle Ages, at a medical school in Salerno, Italy. The emphasis at first was on its medicinal applications rather than the level of intoxication that could be achieved with it. The new beverage became known in Latin as **aqua vitae** ("the water of life"). However, people quickly caught on to its inebriating possibilities, and brandy became the primary distilled liquor in Europe until the middle of the seventeenth century. At that time the Dutch perfected the process of distilling liquor and flavoring it with juniper berries. A new alcoholic beverage was born: gin.

The enormous popularity of gin throughout Europe marked a crucial point in the history of alcohol's effect on European society. Because it was easily produced, cheaper than brandy, and faster-acting than wine, gin became attractive as an alcoholic beverage to all levels of society, particularly the poorer classes of people. By the mid-1700s, alcohol abuse was condemned as a major societal problem, and concerns about drunkenness had become a public issue.

Although gin affected life in many parts of Europe, it was in English cities that the gin epidemic became a genuine crisis. By 1750, gin consumption in England had grown to twenty-two times the level in 1685, and the social devastation was obvious. In London, infant mortality rose during this period, with only one of four baptized babies between 1730 and 1749 surviving to the age of five, despite the fact that mortality rates were falling in the countryside. In one section of the city, as many as one in five houses was a gin shop.

Consumption of other distilled spirits, such as rum and whiskey, added to the overall problem, but gin was undoubtedly the prime culprit. The epidemic of gin drinking in England during the first half of the eighteenth century illustrates how destructive the introduction of a potent psychoactive drug into a newly urban society already suffering from social dislocation and instability can be. The consequences in many ways mirrored the introduction of crack cocaine into the ghettos of the United States during the 1980s.[4]

The social chaos of "Gin Lane" in London, as interpreted by William Hogarth (1697–1764).

Alcohol in Early U.S. History

Judging from the records of Pilgrims aboard the *Mayflower* in 1620, alcohol played a pivotal role in the earliest days of settling the American colonies. William Bradford, historian of the *Mayflower* voyage and later governor of Plymouth Colony in Massachusetts, wrote that in looking for a place to land, they had decided not to "take time for further search or consideration, our victuals [supplies] being much spent, especially our Beere." Evidently, the Pilgrims arrived at Plymouth Rock not only with a passion for freedom but also with a considerable thirst.[5]

To be fair, however, we need to understand that these English settlers, like other travelers at that time, had little choice but to take along alcoholic beverages. Water would have spoiled easily during the sea voyage. Besides, the Pilgrims were not against alcohol per se, merely against the drunken behavior that resulted from its excessive use.

---

aqua vitae (AH-kwa VEE-tay): A brandy, the first distilled liquor in recorded history.

General approval of the moderate use of alcohol was a fact of American life well into the nineteenth century. It is not surprising, therefore, that the social focus for communities in colonial America was the tavern. Not only did taverns serve as the public dispenser of alcoholic beverages, but they also served as the center for local business dealings and town politics. Mail was delivered there; travelers could stay the night; elections were held there. As an institution, the tavern was as highly regarded, and as regularly attended, as the local church.[6]

By today's standards, it is difficult to imagine the extent of alcohol consumption during the early decades of American history. In 1830, the average per capita intake was an immoderate five drinks a day, roughly five times the level of consumption today. It was common to take "whiskey breaks" at 11 A.M. and 4 P.M. each day (except Sunday), much as we take coffee-breaks today. As far as types of liquor were concerned, rum was the favorite in New England and along the North Atlantic coast, but elsewhere whiskey was king. George Washington himself went into the whiskey business at Mount Vernon in 1797, eventually establishing the largest whiskey distillery of his time.[7]

The Rise of Temperance in the United States

In or about 1830, alcohol consumption in the United States started to decrease. This decline coincided with the growing influence of a **temperance movement** among religious leaders, physicians, and social reformers across the nation. Temperance goals originally focused on the moderation, not necessarily the prohibition, of alcohol consumption in society and drew attention to the long-term consequences of chronic alcohol abuse. The distinction between temperate use and total prohibition, however, began to blur over the years. The shift from temperance to prohibition, from 1830 through the beginning of the twentieth century, will be examined in the next chapter.

Patterns of Alcohol Consumption Today

It has been theorized that the earliest systems of agriculture in human history were born of the desire to secure a dependable supply of beer.[8] If this is so, then alcohol, commercialization, and economics have been linked from the very beginning. Today, of course, alcohol is not only a big business, but an enormous business. Americans spend about $108 billion on alcoholic beverages each year. Of this total, $55 billion is spent on beer, $35 billion on liquor, and $18 billion on wine. Approximately $724 million is spent annually to advertise and promote beer alone.[9]

The stainless steel tanks of the world's largest wine maker, the Ernest and Julio Gallo Winery, are located in Modesto, California.

Overall Patterns of Alcohol Consumption

How much do Americans actually drink? From alcohol industry statistics, the current U.S. per capita consumption of pure alcohol has been estimated at approximately 1.3 gallons, roughly equivalent to one-half of an ounce of alcohol each day.

How many drinks does this daily amount add up to? In order to answer this question, we need to consider the amount of pure alcohol that is contained in each type of alcoholic beverage. Table 9.2 shows that a single half-ounce of alcohol is roughly equivalent to any of the following: one 5-ounce glass of wine, one 12-ounce can or bottle of beer, one 12-ounce bottle of wine cooler, or one shot of 80-proof liquor. *All of these quantities are approximately equal in terms of alcohol content, and they are often referred to as "standard drinks."* Based upon equivalencies, the average alcohol consumption per day can be represented as approximately one "standard drink." Bear in mind, however, that the total alcoholic content of a bar drink actually consumed may be difficult to determine with any degree of accuracy. Draft beer is typically dispensed in large glasses that exceed 12 ounces in capacity.

temperance movement: The social movement in the United States, beginning in the nineteenth century, that advocated the renunciation of alcohol consumption.

TABLE 9.2

Alcoholic beverages and their alcohol equivalencies

BEVERAGE	ALCOHOL EQUIVALENCY
1 glass of wine	
5 oz. quantity	5 x .12 = .60 oz. alcohol
12% alcohol concentration	(approx. 1/2 oz.)
1 can of regular beer	
12 oz. quantity	12 x .045 = .54 oz. alcohol
4.5% alcohol concentration	(approx. 1/2 oz.)
1 shot of 80-proof liquor	
1.5 oz. quantity	1.5 x .40 = .60 oz. alcohol
40% alcohol concentration	(approx. 1/2 oz.)
1 bottle of wine cooler	
12 oz. quantity	12 x .05 = .60 oz. alcohol
5% alcohol concentration	(approx. 1/2 oz.)

The bottom line: 1 glass of wine, 1 can of beer, 1 shot of liquor, and 1 bottle of wine cooler contain roughly equivalent amounts of alcohol.

A mixed drink might contain a quantity of liquor that exceeds a standard amount, if the bartender is particularly generous. Therefore, it is quite possible that the overall amount of alcohol consumption will be underestimated.

In addition, statistics based on population averages are often misleading. In looking at any average daily or annual alcohol consumption figures, we need to recognize the enormous disparity in terms of how much alcohol each person consumes during a given year. *Only 30 percent of Americans who drink account for 80 percent of the total consumed each year.* And one-third of that 30 percent, or 10 percent of the drinking population, account for roughly half of the total alcohol consumption. In other words, alcohol drinking by a relatively small proportion of the U.S. population accounts for most of the alcohol consumed.

Looking at the three types of alcohol consumed in the United States, beer consumption represents 88 percent of the overall alcoholic beverage market and a disproportionate share of heavy alcohol drinking. When five or more 12-ounce beers are consumed in a day, there is a stronger association with alcohol-related problems than when there are comparable consumption levels of wine or liquor. We can conclude that beer is the most problematic form of alcohol consumption in the United States today.[10]

Trends in Alcohol Consumption since the Late 1970s

Overall, alcohol consumption levels among Americans steadily declined each year from the late 1970s through the mid-1990s and has remained roughly stable since then. Because a large part of the decline was tied to a growing attention to weight, health, and fitness, the industry responded with the introduction of lighter wines, with fewer calories and a reduced alcohol content, as well as a popular line of wine coolers (wine mixed with sugar and fruit juice), equal in alcoholic content to regular beer. In addition to brands of lighter beers, with an equivalent alcoholic content but fewer calories, there was a growing market for "ice beer," created from a brewing method in which below-freezing temperatures temporarily create crystals and supposedly smooth out the taste.

The Demographics of Alcohol Consumption

Preferences among types of alcoholic beverages are influenced by a host of factors, including age, gender, education, and income. In general, among individuals who drink alcoholic beverages, women are twice as likely as men not to prefer beer, three times as likely as men to prefer wine, and somewhat more likely than men to prefer liquor. The preference for wine and liquor over beer increases as people get older.

Increased years of education are also associated with an increased preference for wine over beer and liquor.

Binge drinking among college students and other young adults is a common social ritual as well as a continuing social concern.

The same is true with income levels, except that the change in preference for liquor is less clear. Individuals earning more than $50,000 prefer wine and beer to liquor, and those earning less than $20,000 prefer beer to liquor and wine. In general, the relationship between personal income and overall alcohol consumption is a curvilinear one: Abstainers and heavy drinkers both earn less than moderate drinkers.[11]

In general, college students consume a large amount of alcohol, though it appears that the establishment of twenty-one as a mandated legal drinking age in all states has delayed the occurrence of *peak* consumption levels to the junior or senior year. Nonetheless, the prevalence of moderate alcohol consumption in college, assessed by those having a drink in the last thirty days, rises substantially from levels encountered in high school.

Among young adults, *binge drinking,* defined for men as having five or more and for women four or more alcoholic drinks in a row, rises sharply from age eighteen, peaks at ages twenty-one to twenty-two, then steadily declines over the next ten years. The prevalence of daily drinking also rises from levels encountered in high school but remains relatively stable through age thirty-two.

Table 9.3 shows the results of a 1997 survey of the drinking habits of more than fifteen thousand college students on 140 U.S. campuses. Overall, 43 percent reported having engaged in binge drinking in a two-week period, 39 percent of the women and 48 percent of the men. The average proportion of binge drinkers on a particular campus ranged from 0 to 80 percent. Not surprisingly, the likelihood of alcohol-related problems increased as a direct function of the level of alcohol consumed. Students who engage in binge drinking are six to ten times more likely than nonbinge drinkers to engage in unsafe sexual behavior, damage property, suffer an injury, drive while drunk, or forget where they were or what they did when they were drinking. These percentages are roughly the same as those reported in a 1993 survey.

The survey also reported that about 79 percent of *nondrinkers* were adversely affected by binge drinking patterns on campus. These reactions, called second-hand

TABLE 9.3

Problems and secondary effects of binge drinking among college students

Percentage of students reporting alcohol-related problems PROBLEM	NONBINGE DRINKERS (1 or more drinks in past year)	OCCASIONAL BINGE DRINKERS (1 or 2 binges in a 2-week period)	FREQUENT BINGE DRINKERS (3 or more binges in 2-week period)
Drove a car after drinking alcohol	20%	43%	59%
Did something I regretted	18	41	66
Forgot where I was or what I did	10	29	56
Argued with friends	10	24	47
Missed class	10	33	65
Engaged in unplanned sexual activity	10	24	45
Did not use protection when having sex	5	10	24
Got into trouble with campus or local police	2	5	15
Percentage of nonbinge drinkers reporting secondary effects, in relation to the binge drinking level of the school SECONDARY EFFECTS	LOW-LEVEL SCHOOLS (fewer than 35% binge drinkers)	MIDDLE-LEVEL SCHOOLS (36–50% binge drinkers)	HIGH-LEVEL SCHOOLS (more than 51% binge drinkers)
Had to take care of a drunken student	37%	50%	60%
Was insulted or humiliated	21	28	35
Had a serious argument or quarrel	15	17	25
Was pushed, hit, or assaulted	8	19	11
Had my property damaged	6	12	20
Experienced an unwanted sexual advance (women only)	20	22	28

Source: Adapted from Wechsler, Henry; Dowdall, George W.; Maener, Gretchen; Gledhill-Hoyt, Jeana; and Hang, Lee (1998). Changes in binge drinking and related problems among American college students between 1993 and 1997: Results of the Harvard School of Public Health College Alcohol Study. *Journal of American College Health, 47,* 57–68.

QUICK CONCEPT  9.1

Understanding Alcoholic Beverages

Check your understanding of the alcohol content of various types of alcoholic beverages by rank ordering the alcohol content of the following five "bar orders," with 1 being the largest amount and 5 being the smallest. Are there any ties?

____ A. three 1-shot servings of liquor and one 5-oz. glass of wine
____ B. two 1-shot servings of liquor
____ C. one 1-shot serving of liquor, one 5-oz. glass of wine, and three 12-oz. beers
____ D. three 5-oz. glasses of wine
____ E. one 1-shot serving of liquor, one 5-oz. glass of wine, and one 12-oz. beer

Answers: 1=C; 2=A; 3=D and E (tie); 5=B

drinking (since the individuals themselves were not drinking), are analogous to the problems of second-hand smoking which will be examined in Chapter 11.[12]

Looking at the early years of teenage drinking, we find that alcohol use has been extensive by the eighth grade. According to the University of Michigan survey, 52 percent of eighth graders reported in 2000 that they had consumed alcohol, 25 percent reported having been drunk at some time in their lives, and 8 percent reported having been drunk in the previous month.[13]

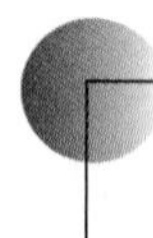

The Pharmacology of Alcohol

Alcohol is a very small molecule, in liquid form, that is moderately soluble in fat and highly soluble in water—all characteristics that make it easily absorbed through the gastrointestinal tract once it is ingested, without needing any digestion. About 20 percent of it is absorbed into the bloodstream directly from the stomach, while the remaining 80 percent is absorbed from the upper portion of the small intestine.

On entering the stomach, alcohol acts initially as an irritant, increasing the flow of hydrochloric acid and pepsin, chemicals that aid digestion. Therefore, in small amounts, alcohol can help digest a meal. In large amounts, however, alcohol will irritate the stomach lining. This is a concern for those already having stomach problems; preexisting ulcers are worsened by drinking alcohol, and heavy alcohol drinking can produce ulcers.

The irritating effect on the stomach explains why the alcohol proceeds on to the small intestine more quickly if alcohol concentrations are high. The stomach is simply trying to get rid of its irritant. Over time, the chronic consumption of alcohol can produce an inflammation of the stomach (gastritis) or the pancreas (pancreatitis).

Because the small intestine assumes the lion's share of the responsibilities and acts extremely rapidly (more rapidly than the stomach), the rate of total alcohol absorption is based largely on the condition of the stomach when the alcohol arrives and the time required for the stomach to empty its contents into the small intestine. If the stomach is empty, an intoxicating effect (the "buzz") will be felt very quickly. If the stomach is full, absorption will be delayed as the alcohol is retained by the stomach along with the food being digested and the passage of alcohol into the small intestine will slow down.

Besides the condition of the stomach, there are other factors related to the alcohol itself and the behavior of the drinker that influence the rate of alcohol absorption. The principal factor is the concentration of alcohol in the beverage being ingested. An ounce of 80-proof (40 percent) alcohol will be felt more quickly than an ounce of wine containing 12 percent alcohol, and of course the level of alcohol in the blood will be higher as well. Also, if the alcoholic beverage is carbonated, as are champagne and other sparkling wines, the stomach will empty its contents faster and effects will be felt sooner. Finally, if the alcohol enters the body at a rapid pace, as when drinks are consumed in quick succession, the level of alcohol in the blood will be higher because the liver cannot eliminate it at a fast enough pace. All other factors being equal, a bigger person requires a larger quantity of alcohol to have equivalent levels accumulating in the blood, simply because there are more body fluids to absorb the alcohol, thus diluting the overall effect.[14]

The Breakdown and Elimination of Alcohol

Its solubility in water helps alcohol to be distributed to all bodily tissues, with those tissues having greater water content receiving a relatively greater proportion of alcohol. The excretion of alcohol is accomplished in two basic ways. About 5 percent will be eliminated by the lungs through exhalation, causing the characteristic "alcohol breath" of heavy drinkers. Breathalyzers, designed to test for alcohol concentrations in the body and used frequently by law-enforcement officials to test for drunkenness, work on this principle. The remaining 95 percent will be eliminated in the urine, after the alcohol has been biotransformed into carbon dioxide and water.[15]

The solubility of alcohol in fat facilitates its passage across the blood-brain barrier (see Chapter 3). As a result, approximately 90 percent of the alcohol in the blood reaches the brain almost immediately. Unfortunately, alcohol passes the blood-placental barrier with equal ease, so that alcohol intake by women during pregnancy affects the developing fetus. As a result, fetal alcohol levels are essentially identical to those of the mother who is drinking.[16] This important matter will be discussed in the next chapter, when we consider a type of mental and physical retardation called *fetal alcohol syndrome*.

The body recognizes alcohol as a visitor with no real biological purpose. It contains calories but no vitamins, minerals, or other components that have any nutritional value. Therefore, the primary reaction is for the body to break it down for eventual removal, through a process called **oxidation.** This biotransformation process consists of two basic steps. First, an enzyme, **alcohol dehydrogenase**, breaks down alcohol into **acetaldehyde.** This enzyme is present in the stomach, where about 20 percent of alcohol is broken down prior to absorption into the bloodstream, and in the liver, where the remaining 80 percent is broken down from accumulations in the blood. Second, another enzyme, **acetaldehyde dehydrogenase,** breaks down acetaldehyde in the liver into **acetic acid.** From there, further oxidation results in oxygen, carbon dioxide, and calories of energy.

The entire process is determined by the speed with which alcohol dehydrogenase does its work, and for a given individual, it works at a constant rate, no matter how much alcohol needs to be broken down. Imagine a bank at which only one teller window stays open, no matter how long the line of customers grows, and you will understand the limitations under which the body is operating.

The specific rate of oxidation is approximately 100 milligrams of alcohol per hour per kilogram of body weight. To put this in perspective, 8 grams of alcohol will be broken down in an hour if you weigh 176 pounds (80 kilograms), and 5 grams of alcohol will be broken down in an hour if you weigh 110 pounds (50 kilograms). Certain conditions and circumstances, however, can alter this basic biotransformation rate (Health Line on page 194).

In terms of alcoholic beverages, the oxidation rate for adults in general is approximately one-third to one-half ounce of pure alcohol an hour. If you sipped (not gulped) slightly less than the contents of one 12-ounce bottle of beer, 4-ounce glass of wine, or any equivalent portion of alcohol (see Table 9.2) very slowly over an hour's time, the enzymes in the stomach and liver would keep up, and you would not feel intoxicated. Naturally, if you consume larger amounts of alcohol at faster rates of consumption, all bets are off.[17]

It is no secret that alcohol consumption is conducive to the accumulation of body fat, most noticeably in the form of the notorious beer belly. It turns out that alcohol does not have significant effects on the biotransformation of dietary carbohydrates and proteins, so a drinking individual who consumes a healthy diet does not have to worry about getting enough nutrients. Alcohol does, however, reduce the breakdown of fat, so that dietary fat has a greater chance of being stored rather than expended. Over time, the accumulation of fat in the liver is particularly serious because it eventually interferes with normal liver function. This condition will be examined in the next chapter as one of the major adverse effects of chronic alcohol consumption on the body.[18]

Measuring Alcohol in the Blood

Alcohol levels in the blood, like levels of any drug, vary considerably not only by virtue of how much is ingested and how long ago but also as a result of differences in an individual's body size and relative proportions of body fat. Consequently, we have to consider a specific ratio referred to as the **blood-alcohol concentration (BAC)** when assessing physiological and psychological effects (an alternative term is blood-alcohol level [BAL]).

---

oxidation: A chemical process in alcohol metabolism.

alcohol dehydrogenase (AL-co-haul DEE-heye-DRAW-juh-nays): An enzyme in the stomach and liver that converts alcohol into acetaldehyde.

acetaldehyde (ASS-ee-TAL-duh-heyed): A by-product of alcohol metabolism, produced through the action of alcohol dehydrogenase.

acetaldehyde dehydrogenase (ASS-ee-TAL-duh-heyed DEE-heye-DRAW-juh-nays): An enzyme in the liver that converts acetaldehyde to acetic acid in alcohol metabolism.

acetic acid (a-SEE-tik ASS-id): A by-product of alcohol metabolism, produced through the action of acetaldehyde dehydrogenase.

blood-alcohol concentration (BAC): The number of grams of alcohol in the blood relative to 100 milliliters of blood, expressed as a percentage.

Health Line

Gender, Race, and Medication: Factors in Alcohol Metabolism

Since enzymes play such a critical role in alcohol breakdown, it is important to consider factors that alter the levels of these enzymes. As mentioned in Chapter 3, two of the factors involve gender and ethnicity. In general, women have about 60 percent less alcohol dehydrogenase in the stomach than men; thus their oxidation of alcohol is relatively slower, even when different body weights have been taken into account.

In addition, about 50 percent of all people of Asian descent have a genetically imposed lower level of acetaldehyde dehydrogenase in the liver. As a consequence, acetaldehyde builds up, causing nausea, itching, facial flushing, and cardiac acceleration. The combination of these symptoms, often referred to as *fast-flushing,* makes alcohol consumption very unpleasant for many Japanese.

It would be reasonable to expect then that those who experienced fast-flushing would drink less alcohol than those who do not. A recent study of Japanese Americans indicates that this is true when you look at a large community sample. For Japanese American college students who have to contend with peer pressure to drink, however, the relationship between the physiological response and the quantity of alcohol consumed is not nearly as strong. For them, environmental factors encourage alcohol consumption, despite their genetically determined predisposition to get sick. In a similar way, the social life of Japanese businessmen has promoted alcohol consumption, though many get sick as a result. A journalist describes the dilemma in present-day Japan in this way:

> *Perhaps in no other nation is drinking so extensively and tightly woven in business. Drinking after work is not only an extension of the company, it is virtually a requirement. Refuse the boss's offer to go out drinking, and your standing in the firm begins to slide.*

Medications can also influence alcohol breakdown by altering levels of alcohol dehydrogenase in the stomach. Aspirin, for example, when taken on a full stomach, reduces enzyme levels by one-half, causing more alcohol to accumulate in the blood. Among women, aspirin has a greater inhibiting effect than among men, so it is possible that enzyme levels may be reduced to nearly zero if a woman is taking aspirin prior to drinking alcoholic beverages. Gastric ulcer medications also inhibit alcohol dehydrogenase and thus increase the physiological impact of alcohol. Any combination of these factors appears to produce additive effects. (See Table 9.5 for other examples of alcohol–medication interactions.)

Sources: Frezza, Mario; DiPadova, Carlo; Pozzato, Gabrielle; Terpin, Maddalena; Baraona, Enrique; and Lieber, Charles S. (1990). High blood alcohol levels in women: The role of decreased gastric alcohol dehydrogenase activity and first-pass metabolism. *New England Journal of Medicine, 322,* 95–99. Gibbons, Boyd (1992, February). Alcohol: The legal drug. *National Geographic Magazine, 181,* p. 27. Goodman, Deborah (1992, January–February). NIMH grantee finds drug responses differ among ethnic groups. *ADAMHA News,* pp. 5,15. Nakawatase, Tomoko V., Yamamoto, Joe, and Sasao, Toshiaki (1993). The association between fast-flushing response and alcohol use among Japanese Americans. *Journal of Studies on Alcohol, 54,* 48–53. Roine, Risto; Gentry, Thomas; Hernandez-Muñoz, Rolando; Baraona, Enrique; and Lieber, Charles S. (1990). Aspirin increases blood alcohol concentrations in humans after ingestion of ethanol. *Journal of the American Medical Association, 264,* 2406–2408.

The BAC refers to the number of grams of alcohol in the blood relative to 100 milliliters of blood, expressed as a percentage. For example, 0.1 gram (100 mg) of alcohol in 100 milliliters of blood is represented by a BAC of 0.10 percent. Table 9.4 shows the BAC levels that can be estimated from one's body weight, number of standard drinks consumed, and hours elapsed since starting the first drink. From these figures, BAC levels are typically considered in terms of three broad categories of behavior: caution (0.01 to 0.05 percent), driving impaired (0.05 to 0.10 percent), and legally drunk (in most states prior to 2002, 0.10 percent and higher). In effect, you need to compute the accumulated BAC levels for your body weight after having a specific number of drinks, then subtract 0.015 percent BAC for each hour since the drinking occurred.[19]

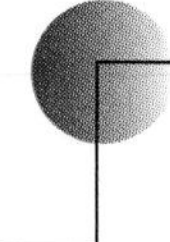

Effects of Alcohol on the Brain

Alcohol is clearly a CNS depressant drug, though it is often misidentified as a stimulant. The reason for this confusion is that alcohol, at low doses, first releases the cerebral cortex from its inhibitory control over subcortical systems in the brain, a kind of double-negative effect. In other words, alcohol is depressing an area of the brain that normally would be an inhibitor, and the result is the illusion of stimulation. The impairment in judgment and thinking (the classic features of being drunk) stems from a loosening of social inhibitions that allow us to be relatively civil and well behaved.

TABLE 9.4

When are you drunk? Calculating your blood-alcohol concentration (BAC) level

WEIGHT (LB.)	STANDARD DRINKS 1	2	3	4	5	6	7	8	9	10
100	.029	.058	.088	.117	.146	.175	.204	.233	.262	.290
120	.024	.048	.073	.097	.121	.145	.170	.194	.219	.243
140	.021	.042	.063	.083	.104	.125	.146	.166	.187	.208
160	.019	.037	.055	.073	.091	.109	.128	.146	.164	.182
180	.017	.033	.049	.065	.081	.097	.113	.130	.146	.162
200	.015	.029	.044	.058	.073	.087	.102	.117	.131	.146
220	.014	.027	.040	.053	.067	.080	.093	.106	.119	.133
240	.012	.024	.037	.048	.061	.073	.085	.097	.109	.122

CAUTION — DRIVING IMPAIRED — LEGALLY DRUNK

Alcohol is "burned up" by your body at .015% per hour, as follows:

No. hours since starting first drink	1	2	3	4	5	6
Percent alcohol burned up	.015	.030	.045	.060	.075	.090

To calculate your BAC level correctly, you must consider the number of standard drinks you have consumed, your body weight, and how much time has passed since the first drink. Note that a BAC level of .10% or higher has been, until recently, the standard for drunk driving in most U.S. states. A BAC level of .08% or higher has been the standard in Alabama, California, Florida, Hawaii, Idaho, Illinois, Kansas, Kentucky, Maine, New Hampshire, New Mexico, North Carolina, Oregon, Texas, Utah, Vermont, Virginia, and the District of Columbia, as well as all of Canada. As of 2002, all U.S. states will have adopted the .08% standard.

Source: Updated from *A primer of drug action,* 8/e by Robert M. Julien © 1998 by W. H. Freeman and Company. Used with permission.

As the BAC level increases, more widespread areas of the brain are affected until an inhibition of the respiratory centers in the medulla becomes a distinct possibility. As with other depressant drugs, acute alcoholic poisoning produces death by asphyxiation. The LD50 level (the lethal dose for 50 percent of the population) for alcohol, at which death is likely to occur, is approximately 0.50 percent. Remember, however, the nature of the LD50 curve (see Chapter 2); deaths can occur at lower concentrations and fail to occur at higher ones.[20]

The effect of alcohol at the neuronal level is less well understood, but the picture is starting to emerge. At present, the leading candidate for a mechanism is the GABA receptor in the brain. This receptor contains three locations: one sensitive specifically to the neurotransmitter GABA, one sensitive to barbiturates, and one sensitive to a type of antianxiety medication (see Chapter 15). The last location is also sensitive to alcohol, and the research suggests that alcohol acts at this site, making it more difficult for the neuron to be stimulated.[21]

More worrisome than alcohol's depressive effects on the brain, however, is its ability to set up a pattern of psychological dependence (see Chapter 3). Since the late 1980s, evidence has accumulated that the reinforcing action of alcohol is a result of its influence on dopamine-releasing neurons in the nucleus accumbens of the brain. The fact that alcohol shares this effect with other abused drugs, including heroin, cocaine, and nicotine, suggests the possibility that treatments for one form of drug abuse might also be useful for others. Chapter 10 will describe the recent research concerning the use of naltrexone, an opiate antagonist, in the treatment of alcohol abuse.[22]

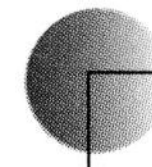

Acute Physiological Effects

Alcohol can produce a number of immediate physiological effects; they will be examined here. The physiological effects resulting from chronic alcohol consumption will be covered in the next chapter.

Toxic Reactions

We need to consider potentially life-threatening situations associated with alcohol as seriously as we would those with any other depressant drug. In general, the therapeutic index for alcohol, as measured by the LD50/ED50 ratio (see Chapter 2), is approximately 6. Because this figure is not very high, caution is strongly advised; the risks in being the "big winner" in a drinking contest should be weighed very carefully. On the one hand, in order to achieve a lethal BAC level of 0.50 percent, a 165-pound man needs to have consumed approximately twenty-three drinks over a four-hour period.[23] On the other hand, consuming ten drinks in one hour, a drinking schedule that achieves a BAC level of 0.35 percent, puts a person in extremely dangerous territory. We need to remember that LD50 is the *average* level for a lethal effect; there is no way to predict where a particular person might be located on the normal curve!

Fortunately, two mechanisms are designed to protect us to a certain degree. First, alcohol acts as a gastric irritant so that frequently the drinker will feel nauseous and vomit. Second, the drinker may simply pass out, and the risk potential from further drinking becomes irrelevant. Nonetheless, there are residual dangers in becoming unconscious; vomiting while in this state can prevent breathing and so death can occur from asphyxiation (Health Alert).

Health Alert

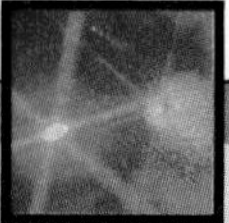

Emergency Signs and Procedures in Acute Alcohol Intoxication

Emergency Signs

- stupor or unconsciousness
- cool or damp skin
- weak, rapid pulse (more than 100 beats per minute)
- shallow and irregular breathing rate, averaging around one every three or four seconds
- pale or bluish skin

Note: Among African Americans, color changes will be apparent in the fingernail beds, mucous membranes inside the mouth, or underneath the eyelids.

Emergency Procedures

- Seek medical help immediately.
- Drinker should lie on his or her side, with the head slightly lower than the rest of the body. This will prevent blockage of the airway and possible asphyxiation if the drinker starts to vomit.
- If drinker is put to bed, maintain some system of monitoring until he or she regains consciousness.

Note: There is no evidence that home remedies for "sobering up," such as cold showers, strong coffee, forced activity, or induction of vomiting, have any effect in reducing the level of intoxication. The only factors that help are the passage of time, rest, and perhaps an analgesic if there is a headache.

Source: Victor, Maurice (1976). Treatment of alcohol intoxication and the withdrawal syndrome: A critical analysis of the use of drugs and other forms of therapy. In Peter G. Bourne (Ed.), *Acute drug abuse emergencies: A treatment manual.* New York: Academic Press, pp. 197–228.

Heat Loss and the Saint Bernard Myth

Alcohol is a peripheral dilator, which means that blood vessels near the skin surface enlarge, leading to overall warmth and redness. This effect is most likely the basis for the myth that alcohol can keep you warm in freezing weather. In actuality, however, alcohol produces a greater heat loss than would be the case without it. In studies conducted of exercising men and women following consumption of alcohol, exaggerated heat loss was significantly greater in men than in women.[24] So if you are marooned in the snow and you see an approaching Saint Bernard with a cask of brandy strapped to its neck, politely refuse the offer. It will not help and could very well do you harm. (But feel free to hug the dog!)

Diuretic Effects

As concentration levels rise in the blood, alcohol begins to inhibit the **antidiuretic hormone (ADH)**, a hormone that normally would act to reabsorb water in the kidneys prior to elimination in the urine. As a result, urine is more diluted and, because large amounts of liquid are typically being consumed at the time, more copious. Once blood alcohol concentrations have peaked, however, the reverse occurs. Water is now retained in a condition called **antidiuresis,** resulting in swollen fingers, hands, and feet. This effect is more pronounced if salty foods (peanuts or pretzels, for example) have been eaten along with the alcohol.

The inhibition of ADH during the drinking of alcoholic beverages can be a serious concern, particularly following vigorous exercise when the body is already suffering from a loss of water and fluid levels are low. Therefore, the advice to the marathoner, whose body may lose more than a gallon of water over the course of a warm three-hour run, is not to celebrate the end of the

antidiuretic hormone (ADH): A hormone that acts to reabsorb water in the kidneys prior to excretion from the body.
antidiuresis: A condition resulting from excessive reabsorption of water in the kidneys.

race with a beer but with nonintoxicating liquids such as Gatorade or similar mineral-rich drinks.[25]

Cardiovascular Effects

Long-term, excessive consumption of alcohol increases the risk of heart disease, elevated blood pressure, and stroke (see Chapter 10). The evidence, however, also indicates that moderate consumption of alcohol (one or two drinks per day) can actually be beneficial to the cardiovascular system, reducing the risk of coronary heart disease and other related cardiovascular problems. When these benefits first came to light in the early 1990s, the focus of attention was on the consumption of wine, particularly red wine. Since then, the research has shown that the moderate consumption of *any* type of alcoholic beverage, beer, wine, or liquor, produces similar effects.

In general, alcohol increases high-density lipoprotein (HDL) cholesterol levels in the blood (the so-called good cholesterol); HDL acts as a protective mechanism against a possible restriction of blood flow through arteries. The greatest benefit applies to those individuals who are at the greatest risk for coronary heart disease as a result of high concentrations of low-density lipoprotein (LDL) cholesterol levels in the blood (the so-called bad cholesterol). It has been estimated that consumption of approximately 8 ounces of wine (a bit less than two standard drinks) causes a 25 percent reduction in risk of coronary heart disease. The fact that alcohol provides the greatest protection against coronary heart disease for those who are at greatest risk helps to explain what has become known as the "French paradox." Until now, it has been difficult to understand why the French, despite their high-fat, cholesterol-elevating diet, do not exhibit the high rate of coronary heart disease that is observed in other groups with similar eating habits. The answer, evidently, is the alcohol they consume.[26]

Even though moderate alcohol use can have some positive effects, it is important to remember that alcohol carries significant negative consequences as well. The consumption of alcohol during pregnancy, even in moderation, greatly increases the risk of retarding the development of the fetus. Therefore, *no amount of alcohol is safe for pregnant women.* In addition, alcohol consumption is problematic for diabetic individuals who have difficulty processing sugars. As will be discussed in the next section of this chapter, alcohol consumption produces acute behavioral effects that are problematic enough to discourage anyone from drinking merely as a way to reduce the chances of a heart attack. Regular exercise and a diet modification to minimize the consumption of highly saturated fats are clearly safer options.[27]

Effects on Sleep

It might seem tempting to induce sleep with a relaxing "nightcap," but in fact the resulting sleep patterns are adversely affected. Alcohol reduces the duration of a phase of sleep called rapid eye movement (REM) sleep (see Chapter 15). Depending on the dose, REM sleep can be either partially or completely suppressed during the night. When alcohol is withdrawn, REM sleep rebounds and represents a higher percentage of total sleep time than before alcohol consumption began. As a result, individuals sleep poorly and experience nightmares.[28]

Interactions with Other Drugs

A very serious concern is the complex interaction of alcohol with many drugs. As noted in Chapter 2, the DAWN reports of emergency room admissions and deaths show an extremely high incidence of medical crises arising from the combination of alcohol not only with prescribed medications but also with virtually all of the illicit drugs on the street. Opiates and opiate-like drugs, marijuana, and many prescription medicines interact with alcohol such that the resulting combination produces effects that are either the sum of the parts or greater than the sum of the parts. In other cases, the ingestion of medications with alcohol significantly lessens the medication's benefits. Anticoagulants, anticonvulsants, and monoamine oxidase inhibitors (used as an antidepressant medication) fit into this second category. Table 9.5 shows a partial listing of major therapeutic drugs that interact with alcohol with undesirable, if not dangerous, outcomes. The complete list is so lengthy that it is fair to say that, whenever any medication is taken, the individual should inquire about possible interactions with alcohol.

Hangovers

About four to twelve hours after heavy consumption of alcohol, usually the next day, unpleasant symptoms of headache, nausea, fatigue, and thirst may occur, collectively known as the *hangover.* At least one such experience has been reported by 40 percent of all men and 27 percent of all women over the age of eighteen.[29] Why these symptoms occur is not at all clear. The probable explanations at present focus on individual aspects of a hangover, though it is likely that several factors contribute to the total phenomenon.

One factor, beyond the simple fact of drinking too much, is the type of alcohol that has been consumed. Among distilled spirits, for example, vodka has a lower probability of inducing hangovers than whiskey. A possible

TABLE 9.5

A partial listing of possible drug–alcohol interactions

GENERIC DRUG (brand name or type)	CONDITION BEING TREATED	EFFECT OF INTERACTION
chloral hydrate (Noctec)	Insomnia	Excessive sedation that can be fatal; irregular heartbeat; flushing
glutethimide (Doriden)	Insomnia	Excessive sedation; reduced driving and machine-operating skills
antihypertensives (Apresoline, Diuril)	High blood pressure	Exaggeration of blood pressure–lowering effect; dizziness on rising
diuretics (Aldactone)	High blood pressure	Exaggeration of blood pressure–lowering effect; dizziness on rising
antibiotics (penicillin)	Bacterial infections	Reduced therapeutic effectiveness
nitroglycerin (Nitro-bid)	Angina pain	Severe decrease in blood pressure; intense flushing; headache; dizziness on rising
warfarin (Coumadin)	Blood clot	Decreased anti-blood clotting effect, easy bruising
insulin	Diabetes	Excessive low blood sugar; nausea; flushing
disulfiram (Antabuse)	Alcoholic drinking	Intense flushing; severe headache; vomiting; heart palpitations; could be fatal
methotrexate	Various cancers	Increased risk of liver damage
phenytoin (Dilantin)	Epileptic seizures	Reduced drug effectiveness in preventing seizures; drowsiness
prednisone (Deltasone)	Inflammatory conditions (arthritis, bursitis)	Stomach irritation
various antihistamines	Nasal congestion	Excessive sedation that could be fatal
acetaminophen (Tylenol)	Pain	Increased risk of liver damage

Sources: National Institute on Alcohol Abuse and Alcoholism (1995, January). Alcohol alert: Alcohol–medication interactions. No. 27, PH355. Bethesda MD: National Institute on Alcohol Abuse and Alcoholism. Office of Substance Abuse Prevention (1988). *The fact is . . . It's dangerous to drink alcohol while taking certain medications.* Rockville MD: National Institute on Drug Abuse. Parker, Christy (1985). *Simple facts about combinations with other drugs.* Phoenix AZ: Do It Now Foundation.

reason is the relatively lower amount of **congeners.** These are substances in alcoholic beverages, including trace amounts of nonethyl alcohol, oils, and other organic matter, that are by-products of the fermentation and distillation processes and give the drinks their distinctive smell, taste, and color. Although no harm is caused by congeners in such minute concentrations, they are still toxic substances, and some adverse effects may show up as a component of the hangover.

Other possible factors include traces of nonoxidized acetaldehyde in the blood, residual irritation in the stomach, and a low blood sugar level rebounding from the high levels induced by the previous ingestion of alcohol. The feeling of swollenness from the antidiuresis, discussed earlier, may contribute to the headache pain. The thirst may be due to the dehydration that occurred the night before.

Numerous "remedies" for the hangover have been concocted over the centuries, but it appears that the best treatment consists of rest, an analgesic medication for the headache (see Chapter 14), and the passage of time. Since the hangover can be considered basically as a collection of symptoms of withdrawal from alcohol, some people have taken to the remedy of consuming more alcohol, a strategy known as "the hair of the dog that bit you." This approach can relieve the symptoms, but it merely delays the inevitable consequences and leads to further alcohol use.

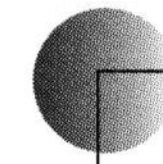

Acute Behavioral Effects

The consumption of alcoholic beverages is so pervasive in American society that it seems almost unnecessary to comment on how it feels to be intoxicated by alcohol. The behavioral effects of consuming alcohol in more than very moderate quantities range from the relatively harmless effects of exhilaration and excitement, talkativeness, slurred speech, and irritability to behaviors that have the potential for causing great harm: uncoordinated movement, drowsiness, sensorimotor difficulties, and stupor.[30] Some of the prominent behavioral prob-

congeners (KON-jen-ers): Nonethyl alcohols, oils, and other organic substances found in trace amounts in some distilled spirits.

lems associated with acute alcohol intoxication will be examined in this section.

Blackouts

A **blackout** is an inability to remember events that occurred during the period of intoxication, even though the individual was conscious at the time. For example, a drinker having too much to drink at a party drives home, parks the car on a nearby street, and goes to bed. The next morning, he or she has no memory of having driven home and cannot locate the car. Owing to the possibility of blackouts, drinkers can be easily misled into thinking that because they can understand some information given to them during drinking, they will remember it later. The risk of blackouts is greatest when alcohol is consumed very quickly, forcing the BAC to rise rapidly.[31]

Driving Skills

There is no question that alcohol consumption significantly impairs the ability to drive or deal with automobile traffic, particularly among young people. In 1999, of the 41,480 traffic fatalities that occurred, 38 percent involved an intoxicated driver or pedestrian showing a BAC level of 0.10 percent or higher and 50 percent showing a BAC level of 0.05 percent. Among fatally injured teenage drivers, more than 60 percent had been drinking prior to the crash.

It is important to recognize that the official state of legal intoxication, defined prior to 2002 as a BAC level of 0.10 percent in most states, does not have to be reached to cause impairment in driving. It has been estimated that the risk of a single-vehicle fatal crash rapidly escalates as alcohol consumption increases. Relative to drivers who have not consumed any alcohol at all, those with BAC levels between 0.02 percent and 0.04 percent have a 40 percent greater risk. When BAC levels are between 0.05 and 0.09 percent, the risk is 11 times greater; when BAC levels are between 0.10 and 0.14 percent, the risk is 48 times greater; when BAC levels are above 0.15 percent, the risk is 380 times greater. Therefore, it is quite possible for an accident to occur even though the driver is not officially "driving while intoxicated" (DWI).[32]

All these statistics could be viewed as correlational and not necessarily proof of a causal relationship between alcohol and automobile accidents, were it not for the data from laboratory-based experiments showing a clear deterioration of sensorimotor skills following the ingestion of alcohol. Reaction times are significantly prolonged, the coordination necessary to steer a car steadily is hampered, and the ability to stay awake when fatigued is impaired following BAC levels as low as 0.03 percent.[33] More important, however, is a major decline in the ability to be aware of peripheral events and stimuli. One researcher in this area expresses the deficit in this way:

Every community has its tragic stories of preventable deaths due to drunk driving.

> *The overwhelming majority of accidents involving alcohol are not accidents in which tracking is the prime error. Contrary to what most people think, it isn't that people are weaving down the road, which is a sign of very high blood alcohol levels; it's that they have failed to see something. They go through a red light, they fail to see a pedestrian or a motorcyclist, they fail to see that the road is curving. Their perceptual and attentive mechanisms are affected very early, after just one drink. These are the things that are the prime causes of accidents.*[34]

Unfortunately, it is the weaving behavior, or other extreme examples of driving impairments, that most often signals the police to stop a car for a possible DWI violation; other impairments frequently go unnoticed.

Increasing the minimum age for alcoholic consumption from eighteen to twenty-one, mandated throughout the United States, has had a major impact on the chances of accident fatalities among young people. On average, fatal nighttime accidents involving eighteen- and nineteen-year-old drivers decreased 13 percent between 1975 and 1984 in twenty-six states that raised the minimum drinking age during that interval. A decrease of 16 percent in nighttime accidents in Michigan following the change in the drinking law was maintained six years later.[35]

blackout: Amnesia concerning events occurring during the period of alcoholic intoxication, even though consciousness had been maintained at that time.

One for the Road

In many states, people convicted repeatedly of drunk-driving offenses can be required to have interlock devices installed in their cars. Each device incorporates a breath analyzer for detecting the presence of alcohol with electronics to disable the car's ignition. A test is required before the car can be started, and the driver must also pull over for occasional retests while the car is moving.

1 The driver enters a four-digit code into a keypad on the handheld sampling unit.

2 When the system is ready for the test, a rectangle appears on a dashboard display.

3 After taking a deep breath, the driver blows steadily into the mouthpiece for two to five seconds, until the rectangle dissappears.

4 The display shows the measured breath alcohol level. Below 0.025, an indicator says that the driver has passed and the car may be started.

5 At 0.025 or above, the vehicle will not start.

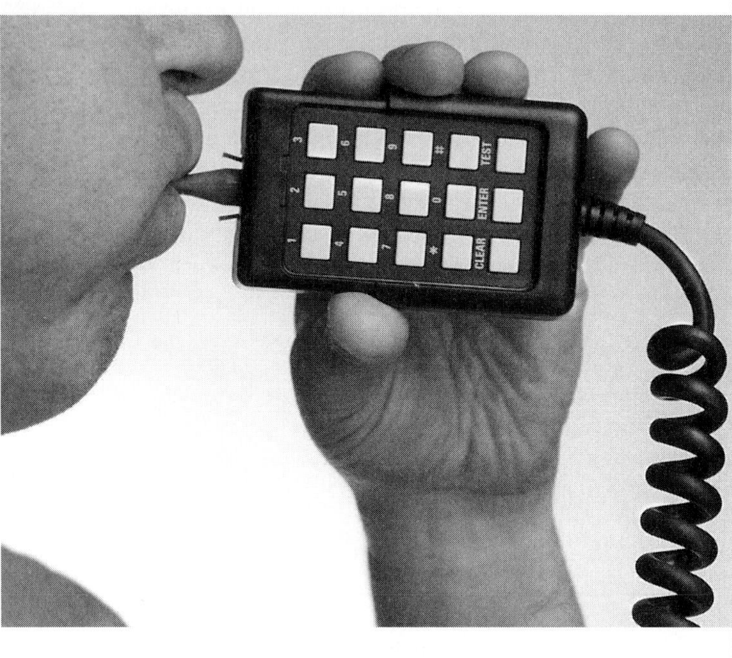

FIGURE 9.1

New devices keep DWI offenders safe by requiring sobriety before starting an automobile.

Source: Bannan, Karen J. (2000, June 15). Device helps keep D.W.I. offenders and others safe. *New York Times,* p. G14.

We have reason to be cautiously optimistic. In U.S. states adopting a 0.08 percent legal BAC limit for driving a motor vehicle, fatalities have declined by approximately 17 percent.[36] Educational programs in schools and communities emphasizing the advantage of "designated drivers," as well as public education and lobbying groups such as Mothers Against Drunk Driving (MADD) and Students Against Drunk Driving (SADD), have had positive effects (see Portrait). In 1982, 30 percent of all drivers involved in a fatal automobile crash were found to be intoxicated (at a BAC level of 0.10 percent or higher). In 1998, the percentage had dropped to 19.

Even so, much work remains to be done, particularly among male drivers, whose involvement in alcohol-related accidents exceeds that of female drivers by a factor of 2:1. A survey conducted in 1996 revealed that 7 percent of males aged twenty-one to thirty-four years reported driving at least once in the past month after having had "too much to drink." Five percent of male drivers aged eighteen to twenty years responded in the same way, despite the fact that sales of alcohol to them are illegal. On a national level, it has been estimated that approximately 500 lives would be saved each year if the legal BAC limit for driving was changed from .10 to .08 percent. As of 2002, all U.S. states will have made this change.[37]

Alcohol, Violence, and Aggression

It is difficult to avoid sweeping generalizations when confronted with statistics about alcohol and violent behavior both in the United States and other countries. In a major study conducted in a community in northwestern

Portrait Candace Lightner—Founder of MADD

In 1980, Candace Lightner's thirteen-year-old daughter, Cari, was killed by a hit-and-run intoxicated driver in California. The driver had been out of jail on bail for only two days, a consequence of another hit-and-run drunk driving crash, and he had three previous drunk driving arrests and two previous convictions. He was allowed to plea bargain to vehicular manslaughter. Although the sentence was to serve two years in prison, the judge allowed him to serve time in a work camp and later a halfway house.

It was appalling to Lightner that drunk drivers, similar to the one who had killed her daughter, were receiving such lenient treatment, with many of them never going to jail for a single day. Lightner quit her job and started an organization that has become a household name: Mothers Against Drunk Driving (MADD).

Since then, MADD has campaigned for stricter laws against drunk driving, and most of the present DWI legislation around the country is a result of its intense efforts. In addition, MADD acts as a voice for victims of drunk-driving injuries and the families of those who have been killed. From a single act of courage, despite enormous grief, Lightner has spawned an organization that boasts more than 3 million members in the United States, with groups in virtually every state and more than four hundred local chapters.

Candace Lightner, founder of MADD

More recently, MADD has set for itself the goal of reducing the number of all traffic fatalities associated with alcohol drinking. In 1992, the percentage was 45; MADD wants it to be 40. These are some of their proposals for change:

1. More effective enforcement of the minimum-drinking-age law.
2. A ".00 percent BAC" criterion for drivers under twenty-one, making it illegal to drive with *any* measurable level of blood alcohol in any state. In 1994, the criterion ranging from 0.00 to 0.02 percent was in effect in seventeen U.S. states and the District of Columbia.
3. Driver's license suspensions for underage persons convicted of purchasing or possession of alcoholic beverages.
4. Alcohol-free zones for youth gatherings.
5. Criminal sanctions against adults who provide or allow alcoholic beverages at events for underage participants.
6. A new minimum BAC level of 0.08 percent for adult drivers in all fifty states. This will have been achieved in 2002.
7. Mandatory alcohol and drug testing for all drivers in all traffic crashes resulting in fatalities or serious bodily injury.
8. Sobriety checkpoints to detect and apprehend alcohol-impaired drivers and as a visible deterrent to drinking and driving.

Source: Information courtesy of Mothers Against Drunk Driving, Dallas, Texas. Interview with Candace Lightner.

Ontario, Canada, reported in 1991, more than 50 percent of the most recent occasions of physical violence were found to be preceded by alcohol use on the part of the assailant and/or the victims themselves.[38] Other studies show from 50 to 60 percent of all murders being committed when the killer had been drinking. About 40 percent of all acts of male sexual aggression against adult women and from 60 to 70 percent of male-instigated domestic violence occur when the offender has been drunk; more than 60 percent of all acts of child molestation involved drunkenness.[39]

Researchers have advanced several theories to account for the linkage between alcohol intoxication and violent behavior. The traditional *disinhibition theory* holds that alcohol on a pharmacological level impairs normal cortical mechanisms responsible for inhibiting the expression of innate or suppressed aggressive inclinations. Another viewpoint, referred to as the *cognitive-expectation theory*, holds that learned beliefs or expectations about alcohol's effects can facilitate aggressive behaviors. This second theory implies that violence is induced by virtue of the act of drinking and one's personal view of how a person is "supposed to respond" rather than by the pharmacological effects of alcohol itself.

Expectations about the consequences of drug-taking behavior or of any behavior at all, as noted in Chapter 3, are studied experimentally through the placebo research design. In the case of the cognitive-expectation theory, it is necessary to use a variation of this design, called the **balanced placebo design.** Subjects are randomly divided

balanced placebo design: An experimental design that can separate psychological effects (due to subjective expectations) and physiological effects (due to the pharmacology of the drug).

into four groups. Two groups are given an alcoholic drink, with one group being told that they are ingesting alcohol and the other that they are ingesting a nonalcohol substitute that tastes and smells like alcohol. Two other groups are given the nonalcohol substitute, with one group being told that they are ingesting this substitute and the other that they are ingesting alcohol.

Studies using the balanced placebo design have shown clearly that beliefs (mind-sets) concerning the effects of drinking are more influential in determining a subject's behavior than the more direct physiological effects of the alcohol. In other words, *what they are told they are consuming is more important than what they consume.* Unfortunately, for a true test of the cognitive-expectation theory, a balanced placebo design cannot be used with BAC levels above 0.035 percent because subjects are no longer fooled by the deception with larger quantities, and most alcohol-associated acts of violence occur with BAC levels at least six times higher.[40]

QUICK CONCEPT  9.2

Understanding the Data from Balanced Placebo Designs

Check your understanding of the balanced placebo design by answering whether the following experimental results reflect (a) psychological effects, (b) physiological effects, or (c) a combination of psychological and physiological effects:

- Scenario 1: Subjects felt sexy after receiving low doses of drug X, regardless of whether or not they knew what they were receiving.
- Scenario 2: Subjects felt sexy if they received low doses of drug X but were told that they did not receive it and also felt sexy if they did not receive low doses of drug X but were told that they did.
- Scenario 3: Subjects felt sexy after being told they would receive low doses of drug X, regardless of whether or not they actually received it.

Answers: Scenario 1. b Scenario 2. c Scenario 3. a

Sex and Sexual Desire

If they were asked, most people would say that alcohol has an enhancing or aphrodisiac effect on sexual desire and performance. The actual effect of alcohol, however, is more complex than these commonly held beliefs express. In fact, it is because of these beliefs that people are frequently more susceptible to the expectations of what alcohol *should* do for them than they are to the actual physiological effects of alcohol.

To examine the complex relationship between alcohol and sex, we need to turn again to studies using the balanced placebo design. The general results from such studies are quite different for men and women. Among men, those who expected to be receiving low levels of alcohol had greater penile responses, reported greater subjective arousal, and spent more time watching erotic pictures, *regardless of whether or not they did indeed receive alcohol.* When alcohol concentrations rise to levels that reflect genuine intoxication, however, the pharmacological actions outweigh the expectations, and the overall effect is definitely inhibitory. Men who are drunk have less sexual desire and a decreased capacity to perform sexually.

In contrast, expectations among women play a lesser role. They are more inclined to react to the pharmacological properties of alcohol itself, but the direction of their response depends on whether we are talking about subjective or physiological measures. For women receiving increasing alcohol concentrations, measures of subjective arousal increase but measures of vaginal arousal decrease. Ironically, the pattern of their responses mirrors Shakespeare's quotation in *Macbeth* that alcohol "provokes the desire, but it takes away from the performance," a comment originally intended to reflect the male point of view.[41]

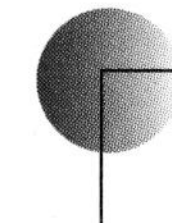

Strategies for Responsible Drinking

The various negative effects of alcohol on physiological responses and behavior have been considered. Yet it is necessary to remember that there are very large numbers of people who drink alcoholic beverages and avoid the adverse effects that have been detailed here. An overwhelming proportion of the population, for example, drink on occasion and have never engaged in any violent or aggressive acts. In addition, they avoid situations (such as driving) in which alcohol consumption would impair their performance and endanger their lives. The issue of responsible drinking is an important one; it may not be easy for us to accomplish but, fortunately, guidelines exist that make it easier.[42] Health Line features some strategies to reduce the problems associated with alcoholic intake.

At the same time, however, we must remember that, regardless of how it is consumed, alcohol remains a drug with a significant potential for dependence. It is not difficult to get hooked. As it has been said, people may plan to get drunk, but no one plans to be an alcoholic. The problems surrounding chronic alcohol abuse and alcoholism will be examined in the next chapter.

Guidelines for Responsible Drinking

- **Know how much you are drinking.** Measure your drinks. Beer is often premeasured (unless you are drinking draft beer from a keg), but wine and liquor drinks frequently are not. Learn what a 5-ounce quantity of wine or a 1½-ounce shot of liquor looks like, and use these measures to guide your drinking.
- **Choose beer or wine over liquor.** Beer especially will make you feel fuller more quickly, with a smaller intake of alcohol. But be careful. A 12-ounce beer is equivalent in alcohol content to a 5-ounce glass of wine or a 1-shot drink of liquor.
- **Drink slowly.** One drink an hour stays relatively even with your body's metabolism of the alcohol you consume. Sipping your drinks is a good strategy for slowing down your consumption. If you are a man, you'll look cool; if you are a woman, you'll look refined.
- **Don't cluster your drinking.** If you are going to have seven drinks during a week, don't drink them all on the weekend.
- **Eat something substantial while you are drinking.** Protein is an excellent accompaniment to alcohol. Avoid salty foods because they will make you thirstier and more inclined to have another drink.
- **Drink only when you are already relaxed.** Chronic alcohol abuse occurs more easily when alcohol is viewed as a way to relax. If you have a problem, seek some nondrug alternative.
- **When you drink, savor the experience.** If you focus on the quality of what you drink rather than the quantity you are drinking, you will avoid drinking too much.
- **Never drink alone.** Drinking cannot be dealt with as a phenomenon of social isolation. Having people around you provides the means to have someone looking out for you.
- **Beware of unfamiliar drinks.** Some drinks, such as zombies and other fruit and rum drinks, are deceptively high in kinds of alcohol that are not easily detected by taste.
- **Never drive a car after having had a drink.** Driving impairment begins after very low quantities of alcohol consumption.
- **Be a good host or hostess.** If you are serving alcohol at a party, do not make drinking the focus of activity. Do not refill your guests' glasses. Discourage intoxication and do not condone drunkenness. Provide transportation options for those who drink at your party. Present nonalcoholic beverages as prominently as alcoholic ones. Prior to the end of the party, stop serving alcohol and offer coffee and a substantial snack, providing an interval of nondrinking time before people leave.
- **Support organizations that encourage responsible drinking.** If you are on a college campus, get involved with the local chapter of BACCHUS (Boost Alcohol Consciousness Concerning the Health of University Students). If there is no chapter, start one.

Sources: Gross, Leonard (1983). *How much is too much? The effects of social drinking.* New York: Random House, pp. 149–152. Hanson, David J., and Engs, Ruth C. (1994). Drinking behavior: Taking personal responsibility. In Peter J. Venturelli (Ed.), *Drug use in America: Social, cultural, and political perspectives.* Boston: Jones and Bartlett, pp. 175–181. *Managing alcohol in your life.* Mansfield MA: Steele Publishing and Consulting.

SUMMARY

What Makes an Alcoholic Beverage?

- Drinkable alcohol is obtained from the fermentation of sugar in some natural products such as grapes, apples, honey, or molasses. The result is some form of wine.
- Beer is obtained from barley, after the starch has first been converted into sugar and then fermented along with other grains and hops, and aged.
- To obtain very strong alcoholic beverages, it is necessary to boil the fermented liquid and condense it later by cooling. This process, called distillation, results in alcohol concentrations of up to 95 percent, and the products are known as distilled spirits or liquors.

Alcohol Use through History

- The history of alcohol use dates back many thousands of years; the process of fermentation is very simple and its discovery was probably accidental.
- Distillation techniques were perfected during the Middle Ages, with brandy being the first distilled spirit. In later centuries, gin gained popularity in Europe, as did whiskey in the United States.

Patterns of Alcohol Consumption Today

- The demographics of alcohol consumption reveal a large disparity in the drinking habits of the population.

About a third do not drink at all, and only about 30 percent of those who drink account for 80 percent of all the alcoholic beverages consumed in the U.S.

- Peak alcohol consumption occurs at ages twenty-one to twenty-two.

The Pharmacology of Alcohol

- Alcohol is a very small molecule, easily soluble in both water and fat. Its absorption into the bloodstream is extremely rapid. The breakdown of alcohol is handled by two special enzymes in the stomach and liver.
- The rate of alcohol biodegradation is constant, so that alcohol can only leave the body at a specific pace, despite the quantity taken in.
- The effective level of alcohol in the body is measured by the blood-alcohol concentration (BAC) level, which must adjust for differences in body weight and the time since ingestion of the last alcoholic beverage.

Effects of Alcohol on the Brain

- Although alcohol affects several neurotransmitters in the brain, it is presently agreed that the principal effect is the stimulation of the GABA receptor.
- Generally, the neural effect of alcohol proceeds downward, beginning with an inhibition of the cerebral cortex, then lower brain sites. Inhibition of respiratory systems in the medulla, usually accomplished at BAC levels in the neighborhood of 0.50 percent, results in asphyxiation and death.

Acute Physiological Effects

- Alcohol at very high levels produces life-threatening consequences and at moderate levels produces a loss of body heat, increased excretion of water, an increase in heart rate and constriction of coronary arteries, disturbed patterns of sleep, and serious interactions with other drugs.

Acute Behavioral Effects

- On a behavioral level, serious adverse effects include blackouts, significant impairment in sensorimotor skills such as driving an automobile, and an increased potential for aggressive acts.
- The relationship between alcohol consumption and sexual desire and performance is a complex one, with differences being observed for men and women.

Strategies for Responsible Drinking

- Despite the potential for alcohol consumption to produce adverse effects, most people can drink in a responsible way that avoids these harmful consequences. However, the risk of alcohol dependence is always present.

KEY TERMS

acetaldehyde, p. 193
acetaldehyde dehydrogenase, p. 193
acetic acid, p. 193
alcohol dehydrogenase, p. 193
antidiuresis, p. 196
antidiuretic hormone (ADH), p. 196
aqua vitae, p. 188
balanced placebo design, p. 201
barley malt, p. 186
blackout, p. 199
blood-alcohol concentration (BAC), p. 193
brewing, p. 186
congeners, p. 198
distillation, p. 186
distilled spirits, p. 187
ethyl alcohol, p. 186
fermentation, p. 186
mash, p. 186
oxidation, p. 193
temperance movement, p. 189

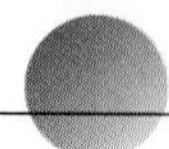

ENDNOTES

1. Pinel, John P. J. (1997). *Biopsychology* (3rd ed.). Boston: Allyn and Bacon, p. 324.
2. Gibbons, Boyd (1992, February). Alcohol: The legal drug. *National Geographic Magazine*, pp. 2–35. Roueché, Berton (1963). Alcohol in human culture. In Salvatore P. Lucia (Ed.), *Alcohol and civilization*. New York: McGraw-Hill, pp. 167–182. Vallee, Bert L. (1998, June). Alcohol in the western world. *Scientific American*, pp. 80–85.
3. McGovern, Patrick E.; Glusker, Donald L.; Exner, Lawrence J.; and Voigt, Mary M. (1996). Neolithic resinated wine. *Nature, 381*, 480–481.

4. Sournia, Jean-Charles (1990). *A history of alcoholism.* Cambridge MA: Basil Blackwell, pp. 14–50. U.S. Department of Health, Education, and Welfare (1978). *Perspectives on the history of psychoactive substance use,* pp. 67–75.
5. Grimes, William (1993). *Straight up or on the rocks: A cultural history of American drink.* New York: Simon and Schuster, p. 36. Musto, David F. (1996, April). Alcohol in American history. *Scientific American,* pp. 78–83.
6. Lender, Mark E., and Martin, James K. (1982). *Drinking in America: A history.* New York: Free Press, pp. 13–14.
7. First in war, peace—and hooch, by George! (2000, December 7). *Newsday,* p. A86. Grimes, *Straight up,* p. 51.
8. Gibbons, Alcohol, p. 7.
9. Ad Age Dataplace: Top ten beer companies (1999, September 27). *Advertising Age,* p. 368. *Standard and Poor's industry surveys: Alcoholic beverages and tobacco* (2000, August 24). Alcohol and tobacco companies see growth, p. 8.
10. Holleran, Joan (1999, May). Drinking up: U.S. alcoholic beverage consumption in gallons per capita by type (beer, wine, distilled spirits) in 1993 and 1998. *Beverage Industry,* pp. 17–21. Rogers, John D., and Greenfield, Thomas K. (1999). Beer drinking accounts for most of the hazardous alcohol consumption reported in the United States. *Journal of Studies on Alcohol, 60,* 732–739.
11. Dawson, Deborah A., Grant, Bridget F., and Chou, Patricia S. (1995). Gender differences in alcohol intake. In Walter A. Hunt and Sam Zakhari (Eds.), *Stress, gender, and alcohol-seeking behavior* (NIAAA Research Monograph 29). Bethesda MD: National Institute on Alcohol Abuse and Alcoholism, pp. 1–21. Heien, Dale (1996). The relationship between alcohol consumption and earnings. *Journal of Studies on Alcohol, 57,* 536–542.
12. Carey, Kate B., and Correia, Christopher J. (1995). Drinking motives predict alcohol-related problems in college students. *Journal of Studies on Alcohol,* 58, 100–105. National Institute on Alcohol Abuse and Alcoholism (1995, July). Alcohol alert: College students and drinking. No. 29, PH357. Bethesda MD: National Institute on Alcohol Abuse and Alcoholism. Wechsler, Henry; Dowdall, George W.; Maener, Gretchen; Gledhill-Hoyt, Jeana; and Hang, Lee (1998). Changes in binge drinking and related problems among American college students between 1993 and 1997: Results of the Harvard School of Public Health College Alcohol Study. *Journal of American College Health,* 47, 57–68.
13. Johnston, Lloyd D. (2000, December 14). "Ecstasy" use rises sharply among teens in 2000; use of many other drugs stays steady, but significant declines are reported for some. News release from the University of Michigan, Ann Arbor, Tables 1 and 2.
14. U.S. Department of Health and Human Services (1990). *Alcohol and health.* (The Seventh Special Report to the U.S. Congress). Rockville MD: National Institute on Alcohol Abuse and Alcoholism.
15. Dubowski, Kurt M. (1991). *The technology of breath-alcohol analysis.* Rockville MD: National Institute on Alcohol Abuse and Alcoholism.
16. Julien, Robert M. (2000). *A primer of drug action* (9th ed.). New York: Worth, p. 95.
17. National Institute on Alcohol Abuse and Alcoholism (1997, January). Alcohol alert: Alcohol metabolism. No. 35, PH371. Bethesda MD: National Institute on Alcohol Abuse and Alcoholism. Friedman, Nancy (1985, August-September). Anatomy of a drink. *Campus Voice,* pp. 61–63. Julien, *A primer of drug action,* pp. 91–97.
18. Suter, Paolo M., Schutz, Yves, and Jequier, Eric (1992). The effect of ethanol on fat storage in healthy subjects. *New England Journal of Medicine,* 326, 983–987.
19. Hawks, Richard L., and Chiang, C. Nora (1986). Examples of specific drug assays. In Richard L. Hawks and C. Nora Chiang (Eds.), *Urine testing for drugs of abuse* (NIDA Research Monograph 73). Rockville MD: National Instititute on Drug Abuse, p. 103. Julien, *A primer of drug action,* pp. 91–97.
20. Levinthal, Charles F. (1990). *Introduction to physiological psychology* (3rd ed.). Englewood Cliffs NJ: Prentice Hall, pp. 181–184.
21. U.S. Department of Health and Human Services (1994). *Alcohol and health.* (The Eighth Special Report to the U.S. Congress). Bethesda MD: National Institute on Alcohol Abuse and Alcoholism, pp. 4–6, 4–7.
22. Blum, Kenneth, and Payne, James E. (1991). *Alcohol and the addictive brain: Hope for alcoholics from biogenetic research.* New York: Free Press. Koob, G. F.; Rassnick, S.; Heinrichs, S.; and Weiss, F. (1994). Alcohol, the reward system and dependence. In B. Jansson, H. Jörnvall, U. Rydberg, L. Terenius, and B. L. Vallee (Eds.), *Toward a molecular basis of alcohol use and abuse.* Basel: Birkhäuser-Verlag, pp. 103–114. Schuckit, Marc A. (1994, August). Naltrexone and the treatment of alcoholism. *Drug Abuse and Alcoholism Newsletter,* San Diego CA: Vista Hill Foundation.
23. Grilly, David M. (1998). *Drugs and human behavior* (3rd ed.). Boston: Allyn and Bacon, p. 140.
24. Luks, Allan, and Barbato, Joseph (1989). *You are what you drink.* New York: Villiard, p. 44.
25. Ibid., pp. 42–43.
26. Berger, Klaus; Ajani, Umed A.; Kase, Carlos S.; Gaziano, J. Michael; Buring, Julie E.; Glynn, Robert J.; Hennekens, Charles H. (1999). Light-to-moderate alcohol consumption and the risk of stroke among U.S. male physicians. *New England Journal of Medicine, 341,* 1557–1564. Hein, Hans O., Suadicani, Poul, and Gyntelberg, Finn (1996). Alcohol consumption, serum low density lipoprotein cholesterol concentration, and risk of ischaemic heart disease: Six year follow up in the Copenhagen male study. *British Medical Journal, 312,* 736–741. Julien, *A primer of drug action* (8th ed.), p. 73. Rimm, Eric B. (2000). Moderate alcohol intake and lower risk of coronary heart disease: Meta-analysis of effects on lipids and haemostatic factors. *Journal of the American Medical Association,* 283, 1269.
27. National Institute on Alcohol Abuse and Alcoholism (1991, July). Alcohol alert: Fetal alcohol syndrome. No. 13, PH297. Bethesda MD: National Institute on Alcohol Abuse

and Alcoholism. Valmadrid, Charles T.; Klein, Ronald; Moss, Scot E.; Klein, Barbara E. K.; and Cruickshanks, Karen J. (1999). Alcohol intake and the risk of coronary heart disease mortality in persons with older-onset diabetes mellitus. *Journal of the American Medical Association, 282,* 239–246.

28. National Institute on Alcohol Abuse and Alcoholism (1998, July). Alcohol Alert: Alcohol and sleep. No. 41. Bethesda MD: National Institute on Alcohol Abuse and Alcoholism.
29. Schuckit, Marc A. (1989). *Drug and alcohol abuse: A clinical guide to diagnosis and treatment* (3rd ed.). New York: Plenum, p. 62.
30. Victor, Maurice (1976). Treatment of alcohol intoxication and the withdrawal syndrome: A critical analysis of the use of drugs and other forms of therapy. In Peter G. Bourne (Ed.), *Acute drug emergencies: A treatment manual.* New York: Academic Press, p. 199.
31. Luks and Barbato, *You are what you drink,* pp. 52–53.
32. National Highway Traffic Safety Administration (1996, July). Fatal accident reporting system. Washington DC: U.S. Department of Transportation. Zador, Paul L. (1991). Alcohol-related relative risk of fatal driver injuries in relation to driver age and sex. *Journal of Studies on Alcohol,* 52, 302–310.
33. National Institute on Alcohol Abuse and Alcoholism (1994, July). Alcohol alert: Alcohol-related impairment. No. 25, PH351. Bethesda MD: National Institute on Alcohol Abuse and Alcoholism.
34. Gross, Leonard (1983). *How much is too much: The effects of social drinking.* New York: Random House, p. 29. Quotation of Dr. Herbert Moskowitz.
35. Fortini, Mary-Ellen (1995). Youth, alcohol, and automobiles: Attitudes and behaviors. In Ronald R. Watson (Ed.), *Alcohol, cocaine, and accidents.* Totowa NJ: Humana Press, pp. 25–39. U.S. Department of Health and Human Services (1990). *Alcohol and health,* pp. 216–217.
36. Hingson, Ralph, Heeren, Timothy, and Winter, Michael (1996). Lowering state legal blood alcohol limits to 0.08%: The effect on fatal motor vehicle crashes. *American Journal of Public Health, 86,* 1297–1299.
37. Liu, Simin; Siegel, Paul Z.; Brewer, Robert D.; Mokdad, Ali H.; Sleet, David A.; and Sardula, Mary (1997). Prevalence of alcohol-impaired driving: Results from a national self-reported survey of health behaviors. *Journal of the American Medical Association, 277,* 122–125. National Highway Traffic Safety Administration (1996, July). National Highway Traffic Administration (1999, March). The relationship of alcohol safety laws to drinking drivers in fatal crashes. Washington DC: U.S. Department of Transportation. Wolfson, Mark; Toomey, Traci L.; Forster, Jean L.; Wagenaar, Alexander C.; McGovern, Paul G.; and Perry, Cheryl L. (1996). Characteristics, policies, and practices of alcohol outlets and sales to underage persons. *Journal of Studies on Alcohol, 57,* 670–674. Zador, Alcohol-related relative risk.
38. Pernanen, Kai (1991). *Alcohol in human violence.* New York: Guilford Press, pp. 192–193.
39. Collins, James J., and Messerschmidt, Pamela M. (1993). Epidemiology of alcohol-related violence. *Alcohol Health and Research World, 17,* 93–100. Goode, Erich (1989). *Drugs in American society* (2nd ed.). New York: McGraw-Hill, p. 118. National Institute on Alcohol Abuse and Alcoholism (1997, October). Alcohol alert: Alcohol, violence, and aggression. No. 38. Bethesda MD: National Institute on Alcohol Abuse and Alcoholism.
40. Pernanen, Kai (1993). Research approaches in the study of alcohol-related violence. *Alcohol Health and Research World, 17,* 101–107. Taylor, Stuart P. (1993). Experimental investigation of alcohol-induced aggression in humans. *Alcohol Health and Research World, 17,* 108–112.
41. Abel, Ernest L. (1985). *Psychoactive drugs and sex.* New York: Plenum Press, pp. 19–54. George, William H., and Norris, Jeanette (1993). Alcohol, disinhibition, sexual arousal, and deviant sexual behavior. *Alcohol Health and Research World, 17,* 133–138.
42. Darby, William, and Heinz, Agnes (1991, January). *The responsible use of alcohol: Defining the parameters of moderation.* New York: American Council on Science and Health, pp. 1–26. Hanson, David J., and Engs, Ruth C. (1994). Drinking behavior: Taking personal responsibility. In Peter J. Venturelli (Ed.), *Drug use in America: Social, cultural, and political perspectives.* Boston: Jones and Bartlett, pp. 175–181.

CHAPTER 10

Chronic Alcohol Abuse and Alcoholism

After you have completed this chapter, you will understand

- Problems surrounding the definition of alcoholism
- The history of attempts to regulate chronic alcohol abuse
- Chronic effects of alcohol
- Patterns of chronic alcohol abuse
- Special problems among the elderly
- Family dynamics in alcoholism
- Genetic and environmental influences in alcoholism
- Approaches to treatment for alcoholism
- Alcoholism in the workplace

When you live in an alcoholic family, you sometimes lie in bed and dream. You dream that your parents are going to quit drinking, that you are going to get closer to them. You are going to have a better life. . . . You picture your parents beginning to care for themselves and for you. You imagine it being beautiful. Your home is clean and organized. Instead of abusing you, or being nice to you just to get rid of you, your parents are helping you with your homework.

—Teens talk about alcohol and alcoholism *(1987)*

Chronic abuse of alcohol has been called the hidden addiction. There is no need to get out on the street and find a pusher; for many people, it is remarkably easy to conceal their problem (at least in the beginning) from family and friends. Alcohol consumption is so tightly woven into the fabric of U.S. social life that it can be difficult to catch on that an individual may be drinking too much too often. All too frequently, chronic abuse of alcohol has been treated as a genteel affair, rarely with the same degree of concern as that associated with the chronic abuse of other drugs. Yet from a pharmacological point of view, it is the same, and we have to realize that fact. This chapter will deal with the very serious consequences of this condition on millions of people and on society at large.

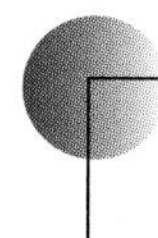

Alcoholism: Stereotypes, Definitions, and Criteria

Close your eyes and try to imagine an alcoholic. You might form an image of someone, probably male, who is down on his heels, perhaps a dirty, skid-row bum with a bottle of cheap wine in his hands, living from day to day in a state of deteriorating health, with no one caring about him except a social worker or police officer or, inevitably, the medical examiner. You would be imagining less than 5 percent of all alcoholics; more than 95 percent of them look quite different. The demographics of alcoholism include every possible category. Alcoholics can be fourteen years old or eighty-four, male or female, professional or blue-collar, urbanite, suburbanite, or rural resident in any community large or small.

What aspects of their behavior tie them all together, allowing us to describe their condition with a single label? Because of the wide diversity of alcoholics, no one has come up with one encompassing definition of alcoholism. Instead, we are left with a set of criteria, basically a collection of signs, symptoms, and behaviors that help us make the diagnosis. A single individual may not fulfill all of these criteria, but if he or she fulfills enough of them, we decide that the standard has been met.

The criteria adopted here focus on four basic life problems that are tied to the consumption of alcohol: (1) problems associated with a preoccupation with drinking, (2) emotional problems, (3) vocational, social, and family problems, and (4) problems associated with physical health.[1] Notice that these criteria make no mention of the cause or causes of alcoholism, only its behavioral, social, and physical consequences. In short, we are recognizing that **alcoholism** is a complex phenomenon with psychological-behavioral components (criteria 1 and 2), social components (criterion 3), and a physical component (criterion 4).

Problems Associated with a Preoccupation with Drinking

The dominant characteristic of alcoholics is their preoccupation with the act of drinking and their incorporation of drinking into their everyday lives. An alcoholic may need a drink prior to a social occasion in order to feel "fortified." With increasing frequency, such a person sees alcohol as a way of dealing with stress and anxiety. Drinking itself becomes a routine, no longer a social, affair. The habit of taking a few drinks on a daily basis on arriving home from work is an example of **symptomatic drinking,** in which alcohol is viewed specifically as a way of relieving tension. Also increasing are incidences of unintentional states of severe intoxication and blackouts of events surrounding the time of drinking, a condition quite different from "passing out" from a high BAC level. One such occurrence may not be a particularly critical sign, but recurrences definitely are.[2]

Traditionally, alcoholism is associated with consumption of a large quantity of alcohol. This sounds pretty obvious and it is true of most alcoholics, but we still have to be careful about overgeneralizing. There are significant differences in the way alcoholics consume their alcohol. Not all of them drink alone or begin every day with a drink. Many of them drink on a daily basis, but others are spree or binge alcoholics who might become grossly intoxicated on occasion and totally abstain from drinking the rest of the time.[3]

Another feature often attributed to alcoholics is the loss of control over their drinking. The alcoholic typically craves a drink and frequently engages in compulsive behavior related to alcohol. There may be a stockpiling of liquor, taking a drink or two before going to a party, or feeling uncomfortable unless alcohol is present. The alcoholic may be sneaking drinks or having drinks that others do not know about, such as surreptitiously having an extra drink or two in the kitchen out of the sight of the party guests.[4] Particularly when the alcoholic is trying to abstain from or reduce the quantity of alcohol consumed,

alcoholism: A condition in which the consumption of alcohol has produced major psychological, physical, social, or occupational problems.
symptomatic drinking: A pattern of alcohol consumption aimed at reducing stress and anxiety.

The typical alcoholic American

Doctor, age 54

Farmer, age 35

Unemployed, age 40

College student, age 19

Counselor, age 38

Retired editor, age 86

Dancer, age 22

Police officer, age 46

Military officer, age 31

Student, age 14

Executive, age 50

Taxi driver, age 61

Homemaker, age 43

Bricklayer, age 29

Computer programmer, age 25

Lawyer, age 52

There's no such thing as typical. We have all kinds.
10 million Americans are alcoholic.
It's our number one drug problem.

Alcoholism affects so many different kinds of people that generalizations about the typical profile of an alcoholic are impossible.

his or her thoughts become focused on the possibility of drinking or ways to rationalize it.[5]

Yet professionals disagree whether all alcoholics are necessarily out of control with respect to alcohol. As discussed later in the chapter, this controversy has major implications for choosing the treatment approach in cases of alcohol abuse. If it is true that even a small amount of alcohol will propel a recovering alcoholic back to alcohol abuse, then a primary focus of treatment should be on no drinking at all, better known as absolute **abstinence.** If it is not true, then there is the possibility of controlled drinking without the fear of "falling off the wagon." The well-known alcohol treatment program Alcoholics Anonymous, for example, functions under the premise that an alcoholic must never drink again, even in minute quantities, if recovery is to be long lasting.

Emotional Problems

Given that alcohol is a depressant drug, it should not be surprising that chronic alcohol intake produces depressive reactions. It has been estimated that between one-third and one-half of all alcoholics experience depressive symptoms sometime in their lives. Only 5 percent, however, show depression prior to the onset of the alcoholic condition. Therefore, the depression is considered to be alcohol-induced, and when the alcoholic abstains from drinking, the depressive symptoms subside.[6]

Vocational, Social, and Family Problems

No one questions the potential problems that chronic alcohol abuse can bring to the maintenance of a job or career, social relationships, and a stable family life. These three areas frequently intertwine, and trouble in one exacerbates the others. A job loss puts stress on marital and family relationships, just as marital and family difficulties put stress on occupational performance.

Numerous clinical studies support the idea of increased domestic instability in the lives of alcoholics, but the true extent of these problems is difficult to assess. Family violence, for example, is frequently examined through cases seen in treatment or social service programs. As a result, these agencies may interpret the domestic behavior of a father not known to have a drinking problem differently from that of a father with a history of alcoholism. A man who drinks heavily and abuses his children may be more likely to be "counted" as an alcoholic than a nonabusive father who consumes just as much alcohol. It is much easier to assess the likelihood of domestic violence or decline in job performance due to acute intoxication than it is to evaluate the influence of chronic abuse of alcohol. Even so, there is no doubt that the cumulative effects of alcoholism on family dynamics are devastating.[7]

Physical Problems

There is also no question that chronic alcohol consumption has a destructive effect on the body. Not surprisingly, a principal site of damage is the brain. Neuroimaging procedures, such as CT and MRI scans, reveal a consistent link between heavy drinking and physical shrinkage of brain matter, particularly in the cerebral cortex, cerebellum, and regions associated with memory and other cognitive functions. These neurological changes are observed even in the absence of other alcohol-related medical conditions such as chronic liver disease.[8]

Hiding the Problems: Denial and Enabling

The major life problems that serve as rough criteria for determining the condition of alcoholism are often not recognized by alcoholics themselves because of their tendency to deny that their drinking is having any influence on their lives or the lives of people around them. When in denial, the alcoholic can be extremely sensitive to any mention of problems associated with drinking. A hangover the next day, for example, is seldom discussed as it would draw attention to the fact that drinking has occurred.[9]

Denial can also be manifest among the people around the alcoholic. Members of an alcoholic's family, for example, may try to function as if life were normal. Through their excuse making and efforts to undo or cover up the frequent physical and psychological damage the alcoholic causes, they inadvertently prevent the alcoholic from seeking treatment or delay that treatment until the alcoholism is more severe. These people are referred to as **enablers** because they enable the alcoholic to function as an alcoholic as opposed to a sober person. Both processes of denial and enabling present major difficulties not only in establishing problem-oriented criteria for diagnosing alcoholism but also in introducing necessary

abstinence: The complete avoidance of some consumable item or behavior.

enablers: Individuals whose behavior consciously or unconsciously encourages another person's continuation in a pattern of alcohol or other drug abuse.

A Self-Administered Short Michigan Alcoholism Screening Test (SMAST)

The Michigan Alcoholism Screening Test (MAST), twenty-four questions to be answered in ten to fifteen minutes, is designed as a structured interview instrument to detect alcoholism. A shorter thirteen-question version (SMAST), shown here, has approximately the same level of reliability and validity. Score one point for each response that matches the one in parentheses. According to the authors of the test, a total score of 0 or 1 indicates a nonalcoholic, 2 a possible alcoholic, and 3 or more an alcoholic.

1. Do you feel you are a normal drinker? (By normal we mean you drink less than or as much as most other people.) (NO)
2. Does your wife, husband, a parent, or other near relative ever worry or complain about your drinking? (YES)
3. Do you ever feel guilty about your drinking? (YES)
4. Do friends or relatives think you are a normal drinker? (NO)
5. Are you able to stop drinking when you want to? (NO)
6. Have you ever attended a meeting of Alcoholics Anonymous? (YES)
7. Has drinking ever created problems between you and your wife, husband, a parent, or other near relative? (YES)
8. Have you ever gotten into trouble at work because of drinking? (YES)
9. Have you ever neglected your obligations, your family, or your work for two or more days in a row because you were drinking? (YES)
10. Have you ever gone to anyone for help about your drinking? (YES)
11. Have you ever been in a hospital because of drinking? (YES)
12. Have you ever been arrested for drunken driving, driving while intoxicated, or driving under the influence of alcoholic beverages? (YES)
13. Have you ever been arrested, even for a few hours, because of other drunken behavior? (YES)

Source: Selzer, Melvin L., Vinokur, Amiram, and van Rooijen, Louis (1975). A self-administered Short Michigan Alcoholism Screening Test (SMAST). *Journal of Studies on Alcohol, 36,* 117–126.

interventions. Denial and enabling are clearly relevant processes in the area of alcoholism, but it is not difficult to see how they present problems with regard to *any* form of drug abuse (see Chapter 17).

Health Line provides a useful self-survey for determining the signs of potential alcoholism. You may want to try it out on yourself and people that you know.

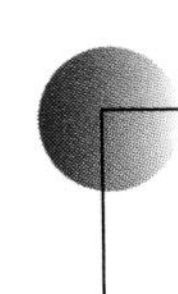

Alcohol Abuse and Alcohol Dependence: The Professional's View

As you can see, the criteria commonly employed in determining the presence of alcoholism are at times quite murky, and often there are nearly as many counterexamples to each of the criteria as there are examples. The American Psychiatric Association, through its Diagnostic and Statistical Manual, fourth edition (DSM-IV), has attempted to put together as many common features as possible and has established two basic syndromes. It is important to understand these technical definitions, because professionals in the field of alcoholism commonly use the DSM-IV either in their research or in clinical work.[10]

The first syndrome, referred to as **alcohol abuse,** is characterized as either (1) the continued use of alcohol for at least one month despite the knowledge of having a persistent or recurring physical problem or some difficulty in social or occupational functioning, or (2) the recurring use of alcohol in situations (such as driving) when alcohol consumption is physically hazardous.

The second syndrome, referred to as **alcohol dependence,** is characterized as alcohol abuse that also involves any three of the following seven situations:

- consuming alcohol in amounts or over a longer period than the person intends
- a persistent desire, or one or more unsuccessful attempts, to cut down or control drinking

alcohol abuse: A syndrome characterized primarily by the continued use of alcohol despite the drinker's knowledge of having a persistent physical problem or some social or occupational difficulty.
alcohol dependence: A syndrome in which alcohol abuse involves a variety of significant physical, psychological, social, and behavioral problems.

QUICK CONCEPT  10.1

Understanding the Psychology of Alcoholism

Check your understanding of the psychological aspects of alcoholism by matching the quotations or behavioral descriptions (on the left) with the appropriate term (on the right).

1. Brad tries to call his estranged wife on the telephone. She hangs up on him. Now angry and frustrated, Brad takes a drink.
2. Mary stays sober during the work week, but on the weekend she downs at least two quarts of vodka.
3. "Despite what my family says, I am convinced I am not an alcoholic."
4. "If I'm with her when she's drinking, I can make sure she doesn't overdo her drinking."
5. "I'm going to the theater later. I don't think there will be any liquor there so I had better have a couple of drinks before I go."

a. denial
b. enabling
c. out-of-control drinking
d. spree or binge drinking
e. symptomatic drinking

Answers: 1. e 2. d 3. a 4. b 5. c

- a great deal of time spent drinking or recovering from the effects of drinking
- alcohol consumption continuing despite knowledge that drinking either causes or exacerbates recurrent physical or psychological problems
- important social, occupational, or recreational activities given up or reduced because of alcohol
- marked tolerance or the need to drink more than before to achieve previous levels of intoxication
- symptoms of alcohol withdrawal or the consumption of alcohol in order to relieve or avoid withdrawal symptoms

Obviously, individuals fitting the second definition are considered more greatly impaired than those fitting the first. That distinction was also true with regard to the more general criteria for substance abuse and substance dependence (see Chapter 2). Approximately 4 percent of U.S. adults are alcohol abusers, and 6 percent are alcohol dependent.[11]

The History of Efforts to Regulate Chronic Alcohol Abuse

In the late 1700s, prominent physicians, writers, and scientists began to consider the long-term adverse effects of alcohol consumption and tried to formulate some kind of social reform to mitigate them. The goal at that time was to reduce the consumption of distilled spirits (liquor) only. It was a temperate attitude toward drinking (hence the phrase "temperance movement") rather than an insistence on the total prohibition of alcohol.

In the United States, where the temperance movement was to be stronger than anywhere else, its most influential spokesman was Benjamin Rush, a physician, Revolutionary War hero, and signer of the Declaration of Independence. In his 1785 pamphlet *An inquiry into the effects of ardent spirits on the human mind and body*, Rush vividly described the range of mental and physical dangers associated with alcohol abuse:

> *Strong liquor is more destructive than the sword. The destruction of war is periodic whereas alcohol exerts its influence upon human life at all times and in all seasons. . . . A nation corrupted by alcohol can never be free.*[12]

Rush's efforts did not have a major impact on the drinking habits of American society during his lifetime. As described in Chapter 9, alcohol consumption in the United States at that time was enormous and continued to rise until about 1830. Rush's words, however, served as an inspiration to political and religious groups around the country who saw alcohol abuse in social and moral terms. In their view, drunkenness led to poverty, a disorderly society, and civil disobedience. In short, it was unpatriotic at best and subversive at worst. When we hear the phrase "demon rum," we have to recognize that many Americans during the nineteenth century took the phrase quite literally. Liquor was demonized as a direct source of evil in the world. The idea, like any other form of scapegoating, spread like wildfire. In 1831, the American Temperance Society reported that nearly 2 million Americans had renounced strong liquor and more than eight hundred societies had been established. By the 1850s, twelve U.S. states and two Canadian provinces had introduced legislation forbidding the sale of "alcoholic" (distilled) drink.

Whether or not they may have been justified in doing so, temperance groups took credit for a drastic change that was occurring in the levels of alcohol consumption in the United States. From 1830 to 1850, consumption of all types of alcohol plummeted from an annual per capita level of roughly 7 gallons to roughly 2 gallons, approximately 50 percent higher than today's consumption level (see Chapter 9). It is quite possible that this decline encouraged the temperance movement to formulate its ultimate goal, a prohibition of alcohol consumption in any form.

The Road to National Prohibition

A major development in the temperance movement was the formation in 1873 of a women's organization called the Woman's Christian Temperance Union (WCTU). Almost from the beginning, its primary target was a highly visible fixture of late nineteenth-century American life: the saloon. These establishments were now vilified as the source of all the troubles alcohol could bring. It is not difficult to imagine how the saloon would have been seen as a significant threat to American women in general.

> *Bars appeared to invite family catastrophe. They introduced children to drunkenness and vice and drove husbands to alcoholism; they also caused squandering of wages, wife beating, and child abuse; and, with the patron's inhibitions lowered through drink, the saloon led many men into the arms of prostitutes (and not incidentally, contributed to the alarming spread of syphilis).*[13]

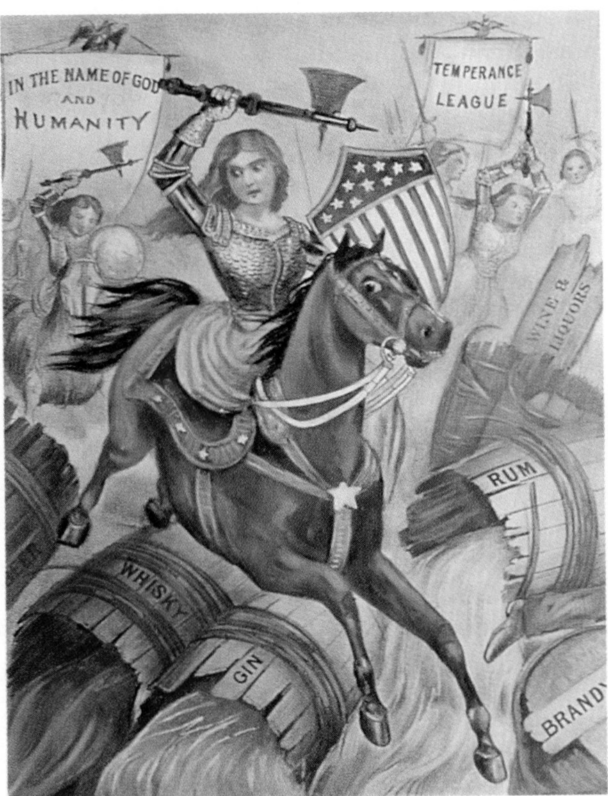

Even though this 1874 engraving shows a temperance crusader in full battle regalia, relatively few temperance activists resorted to physical violence.

No wonder the WCTU hated the saloon, and no saloon in the country was safe from their "pray-in" demonstrations, vocal opposition, and in some cases violent interventions. Their influence eventually extended into every aspect of American culture. The WCTU and other antialcohol forces, such as the newly formed Anti-Saloon League and National Prohibition Party, were soon electing congressional candidates pledged to enact national legislation banning alcohol consumption throughout the land.

The Beginning and Ending of a "Noble Experiment"

In December 1917, Congress passed a resolution "prohibiting the manufacture, sale, transportation, or importation of intoxicating liquors," the simple wording that would form the basis for the Eighteenth Amendment to the U.S. Constitution. (Notice that it did not forbid purchase or use of alcohol). The Volstead Act of 1919 set up the enforcement procedures. By the end of the year, the necessary thirty-six states had ratified the amendment, and Prohibition took effect in January 1920.

Despite its lofty aims, Prohibition was doomed to failure. In the countryside, operators of illegal stills (called "moonshiners" because they worked largely at night) continued their production, despite the efforts of an occasional half-hearted raid by Treasury agents (known as "revenooers"). The major cities became centers of open defiance. Liquor, having been smuggled into the country, flowed abundantly as saloons turned into speakeasies and operated in violation of the law.

The early years of Prohibition did, however, show positive effects in the area of public health. Alcohol-related deaths, cirrhosis of the liver, mental disorders, and alcohol-related crime declined in 1920 and 1921, but in a few years, the figures began to creep up again and the level of criminal activity associated with illegal drinking was clearly intolerable.[14] By the end of the decade, for the vast majority of Americans, it had become obvious that the experiment was not working.

In 1933, President Franklin D. Roosevelt, having run on a platform to repeal the Volstead Act, signed the necessary legislation that became the Twenty-first Amendment; ratification was swift. Alcohol was restored as a legal commodity and its regulation was returned once more to local authorities. Since that time, state prohibition laws have gradually been repealed, with Mississippi in 1966 being the last state to do so.

Present-Day Regulation by Taxation

One immediate benefit of repealing Prohibition was the return of federal revenue from taxes on alcohol. In 1933 alone, such taxes brought in $500 million, which was used to finance social programs during the Depression. The concept of collecting taxes on the basis of alcohol consumption dates back to the very beginning of the United States as a nation. In 1794, the newly formed U.S. Congress passed a law requiring an excise tax on the sale of whiskey. After a short-lived Whiskey Rebellion in which President Washington had to order federal militia to subdue Appalachian farmers who had refused to pay the new tax, the practice of taxing alcohol was accepted and has continued to the present day as a legal way of raising tax money.

Taxes on alcohol sales have been an indirect mechanism for regulating the consumption of alcohol by increasing its price, not unlike taxes on tobacco products (see Chapter 11). Governmental revenue from alcohol sales alone amounts to more than $7 billion. Today, alcoholic beverages are one of the most heavily taxed consumer products. Approximately 42 percent of the retail price of an average bottle of distilled spirits, for example, is earmarked for federal, state, or local taxes.[15]

Should the price of alcohol be used to affect the pattern of consumption? As noted in Chapter 9, alcohol consumption rates have declined over the last decade or so, in part as a result of changing attitudes toward personal health and dieting. The alcohol beverage industry is quick to blame the governmental taxes for decreasing their retail sales and often observes that because of reduced sales, the net income to the government actually ends up less than before the tax increase. Those in favor of these taxes, however, argue that the nation's taxation policy with regard to alcohol and other legal psychoactive drugs (such as nicotine) that have negative consequences on society is an appropriate option of government.

It has been proposed that alcohol taxes be set high enough to begin to offset the total societal costs resulting from alcohol abuse. This approach would place a type of "user fee" on the consumption of alcohol. It has been estimated that if the average tax on a gallon of pure alcohol were raised from $35 to about $80, not only would consumption rates decline significantly but the tax revenue on the sales that remain would be substantial enough to pay the health-care costs of patients whose medical expenses arise from alcohol-related illnesses. However, there is also the possibility that raising the costs of alcohol might lead to the development of a black market for its purchase, little change in alcohol consumption, and a net decline in tax revenues.[16]

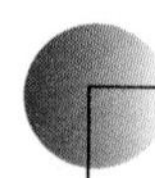

Chronic Effects of Alcohol

This section will deal with what we know about the consequences of long-term (chronic) consumption of alcohol over and above the acute effects that were discussed in the last chapter.

Tolerance and Withdrawal

As with other CNS depressants, alcohol consumption over a period of time will result in a tolerance effect. On a metabolic level, alcohol dehydrogenase activity during tolerance becomes higher in the stomach and liver, allowing the alcohol to leave the body somewhat faster; on a neural level, the brain is less responsive to alcohol's depressive effects.[17] Therefore, if alcohol consumption remains steady, the individual feels less of an effect.

As a result of tolerance and the tendency to compensate for it in terms of drinking a greater quantity, the chronic alcohol abuser is subject to increased physical risks. There is a serious behavioral risk as well; for example, an alcohol-tolerant drinker may consider driving with a BAC level that exceeds the standard for drunk driving, thinking he or she is not intoxicated and hence not impaired. A person's driving ability, under these circumstances, will be substantially overestimated.

An alcohol-dependent person's abrupt withdrawal from alcohol can result in a range of serious physical symptoms, beginning from six to forty-eight hours after the last drink, but estimates vary as to how many people are typically affected. Among hospitalized patients, only 5 percent appear to show withdrawal symptoms, whereas other studies of alcoholics using outpatient facilities have estimated the percentage to be as high as 18. Although the exact incidence may be somewhat unclear, there is less disagreement as to what takes place. Physical withdrawal effects are classified in two clusters of symptoms.

alcohol withdrawal syndrome: The more common of two general reactions to the cessation of alcohol consumption in an alcoholic. It is characterized by physiological discomfort, seizures, and sleep disturbances.

The first cluster, called the **alcohol withdrawal syndrome,** is the more common of the two. It begins with insomnia, vivid dreaming, and a severe hangover; these discomforts are followed by tremors (the "shakes"), sweating, mild agitation, anxiety (the "jitters"), nausea, and vomiting, as well as increased heart rate and blood pressure. In some patients, there are also brief tonic-clonic (grand mal) seizures, as the nervous system rebounds from the chronic depression induced by alcohol. The alcohol withdrawal syndrome usually reaches a peak from twenty-four to thirty-six hours after the last drink and is over after forty-eight hours.

The second cluster, called **delirium tremens (DTs),** is much more dangerous and is fortunately less common. The symptoms include extreme disorientation and confusion, profuse sweating, fever, and disturbing nightmares. Typically, there are also periods of frightening hallucinations, when the individual might experience seeing snakes or insects on the walls, ceiling, or his or her skin. These effects generally reach a peak three to four days after the last drink. During this time, there is the possibility of life-threatening events such as heart failure, dehydration, or suicide, so it is critical for the individual to be hospitalized and under medical supervision at all times. The current medical practice for treating individuals undergoing withdrawal is to administer antianxiety medication (see Chapter 15) to relieve the symptoms. After the withdrawal period has ended, the dose levels of the medication are gradually reduced and discontinued.[18]

(a)

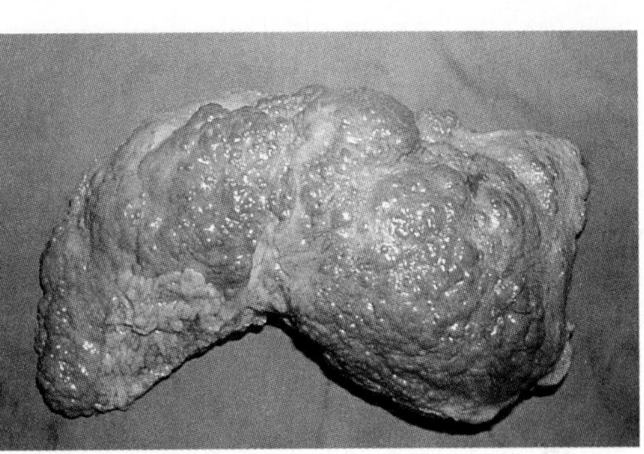

(b)

FIGURE 10.1

The dramatic difference between a healthy liver (a) and a cirrhotic liver (b).

Liver Disease

Chronic consumption of alcohol produces three forms of liver disease. The first of these is a **fatty liver,** resulting from an abnormal concentration of fatty deposits inside liver cells. Normally, the liver breaks down fats adequately, but when alcohol is in the body the liver breaks down the alcohol at the expense of fats. As a result, fats accumulate and ultimately interfere with the functioning of the liver. The condition is fortunately reversible, if the drinker abstains. The accumulated fats are gradually metabolized, and the liver returns to normal.

The second condition is **alcoholic hepatitis,** an inflammation of liver tissue causing fever, jaundice (a yellowing of the skin), and abdominal pain, resulting at least in part from a lower functioning level of the immune system. It is also reversible with abstinence, though some residual scarring may remain.

The third and most serious liver condition is **alcoholic cirrhosis,** characterized by the progressive development of scar tissue that chokes off blood vessels in the liver and destroys liver cells by interfering with the cell's utilization of oxygen. At an early stage, the liver is enlarged from the accumulation of fats, but at later stages it is shrunken as liver cells begin to degenerate (Figure 10.1). Though abstinence helps to prevent further liver degeneration when cirrhosis is diagnosed, the condition is not reversible except by liver transplantation surgery.

delirium tremens (DTs): The less common of two general reactions to the cessation of drinking in an alcoholic. It is characterized by extreme disorientation and confusion, fever, hallucinations, and other symptoms.
fatty liver: A condition in which fat deposits accumulate in the liver as a result of chronic alcohol abuse.
alcoholic hepatitis (AL-co-HAUL-ik hep-ah-TEYE-tus): A disease involving inflammation of the liver as a result of chronic alcohol abuse.
alcoholic cirrhosis (AL-co-HAUL-ik seer-OH-sis): A disease involving scarring and deterioration of liver cells as a result of chronic alcohol abuse.

Prior to the 1970s, alcoholic cirrhosis was attributed to nutritional deficiencies that are often associated with an alcoholic's diet. We know now that, although nutritional problems play a role, alcohol itself is toxic to the liver. After a pattern of heavy alcohol consumption of many years, it is possible to develop cirrhosis, even when nutrition is adequate. A major cause of liver cell damage is the toxic accumulation of free radicals, molecule fragments that are by-products of acetaldehyde, the enzyme involved in alcohol breakdown (Chapter 9).

Cirrhosis is ranked as the ninth leading cause of death in the United States, with most deaths occurring in people forty to sixty-five years old. Daily drinkers are at a higher risk of developing cirrhosis than binge drinkers, though this risk may be the result of the relatively larger quantity of alcohol consumed over a long period of time. Generally, patients showing liver damage have been drinking for ten to twenty years. Only 10 to 20 percent of all heavy drinkers develop cirrhosis, however, in contrast to 90 to 100 percent who show evidence of either fatty liver or hepatitis. There may be a genetic predisposition for cirrhosis that puts a subgroup of alcoholics at increased risk.[19]

Cardiovascular Problems

About one in every four alcoholics develops cardiovascular problems due to the chronic consumption of alcohol. The effects include inflammation and enlargement of the heart muscle, poor blood circulation to the heart, irregular heart contractions, fatty accumulations in the heart and arteries, high blood pressure, and brain hemorrhage.[20]

Cancer

Chronic alcohol abuse is associated with the increased risk of several types of cancers, in particular cancers of the esophagus, pharynx, and larynx. Nearly 50 percent of all such cancers are associated with heavy drinking. If alcohol abusers also smoke cigarettes, the increased risk is even more dramatic. An increased risk of liver cancer is also linked to chronic alcoholic abuse, whether or not cirrhosis is also present. In addition, an association has been made between alcohol consumption and breast cancer in women, a 41 percent greater risk being observed (relative to nondrinkers) in women who consume from two to five drinks per day. However, there is either a weaker association or no association at all with cancers of the stomach, colon, pancreas, or lungs.

Alcohol is not technically considered a carcinogen (a direct producer of cancer), so why the risks are increased in certain cancer types is at present unknown. It is possible that the increased risk is a combined result of alcohol enhancing the carcinogenic effects of other chemicals and, as is true with the development of hepatitis, depressing the immune system. With a reduced immune response, the alcoholic may have a lowered resistance to the development of cancerous tumors.[21]

Wernicke-Korsakoff Syndrome

Chronic alcohol consumption can produce longer-lasting deficits in the way an individual solves problems, remembers information, and organizes facts about his or her identity and surroundings. These cognitive deficits are commonly referred to collectively as **alcoholic dementia** and are associated with a structural loss of brain tissue. Specifically, there is an enlargement of brain ventricles (the interior fluid-filled spaces within the brain), a widening of fissures separating sections of cerebral cortex, and a loss of acetylcholine-sensitive receptors. The combination of these effects results in a net decrease in brain mass. CT scans and MRI scans, two imaging techniques that reveal the structural features of the brain, show that the degree of enlargement of the ventricles correlates with a decline in overall intelligence, verbal learning and retention, and short-term memory, particularly for middle-aged and elderly alcoholics.

From 50 to 75 percent of all detoxified alcoholics and nearly 20 percent of all individuals admitted to state mental hospitals show signs of alcohol-related dementia. Through abstinence, it is possible to reverse some of the cognitive deficits and even some of the abnormalities in the brain, depending on the age of the alcoholic when treatment begins. As you might suspect, younger alcoholics respond better than older ones.[22]

A more severe form of cognitive impairment related to chronic alcohol consumption is a two-stage disease referred to as **Wernicke-Korsakoff syndrome**. In the

---

alcoholic dementia (AL-co-HAUL-ik dih-MEN-chee-ah): A condition in which chronic alcohol abuse produces cognitive deficits such as difficulties in problem solving and memory.

Wernicke-Korsakoff syndrome (VERN-ih-kee KOR-sa-kof SIN-drohm): A condition resulting from chronic alcohol consumption, characterized by disorientation, cognitive deficits, amnesia, and motor difficulty.

---

first stage, called *Wernicke's encephalopathy* or simply *Wernicke's disease*, the patient shows confusion and disorientation, abnormal eye movements, and difficulties in movement and body coordination. These neurological problems arise from a deficiency in Vitamin B_1 (**thiamine**), a necessary nutrient for glucose to be consumed by neurons in the brain. Extreme alcoholics may go days or weeks at a time eating practically nothing and receiving calories exclusively from drinking alcoholic beverages. As a result of thiamine deficiency, large numbers of neurons die in areas of the brain specifically concerned with thinking and movement. About 15 percent of patients with Wernicke's disease, however, respond favorably to large amounts of thiamine supplements in combination with abstinence from alcohol, restoring their previous level of orientation, eye movements, and coordination.

Many Wernicke's disease patients, whether or not they recover from confusion and motor impairments, also display a severe form of chronic amnesia and general apathy called *Korsakoff's psychosis*. Specifically, such patients cannot remember information that has just been presented to them and have only a patchy memory for distant events that occurred prior to their alcoholic state. They frequently attempt, through a behavior called **confabulation,** to compensate for their gaps in memory by telling elaborate stories of imagined past events, as if trying to fool others into thinking that they remember more than they actually do.

Thiamine deficiency is linked to Korsakoff's psychosis as well. About 20 percent of patients completely recover and 60 percent partially recover their memory after being treated with thiamine supplements. Yet the remaining 20 percent, generally the most severely impaired patients and those with the longest history of alcohol consumption, show little or no improvement and require chronic institutionalization.[23]

Fetal Alcohol Syndrome

The disorders just reviewed have generally been associated with consumption of large quantities of alcohol over a long period of time. In the case of the adverse effects of alcohol during pregnancy on unborn children, we are dealing with a unique situation. First of all, we need to recognize the extreme susceptibility of a developing fetus to conditions in the mother's bloodstream. In short, if the mother takes a drink, the fetus takes one too. And to make matters worse, the fetus does not have sufficient levels of acetaldehyde to break down the alcohol properly; thus the alcohol stays in the fetus's system longer than in the mother's. In addition, the presence of alcohol coincides with a period of time in prenatal development when critical processes are occurring that are essential for the development of a healthy, alert child.

Although it has long been suspected that alcohol abuse among pregnant women might present serious risks to the fetus, a specific syndrome was not established until 1973, when Kenneth L. Jones and David W. Smith described a cluster of characteristic features in children of alcoholic mothers that has since been defined as **fetal alcohol syndrome (FAS).**[24] Their studies, and research conducted since then, have clearly shown that alcohol is **teratogenic;** that is, it produces specific birth defects in offspring by disrupting fetal development during pregnancy, even when differences in prenatal nutrition have been accounted for. Later in life, FAS children show deficits in short-term memory and problem solving and exhibit signs of hyperactivity in school. These problems continue into adulthood.[25]

Present-day diagnoses of FAS are made on the basis of three groups of observations: (1) prenatal or postnatal growth retardation in which the child's weight or length is below the 10th percentile, (2) evidence of CNS abnormalities or mental retardation, and (3) a characteristic skull and facial appearance that includes a smaller-than-normal head, small wide-set eyes, drooping eyelids, a flattening of the vertical groove between the mouth and nose, a thin upper lip, and a short upturned nose. If only some of these characteristics are observed, the condition is referred to as possible **fetal alcohol effect (FAE).**

The incidence of FAS is approximately one to two cases per thousand live births in the general U.S. population, but the rates vary greatly within that population. When studies concern only heavy-drinking alcoholic

---

thiamine (THEYE-ah-meen or THEYE-ah-min): Vitamin B_1.
confabulation: The tendency to make up elaborate past histories to cover the fact that long-term memory has been impaired.
fetal alcohol syndrome (FAS): A serious condition involving mental retardation and facial-cranial malformations in the offspring of an alcoholic mother.
teratogenic (TER-ah-tuh-JEN-ik): Capable of producing specific birth defects.
fetal alcohol effect (FAE): A cognitive deficiency in the offspring of an alcoholic mother. It is considered less serious than fetal alcohol syndrome.

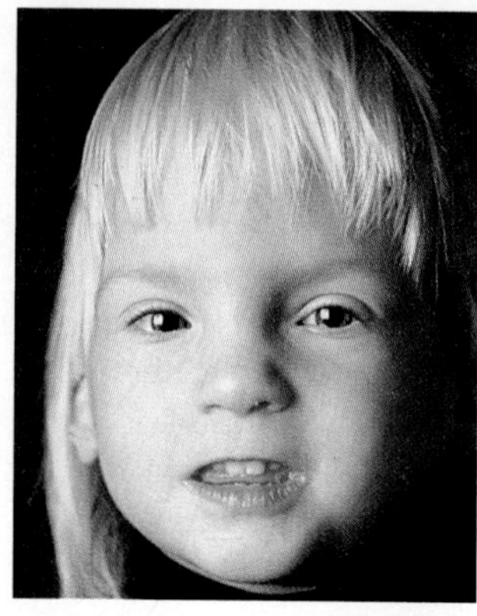

The face of a child with fetal alcohol syndrome, showing the wide-set eyes and other features that are characteristic of this condition.

mothers, the prevalence rate rises to approximately twenty-nine per thousand. Studies have also shown that African American and Native American women are more vulnerable to both FAS and FAE than women in other ethnic and racial categories, despite similar patterns of drinking behavior and other key factors such as nutrition. These differences suggest that a genetic factor may be contributing to the increase in risk.[26]

We do not know at present how alcohol causes FAS or FAE, except that the greatest risk is in the first trimester of pregnancy, especially the third week of gestation when craniofacial formation and brain growth are prominent developmental milestones. Binge drinking during this time appears to be very damaging to the fetus. For example, if two mothers consumed a similar overall quantity of alcohol during their pregnancies but Mother A consumed one drink on each of seven days in a week and Mother B consumed all seven drinks on two weekend evenings, then Mother B would have run a far greater risk to her child than Mother A.[27]

Although not all alcoholic mothers will give birth to babies with FAS or FAE, the research findings are clear: Risks are greatly increased when excessive drinking is taking place. Although an occasional drink may have minimal effects, no one has determined a "safe" level of drinking during pregnancy that would make this behavior risk-free. The objective of prevention, therefore, is to educate women to the dangers of drinking at any level and to encourage complete abstinence from alcohol (as well as other psychoactive drugs) during their pregnancy. Since 1989, all containers of alcoholic beverages must contain two warning messages, one of which is that "according to the Surgeon General, women should not drink alcoholic beverages during pregnancy because of the risk of birth defects."

Fortunately, the public is aware of the problem and the number of women who consume alcohol during pregnancy has declined over the last twenty-five years. In some instances, it has been possible to affect prenatal exposure to alcohol in a positive way through broad social change. For example, in 1978, a change in social policy among members of a Southwestern Plains Native American tribe, shifting the distribution of mineral-rights income toward social programs on the reservation, resulted in the prevalence rate for FAS decreasing from fourteen per thousand live births to none at all. A combined prevalence rate of FAS and FAE decreased from twenty-seven per thousand live births to five. The potential influence of sociocultural factors in altering alcohol consumption patterns needs to be examined closely in all high-risk populations.[28]

The bad news, however, is that the rates of alcohol consumption among several other high-risk populations in the United States, such as pregnant smokers, unmarried women, women under the age of twenty-five, and women with the fewest years of education, have remained unchanged. Twenty percent of pregnant women nationwide continue to consume alcohol, with the percentage rising to 37 among smokers. A 1995 survey by the Centers for Disease Control and Prevention found that 3.5 percent of pregnant women admitted to having seven or more drinks per week or binging on five or more drinks at once within the previous month.[29]

Until these statistics improve, FAS and FAE will continue to be the third leading cause of mental retardation not only in the United States but in the entire Western world, exceeded only by Down syndrome and spina bifida. The fact that the development of alcohol-related fetal defects is entirely preventable makes the incidence of these conditions all the more tragic (Health Line).

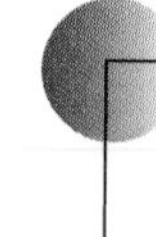

Patterns of Chronic Alcohol Abuse

When we consider the range of direct and indirect costs to society that result from chronic abuse of alcohol, the price we pay is enormous. These costs include the expense of treatment for alcoholism and of medical intervention for alcohol-related diseases, lost productivity from absenteeism and decreases in worker performance, treatment for alcohol-related injuries, and the lost value of future earnings of individuals who die prematurely because of alcoholism. The total costs in the United States are estimated to exceed $150 billion annually, even without taking into consideration the incalculable costs of

The TWEAK Alcoholism Screening Instrument for Pregnant Women

One of the difficulties in getting information about possible alcoholic behavior is the tendency for the individual to deny that alcohol abuse is going on. It is especially important to find out whether or not pregnant women are engaging in this behavior. The following is a brief screening questionnaire, called the TWEAK, that provides personal information about drinking problems, without asking about them in a direct fashion. There are five basic questions (one question for each letter in the acronym TWEAK), with the first question presented in two alternative forms. The choice of whether to ask Question 1a or 1b is left to the health professional collecting the information.

1a. How many drinks does it take before you begin to feel the first effects of alcohol? (T—it asks about tolerance in terms of an initial state of intoxication)
1b. How many drinks does it take before the alcohol makes you fall asleep or pass out? Or, if you never drink until you pass out, what is the largest number of drinks you have? (T—it asks about tolerance in terms of an extreme level of intoxication)
2. Have your friends or relatives worried or complained about your drinking in the past year? (W—it asks about the extent of worry about one's drinking)
3. Do you sometimes take a drink in the morning when you first get up? (E—it refers to an "eye opener")
4. Are there times when you drink and afterward you can't remember what you did or said? (A—it refers to amnesia or a blackout episode)
5. Do you sometimes feel the need to cut down on your drinking? (K—it refers to the need to cut down on the level of alcohol consumption)

Three drinks or more is considered a positive answer to Question 1a; five drinks or more is considered a positive answer to Question 1b. Positive answers count for two points in Questions 1 and 2, and one point each for Questions 3, 4, and 5. A score of 3 or more, out of a maximum of 7, is interpreted as an indication of a possible alcohol problem.

Researchers have found that TWEAK scores can accurately identify up to 77 percent of women who are problem drinkers (an indication of the sensitivity of the questionnaire) and up to 93 percent of women who are not (an indication of the specificity of the questionnaire). Other short surveys are available, but they do not differentiate the two groups as well as the TWEAK. Using this instrument is a major step toward preventing FAS by identifying those women whose drinking during pregnancy will have adverse effects on the developing fetus.

Sources: Bradley, Katharine A.; Boyd-Wickizer, Jodie; Powell, Suzanne H.; and Burman, Marcia L. (1998). Alcohol screening questionnaires in women: A critical review. *Journal of the American Medical Association, 280,* 166–171. Parsons, Oscar A. (1996). Alcohol abuse and alcoholism. In Russell L. Adams, Oscar A. Parsons, Jan L. Culbertson, and Sara Jo Nixon (Eds.), *Neuropsychology for clinical practice: Etiology, assessment, and treatment of common neurological disorders.* Washington DC: American Psychological Association, pp. 175–201.

human suffering that are involved in the estimated 125,000 alcohol-related deaths each year.[30]

The Demographics of Alcoholism

As mentioned earlier, alcoholics can be found in every age, gender, racial, ethnic, and religious group, and in all socioeconomic levels and geographic regions of the country. Nonetheless, large differences in prevalence exist within these categories. For example, men outnumber women in the incidence of alcoholism by about six to one, with men tending to be steadier from day to day in their consumption of alcohol and women tending to abstain from drinking for lengths of time and to binge once they start drinking again. Overall, women are more vulnerable to alcohol-related organ damage. Whether this higher risk is a result of differences in the pattern of drinking or in differences in the way alcohol is processed in a woman's body is at present unknown.[31]

Figure 10.2 shows that, when the severity of alcohol problems is measured by the rate of alcohol-related deaths from disease or injury, the highest levels in the United States generally occur in the South, the West, and Alaska.[32] For a discussion of some of the other demographic differences, see Chapter 9.

Alcohol Abuse among the Elderly

There is a widely held belief that alcohol abuse is not much of a problem with the elderly. Unfortunately, that is a myth. On the basis of careful studies addressing the problem of

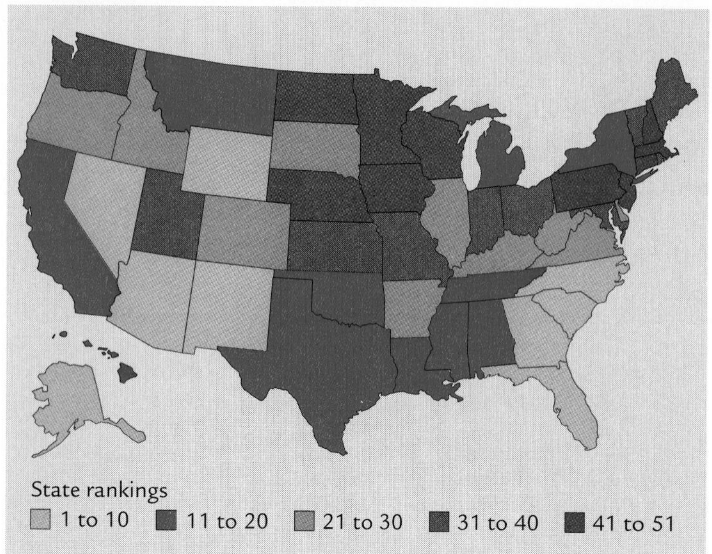

FIGURE 10.2

The fifty U.S. states and the District of Columbia ranked from 1 to 51 (1 being the highest) in terms of deaths resulting from any alcohol-related disease or injury.

Source: Caces, M. F., et al. (1991). Comparative alcohol-related mortality statistics in the United States by state, 1979–1985. *Alcohol Health and Research World, 15,* 166.

chronic alcohol abuse among the elderly, it has been estimated that between 2 and 10 percent of the elderly population have alcohol problems, with the percentage rising to nearly 50 among those residing in nursing homes. An analysis of Medicare records has indicated that more people over the age of sixty-five are hospitalized each year for alcohol-related problems than for heart attacks.[33]

One of the reasons for the underreporting of this problem is that we typically use the quantity of alcohol consumed as a primary index of alcoholism, and alcohol consumption does indeed decline with age. Yet, because of the changes in alcohol biotransformation over a lifetime, three drinks consumed at age sixty can be equivalent in their effects to four times as many drinks for someone at age twenty. In addition, the indications of social and occupational problems, traditionally part of the criteria for alcoholism, are often irrelevant for an elderly drinker. There is no incidence of drunk driving if the person is no longer driving, no job supervisor to notice a decline in work performance, and frequently no spouse to complain of social difficulties. Finally, the occurrence of blackouts or symptoms of Wernicke-Korsakoff syndrome may be misdiagnosed simply as an indication of senility or the onset of Alzheimer's disease.

A number of problems particularly affect the elderly who chronically abuse alcohol. One problem is the risk of the alcohol interacting with the many medications that the elderly typically take. Another is the risk of complications in already existing medical conditions of heart disease and gastrointestinal disorders.

There is growing recognition that treatment programs for alcoholism ought to be tailored to the elderly person's special needs; frequently the traditional treatment programs that benefit much younger individuals do not work well with older people. Many seniors were brought up in an era when highly negative attitudes toward drinking prevailed, so if they are drinking themselves, they feel stigmatized and resist treatment. On a brighter note, however, it has been found that, when treatment programs are designed specifically with the elderly in mind, older alcoholics will often respond well to treatment.[34]

The Family Dynamics of Alcoholism: A Systems Approach

Alcoholism, like any form of drug abuse, is an especially traumatizing experience for the families involved. For every one person who has a problem with alcohol, there are, on average, at least four others who are directly affected on a day-to-day basis. It is therefore important to examine some of these effects on particular family members. Since the 1950s, a **systems approach** has advocated looking at how the alcoholic and other members of the family interact.[35] We discussed one of these aspects earlier in the chapter in connection with the adverse effects of enabling behavior on the alcoholic. Another important aspect related to an alcoholic's family is the possibility of codependency.

Beginning in the early 1980s, the concept of **codependency** has gained widespread attention as a way of understanding people who live on a day-to-day basis with

systems approach: A way of understanding a phenomenon in terms of complex interacting relationships among individuals, family, friends, and community.

codependency: A concept that individuals who live with a person having an alcohol (or other drug) dependence suffer themselves from difficulties of self-image and social independence.

an alcoholic or any individual with a drug dependence. Definitions vary but most identify four essential features. In members of the family of an alcoholic, therapists have observed (1) an overinvolvement with the alcoholic, (2) obsessive attempts to control the alcoholic's behavior, (3) a strong reliance upon external sources of self-worth, through the approval of others, and (4) an attempt to make personal sacrifices in an effort to improve the alcoholic's condition.[36]

In the mind of a codependent, it is not considered OK to have one's own feelings, not OK to have problems of one's own, and not OK to enjoy oneself. If people in a relationship with a codependent act badly, the codependent believes that he or she is responsible for their behavior. Because codependency is considered to be a learned pattern of thinking rather than an innate trait, the goal of therapy is to teach the codependent person to detach himself or herself from the alcoholic and begin to meet his or her needs rather than to be controlled by the value judgments of others.[37]

Professionals, however, have questioned the validity of the codependency concept. They have argued that by labeling a person a codependent, the therapist is promoting feelings of helplessness or victimization in these individuals that might not have existed before. Indeed, the idea of codependency might diminish the person's incentive to begin efforts to take control over his or her life by reinforcing the feeling that he or she is "doomed to suffer." Critics have also pointed out that actual patterns of codependency may not be specific to particular individuals but rather are common to practically everyone. Codependency may simply reflect the problems of living in modern society, only now we have found language to explain our own failures by blaming other people.[38]

Children of an Alcoholic Parent or Parents

Considering the immense impact that our parents have in our lives, it is understandable that an alcoholic family will have distinct negative consequences on the psychological development of the children in that family. As a result, **children of alcoholics (COAs)** have a higher statistical risk of becoming alcoholics than do children of nonalcoholics. Whether this increased risk is genetically or environmentally based is a complex issue that will be reviewed in the next section.

An equally important and independent risk factor, however, may be the specific behavioral and physiological reactions a person has to alcohol itself. Men who at age twenty have a relatively low response to alcohol, in that they need to drink more than other people to feel intoxicated, carry a higher risk of becoming alcoholic by the time they are thirty, regardless of their pattern of drinking at an earlier age and regardless of their parents' drinking. Sons of alcoholics having a low response to alcohol have a 60 percent chance of becoming alcoholics, compared to a 42 percent chance for sons of alcoholics in general. Sons of nonalcoholics having a low response to alcohol have a 22 percent chance of becoming alcoholics, compared to an 8–9 percent chance for sons of nonalcoholics in general.

The combination of these two risk factors—family history and a low response to alcohol—is obviously the worst scenario for a development of alcoholism, at least in males. Nonetheless, we should remember that a large proportion of people still *do not* become alcoholics, even with both risk factors present. The question of what protective factors may contribute to the resiliency of high-risk individuals with regard to alcoholism is a major subject of current research.[39]

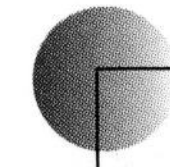

The Genetics of Alcoholism

For centuries, alcoholism has appeared to run in families. Today, this casual observation has led to a specific question: To what extent is alcoholism genetically determined (through the genes of the parents) and to what extent is it environmentally determined (through the living conditions in which the offspring have been brought up)? One approach is to examine the inheritance pattern in a family tree. It is impossible, however, to tease out the separate genetic (nature) and environmental (nurture) factors from information of this kind.

For more precise answers, one option is to turn to cases of adoption in which children can be compared to either their biological or adoptive parents. In 1981, an extensive research study in Sweden looked at the adoption records of approximately three thousand children who had alcoholic biological parents but lived with nonalcoholic adoptive parents. The results showed that a larger percentage of these children become alcoholics than would be seen in the general population. The greater

children of alcoholics (COAs): Individuals who grew up in a family with either one or two alcoholic parents.

incidence was present even when the children had been raised by their adoptive parents immediately after being born, indicating that a strong genetic component was operating.

There were, however, two subgroups among those children who eventually became alcoholics. One subgroup, called *Type 1 alcoholics*, developed problem drinking later in life and generally functioned well in society. In addition to a genetic predisposition toward alcoholism, there was for this subgroup a strong environmental factor as well. Whether or not the child was placed in a middle-class or poor adoptive family influenced the final outcome. A second subgroup, called *Type 2 alcoholics*, developed alcoholism earlier in life and had significant antisocial patterns of behavior. A strong genetic component was operating in this subgroup, and because the socioeconomic status of the adoptive family made no difference in the outcome, we can conclude that environmental factors played a negligible role. Table 10.1 gives a more complete picture of the characteristics associated with Type 1 and Type 2 alcoholics.[40]

TABLE 10.1

Two types of alcoholics

CHARACTERISTICS	TYPE 1	TYPE 2
Usual age at onset	(late onset) after 25	(early onset) before 25
Inability to abstain	infrequent	frequent
Fights and arrests when drinking	infrequent	frequent
Psychological dependence (loss of control)	infrequent	frequent
Guilt and fear about alcoholism	frequent	infrequent
Novelty-seeking personality	low	high
Tendency to use alcohol to escape negative feelings	high	low
Tendency to use alcohol to achieve positive feelings	low	high
Gender	male and female	male only
Extent of genetic influences	moderate	high
Extent of environmental influences	high	low
Serotonin abnormalities in the brain	absent	present

Source: Updated from Cloninger, C. Robert (1987). Neurogenetic adaptive mechanisms in alcoholism. *Science, 236,* 410–416.

The study of twins is another source of information about the genetic and environmental influences in alcoholism. Probably the most important piece of data is the **concordance rate** for alcoholism in pairs of identical twins—that is, how likely one member of a pair is to be alcoholic if the other one is. The concordance rate has been found to be only 58 percent. If genetics were the whole story in determining the incidence of alcoholism, the concordance rate would have been 100 percent.

If we look closely at the type of alcoholic involved and whether the alcoholic is male or female, the data from twin studies are similar to those found in the adoption research. A study conducted in 1992, for example, found that the concordance rate for identical twins was significantly higher than the concordance rate for fraternal twins when one member of the pair was a male alcoholic whose drinking problems started in adolescence (in other words, a Type 2 alcoholic). For female and male alcoholics whose drinking problems started after adolescence (the Type 1 subgroup), a comparison of concordance rates shows that genetic factors played a lesser role.[41]

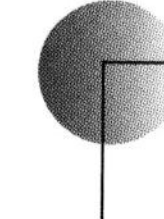

The Concept of Alcoholism as a Disease

In contrast to the days when alcoholism was considered a moral failure or worse, the majority opinion today is that alcoholism is best characterized as a disease and that the alcoholic should be treated rather than punished. This viewpoint has evolved over the years, originating from the writings of E. M. Jellinek in the late 1940s. Jellinek proposed that alcohol dependence progressed through a natural sequence of stages, much as a physical illness develops.[42] In more recent interpretations, the disease concept has moved away from the idea that all alcoholics follow a common path (many of Jellinek's ideas have not been confirmed) to a more general focus on the biological factors that might differentiate alcoholics from nonalcoholics. In addition, the

concordance rate: The likelihood that one member of a twin or family relation will have a condition if the other one has it.

disease concept has led to the idea that the alcoholics are fundamentally out of control and abstinence is the only answer to their recovery.[43]

Since 1957, the American Medical Association has defined alcoholism as a disease, and numerous other health organizations have adopted a similar position. As reasonable as this position might sound, the disease concept has created something of a dilemma among professionals concerned with the treatment of alcohol abuse. It places the burden on physicians to deal with the alcoholic through medical interventions, and unfortunately the medical profession is frequently ill-equipped to help. A study in 2000, for example, found that 94 percent of a group of primary care physicians failed to make a correct diagnosis of early stage alcohol abuse when presented with symptoms typical of this condition. Only a small percentage, approximately one out of five, considered themselves "very prepared" to diagnose alcoholism in the first place.[44]

Important legal considerations also cloud this issue. Can we say, for example, that an alcoholic is legally absolved from a crime or a legal obligation because he or she is afflicted with this disease? These and related issues will be explored later in the chapter in Health Line and in Point/Counterpoint on page 287.

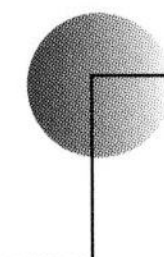

Approaches to Treatment for Alcoholism

Alcoholism, as should be clear at this point, is a study in diversity, and it makes sense that there might be some advantage in matching alcoholics with certain characteristics to specific forms of treatment. One treatment program might be best suited for one subgroup, another for another subgroup. As reasonable as this hypothesis sounds, however, a major study begun in the late 1980s and completed in 1997 has shown little or no benefit in patient–treatment matching. Apparently, no one treatment approach is overwhelmingly superior to others.[45] In this section, we will examine forms of alcoholism treatment as classified into two broad areas: biological interventions, which involve medications, and psychosocial interventions such as Alcoholics Anonymous and other self-help programs.

Biologically Based Treatments

The use of **disulfiram** (brand name: Antabuse) is based on the idea that if a drug induces an aversive reaction in alcoholics when alcohol is consumed, then consumption will be avoided and the problems of alcoholism will be reduced. Disulfiram, taken orally as a pill once each day, inhibits alcohol dehydrogenase, allowing acetaldehyde to build up in the bloodstream. As a result, individuals who consume alcohol in combination with disulfiram experience a flushing of the face, rapid heart rate and palpitations, nausea, and vomiting. These effects occur not only by consuming alcoholic beverages but by ingesting alcohol in other forms such as mouthwashes, cough mixtures, and even by the absorption of aftershave lotions and shampoos through the skin.

Clearly the symptoms caused by a combination of disulfiram and alcohol can be a powerful short-term deterrent to alcoholic drinking, but the question is whether or not this kind of aversion therapy is an effective treatment over the long run. Careful studies in which disulfiram has been administered to large numbers of alcoholics indicate that it is not effective when it is the sole treatment. One major problem is that alcoholics must take the drug regularly every day, and because disulfiram does nothing to reduce the alcoholic's craving for alcohol, compliance rates are low.

The consensus among professionals in this field is that disulfiram can be useful in a subgroup of higher-functioning alcoholics with exceptionally high motivation to quit drinking; for others, disulfiram can be useful as a transitional treatment until other support programs are in place. In the future, a transdermal patch for the slow absorption of disulfiram through the skin, such as the ones currently available for nicotine, may be feasible. Physicians and drug counselors could assure compliance by checking the continued presence of the patch on the alcoholic's skin, particularly if the patch were designed so that the user could not repeatedly remove and reapply it.[46]

disulfiram (deye-SULL-fih-ram): A medication that causes severe physical reactions and discomfort when combined with alcohol. Brand name is Antabuse.
naltrexone (nal-TREX-ohn): A long-lasting opiate antagonist, available since 1994 for the treatment of alcoholism. Brand name is ReVia.
nalmefene (nal-MEH-feen): A long-lasting opiate antagonist, similar to naltrexone, currently in development for the treatment of alcoholism.

A more direct approach to treatment than aversion therapy is to reduce the actual craving for alcohol on a physiological level. As noted in Chapter 9, there is a strong suspicion that alcohol dependence is related to activity in the receptors of the same dopamine-releasing neurons in the brain that have been implicated in heroin abuse. In other words, heroin abuse and alcohol abuse might share the same neural mechanisms in the brain.

Based upon this idea, it makes sense that a drug that is known to inhibit opiate receptors in the brain would be useful in the treatment of alcoholism. In 1994, the opiate-antagonist **naltrexone** (brand name: ReVia) was approved for use. Research has shown that naltrexone treatment substantially reduces the incidence of relapses and feelings of craving, when combined with traditional counseling and rehabilitative services. Another related drug, **nalmefene,** is currently in clinical trials and shows great promise.

An alternative approach has focused on the role of serotonin levels in the brains of alcoholics. Since early onset (Type 2) alcoholism differs from late-onset (Type 1) alcoholism due to its association with serotonin abnormalities in the brain (see Table 10.1), a drug that reduces serotonin levels such as ondansetron (brand name: Zofran), typically used as an antinausea medication, should be beneficial in treating this subgroup. A recent study has confirmed this prediction. Among Type 2 alcoholics, Zofran significantly reduced their drinking behavior and provided a longer period of abstinence.[47]

A diverse group of men and women at a typical Alcoholics Anonymous meeting.

TABLE 10.2

The famous Twelve Steps of Alcoholics Anonymous

1. We admitted we were powerless over alcohol—that our lives had become unmanageable.
2. Came to believe that a Power greater than ourselves could restore us to sanity.
3. Made a decision to turn our will and our lives over to the care of God *as we understood Him.*
4. Made a searching and fearless moral inventory of ourselves.
5. Admitted to God, to ourselves, and to another human being the exact nature of our wrongs.
6. Were entirely ready to have God remove all these defects of character.
7. Humbly asked Him to remove our shortcomings.
8. Made a list of all persons we had harmed and became willing to make amends to them all.
9. Made direct amends to such people wherever possible, except when to do so would injure them or others.
10. Continued to make moral inventory and when we were wrong promptly admitted it.
11. Sought through prayer and meditation to improve our conscious contact with God *as we understood Him,* praying only for knowledge of His will for us and the power to carry that out.
12. Having had a spiritual awakening as a result of these steps, we tried to carry this message to alcoholics, and to practice these principles in all our affairs.

Source: The Twelve Steps are reprinted and adapted with permission of Alcoholics Anonymous World Services, Inc. Permission to reprint this material does not mean that AA has reviewed or approved the contents of this publication, nor that AA agrees with the views expressed herein. AA is a program of recovery from alcoholism *only.* Use of Twelve Steps in connection with programs and activities that are patterned after AA, but that address other problems, does not imply otherwise.

Alcoholics Anonymous

The best-known treatment program for alcoholism is **Alcoholics Anonymous (AA).** Founded in 1935, this organization has been conceived basically as a fellowship of alcoholics who wish to rid themselves of their problem drinking by helping one another maintain sobriety. The philosophy of AA is expressed in the famous Twelve Steps (Table 10.2). Members must have acknowledged that

Alcoholics Anonymous (AA): A worldwide organization devoted to the treatment of alcoholism through self-help groups and adherence to its principles.

Drugs . . . in Focus

Is Controlled Drinking Possible for Alcoholics?

One of the most intensely debated questions in the field of alcoholism treatment has been whether it is possible for alcoholics to achieve a level of "controlled drinking" without falling back into a state of alcohol dependence.

On one side are well-entrenched organizations such as Alcoholics Anonymous and the National Institute on Alcohol Abuse and Alcoholism, as well as many other organizations, which assert that alcoholism is an irreversible disease, that abstinence is the only answer, and that even the slightest consumption of alcohol will trigger a cascade of problems that the alcoholic is constitutionally incapable of handling.

On the other side are groups, represented in greater numbers in Canada and Europe than in the United States, asserting that uncontrolled drinking is a reversible behavioral disorder and that for many alcoholics the promotion of total abstinence as a treatment goal is a serious obstacle to their success in rehabilitation. The organization Moderation Management is an example of this type of therapeutic approach.

Some of the early controlled-drinking studies had enough methodological flaws that the abstinence-only group could be justified in denouncing them. But later research, using carefully randomized assignment of alcoholic subjects to either an abstinence-oriented treatment or a controlled-drinking one, has shown that long-term results are comparable for either group. This is not to say that the prospects are wonderful for either of them; the odds are still higher *against* long-term recovery from alcoholism than *for* it, no matter what the treatment. But it does appear that controlled drinking can occur.

How many alcoholics can manage to achieve a continued level of nonproblem drinking? Percentages vary from 2 to 10 to 15, though the lower figure is probably more accurate for those individuals with severe alcoholic difficulties. Perhaps a more important point is that no one knows how to predict whether or not an alcohol abuser will be one of that small number of successful controlled drinkers. Obviously, most alcoholics are convinced that they will be the lucky ones. How does an alcoholism-treatment counselor handle this? A prominent expert offers one strategy:

> *My own perspective is that there is little sense in losing a client by a standoff on this issue. . . . It has been my clinical experience that an unsuccessful trial at "controlled drinking" may be a more persuasive confrontation of the need for abstinence than any amount of argumentation between therapist and client.*

Sources: Goode, Erich (1999). *Drugs in American society* (5th ed.). Boston: McGraw-Hill College, p. 194. Hester, Reid K., and Miller, William R. (1989). Self-control training. In Reid K. Hester and William R. Miller (Eds.), *Handbook of alcoholism treatment approaches.* New York: Pergamon Press, pp. 141–149. Miller, William R. (1989). Increasing motivation for change. In Reid K. Hester and William R. Miller (Eds.), *Handbook of alcoholism treatment approaches.* New York: Pergamon Press, p. 77. Sobell, Mark B., and Sobell, Linda C. (1978). *Behavioral treatment of alcohol problems: Individualized therapy and controlled drinking.* New York: Plenum.

they were "powerless over alcohol" and their lives became unmanageable, and to have turned their will and their lives over "to the care of God *as we understood Him.*" As the steps indicate, there is a strong spiritual component to the AA program, though the organization vigorously denies that religious doctrine prevails.

AA functions as a type of group therapy with each member oriented toward a common goal: the maintenance of abstinence from alcohol despite a powerful and continuing craving for it. All meetings are completely anonymous (only first names are used in all communications), and the proceedings are dominated by members recounting their personal struggles with alcohol, their efforts to stop drinking, and their support for fellow alcoholics in their own struggles. New members are encouraged to pair up with a sponsor, typically a more experienced AA member who has successfully completed the Twelve Steps and can serve as a personal source of support on a day-to-day basis. According to AA, no alcoholic is ever cured, only recovered, and the process of recovery continues throughout that person's life. Alcoholism, in its view, is a disease, and relapse from sobriety can occur at any moment (Drugs . . . in Focus).

AA has grown to more than 95,000 groups around the world and an estimated two million members, though it is difficult to get a precise count since the organization is deliberately structured very loosely. Perhaps more important than its size is the powerful impact it has made not only on the way we deal with alcoholism but also on the way we consider treatment for any compulsive behavior. Over the years, the twelve-step program has

Portrait Bill W. and Dr. Bob—Founders of Alcoholics Anonymous

The backgrounds of William Griffith Wilson and Dr. Robert Smith, when they met in the spring of 1935, could not have been more different, but they shared an important common thread. They were both alcoholics, and their lives had come apart because of it. Wilson had gone from being a successful businessman, whose investments on Wall Street during the 1920s had made him rich, to a penniless failure after losing his entire fortune in the 1929 crash. Whether rich or poor, he had been a drunk, but his poverty made the condition worse. In 1934 Wilson was admitted to Towns Hospital in New York City and agreed to subject himself to the "belladonna cure," a treatment based on his receiving morphine and the powerful hallucinogen belladonna. Under the influence of this combination of drugs, Wilson experienced "his spiritual awakening." He later wrote,

> *In the wake of my spiritual experience there came a vision of a society of alcoholics. If each sufferer were to carry the news of the scientific hopelessness of alcoholism to each new prospect, he might be able to lay every newcomer wide open to a transforming spiritual experience.*

For several months following his new-found mission in life, Wilson sought out drunks to "work on." On a trip to Akron, Ohio, where he was seeking a new job, he was introduced by mutual friends to a proctologist and surgeon named Dr. Robert Smith.

Bill W., cofounder of Alcoholics Anonymous

Smith's alcoholism had wrecked a distinguished medical career, and in 1935, he was in severe financial straits. Wilson's determination combined with Smith's desperation led to their taking on the task of keeping each other sober and helping others do the same. On June 10, 1935 (the official date of the founding of Alcoholics Anonymous), Smith took his last drink. By 1939, Wilson had completed the writing of the Twelve Steps and an extended explanation of the AA philosophy, known today as the Big Book. Wilson and Smith had discovered that they were most successful in keeping alcoholics abstinent when they attended meetings on a regular basis and were assured of complete privacy and anonymity. Wilson became Bill W., and Smith became Dr. Bob.

It was not until the 1940s that AA started to be nationally known. The *Saturday Evening Post,* one of the leading magazines of the day, gave them their first real publicity break, publishing an article about the organization that generated an avalanche of responses and a dramatic increase in membership. During this time, a prayer was composed that would eventually be repeated millions of times in AA meetings throughout the world: "God grant me the serenity to accept the things I cannot change, the courage to change the things I can, and the wisdom to know the difference."

Sources: Alcoholics Anonymous comes of age: A brief history of AA (1959). New York: Alcoholics Anonymous World Services. Alibrandi, Lucinda A. (1982). The fellowship of Alcoholics Anonymous. In E. Mansell Pattison and Edward Kaufman (Eds.), *The encyclopedic handbook of alcoholism.* New York: Gardner Press, p. 979.

become a generic concept, as the precepts and philosophy of AA have been widely imitated. We now have Al-Anon for the spouses and family of alcoholics going through the AA program and Alateen as a specialized AA program for teenage alcoholics, as well as Gamblers Anonymous, Nicotine Anonymous, Narcotics or Cocaine Anonymous, and Overeaters Anonymous.

Despite its stature as an approach to treatment, however, there are relatively few scientific appraisals of the overall effectiveness of AA. One of the principal problems is the anonymity that is guaranteed to all members, making it difficult to conduct well-controlled follow-up studies on how well AA members are doing. Nonetheless, AA is widely regarded in the field of alcohol rehabilitation as a beneficial self-help approach, particularly when it is combined with other treatments such as individual counseling and medical interventions.[48]

Rational Recovery

In contrast to AA, the self-help program **Rational Recovery (RR)** assumes that people do not need to believe they are "powerless over alcohol" or submit to "a Power greater than ourselves" (excerpts taken from the Twelve Steps) in order to recover from alcoholism. Instead, the dominant philosophy is that individuals have the power them-

Rational Recovery (RR): An alcoholism and other drug-abuse treatment program emphasizing a nonspiritual philosophy and a greater sense of personal control in the abuser.

The Non-Disease Model of Alcoholism and Other Patterns of Drug Abuse

Despite the "official" description of alcoholism as a disease by the American Medical Association and many international health organizations, the concept of alcoholism as a disease remains controversial and continues to attract vigorous criticism. As Erich Goode has put it, the non-disease theorists assert that alcoholics (as well as other drug abusers) are ". . . not 'sick,' but are rational, problem-solving human beings attempting to carve out a meaningful existence in a harsh and seemingly unyielding environment." Others have warned that the disease model encourages alcoholics to assume a passive stance, depending solely on the advances of modern medicine to save the day, and that acceptance of the disease model often leads to making excuses for one's behavior rather than changing it. As a one-liner expresses it, "There's nothing wrong with being an alcoholic, if you're doing something about it."

The "disease versus non-disease" debate has inevitable consequences for the ways in which we choose to respond to the problem. Non-disease theorists view the prevailing majority opinion as unfortunately leading to a marginalization of alcoholics, reducing them to a small group of afflicted, biologically predestined individuals, rather than seeing these people in the context of the way all of us behave to one degree or another. In the words of non-disease advocate Stanton Peele, this attitude fosters a "coercive, one-size-fits-all . . . disease treatment system of hospitals, Alcoholics Anonymous, and the 12 steps, which are increasingly administered within the framework of the law enforcement system." He views the disease model as leading to the assumption that all drinking must cease (a position held by AA), instead of to encouragement of controlled levels of drinking, as advocated by Moderation Management (MM). He also argues that, without the disease model of alcoholism and other drug abuse, it is possible to focus on "the larger question of why some people seek to close off their experience through a comforting, but artificial and self-consuming relationship with something external to themselves. In itself, the choice of object is irrelevant to this universal process of becoming dependent."

Further discussion of the disease model of alcoholism can be found in the form of a simulated debate in Point/Counterpoint on page 287.

Sources: Goode, Erich (1999). *Drugs in American society.* New York: McGraw-Hill College, quotation on p. 350. Kinney, Jean, and Leaton, Gwen (1995). *Loosing the grip: A handbook of alcohol information.* St. Louis: Mosby, pp. 60–62. Peele, Stanton (1995). Assumptions about drugs and the marketing of drug policies. In W. K. Bickel and R. J. DeGrandpre (Eds.), *Drug policy and human nature.* New York: Plenum, pp. 199–220, first quotation on p. 214. Peele, Stanton, and Brodsky, Archie (1975). *Love and addiction.* New York: Taplinger Publishing, second quotation on p. 55. Walters, Glenn D. (1999). *The addiction concept: Working hypothesis or self-fulfilling prophesy?* Needham Heights MA: Allyn and Bacon, pp. 20–22.

selves to overcome anything, including drinking. The strategy is based on Rational Emotive Therapy (RET), developed by the psychologist Albert Ellis, which emphasizes the rooting out of irrational thoughts, emotions, and beliefs that prevent the achievement of personal goals.

Another major difference is that RR insists on professional involvement in its program, with a professional adviser (often a clinical psychologist) assisting members in learning the fundamentals of RET. No reference is made to God or a higher power; in fact, RR points out that the objective is "NHP (no higher power) sobriety." The goal in RR is that within a year and a half members will be able to maintain sobriety without going to RR meetings. In contrast, AA members are encouraged to continue going to meetings for the rest of their lives.

Since 1990, there has been increased interest in a secular (nonreligious) approach to self-help alcoholism treatment such as that practiced by RR. Other examples of this approach are Men for Sobriety (MFS), Women for Sobriety (WFS), Moderation Management (MM), and Secular Organization for Sobriety (SOS). Nonetheless, recent research has indicated that alcoholics benefit from participation in AA programs, regardless of their religious beliefs.[49]

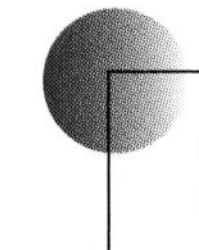

Alcoholism in the Workplace

Considering the adverse impact of alcoholism on worker productivity, it makes sense that corporations, hospitals, the armed services, and many other large

QUICK CONCEPT  10.2

Understanding Alcoholics Anonymous

Check your understanding of the principles and philosophy of Alcoholics Anonymous by checking off whether or not the following statements would be ascribed to by Alcoholics Anonymous.

1. I have always had the power to control my drinking. ❑ yes ❑ no
2. I must put myself in the hands of a Higher Power if I am to be sober for the rest of my life. ❑ yes ❑ no
3. It is possible to be cured of alcoholism. ❑ yes ❑ no
4. I am capable of having a drink once in a great while without slipping back into alcoholism. ❑ yes ❑ no
5. The more meetings I attend, the better chance I have of remaining sober. ❑ yes ❑ no

Answers: 1. no 2. yes 3. no 4. no 5. yes

organizations should profit by instituting programs of their own for employees needing help. These efforts, referred to as **employee assistance programs (EAPs),** have grown enormously over the past twenty years; today it is estimated that about 40 percent of the U.S. work force is covered by EAPs at their place of employment. EAPs in the context of drug abuse treatment and prevention will be examined in Chapter 17.[50]

employee assistance programs (EAPs): Corporate or institutional programs for workers or employees to help them with alcohol or other drug-abuse problems.

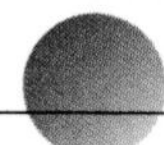

SUMMARY

Alcoholism: Stereotypes, Definitions, and Criteria

- Alcoholism is a multidimensional condition that is typically defined in terms of four major criteria: (1) problems associated with a preoccupation with drinking, (2) emotional problems, (3) vocational, social, and family problems, and (4) physical problems. Not all criteria have to be met, however, for alcoholism to be diagnosed.

The History of Efforts to Regulate Chronic Alcohol Abuse

- An appreciation of the adverse consequences of chronic alcohol abuse started in the late 1700s and took root in the United States as a temperance movement. This movement addressed its concerns primarily toward the drinking of distilled spirits.
- The differentiation among forms of alcohol drinking became blurred during the nineteenth century, as temperance advocates began to promote a total ban on alcohol consumption. National Prohibition was the law in the United States from 1920 to 1933.
- Since the end of Prohibition, government regulation has been carried out chiefly through education and the taxation of alcohol.

Chronic Effects of Alcohol

- Physical effects of alcoholism include tolerance and withdrawal, liver disease, cardiovascular disease, cancer, and neurological disorders such as Wernicke-Korsakoff syndrome.
- A particular concern is the development of fetal alcohol syndrome (FAS) in the offspring of alcoholic mothers.
- The concept of codependency has helped shed light on the specific effects of alcoholism on spouses and other family members. The children of alcoholics (COAs) have been considered particularly vulnerable,

along with individuals who have a relatively low response to the intoxicating effects of alcohol.

The Genetics of Alcoholism

- Studies of adoptions and twins have provided information about the relative influences of genetics and environment on the development of alcoholism.
- A distinction has been made between a male or female alcoholic with drinking problems occurring late in life (Type 1) and a male alcoholic with drinking problems occurring in adolescence (Type 2). The latter subgroup appears to have a greater genetic component in the inheritance pattern.

Approaches to Treatment for Alcoholism

- Approaches include biologically based treatments, such as the administration of disulfiram (Antabuse) or naltrexone (ReVia), and psychosocial treatments, such as the self-help programs of Alcoholics Anonymous (AA).
- Objections to certain aspects of the AA philosophy have promoted the growth of other self-help organizations such as Rational Recovery (RR).
- Corporations and other large organizations have instituted employee assistance programs (EAPs) to help workers with problems of alcohol abuse or other forms of drug abuse.

KEY TERMS

abstinence, p. 210
alcohol abuse, p. 211
alcohol dependence, p. 211
alcohol withdrawal syndrome, p. 214
alcoholic cirrhosis, p. 215
alcoholic dementia, p. 216
alcoholic hepatitis, p. 215
Alcoholics Anonymous (AA), p. 224
alcoholism, p. 208
children of alcoholics (COAs), p. 221
codependency, p. 220
concordance rate, p. 222
confabulation, p. 217
delirium tremens (DTs), p. 215
disulfiram, p. 223
employee assistance programs (EAPs), p. 228
enablers, p. 210
fatty liver, p. 215
fetal alcohol effect (FAE), p. 217
fetal alcohol syndrome (FAS), p. 217
nalmefene, p. 223
naltrexone, p. 223
Rational Recovery (RR), p. 226
symptomatic drinking, p. 208
systems approach, p. 220
teratogenic, p. 217
thiamine, p. 217
Wernicke-Korsakoff syndrome, p. 216

ENDNOTES

1. Goodwin, Donald W., and Gabrielli, William F. (1997). Alcohol: Clinical aspects. In Joyce H. Lowinson, Pedro Ruiz, Robert B. Millman, and John G. Langrod (Eds.), *Substance abuse: A comprehensive textbook.* Baltimore: Williams and Wilkins, pp. 142–148. Julien, Robert M. (2001). *A primer of drug action* (9th ed.). New York: Worth, pp. 108–110.
2. Hoff, Ebbe Curtis (1974). *Alcoholism: The hidden addiction.* New York: Seabury Press, pp. 75–88.
3. Hofmann, Frederick G. (1983). *A handbook on drug and alcohol abuse* (2nd ed.). New York: Oxford University Press, p. 99.
4. Hoff, *Alcoholism*, pp. 78–79.
5. Drobes, David J., and Thomas, Suzanne E. (1999). Assessing craving for alcohol. *Alcohol Research and Health, 23*, 179–186. Ludwig, Arnold M. (1988). *Understanding the alcoholic's mind: The nature of craving and how to control it.* New York: Oxford University Press.
6. Schuckit, Marc A. (1995). *Drug and alcohol abuse: A clinical guide to diagnosis and treatment* (4th ed.). New York: Plenum, pp. 55–96.
7. Maiden, R. Paul (1997). Alcohol dependence and domestic violence: Incidence and treatment implications. *Alcohol Treatment Quarterly, 15*, 31–50. U.S. Department of Health and Human Services (1990). *Alcohol and health* (Seventh Special Report to the U.S. Congress). Rockville MD: National Institute on Alcohol Abuse and Alcoholism, p. 174.
8. Hofmann, *Handbook on drug and alcohol abuse*, pp. 98–99. National Institute on Alcohol Abuse and Alcoholism (2000). Alcohol alert: Imaging and alcoholism: A window on the brain. No. 47. Rockville MD: National Institute on Alcohol Abuse and Alcoholism.
9. Fishbein, Diana H., and Pease, Susan E. (1996). *The dynamics of drug abuse.* Needham Heights MA: Allyn and Bacon, pp. 122–124.

10. American Psychiatric Association (1994). *Diagnostic and statistical manual of mental disorders* (4th ed.). Washington DC: American Psychiatric Association, pp. 181–183, 194–196.
11. National Institute on Alcohol Abuse and Alcoholism (1995, October). Alcohol alert: Diagnostic criteria for alcohol abuse and dependence. No. 30. Bethesda MD: National Institute on Alcohol Abuse and Alcoholism.
12. Quoted in Sournia, Jean-Charles (1990). *A history of alcoholism.* Cambridge MA: Basil Blackwell, p. 29.
13. Lender, Mark E., and Martin, James R. (1982). *Drinking in America: A history.* New York: Free Press, p. 107.
14. Sournia, *History of alcoholism*, p. 122.
15. *Standard and Poor's Industry Surveys* (1997, January 23). Alcoholic beverages and tobacco, p. 15. *Standard and Poor's Industry Surveys* (1997, September 11). Alcoholic beverages and tobacco, p. 16.
16. Chaloupka, Frank J. (1993). Effects of price on alcohol-related problems. *Alcohol Health and Research World, 17,* 46–53.
17. Schuckit, *Drug and alcohol abuse*, pp. 79–80.
18. Sellers, Edward M., and Kalant, Harold (1982). Alcohol withdrawal and delirium tremens. In E. Mansell Pattison and Edward Kaufman (Eds.), *Encyclopedic handbook of alcoholism.* New York: Gardner Press, pp. 147–166.
19. National Institute on Alcohol Abuse and Alcoholism (1993, January). Alcohol alert: Alcohol and the liver. No. 19. Bethesda MD: National Institute on Alcohol Abuse and Alcoholism. National Institute on Alcohol Abuse and Alcoholism (1998). Alcohol alert: Alcohol and the liver: Research update. No. 42. Rockville MD: National Institute on Alcohol Abuse and Alcoholism.
20. Brands, Bruna; Sproule, Beth; and Marshman, Joan (Eds.) (1998). *Drugs and drug abuse: A reference text* (3rd ed.). Toronto: Addiction Research Foundation, p. 271.
21. Smith-Warner, Stephanie A.; Spiegelman, Donna; Shiaw-Shyuan, Yuan; Van den Brandt, Piet A.; Folsom, Aaron R.; Goldbohm, Alexandra; Graham, Saxon; Holmberg, Lars; Howe, Geoffrey R.; et al. Alcohol and breast cancer in women: A pooled analysis of cohort studies. (1998). *Journal of the American Medical Association, 279,* 535–540.
22. U.S. Department of Health and Human Services. *Alcohol and health,* pp. 123–124.
23. Kalat, James W. (1998). *Biological psychology* (6th ed.). Pacific Grove CA: Brooks-Cole, p. 354. McEvoy, Joseph P. (1982). The chronic neuropsychiatric disorders associated with alcoholism. In E. Mansell Pattison and Edward Kaufman (Eds.), *Encyclopedic handbook of alcoholism.* New York: Gardner Press, pp. 167–179.
24. Armstrong, Elizabeth M. (1998). Diagnosing moral disorder: The discovery and evolution of fetal alcohol syndrome. *Social Science and Medicine, 47,* 2025–2042. Gabriel, Kara; Hofmann, Candace; Glavas, Maria; and Weinberg, Joanne (1998). The hormonal effects of alcohol use on the mother and fetus. *Alcohol Health and Research World, 22,* 170–177. Jones, Kenneth L., and Smith, David W. (1973). Recognition of the fetal alcohol syndrome in early infancy. *Lancet, 2,* 999–1001. Jones, Kenneth L.; Smith, David W.; Ulleland, Christy N.; and Steissguth, Ann P. (1973). Pattern of malformation in offspring of chronic alcoholic mothers. *Lancet, 1,* 1267–1271. Young, Nancy K. (1997). Effects of alcohol and other drugs on children. *Journal of Psychoactive Drugs, 29,* 23–42.
25. Olson, Heather C.; Feldman, Julie, J.; Streissguth, Ann P.; Sampson, Paul D.; and Bookstein, Fred L. (1998). Neuropsychological deficits in adolescents with fetal alcohol syndrome: Clinical findings. *Alcoholism: Clinical and Experimental Research, 22,* 1998–2012. Phelps, LeAdelle (1995). Psychoeducational outcomes of fetal alcohol syndrome. *School Psychology Review, 24,* 200–212.
26. Institute of Medicine (U.S.), Committee to study fetal alcohol syndrome (1995). *Fetal alcohol syndrome: Diagnosis, epidemiology, prevention, and treatment.* Washington DC: National Academy Press. Ma, Grace X.; Toubbeh, Jamil; Cline, Janette; and Chisholm, Anita (1998). Fetal alcohol syndrome among Native American adolescents: A model prevention program. *Journal of Primary Prevention, 19,* 43–55.
27. National Institute on Alcohol Abuse and Alcoholism (1991, July). Alcohol alert: Fetal alcohol syndrome. No. 13. Bethesda MD: National Institute on Alcohol Abuse and Alcoholism. U.S. Department of Health and Human Services. *Alcohol and health,* pp. 139–161. U.S. Department of Health and Human Services. *Alcohol research,* p. 52.
28. May, Philip A. (1991). Fetal alcohol effects among North American Indians. *Alcohol Health and Research World, 15,* 239–248.
29. Alcohol alert: Fetal alcohol syndrome. Serdula, Mary; Williamson, David F.; Kendrick, Juliette S.; Anda, Robert F.; and Byers, Tim (1991). Trends in alcohol consumption by pregnant women. *Journal of the American Medical Association, 265,* 876–879.
30. National Institute on Drug Abuse and National Institute on Alcohol Abuse and Alcoholism (1998). *Economic costs of alcohol and drug abuse in the United States—1992.* Rockville MD: National Institutes of Health.
31. Cloninger, C. Robert (1987). Neurogenetic adaptive mechanisms in alcoholism. *Science, 236,* 410–416. Guze, Samuel B.; Cloninger, C. Robert; Martin, Ronald; and Clayton, Paula J. (1986). Alcoholism as a medical disorder. *Comprehensive Psychiatry, 27,* 501–510. National Institute on Alcohol Abuse and Alcoholism (1999). Alcohol alert: Are women more vulnerable to alcohol's effects? Rockville MD: National Institute on Alcohol Abuse and Alcoholism.
32. Caces, M. F.; Stinson, Frederick S.; Elliott, Steven D.; and Noble, John A. (1991). Comparative alcohol-related mortality statistics in the United States by state, 1979–1985. *Alcohol Health and Research World, 15,* 161–168.

33. Maletta, Gabe J. (1982). Alcoholism and the aged. In E. Mansell Pattison and Edward Kaufman (Eds.), *Encyclopedic handbook of alcoholism.* New York: Gardner Press, pp. 779–791.
34. Fleming, Michael F.; Manwell, Linda, B.; Barry, Kristen L.; Adams, Wendy; and Stauffacher, Ellyn A. (1999). Brief physician advice for alcohol problems in older adults: A randomized community-based trial. *Journal of Family Practice, 48,* 378–384. Graham, Kathryn; Della Clarke, Christine B.; Carver, Virginia; Dolinki, Louise; Smythe, Cynthia; Harrison, Susan; Marshman, Joan; and Brett, Pamela (1996). Addictive behaviors in older adults. *Addictive Behaviors, 21,* 331–348.
35. DiNitto, Diana M., and McNeece, C. Aaron (1994). *Chemical dependency: A systems approach.* Englewood Cliffs NJ: Prentice-Hall, pp. 214–239.
36. Doweiko, Harold E. (1993). *Concepts of chemical dependency* (2nd ed.). Pacific Grove CA: Brooks-Cole, p. 265.
37. Beattie, Melody (1989). *Beyond codependency.* New York: Harper and Row, pp. 15–16, 84–85. Whitfield, Charles L. (1997). Co-dependence, addictions, and related disorders. In Lowinson et al. (Eds.), *Substance abuse: A comprehensive textbook.* Baltimore: Williams and Wilkins, pp. 672–683.
38. Doweiko, *Concepts of chemical dependency,* pp. 269–271, 282–284.
39. Erblich, Joel, and Earleywine, Mitchell (1999). Children of alcoholics exhibit attenuated cognitive impairment during an ethanol challenge. *Alcoholism: Clinical and Experimental Research, 23,* 476–482. Hussong, Andrea M., and Chassin, Laurie (1997). Substance use initiation among adolescent children of alcoholics: Testing protective factors. *Journal of Studies on Alcohol, 58,* 272–279. Hussong, Andrea M., Curran, Patrick J., and Chassin, Laurie (1998). Pathways of risk for accelerated heavy alcohol use among adolescent children of alcoholic parents. *Journal of Abnormal Child Psychology, 26* , 453–466. Schuckit, Marc A., and Smith, Tom L. (1997). Assessing the risk for alcoholism among sons of alcoholics. *Journal of Studies on Alcohol, 58,* 141–145.
40. Cloninger, Neurogenetic adaptive mechanisms. Cloninger, C. Robert, Gohman, M., and Sigvardsson, S. (1981). Inheritance of alcohol abuse: Cross fostering analysis of adopted men. *Archives of General Psychiatry, 38,* 861–868.
41. McGue, Matt, Pickens, Roy W., and Svikis, Dace S. (1992). Sex and age effects on the inheritance of alcohol problems: A twin study. *Journal of Abnormal Psychology, 101,* 3–17. Schuckit, Marc A. (1987). Biological vulnerability to alcoholism. *Journal of Counseling and Clinical Psychology, 55,* 301–399.
42. Jellinek, E. M. (1952). Phases of alcohol addiction. *Quarterly Journal of Studies in Alcohol, 13,* 672. Jellinek, E. M. (1960). *The disease concept of alcoholism.* New Haven CT: Hillhouse Press. Vaillant, George E. (1995). *The natural history of alcoholism revisited.* Cambridge MA: Harvard University Press.
43. George, William H., and Marlatt, G. Alan. (1983). Alcoholism: The evolution of a behavioral perspective. In Marc Galanter (Ed.), *Recent developments in alcoholism.* Vol. 1. New York: Plenum, pp. 105–138.
44. Fingarette, Herbert. (1988, November/December). Alcoholism: The mythical disease. *Utne Reader, 30,* 66. Maltzman, Irving (1994). Why alcoholism is a disease. *Journal of Psychoactive Drugs, 26,* 13–31. National Center on Addiction and Substance Abuse at Columbia University (2000, May). *Missed opportunity: National survey of primary care physicians and patients on substance abuse.* New York: National Center on Addiction and Substance Abuse at Columbia University.
45. Project MATCH Research Group (1997). Matching alcoholism treatments to client heterogeneity: Project MATCH posttreatment drinking outcomes. *Journal of Studies on Alcohol, 58,* 7–29.
46. Banys, Peter (1988). The clinical use of disulfiram (Antabuse): A review. *Journal of Psychoactive Drugs, 20,* 243–261. Schuckit, *Drug and alcohol abuse,* pp. 266–268.
47. Garbutt, James C.; West, Suzanne L.; Carey, Timothy S.; Lohr, Kathleen N.; and Crews, Fulton T. (1999). Pharmacological treatment of alcohol dependence: A review of the evidence. *Journal of the American Medical Association, 281,* 1318–1325. Johnson, Bankole A., et al. (2000, August 23/30). Ondansetron for reduction of drinking among biologically predisposed alcoholic patients. *Journal of the American Medical Association, 284,* 963–971. Mason, Barbara J.; Salvato, Fernando R.; Williams, Lauren D.; and Ritvo, Eva C. (1999). A double-blind, placebo-controlled study of oral nalmefene for alcohol dependence. *Archives of General Psychiatry, 56,* 719–724. Volpicelli, Joseph R.; Alterman, Arthur I.; Hayashida, Motoi; and O'Brien, Charles P. (1992). Naltrexone in the treatment of alcohol dependence. *Archives of General Psychiatry, 49,* 876–880.
48. Hopson, Ronald E., and Beaird-Spiller, Bethany (1995). Why AA works: A psychological analysis of the addictive experience and the efficacy of Alcoholics Anonymous. *Alcoholism Treatment Quarterly, 12,* 1–17. Nace, Edgar P. (1997). Alcoholics Anonymous. In Lowinson et al. (Eds.), *Substance abuse: A comprehensive textbook.* Baltimore: Williams and Wilkins, pp. 383–390.
49. Ellis, Albert, and Velten, Emmett (1992). *When AA doesn't work for you: Rational steps to quitting alcohol.* Fort Lee NJ: Barricade Press. Horvath, Arthur T. (1997). Alternative support groups. In Lowinson et al. (Eds.), *Substance abuse: A comprehensive textbook.* Baltimore: Williams and Wilkins, pp. 390–396. Kaskutas, Lee A. (1996). A road less traveled: Choosing the "Women for Sobriety" program. *Journal of Drug Issues, 26,* 77–94. Schmidt, Eric (1996). Rational recovery: Finding an alternative for addiction treatment. *Alcoholism Treatment Quarterly, 14,* 47–57. Winzelberg, Andrew, and Humphreys, Keith (1999). Should patients' religiosity influence clinicians' referral to 12-step self-help groups? Evidence from a study of 3,018

male substance abuse patients. *Journal of Consulting and Clinical Psychology*, 67, 790–794.

50. Ames, Genevieve M., Grube, Joel W., and Moore, Roland S. (1997). The relationship of drinking and hangovers to workplace problems: An empirical study. *Journal of Studies on Alcohol*, 58, 37–47. Blum, Terry C., Roman, Paul M., and Martin, Jack K. (1993). Alcohol consumption and work performance. *Journal of Studies on Alcohol*, 54, 61–70. U.S. Department of Health and Human Service. *Alcohol and health*, pp. 252–254. National Institute on Alcohol Abuse and Alcoholism (1999). Alcohol alert: Alcohol and the workplace. No. 44. Rockville MD: National Institute on Alcohol Abuse and Alcoholism.

CHAPTER 11

Nicotine and Tobacco

After you have completed this chapter, you will understand

- The story of tobacco through history
- The present-day tobacco industry
- The main culprits: carbon monoxide, tar, and nicotine
- Nicotine as a stimulant drug
- Nicotine and smoking dependence
- Adverse health consequences from smoking
- Patterns of tobacco use
- Strategies for people who want to stop smoking

Mark Twain is supposed to have said that quitting smoking was the easiest thing he ever did and that he should know because he had done it a thousand times. Well, I should know too. It seems that I've tried to quit a million times. I realize it's not good for me; I'm no fool. But you have to know that when I wake up in the morning, all I can think about is that first cigarette. Without it, my day doesn't begin.

—*Anonymous*

In some ways, our attitudes toward tobacco have not changed. Many people still find tobacco smoke and the behavior of smoking as personally objectionable as they did in the sixteenth century when tobacco was first introduced to the western world, and, judging from the opening quotation, people today have as much difficulty quitting as they did in Mark Twain's time. In other ways, however, the times have definitely changed. For almost fifty years, until the middle 1960s, lighting up and smoking a cigarette was an unquestionable sign of sophistication. There was little or no public awareness that any harm would come of it. It was an era before surgeon general's reports, National Smokeout Days, and no-smoking sections in restaurants.

Today, it is no longer a matter of debate that tobacco smoking is a major health hazard, not only to the person doing the smoking but also to society at large. These concerns are based not on public attitudes that can change over time but on solid scientific fact. It is also no longer a matter of debate that the main psychoactive ingredient in tobacco, nicotine, is a major dependence-producing drug.

Yet we need to recognize that tobacco products are legally sanctioned commodities with an economic significance, both to the United States and the world, that cannot be ignored. How did we arrive at this paradoxical point, and what lies ahead? This chapter will explore what we now know about the effects of tobacco smoking and other forms of tobacco consumption, the impact these behaviors have had on U.S. society, and the ways in which society has dealt with the issue of tobacco over the years. It will also consider current approaches toward helping people who choose to stop smoking and preventing the adverse consequences.

Tobacco Use through History

Shortly after setting foot on the small island of San Salvador on October 12, 1492, Christopher Columbus received from the inhabitants a welcoming gift of large, green, sweet-smelling tobacco leaves. Never having seen tobacco before, Columbus did not know what to make of this curious offering, except to observe in his journal that the leaves were greatly prized by the "Indians." In the first week of November, two members of the expedition ventured to the shores of Cuba, searching at Columbus's insistence for the great khan of Cathay (China). They found no evidence of the khan but did return with reports of natives who apparently were "drinking smoke." They rolled up tobacco leaves in the dried corn leaves or stuffed them into hollow reeds, lit them with fire, and then inhaled the smoke through the nose and mouth. It was a totally bizarre scene to these European observers; one interpretation was that the natives were perfuming themselves in some exotic ritual.

Before long, Columbus's men tried "tobacco drinking" themselves. One sailor in particular, Rodrigo de Jerez, became quite fond of the practice. He was, in fact, history's first documented European smoker, though he lived to regret it. When Rodrigo returned to Spain, he volunteered to demonstrate the newfound custom to his neighbors, who instead of being impressed thought that anyone who could emit smoke from the nose and mouth without burning had to be possessed by the Devil. A parish priest turned Rodrigo over to the Inquisition, which sentenced him to imprisonment for witchcraft. He spent several years in jail, presumably without a supply of tobacco. Rodrigo may therefore also be remembered as the first European smoker to quit cold turkey.[1]

In 1560, the year historians mark as the year tobacco was officially introduced to Europe, a Spanish physician brought some tobacco plants back from the New World and presented them to King Philip II of Spain. Meanwhile, in England, both Sir Francis Drake on his return from his voyage around the world and Sir Walter Raleigh on his return from the new colony of Virginia championed the use of tobacco. Suddenly, the practice of smoking tobacco through long, elaborate pipes became fashionable among the aristocracy.

Not everyone, however, was enthusiastic about this new fad of smoking. Predating a modern-day surgeon general's report by more than 350 years, King James I of England issued a lengthy statement in 1604 condemning tobacco use. Referring to tobacco as a "stinking weede," he characterized smoking as "a custom loath-

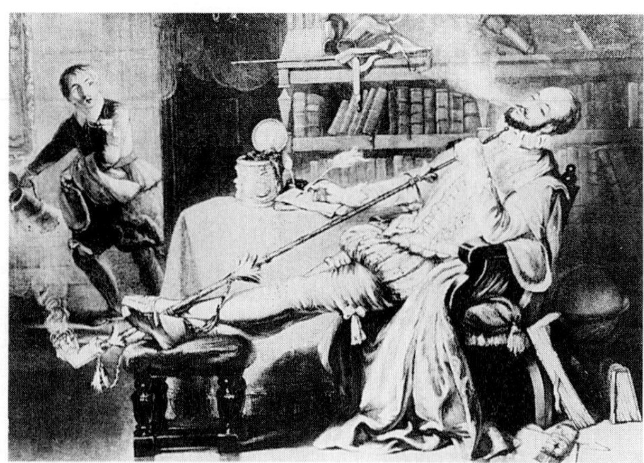

Sir Walter Raleigh (1552–1618) relaxes with a long smoking pipe as his servant rushes in to extinguish the fire with a pail of beer.

some to the eye, hateful to the nose, harmful to the brain, [and] dangerous to the lung." In the first recorded comment on its potential for causing dependence, the king observed that "he that taketh tobacco saith he cannot leave it, it doth bewitch him."

Politics, Economics, and Tobacco

Elsewhere in the world, during the early seventeenth century, the condemnation of tobacco became extreme. In Russia, conservatives in power saw tobacco use as one more piece of detestable evidence that their country was going "Western" and penalties for smoking included whipping, public torture, exile to Siberia, and death. Turkey, Japan, and China tried similar tactics, but, not surprisingly, tobacco use continued to spread.[2]

By the end of the seventeenth century even the fiercest opponents of tobacco had to concede that it was here to stay. A sultan of Turkey in 1648 became a smoker himself, and naturally penalties for tobacco use vanished overnight; Czar Peter the Great in 1689 pledged to open up Russia to the West, and tobacco suddenly became a welcome symbol of modernism; Japan and China stopped trying to enforce a prohibition that citizens obviously did not want. Even England's James I, despite his personal dislike for tobacco, soon recognized the attractive prospect of sizable revenue from taxes imposed on this popular new commodity.[3]

Snuffing and Chewing

One form of tobacco use observed by the early Spanish explorers was the practice of grinding a mixture of tobacco into a fine powder (**snuff**), placing or sniffing a pinch of it into the nose, and exhaling it with a sneeze. By the 1700s, this custom, called **snuffing**, overtook smoking as the dominant form of tobacco use. Among French aristocrats, both men and women, expensive snuffs, perfumed with exotic scents and carried in jeweled and enameled boxes, became part of the daily routine at the court in France and then in the rest of Europe. There were snuffs for the morning, snuffs for the afternoon, and snuffs for after dinner; some were designed for the ladies, the aged, novices, and the advanced. Sneezing was considered to clear the head of "superfluous humours," invigorate the brain, and brighten the eyes. In an era when bad smells were constant features of daily living, snuffing brought some degree of relief, not to mention a very effective way of sending nicotine to the brain (see Chapter 3).

Because of their dominance in the rapidly expanding tobacco market, the English colonies in America, particularly Virginia, prospered greatly. England enjoyed a profitable tobacco trade, but you might say that their development of colonial tobacco growing eventually backfired. In 1777, when Benjamin Franklin was sent as an envoy to France to gain support against the British in the American War for Independence, a key factor in his success was an offer to deliver prime Virginia tobacco in return for French money. The French agreed, and the rest is history. Had it not been for American tobacco, there might not have been a United States of America at all.[4]

In the United States, snuffing was soon replaced by a more rough-and-ready method for using tobacco: chewing. The practice was not totally new; early Spanish explorers had found the natives chewing tobacco as well as smoking it from the earliest days of their conquest, though North American tribes preferred smoking exclusively. Chewing tobacco had the advantage of freeing the hands for work, and its low cost made it a democratic custom befitting a vigorous new nation in the nineteenth century.

However, the need to spit out tobacco juices on a regular basis raised the tobacco habit to unimaginable heights of gross behavior. It was enough to make the objections to smoke and of possible fire fade into insignificance; now the problem was a matter of public health. Tobacco spitting became a major cause behind the spread of infectious diseases such as tuberculosis. Adding to the picture was the likelihood that a person's accuracy in targeting the nearest spittoon was inevitably compromised by his level of alcohol consumption, which was setting all-time highs during this period (see Chapter 9). Charles Dickens, on his travels through the United States, commented in 1842 that the demise of the once-handsome carpet in the U.S. Senate chamber was personally depressing:

> *Washington may be called the head-quarters of tobacco-tinctured saliva. . . . In all the public places of America, this filthy custom is recognized. In the courts of law, the judge has his spittoon, the crier his, the witness his, and the prisoner his, while the jurymen and spectators are provided for.*[5]

A present-day baseball dugout seems, by comparison, to be a model of decorum. The growth in the popularity of smokeless tobacco since the 1970s will be examined in a later section.

---

snuff: A quantity of finely shredded or powdered tobacco. Modern forms of snuff are available in either dry or moist forms.

snuffing: The ingestion of snuff either by inhalation or absorption through tissue in the nose.

Cigars and Cigarettes

By the time of the American Civil War, the fashion in tobacco use began to shift once more, as its overall popularity continued to soar. Although the plug of tobacco suitable for chewing was still a major seller and would remain so until the early twentieth century, two new trends developed, particularly in the growing industrial cities. One was the popularity of smoking **cigars** (commonly known as "seegars"), tight rolls of dried tobacco leaves. New innovations in curing (drying) tobacco leaves had produced a milder and lighter-quality leaf that was more suitable for smoking than the older forms that had been around since the colonial period. North Carolina, with its ideal soil for cultivating this type of tobacco, began to dominate as the tobacco-growing center of the United States; it continues to do so today. With the advent of cigars, tobacco consumers could combine the feeling of chewing (since the cigar remained in the mouth for a relatively long period of time) and the effects of ingesting tobacco smoke.

The other trend was the introduction of **cigarettes,** rolls of shredded tobacco wrapped in paper. They had become popular among British soldiers returning from the Crimean War in 1856, who had adopted the practice from the Turks. All of Europe took to cigarettes immediately, but the United States proved a harder sell. Part of the problem was the opposition of a well-entrenched U.S. cigar industry, which did not look kindly on an upstart competitor. Cigar makers did not discourage the circulation of rumors that cigarettes were being adulterated with opium, which accounted for people getting hooked on them (obviously nicotine could not possibly have been a factor), or that the cigarette paper wrapping was actually soaked in arsenic or white lead. There were other accusations that cigarette factory workers were urinating on the tobacco to give it an extra "bite" and that Egyptian brands were mixed with crushed camel dung.[6]

An even greater marketing problem than unsubstantiated rumors, however, was the image of cigarette smoking itself. A cigarette was looked upon as a dainty, sissy version of the he-man cigar; cigars were fat, long, and dark whereas cigarettes were slender, short, and light. Well into the beginning of the twentieth century, this attitude persisted. This is what John L. Sullivan, champion boxer and symbol of American masculinity, thought of cigarettes in 1904:

> *Who smokes 'em? Dudes and college stiffs—fellows who'd be wiped out by a single jab or a quick undercut. It isn't natural to smoke cigarettes. An American ought to smoke cigars. . . . It's the Dutchmen, Italians, Russians, Turks, and Egyptians who smoke cigarettes and they're no good anyhow.*[7]

The public image of the cigarette would eventually change dramatically; until then cigarette manufacturers had to rely instead on a distinct marketing advantage: low cost. In 1881, James Bonsack patented a cigarette-making machine that transformed the tobacco industry. Instead of producing at most 300 cigarettes an hour by hand, three machine operators could now turn out 200 a minute, or roughly 120,000 cigarettes a day. This is a snail's pace compared to the present state-of-the-art machines capable of producing 10,000 cigarettes a minute, but in those days the Bonsack machine was viewed as an industrial miracle. Cigarette prices by the end of the 1800s were as cheap as twenty for a nickel.[8]

Tobacco in the Twentieth Century

At the beginning of the twentieth century, Americans could choose from a variety of ways to satisfy their hunger for tobacco. Cigars and pipes were still the dominant form of tobacco use. Plugs of chewing tobacco were still enjoyed by many and spittoons were still in evidence, but with the new emphasis on social manners and crackdowns by public health officials concerned with major epidemics of infectious diseases, their days were numbered in the big cities. Chewing remained popular, however, in rural towns of America, and present-day sales are concentrated in these regions.

The future seemed to favor the cigarette for two basic reasons. First, a growing number of women began to challenge the idea of masculine domination, and smoking tobacco was one of the privileges of men that women now wanted to share. Not that women smoking was met with immediate acceptance; in one famous case in 1904, a New York City woman was arrested for smoking in public. Nonetheless, as smoking among women became more common, the mild-tasting, easy-to-hold cigarette was the perfect option for them. By the 1920s, advertising slogans such as "Reach for a Lucky instead of a sweet" (a clever effort to portray cigarette smoking as a weight-control aid) as well as endorsements by glamorous celebrities were being designed specifically for the women's market. A second factor was World War I, during which

cigars: Tightly rolled quantities of dried tobacco leaves.
cigarettes: Rolls of shredded tobacco wrapped in paper, today usually fitted at the mouth end with a filter.

Cigarette advertisements drew on an association with glamorous women and Hollywood celebrities.

time cigarettes were a logical form of tobacco to take along to war. Times of tension have always been times of increased tobacco use. When the war was over, the cigarette was, in the words of one historian, "enshrined forever as the weary soldier's relief, the worried man's support, and the relaxing man's companion."[9]

Cigarettes really came into their own in the 1920s, with the introduction of heavily advertised brand names and intense competition among American tobacco companies. Some of the major brand names introduced during this period were Camel, Chesterfield, Lucky Strike, Philip Morris, and Old Gold. Cigarette sales in the United States increased from $45 billion in 1920 to $80 billion in 1925 and $180 billion by 1940.[10]

Health Concerns and Smoking Behavior

A combination of promotion through mass media advertising and the implied endorsement of smoking by glamorous people in the entertainment industry and sports celebrities enabled the tobacco industry, now dominated by cigarettes, to increase its volume of sales from the 1940s to the 1980s by a steady 9 billion cigarettes each year. The peak in domestic sales was reached in 1981, when approximately 640 billion were sold. Owing to the increase in population, however, per capita consumption in the United States had peaked in 1963 at approximately 4,300 cigarettes per year (roughly twelve cigarettes per day).

Beginning in 1964, per capita consumption began a steady decline, with the present level at approximately 2,100 cigarettes per year (roughly six cigarettes per day). The year of the turnaround in per capita consumption is significant because it coincided with the surgeon general's first report on smoking and health. For the first time, the federal government asserted publicly what had been suspected for decades, that tobacco smoking was linked to cancer and other serious diseases. From the standpoint of tobacco use in America, the surgeon general's report had three major effects. First, in the month or so immediately after the report was released, there was a dramatic dip (approximately 25 percent) in per capita consumption levels. Although succeeding months in 1964 showed a bounce upward, most likely reflecting the fact that many people who tried to quit had only temporary success, the long-term trend in U.S. tobacco consumption from that point on would never be upward again.

As evidence of health risks accumulated, restrictions on public consumption were instituted. In 1971, all television advertising for tobacco was banned, and in 1984, a rotating series of warning labels (already on all packages of tobacco products since 1966) were required on all print advertisements and outdoor billboards.[11]

A second major effect was the change in the types of cigarettes smoked by the average smoker. In the 1950s, more and more cigarette smokers chose to smoke filtered as distinct from unfiltered cigarettes, in an effort to ingest less of the toxins in tobacco. By the 1990s, about 95 percent of all smokers were using filtered brands.[12]

Unfortunately, the dominance of filtered cigarettes has not lessened the health consequences of smoking, only created the illusion of having done so. One problem is that when filtered cigarettes were introduced, the industry changed the formulation of the cigarette tobacco, substituting a stronger blend of tobacco with an increased tar content. Tar, as will be shown, represents a major factor in smokers' health problems, but it is also the primary source of a cigarette's flavor.

In short, a higher-tar blend of tobacco was used to satisfy the consumer, even though it essentially counteracted the point of using a filter in the first place or even made matters worse. As a result of a stronger "filter blend" formula in the cigarette, **sidestream smoke,** the smoke directly inhaled by a nonsmoker from a burning cigarette, ends up more toxic when originating from a filtered cigarette than it is from an unfiltered one. In principle, a cigarette filter should allow a flow of air through small holes in the filter itself. Because a smoker typically holds the cigarette with the fingers covering these holes, however, little or no filtering is accomplished.

From the standpoint of profits, filtered cigarettes were a boon to the tobacco industry. Filters were only paper and therefore cost considerably less than filling the same space with tobacco. One prominent brand went one step further by recessing its filter "a neat, clean, quarter inch away," giving the further illusion of filtering away impurities but actually only creating air space.[13]

A third consequence was a direct response to the assertion by the surgeon general that tar and nicotine were specifically responsible for increased health risks from smoking. New cigarette brands were introduced that were low in tar and nicotine (T/N), and the Federal Trade Commission began to issue a listing of tar and nicotine levels in major commercial brands. As later surgeon general's reports have indicated, however, smokers can essentially cancel out the benefits of switching to low T/N brands by varying the manner in which they smoke a low T/N cigarette. Smokers take more puffs, inhale more deeply, and smoke more of the cigarette when it has a lower T/N level in order to maintain the same amount of nicotine (the same number of nicotine "hits"). In addition, a greater number of low T/N cigarettes have to be smoked to satisfy the smoker's needs, a fact that has obvious implications for tobacco sales.[14]

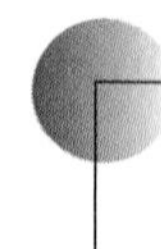

Tobacco Today: An Industry on the Defensive

The tobacco industry in the United States, since the early 1990s, has faced continuing challenges from federal governmental agencies, as well as individuals and groups who have sued tobacco companies for damages resulting from their ingestion of tobacco products. As a result, at the beginning of the new millennium, the legal and economic status of the tobacco industry has been altered significantly. In 1993, the U.S. Environmental Protection Agency (EPA) announced its conclusion from available research that **environmental tobacco smoke (ETS),** the sidestream smoke in the air that is inhaled by nonsmokers as a result of tobacco smoking, causes lung cancer. Since then, most U.S. states, cities, and communities have enacted laws mandating smoke-free environments in all public and private workplaces, unless ventilated smoking rooms have been provided. It is now typical for restaurants, hotels, and other commercial spaces to be at least partially smoke-free. In 1994, congressional hearings were held on allegations that during the 1970s tobacco companies had suppressed research data obtained in their own research laboratories regarding the hazards of cigarette smoking. More recently, the Philip Morris company issued a statement, formally admitting that "there is overwhelming medical and scientific consensus that cigarette smoking causes cancer, heart disease, emphysema, and other serious diseases" and that "cigarette smoking is addictive, as that term is most commonly used today." This new stance is a complete reversal of the industry's 1994 congressional testimony regarding tobacco use.

The Tobacco Settlement

In 1998, the major American tobacco corporations entered into an agreement with all fifty U.S. states to resolve claims that the states should be compensated for the costs of treating people with smoking-related illnesses. Under the terms of the settlement, the tobacco industry will pay the states approximately $246 billion over twenty-five years. The tobacco industry also agreed to refrain from marketing tobacco products to those under eighteen and pay $24 million a year over a decade for a research foundation dedicated toward finding ways to reduce smoking among youths. In contrast to earlier proposed settlements, however, tobacco corporations under this agreement would not be penalized if levels of under-age smoking did not decline over that period of time. In addition, the settlement did not prevent individuals or groups of individuals from suing tobacco corporations in separate actions. The cost of the settlement has been borne largely through an increase in cigarette prices, amounting to about thirty-five cents a pack.

Whether the tobacco settlement will produce a decline in smoking levels in general, or among young people in particular, remains to be seen. While providing the states with a considerable monetary windfall, it is unclear how much of the compensation funds will directly benefit

sidestream smoke: Tobacco smoke that is inhaled by nonsmokers from the burning cigarettes of nearby smokers. Also referred to as environmental tobacco smoke.

environmental tobacco smoke (ETS): Tobacco smoke in the atmosphere as a result of burning cigarettes; also called sidestream or secondary smoke.

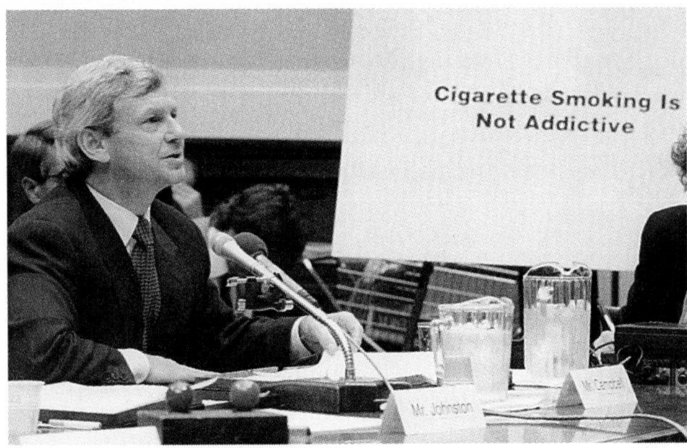

In 1994, tobacco industry executives testified before a congressional committee in defense of cigarette smoking and other tobacco use. In 1999, the Philip Morris company formally reversed its earlier position that smoking was not addictive.

smoking prevention programs. It is also unclear whether tobacco corporations will find themselves paying additional money in the future to individuals or groups of individuals currently suing them for health-related damages.[15]

Federal Regulation of Nicotine as a Drug

In 1996, the FDA declared its regulatory authority over tobacco products, asserting that nicotine was a drug and that tobacco products were essentially "drug-delivery devices." Under FDA rules, the government was authorized to restrict access to cigarette vending machines, require tobacco customers to show proof that they are at least eighteen years old, limit advertisements on billboards and print publications to black-and-white text-only messages, keep billboards away from areas around schools and playgrounds, and prohibit promotional merchandise aimed at young people. The FDA did not exclude, at that time, the possibility of future regulations over the character of tobacco products themselves.

In 1998, however, a federal appeals court ruled against the FDA's action, arguing that the agency had overstepped its authority by acting without specific authorization from Congress. Two years later, the U.S. Supreme Court agreed with the lower court's ruling, a decision that has renewed the intense debate over the future of tobacco regulation in the United States.[16]

Tobacco Regulation and Economics

Some have argued that an effective way to reduce the rate of smoking is to making smoking more expensive. Why not increase cigarette taxes, the logic goes, when cigarette smoking contributes so substantially to major disease? The prospect of reducing cigarette sales by increasing cigarette taxation is supported by data from U.S. states and other countries where tobacco excise taxes have been increased. As a rule of thumb, for every 10 percent increase in the retail price of cigarettes, consumption has fallen by 2 to 3 percent. Public health officials have estimated that an increase of $1.50 to $2.00 a pack would be required to reduce smoking by as much as 50 percent over several years, particularly with respect to smoking among young people whose financial resources are the most limited. So far, increases in cigarette prices due to the 1998 settlement and increases in even the highest-taxing U.S. states have not combined to reach the lower limit of this range.

It should be noted that policy decisions regarding smoking in the United States concern tobacco products sold only within the United States. As will be discussed later in the chapter, many other nations have substantially higher prevalence rates for cigarette smoking, and their governments have taken far fewer steps toward instituting policies to reduce smoking behavior. For American tobacco corporations, an expanding global marketplace for U.S. cigarettes has given them the opportunity for an increase in profits from foreign sales that has largely compensated for the financial losses from a decline in domestic sales. Moreover, in a larger sense, cigarette sales abroad represent a major component of overall U.S. foreign trade. In recent years, U.S. exports of tobacco products have exceeded imports by approximately $2 billion, creating a significant trade surplus. Therefore, the U.S. trade deficit (defined as an excess of imports over exports) would be considerably worse than it is today, were it not for the export of tobacco products to other nations.[17]

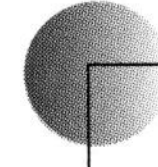

What's in Tobacco?

When a smoker inhales from a lit cigarette, the temperature at the tip rises to approximately 1,700 degrees Fahrenheit (926 degrees Centigrade), as oxygen is drawn through the tobacco, paper, and other additives. This is the reason for the bright glow as a smoker inhales from a cigarette. At this intense heat, more than four thousand separate compounds are oxidized and released through cigarette smoke. The smoker inhales the result as **mainstream smoke,** usually screened through the cigarette

mainstream smoke: The smoke inhaled directly from cigarettes or other tobacco products.

filter and cigarette paper. As mentioned earlier, the sidestream smoke that is released from the burning cigarette tip itself is unfiltered, and because it is a product of a slightly less intense burning process occurring between puffs, more unburned particles are contained in the smoke.

In general, we can speak of two components in tobacco smoke. The **particulate phase,** consisting of small particles (one micrometer or larger in diameter) suspended in the smoke, includes water droplets, nicotine, and a collection of compounds that will be referred to collectively as **tar.** The particles in tar constitute the primary source of carcinogenic compounds in tobacco. The second component is the **gaseous phase,** consisting of gas compounds in the smoke, including carbon dioxide, carbon monoxide, ammonia, hydrogen cyanide, acetadehyde, and acetone. Among these gases, carbon monoxide is clearly the most toxic.

This diverse collection of physiologically active toxins is quite unique to tobacco. One way of putting it is that the fifty thousand to seventy thousand puffs per year that a one-pack-a-day cigarette smoker takes in amounts to a level of pollution far beyond even the most polluted urban environment anywhere in the world.[18] The following discussion will focus on three of the most important compounds in tobacco smoke: carbon monoxide, tar, and nicotine.

Carbon Monoxide

As most people know, **carbon monoxide** is an odorless, colorless, tasteless but extraordinarily toxic gas. It is formed when tobacco burns because the oxidation process is incomplete. In that sense, burning tobacco is similar to an inefficient engine, like a car in need of a tune-up. The danger in carbon monoxide is that it easily attaches itself to hemoglobin, the pigment inside red blood cells, occupying those portions of the hemoglobin molecule normally reserved for the transport of oxygen from the lungs to the rest of the body. Carbon monoxide has about a two hundred times greater affinity for hemoglobin than does oxygen, so oxygen does not have much of a chance. Carbon monoxide is also more resistant to detaching itself from hemoglobin, so there is an accumulation of carbon monoxide over time.

The ultimate result of carbon monoxide is a subtle but effective asphyxiation of the body from a lack of oxygen. Generally, people who smoke a pack a day accumulate levels of carbon monoxide in the blood of 25 to 35 parts per million blood components (p.p.m.), with levels of 100 p.p.m. for short periods of time while actually smoking. Of course, greater use of tobacco produces proportionally higher levels of carbon monoxide. Carbon monoxide is the primary culprit in producing cardiovascular disease among smokers, as well as in causing deficiencies in physiological functioning and behavior.[19]

Tar

The quantity of tar in a cigarette varies from levels of 12 to 16 mg per cigarette to less than 6 mg. It should also be noted that the last third of each cigarette contains 50 percent of the total tar, making the final few puffs far more hazardous than the first ones.

The major problem with tar lies in its sticky quality, not unlike that of the material used in paving roads, which allows it to adhere to cells in the lungs and the airways leading to them. Normally, specialized cells with small hairlike attachments called **cilia** are capable of removing contaminants in the air that might impede the breathing process. These cilia literally sweep the unwanted particles upward to the throat, in a process called the **ciliary escalator,** where they are typically swallowed, digested, and finally excreted from the body through the gastrointestinal system. Components in tar alter the coordination of these cilia so that they can no longer function effectively. The accumulation of sticky tar on the surface of the cells along the pulmonary system permits carcinogenic compounds that would normally have been eliminated to settle on the tissue. As will be discussed later, the resulting cellular changes produce lung cancer, and similar carcinogenic effects in other tissues of the body produce cancer in other organs.[20]

particulate phase: Those components of smoke that consist of particles.
tar: A sticky material found in the particulate phase of tobacco smoke and other pollutants in the air.
gaseous phase: The portion of tobacco smoke that consists of gases.
carbon monoxide: An extremely toxic gas that prevents blood cells from carrying oxygen from the lungs to the rest of the body.
cilia: Small hair cells.
ciliary escalator: The process of pushing back foreign particles that might interfere with breathing upward from the air passages into the throat, where they can be swallowed and excreted through the gastrointestinal tract.

Nicotine

Nicotine is a toxic, dependence-producing psychoactive drug found exclusively in tobacco. It is an oily compound varying in hue from colorless to brown. A few drops of pure nicotine, about 60 mg, on the tongue would quickly kill a healthy adult, and it is commonly used as a major ingredient in insecticides and pesticides of all kinds. Cigarettes, however, contain from 0.5 to 2.0 mg of nicotine (depending on the brand), with about 20 percent being actually inhaled and reaching the bloodstream. This means that 2 to 8 mg of nicotine are ingested per day for a pack-a-day smoker, and 4 to 16 mg of nicotine for a smoker of two packs a day.[21]

Inhaled nicotine from smoking is absorbed extremely rapidly and easily passes through the blood-brain barrier, as well as through the blood-placental barrier in pregnant women, in a few seconds. The entire effect is over in a matter of minutes. By the time a cigarette butt is extinguished, nicotine levels in the blood have peaked, and its breakdown and excretion from the body are well underway. The elimination half-life of nicotine is approximately two to three hours.

The speed of nicotine absorption would ordinarily be much slower if it were not for the presence of ammonia as an additive in the tobacco blend. The combination of nicotine and ammonia changes the naturally acidic nicotine into an alkalinic free-base form that more easily passes from body tissues into the bloodstream. As a result, ammonia increases the availability of nicotine in the blood, much as the addition of alkaline materials like baking soda converts cocaine into crack cocaine (see Chapter 4). The information that ammonia had been introduced into the manufacture of cigarette tobacco during the 1970s, in an apparent effort to increase the "kick" of nicotine, came to light in 1995 and was confirmed by tobacco company documents released in 1998.[22]

The primary effect of nicotine is to stimulate CNS receptors that are sensitive to acetylcholine (see Chapter 3). These receptors are called *nicotinic receptors* because they are excited by nicotine. One of the effects of activating them is the release of adrenalin, which increases blood pressure and heart rate. Another effect is to inhibit activity in the gastrointestinal system. At the same time, however, as most smokers will tell you, a cigarette is a relaxing factor in their lives. Part of this reaction may be due to an effect on the brain that promotes a greater level of clear thinking and concentration; another part may relate to the fact that nicotine, at moderate doses, serves to reduce muscle tone so that muscular tightness is decreased. Research has shown that cigarette smoking helps to sustain performance on monotonous tasks and to improve short-term memory. We can assume that it is the nicotine in cigarettes and other tobacco products that is responsible because nicotine tablets have comparable behavioral effects.[23]

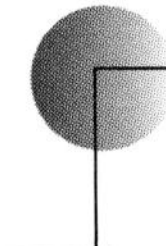

The Dependence Potential of Nicotine

Historically, the dependence potential of nicotine has been demonstrated at times in which the usual availability of tobacco has suddenly been curtailed. In Germany following the end of World War II, for example, cigarettes were rationed to two packs a month for men and one pack a month for women. This "cigarette famine" produced dramatic effects on the behavior of German civilians. Smokers bartered their food rations for cigarettes, even under the extreme circumstances of chronic hunger and poor nutrition. Cigarette butts were picked from the dirt in the streets by people who admitted that they were personally disgusted by their desperation. Some women turned to prostitution to obtain cigarettes, while alcoholics of both sexes testified that it was easier to abstain from drinking alcohol than it was to abstain from smoking.[24]

It is now known that nicotine stimulates the release of dopamine in the nucleus accumbens, the same area of the brain responsible for the reinforcing properties of opiates, cocaine, and alcohol.[25] In addition, several behavioral factors combine with this physiological effect to increase the likelihood that a strong dependence will be created. One of these factors is the speed with which smoked nicotine reaches the brain. The delivery time has been estimated as five to eight seconds. A second factor is the wide variety of circumstances and settings surrounding the act of smoking that later come to serve as learned rewards. A smoker may find, for example, that the first cigarette with a cup of coffee in the morning (a source of another psychoactive drug, caffeine) is strongly reinforcing. A major reseacher on addictions has expressed it in this way:

> *Smoking . . . comes to be rewarded by the enjoyment of oral, manual, and respiratory manipulations involved in the process of lighting, puffing, and handling cigarettes, the pleasure and relaxation*

nicotine: The prime psychoactive drug in tobacco products.

associated with using alcohol, finishing a good meal, . . . and the perceived diminution of unpleasant affective [emotional] states of anxiety, tension, boredom, or fatigue. . . . No other substance can provide so many kinds of rewards, is so readily and cheaply available, and can be used in so many settings and situations.[26]

A third factor is the sheer number of times the smoker experiences a dose of nicotine. When you consider that a smoker takes from one to two hundred puffs each day from the twenty cigarettes that represent a pack-a-day pattern of smoking, you realize that smoking is a highly practiced, overlearned behavior.[27]

The Titration Hypothesis of Nicotine Dependence

There is considerable evidence that smokers adjust their smoking behavior to obtain a stable dose of nicotine from whatever cigarettes they are smoking, an idea called the **titration hypothesis.** When exposed to cigarettes of decreasing nicotine content, smokers will smoke a greater number of them to compensate and will increase the volume of each puff. When they inhale more puffs per cigarette, a greater interval of time will elapse before they light up another one. If they are given nicotine gum to chew, the intensity of their smoking behavior will decline, even though they have not been told whether the gum contains nicotine or is a placebo. All these studies indicate that experienced smokers arrive at a consistent "style" of smoking that provides their bodies with a relatively constant level of nicotine.[28]

Tolerance and Withdrawal

First-time smokers often react to a cigarette with a mixture of nausea, dizziness, or vomiting. These effects typically disappear as tolerance develops in the nicotinic receptors in the brain. Other physiological effects, such as increases in heart rate, tremors, and changes in skin temperature, show weaker tolerance effects or none at all. The strongest dependence-related effect of cigarette smoking can be seen in the symptoms of withdrawal that follow the discontinuation of smoking. Within about six hours after the last cigarette, a smoker's heart rate and blood pressure will decrease. Over the next twenty-four hours, common symptoms will include headache, an inability to concentrate, irritability, drowsiness, and fatigue, as well as insomnia and other sleep disturbances. Most striking of all are the strong feelings of craving for a cigarette. Ex-smokers can attest to cravings that slowly diminish but nonetheless linger on for months, and in some cases, for years.[29]

Nicotine dependence, as demonstrated, is the central factor in the continuation of smoking behaviors. The level of dependence is significant, even when compared to dependence levels of illicit drugs available on the street. In a study of people who smoked and were also in some form of drug-abuse treatment, 74 percent judged the difficulty of quitting smoking to be at least as great as the difficulty in stopping their drug of choice. One in three considered it "much harder" to quit smoking.[30]

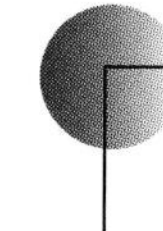

Health Consequences of Tobacco Use

The adverse health consequences of tobacco use can be classified in three broad categories: cardiovascular disease, respiratory disease, and cancer. In addition, there are also special health difficulties that smoking can bring to women and hazards from using smokeless tobacco. An enormous literature on the adverse effects of tobacco use has grown steadily since the original surgeon general's report in 1964, though by that time more than thirty thousand research studies had been conducted on the question.

Beyond all the reports, however, are the sheer numbers of people who are affected. In the United States alone, among the estimated 520,000 deaths each year that are attributed to substance abuse of one kind or another, approximately 430,000 of them (more than the total number of Americans who died in World War II) are specifically tied to cigarette smoking. The medical community considers these deaths to be premature deaths because they are entirely preventable; these people would have been alive if their behaviors had been different.

The numbers are simple, and staggering: Smoking-related deaths account for at least one out of every five deaths in the United States every year, nearly 1,200 deaths each day. A person's life is shortened by fourteen minutes every time a cigarette is smoked. Smoking two packs a day for twenty years reduces one's lifespan by approximately eight years. Unlike alcohol, which presents no significant health hazards when consumed in moderation, tobacco is a dangerous product *when used as intended* (Figure 11.1).[31]

titration hypothesis: The idea that smokers will adjust their smoking of cigarettes so as to maintain a steady input of nicotine into the body.

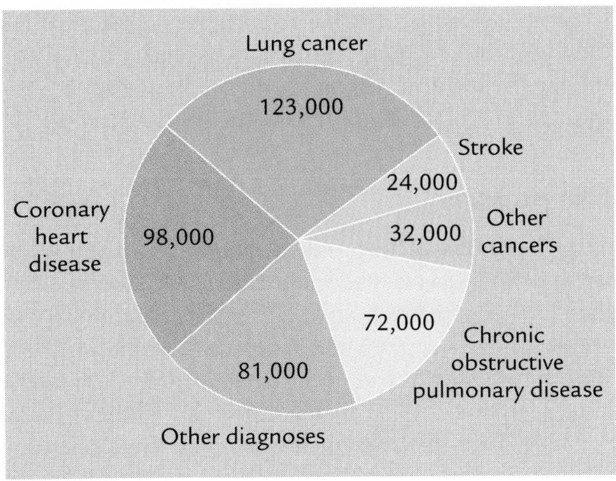

FIGURE 11.1

The distribution of approximately 430,000 U.S. deaths attributed each year to cigarette smoking.

Source: Centers for Disease Control and Prevention (1999, March 3). *Morbidity and Mortality Weekly Report.* Atlanta: Centers for Disease Control and Prevention.

Cardiovascular Disease

Cardiovascular disease includes a number of specific conditions. Some of these diseases are **coronary heart disease (CHD)**, in which damage to the heart is incurred due to the restriction of blood flow through narrowed or blocked coronary arteries; **arteriosclerosis,** in which the walls of arteries harden and lose their elasticity; **atherosclerosis,** in which fatty deposits inside arteries impede blood flow; and stroke, in which interruption or reduction in blood flow causes damage to the brain. In all these diseases, cigarette smoking increases the risk dramatically.

We know now that smoking is responsible for approximately 30 percent of all CHD deaths. The risk of CHD doubles if you smoke and quadruples if you smoke heavily. On average, smoking also raises the risk of a sudden death (such as from a fatal heart attack) by two to four times, with the degree of risk increasing as a direct function of how many cigarettes are smoked per day. To put it even more boldly, it has been estimated that, unless smoking patterns change dramatically in the future, about 10 percent of all Americans now alive may die prematurely from some form of heart disease as a result of their smoking behavior. Yet, strangely enough, a recent study has shown that only 29 percent of current smokers and only 39 percent of heavy smokers believe that they have a higher-than-average risk of a heart attack.[32]

These statistics are strengthened by the understanding we have of how cigarette smoking actually produces these dangerous cardiovascular conditions. The major villains are nicotine and carbon monoxide. Nicotine, as a stimulant drug, increases the contraction of heart muscle and elevates heart rate. At the same time, it causes a constriction of blood vessels, leading to a rise in blood pressure, and also increases *platelet adhesiveness* in the blood. As a result of a greater adhesiveness, platelets clump together and increase the risk of developing a blood clot. If a clot forms within coronary arteries, a heart attack can occur; a clot traveling into the blood vessels of the brain can produce a stroke. Finally, nicotine increases the body's serum cholesterol and fatty deposits, leading to the development of atherosclerosis. While nicotine is doing its dirty work, carbon monoxide makes matters worse. A lack of oxygen puts further strain on the ability of the heart to function under already trying circumstances.[33]

Respiratory Diseases

The general term **chronic obstructive pulmonary disease (COPD)** refers to several conditions in which breathing is impaired because of some abnormality in the air passages either leading to or within the lungs. In the United States, 80 to 90 percent of all such cases are the result of cigarette smoking. With the exception of a rare genetic defect, cigarette smoking is the only established cause for clinically significant COPD.

Two examples of COPD are **chronic bronchitis,** in which excess mucus builds up in air passages, leading to an inflammation of bronchial tissue, and **emphysema,** in

coronary heart disease (CHD): Disease that damages the heart as a result of a restriction of blood flow through coronary arteries.

arteriosclerosis (ar-TEER-ee-oh-scluh-ROH-sis): A disease in which blood flow is restricted because the walls of arteries harden and lose their elasticity.

atherosclerosis (ATH-er-oh-scluh-ROH-sis): A disease in which blood flow is restricted because of the buildup of fatty deposits inside arteries.

chronic obstructive pulmonary disease (COPD): A group of diseases characterized by impaired breathing due to an abnormality in the air passages.

chronic bronchitis: A respiratory disease involving inflammation of bronchial tissue following a buildup of excess mucus in air passages.

emphysema (EM-fuh-SEE-mah): An enlargement of air sacs in the lungs and abnormalities in the air sac walls, causing great difficulty in breathing.

which air sacs in the lungs are abnormally enlarged and the air sac walls either become inelastic or rupture, leading to extreme difficulty in inhaling oxygen and exhaling carbon dioxide. In the case of advanced emphysema, more than 80 percent of a patient's energy is required merely to breathe. Either disease or a combination of the two causes more than seventy thousand deaths each year, and many additional thousands are forced to lead increasingly debilitating lives, gasping and struggling each day to breathe:

> *Many of [the thousands of people with COPD] are attached to oxygen tanks, imprisoned at home or in the hospital because they are too weak to breathe on their own. Often their friends or family members will pound on their backs, temporarily freeing the lungs of the yellow mucus that impedes their breathing every day.*[34]

Pulmonary damage, however, is not limited to adults who have been smoking for many years. Cigarette smoking is also associated with airway obstruction and slower growth of lung function in younger populations. Adolescents who smoke five or more cigarettes a day are 40 percent more likely to develop asthma and 30 percent more likely to have symptoms of wheezing but not asthma than those who do not smoke. Girls show a greater loss of pulmonary function than boys in the smoking group, even though boys report that they smoke more cigarettes.[35]

Lung Cancer

At the beginning of the twentieth century, lung cancer was a rare disease, and its steady increase in U.S. society since then has been in direct proportion to the availability of cigarettes. Today, nearly 90 percent of the more than 140,000 lung cancer deaths each year have been determined by the American Cancer Society to be caused by cigarette smoking. These facts are made even more tragic when you consider that the survival rate for one year after a diagnosis of lung cancer is only approximately 25 percent, and about 87 percent of lung cancer patients die within five years of initial diagnosis. While there has been a steady decrease in deaths from lung, tracheal, and bronchial cancer among African-American males since 1990, there still remains an approximately 35 percent greater mortality rate in this group, relative to white males (Figure 11.2).

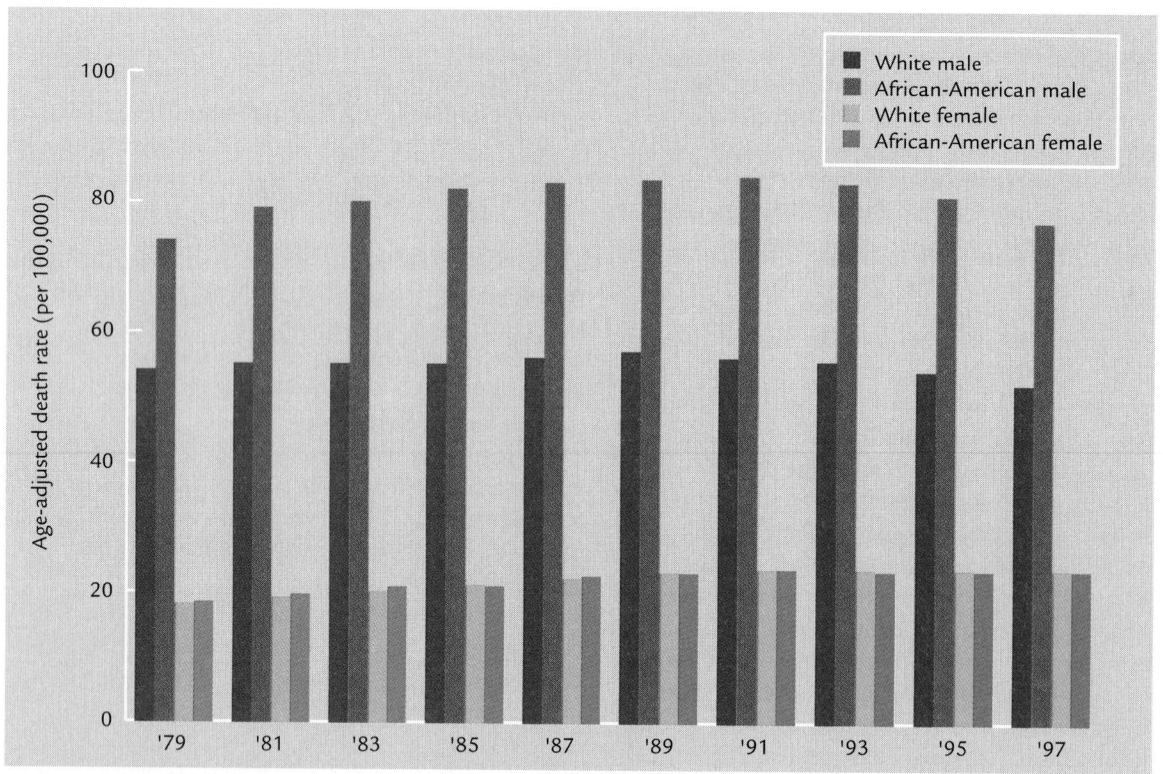

FIGURE 11.2

The trends in death rate due to lung, tracheal, and bronchial cancer, 1979–1997.
Source: National Center for Health Statistics, Centers for Disease Control and Prevention.

Another important change has occurred over the years with respect to this disease. Lung cancer was once considered a "man's disease." More recently, however, increasing numbers of women have contracted lung cancer as a result of their increased level of cigarette smoking. Since 1988, lung cancer has exceeded breast cancer as the leading cause of cancer deaths among women.

As discussed earlier in the chapter, the exposure to tar in cigarette smoke disrupts the necessary action of ciliary cells in the bronchial tubes leading to the lungs. Without their protective function, the lungs are open to attack. Several carcinogenic compounds in the smoke can now enter the lungs and stimulate the formation of cancerous growths, **carcinomas,** in lung tissue. One of these compounds, *benzopyrene,* has been found to cause genetic mutations in cells that are identical to the mutations observed in patients who have developed carcinomas in their lungs. This finding is important because it establishes a causal link between a specific ingredient in tobacco smoke and human cancer.[36]

Health Alert

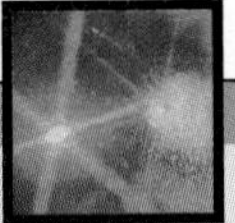

Signs of Trouble from Smokeless Tobacco

- Lumps in the jaw or neck area
- Color changes or lumps inside the lips
- White, smooth, or scaly patches in the mouth or on the neck, lips, or tongue
- A red spot or sore on the lips or gums or inside the mouth that does not heal in two weeks
- Repeated bleeding in the mouth
- Difficulty or abnormality in speaking or swallowing

Any of these signs should be reported to a physician as soon as possible. In the meantime, and in the future, use of smokeless tobacco should be discontinued.

Source: Payne, Wayne A., and Hahn, Dale B. (1992). *Understanding your health.* St. Louis: Mosby Year Book, p. 278.

Other Cancers

Certainly lung cancer is the best-known and most common example of smoking-related cancers; unfortunately, other organs are affected in a similar way. In the United States, approximately 30 percent of cancer deaths *of all types* have been linked to smoking. It has been estimated that smokers increase their risk by two to twenty-seven times for cancer of the larynx, thirteen times for mouth or lip cancer, two to three times for bladder cancer, two times for pancreatic cancer, and five times for cancers of the kidney or uterine cervix.[37]

Despite a widespread belief to the contrary, using smokeless tobacco, in the form of chewing tobacco or snuff, does not prevent the user from incurring an increased risk of cancer. Continuing contact with tobacco in the mouth has been shown to produce precancerous cell changes, as revealed by **leukoplakia** (white spots) and **erythroplakia** (red spots) inside the mouth and nasal cavity. Even though smokeless tobacco obviously avoids the problems associated with tobacco smoke, it does not prevent the user from being exposed to carcinogens, specifically a class of compounds called **nitrosamines** that are present in all tobacco products. As a result of federal legislation enacted in 1986, all forms of smokeless tobacco must contain, on the package, a set of specific warnings that these products may cause mouth cancer as well as gum disease and tooth loss (Health Alert). To reinforce the idea that dangers are still present in smokeless tobacco, one of these warnings reads: "This product is not a safe alternative to cigarette smoking."

Special Problems for Women

The range of health risks to a developing fetus and to the newborn when the mother smokes during pregnancy has been listed in Chapter 2. To these concerns, an important addition is the toxic interaction of tobacco smoke with birth control pills. Women who smoke have a more than three times greater risk of dying from stroke due to brain hemorrhaging and an almost two times greater risk of dying from a heart attack. If they are using birth control pills as well, the risk increases to twenty-two times and twenty times, respectively.[38]

carcinomas (CAR-sih-NOH-mas): Cancerous tumors or growths.

leukoplakia (LOO-koh-PLAY-kee-ah): Small white spots inside the mouth and nasal cavity, indicating precancerous tissue.

erythroplakia (eh-RITH-ro-PLAY-kee-ah): Small red spots inside the mouth and nasal cavity, indicating precancerous tissue.

nitrosamines (nih-TRAW-seh-meens): A group of carcinogenic compounds found in tobacco.

DRUGS . . . IN FOCUS

Who Has the Right: Smokers or Nonsmokers?

Since the 1980s, an increasingly thorny issue that divides worker against worker, restaurant patron against restaurant patron, and nearly anyone who ventures out of his or her home is the question of smokers' rights versus nonsmokers' rights. On the one hand, smokers argue that smoking is a personal freedom and that nonsmokers are restricting that freedom. On the other hand, nonsmokers, armed with increasing facts to back them up, argue that we are talking about a genuine hazard to the public health, not merely an objection based on the smell of smoke or the cleanliness of ashtrays. To quote a line from the self-styled Nonsmoker's Bill of Rights, "Nonsmokers have the right to breathe clean air, free from harmful and irritating tobacco smoke. This right supersedes the right to smoke when the two conflict."

As we are all aware, the balance of public sentiment has tilted increasingly toward the side of the nonsmoker. Anyone in an airport will have no difficulty observing the feverish last-minute smokers, getting in that last cigarette before the start of a nonsmoking flight, or the pained look on their faces when confronted by the ubiquitous no-smoking sign. Perhaps the most concrete development was the decision by the Chrysler Corporation to design the 1995 and subsequent Chrysler Cirrus and Dodge Stratus automobiles without ashtrays or cigarette lighters. Smokers are able to order these items on these models only as an option. Smoking is no longer standard.

Source: Bennet, James (1994, January 5). In new Chrysler, ashtrays will be just an option. *New York Times,* pp. A1, D26.

The Hazards of Environmental Smoke

In the early days of development of methods for detecting nicotine in the bloodstream, scientists were puzzled to find traces of nicotine in nonsmokers. They suspected at first that there was some flaw in their analysis but later had to conclude that their measurements were indeed accurate. Nonsmokers testing positive had shared car rides or workplaces with smokers shortly before their tests. Today, a large body of evidence indicates not only the presence of tobacco smoke compounds in the bodies of nonsmokers but also the significant health risks that such "involuntary smoking" can provoke. In other words, environmental tobacco smoke is a hazard even to the health of people who are not actively smoking.

Approximately 85 percent of the smoke in an average room where people are smoking cigarettes is generated by sidestream smoke, and about three-fourths of the nicotine originating from these cigarettes ends up in the atmosphere. In some cases, the carcinogens released in ETS are so potent that they are dangerous even in their diluted state. For example, N-nitrosamine (an example of a group of carcinogens mentioned earlier in connection with smokeless tobacco) is so much more concentrated in sidestream smoke than in mainstream smoke that nonsmokers will end up inhaling as much of it after one hour in a very smoky room as will a smoker after smoking ten to fifteen cigarettes.[39]

Overall, nonsmoking wives of husbands who smoke have a 30 percent increased chance of lung cancer compared with women whose husbands do not smoke; if the husband is a heavy smoker, then the wife's risk increases by two to three times. If both spouses smoke, of course, they are susceptible to the effects of both ETS and their own mainstream smoke. Exposure to ETS among women who have never smoked has been found to double their risk of experiencing a heart attack. Children are also vulnerable, with a greater chance of developing colds, asthma, bronchitis, chronic coughs, ear infections, and reduced lung functioning if their parents smoke. (See Drugs . . . in Focus.)[40]

QUICK CONCEPT  11.1

Understanding the Effects of Tobacco Smoking

Check your understanding of the effects of tobacco smoking by associating each of the following physical effects with (a) carbon monoxide, (b) tar, or (c) nicotine. It is possible to have a combination of two factors as the correct answer.

1. a decrease in oxygen in the body
2. physical dependence
3. cellular changes leading to cancer
4. cardiovascular disease
5. chronic bronchitis

Answers: 1. a 2. c 3. b 4. a and c 5. b

Patterns of Smoking Behavior and Use of Smokeless Tobacco

In 1965, about 40 percent of all American teenagers and adults smoked cigarettes, and it is estimated that more than 50 percent did in the 1940s. In 1999, however, according to the National Household Survey on Drug Abuse, approximately 26 percent smoked a cigarette within the past month, qualifying as regular smokers. Though this percentage is significantly less than it had been, we are still considering a very large number of people. Extrapolating to the U.S. population, a 26 percent prevalence rate corresponds to approximately 57 million people. A steady decline in the percentage of American smokers stopped around 1991, and the prevalence rate has declined only slightly since then. An exception, however, can be seen in college students. From 1993 to 1997, the percentage in this group smoking cigarettes in the last month rose from 22 percent to 29 percent, from below the national average to above it, with the largest increases among females. Recent surveys reveal that 46 percent of college students have used a tobacco product in the past year and 33 percent use it currently. Cigarette smoking accounts for most of the tobacco use in this group.[41]

To look at prevalence rates among younger people, we turn to the results of the University of Michigan survey. Among high school seniors in 2000, about 31 percent had smoked within the last thirty days, about 21 percent smoked on a daily basis during that time, and 11 percent smoked at least half a pack a day.[42]

The Youngest Smokers

The University of Michigan survey also gives us an idea of the pattern of smoking among students at the junior high school level. In 2000, 41 percent of eighth graders reported that they had tried cigarettes in their lifetime, and about 15 percent said that they had smoked at least once in the prior month. Approximately 7 percent of all eighth graders smoked on a daily basis, and 3 percent smoked at least a half a pack a day.

The peak years for starting to smoke were reported in the survey to be in the sixth and seventh grade, but a significant number of eighth graders who were regular smokers said that they had started earlier. About 16 percent have reported that they had begun prior to the sixth grade; in fact, about 8 percent have reported that they had started prior to the fifth grade. A recent study of sixth-through-eighth-graders (ages eleven to thirteen) has found that 9 percent of those in this age group smoke cigarettes on a regular basis.[43]

Attitudes toward Smoking among Young People

A particularly discouraging aspect of current statistics about smoking concerns the percentage of young people reporting that cigarette smoking does not present a great risk to their health. About 27 percent of high school seniors in 2000 perceived smoking one or more packs of cigarettes a day as not presenting a great risk to their health. This attitude exists in the context of a barrage of information directed to them regarding the adverse consequences of smoking.

Statistics with respect to attitudes among eighth graders are, unfortunately, even worse than those for high school seniors. More than four out of every ten eighth graders (41 percent) in 2000 considered smoking one or more packs a day not to be presenting a great risk. This finding is especially troubling, given the substantial potential for nicotine dependence and the consistent finding that a large proportion of adult smokers began to smoke at approximately this time in their lives. It has been

The nine-year Joe Camel advertising campaign ended in 1997, as opposition mounted against tobacco promotions targeting youth. Here is a parody of the Camel campaign, through the eyes of Garry Trudeau, creator of Doonesbury.

Cigarette smoking among minors is a continuing social problem.

estimated that between 80 and 90 percent of regular smokers begin to smoke by the age of eighteen.[44]

In 1997, the FDA established eighteen as the national minimum age at which tobacco products could be purchased and required vendors to verify the ages of purchasers up to the age of twenty-seven in an effort to reduce the access of young people to tobacco. The prospects of enforcing this regulation to the extent necessary to achieve its goal, however, are dim. In a study that examined tobacco sales in a community in Massachusetts, an 82 percent vendor compliance with the minimal age requirement was found to have been achieved, based on the number of sale refusals to underage volunteers who attempted to purchase a pack of cigarettes. Even so, adolescents in the community reported no difference in their perceived access to cigarette purchases or their rate of smoking, relative to other young people living in other communities which had not instituted sales restrictions. The new federal regulation has set a goal of 80 percent compliance on the part of vendors. On the basis of this research, compliance levels clearly need to be much higher than 80 percent if we are to see a reduction in tobacco sales to underage purchasers and a reduction in their rates of smoking.[45]

Use of Smokeless Tobacco

Smokeless tobacco is ingested, as the name implies, by absorption through the membranes of the mouth rather than by inhalation of smoke into the lungs (Table 11.1). The two most common forms are the traditional loose-leaf chewing tobacco (brand names include Red Man and Beech Nut) and moist, more finely shredded tobacco called **moist snuff** or simply snuff (brand names include Copenhagen and Skoal). Snuff, by the way, is no longer sniffed into the nose, as in the eighteenth century, but rather placed inside the cheek or alongside the gum under the lower lip. Some varieties of snuff are available in a small absorbent-paper sack (like a tea bag), so that the tobacco particles do not get stuck in the teeth. The practice is called "dipping."

TABLE 11.1

Forms of smokeless tobacco

TYPE	DESCRIPTION
Chewing tobacco	
Loose-leaf	Made of cigar-leaf tobacco, sold in small packages, heavily flavored or plain
Fine-cut	Similar to loose-leaf but more finely cut so that it resembles snuff
Plug	Leaf tobacco pressed into flat cakes and sweetened with molasses, licorice, maple sugar, or honey
Twist	Made of stemmed leaves twisted into small rolls and then folded
(Chewing tobacco is not really chewed but rather held in the mouth between the cheek and lower jaw.)	
Snuff	
Dry, moist, sweetened, flavored, salted, scented	
(A pinch of snuff, called a *quid,* is typically tucked between the gum and the lower lip. Moist varieties are currently the most popular.)	

Source: Adapted from Popescu, Cathy (1992). The health hazards of smokeless tobacco. In Kristine Napier (Ed.), *Issues in tobacco.* New York: American Council on Science and Health, pp. 11–12.

Since the 1970s, smokeless tobacco has increased in popularity among young males, particularly in rural communities in the South and North Central regions of the United States. In these areas, up to 12 percent of high school seniors report using smokeless tobacco within the past 30 days and 5 percent report using it on a daily basis. Prevalence rates for those living in rural communities are about twice as high as for those living in large cities when reporting use in the past 30 days and about ten times higher when reporting daily use.[46]

Currently, the form of smokeless tobacco showing the most consistent gains in recent sales is moist snuff, with some brands sold in cherry or wintergreen flavors. As

moist snuff: Damp, finely shredded tobacco, typically placed against the gum under the lower lip.

with cigarette tobacco, variations in the alkalinity of different brands of moist snuff allow for different percentages of the nicotine in the tobacco to be absorbed through the membranes of the mouth. Thus, snuff users typically start with brands that release relatively low levels of nicotine, then "graduate" to more potent brands. The most potent brand on the current market, Copenhagen, is also the best-selling snuff in the United States.[47]

Despite continuing warnings that smokeless tobacco presents great risk to one's health, its popularity continues. As stated earlier, while smokeless tobacco presents no immediate danger to the lungs, there are substantial adverse effects on other organs of the body. At the very least, regular use of smokeless tobacco increases the risk of gum disease, damage to tooth enamel, and eventually the loss of teeth. More seriously, the direct contact of the tobacco with membranes of the mouth allows carcinogenic nitrosamines to cause tissue changes that can lead to oral cancer. Delay in the treatment of oral cancer increases the likelihood of the cancer spreading to the jaw, pharynx, and neck. When swallowed, saliva containing nitrosamines can produce stomach and urinary tract cancer. All the negative consequences of ingesting nicotine during tobacco smoking are also present in the use of smokeless tobacco.[48]

Cigars and Flavored Cigarettes

For a brief time in the 1990s, there was a resurgence in the popularity of cigars, spurred on by images of media stars, both male and female, who had taken up cigar smoking as the tobacco use of choice. The cigar suddenly was fashionable. This is one writer's description of cigar smoking during this time:

> *Pin-striped fat cats, Wall Street wanna-bes, irony-drenched Gen-Xers and just plain folks-with-smokes crowd the wood-paneled, leather-chaired cigar bars and "humidor societies" that have popped up in just about any city you can name.*[49]

By the end of the decade, however, the cigar-smoking craze had "gone up in smoke." While part of the problem related to changing market conditions for imported cigars, a major contributing factor was the increasing recognition that cigars could not be regarded as a safe alternative to cigarettes. Cigar smoke is more alkaline than cigarette smoke, so the nicotine content in cigars can be absorbed directly through tissues lining the mouth rather than requiring inhalation into the lungs. In addition, due to the tar content, the risk of lung cancer is five times higher for those who smoke cigars, eight times higher for those smoking three or more cigars a day, and eleven times higher for those inhaling the smoke of cigars, relative to nonsmokers. Regular cigar smokers have a doubled risk, relative to nonsmokers, for cancers of the mouth, throat, and esophagus; they also incur a 45 percent higher risk of COPD and a 27 percent higher risk of coronary heart disease (Portrait). Major cigar manufacturers have now agreed to place warning labels on their products, alerting consumers to the risk of mouth and throat cancer, lung cancer and heart disease, and hazards to fertility and unborn children.[50]

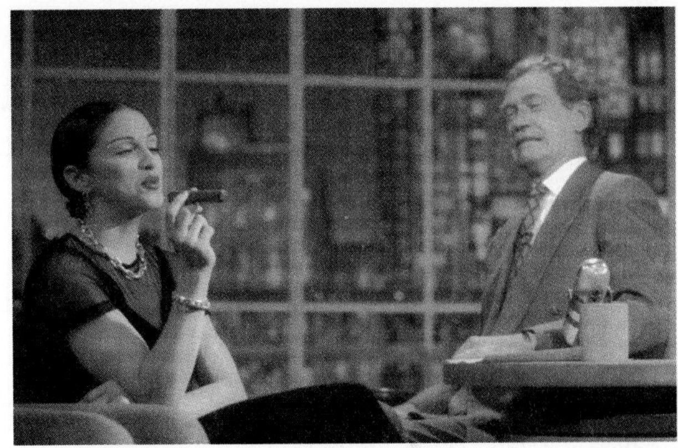

Madonna's cigar smoking on the David Letterman show reflected the glamorization of cigars in the 1990s.

More recently, another phenomenon in tobacco use is worth noting: the discovery of flavored cigarettes. Hand-rolled cigarettes from India, flavored with cinnamon, orange, strawberry, or chocolate, called *bidis* (pronounced BEE-dees), and clove-flavored cigarettes from Indonesia, called *kreteks* (pronounced KRAY-teks) have become choices among middle-school students. While only 2 percent of these young people smoke flavored cigarettes, there are significant health concerns because these tobacco products are unfiltered, contain significantly higher nicotine and tar concentrations than traditional American brands, and require more vigorous puffing, thus pulling a greater amount of smoke into the lungs.[51]

Tobacco Use around the World

Tobacco smoking has never been limited to North America, but until recently much of that smoking has been independent of American tobacco corporations. Today, the picture has changed dramatically. Overall, U.S. cigarette exports increased 200 percent from 1985 to 1991. During this brief period, cigarette exports to Japan increased more than 700 percent, from 6.5 billion cigarettes to 54 billion, and more than 1,200 percent to South Korea, from 300 million cigarettes to 4 billion. We have to recognize, however, that though the percentage of imported cigarettes

Portrait Sigmund Freud—Nicotine Dependence, Cigars, and Cancer

Probably the best-known photograph of Sigmund Freud, founder of psychoanalysis and one-time proponent of cocaine (see Chapter 4), shows him with a cigar in hand. Given that Freud typically smoked twenty cigars each day, it is not surprising that he did not set it aside merely to have his picture taken. But there is a story behind this photograph, a lesson about the power of smoking over the will to stop and the tragic health consequences when the will succumbs.

In 1923, at the age of sixty-seven, Freud noted sores on his palate and jaw that failed to heal, a sign of oral cancer. Surgery was indicated and fortunately successful in removing the cancerous tissue. This would be only the first of thirty-three surgical operations on the jaw and oral cavity that Freud was to endure for the remaining sixteen years of his life. As the leukoplakia and finally genuine carcinomas returned to his mouth, he was repeatedly warned by specialists that his practice of smoking cigars was the root of his problems and that he must stop. Despite these warnings, Freud kept on smoking.

Sigmund Freud

Freud tried very hard to stop; indeed, sometimes he would not smoke for a few weeks at a time. In addition to his problems with cancer, he suffered from chest pains called "tobacco angina." In 1936, the angina became acutely painful and as his biographer, Ernest Jones, has noted, "It was evidently exacerbated by nicotine since it was relieved as soon as he stopped smoking."

By this time, Freud's jaw had been entirely removed and an artificial jaw substituted in its place. He was almost constantly in pain, often could not speak, and sometimes could not eat or swallow. Despite the agony, Freud still smoked a steady stream of cigars until he finally died at the age of eighty-three.

Here was a man whom many consider to be one of the intellectual giants of the twentieth century. Yet the giant was a slave to his cigars.

Source: Brecher, Ruth; Brecher, Edward; Herzog, Arthur; Goodman, Walter; Walker, Gerald; and the Editors of *Consumer Reports* (1963). *The Consumer Union's report on smoking and the public interest.* Mount Vernon NY: Consumer Union, pp. 91–95.

into Asian countries has risen, the American presence still represents only a relatively small percentage of total cigarette sales in these nations.

Unfortunately, the prevalence rate of smoking in these countries far exceeds that of the United States, coupled with substantially less public concern for the consequences of smoking on health. In Japan, for example, 59 percent of all adult men smoke cigarettes (Figure 11.3). No-smoking sections in restaurants and offices are uncommon; approximately half a million outdoor vending machines allow minors to purchase cigarettes easily, though officially such sales are illegal, and there is little or no governmental opposition to smoking in general. The Japanese currently enjoy the longest life expectancy in the world, but health officials are concerned that this status is certain to change over the next twenty years. Deaths from lung, tracheal, and bronchial cancer among the Japanese have risen dramatically since 1980, and there is no indication that this trend will moderate in the future.[52]

Perhaps nowhere in the world is the impact of cigarette smoking on public health more evident than in present-day China. Because of its huge population, an estimated 300 million Chinese smokers, out of a population of 900 million adults, accounts for 30 percent of the world's total consumption of tobacco. Approximately 61 percent of all Chinese men smoke regularly, as do approximately 7 percent of all Chinese women. This disparity, however, is rapidly shrinking, and overall prevalence rates will surely climb as more young Chinese women begin to view smoking as a symbol of independence and power.

On the basis of these figures, the World Health Organization predicts that more than 2 million Chinese will die of tobacco-related illnesses annually by the year 2025, nearly four times the number in 1997. By the middle of the twenty-first century, if current trends continue, the annual death toll will reach 3 million. Presently, high import tariffs on American cigarettes have kept the Chinese tobacco market almost completely controlled by government-owned tobacco companies, but American tobacco companies may play a larger role in the future if trade policies change.[53]

Quitting Smoking: The Good News and the Bad

Given the grim story of all the documented health risks associated with tobacco, it is at least reassuring to know that if a smoker does succeed in quitting, some of the damage can be undone. Here are the benefits:

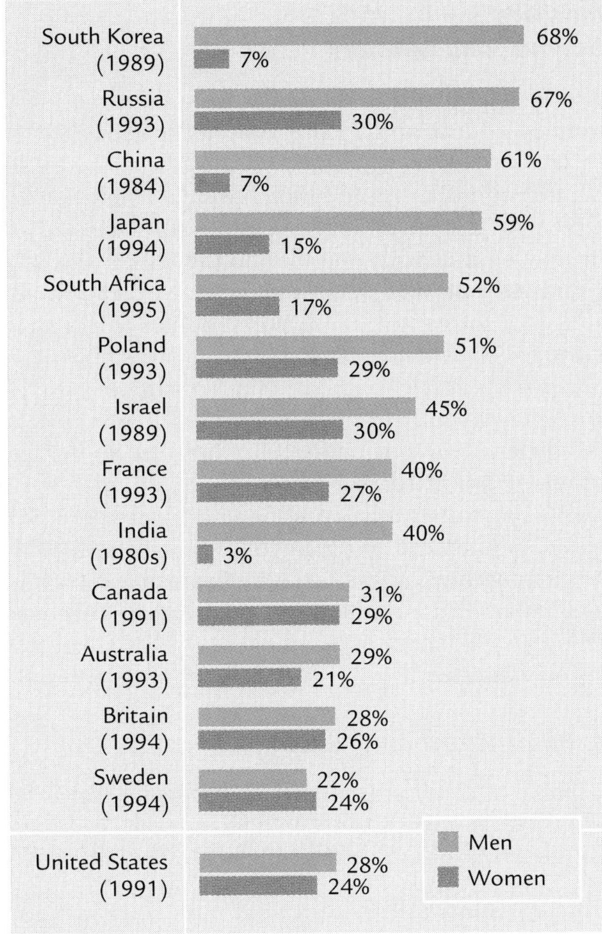

FIGURE 11.3

Smoking rates for men and women over fifteen years old in selected countries.
Source: World Health Organization. Copyright © 1997 by The New York Times Company. Reprinted by permission.

- Within 8 hours—Carbon monoxide levels in the blood drop to normal.
- Within 24 hours—Chances of a heart attack decrease.
- Within 2 weeks to 3 months—Circulation improves. Lung function increases by up to 30 percent.
- Within 1 to 9 months—Coughing, sinus congestion, fatigue, and shortness of breath decrease. Cilia regain normal function in the lungs, increasing ability to handle mucus, clean the lungs, and reduce infection.
- Within 1 year—Excess risk of coronary heart disease is half that of a smoker's.
- Within 5 to 10 years—Risk of stroke is reduced to that of a nonsmoker's.
- Within 10 years—Lung cancer death rate is about half that of a continuing smoker's.
- Within 15 years—Risk of coronary heart disease is equal to that of a nonsmoker's.[54]

The Bad News: How Hard It Is to Quit

The advantages of quitting are real and most people are aware of them, but the fact remains that, in the words of the surgeon general's report in 1988, "The pharmacologic and behavioral processes that determine tobacco addiction are similar to those that determine addiction to drugs such as heroin and cocaine."[55] It may be easy to quit smoking for a short while but it is very difficult to avoid a relapse, as any former or present smoker will tell you.

Yet millions of people do manage to quit and remain abstinent from smoking for at least a year. The estimated number of Americans who have done so exceeds 50 million, nearly half of all living adults who ever smoked in their lives. Research studies on smoking cessation indicate that there are no gender differences with regard to the likelihood that a person will quit smoking for one to four years, though men are more likely than women to have been abstinent for five years or more. The fact that a higher level of smoking is consistently related to a lower level of education and family income makes it vital that smoking-cessation programs be available to those who ordinarily would not be able to afford them. Unfortunately, smoking rates among people who did not complete high school have decreased more slowly since the 1970s than those among college graduates.[56]

The options available to smokers who want to quit are numerous. In addition to behaviorally oriented social support groups (Smokers Anonymous, SmokeEnders, Smoke-Stoppers), individual counseling, hypnosis, and acupuncture, specific prescription drugs can help reduce the withdrawal symptoms and feelings of nicotine craving. One example is a sustained-release form of the antidepressant drug bupropion. Originally marketed as a treatment for depression under the name Wellbutrin, it was approved by the FDA in 1997 for use as an aid for smoking cessation and renamed Zyban when marketed for this purpose. Doctors recommend taking Zyban daily for a week prior to the last cigarette in order to allow drug levels to build up in the bloodstream and buffer the loss of nicotine when smoking stops. About 44 percent of individuals taking Zyban have refrained from smoking after seven weeks, and 23 percent remain so after one year, roughly twice the percentage of those who receive a placebo. Since 1999, the costs of all prescription medications and quit-smoking programs have been tax-deductible as medical expenses.[57]

Health Line: Ten Tips on How to Succeed When Trying to Quit Smoking

- Choose a quit date and stick to it.
- Remember that you are dependent, physiologically and psychologically, on nicotine and that the first few days without cigarettes will be the hardest.
- Change the habits that are associated with smoking. If you have had a cigarette with your morning coffee, drink orange juice instead.
- Tell all the people you know that you are quitting and ask for their support.
- Drink lots of water and brush your teeth frequently to rid yourself of the taste of tobacco.
- Never carry matches or a lighter with you. Put away your ashtrays or fill them with something else.
- Spend time with people who don't smoke.
- Keep a supply of sugarless gum, celery sticks, or hard candy on hand to use as a cigarette substitute.
- If you have an uncontrollable urge to light up, take ten deep breaths instead. Hold the last breath, then exhale slowly, and tell yourself you have just had a cigarette.
- Think about all the money you are saving by not buying cigarettes. A simple calculation will convince you that the amount saved in five years from just a moderate level of smoking (say half a pack a day) is more than $2,000.

Source: Updated from American Cancer Society (1986). *Breaking free.* Atlanta: American Cancer Society, p. 9.

Nicotine Gums, Patches, Sprays, and Inhalers

The long-term goal in quitting smoking is to withdraw from dependence-producing nicotine altogether and to be totally free of any hazard associated with tobacco. In the meantime, however, it is possible to employ an alternate route of ingestion for nicotine that avoids inhaling carbon monoxide and tar into the lungs. Chewing gum containing nicotine (brand name: Nicorette), available since the early 1970s as a prescription drug, is now marketed on a nonprescription basis. Transdermal nicotine patches are marketed on a nonprescription basis as well. Prescription nicotine-substitute options include a nasal spray (brand name: Nicotrol NS) and an oral inhalation system (brand name: Nicotrol Inhaler) in which nicotine is inhaled from a cartridge through a plastic mouthpiece. With any of these nicotine-substitute approaches, behavioral counseling is advised while nicotine levels are gradually reduced. Behavioral counseling greatly increases the smoker's chance of becoming an ex-smoker.[58]

A Final Word on Quitting

It should be emphasized, however, that approximately 90 percent of all smokers who quit do so on their own, without any professional or outside help, by simply quitting cold turkey and deciding to forgo all cigarettes in the future. Abrupt and total withdrawal from nicotine produces withdrawal symptoms that subside more quickly and are no worse than those experienced after a gradual withdrawal.[59] It is when these efforts have failed that alternative ap-

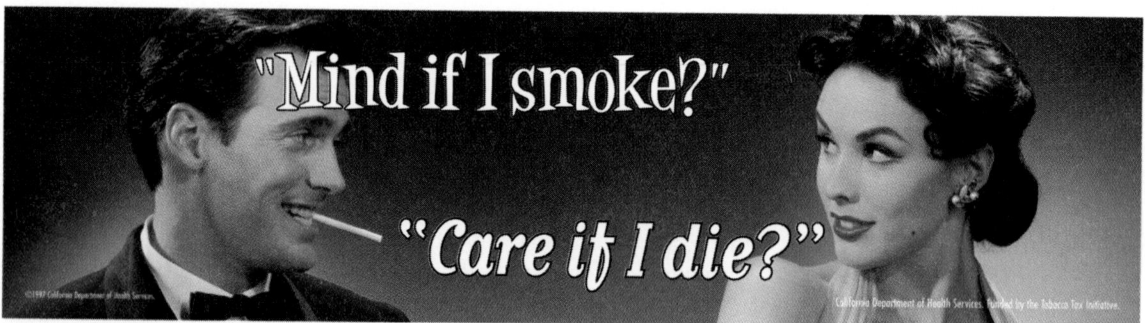

Part of California's antismoking campaign, this billboard focuses on the dangers of environmental tobacco smoke. Researchers have found that this approach reduces the desire among adolescents to start smoking.

Source: California Department of Health Services.

proaches need to be considered. Health professionals emphasize that if one treatment strategy does not work out, the smoker should try another. The long-term consequences of failure are just too great (Health Line). The best option, of course, is never to start in the first place, which brings us back to the teenage years, when virtually all adult smokers pick up the habit. The challenge in this area of public health, as we begin the twenty-first century, will be the communication of effective messages that prevent the initiation of cigarette smoking as well as other forms of tobacco use by young people (see Chapter 18).[60]

SUMMARY

Tobacco through History

- Tobacco use originated among the original inhabitants of North and South America, and its introduction to Europe and the rest of the world dates from the first voyage of Columbus. Europeans used tobacco initially in the form of pipe smoking and later in the form of snuff.
- In the nineteenth-century United States, the most popular form was tobacco chewing and later cigar smoking. It was not until the late nineteenth century and early twentieth century that cigarette smoking became popular.

Health Concerns and Smoking Behavior

- The 1964 surgeon general's report, the first official statement on the connection between smoking and adverse health consequences, produced a general reversal in the previously climbing per capita consumption of cigarettes.
- Since 1964, the surgeon general's reports have solidified the position that nicotine is a clearly addicting component of tobacco and that tobacco use, whether in a smoked or smokeless form, causes significant health risks.
- Since 1964, there has been increased use of filtered, low-tar, and low-nicotine cigarettes.

Tobacco Today: An Industry on the Defensive

- Since the early 1990s, most U.S. states, cities, and communities have enacted laws mandating smoke-free environments in all public and private workplaces. It is now typical for restaurants, hotels, and other commercial spaces to be at least partially smoke-free.
- Additional pressure on the tobacco industry has come from proposals to increase the federal excise tax on tobacco products.
- Increased public pressure since the mid-1990s has resulted in a greatly limited marketing approach for tobacco products, particularly with respect to sales to young people.
- In 1998, the major American tobacco corporations entered into a $246 billion settlement agreement with all 50 U.S. states to resolve claims that the states should be compensated for the costs of treating people with smoking-related illnesses.

What's in Tobacco?

- The principal ingredients consumed during the smoking of tobacco are nicotine, tar, and carbon monoxide.
- The smoker inhales smoke in the form of mainstream smoke (through the cigarette itself) and sidestream smoke (released from the cigarette tip into the air).

The Dependence Potential of Nicotine

- Nicotine ingestion produces both tolerance effects and physical withdrawal symptoms. A prominent feature of nicotine withdrawal is the strong feeling of craving for a return to tobacco use.
- Smokers typically adjust their smoking behavior to obtain a stable dose of nicotine.

Health Consequences from Tobacco Use

- Tobacco smoking produces an increased risk of cardiovascular disease such as coronary heart disease and stroke, lung cancer and other forms of cancer, and respiratory diseases such as chronic bronchitis and emphysema.

- In addition to the hazards to the smoker through the inhalation of mainstream smoke, there are hazards to the developing fetus when the mother is smoking and hazards to nonsmokers who inhale sidestream smoke (environmental tobacco smoke).

Patterns of Smoking Behavior and Use of Smokeless Tobacco

- In the late 1990s, the prevalence rate for smoking in the United States was approximately 26 percent.
- The peak years for smokers to start are in the sixth and seventh grades of school.
- A disturbingly high percentage of students think that cigarette smoking does not present "great risk" to their health, despite well-publicized information regarding adverse affects.
- A global trend of unabated smoking rates in Japan, China, and elsewhere threatens the future health of huge populations of people worldwide.

Quitting Smoking: The Good News and the Bad

- Research has clearly shown that when people quit smoking, many health risks diminish rapidly. Unfortunately, nicotine dependence is very strong, and it is difficult to quit smoking permanently.
- Present-day approaches toward smoking cessation include behavioral treatment programs, hypnosis, acupuncture, and prescription drugs to reduce withdrawal symptoms and craving, as well as a variety of nicotine substitutes.

KEY TERMS

arteriosclerosis, p. 243
atherosclerosis, p. 243
carbon monoxide, p. 240
carcinomas, p. 245
chronic bronchitis, p. 243
chronic obstructive pulmonary disease (COPD), p. 243
cigarettes, p. 236
cigars, p. 236
cilia, p. 240
ciliary escalator, p. 240
coronary heart disease (CHD), p. 243
emphysema, p. 243
environmental tobacco smoke (ETS), p. 238
erythroplakia, p. 245
gaseous phase, p. 240
leukoplakia, p. 245
mainstream smoke, p. 239
moist snuff, p. 248
nicotine, p. 241
nitrosamines, p. 245
particulate phase, p. 240
sidestream smoke, p. 238
snuff, p. 235
snuffing, p. 235
tar, p. 240
titration hypothesis, p. 242

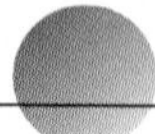

ENDNOTES

1. Brooks, Jerome E. (1952). *The mighty leaf: Tobacco through the centuries.* Boston: Little, Brown, pp. 11–14. Fairholt, Frederick W. (1859). *Tobacco: Its history and associations.* London: Chapman and Hill, p. 13.
2. Brooks, *The mighty leaf,* pp. 74–80. White, Jason M. (1991). *Drug dependence.* Englewood Cliffs NJ: Prentice Hall, pp. 32–33.
3. Austin, Gregory A. (1978). *Perspectives on the history of psychoactive substance use.* Rockville MD: National Institute on Drug Abuse, pp. 1–12.
4. Brooks, *The mighty leaf,* p. 181. Lehman Brothers (1955). *About tobacco.* New York: Lehman Brothers, pp. 18–20.
5. Quotation from Dickens, Charles (1842). *American notes.* Cited in Brooks, *The mighty leaf,* pp. 215–216.
6. Tate, Cassandra (1989). In the 1800s, antismoking was a burning issue. *Smithsonian, 20* (4), 111.
7. Quotation originally in Bain, John, and Werner, Carl (1905). *Cigarettes in fact and fancy.* Boston: H. M. Caldwell. Cited in Brooks, *The mighty leaf,* p. 259.
8. Kluger, Richard (1996). *Ashes to ashes: America's hundred-year cigarette war, the public health, and the "unabashed" triumph of Philip Morris.* New York: Knopf. Lehman Brothers, *About tobacco,* pp. 24–27. Slade, John (1992). The tobacco epidemic: Lessons from history. *Journal of Psychoactive Drugs, 24,* 99–109.
9. Lehman Brothers, *About tobacco,* p. 30.
10. Ibid., p. 31.
11. U.S. Department of Health and Human Services (1991). *Strategies to control tobacco use in the United States: A blueprint for public health action in the 1990s* (NIH Smoking and Tobacco Control Monograph No. 1). Bethesda MD: National Cancer Institute.

12. Federal Trade Commission Report to Congress (1992). Pursuant to the Federal Cigarette Labeling and Advertising Act, p. 31.
13. Short, J. Gordon (1990, fall). The golden leaf. *Priorities*, p. 10.
14. Gerstein, Dean R., and Levison, Peter K. (Eds.) (1982). *Reduced tar and nicotine cigarettes: Smoking behavior and health.* Washington DC: National Academy Press. Mann, Charles K. (1975). *Tobacco: The ants and the elephants.* Salt Lake City UT: Olympus Publishing, pp. 91–109.
15. Meier, Barry (1998, November 14). Cigarette makers and states draft a $206 billion deal. *New York Times*, pp. A1, A9.
16. Biskupic, Joan (2000, March 22). FDA can't regulate tobacco, Supreme Court rules 5 to 4. *Washington Post*, p. A1. Greenhouse, Linda (1999, December 2). Justices skeptical of U.S. effort for jurisdiction over cigarettes. *New York Times*, pp. A1, A32.
17. Alcoholic beverages and tobacco (1997, September 11). *Standard and Poor's Industry Surveys*, p. 10. Cox, Matthew (1999, December 18). Cigarette tax hike deal: Health plan calls for 55-cent jump. *Newsday*, p. A5.
18. Payne, Wayne A., and Hahn, Dale B. (1992). *Understanding your health.* St. Louis: Mosby Year Book, p. 270.
19. Schlaadt, Richard G. (1992). *Tobacco and health.* Guilford CT: Dushkin Publishing, p. 41.
20. Gahagan, Dolly D. (1987). *Switch down and quit: What the cigarette companies don't want you to know about smoking.* Berkeley CA: Ten Speed Press, p. 44. Payne and Hahn, *Understanding your health*, pp. 273–275.
21. Jacobs, Michael R., and Fehr, Kevin O'B. (1987). *Drugs and drug abuse: A reference text* (2nd ed.). Toronto: Addiction Research Foundation, pp. 417–425. Julien, Robert M. (2001). *A primer of drug action* (9th ed.). New York: Worth, p. 229.
22. Meier, Barry (1998, February 23). Cigarette maker manipulated nicotine, its records suggest. *New York Times*, pp. A1, A15. Pankow, J. F.; Mader, B. T.; Isabelle, L. M.; Luo, W. T.; Pavlick, A.; and Liang, C. K. (1997). Conversion of nicotine and tobacco smoke to its volatile and available free-base form through the action of gaseous ammonia. *Environmental Science & Technology*, *31*, 2428–2433. Schmitz, Joy M., Schneider, Nina G., and Jarvik, Murray E. (1997). Nicotine. In Joyce H. Lowinson, Pedro Ruiz, Robert B. Millman, and John G. Langrod (Eds.), *Substance abuse: A comprehensive textbook.* Baltimore: Williams and Wilkins, pp. 276–294.
23. American Lung Association (1989). *Facts about . . . nicotine addiction and cigarettes.* New York: American Lung Association. Julien, *A primer of drug action*, p. 231. Parrott, Andy C. (1999). Does cigarette smoking *cause* stress? *American Psychologist*, *54*, 817–820. Phillips, Sarah, and Fox, Pauline (1998). An investigation into the effects of nicotine gum on short-term memory. *Psychopharmacology*, *140*, 429–433. Schuckit, Marc A. (1995). *Drug and alcohol abuse: A clinical guide to diagnosis and treatment* (4th ed.). New York: Plenum, p. 260.
24. Brecher, Edward M., and the editors of *Consumer Reports* (1972). *Licit and illicit drugs.* Boston: Little, Brown, pp. 220–228.
25. Pontieri, Francesco E.; Tanda, Gianluigi; Orzi, Francesco; and DiChiara, Gaetano (1996). Effects of nicotine on the nucleus accumbens and similarity to those of addictive drugs. *Science*, *382*, 255–257.
26. Lichtenstein, Edward, and Brown, Richard A. (1980). Smoking cessation methods: Review and recommendations. In William R. Miller (Ed.), *The addictive behaviors: Treatment of alcoholism, drug abuse, smoking, and obesity.* New York: Pergamon Press, pp. 169–206. Quotation on p. 173.
27. Ibid., pp. 172–173.
28. Herning, Ronald I., Jones, Reese T., and Fischman, Patricio (1985). The titration hypothesis revisited: Nicotine gum reduces smoking intensity. In John Grabowski and Sharon M. Hall (Eds.), *Pharmacological adjuncts in smoking cessation* (NIDA Research Monograph 53). Rockville MD: National Institute on Drug Abuse, pp. 27–41. Jarvik, Murray E. (1979). Biological influences on cigarette smoking. In Norman A. Krasnegor (Ed.), *The behavioral aspects of smoking* (NIDA Research Monograph 26). Rockville MD: National Institute on Drug Abuse, pp. 7–45.
29. Jarvik, Biological influences, pp. 25–29. Schuckit, *Drugs and alcohol abuse*, pp. 264–265.
30. Koslowski, Lynn T.; Wilkinson, Adrian; Skinner, Wayne; Kent, Carl; Franklin, Tom; and Pope, Marilyn. (1989). Comparing tobacco cigarette dependence with other drug dependencies. *Journal of the American Medical Association*, *261*, 898–901.
31. Julien, *A primer of drug action*, p. 236. Roper, W. L. (1991). Making smoking prevention a reality. *Journal of the American Medical Association*, *266*, 3188–3189.
32. Ayanian, John Z., and Cleary, Paul D. (1999). Perceived risks of heart disease and cancer among cigarette smokers. *Journal of the American Medical Association*, *281*, 1019–1021. Howard, George; Wagenknecht, Lynne E.; Burke, Gregory L.; Diez-Roux, Ana; Evans, Gregory W.; McGovern, Paul; Nieto, Javier; and Tell, Grethe S. (1998). Cigarette smoking and progression of atherosclerosis. *Journal of the American Medical Association*, *279*, 119–124. U.S. Department of Health and Human Services, Public Health Service, Office of Smoking and Health (1983). *The health consequences of smoking: Cardiovascular disease* (A report of the surgeon general) Rockville MD: U.S. Public Health Service, pp. 63–156.
33. Payne and Hahn, *Understanding your health*, pp. 272–273.
34. Schlaadt, *Tobacco and health*, p. 52.
35. Gold, Diane R.; Wang, Xiaobin; Wypij, David; Speizer, Frank E.; Ware, James H.; and Dockery, Douglas W. (1996). Effects of cigarette smoking on lung function in adolescent boys and girls. *New England Journal of Medicine*, *335*, 931–937. U.S. Department of Health and Human Services, Public Health Service, Office of Smoking and Health (1984). *The health consequences of smoking: Chronic obstructive lung disease* (A report of the surgeon general). Rockville MD: U.S. Public Health Service, pp. 329–360.
36. American Cancer Society (1998). *Trends in lung cancer rates, 1974–1994.* Atlanta: American Cancer Society. Denissenko, Mikhail F.; Pao, Annie; Tang, Moon-Shong; and

Pfeifer, Gerd P. (1996). Preferential formation of benzopyrene adducts at lung cancer mutational hotspots in *P53. Science, 274,* 430–432.

37. Schuckit, *Drug and alcohol abuse,* pp. 267–268.
38. U.S. Department of Health and Human Services, Public Health Service, Office of Smoking and Health (1980). *The health consequences of smoking for women* (A report of the surgeon general). Rockville MD: U.S. Public Health Service, pp. 98–101.
39. Davis, Ronald M. (1998). Exposure to environmental tobacco smoke: Identifying and protecting those at risk. *Journal of the American Medical Association, 280,* 1947–1949. Ginzel, K. H. (1992). The ill-effects of second hand smoke. In Kristine Napier (Ed.), *Issues in tobacco.* New York: American Council on Science and Health, pp. 6–7.
40. Fielding, Jonathan E., and Phenow, Kenneth J. (1989). *Health effects of involuntary smoking.* Atlanta GA: American Cancer Society. Kawachi, Ichiro; Colditz, Graham A.; Speizer, Frank E.; Manson, JoAnn E.; Stampfer, Meir J.; Willett, Walter C.; and Hennekens, Charles H. (1997). A prospective study of passive smoking and coronary heart disease. *Circulation, 95,* 2374–2379. Nafstad, Per; Fugelseth, Drude; Qvigstad, Erik; Zahlsen, Kolbjørn; Magnus, Per, and Lindenmann, Rolf (1998). Nicotine concentration in the hair of nonsmoking mothers and size of offspring. *American Journal of Public Health, 88,* 120–124.
41. Rigotti, Nancy A., Lee, Jae Eun, and Wechsler, Henry (2000). U.S. college students' use of tobacco products. *Journal of the American Medical Association, 284,* 699–705. Substance Abuse and Mental Health Services Administration (2000). *Summary of findings from the 1999 National household survey on drug abuse.* Rockville MD: Substance Abuse and Mental Health Services Administration, Office of Applied Studies, Tables G.21, G.22. Wechsler, Henry, Rigotti, Nancy A., and Gledhill-Hoyt, Jeana (1998). Increased levels of cigarette use among college students: A cause for national concern. *Journal of the American Medical Association, 280,* 1673–1678.
42. Johnston, Lloyd D. (2000, December 14). Cigarette use and smokeless tobacco use decline substantially among teens. News release from the University of Michigan, Ann Arbor, Table 1.
43. Centers for Disease Control and Prevention (2000, January 28). Tobacco use among middle and high school students—United States, 1999. *Morbidity and Mortality Weekly Report, 49,* 49–52. Johnston, Cigarette use, Table 1. Johnston, Lloyd D., O'Malley, Patrick M., and Bachman, Jerald G. (1999). *National survey results on drug use from the Monitoring the Future Study, 1975–1998.* Bethesda MD: National Institute on Drug Abuse, Table 6-1.
44. Johnston, Cigarette use, Table 4.
45. Emmons, Karen M.; Wechsler, Henry; Dowdall, George; and Abraham, Melissa (1998). Predictors of smoking among U.S. college students. *American Journal of Public Health, 88,* 104–107. Pierce, John P.; Choi, Won S.; Gilpin, Elizabeth A.; Farkas, Arthur J.; and Berry, Charles C. (1998). Tobacco industry promotional cigarettes and adolescent smoking. *Journal of the American Medical Association, 279,* 511–515. Rigotti, Nancy A.; DiFranza, Joseph R.; Chang, YuChiao; Tisdale, Thelma; Kemp, Becky; and Singer, Daniel E. (1997). The effect of enforcing tobacco-sales laws on adolescents' access to tobacco and smoking behavior. *New England Journal of Medicine, 337,* 1044–1057.
46. Johnston, O'Malley, and Bachman, *Monitoring the Future,* Tables 4-7 and 4-8.
47. Freedman, Alix M. How a tobacco giant doctors snuff brands to boost their "kick." (1994, October 26). *Wall Street Journal,* pp. A1, A14.
48. Boyle, Raymond G.; Stilwell, Jean; Vidlak, Lori M.; and Huneke, Joleen T. (1999). "Ready to quit chew?" Smokeless tobacco cessation in rural Nebraska. *Addictive Behaviors, 24,* 293–297. U.S. Department of Health and Human Services, Public Health Service, Office of Smoking and Health (1986). *The health consequences of smokeless tobacco* (A report of the advisory committee to the surgeon general). Rockville MD: Public Health Service.
49. Hamilton, Kendall (1997, July 21). Blowing smoke. *Newsweek,* pp. 54–60. Quotation on p. 56.
50. Ackerman, Elise (1999, November 29). The cigar boom goes up in smoke. *Newsweek,* p. 55. Baker, Frank, et al. (2000). Health risks associated with cigar smoking. *Journal of the American Medical Association, 284,* 735–740. Brody, Jane (1996, May 29). Personal health: Smokescreen of glamour hides dangers of cigars. *New York Times,* p. C9. Henderson, Charles W. (2000, March 6). Cigars increase risk fivefold. *Health Letter on the CDC,* NewsRx.com.
51. Noble, Holcomb B. (2000, January 28). One of eight middle-school students has smoked or chewed tobacco, survey finds. *New York Times,* p. A20. Small Indian cigarettes light up teen smokers (1999, May 11). *Newsday,* p. A49.
52. American Cancer Society. *Cancer facts and figures 1993,* p. 22. Sterngold, James (1993, October 17). When smoking is a patriotic duty. *New York Times,* Sect. 3, pp. 1, 6. Watts, Jonathan (1999). Smoking, sake, and suicide: Japan plans a healthier future. *The Lancet, 354,* p. 843.
53. Collins, Glenn (1998, November 20). U.S. tobacco industry looks longingly at Chinese market, but in vain. *New York Times,* p. A16. Rosenthal, Elisabeth, and Altman, Lawrence K. (1998, November 30). China, a land of heavy smokers, looks into abyss of fatal illness. *New York Times,* pp. A1, A16. Tyler, Patrick E. (1996, March 16). In heavy smoking, grim portent for China. *New York Times,* pp. 1, 5. Yuan, Jian-Min; Ross, Ronald K.; Wang, Xue-Li; Gao, Yu-Tang; Henderson, Brian E.; and Yu, Mimi C. (1996). Morbidity and mortality in relation to cigarette smoking in Shanghai, China: A prospective male cohort study. *Journal of the American Medical Association, 275,* 1646–1650.
54. American Cancer Society, Atlanta. Cited in *The world almanac and book of facts 2000* (1999). Mahwah NJ: Primedia Reference, p. 733.

55. U.S. Department of Health and Human Services, Public Health Service, Office of Smoking and Health (1988). *The health consequences of smoking: Nicotine addiction* (A report of the surgeon general). Rockville MD: Public Health Service, p. 9.
56. Ehrich, Beverly, and Emmons, Karen M. (1994). Addressing the needs of smokers in the 1990s. *The Behavior Therapist, 17* (6), 119–122. U.S. Department of Health and Human Services, Public Health Service, Office of Smoking and Health (1990). *The health benefits of smoking cessation* (A report of the surgeon general). Atlanta: Office of Smoking and Health, pp. 610–611.
57. Benowitz, Neal L. (1997). Treating tobacco addiction—Nicotine or no nicotine? *New England Journal of Medicine,* 337, 1230–1231. Smoking treatments deductible (1999, June 11). *Newsday,* p. A66.
58. Fiscella, Kevin, and Franks, Peter (1996). Cost-effectiveness of the transdermal nicotine patch as an adjunct to physician's smoking cessation counseling. *Journal of the American Medical Association,* 275, 1247–1251. Hughes, John R.; Goldstein, Michael G.; Hurt, Richard D.; and Shiffman, Saul (1999). Recent advances in the pharmacotherapy of smoking. *Journal of the American Medical Association, 281,* 72–76. Noble, Holcomb B. (1999, March 2). New from the war to stop smoking: Success. *New York Times,* pp. F1–F2.
59. Jarvik, Biological influences, p. 32.
60. Goldman, Lisa K., and Glantz, Stanton A. (1999). Evaluation of antismoking advertising campaigns. *Journal of the American Medical Association,* 279, 772–777.

CHAPTER 12

Caffeine

After you have completed this chapter, you will understand

- The sources of caffeine: coffee, tea, chocolate, soft drinks, and medications
- How coffee is decaffeinated
- The effects of caffeine on the body
- The effects of caffeine on human behavior and performance
- Health considerations when consuming caffeine
- The medical uses of theophylline
- The effects of caffeine on kids

For a while, Steve couldn't understand why he was suffering those headaches. Every Saturday afternoon, sometimes earlier in the day, he would get a pounding headache and feel grumpy and out of sorts. Then it occurred to him. On the weekends at home, he was able to sleep late and drank decaffeinated coffee instead of his regular brew at the office. He realized that he was going through caffeine withdrawal. I had better cut down, he said to himself. Or switch to regular on the weekends.

If you enjoy a cup of caffeinated coffee or caffeinated tea, a wedge of chocolate, or a glass of some soft drink, you may be surprised to know that you are engaging in the most popular form of drug-taking behavior in the world. To varying degrees, all these products contain caffeine, a psychoactive stimulant drug. It should be added, however, that you need not be overly concerned. Among the range of psychoactive stimulants that exist (the major ones were examined in Chapters 4 and 11), caffeine is considerably weaker than most and the research shows that it is relatively benign. Nonetheless, as will be shown, caffeine can be a dependence-producing drug, and several precautions against its use should be heeded.

Caffeine belongs to a family of stimulant compounds called **xanthines.** Two other major examples of xanthines, **theobromine** (found in chocolate) and **theophylline** (found in small amounts in tea), also have stimulating effects. In general, theophylline and caffeine have approximately equal stimulatory effects; theobromine is only about one-tenth as strong. The focus of this chapter will be on what we know about caffeine itself, beginning with a look at three natural sources of caffeine: coffee, tea, and chocolate.

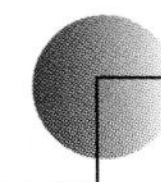

Coffee

We do not know exactly when coffee drinking began, but we do know that the plant ***Coffea arabica,*** from which coffee beans were first harvested, originated in Ethiopia, and its cultivation spread to Yemen and Arabia at some time between the eleventh and the fifteenth century. Coffee has been called "the wine of Islam," suggesting that it was viewed as a substitute for alcoholic beverages, which are forbidden by the Koran. A popular legend concerning the beginnings of coffee drinking has it that a young Yemenite or Ethiopian goatherd named Khaldi, while tending his flock, noticed that his goats were unusually hyperactive and unable to sleep after nibbling some red berries in the field. Khaldi tried some himself and, on feeling as exhilarated as his goats, took the berries to the local Islamic monastery. The chief holy man there prepared a beverage from these berries and found the effect to be so invigorating that he was able to stay awake during a long night of prayers in the mosque. According to this legend, the fame of the "wakeful monastery" and its remarkable potion spread through the whole kingdom and to other countries of the region.[1]

At first, coffee was banned on religious grounds because some Islamic clerics considered it to be as much an intoxicant as an alcoholic beverage, but the disputes were eventually settled and coffee drinking became a fixture of daily life. In the words of one historian, "The growth of coffee and its use as a national beverage became as inseparably connected with Arabia as tea is with China."[2]

Coffee in Britain and North America

The practice of coffee drinking reached England in the middle of the seventeenth century, just in time to be associated with one of the most turbulent periods of political, social, economic, and religious unrest in its history. Establishments specializing in the sale of coffee, known as coffee houses, became the sites of heated debates about the great issues of the day. The idea of constitutional self-government, the divine right of the monarchs to rule their countries, and religious feuds between English Catholics and Protestants were some of these social questions.

It was in coffee houses that intellectuals met and argued their respective points of view. In fact, until the end of the eighteenth century, when tea began to replace coffee as the dominant British drink, coffee was the principal alternative social beverage to alcohol. The British coffee house enjoyed the reputation of being a place where men (women rarely frequented them, though they often managed them) could socialize with one another and enjoy a nonintoxicating beverage in sober company. The emphasis was on keeping a clear head, which was certainly not likely after an hour or two at the local tavern. In fact, historians have credited coffee houses with helping to moderate the widespread drunkenness that was rampant as a result of the "gin epidemic" in England during the 1700s (see Chapter 9). A popular nickname for coffee houses was penny universities, since the conversation there was considered to be as stimulating as a university education and a lot cheaper.[3]

caffeine: A xanthine stimulant found in coffee, tea, chocolate, soft drinks, and several medications.

xanthines (ZAN-theens): A family of CNS stimulant drugs that includes caffeine, theophylline, and theobromine.

theobromine (THEE-oh-BROH-meen): A xanthine stimulant found in chocolate.

theophylline (THEE-oho-FILL-lin): A xanthine stimulant found in small amounts in tea. It is used as an anti-asthma medication.

Coffea arabica (air-ah-BEE-kah): A type of coffee bean native to the Middle East but now grown principally in South America. It is typically referred to simply as arabica.

Coffee houses in colonial America served a similar purpose. One such political gathering place, the Green Dragon in Boston, was the setting for the meetings of John Adams, Paul Revere, and their compatriots as they planned their strategy against the British. After the Revolutionary War, coffee emerged as the American national drink, especially after 1830 when alcohol consumption began to decline (see Chapter 9). During the settling of the American frontier, coffee was an indispensable provision for the long trek westward. By 1860, Americans were consuming three-fourths of the world's entire production of coffee.

Today, the United States remains the world's top importer of coffee, with about one-half originating in Brazil and Colombia. However, U.S. per capita coffee consumption ranks only in the top twenty among nations of the world, behind most countries of Western Europe and Scandinavia. Since roughly 1960, coffee consumption has gradually declined as American drinking habits have shifted to an increased consumption of colas, particularly among young adults. If present trends continue, cola drinks will soon surpass coffee as the country's primary source of caffeine. In the meantime, the types of coffee that Americans consume have become more and more sophisticated. As one writer has put it:

> *. . .We no longer boil grounds campfire style or percolate them genteel style in the pot. And we have a taster's dream choice of beans, roasts, grinds, and brewing equipment. Even our lingo has changed—from "Gimme a cuppa joe" to "Give me an iced short schizo skinny hazelnut cappuccino with wings." (Translation: a small iced hazelnut coffee with one shot of regular and one of decaf, plus skim milk with foam, to go.)*[4]

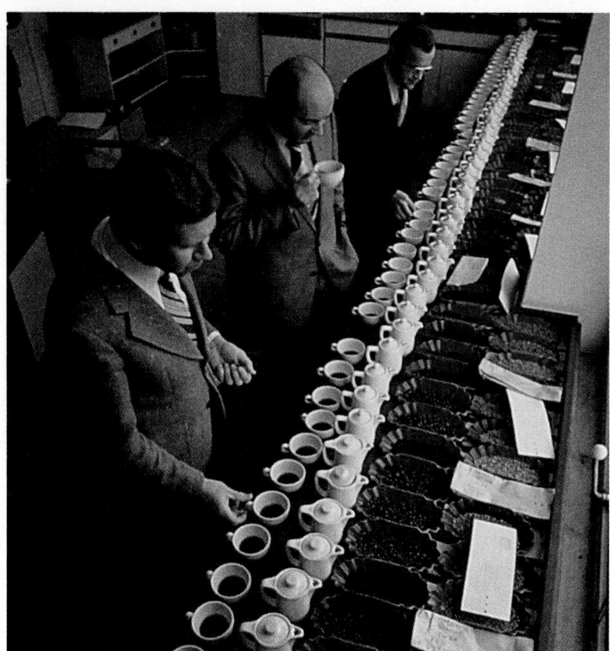

Expert coffee tasters in a German coffee company sample the possibilities before deciding on a particular blend.

Major Sources of Coffee

Two species of coffee beans dominate the world market. *Coffea arabica*, the original coffee bean as far as Westerners are concerned, is grown mostly in Brazil and Colombia, having been brought to South America by the French in the early 1700s. Another major species, ***Coffea robusta***, is grown primarily in formerly Dutch plantations on the Indonesian island of Java (hence, the popular phrase "a cup of Java" for a drink of coffee); some is also produced in Brazil and the Ivory Coast and other countries in Africa. *Coffee arabica* beans represent about 70 percent of the world's coffee production.

Coffee blends are generally combinations of these two types of beans, with the ratio dictated by local tastes and economic concerns. Robusta beans are considered by coffee experts to be inferior to arabica beans because of their relatively harsher taste, but robusta beans have approximately twice the caffeine content and are cheaper to buy.

How Coffee Is Made

The preparation of today's coffee begins by separating the coffee bean from the ripened berry of the coffee plant, which is accomplished in two basic ways. The dry method is a variation of the most ancient and primitive tradition. Freshly picked berries are spread out to dry in the sun for two to three weeks or dried in special heating machines. Afterward, the dried husks are removed mechanically or by hand to yield green coffee beans. Brazilian arabica beans are prepared by the dry method, as are almost all robusta beans. If the wet method is employed, coffee berries are soaked in water for about twenty-four hours, later washed and then dried in the sun. All arabica beans, except for those grown in Brazil, are prepared by the wet method.

Which of the two methods yields better-tasting coffee is frequently debated among coffee lovers, but no one questions the fact that more can go wrong with the dry

***Coffea robusta* (row-BUS-tah):** A type of coffee bean grown principally in Indonesia, Brazil, and Africa.

method. When the berries are dried immediately after picking, the whole process takes much longer. There is a chance, for example, that a few rotting berries could impart a foul taste to other berries and ruin the crop. It is less expensive, however, and is tailored to the conditions of a less industrialized nation.

Whether it is prepared wet or dry, the result is a green coffee bean, with a shelf life of a year or more. Assuming these beans are not to be decaffeinated, the next step is roasting, in which the beans are heated to approximately 400 to 500 degrees Fahrenheit for five minutes or so. The longer the roasting time, the darker the roasted bean and the stronger the flavor once the beans are ground. According to coffee experts, roasted coffee beans reach the peak of flavor from twenty-four to seventy-two hours after roasting, depending on the variety of bean. After a week or two, roasted beans are no longer considered fresh. It is important to grind and consume the coffee, they say, within a week for optimal results.[5] These guidelines apply, of course, to coffee from beans that are sold by specialty stores; most U.S. consumers buy their coffee in vacuum-packed cans that prolong the freshness.

Instant coffee, a form of coffee that represents about a third of total U.S. coffee consumption, is made either by the spray-dried method, in which brewed coffee is dried by hot air, or by the freeze-dried method, in which brewed coffee is frozen and the water separates itself from the solids in the coffee. These solids are later granulated or converted into flakes. The freeze-dried method is the more expensive of the two, but the consensus is that it yields a better-tasting instant coffee.[6]

The Caffeine Content in Coffee

A caffeine content in a "standard" 5-ounce cup of coffee can range from about 29 to 176 milligrams (mg) depending on the method of brewing, the amount of coffee used, the brand of coffee, and the brewing time. Roughly speaking, the caffeine content in coffee can be estimated to be about 100 mg. Comparable amounts of instant coffee have about 60 mg of caffeine, percolated coffee has about 85 mg, and drip-brewed coffee has about 112 mg. Caffeine is the only xanthine found in coffee (Drugs . . . in Focus).[7]

DRUGS . . . IN FOCUS

Why There Are No (Live) Flies in Your Coffee

Chemical compounds found naturally in plants are generally there for a purpose, though it may take a while for scientists to figure out what that purpose may be. In the case of plants containing xanthines, the benefit lies in the area of insect control.

We now know that xanthines interfere with an insect's ability to feed on a plant because they increase the level of octopamine, an excitatory chemical in the nervous systems of invertebrates. As a result, contact with xanthine-containing plants causes insects to become overly stimulated and die. Fortunately, octopamine plays little or no role in mammalian nervous systems. One extra benefit in knowing how xanthines affect insects is the possibility in the future of developing xanthine-based pesticides that are effective on insects, without affecting human beings.

Source: Nathanson, James A. (1984). Caffeine and related methylxanthines: Possible naturally occurring pesticides. *Science, 226,* 184–187.

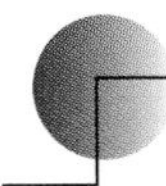

Tea

By the standard of historical records, tea is the world's oldest caffeine-containing beverage. The legendary Chinese emperor Shen Nung is credited with its discovery in 2737 B.C., along with other stimulants such as the antiasthma medication we now know as ephedrine (see Chapter 4) and marijuana (see Chapter 7). Tea is a brew of leaves from the ***Camellia sinensis*** (tea plant), a large evergreen tree that is typically trimmed back to look more like a bush. The word *sinensis* refers to its origin in China.[8]

Dutch traders brought tea from Asia to Western Europe in the early 1600s, where it met with mixed reviews. The Germans tried tea drinking for a while but then returned to beer; the French also tried it but then returned to coffee and wine. The Chinese traded directly with the Russians, who loved it and made tea drinking a national pastime, sipping hot tea from glasses through a sugar cube held between the teeth. Giant tea urns, called samovars, kept tea available for drinking throughout the day.

Tea in Britain and North America

The principal Dutch success with tea in Europe was in Britain, where it eventually became the national drink.

Camellia sinensis: The plant from which tea leaves are obtained.

Chinese tea, as noted in Chapter 5, was in such great demand by the British that the Chinese were forced to trade their tea in exchange for opium imported by the British into their own country. By 1842, the problems with this odd arrangement escalated into the Opium War, pitting China against Britain and later France and the United States.

By the end of the nineteenth century, however, China was no longer the principal source for British tea. Tastes had changed, away from the subtle flavor of Chinese green tea leaves and toward a stronger, blacker tea that was being grown in India and Ceylon (now Sri Lanka). It also did not hurt that a greater number of cups could be made from a pound of Indian or Ceylonese tea, making it more economical for the average consumer. Today's teas are blends of black tea leaves, chiefly from India, Sri Lanka, and Indonesia, though there is a growing market for green tea from China and Kenya.[9]

We do not know whether the gentlemen at the Green Dragon coffee house in Boston were drinking coffee or tea during the months of growing unrest and resentment against the British prior to the beginning of the Revolutionary War, but it is quite likely that much of the talk concerned tea. In 1773, the British government had decided to allow British agents to sell cheap tea directly to the American colonies, bypassing American tea merchants in the process. In the eyes of the Americans, the policy was another instance of British tyranny and one more reason why the colonies should be independent.

We do know what happened next. On the night of December 16, 1773, while three British ships loaded with chests of British tea lay at anchor in Boston harbor, fifty to sixty colonists, supposedly dressed as Indians (this part is disputed), boarded the vessels and proceeded to break open the tea chests and dump the contents into the water. Thus, the Boston Tea Party entered the pages of history. Strangely enough, the initial reaction to this event in British newspapers did not focus on the political ramifications but rather on the pharmacological effect of the tea on the unfortunate fish in Boston harbor. One report said that the fish "had contracted a disorder not unlike the nervous complaints of the body." Assuming this story is true, we can only conclude that all that tea had given the fish a large dose of caffeine.[10]

Largely as a result of continuing anti-British sentiment during the early history of the United States, drinking tea was viewed as unpatriotic, and coffee became the preferred beverage. Today, American consumption of tea is only approximately one-eighth that of Ireland and Great Britain, who lead the world as you might suspect in per capita tea drinking. More than 80 percent of all tea consumed in the United States is in the form of iced tea, a beverage that was introduced at the Louisiana Purchase Exposition in St. Louis in the summer of 1904.

An engraving depicting American colonists at the Boston Tea Party, 1773.

The Chemical Content in Tea

Tea contains two xanthines, caffeine and theophylline. The caffeine content of a 5-ounce cup of tea is approximately 60 mg, the same level as a comparable cup of instant coffee. This comparison, however, applies to a medium brew of tea. If the tea is a strong brew, the caffeine content approaches that of regular coffee, especially if the tea is produced in Britain rather than the United States. A strong brew of Twining's English Breakfast tea, for example, contains approximately 107 mg of caffeine, a larger dose than many regular brewed coffees and certainly greater than instant coffee.[11]

The other xanthine found in tea, theophylline, is found in much smaller concentrations than caffeine. As will be noted later, its bronchodilating effect is clinically useful for the treatment of asthma and other respiratory problems.

A recently recognized group of nonxanthine chemicals in tea, called *polyphenols,* appears to have beneficial effects in the prevention of heart disease, inflammatory disorders, and some forms of cancer. Polyphenols are plentiful in green tea and, to a lesser degree, black or pekoe tea. Although both types of tea are harvested from the *Camellia sinensis* plant, they are processed differently. Black tea leaves are fermented prior to drying, whereas green tea leaves are not. During the fermentation process, black tea loses most of its polyphenols and therefore its potential health benefits.[12]

Chocolate

Chocolate comes from **cocoa bean pods** growing directly on the trunk and thick main branches of cacao trees. Cacao trees are native to Mexico and Central America, but now they are grown in tropical regions of the Caribbean, South America, Africa, and Asia. The leading exporters of cocoa beans to the United States are Indonesia, the Ivory Coast, Brazil, the Dominican Republic, and Malaysia, in that order.[13]

According to a popular legend, chocolate was a gift from the Aztec god Quetzalcoatl to give humans a taste of paradise. At the time of Hernando Cortés's expedition to Mexico in 1519, chocolate (*xocoatl* or *chocolatl* as the Aztecs called it) was a prized beverage, to be enjoyed only by the rulers and the upper classes of society. The Aztec emperor Montezuma II drank a cocoa-derived mixture flavored with spices and presumably liked it so much that he consumed fifty cups daily. But it was very different from the chocolate we know today. The original version was a cold, thick, frothy, souplike concoction that was eaten with a spoon. Most significant, it was bitter in taste because the Aztecs had no knowledge of sugarcane and therefore no way to sweeten it. Reluctantly, Cortés took some cocoa bean pods back to Spain in 1528.

Once home, Cortés prepared chocolate as he had learned it from the Aztecs, but with an important difference: the addition of sugar. Now, in a sweetened form called *molinet*, chocolate became an instant success, and a closely guarded secret that the Spanish emperor Charles V and his royal court wanted to keep to themselves. Inevitably, however, word leaked out to the other royal courts of Europe that the Spanish were enjoying an exotic new drink that came from the New World.

The official unveiling of sweet chocolate coincided with a royal wedding. When the fourteen-year-old Spanish princess arrived in Paris to marry the fourteen-year-old Louis XIII of France in 1615, she carried with her a betrothal gift of Spanish chocolate. It was the beginning of the traditional connection of chocolate with romance. Later, in 1660, a similar betrothal gift at the wedding of another Spanish princess and Louis XIV of France sealed its reputation as the gift of love. It also has not hurt chocolate's image that the eighteenth-century Italian lover Casanova credited his considerable sexual prowess to a habit of drinking chocolate each morning.

Chocolate took its place in England not so much as a symbol of romance but as simply another good-tasting beverage that could be sold in the growing number of coffee houses in English cities. From the beginning, chocolate was sold in shops rather than hidden away behind palace walls. It was not cheap, but at least it was available to all who could afford to buy it. By 1700, the specialty chocolate house rivaled the coffee house as a place to gather and discuss current events.

How Chocolate Is Made

From the days of pre-Columbian America to the early part of the nineteenth century, the method for preparing chocolate did not fundamentally change, except for the addition of such ingredients as sugar. In 1828, however, something did change. To appreciate what transpired, it is important to understand the nature of chocolate itself and the ways it can be processed.

Once cocoa beans are roasted, they can be heated in a machine to such temperatures that the natural fat within the beans, called **cocoa butter,** melts. The result is a deep-colored chocolaty-smelling paste called **chocolate liquor.** When it later cools and hardens, the paste is often called **baking chocolate.** As chocolate, it is as pure as you can get, but since it has an "extrabittersweet" flavor, it is not yet good enough to eat.

The real innovation in chocolate processing came in 1828, when a Dutch chemist, Coenraad van Houten, invented a screw press to squeeze the cocoa butter out of the hardened chocolate liquor. Surprisingly, pure cocoa butter is not brown but white in color; in fact, "white chocolate" is essentially pure cocoa butter with added ingredients. What is left after the cocoa butter has been removed from the chocolate liquor is a dry, dark-colored, cakelike substance that can be crushed into a powder. This powder can be mixed with sugar and other flavorings, and hot milk or water can be added to make cocoa.

To make chocolate as we know it, several additional processing steps are required, many of which were developed by the Swiss chocolatier Rodolphe Lindt in 1879. A ratio of cocoa liquor and cocoa butter is combined with milk, sugar, and vanilla to make milk chocolate. Just how

cocoa bean pods (COH-coh): Parts of the cacao tree that are the raw material for cocoa and chocolate. Not to be confused with coca, the source of cocaine.
cocoa butter: The fat content of the cocoa bean.
chocolate liquor (lih-KOOR): A deep-colored paste made when roasted cocoa beans are heated so that the cocoa butter in the beans melts.
baking chocolate: A hardened paste, consisting of chocolate liquor, produced by heating roasted cocoa beans.

Chocolate and Heart Disease: Some Good News

Are we running any risk to our health by indulging in our obvious love for chocolate? It is true that chocolate is rich in saturated fatty acids, villains when it comes to raising cholesterol and clogging our coronary arteries. Yet the particular saturated fatty acid in the cocoa butter of chocolate turns out to be quite benign. The main component of cocoa butter is a fatty acid known as stearic acid, which is rapidly converted in the liver to oleic acid, a monounsaturate that neither raises nor lowers serum cholesterol.

One study found that healthy young men on a twenty-six-day diet in which a total of 37 percent of calories came from fat and 81 percent of those fat calories came from cocoa butter had no increase in their serum cholesterol, and their cholesterol levels were no higher than if they had been on a comparable diet in which the fat came from olive oil.

Recent evidence suggests that chocolate may even *protect* arteries from disease. Cocoa powder, it has been discovered, has a concentration of compounds called *flavonoids* that are known to function as antioxidants in the bloodstream. The greater the level of antioxidants, the lower the probability that artery-clogging cells will develop. A 1.5-ounce piece of chocolate (or 3 tablespoons of cocoa powder) contains approximately the same amount of flavonoids as 5 ounces of red wine, another product with proven antioxidant properties (see Chapter 9).

This is not to say that chocolate should now be viewed as a health food. Milk chocolate contains by definition (and by law) a minimal amount of milk-derived butterfat in addition to cocoa butter. Some chocolates also contain palm oil or coconut oil, two saturated fats that *do* raise cholesterol levels. And no one should expect to lose weight on a chocolate diet. Even so, nutritionists are concluding that there is little harm in eating two or three chocolate bars a week, which is welcome news for chocolate lovers everywhere.

Sources: Raloff, Janet (2000, March 18). Chocolate hearts: Yummy and good medicine? *Science News*, pp. 188–189. Waterhouse, Andrew J., Shirley, Joseph R., and Donovan, Jennifer I. (1996). Antioxidants in chocolate. *Lancet, 348,* 834.

much cocoa butter is added depends on the type of chocolate that is wanted—the more cocoa butter, the sweeter the result. Fortunately, unlike other fats, cocoa butter almost never goes rancid. In other words, milk chocolate keeps. It might turn white after a while, but that simply means that the cocoa butter is starting to separate from the mixture. It is all right to eat, though chocolate connoisseurs would surely disagree. All that is needed to produce commercial chocolate is to refine the texture to achieve that degree of smoothness the world has come to know and love (Health Line).[14]

The Chocolate Industry Today

Present-day domestic sales of chocolate bars in the United States are dominated by Hershey Chocolate USA and M&M/Mars, together holding approximately 80 percent of the market (see Portrait). Overall, the annual per capita consumption of chocolate in the United States is slightly more than 12 pounds, which puts the country eighth among chocolate-loving nations of the world. The champion, not surprisingly, is Switzerland, where the per capita consumption of chocolate is approximately 22 pounds a year. Germany and Belgium/Luxembourg are runners-up with per capita consumptions of about 21 pounds per year.[15]

The Xanthine Content in Chocolate

The amounts of xanthines are much smaller in chocolate than in coffee or tea. A typical 1-ounce piece of milk chocolate, for example, contains about 6 mg of caffeine and about 44 mg of theobromine. With theobromine packing about one-tenth the stimulant power of caffeine, we can approximate the total effect of this quantity of chocolate to be roughly equivalent to 10 mg of caffeine. Of course, eating more than 1 ounce will change these figures (a typical chocolate bar is approximately 1.5 ounces), but even so, it is unlikely that chocolate will keep you up at night.[16]

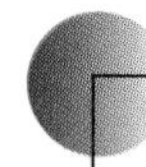

Soft Drinks

The fourth and final major source of caffeine in our diet is soft drinks. Table 12.1 shows the caffeine content of prominent soft-drink brands. Although most of the caffeinated drinks are colas, it is possible for a noncola to be caffeinated as well. The reason is that more than 95 percent of the caffeine in caffeinated soft drinks is added by the manufacturer during production; less than 5 percent actually comes from the West African kola nut, from which cola gets its name.

Portrait: Milton S. Hershey and the Town Built on Chocolate

When Milton Hershey made a decision in 1893 to go into the chocolate business, he was already an experienced confectioner with a prosperous caramel company in Lancaster, Pennsylvania, to his credit. But he could see that the future was in chocolate. New German-built machinery was now available to mass-produce milk chocolate. Hershey wanted to be in the business on the ground floor.

He bought the equipment and started to experiment on a special recipe, using fresh milk from the local dairy farms instead of powdered milk. The proportion of milk and sugar, the blend of cocoa beans, and the roasting time are secrets to this day. All we know is that somehow Hershey figured out a recipe that was a winner. The new Hershey bar was an instant hit.

By 1903, the Hershey chocolate business had become so successful that it needed a new factory. Defying conventional wisdom, however, Hershey did not look for a town or city for the factory but rather went into the surrounding countryside. He bought a thousand acres of prime Pennsylvania Dutch farmland, built his factory, then decided to build a town around it.

Milton Hershey

By 1930, the town of Hershey had grown to include residents beyond the six thousand factory workers. The Hershey business was now worldwide, with its chocolate kisses and chocolate syrup in addition to other products. During hard economic times, in order to maintain employment, Hershey went on a construction spree. He built the famous Hershey Hotel, Hershey Gardens, a football stadium and sports arena, and a convention center. Because he was childless, he turned his attention to building a Milton Hershey school for orphaned boys and girls.

Milton Hershey died in 1945 at the age of eighty-eight, but his corporate heirs continued in his spirit. Today, there is the Milton S. Hershey Medical Center of the Pennsylvania State University, endowed by the Hershey Company. And of course there is Hersheypark, a continuation of an old amusement park Hershey had built in 1905, all powered by a best-selling chocolate bar and a man with a very sweet dream.

Source: Morton, Marcia, and Morton, Frederic (1986). *Chocolate: An illustrated history.* New York: Crown Publishers, pp. 89–125.

In general, the United States leads the world in per capita consumption of soft-drink products, nearly 56 gallons annually or the equivalent of 2–3 eight-ounce servings each day. Beverages with high levels of caffeine, either citrus-flavored noncolas (such as Mountain Dew) or colas (such as Jolt), presently constitute a relatively small proportion of total soft-drink sales, but they have been the fastest growing segment of the beverage industry since 1991. The concern that these beverages might be a problem for young drinkers who are attracted to

TABLE 12.1

Caffeine levels and domestic U.S. market share of leading brands of soft drinks

BRAND NAME	PERCENTAGE OF MARKET (1999)	CAFFEINE CONTENT (mg/12 oz.)	BRAND NAME	PERCENTAGE OF MARKET (1999)	CAFFEINE CONTENT (mg/12 oz.)
Coca-Cola Classic	20.3%	45.6	Others (cola, citrus, orange, root beer, etc.)	27.3	
Pepsi-Cola	14.1	38.4	Go Go	n/a	112
Diet Coke	8.5	45.6	Guts	n/a	54
Mountain Dew	7.1	54.0	Jolt	n/a	72
Sprite	6.7	none	Josta	n/a	58
Dr. Pepper	6.2	40.0	$Krank_2O$	n/a	71
Diet Pepsi	4.7	38.4	Red Bull	n/a	116
7Up	2.0	none	Surge	n/a	51
Caffeine-free Diet Coke	1.7	none	XTC	n/a	70
Minute Maid	1.3	none			

Sources: Barboza, David (1997, August 22). More hip, higher hop. *New York Times*, pp. D1, D5. Sales figures from *Beverage World* (2000) Web site.

QUICK CONCEPT  12.1

Understanding Caffeine Levels in Foods and Beverages

Check your understanding of the relative amounts of caffeine in various foods and beverages by rank ordering the following caffeine-containing foods or beverages, from 1 (most) to 6 (least). If any examples have caffeine levels close enough to be considered a tie, indicate this in your ranking.

_____ a. a 1-ounce bar of milk chocolate

_____ b. a 5-ounce cup of drip-brewed coffee

_____ c. a 5-ounce cup of tea

_____ d. a 12-ounce can of Coca-Cola

_____ e. a 5-ounce cup of instant coffee

_____ f. a 5-ounce cup of decaffeinated coffee

Answers: a. 5 b. 1 c. 2 (tie) d. 4 e. 2 (tie) f. 6

these products as stimulants will be explored in a later section.[17]

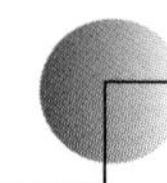

Caffeine from Medications

Caffeine is sold purely as a stimulant in over-the-counter (OTC) drugs such as NoDoz and Vivarin tablets and as one of several ingredients in a number of other products ranging from pain relievers and cold remedies to diuretics and weight-control aids. As Table 12.2 shows, the equivalent caffeine level in these products ranges approximately from that of one-third of a cup to two cups of regular coffee.

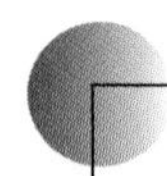

The Era of Decaffeination

Public concerns about adverse effects of caffeine and a general increase in consciousness about health have led to a steady increase in decaffeinated consumer products, particularly coffee. Since 1960, the percentage of decaffeinated coffee in total coffee sales has risen dramatically. Unfortunately, as most coffee lovers know, decaffeination greatly reduces coffee flavor.

One of the reasons for the loss in flavor is the choice of beans being decaffeinated. Typically, only the robusta species of coffee bean is decaffeinated, not only because it costs less but also because its harsher flavor can better withstand the decaffeination process.[18]

Another reason stems from the major technique employed in decaffeination, known as the *water method.* In this technique, the beans are first steamed and then soaked in water. The soaking removes the caffeine but also all the other solids in the coffee beans that give them a rich flavor. The water is removed, the caffeine is removed from the water, and the remaining water is returned to soak the still-wet beans, in an effort to reintroduce some of the lost flavor. Most coffee experts consider the coffee bean that has been "naturally decaffeinated" in this way to bear only a pale resemblance to its former self. Coffee manufacturers tend to roast the decaffeinated beans longer (some say that they are then overroasted) to produce extra body and flavor.

Recently, a new technique of using carbon dioxide to loosen the chemical bonds that hold caffeine to the coffee bean has been developed, and decaffeinated coffees produced in this way are available in a few selected brands. The flavor is significantly superior to coffee decaffeinated by the water method.[19]

TABLE 12.2

Caffeine content in common over-the-counter medications

MEDICATION	CAFFEINE PER TABLET OR CAPSULE (in milligrams)	CAFFEINE PER RECOMMENDED DOSAGE (in milligrams)
Stimulants		
NoDoz	100	200
Vivarin	200	200
Pain relievers		
Anacin	32	64
Excedrin	65	130
Midol	32	64
Vanquish	33	66
Cold remedies		
Coryban-D	30	30
Dristan	16	32
Triaminicin	30	30
Diuretics		
Aqua-Ban	100	200

Note: Caffeine is also found in prescription remedies for migraine (Cafergot and Migral) and in pain relievers (Darvon Compound and Fiorinol).

Source: Updated from Gilbert, Richard J. (1986). *Caffeine: The most popular stimulant.* New York: Chelsea House Publishers, p. 51.

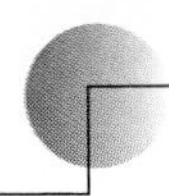

Caffeine as a Drug

When ingested orally, caffeine is absorbed in about thirty to sixty minutes. Caffeine levels peak in the bloodstream in one hour, and reactions in the central nervous sytem peak in about two hours. Many coffee drinkers notice a boost of energy, or "buzz," almost immediately, but this effect is attributable either to the sugar in the coffee or a conditioned learning effect, not to the caffeine itself. From three to seven hours after caffeine is consumed, approximately half of it still remains in the bloodstream.

The biotransformation of caffeine and the time it takes to eliminate it vary according to a number of factors. For example, women in late stages of pregnancy and those using oral contraceptives eliminate caffeine from their systems more slowly than either men or women in general. Infants and the elderly also show a slower elimination of caffeine. In contrast, smokers eliminate caffeine about 100 percent more quickly than nonsmokers. As a result, smokers on average experience the effect of the caffeine they consume for a relatively shorter period of time; it is possible that smokers tend to drink more caffeinated coffee than nonsmokers in order to compensate for their faster elimination of caffeine.[20]

Effects of Caffeine on the Body

The stimulant effects of caffeine, as well as those of the other xanthines, are a result of its ability to block the effects of an inhibitory neurotransmitter called **adenosine.** Normally, adenosine binds to receptors on the surface of cells and, consequently, produces sleepiness, dilation of blood vessels, and constriction of bronchial passageways. It also protects the body against seizures, slows down the body's reaction to stress, and lowers heart rate, blood pressure, and body temperature.

By inhibiting the effects of adenosine, caffeine and other xanthines cause the opposite responses to occur, though the actual results are complex. In general, peripheral blood vessels are dilated, while cerebral blood vessels in the head are constricted. Because dilated blood vessels in the head can frequently result in headache pain, caffeine can help headache sufferers, and that is why it is found in many over-the-counter pain relievers. Heart rate is slightly elevated when caffeine is consumed, but the effect is dose-dependent and often is not observed at all.

The fact that caffeine has a bronchodilating effect makes it helpful in treating asthmatic conditions in which the bronchial passageways are abnormally constricted. Theophylline, however, has a stronger bronchodilating effect than caffeine and as a result can be prescribed at lower doses. Caffeine is effective, but patients often report unpleasant side effects of "jitteriness" before their asthmatic condition improves.[21]

Effects of Caffeine on Behavior

A major effect of caffeine as well as other xanthines is to excite neuronal activity in the brain. As the dose increases, the effects expand from the cerebral cortex downward to lower systems in the brain and finally to the spinal cord. The behavioral consequence of this excitation is a feeling of mental alertness and lack of fatigue. On the basis of these effects, you might expect that caffeine would also improve human performance, but reports in this regard are quite mixed. Subjects in controlled experimental settings feel stimulated and more alert, but whether their performance improves after caffeine depends on the type of task, their personal characteristics, and even the time of day when the experiment is conducted.

Nonetheless, it is possible to make some generalizations about caffeine's effect on performance. In general, caffeine increases vigilance and attentiveness in tasks at which subjects become easily bored, and it decreases the response time to simple visual or auditory signals. For more complex tasks in which subjects need to make decisions or in situations that require motor coordination, however, caffeine either has little effect or can be disruptive. Most reports of improvements under caffeine involve conditions in which the subject is already either bored or fatigued. In these circumstances, caffeine helps either to maintain a level of performance that would otherwise have declined or to restore performance from a state degraded by boredom or fatigue.[22]

There is less disagreement as to the impact of caffeine on sleep. The most obvious effect is a lengthening of the time it takes to fall asleep and a decrease in the quality of sleep once it comes. Generally, studies investigating caffeine effects have involved coffee drinking, and the sleep effects are seen more strongly in nondrinkers of coffee than in habitual heavy coffee drinkers.[23]

As a final note, it is important to emphasize an effect that caffeine does *not* produce: the supposed ability to sober up a person recently intoxicated with alcohol.

adenosine (a-DEN-oh-seen): An inhibitory neurotransmitter that is blocked, or neutralized, by caffeine and other xanthines. The action on adenosine receptors in the body is the basis for the stimulant properties of these drugs.

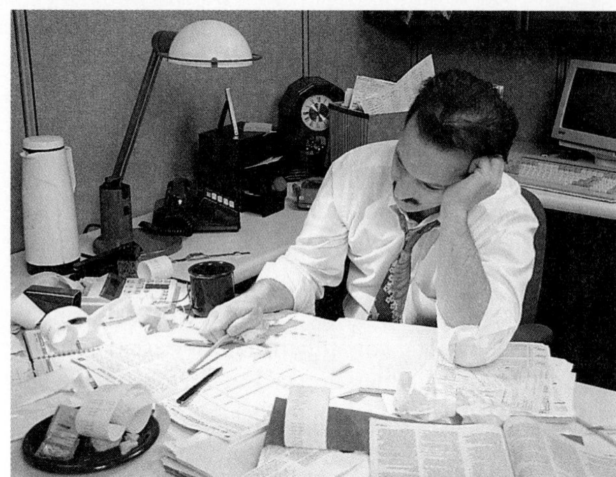

Caffeine is typically most effective to ward off sleep and improve performance on tedious tasks, both at home and in the workplace.

Despite the widespread notion that a cup of strong black coffee will help someone who is drunk, the evidence is simply not there. The only result is that you will have a more alert drunk on your hands. The behavioral consequences of alcohol intoxication (see Chapter 9), such as impaired judgment and poor perceptual-motor skills, remain the same.

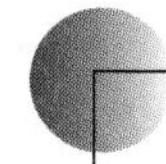

Health Risks

Studies investigating the health consequences of caffeine consumption have been conducted for more than a century, and the conclusions have varied considerably.

Cardiovascular Effects

Because it is known that caffeine stimulates cardiac muscle as well as skeletal muscle throughout the body, it is only natural to be concerned with the possibility that caffeine consumption would be a risk factor for a heart attack or cardiac arrhythmia (irregular heart beat). In 1973, a great deal of publicity was generated by a study called the Boston Collaborative Drug Surveillance Program in which a large number of individuals at Boston metropolitan hospitals were surveyed as to their use of many different drugs, including caffeine, and the incidence of various disease states. The researchers reported that the consumption of more than six cups of caffeinated coffee a day more than doubled the risk of a heart attack.[24] Further studies, however, have failed to find any connection at all between caffeine and heart attacks.

What do we do when the medical literature is so inconclusive and contradictory? First of all, in caffeine studies that show some cardiovascular health risk, the consumption levels are rather high (five to six cups or more a day). Drinking less caffeine has not been identified as a risk factor. Even so, potential health problems associated with caffeine consumption have to be considered in the context of other behaviors. As a pharmacologist has put it,

> *In both males and females without heart disease, the use of caffeinated coffee and the total daily intake of caffeine do not appreciably increase the risk of coronary artery disease or stroke. . . . Coffee consumption is strongly associated with cigarette smoking, and increased rates of coronary heart disease in heavy coffee drinkers who smoke occur as a result of the cigarette smoking, not the caffeine consumption.*[25]

At the same time, we should be aware that a four-year-old child drinking a 20-ounce cola drink is consuming a high dose of caffeine, and we should not be surprised that marked behavioral and physiological effects will follow.

Osteoporosis and Bone Fractures

A 1990 study analyzing caffeine consumption and incidence of hip fractures among more than three thousand elderly men and women found that those who reported drinking 2.5 to 3 cups of caffeinated coffee or 5 to 6 cups of caffeinated tea per day had a 69 percent greater risk of osteoporosis (bone loss and brittleness) than caffeine abstainers. Those who reported drinking more than 3.5 cups of caffeinated coffee or 7 cups of caffeinated tea had an 82 percent greater risk. Because one of the effects of caffeine is to increase the urinary excretion of calcium and to inhibit the absorption of calcium from the diet in the elderly, it makes sense that there might be an adverse effect on bone tissue in this age group.[26]

Breast Disease

A 1981 report indicated a relationship between caffeine consumption and the formation of benign (that is, noncancerous) lumps in the breasts called *fibrocystic lesions.* However, the study was severely criticized as not being based on randomized sampling nor having methodological controls that would shield the researchers from imposing their bias in observing fibrocystic lesion cases. More recent and carefully executed studies show no relationship between the incidence of this frequently painful condition and caffeine consumption.[27] There is disagreement about whether women who already have fibrocystic lesions might show improvement by abstaining from caffeinated products; a 1985 report indicates that abstinence is helpful, whereas subsequent reports indicate that there is no benefit.[28]

Cancer

A 1971 study indicated an association between caffeine consumption and urinary-tract cancer, and a 1981 study indicated an association with pancreatic cancer. In both studies, the conclusions were based on methodologically flawed designs, and presently the medical consensus is that caffeine consumption is not causally related to these or any other types of cancer.[29]

Effects during Pregnancy and Breastfeeding

At one time, caffeine use was suspected to be linked to infertility in women. A study in 1990 reported that women who consumed three cups of coffee a day reduced their chances of getting pregnant by 25 percent. A more recent study in 1998, however, has found no relationship between caffeine intake and infertility.[30]

Nonetheless, there can be potential problems later in pregnancy. Caffeine consumption (more than three or four cups of coffee a day) during the first three months of pregnancy is related to a greater incidence of low birth weight in the newborn, though the incidence of premature birth or birth defects is not increased. There is also a relationship between very high levels of caffeine consumption (more than six cups of coffee per day) during pregnancy and an increased risk of miscarriage. Therefore, the cautionary advice of the FDA is warranted: Women should abstain from caffeine if at all possible during pregnancy.[31]

Afterward, in the case of breastfeeding, it is also a good idea to continue a caffeine-free diet. Enzymes that normally break down caffeine in the liver are not present in the liver of a newborn baby, and as a consequence the elimination half-life of caffeine is much longer than in the adult, up to eighty-five hours. Though there is no evidence of specific harm from having a stimulant such as caffeine in the nervous system for such intervals of time, it seems to be a situation that might well be avoided.[32]

Panic Attacks

Consumption of caffeine equivalent to about four to five cups of coffee a day has been associated with the onset of panic attacks in those individuals suffering from a panic disorder. This finding is consistent with the known effects of caffeine as a CNS stimulant. Any person with a history of panic attacks should be careful to avoid caffeine, and mental health professionals should be aware of the possibility that caffeine consumption could trigger a panic episode.[33]

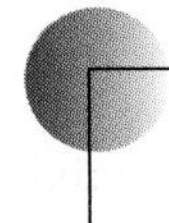

Dependence, Acute Toxicity, and Medical Applications

More than 85 percent of people in the United States consume caffeine in one form or another each day. In 1985, 401 men and women, all employees of the state of New York, were asked about their caffeine consumption over the previous seventy-two-hour period, including all foods, beverages, and medications that might contain caffeine. Only eleven of them did not consume any caffeine at all, and the average caffeine consumption level was about 400 mg.[34] This was neither a random nor a very large sample, but the results nonetheless illustrate the basic point made at the opening of this chapter: Caffeine consumption is a cultural norm in the United States and the rest of the world. The fact that caffeinated beverages in particular are embedded in the diet of this country makes it difficult to think of caffeine as a drug, much less one that could cause dependence. "People say they're addicted to caffeine and laugh," a prominent caffeine researcher has said. "They wouldn't say the same thing about heroin."[35]

Tolerance

When individuals who do not usually use caffeine are administered repeated doses equivalent to amounts that would ordinarily be acquired from the diet, the initial increases in heart rate and blood pressure start to decline after approximately seventy-two hours.[36] In other words, with respect to the cardiovascular effects of caffeine, a classic tolerance effect, as defined in Chapter 2, can be observed.

With respect to the behavioral and psychological effects of caffeine, tolerance effects are more difficult to evaluate, despite the fact that most of us have noticed at some time in our lives that caffeine was having a progressively smaller effect on us as we started to be habitual caffeine consumers. The problem appears to be that once we are in a laboratory setting, most of us are already tolerant to the effects of caffeine. Recent studies that have specifically controlled for variations in the subject's recent dietary intake of caffeine have shown tolerance effects for dosage levels as low as 100 mg, the equivalent of one to two cups of coffee.

Withdrawal

A stronger case for caffeine being a drug that produces physical dependence is contained in the research findings concerning withdrawal. As you may have encountered yourself, a sudden cessation in the intake of coffee or other caffeinated products results in symptoms of headache, impaired concentration, drowsiness, irritability, muscle aches, and other flu-like symptoms. A headache is a typical withdrawal symptom, usually appearing from twelve to eighteen hours after the last dose of caffeine, peaking over the next two days or so, and persisting in some individuals for up to a week. As you would expect, a reintroduction of caffeine causes the withdrawal symptoms to disappear. One study on the pattern of withdrawal symptoms from caffeine found significant symptoms even when subjects had been consuming as little as 100 mg per day.[37]

Craving

The case for physical dependence is clear; the case for psychological dependence, however, is presently uncertain. We do not know if the tendency to have that next cup of coffee or other caffeinated product is a matter of desiring to have it or an effort to avoid withdrawal symptoms that would ensue if we did not have it.

Acute Toxicity of Caffeine

Too much caffeine can produce toxic effects on the body, but the amount that might do so is substantial and generally beyond what we typically consume. Approximately 1,000 mg of caffeine (equivalent to about ten cups of caffeinated coffee), consumed over a short period of time, results in extreme nervousness and agitation, muscle hyperactivity and twitching, profound insomnia, heart palpitations and arrhythmias, gastrointestinal upset, nausea, and diarrhea. The condition is referred to as **caffeinism.** In a few individuals, particularly those who do not typically ingest caffeine, these symptoms might arise from a much lower dose level. There is also growing concern that caffeine use might magnify emotional difficulties in mental health patients and reduce the benefits of medications that they are taking.

While caffeinism is not officially recognized as a psychological disorder by the American Psychiatric Association, the DSM-IV manual defines a condition called *acute caffeine intoxication*, resulting from a caffeine intake in excess of 250 mg and producing caffeinism-like symptoms that cause "significant distress or impairment in social, occupational, or other important areas of functioning." It is admittedly unusual to observe such behaviors from a caffeine level equivalent to two or three cups of coffee, but as the dose rises above this level, the probability of observing a toxic reaction can be expected to increase.[38]

The adult lethal dose is approximately 5 to 10 grams (5,000 to 10,000 mg), which is equivalent roughly to somewhere between forty and eighty cups of caffeinated coffee. The lowest caffeine dose known to have been fatal in an adult is 3.2 grams (3,200 mg), administered mistakenly by a nurse who believed the syringe contained another drug. Lethal doses for children are lower, and a number of accidental deaths have resulted from eating large quantities of caffeine-containing medications.[39]

Medications Based on Xanthines

Owing to the superiority of theophylline over caffeine in its ability to relax smooth muscle, theophylline has been used medically to treat a number of clinical conditions. Its application as a bronchodilator for asthmatics has been mentioned earlier. One particular medication, aminophylline, combines theophylline with methyledi-amine, an inert compound that increases the absorption of theophylline and enhances its clinical benefit. Because theophylline also stimulates cardiac muscle, it is sometimes prescribed for patients with congestive heart disease (Table 12.3).

Kids and Caffeine: A Special Concern

There is little doubt that caffeine consumption among young people in the United States under the age of eighteen has risen significantly in the last decade or so. One reason has to do with the consumption of caffeinated soft drinks. It has been estimated that teenagers consume about sixty-four gallons of soft drinks each year, largely in caffeinated forms. Mega-sized soft drinks, sometimes with free refills, are standard offerings in fast-food restaurants and convenience stores; soft-drink vending machines that provide twenty-ounce bottles, instead of twelve-ounce cans, are not uncommon. Another major opportunity for

caffeinism: A dangerous state of overstimulation from a very large dose of caffeine.

TABLE 12.3

Some examples of xanthine-based medications		
MEDICATION	BRAND NAME	MANUFACTURER
theophylline	Aerolate	Fleming
	Slo-Bid, Slo-Phyllin	Rhone-Poulenc Rorer
	Uni-Dur	Key Pharmaceuticals
	Theolair tablets	3M Pharmaceuticals
	Uniphyl	Purdue Frederick
aminophylline	Aminophylline oral solution	Roxane

Source: Physicians' desk reference (54th ed.) (2000). Montvale NJ: Medical Economics Company.

The large doses of caffeine ingested by young people on a daily basis have raised health concerns.

caffeine consumption in this age group comes from patterns of coffee drinking at coffee bars, where highly caffeinated espresso drinks served sweet and cold are increasingly popular. While the level of caffeine intake in multiple soft drinks and coffee may be equivalent to levels experienced by many adults, the physiological and behavioral effects are actually greater, since body weight in a younger population is only one-half to two-thirds that of an adult. In other words, the dosage level of caffeine, expressed as milligrams per kilogram (mg/kg), ends up exceeding levels typically ingested by adults.

The extent of caffeine consumption in this population raises some significant health concerns. Drinking caffeinated beverages instead of milk can result in deficient levels of calcium and phosphorus, minerals that are needed for normal bone growth during adolescence. While research is presently lacking as to whether significant caffeine consumption in the early years will lead to osteoporosis in adulthood, the research showing an increased risk among the elderly suggests that a similar risk might exist for younger people as well. On a behavioral level, there are concerns about hyperactivity, nervousness, and anxiety among young people who ingest large amounts of caffeine, as well as decreased attention span and lower proficiency in school when experiencing symptoms of caffeine withdrawal. Unfortunately, very few studies exist that have specifically investigated short-term or long-term effects of caffeine on children and teenagers.[40]

SUMMARY

- Caffeine belongs to a family of stimulant drugs called xanthines. It is found in coffee, tea, chocolate, many soft drinks, and some medications.
- Other xanthines are theophylline (found in tea) and theobromine (found in chocolate).

Coffee

- Coffee drinking originated in the Middle East and later was introduced to England in the seventeenth century. Coffee houses in Britain and in colonial America sprang up as establishments where political and social discussions could be held.
- Today's coffee comes from a mixture of arabica and robusta beans, imported largely from Brazil, Colombia, Indonesia, and several nations in Africa.
- On average, a 5-ounce cup of coffee contains roughly 100 mg of caffeine, with the actual level determined by the type of coffee beans used and the method of brewing.

Tea

- Tea drinking originated in China and later was introduced to Europe by Dutch traders in the early seventeenth century. It became most popular in Britain and Russia. Today, tea consumption is greatest in Britain and Ireland.
- On average, a 5-ounce cup of tea contains roughly 60 mg of caffeine, with the actual level determined by the method of brewing and brand.

Chocolate

- Chocolate originated in pre-Columbian Central America and was introduced to Europe by the return of Cortés to Spain in 1528. Its popularity spread across Europe in the seventeenth century. By the 1880s, techniques for present-day milk chocolate had been perfected.
- The caffeine level in chocolate is relatively low, roughly 6 mg per ounce.

Soft Drinks

- Caffeinated colas have most of the caffeine content added to the beverage during production. Levels of caffeine in these beverages are approximately 38–45 mg per 12 ounces.

Caffeine from Medications

- As a drug, caffeine and other xanthines are stimulants of the CNS and of peripheral musculature. Theophylline, in particular, has a strong bronchodilating effect and is useful for treating asthmatic conditions.

Caffeine as a Drug

- The behavioral effects of caffeine can be characterized principally as a reduction in fatigue and boredom, as well as a delay in the onset of sleep.
- Health risks from moderate consumption of caffeine are not clinically significant, except for the adverse effects of fetal development during pregnancy, the development of bone loss among the elderly, possibly an adverse effect on cardiac condition of patients already suffering from cardiovascular disease, and the aggravation of panic attacks among patients with this disorder.
- Continued consumption of caffeine produces tolerance effects; when caffeine consumption ceases, withdrawal symptoms are observed. High levels of caffeine consumption can produce toxic effects, though deaths are extremely rare.

Kids and Caffeine

- Young people in the United States ingest increasingly large quantities of caffeine through the drinking of caffeinated soft drinks and coffee. The actual dosage level is substantial since body weight is less than that of an adult.
- Health concerns regarding caffeine consumption in this population include potential deficiencies in calcium and phosphorus for normal bone growth as well as behavioral problems such as hyperactivity, nervousness, and anxiety.

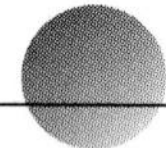

KEY TERMS

adenosine, p. 267
baking chocolate, p. 263
caffeine, p. 259
caffeinism, p. 270
Camellia sinensis, p. 261
chocolate liquor, p. 263
cocoa bean pods, p. 263
cocoa butter, p. 263
Coffea arabica, p. 259
Coffea robusta, p. 260
theobromine, p. 259
theophylline, p. 259
xanthines, p. 259

ENDNOTES

1. Austin, Gregory A. (1978). *Perspectives on the history of psychoactive substance use.* Rockville MD: National Institute on Drug Abuse, p. 50. Jacob, Heinrich E. (1935). *Coffee: The epic of a commodity.* New York: Viking Press, pp. 3–10.
2. Robinson, Edward F. (1893). *The early history of coffee houses in England.* London: Kegan Paul, p. 26. Cited in Edward M. Brecher, and the editors of Consumer Reports (1972), *Licit and illicit drugs.* Boston: Little Brown, p. 197.
3. Ukers, William H. (1935). *All about coffee.* New York: Tea and Coffee Trade Journal Co., p. 61. Wellman, Frederick L. (1961). *Coffee: Botany, cultivation, and utilization.* New York: Interscience Publishers, p. 22 or 23.
4. Fussell, Betty (1999, September 5). The world before Starbucks. *New York Times Book Review*, p. 26, quotation on p. 26. International Coffee Organisation, London, 1999. Pendergrast, Mark (1999). *Uncommon grounds: The history of coffee and how it transformed our world.* New York: Basic

Books. Starbird, Ethel A. (1981, March). The bonanza bean: Coffee. *National Geographic Magazine*, pp. 398–399.

5. Spiller, Monica A. (1998). The coffee plant and its processing. In Gene A. Spiller (Ed.), *Caffeine.* Boca Raton FL: CRC Press, pp. 79–95. Svicarovich, John; Winter, Stephen; and Ferguson, Jeff (1976). *The coffee book: A connoisseur's guide to gourmet coffee.* Englewood Cliffs NJ: Prentice-Hall, pp. 21–31.
6. Davids, Kenneth (1976). *Coffee: A guide to buying, brewing, and enjoying.* San Francisco: 101 Productions, pp. 161–166. *U.S. Winter Coffee Drinking Study* (1998). New York: National Coffee Association of USA, Inc.
7. Barone, J. J., and Roberts, H. (1984). Human consumption of caffeine. In Peter B. Dews (Ed.), *Caffeine: Perspectives from recent research.* Berlin: Springer-Verlag, pp. 60–63.
8. Shalleck, Jamie (1972). *Tea.* New York: Viking Press.
9. Maitland, Derek (1982). *5000 years of tea: A pictorial companion.* Hong Kong: CFW Publications Limited, pp. 80–89.
10. Gilbert, Richard (1986). *Caffeine: The most popular stimulant.* New York: Chelsea House, p. 23.
11. Groisser, Daniel S. (1978). A study of caffeine in tea. *American Journal of Clinical Nutrition, 31,* 1727–1731.
12. Haqqi, Tariq M.; Anthony, Donald D.; Gupta, Sanjay; Ahmad, Nihal; Lee, M.-S.; Kumar, Ganesh K.; and Mukhtar, Hasan (1999). Prevention of collagen-induced arthritis in mice by a polyphenolic fraction from green tea. *Proceedings of the National Academy of Sciences,* 96, 4524–4529. Steinman, David (1994, March–April). Why you should drink green tea. *Natural Health, 24,* 56–57.
13. U.S. Department of Agriculture, Foreign Agricultural Service, 1992 data. Information courtesy of the Chocolate Manufacturers Association, McLean, Virginia.
14. Morton, Marcia, and Morton, Frederic (1986). *Chocolate: An illustrated history.* New York: Crown Publishers, pp. 77–87.
15. Brody, Jane E. (1994, February 14). Hearts may safely flutter over valentine chocolates. *New York Times,* pp. A1, A15. Information for 1998 courtesy of the CAOBISCO Secretariat, Brussels, and the U.S. Department of Commerce, Washington DC. *The market share reporter 2000* (1999). Detroit MI: Gale Group, p. 367.
16. Apgar, Joan L., and Tarka, Stanley M. (1998). Methylzanthine composition and consumption patterns of cocoa and chocolate products. In Gene A. Spiller (Ed.), *Caffeine.* Boca Raton FL: CRC Press, pp. 163–192. Spiller, Gene A. (1984). *The methylxanthine beverages and foods: Chemistry, consumption, and health effects.* New York: A. R. Liss, pp. 171–172.
17. Barboza, David (1997, August 22). More hip, higher hop. *New York Times,* p. D1, D5. Lazarus, George (2000, February 14). There's nothing flat about love of soft drinks. *Chicago Tribune,* Section 3, p. 4.
18. Kummer, Corby (1990, July). Is coffee harmful? *Atlantic,* 266, pp. 92–96.
19. DeMers, John (1986). *The community kitchen's complete guide to gourmet coffee.* New York: Simon and Schuster, pp. 85–89. Kummer, Is coffee harmful? pp. 92–96.
20. Gilbert, *Caffeine,* pp. 76–79. Julien, Robert M. (2001). *A primer of drug action* (9th ed.). New York: Worth, p. 222. Quinlan, Paul, Lane, Joan, and Aspinall, Laurence (1997). Effects of hot tea, coffee and water ingestion on physiological responses and mode: The role of caffeine, water, and beverage type. *Psychopharmacology, 134,* 164–173.
21. Schiwall, S. I. (1986, November). Asthma relief that's brewed by the cup. *Prevention,* 38, 127. Spiller, Gene A. (1998). Basic metabolism and physiological effects of the methylxanthines. In Gene A. Spiller (Ed.), *Caffeine.* Boca Raton FL: CRC Press, pp. 225–231.
22. Curatolo, Peter W., and Robertson, David (1983). The health consequences of caffeine. *Annals of Internal Medicine,* 98, 641–653. Durlach, Paula J. (1998). The effects of a low dose of caffeine on cognitive performance. *Psychopharmacology, 140,* 116–119. Sawyer, Deborah A., Julia, Harry L., and Turin, Alan C. (1982). Caffeine and human behavior: Arousal, anxiety, and performance effects. *Journal of Behavioral Medicine,* 5, 415–439. Smith, Barry D., and Tola, Kenneth (1998). Caffeine: Effects on psychological functioning and performance. In Gene A. Spiller (Ed.), *Caffeine.* Boca Raton FL: CRC Press, pp. 251–299.
23. Curatolo and Robertson, Health consequences of caffeine, p. 644.
24. Jick, Hershel; Miettinen, Olli S.; Neff, Raymond K.; Shapiro, Samuel; Heinonen, Olli; and Slone, Dennis (1973). Coffee and myocardial infarction. *New England Journal of Medicine,* 289, 63–67.
25. Julien, Robert M. (1998). *A primer of drug action* (8th ed.). New York: Freeman, p. 163.
26. Bruce, Bonnie, and Spiller, Gene A. (1998). Caffeine, calcium, and bone health. In Gene A. Spiller (Ed.), *Caffeine.* Boca Raton FL: CRC Press, pp. 345–356. Kiel, Douglas P.; Felson, David T.; Hannan, Marian T.; Anderson, Jennifer J.; and Wilson, Peter W. F. (1990). Caffeine and the risk of hip fracture: The Framingham study. *American Journal of Epidemiology,* 132, 675–684.
27. Levinson, Wendy, and Dunn, Patrick M. (1986). Nonassociation of caffeine and fibrocystic breast disease. *Archives of Internal Medicine, 146,* 1773–1775. Minton, John P.; Foecking, M. K.; Webster, J. T.; and Matthews, R. H. (1979). Caffeine, cyclic nucleotides, and breast diseases. *Surgery, 86,* 105–109. Russell, Linda C. (1989). Caffeine restriction as initial treatment for breast pain. *Nurse Practitioner, 14,* 36–37.
28. Julien, *A primer of drug action* (8th ed.), p. 162.
29. Curatolo and Robertson, Health consequences of caffeine, p. 647.
30. Caan, Bette, Quesenberry, Charles P., and Coates, Ashley, O. (1998). Differences in fertility associated with caffeinated beverage consumption. *American Journal of Public Health,* 88, 270–274. Joesoef, M. Riduan; Beral V.; Rolfs, Robert T.; Aral, Sevgio O.; and Cramer, Daniel W. (1990). Are caffeinated beverages risk factors for delayed conception? *Lancet,* 335, 136–137.
31. Fenster, Laura; Eskenazi, Brenda; Windham, Gayle C.; and Swan, Shanna H. (1991). Caffeine consumption during

pregnancy and fetal growth. *American Journal of Public Health, 81,* 458–461. Infante-Rivard, Claire; Fernandez, Alberto; Gauthier, Robert; David, Michele; and Rivard, Georges-Etienne (1993). Fetal loss associated with caffeine intake before and during pregnancy. *Journal of the American Medical Association, 270,* 2940–2943. Klebanoff, Mark A.; Levine, Richard J.; DerSimonian, Rebecca; Clemens, John D.; and Wilkins, Diana G. (1999). Maternal serum paraxanthine, a caffeine metabolite, and the risk of spontaneous abortion. *New England Journal of Medicine, 341,* 1639–1644.

32. Gilbert, *Caffeine,* pp. 78–79.
33. Charney, Dennis S., Heniger, George R., and Jatlow, Peter L. (1985). Increased anxiogenic effects of caffeine in panic disorders. *Archives of General Psychiatry, 42,* 233–243. Clay, Rebecca A. (1996, August). Coffee's jittery high can thwart treatment plans. *APA Monitor* (American Psychology Association, Washington DC), p. 12.
34. Weidner, Gerdi, and Istvan, Joseph (1985). Dietary sources of caffeine. *New England Journal of Medicine, 313,* 1421.
35. DeAngelis, Tori (1994, February). People's drug of choice offers potent side effects. *APA Monitor* (American Psychological Association, Washington DC), p. 16. Quotation by Dr. John Hughes.
36. Robertson, David; Wade, Dawn; Workman, Robert; and Woosley, Raymond L. (1981). Tolerance to the humoral and hemodynamic effects of caffeine in man. *Journal of Clinical Investigation, 67,* 1111–1117.
37. Griffiths, Roland R., and Woodson, Phillip P. (1988). Caffeine physical dependence: A review of human and animal laboratory studies. *Psychopharmacology, 94,* 437–451. Phillips-Bute, Barbara G., and Lane, James D. (1998). Caffeine withdrawal symptoms following brief caffeine deprivation. *Physiology and Behavior, 63,* 35–39. Schuh, Kory J., and Griffiths, Roland R. (1997). Caffeine reinforcement: The role of withdrawal. *Psychopharmacology, 130,* 320–326.
38. American Psychiatric Association (1994). *Diagnostic and statistical manual of mental disorders (DSM-IV)* (4th ed.). Washington DC: American Psychiatric Association, pp. 212–215. Greden, John F., and Walters, Adale (1997). Caffeine. In Joyce H. Lowinson, Pedro Ruiz, Robert B. Millman, and John G. Langrod (Eds.), *Substance abuse: A comprehensive textbook.* Baltimore: William and Wilkins, pp. 294–307. Larson, Cynthia A., and Carey, Kate B. (1998). Caffeine: Brewing trouble in mental health settings? *Professional Psychology, 29,* 373–376.
39. Gilbert, *Caffeine,* pp. 108–109.
40. Bernstein, Gail A.; Carroll, Marilyn E.; Dean, Nicole W.; Crosby, Ross D.; Perwien, Amy R.; and Benowitz, Neal L. (1998). Caffeine withdrawal in normal school-age children. *Journal of the American Academy of Child and Adolescent Psychiatry, 37,* 858–865. Cordes, Helen (1998, April 27). Generation wired: Caffeine is the new drug of choice for kids. *The Nation,* pp. 11–16. Skinner, Jean D.; Carruth, Betty Ruth; Houck, Kelly S.; Morris, Melissa; et al. (2000). Caffeine intake in young children differs by family socioeconomic status. *Journal of the American Dietetic Association, 100,* 229–231. Van Tine, Julia (1998, December). The buzz on kids and caffeine. *Prevention,* p. 32.

CHAPTER 13

Glues, Solvents, and Other Inhalants

After you have completed this chapter, you will understand

- The history of psychoactive inhalants
- The acute effects and dangers of glue, solvent, or aerosol spray inhalation
- Patterns of inhalant abuse and its chronic effects
- Society's response to concerns about inhalant abuse
- The abuse of amyl nitrite and butyl nitrite

"I remember," Julio says, taking quick, nervous puffs from his cigarette, "when I was a little kid, maybe eight or nine, and I used to take the garbage out for my mother, I'd always see tubes from airplane glue under the stairwell in our apartment house and in the alley out back. At first, glue just meant building models to me. But I'd see people sniffing it, under the stairwell. I was curious, and one day I tried it. It made me feel like I was in a trance. It wasn't really exciting, but I did it again and again until we moved, and in the new neighborhood people weren't into glue and I didn't see the empty tubes to remind me anymore."[1]

Sometimes, psychoactive drugs do not originate in a pharmacy or a liquor store or even on the street. They can be found under the sink, in kitchen or bathroom cabinets, in the basement, or in the garage. Ordinary household products frequently have the potential for giving euphoriant effects if they are sniffed or inhaled. When you consider that these substances are readily available to anyone in a family, including its youngest members, the consequences of their abuse become particularly troubling. This chapter will concern itself with glues, solvents, and other inhalant products, as dangerous recreational drugs.

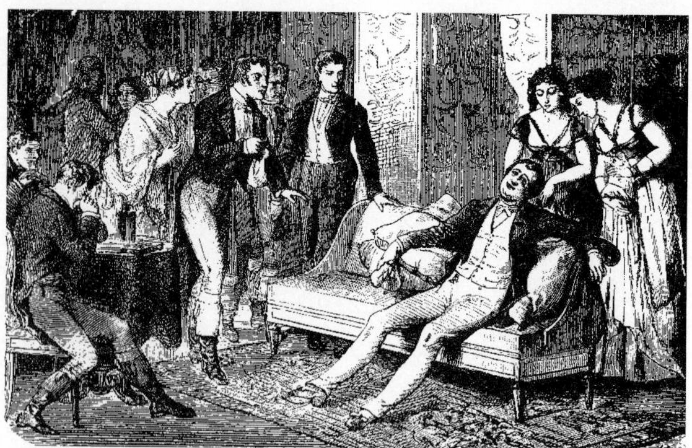

Inhalation of nitrous oxide provided an extra measure of frivolity in an evening of entertainment in the early nineteenth century.

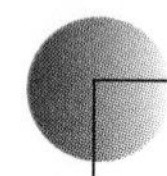

Inhalants through History

The mind-altering effects of substances inhaled into the lungs have been known since the beginnings of recorded history. Burnt spices and aromatic gums were used in acts of worship in most parts of the ancient world; exotic perfumes were inhaled during Egyptian worship as well as in Babylonian rituals. Inhalation effects also figured prominently in the famous rites of the oracle at Delphi in ancient Greece, where trances induced by the inhaling of vapors led to mysterious utterances that were interpreted as prophecies.[2]

Whether any of these phenomena were the result of genuine psychoactive effects rather than of placebo effects is difficult to tell, since it is not known what substances were involved. It was not until the latter part of the eighteenth century that reports about the inhalation of specific drugs began to appear. The two most prominent examples were cases involving nitrous oxide and ether. These anesthetic drugs were first used as surgical analgesics in the 1840s, but they had been synthesized decades earlier. From the very start, the word spread of recreational possibilities.

Nitrous Oxide

The British chemist Sir Humphrey Davy synthesized the gas **nitrous oxide** in 1798 at the precocious age of nineteen. He immediately observed the pleasant effects of this "laughing gas" and proceeded to give nitrous-oxide parties for his literary and artistic friends. By the early 1800s, recreational use of nitrous oxide became widespread both in England and the United States as a nonalcoholic avenue to drunkenness. In the 1840s, public demonstrations were held in cities and towns, as a traveling show, by entrepreneurs eager to market the drug commercially.

It was at such an exhibition in Hartford, Connecticut, that a young dentist, Horace Wells, got the idea for using nitrous oxide as an anesthetic. One of the intoxicated participants in the demonstration had stumbled and fallen, receiving in the process a severe wound to the leg. Seeing that the man showed no evidence of pain despite his injury, Wells was sufficiently impressed to try out the anesthetic possibilities himself. The next day, he underwent a tooth extraction while under the influence of nitrous oxide. He felt no pain during the procedure, and nitrous oxide has been a part of dental practice ever since, though recently its role as a routine anesthesia has become a matter of controversy.[3]

During the 1960s, nitrous-oxide inhalation reappeared as a recreational drug. Tanks of compressed nitrous oxide were diverted for illicit use, and health professionals, like their counterparts one hundred years earlier, were reportedly hosting nitrous oxide parties. Small cartridges of nitrous oxide called **whippets**, generally used by restaurants to dispense whipped cream, became available through college campus "head shops" and mail-order catalogs. The customary pattern of nitrous-oxide abuse was to fill a balloon from these cylinders and inhale the gas from the balloon. The result was a mild euphoric high that lasted for a few minutes and a sense of well-being that lingered for several hours. Sometimes, there would be a loss of consciousness for a few seconds and an experience of "flying." Once consciousness returned, there was the possibility of sensory distortions,

nitrous oxide (NEYE-trus OX-eyed): An analgesic gas commonly used in modern dentistry. It is also referred to as laughing gas.

whippets: Small canisters containing pressurized nitrous oxide.

nausea, or vomiting. Ordinary cans of commercial whipped cream, in which nitrous oxide is the propellant gas, currently provide easy access to this inhalant.

Nitrous oxide itself is a nontoxic gas, but its inhalation presents serious risks. As with any euphoriant drug, the recreational use of nitrous oxide can be extremely dangerous when a person is driving under its influence. In addition, if nitrous oxide is inhaled through an anesthetic mask and the mask is worn over the mouth and nose, without the combination of oxygen, the consequences can be lethal. Nitrous oxide dilutes the air that a person breathes. Unless there is a minimum of 21 percent oxygen in the mixture, reproducing the 21 percent oxygen content in the air, a lack of oxygen (called **hypoxia**) will produce suffocation or irreversible brain damage.[4]

Ether

As was true of nitrous oxide, **ether** came into use well before its anesthetic effects were appreciated by the medical profession. It was introduced by Friedrich Hoffmann at the beginning of the 1700s, under the name Anodyne, as a liquid "nerve tonic" for intestinal cramps, toothaches, and other pains. Whether it was swallowed or inhaled (it evaporated very quickly), ether also produced effects that resembled intoxication from alcohol. In fact, during the mid-1800s, when the combination of a heavy tax on alcohol and an anti-alcohol temperance campaign in England and Ireland forced people to consider alternatives to alcoholic beverages, both ether drinking and ether inhalation became quite popular. It was used for the same purpose later in the United States during the Prohibition years and in Germany during World War II when alcohol was rationed. Ether's flammability, however, made its recreational use highly dangerous.[5]

TABLE 13.1

Common household products with abuse potential as inhalants
Gasoline
Hobby glues and cements
Paint thinners
Lacquers and enamels
Varnishes and varnish removers
Cigarette or charcoal lighter fluid
Fingernail polishes and polish remover
Stain removers, degreasers, and other dry-cleaning products
Upholstery protection spray products (e.g., Scotchgard*)
Windshield de-icers
Disinfectants
Fire extinguishing volatile chemicals
Typewriter correction fluid
Permanent felt marker ink
Aerosol hair sprays
Vegetable frying pan lubricants
Spray deodorants
Spray paints
Whipped cream propellants
Freon

Note: The above is a partial list. New products are continually being introduced.

*Scotchgard is a registered product of the 3M Corporation.

Glue, Solvent, and Aerosol Inhalation

The abuse of nitrous oxide and ether may have a relatively long history, but the more familiar reports of inhalation abuse involving glue and solvent chemicals have only appeared since the late 1950s. Table 13.1 lists some of the common products that have been subject to abuse, including glues, paint thinners, lighter fluid, and stain removers. In addition, many aerosol products are also inhalable: hair sprays, deodorants, vegetable lubricants for cooking, and spray paints. Unfortunately, new products are continually being introduced for genuinely practical uses, with little awareness of the consequences should someone inhale their ingredients on a recreational basis (Table 13.2). There are also significant problems associated with occupational exposure to solvent vapors. In a recent study, one hundred and twenty-five pregnant women who had been exposed to solvent products at the workplace were studied over a nine-year period. There was a thirteen-times greater risk of birth defects among the exposed group, relative to controls. Occupations of these women included factory workers, laboratory technicians, artists, printing industry workers, chemists, and painters.[6]

The Abuse Potential of Inhalants

Commercial glues, solvents, and aerosol sprays are prime candidates for drug abuse for a number of reasons. First

hypoxia (heye-POX-ee-ah): A deficiency in oxygen intake.

ether (EE-ther): An anesthetic drug, first introduced to surgical practice by William T. Morton in the 1840s. It is highly flammable.

TABLE 13.2

Household products with abuse potential and their ingredients

HOUSEHOLD PRODUCT	POSSIBLE INGREDIENTS
Glues, plastic cements, and rubber cements	Acetates, acetone, benzene, hexane, methyl chloride, toluene, trichloroethylene
Cleaning solutions	Carbon tetrachloride, petroleum products, trichloroethylene
Nail polish removers	Acetone
Lighter fluids	Butane, isopropane
Paint sprays, paint thinners, and paint removers	Acetone, butylacetate, methanol, toluene
Other petroleum products	Acetone, benzene, ether, gasoline, hexane, petroleum, tetraethyl lead, toluene
Typewriter correction fluid	Trichloroethylene
Hair sprays	Butane, propane
Deodorants, air fresheners	Butane, propane
Whipped cream propellants	Nitrous oxide

Source: Sharp, Charles W., and Rosenberg, Neil L. (1997). Inhalants. In Joyce H. Lowinson, Pedro Ruiz, Robert B. Millman, and John G. Langrod (Eds.), *Substance abuse: A comprehensive textbook* (3rd ed.). Baltimore: Williams and Wilkins, p. 248.

of all, because they are inhaled into the lungs, the feeling of intoxication occurs more rapidly than with orally administered alcohol. "It's a quicker drunk," in the words of one solvent abuser.[7] The feeling is often described as a "floating euphoria," similar to the effect of alcohol but with a shorter course of intoxication. The high is over in an hour or so, and the hangover is considered less unpleasant than that following alcohol consumption. Second, the typical packaging of inhalant products makes them easy to carry around and conceal from others. Even if they are discovered, many of the products are so common that it is not difficult to invent an excuse for having them on hand.

Finally, most inhalants are easily available in hardware stores, pharmacies, and supermarkets, where they can be bought cheaply or stolen. Among some inhalant abusers, shoplifting these products from open shelves is not only routine but expected. Inhalants are even more widely available than alcohol in poor households; liquor may be in short supply but gasoline, paints, or aerosol products are usually around the house or garage.[8] All these factors contribute to the considerable potential for inhalant abuse.

Acute Effects of Glues, Solvents, and Aerosols

The fumes from commercial inhalant products fall into the general category of depressant drugs, in that the central nervous system is inhibited after they are inhaled. Brain waves, measured objectively through an electroencephalograph (EEG), slow down. Subjectively, the individual feels intoxicated within minutes after inhalation. The most immediate effects include giddiness, euphoria, dizziness, and slurred speech, lasting for fifteen to forty-five minutes. This state is followed by one to two hours of drowsiness and sometimes a loss of consciousness. Along with these effects are occasional experiences of double vision, ringing in the ears, and hallucinations.[9]

The Dangers of Inhalant Abuse

We should realize that inhalant abuse often involves concentrations of glue and solvent products that are usually fifty to a hundred times greater than the maximum allowable concentration of exposure in industry. The health of the inhalant abuser, therefore, is obviously at risk (Health Alert).

The dangers of inhalant abuse lie not only in the toxic effects of the inhaled compound on body organs but in the behavioral effects of the intoxication itself. Inhalant-produced feelings of euphoria include feelings of recklessness and omnipotence. There have been instances of young inhalant abusers leaping off roof tops in an effort to fly, running into traffic, lying on railroad tracks, or incurring severe lacerations when pushing their hand through a glass window that has been perceived as open. The hallucinations that are sometimes experienced carry their own personal risks. Walls may appear to be closing in or the sky may seem to be falling. Ordinary objects may be perceived to be changing their shape, size, or color. Any one of these delusions can easily lead to impulsive and potentially destructive behavior.[10]

There are also hazards in the ways in which inhalants are administered. While solvents are sometimes inhaled from a handkerchief or from the container in which they were originally acquired ("huffing"), glues and similar vaporous compounds are often squeezed into a plastic bag and inhaled while the bag is held tightly over the nose and mouth ("bagging"). Potentially, a loss of consciousness can result in hypoxia and asphyxiation. Choking can occur if there is vomiting while the inhaler is unconscious. In an early investigation in the 1960s of nine documented deaths attributed to glue inhalation, at least six were caused specifically by a lack of oxygen.[11] Another danger

Health Alert

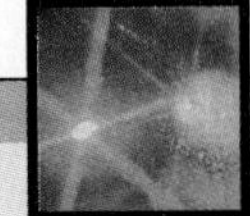

The Signs of Possible Inhalant Abuse

- Headaches and dizziness
- Light sensitivity (from dilation of the pupils)
- Reddened, irritated eyes and rash around the mouth
- Double vision
- Ringing in the ears (tinnitus)
- Sneezing and sniffling
- Coughing and bad breath
- Nausea, vomiting, and loss of appetite
- Diarrhea
- Chest pains
- Abnormal heart rhythm (cardiac arrhythmia)
- Muscle and joint aches
- Slurred speech and unsteady muscle coordination
- Chemical odor or stains on clothing or body
- Rags, empty aerosol cans and other containers
- Plastic and paper bags found in closets and other hidden places

Sources: Fox, C. Lynn, and Forbing, Shirley, E. (1992). *Creating drug-free schools and communities.* New York: HarperCollins, p. 37. Schuckit, Marc A. (1995). *Drug and alcohol abuse: A clinical guide to diagnosis and treatment* (4th ed.). New York: Plenum Medical Book Co., p. 219.

lies in the inhalation of freon, a refrigerant gas so cold that the larynx and throat can be frozen upon contact.

The toxic effects of inhalant drugs themselves depend on the specific compound, but the picture is complicated by the fact that most products subject to inhalant abuse contain a variety of compounds and in some cases the list of ingredients on the product label is incomplete. Therefore, often we do not know if the medical symptoms resulted from a particular chemical or its interaction with others. Nonetheless, there are specific chemicals that have known health risks. The most serious concern involves sudden-death cases, brought on by cardiac dysrhythmia, that have been reported following the inhalation of propane and butane, commonly used as a propellant for many commercial products.

In 1991, a total of 56 solvent-abuse deaths were reported in the United States and 122 in England. The number of deaths in England was about twice that in the United States, but in fact the death rate was actually twenty times higher, taking into account the population difference between the two nations.[12] Besides butane and propane, other inhalant ingredients that present specific hazards are *acetone, benzene, hexane, toluene,* and *gasoline.*

- *Acetone:* **Acetone** inhalation causes significant damage to the mucous membranes of the respiratory tract.
- *Benzene:* Prolonged exposure to **benzene** has been associated with carcinogenic (cancer-related) disorders, specifically leukemia, as well as anemia. Benzene is generally used as a solvent in waxes, resins, lacquers, paints, and paint removers.
- *Hexane:* The inhalation of **hexane,** primarily in glues and other adhesive products, has been associated with peripheral nerve damage leading to muscular weakness and muscle atrophy. There is a latency period of a few weeks before the symptoms appear.
- *Toluene:* **Toluene** inhalation through glue sniffing has been associated with a reduction in short-term memory, anemia, and a loss of hearing, as well as dysfunctions of the cerebellum that result in difficulties in movement and coordination. Toluene has also been implicated as a principal factor in cases of lethal inhalation of spray paints and lacquers, though it is difficult to exclude the contribution of other solvents in these products.
- *Gasoline:* Concentrated vapors from gasoline can be lethal when inhaled. Medical symptoms from gasoline inhalation are also frequently attributed to gasoline additives that are mixed in the fuel. The additive **triorthocresyl phosphate (TCP),** in particular, has been associated with spastic muscle disorders and liver problems. Lead content in gasoline is generally linked to long-term CNS degeneration, but fortunately leaded

acetone (ASS-eh-tohn): A chemical found in nail polish removers and other products.
benzene: A carcinogenic (cancer-producing) compound found in many solvent products, representing a serious health risk when inhaled.
hexane: A dangerous compound present in many glues and adhesive products. Inhalation of these products has been associated with muscular weakness and atrophy.
toluene (TOL-yoo-ene): A compound in glues, cements, and other adhesive products. Inhalation of these products results in behavioral and neurological impairments.
triorthocresyl phosphate (TCP) (tri-OR-thoh-CREH-sil FOS-fate): A gasoline additive. Inhalation of TCP-containing gasoline has been linked to spastic muscle disorders and liver problems.

gasoline is no longer commonly available in the United States. On the other hand, present-day gasoline mixtures contain large amounts of toluene, acetone, and hexane to help achieve the "anti-knock" quality that lead had previously provided.[13]

Patterns of Inhalant Abuse

Among all the psychoactive drugs, inhalants are associated most closely with the young and often the very young. For those who engage in inhalant abuse, these compounds frequently represent the first experience with a psychoactive drug, preceding even alcohol or tobacco. Overall, inhalant abuse ranks as the fourth highest incidence of drug experimentation among secondary school students, surpassed only by alcohol, tobacco, and marijuana (in that order). Most of these drug abusers, however, are younger than secondary school age: often they are between eleven and thirteen years old. The University of Michigan survey of 2000 found that almost one out of five eighth-grade students (18 percent) had used inhalants at some previous time. About 9 percent reported that they had used inhalants within the past year, and 5 percent within the past month. Inhalants are the only class of drugs for which the incidence of usage in the eighth grade significantly exceeds the incidence in the tenth and twelfth grades. Evidently, awareness of this form of drug-taking activity is quite extensive in the later elementary and middle school student population. According to a recent survey, almost two-thirds of ten- to seventeen-year-olds know the meaning of "huffing" and report that they were about twelve years of age when they first knew of classmates abusing inhalants.[14]

In other cultures and under different circumstances, inhalant abuse affects even younger children and a wider proportion of that age group. In Mexico City, among street children as young as eight or nine who live without families in abandoned buildings, rates of inhalant abuse are extremely high, with 22 percent reporting some form of solvent inhalation on a daily basis. Inhalant abuse is reported to be commonplace among street children in Rio de Janeiro and other major cities in Central and South America and Asia (Drugs . . . in Focus).[15]

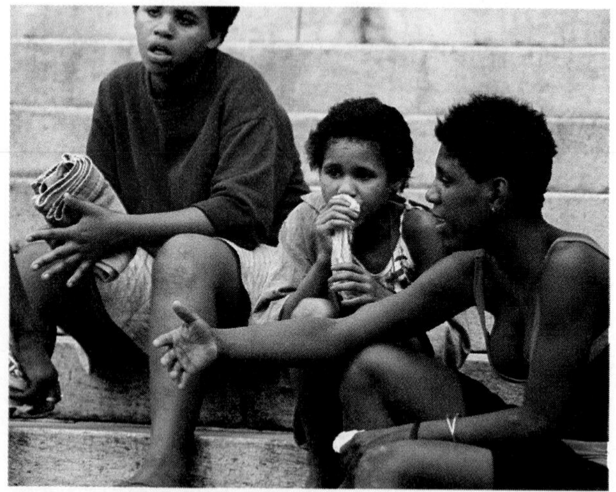

A group of abandoned Brazilian children inhale glue from bags in Rio de Janeiro. The dazed expression is a typical sign of inhalant intoxication.

DRUGS . . . IN FOCUS

Resistol and *Resistoleros* in Latin America

In the cities of Central and South America, the street children are referred to as *resistoleros,* a name derived from their frequent habit of sniffing a commercial brand of shoemaker's glue called Resistol. Granted, many cases of inhalant abuse among the hundreds of thousands of children in Latin America do not specifically involve Resistol; nevertheless, the frequency of Resistol abuse and the fact that Resistol dominates the market in commercial solvent-based adhesives have focused attention on the company that manufactures it, the H. B. Fuller Company of St. Paul, Minnesota.

Concern for the welfare of these children has also spotlighted a thorny ethical issue: Should a corporation accept the social responsibility when widespread abuse of its product exists, either in the United States or elsewhere in the world? Testor Corporation in 1969 added a noxious ingredient to discourage abuse of its model glue; in 1994, a German chemical company marketing a Resistol rival stopped its distribution in this region. For its part, Fuller did modify the formulation of Resistol in 1992, replacing the sweet-smelling but highly toxic toluene with a slightly less toxic chemical, cyclohexane. However, it continues to sell Resistol, claiming that its legitimate uses benefit the economies of regions where it is marketed. Moreover, the company has funded community programs for homeless children throughout Central America and has restricted its Resistol marketing efforts to large industrial customers rather than small retailers. Unappeased, foes continue to press Fuller to discontinue the product entirely.

Source: Henriques, Diana B. (1995, November 26). Black mark for a "good citizen." Critics say H. B. Fuller isn't doing enough to curb glue-sniffing. *New York Times,* Section 3, pp. 1, 11.

Inhalant abuse, on an experimental basis, is not restricted by social or geographic boundaries (Portrait). Chronic inhalant abuse, however, is overrepresented among the poor and those youths suffering emotional challenges in their lives and seeking some form of escape. Studies of young inhalant abusers show high rates of delinquency, poor school performance, and emotional difficulties. They often come from disorganized, multi-problem homes in which the parents are actually or effectively absent or else engage themselves in abuse of alcohol or some other substance.[16] The diversity of ethnic subgroups showing high prevalence rates for inhalant abuse include such disparate groups as Latino children in a rural community in the Southwest, Native American children on U.S. reservations, and white children in an economically disadvantaged neighborhood in Philadelphia.

Whatever the ethnic identity of the chronic inhalant abuser, a critical factor is peer influence. Most studies indicate that glue, solvent, or aerosol inhalation is generally experienced in small groups, often at the urging of friends or relatives. Young inhalant abusers tend to be more alienated than others at this age, and the feelings of alienation can be an important factor in leading a youth to others who are also alienated, thus creating a cluster of peers who engage in this form of drug-taking behavior. One survey among Native American youth, for example, found that when friends strongly encouraged inhalant use or would not try to stop it, 84 percent of the sample reported having tried inhalants and 41 percent reported having used them recently. In contrast, when friends discouraged inhalant use or were perceived as applying strong sanctions against it, only 19 percent reported having tried inhalants and only 3 percent had used them recently.[17]

Questions about Chronic Inhalant Abuse

The long-term effects of inhalant abuse are not well documented, owing to the fact that inhalant abuse frequently does not extend over more than a year or two in a person's life and may occur only sporadically. There have been reports of cases showing a tolerance to the euphoriant effects of glues and gasoline. Although it is difficult to determine the dosages that are involved with these tolerance

Portrait Scott Pecor—The Scotchgard High

On a secluded beach in south Florida, a group of friends would meet on a weekend and pass around the $5 spray can of Scotchgard, a substance that is sprayed on upholstery and carpets to prevent stains from spills. A saturated washcloth held against the mouth for a few seconds was all it would take to get a few minutes of tingling and intoxication. There would be no worry about beer cans or liquor bottles that their parents might discover, no need for a fake ID to buy it, no telltale signs to give them away.

"That's all that you really needed to get high," Courtney Knief, a fifteen-year-old girl from Fort Pierce, later recalled. She doesn't, however, sniff Scotchgard anymore.

"It killed my boyfriend and my best friend. I had no idea somebody could die from it. I wish I would have had the sense to open my eyes and say hey this is stupid."

Courtney's boyfriend was sixteen-year-old Scott Pecor of nearby Port St. Lucie, who had died of heart failure from a large dose of inhaled Scotchgard. His older brother had found him unconscious in his backyard and had found the near-empty can on the family's couch. Scott and Courtney had been "huffing" Scotchgard for about three months; they had gotten high three days before he died.

Family and friends comfort each other at Scott Pecor's funeral in 1991

Scott was a soccer player and honors student in his high school, with aspirations to be an architect. He wasn't an angry or rebellious kid, his parents say. Without any signs of overt drunken behavior or obvious aftereffects, Scott's inhalant abuse went totally unnoticed by them.

From 1989 to 1991, the local medical examiner had recorded three teenage deaths in three nearby counties. One boy died after inhaling butane lighter refills, another from inhaling paint thinner. Scott was the first casualty from Scotchgard itself, though the manufacturer, the 3M Company of Minneapolis, reported that from 1989 to 1991 more than twenty people died from inhaling the fabric protector.

Unfortunately, the dangers of inhalants are not fully appreciated. In a 1990 school district survey in a Florida county immediately south of where Scott lived, 10 percent of seventh graders indicated that inhalants were not perceived as harmful and between 8 and 10 percent of them reported having used them. Scotchgard and Freon were current favorites.

Source: Hiaasen, Rob (1991, March 29). The newest deadly high. *Palm Beach Post*, p. 1D.

effects, it appears that individuals exposed only to low concentrations for brief periods of time or high levels occasionally do not show tolerance to the inhalants.

Inhalant dependence occurs frequently. Inhalant abusers have been reported as feeling restless, irritable, and anxious when prevented from inhaling glues, solvents, or aerosols. Physiological withdrawal symptoms are only rarely observed among inhalant abusers but are frequently observed among animals in laboratory studies, so the question of whether physical dependence exists has yet to be definitively answered.[18]

A Gateway for Future Drug Abuse?

The young age at which inhalant abuse occurs leads to the question of whether there is a causal link between inhalant abuse and later abuse of other drugs. Without a doubt, some youths will subsequently replace inhalants with alcohol, marijuana, and other recreational drugs, but the experience of inhalants cannot be considered to lead, per se, to other drug experimentation or long-term abuse. This is how one author has put it:

> *The socially and emotionally healthy juvenile casually experimenting with solvent sniffing does not bear any greater potential for heroin addiction than had he not sniffed solvents. Conversely, the disturbed youth from a broken home, who is frequently exposed to pushers, probably bears the same high risk of ultimate narcotic abuse whether or not he sniffs glue. Regardless of surrounding circumstances, however, any significant resort to intoxicating substances in childhood should be carefully noted as a potential warning of a growing emotional disturbance or as a predictor of a future drug-dependent personality.*[19]

A similar "gateway argument" with respect to marijuana was presented in Chapter 7.

SNIFFING CORRECTION FLUID
CAN STOP YOUR HEART.

Poster images represent a growing national effort to prevent inhalation abuse.

Responses of Society to Inhalant Abuse

> *Sniffing gasoline or paint is a grubby, dirty, cheap way to get high. Inhalant users are, therefore, likely to be the social rejects, the emotionally disturbed, the disadvantaged minorities, the maladjusted, as well as angry and alienated. There is nothing attractive, exciting, or appealing about inhalant use or inhalant users. . . .*[20]

Certainly, the concern about inhalant abuse takes a backseat to more widely publicized concerns about cocaine and heroin abuse. Despite the relatively low priority given to inhalant abuse, however, steps have been taken to reduce some of its hazards. One major approach has been to restrict the availability and sales of glues to young people, a strategy that, as you might predict, has met with mixed success. Some U.S. cities have restricted sales of plastic cement unless it is purchased with a model kit, but such legislation is largely ineffective when model kits themselves are relatively inexpensive. As with the official restriction of sales of alcohol and tobacco to minors, young people can find a way around these laws.

More direct action has been taken since 1969 by the Testor Corporation, a leading manufacturer of plastic cement for models, by incorporating **oil of mustard** into the formula. This additive produces severe nasal irrita-

oil of mustard: An additive in Testor brand hobby-kit glues that produces nasal irritation when inhaled, thus reducing the potential for inhalant abuse.

tion similar to the effect of horseradish, while not affecting its use as a glue or the effect on the user who does not inhale it directly. Other brands of glues and adhesives, however, may not contain oil of mustard and as a result could still be available for abuse, and additives in general would not be desirable for certain products that are used for cosmetic purposes.

In an additional step taken to reduce inhalant abuse, concentrations of benzene in many household products sold in the United States have been reduced or eliminated, though it is difficult to determine the exact composition of solutions merely by inspecting the label. Standards for products manufactured and sold in foreign countries are typically far less stringent.[21]

Beyond the difficulty in identifying the toxicity of specific solvent compounds, there is the overriding general problem of the enormous variety and easy availability of solvent-containing products. As one researcher has lamented, "If sales of gold paint or paint thinner are curtailed, people may choose to use typewriter correction fluid, or shoe polish or nail polish remover, or hundreds of other items that have legitimate uses in everyday life."[22]

Ultimately, some sort of educational strategy must be coordinated that is targeted at children in the elementary grades in school and their parents at home. Different countries have differing educational approaches, ranging from nonalarmist, low-key programs to those urging absolute abstinence, and it is not clear which strategy is most effective in controlling inhalant abuse. A National Inhalants and Poisons Awareness Week is currently held each year in March, to promote greater efforts to inform the public about this problem.[23]

In the meantime, attention has zeroed in on abusive inhalation of two specific products, amyl nitrite and butyl nitrite, affecting an entirely different population from the one traditionally associated with glue, solvent, or aerosol inhalants. Like nitrous oxide and ether, these nitrites have been around for some time, but their abuse has been relatively recent.

Amyl Nitrite and Butyl Nitrite Inhalation

Amyl and butyl nitrites were first identified in the nineteenth century. When inhaled, they produce an intense vasodilation, a relaxation of smooth muscle, a fall in blood pressure, and a reflex increase in heart rate. Since 1867, **amyl nitrite** has been used medically, on a prescription basis, in the treatment of angina pain in heart patients and as an antidote to cyanide poisoning. **Butyl nitrite** produces similar therapeutic effects but has never been used on a clinical basis.

News of the recreational potential of nitrite inhalation began to spread in the 1960s and reached a peak in the 1970s, particularly within the homosexual community, as it was recognized that the vasodilation of cerebral blood vessels produced a euphoric high, anal sphincter muscles were relaxed, and vasodilation of genital blood vessels enhanced sexual pleasure (Table 13.3). By 1979, more than 5 million people in the United States were using amyl or butyl nitrites more than once a week. The concern, however, that nitrites might be linked to the development of **Kaposi's sarcoma,** a rare form of cancer affecting the immune system, frequently observed in AIDS patients, has led to a significant decline in their popularity, although they continue to be abused.[24]

Patterns of Nitrite Inhalation Abuse

Amyl nitrite is often referred to as "poppers" or "snappers" because it is commonly available in a mesh-covered glass ampule and there is a popping sound as the ampule is broken and the vapors of the nitrite are inhaled as they are released into the air. It is quick-acting, with vasodilatory effects appearing within thirty seconds. Light-headedness, a flushing sensation, blurred vision, and euphoria last for about five minutes, followed by headache and nausea. Butyl nitrite follows a similar time course in its effects and is available in pornography shops and mail-order catalogs. Many of the various "trade names" for butyl nitrite (Table 13.4) refer to its supposed sexual benefits as well as the fact that its vapors emit a strong odor resembling that of sweaty socks.

Frequently identified with homosexual activity, cases of nitrite inhalation have also been found among

amyl nitrite (AY-mil NEYE-trite): An inhalant drug that relaxes smooth muscle and produces euphoria. Clinically useful in treating angina pain in cardiac patients, it is also subject to abuse.

butyl nitrite (BYOO-til NEYE-trite): An inhalant drug, similar in its effects to amyl nitrite. It is commonly abused as it induces feelings of euphoria.

Kaposi's sarcoma: A form of cancer affecting the immune system and associated with AIDS.

TABLE 13.3

A chronology of nitrite inhalation abuse

DATE	EXAMPLE OF INHALATION	DATE	EXAMPLE OF INHALATION
1859	Flushing of skin with amyl nitrite first described	1976	$50 million sales reported in nitrites in one U.S. city
1867	First therapeutic use of amyl nitrite for angina pain	1977	Nitrite inhalation predominant among homosexual men
1880s	Butyl nitrite studied but not used clinically	1979	More than 5 million people estimated to have used nitrites more than once per week
1960	Amyl nitrite prescription requirement eliminated by FDA		19 cases of Kaposi's sarcoma found in retrospect
1963	First reports of recreational use of nitrites	1980	56 cases of Kaposi's sarcoma reported
1960s	Widespread recreational use of nitrites among young adults	1981	Increased suspicions of a link between nitrite use and Kaposi's sarcoma
1969	Amyl nitrite prescription requirement reinstated	1985	Concerns about AIDS and HIV infection beginning to receive widespread media attention
1970	Street brands of butyl nitrite beginning to be widely available	1990s to present	Nitrite inhalation abuse greatly reduced among nonhomosexual populations
1974	Popper craze beginning		

Source: Updated from Newell, Guy R., Spitz, Margaret R., and Wilson, Michael B. (1988). Nitrite inhalants: Historical perspective. In Harry W. Haverkos and John A. Dougherty (Eds.), *Health hazards of nitrite inhalants* (NIDA Research Monograph 83). Rockville MD: National Institute of Drug Abuse, p. 6.

heterosexual adolescents, for whom the primary attraction is a feeling of general euphoria. The University of Michigan survey began looking at prevalence rates for nitrite inhalation in 1979. In that year, approximately 11 percent of high school seniors reported having tried nitrite inhalants at least once in their lifetime. By 2000, the rate had dropped substantially to less than 1 percent.[25]

Health Risks in Nitrite Inhalation Abuse

Nitrites increase intraocular pressure and as a result are associated with the development of glaucoma. Blood-cell abnormalities are also observed. The primary concern, however, surrounds the potential carcinogenic effects of nitrites. Studies of individuals with Kaposi's sarcoma have showed a high incidence of nitrite inhalation. Although it is now known that AIDS is produced by an infection of the human immunodeficiency virus (HIV), the growing consensus is that nitrite inhalation is a cofactor in the suppression of the immune system that is characteristic of AIDS and increases the risk of Kaposi's sarcoma.[26]

TABLE 13.4

"Brand names" for butyl nitrite

Aroma of Men	Hardware	Mama Poppers
Ban Apple Gas	Heart On	Oz
Bang	Highball	Quick Silver
Bullet	Jac Aroma	Rush
Climax	Lightning Bolt	Satan's Scent
Crypt Tonight	Liquid Increase	Thrust
Discorama	Locker Room	Toilet Water

Source: Maickel, Roger P. (1988). The fate and toxicity of butyl nitrites. In Harry W. Haverkos and John A. Dougherty (Eds.), *Health hazards of nitrite inhalants* (NIDA Research Monograph 83). Rockville MD: National Institute on Drug Abuse, p. 16.

QUICK CONCEPT CHECK 13.1

Understanding the History of Inhalants

Check your understanding of the history of inhalant drugs by indicating whether a particular substance was used (a) first recreationally, then as an application in medicine; (b) first as an application in medicine, then recreationally; or (c) recreationally, with no known application in medicine.

1. amyl nitrite
2. hexane
3. nitrous oxide
4. toluene

Answers: 1. b 2. c 3. a 4. c

SUMMARY

Glue, Solvent, and Aerosol Inhalation

- Present-day inhalant abuse involves a wide range of commercial products: gasoline, glues and other adhesives, household cleaning compounds, aerosol sprays, and solvents of all kinds.
- These products are usually cheap, readily available, and easily concealable, and their intoxicating effects when inhaled are rapid. All of these factors make inhalants prime candidates for abuse.
- The principal dangers of inhalant abuse lie in the behavioral consequences of intoxication and in the possibility of asphyxiation when inhalants are administered by an airproof bag held over the nose and mouth.
- Specific toxic substances contained in inhalant products include acetone, benzene, hexane, toluene, and gasoline.

Patterns of Inhalant Abuse

- Inhalant abuse respects no social or geographic boundaries, though prevalence rates are particularly high among poor and disadvantaged populations.
- Research studies indicate the presence of psychological dependence rather than physical dependence in inhalant abuse behavior.
- Tolerance effects are seen for chronic inhalant abusers when the inhalant concentration is high and exposure is frequent.

Responses of Society to Inhalant Abuse

- Concern about the dangers of inhalant abuse has led to restriction of the sale of model-kit glues to minors and a modification of the formulas for model-kit glue in order to lessen the popularity of deliberate inhalation.
- There are so many products currently on the open market that contain volatile chemicals that a universal restriction of abusable inhalants is practically impossible.

Amyl Nitrite and Butyl Nitrite Inhalation

- Two types of inhalants, amyl nitrite and butyl nitrite, appeared on the scene in the 1960s, reaching a peak in the late 1970s. Although they are chiefly identified with homosexual individuals, populations of heterosexual adolescents and young adults have also engaged in this form of inhalant abuse.
- These nitrites are recognized now as a cofactor in the development of Kaposi's sarcoma, a form of cancer associated with AIDS.

KEY TERMS

acetone, p. 279
amyl nitrite, p. 283
benzene, p. 279
butyl nitrite, p. 283
ether, p. 277
hexane, p. 279
hypoxia, p. 277
Kaposi's sarcoma, p. 283
nitrous oxide, p. 276
oil of mustard, p. 282
toluene, p. 279
triorthocresyl phosphate (TCP), p. 279
whippets, p. 276

ENDNOTES

1. Quotation from Silverstein, Alvin, Silverstein, Virginia, and Silverstein, Robert (1991). *The addictions handbook.* Hillside NJ: Enslow Publishers, p. 51.
2. Preble, Edward, and Laury, Gabriel V. (1967). Plastic cement: The ten cent hallucinogen. *International Journal of the Addictions, 2,* 271–281.
3. Gillman, Mark A., and Lichtigfeld, Frederick J. (1997). Clinical role and mechanisms of action of analgesic nitrous oxide. *International Journal of Neuroscience, 93,* 55–62. Nagle, David R. (1968). Anesthetic addiction and drunkenness. *International Journal of the Addictions, 3,* p. 33.
4. Julien, Robert M. (2001). *A primer of drug action* (9th ed.). New York: Worth, pp. 121–122. Layzer, Robert B. (1985). Nitrous oxide abuse. In Edmond I. Eger (Ed.), *Nitrous oxide/N_2O.* New York: Elsevier, pp. 249–257. Morgan, Roberta (1988). *The emotional pharmacy.* Los Angeles: Body Press, pp. 212–213.
5. Nagle, Anesthetic addiction and drunkenness, pp. 26–30.

6. Khattak, Sohail; K-Moghtader, Guiti; McMartin, Kristen; Barrera, Maru; Kennedy, Debbie; and Koren, Gideon (1999). Pregnancy outcome following gestational exposure to organic solvents. *Journal of the American Medical Association, 281,* 1106–1109.
7. Cohen, Sidney (1977). Inhalant abuse: An overview of the problem. In Charles W. Sharp and Mary Lee Brehm (Eds.), *Review of inhalants: Euphoria to dysfunction* (NIDA Research Monograph 15). Rockville MD: National Institute on Drug Abuse, p. 7.
8. Ibid., pp. 6–8.
9. Schuckit, Marc A. (1995). *Drug and alcohol abuse: A clinical guide to diagnosis and treatment* (4th ed.). New York: Plenum Medical Book Co., pp. 217–225. Sharp, Charles W., and Rosenberg, Neil L. (1997). Inhalants. In Joyce H. Lowinson, Pedro Ruiz, Robert B. Millman, and John G. Langrod (Eds.), *Substance abuse: A comprehensive textbook.* Baltimore: Williams and Wilkins, pp. 246–264.
10. Winger, Gail, Hofmann, Frederick G., and Woods, James H. (1992). *A handbook on drug and alcohol abuse: The biomedical aspects* (3rd ed.). New York: Oxford University Press, pp. 90–91.
11. Brecher, Edward M., and the editors of *Consumer Reports* (1972). *Licit and illicit drugs.* Boston: Little, Brown, p. 331.
12. Karch, Steven B. (1996). *The pathology of drug abuse* (2nd ed.). Boca Raton FL: CRC Press, pp. 431–437. Siegel, Earl, and Wason, Suman (1992). Sudden sniffing deaths following inhalation of butane and propane: Changing trends. In Charles W. Sharp, Fred Beauvais, and Richard Spence (Eds.), *Inhalant abuse: A volatile research agenda* (NIDA Research Monograph 129). Rockville MD: National Institute on Drug Abuse, pp. 193–201.
13. Brands, Bruna, Sproule, Beth, and Marshman, Joan (1998). *Drugs and drug abuse: A reference text.* Toronto: Addiction Research Foundation, pp. 469–471. Bruckner, James V., and Peterson, Richard G. (1977). Toxicology of aliphatic and aromatic hydrocarbons. In Charles W. Sharp and Mary L. Brehm (Eds.), *Review of inhalants: Euphoria to dysfunction* (NIDA Research Monograph 15). Rockville MD: National Institute on Drug Abuse, pp. 124–163. Comstock, Eric G., and Comstock, Betsy S. (1977). Medical evaluation of inhalant abusers. In Charles W. Sharp and Mary L. Brehm (Eds.), *Review of inhalants: Euphoria to dysfunction* (NIDA Research Monograph 15). Rockville MD: National Institute on Drug Abuse, pp. 54–80. Garriott, James C. (1992). Death among inhalant abusers. In Charles W. Sharp, Fred Beauvais, and Richard Spence (Eds.), *Inhalant abuse: A volatile research agenda* (NIDA Research Monograph 129). Rockville MD: National Institute on Drug Abuse, pp. 171–193. Jacobs, Michael R., and Fehr, Kevin O'B. (1987). *Drugs and drug abuse: A reference text* (2nd ed.). Toronto: Addiction Research Foundation, pp. 322–323.
14. Edwards, Ruth W., and Oetting, E. R. (1995). Inhalant use in the United States. In Nicholas Kozel, Zili Sloboda, and Mario De La Rosa (Eds.), *Epidemiology of inhalant abuse: An international perspective* (NIDA Research Monograph 148). Rockville MD: National Institute on Drug Abuse, pp. 8–28. Inhalant abuse increases among nation's youth (2000, May). *Nation's Health,* p. 5. Johnston, Lloyd D. (2000, December 14). "Ecstasy" use rises sharply among teens in 2000; use of many other drugs stays steady, but significant declines are reported for some. News release from the University of Michigan, Ann Arbor, Tables 1 and 2. Preboth, Monica (2000, February 15). Prevalence of inhalant abuse in children. *American Family Physician,* p. 1206.
15. Howard, Matthew O.; Walker, R. Dale; Walker, Patricia S.; Cottler, Linda B.; and Compton, Wilson M. (1999). Inhalant use among urban American Indian youth. *Addiction, 94,* 83–95. Kin, Foong, and Navaratnam, Vis (1995). An overview of inhalant abuse in selected countries of Asia and the Pacific region. In Nicholas Kozel, Zili Sloboda, and Mario De La Rosa (Eds.), *Epidemiology of inhalant abuse: An international perspective* (NIDA Research Monograph 148). Rockville MD: National Institute on Drug Abuse, pp. 29–49. Leal, Hermán; Mejía, Laura; Gómez, Lucila; and Salina de Valle, Olga (1978). Naturalistic study on the phenomenon of inhalant use in a group of children in Mexico City. In Charles W. Sharp and L. T. Carroll (Eds.), *Voluntary inhalation of industrial solvents.* Rockville MD: National Institute on Drug Abuse, pp. 95–108. Medina-Mora, María Elena, and Berenzon, Shoshana (1995). Epidemiology of inhalant abuse in Mexico. In Nicholas Kozel, Zili Sloboda, and Mario De La Rosa (Eds.), *Epidemiology of inhalant abuse: An international perspective* (NIDA Research Monograph 148). Rockville MD: National Institute on Drug Abuse, pp. 136–174. Surratt, Hilary L., and Inciardi, James A. (1996). Drug use, HIV risks, and prevention/intervention strategies among street youths in Rio de Janeiro, Brazil. In Clyde B. McCoy, Lisa R. Metsch, and James A. Inciardi (Eds.), *Intervening with drug-involved youth.* Thousand Oaks MI: Sage Publications, pp. 173–190.
16. Hofmann, *Handbook on drug and alcohol abuse,* p. 134. Howard, Matthew O., and Jenson, Jeffrey M. (1998). Inhalant use among antisocial youth: Prevalence and correlates. *Addictive Behaviors, 24,* 59–74. Mackesy-Amiti, Mary Ellen, and Fendrich, Michaeal (1999). Inhalant abuse and delinquent behavior among adolescents: A comparison of inhalant users and other drug users. *Addiction, 94,* 555–564.
17. Oetting, E. R., Edwards, Ruth W., and Beauvais, Fred (1988). Social and psychological factors underlying inhalant abuse. In Raquel A. Crider and Beatrice A. Rouse (Eds.), *Epidemiology of inhalant abuse: An update* (NIDA Research Monograph 85). Rockville MD: National Institute on Drug Abuse, pp. 172–203.
18. Hofmann, *Handbook on drug and alcohol abuse,* pp. 138–139. Karch, *The pathology of drug abuse,* p. 432. Korman, Maurice (1977). Clinical evaluation of psychological factors. In Charles W. Sharp and Mary Lee Brehm (Eds.), *Review of inhalants: Euphoria to dysfunction* (NIDA Research Monograph 15). Rockville MD: National Institute on Drug Abuse, pp. 30–53.
19. Hofmann, *Handbook on drug and alcohol abuse,* p. 134.
20. Oetting, Edwards, and Beauvais, Social and psychological factors, p. 197.
21. Sharp, Charles W. (1977). Approaches to the problem. In Charles W. Sharp and Mary Lee Brehm (Eds.), *Review of*

inhalants: Euphoria to dysfunction (NIDA Research Monograph 15). Rockville MD: National Institute on Drug Abuse, pp. 226–242.
22. Kerner, Karen (1988). Current topics in inhalant abuse. In Raquel A. Crider and Beatrice A. Rouse (Eds.), *Epidemiology of inhalant abuse: An update* (NIDA Research Monograph 85). Rockville MD: National Institute on Drug Abuse, p. 20.
23. Information courtesy of the National Inhalant Prevention Coalition, Austin TX.
24. Newell, Guy R., Spitz, Margaret R., and Wilson, Michael B. (1988). Nitrite inhalants: Historical perspective. In Harry W. Haverkos and John A. Dougherty (Eds.), *Health hazards of nitrite inhalants* (NIDA Research Monograph 83). Rockville MD: National Institute on Drug Abuse, pp. 1–14.
25. Johnston, Table 4.
26. Haverkos, Harry W. (1988). Epidemiological studies—Kaposi's sarcoma vs. opportunistic infections among homosexual men with AIDS. In Harry W. Haverkos and John A. Dougherty (Eds.), *Health hazards of nitrite inhalants* (NIDA Research Monograph 83). Rockville MD: National Institute on Drug Abuse, pp. 96–105.

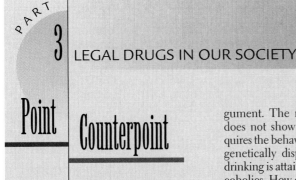

PART 3 LEGAL DRUGS IN OUR SOCIETY

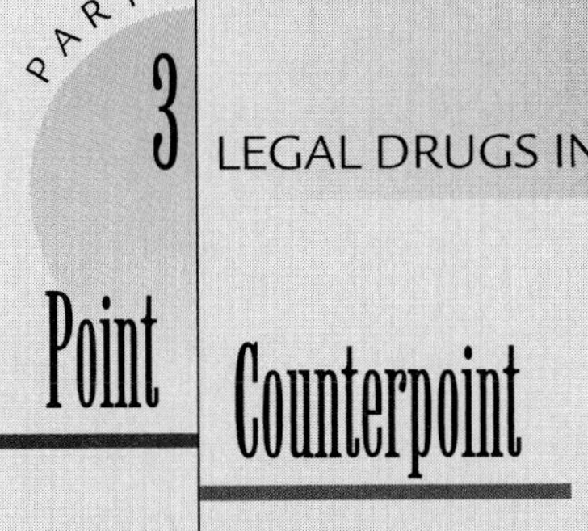

Should Alcoholism Be Viewed as a Disease?

The following viewpoints on whether or not alcoholism is a disease represent both sides of this controversial issue. Read them with an open mind. Don't think you have to come up with the final answer, nor should you necessarily agree with the last argument you read. Many of the ideas in this feature come from the sources listed.

POINT

Alcohol abuse has recently been defined by the National Institute of Alcohol Abuse and Alcoholism (NIAAA) as having three criteria: a preoccupation with drinking alcohol, a pattern of compulsive use despite the adverse consequences, and a pattern of relapse to alcohol use. Alcoholics cannot control their drinking; that is their disease. Give a drink to a person who is genetically vulnerable to alcohol and the consumption of alcohol will make that person an alcoholic, just as a person infected with a type of bacteria might acquire an infectious disease.

COUNTERPOINT

First of all, you're taking considerable liberties with the bacterial infection argument. The research on alcoholism does not show that everyone who acquires the behaviors of alcohol abuse was genetically disposed to it. Controlled drinking is attainable for at least some alcoholics. How do you separate the alcoholics who respond less to genetic factors than to environmental ones and seem to retain some degree of control over their drinking from those individuals who do not? Besides, we are not talking about alcohol as some invisible bacteria floating around, waiting to "infect" people without their knowledge. Alcoholics become alcoholic because they consume a substance that later on they no longer can handle. At one time in their lives, they chose to have that first drink; no one person or thing made them do it.

POINT

We accept the fact that the alcoholic is responsible for "that first drink," but we assert that the consequences are not voluntary. The alcoholic is powerless over alcohol, not over his or her alcoholism. The situation is similar to a diabetic being in control over whether or not a treatment of insulin injections should be taken. The alcoholic can seek treatment.

COUNTERPOINT

You can't have it both ways. Being responsible for the treatment of the disease is not the same as being powerless in the face of alcoholism (one of the main assumptions of Alcoholics Anonymous). Even the Supreme Court has trouble wrestling with the issue. In 1988, it ruled that two alcoholics could not be excluded from claiming educational benefits normally accorded to veterans just because their alcoholism prevented them from applying in the time allowed. The Veterans Administration had refused them, claiming that alcoholism, without physical or mental disorders, is an example of "willful misconduct."

POINT

Not exactly. The Court ruled that the source of the "willful misconduct" was the disease of alcoholism. In doing so, they actually reconfirmed the concept of alcoholism as a disease. The courts typically do not excuse the alcoholic from the consequences of the condition. Instead, they give the person a choice of being punished for his or her offenses or accepting a program of rehabilitation. We cannot go back to the days when drinking too much was considered a moral deficiency.

COUNTERPOINT

If alcoholism is a disease, then it's a very strange one. It may be in a category all its own.

Critical Thinking Questions for Further Discussion

1. Is alcoholism different from other forms of drug abuse? Would we support moderate use of drugs other than alcohol? Why or why not?
2. Would our social response to alcoholism be different if alcohol were an illicit substance?

Sources: Holden, Constance (1987). Is alcoholism a disease? *Science, 238,* 1647. Maltzman, Irving (1994). Why alcoholism is a disease. *Journal of Psychoactive Drugs, 26,* 13–31. Miller, Norman, and Toft, Doug (1990). *The disease concept of alcoholism and other drug addiction.* Center City MN: Hazelden Foundation.

Prescription Drugs, Over-the-Counter Drugs, and Dietary Supplements

After you have completed this chapter, you will understand

- The distinction between prescription and OTC drugs
- The evolution of U.S. drug regulations
- FDA procedures for approving new drugs
- Prescription drugs changing to OTC drugs
- Types of OTC analgesic drugs
- Weight-loss aids, sleep aids, and cough-and-cold remedies
- The pharmaceutical industry today
- Dietary supplements

The little English graveyard alongside the old church contained a dozen or so monuments, their inscriptions nearly worn away by more than two centuries of wind and rain. Each epitaph told a bit about a life remembered. One was in rhyme:

> Here lies the body of Mary Ann Lauders,
> died of drinking Cheltenham waters.
> If she had stuck to Epsom salts,
> she wouldn't be lying in these here vaults.

I wondered what Mary's family might have done today. Would they have sued Cheltenham for promoting a pharmaceutical product that was neither safe nor effective? Would the British equivalent of the FDA have shut them down? And who says that Epsom salts are any more effective? Where are the clinical test results? Was there a placebo control?

The next time you are in a pharmacy or drug store, take a minute to look around you. Besides the overwhelming variety of cosmetics, shaving creams, toothpastes, deodorants, and all the other products that have become part of our daily lives, three broad categories of products are available for purchase as medicines.

The first group of medicinal products, roughly 2,500 of them, placed mostly out of view and behind the pharmacist's counter, are **prescription drugs.** Their purchase and use require the submission of a written prescription form with an appropriate signature (or a doctor's phone call) that certifies that you are taking one of these drugs for a medical condition and at a dosage level appropriate for that condition. The amount of the drug that you are allowed to purchase at any one time is specified, and a limit on the number of prescription renewals offers some control over that drug's use over an extended period of time. By law, only licensed physicians or dentists are permitted to write (or call in) prescriptions for their patients, and only registered pharmacists are permitted to fill these prescriptions and dispense these drugs to the consumer.

The second group of products, roughly 300,000 of them, are **over-the-counter (OTC) drugs.** In contrast to prescription drugs, OTC drugs are available to you right off the shelves that line the aisles of the store, and their use is limited only by your ability to pay for them. With OTC drugs, you are your own physician. In most cases, you have diagnosed the ailment yourself and determined the course of treatment. Recommended doses are clearly printed on the label, and you may get some guidance from the pharmacist; however, there is no direct medical supervision over the dosage level that you actually consume at any given time. No one will tell you when to stop using these drugs or whether they were appropriate to take in the first place. Given the almost total absence of supervision over the personal use of OTC drugs, some basic safeguards are needed. Are the drugs safe to use, if taken at the dosage levels listed on the package? Are they effective in helping you in the way they claim?

In the United States, the regulation of both prescription and OTC drugs has been assigned to the U.S. Food and Drug Administration. The FDA is responsible for determining whether an existing prescription drug should continue to be available for public use and whether a newly developed drug can pass established standards of safety and effectiveness to be marketed as a prescription drug. The agency also oversees the safety and effectiveness of OTC drugs. By necessity, according to FDA standards, the strength and concentration of active ingredients in OTC drugs must have a greater margin of safety than active ingredients in prescription drugs to justify their wide availability to the general public under such unsupervised circumstances.

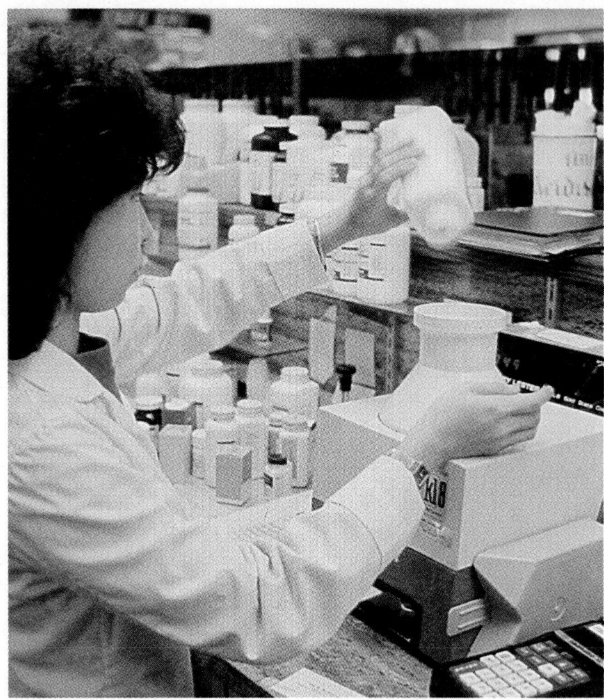

Pharmacists are specially trained to dispense approximately 2,500 different prescription drugs.

No drug, however, is totally free of potentially toxic effects, despite exhaustive efforts to assure the safety of prescription and OTC drugs. The potential for misuse of OTC drugs is a particular concern. It is important, therefore, to review four major classes of OTC drugs for which a potential for misuse exists: analgesics, weight-loss aids, sleep aids, and cough-and-cold remedies.

In contrast to prescription drugs and OTC drugs, a third group of products, dietary supplements, are relatively new. They currently occupy a relatively small, though increasing, amount of shelf space. Dietary supplements are generally available to the public in the form of vitamin or herbal preparations. While they are marketed in a similar manner as OTC drugs, there is an important difference. As defined by the Dietary Supplement

prescription drugs: Drugs available to the public only when approved by a medical professional and dispensed by a licensed pharmacist.
over-the-counter (OTC) drugs: A class of medicinal drugs available to the public without the requirement of a prescription.

Health and Education Act in 1994, dietary supplement labels must specify that the product has *not* been evaluated by the FDA and that the claims of benefit from using the product are limited only to helping certain common physical conditions associated with different stages of life (adolescence, pregnancy, menopause, and aging). Dietary supplement manufacturers are not allowed to claim benefits with respect to the diagnosis, treatment, cure, or prevention of more uncommon conditions or diseases. Two prominent dietary supplements marketed for psychoactive applications, gingko biloba and ginseng, will be reviewed in this chapter.

How the Regulation of Prescription and OTC Drugs Began

We take for granted that the ingredients in drugs commercially available to us through drugstores, pharmacies, and supermarkets are pure and unadulterated. We assume that they will not harm us when we use them as directed and that they will reliably produce the benefits claimed on the package. Prior to 1906, no such assumptions could have been made. First of all, the consumer of any of the fifty thousand or so patent medicines available for purchase had no guarantee about what he or she was getting. Consumers could order, for example, the White Star Secret Liquor Cure from the 1897 Sears, Roebuck catalog (see Chapter 5) and not be told that they would be consuming opium. The manufacturer was under no obligation to inform the buyer of that fact, or anything else for that matter.

As a response to public outcry over the unregulated patent medicines flooding the market, as well as publicity about the terrible conditions in the meatpacking industry, Congress enacted the Pure Food and Drug Act in 1906. This legislation set out to assure that all foods and drugs in the United States would be inspected for purity and consistency. In addition, all active ingredients in drugs had to be clearly and accurately identified on the label. The 1906 act did not, however, guarantee any more protection than that. Until 1938, drugs could still be useless and/or dangerous as long as the label listed the ingredients in a correct manner.

As often happens, it took another national crisis to generate further action. In September 1937, a syrup for sore throats called Elixir Sulfanilamide, manufactured in a small factory in Tennessee, was found to be the cause of 107 deaths throughout the United States. Many of those affected were children. The reason for the tragic results was quickly determined to be the fact that the sulfanilamide component (in itself a useful antibiotic) had been dissolved in a solution containing diethylene glycol, a close relative to present-day antifreeze. Obviously, the product had not been adequately tested for safety.

Luckily, the FDA was able to seize the entire stock, and it was taken off the market before any more deaths occurred. But the FDA acted not because Elixir Sulfanilamide had been judged unsafe (under the 1906 law, the FDA would not have been able to act on these grounds) but because the preparation had been mislabeled. Technically, an elixir had to contain some quantity of ethyl alcohol (see Chapter 9), and Elixir Sulfanilamide had none. Hence, the law had been broken![1]

After this incident, the American public sent a clear message to Washington that they would no longer tolerate the marketing of unsafe drugs. President Roosevelt signed into law the Federal Food, Drug, and Cosmetic (FDC) Act, which has served to the present-day as the basic food and drug law in the United States. Taking effect in 1938, this law mandated that all ingredients in cosmetic products had to be accurately identified, and drug companies were henceforth required to demonstrate by research studies that new drugs were safe (when used as directed) before they could be marketed commercially. A 1951 amendment to the FDC Act established a clear distinction between prescription and OTC drugs. By that point, the FDA had grown in stature and power as the official guardian of the public interest with regard to food, drugs, and cosmetics.

The final element of governmental control took effect in 1962, once again as a reaction to a well-publicized health emergency. In the late 1950s, a drug called **thalidomide** had been marketed by a West German pharmaceutical company and used by thousands of pregnant women in Europe, Canada, Australia, and South America as a sedative and treatment for the discomforts of morning sickness. In 1960, a U.S. pharmaceutical company applied to the FDA for approval to market thalidomide in the United States. Despite pressure to do so, the FDA refused the application. Scattered reports had been noted of the incidence of deformities among babies of mothers who had been taking thalidomide (Portrait). By 1962, Americans learned of the enormity of the tragedy and how close they had come to being affected themselves. Thousands of

thalidomide (tha-LID-oh-meyed): A highly teratogenic (birth-defect-producing) drug.

Portrait: Frances Kelsey—Saving a Generation of American Babies

In October 1961, a new medical officer at the FDA's Division of New Drugs, Dr. Frances Kelsey, was assigned the task of supervising the approval for a new drug called thalidomide. Introduced by a German pharmaceutical company in 1958, the drug had been hailed as "the tranquilizer of the future." Even massive doses of thalidomide couldn't kill you. Virtually all the countries of the world had accepted thalidomide for marketing within their own borders; only France, Israel, and the United States were holding out. At that time, the FDA had to reject the application for a new drug in sixty days or automatically allow it to be approved and marketed. Merrell Pharmaceuticals had sponsored the application for thalidomide and was anxiously awaiting the results. But Kelsey kept on stalling; after each sixty-day period, she would routinely reject the application as "incomplete."

As Kelsey studied the data, something seemed wrong about thalidomide. One of its side effects, of minor importance by itself, was a mild neuritis, or "tingling of the nerves." It reminded her of research she had conducted fifteen years earlier in which she had observed that neuritis of this type in pregnant animals resulted in deformed offspring. None of the experimental animal data, however, had shown anything even resembling birth defects. It remained simply her gut instinct to wait a little longer, just to be sure.

Frances Kelsey

In retrospect, seldom had a wait been more worthwhile. Within a year of thalidomide's introduction in Germany, an extremely rare birth deformity began to appear. Babies were born with short, finlike flaps instead of normal arms and legs, victims of a disorder called *phycomelia*. The number of cases of phycomelia had mysteriously increased from 12 in 1959, to 83 in 1960, to 302 in 1961. A German pediatrician offered the theory that these horrible deformities were tied to the taking of thalidomide by pregnant women. By 1962, it was clear that the drug was indeed the culprit.

It has been estimated by the FDA that more than ten thousand babies in twenty countries were victims of thalidomide. But American children never had to experience this tragedy, thanks to one woman who listened to her suspicions and was brave enough to say no. In 1962, President John F. Kennedy awarded Kelsey the President's Gold Medal for Distinguished Service, in honor of her heroic stance.

Today, thalidomide is used only in extremely restricted applications and is never given to fertile women on the off chance that they might be pregnant. Ironically, this highly teratogenic (birth-defect–causing) drug is one of the few treatments available for leprosy. It has also been found to be beneficial in the treatment of multiple myeloma, a form of bone-marrow cancer.

Sources: Editorial: Thalidomide—A revival story (1999). *New England Journal of Medicine, 341,* 1606–1609. Patrick, William (1988). *The Food and Drug Administration.* New York: Chelsea House, pp. 41–42.

babies around the world were born armless, legless, or both because of this drug.

Though the Kefauver-Harris Amendment of 1962 was a direct consequence of the thalidomide crisis, the FDA had in fact been acting on the basis of statutes that already existed. The safety of new drugs had to be assured by an FDA approval process, which is precisely what the FDA carried out. Nonetheless, the American public, anxious because it had barely avoided a major catastrophe, was insistent that the FDA be given broader powers. As a result of the 1962 amendment, drug companies were required to prove that new drugs were *effective* as well as safe. The concern until then had been only the matter of safety.

An important additional feature of the new regulations, however, did affect the maintenance of drug safety. Once new drugs were approved, drug companies were required to send reports to the FDA on a regular basis, informing the agency of any adverse reactions experienced by their users. As a result, any unforeseen difficulties with FDA-approved drugs could be recognized and appropriate measures could then be taken.

The FDA continues to prosecute violators of the drug laws, but enforcement is no longer its sole mission. Regulations since 1938 have allowed the FDA a more active role in preventing problems from arising in the first place (Table 14.1).[2] A major part of this preventive approach is the set of procedures required for the approval of new prescription drugs and the setting of standards for OTC drugs.

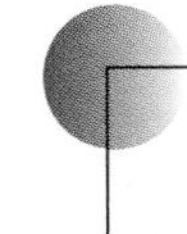

Procedures for Approving Prescription and OTC Drugs

The current process for introducing a new prescription drug on the market consists of a number of stages or phases of approval required by the FDA. It begins in

TABLE 14.1

Major regulatory laws of the FDA since 1938

ACT OR AMENDMENT	YEAR	EFFECT
Color Additive Amendment	1960	Regulated the safe use of color additives in drugs and food
Hazardous Substances Labeling Act	1960	Required warning labels on all products intended for home use
Kefauver-Harris Amendment	1962	Required that new drugs be effective as well as safe
Child Protection Act	1966	Regulated the safety of toys sold across state lines
Medical Device Amendment	1976	Required that any health-care product or device be effective and safe
Instant Formula Act	1980	Regulated the contents of baby-formula preparations
Antitampering Act	1983	Required tamper-resistant packaging for all OTC products
Orphan Drug Act	1983	Allowed drug companies to take tax credits for developing new drugs with low potential for profits
Prescription Drug User Fee Act	1992	Increased FDA efficiency in the review of new drug applications
Dietary Supplement Health and Education Act	1994	Set guidelines for the marketing of vitamin and herbal preparations
FDA Modernization Act	1997	Streamlined procedures for approval of new drugs, food labels, and medical devices

Source: Patrick, William (1988). *The Food and Drug Administration.* New York: Chelsea House, pp. 37–49. Updated with information from the U.S. Food and Drug Administration, Washington DC.

the laboratories of the drug companies themselves, with the identification of the composition of a new compound, a purification of its active ingredients, and a preliminary determination of any possible toxic effects. Extensive tests in two or more species of laboratory animals are carried out to establish the LD50 dosage of the compound, the concentration that leads to death in 50 percent of the animals studied (see Chapter 2). Specific tests are also made on pregnant animals to determine whether administration of the compound might produce birth defects. If the intention is to market the compound as a drug for chronic disorders, the toxicity studies need to be extended over a period of time that simulates the projected duration that the drug might be used by human patients.

After these preliminary studies are completed and the new drug has been determined to be safe with animals, the drug company then notifies the FDA, through an application known as a Notice of Claimed Investigational Exemption for a New Drug (IND), that this compound has promise as a new prescription drug and that permission is now requested to conduct testing in humans.

Phases of Clinical Studies for Prescription Drugs

At this point, drug-testing procedures focus on the question of whether the compound will be effective as a medicinal drug, although safety considerations are noted as well. A sequence of four stages of clinical testing is now begun, with each stage dependent on the success of the preceding one.

- In the first stage of clinical studies, called **Phase 1 trials,** healthy volunteers (frequently prison inmates or medical students) are administered the drug, and certain pharmacological questions are answered. How quickly is the new drug absorbed and eliminated? Are any side effects observed? What range of dosages is safe for use? Do any specific schedules for administration (one large dose per day versus three small ones) minimize any adverse effects?
- In the second stage of clinical studies, called **Phase 2 trials,** the new drug is tested on a small number of human patients who have the medical condition or illness that the drug is intended to treat. Researchers are careful to select only those patients who are free of other health problems, so that any improvements will be identified as a genuine effect on the illness in question. It should not be surprising that all these clinical studies are conducted in a double-blind fashion. Neither the researchers nor the patients are aware of whether the new drug or a look-alike placebo (see Chapter 3) is being administered. As a result, positive effects (if any) are attributed to the therapeutic prop-

Phase 1 trials: The first stage of clinical testing, in which an experimental drug is administered to healthy volunteers to check on possible side effects and to determine patterns of absorption and elimination.
Phase 2 trials: The second stage of clinical testing, in which an experimental drug is given to a small population of patients having the medical condition for which the drug is considered a possible treatment.

Widening the Population during Drug Testing

Traditionally, clinical trials for potential new drugs have been conducted on young men. In 1977, the FDA banned women from taking part in most of the clinical trials for new drugs on the grounds that there might be harm to the fetus if a woman became pregnant during testing. Since 1993, however, the ban has been lifted. Possible risks for pregnant women are still a matter of great concern, but equal consideration is now directed to the need for gender-specific data on a future drug. As a result, it is now possible to know about any adjustment in dosage or administration that might optimize the drug's effect for women, as well as men.

A related matter is the smaller amount of attention that has been paid to the possibility that either elderly or very young patients might have responses to a prescription drug substantially different from those of young adults. It is not simply a matter of giving a lower level of the recommended "adult dose" to these populations. The elderly and children often metabolize drugs in unique ways, so that some prescription drugs may not be appropriate for them at any dose level. Since 1999, drug manufacturers must conduct prescription drug testing in children if the medication is to be used by a significant number of young patients. In addition, drug companies are required to conduct new studies of some drugs already in wide use among children.

Sources: Editorial: Drug safety for children (1999, January 1). *New York Times,* p. A18. Testing drugs in older people (1990, November). *FDA Consumer,* pp. 24–27.

erties of the drug, free of any expectations or biases that the researchers or patients may have had.

- Phase 2 trials are conducted on a population of up to several hundred patients. If successful, the third clinical stage, called **Phase 3 trials,** is undertaken. At this point, the safety, effectiveness, and proper dosage levels are investigated in a population of several thousand patients. A closer examination of possible side effects (some of which may be observed only rarely) is carried out, and further fine tuning is made in the recommended usage of the drug (Health Line).
- After all three stages of clinical trials have been completed, a process that takes three years or more (Figure 14.1), and the drug company considers the results satisfactory, a New Drug Application (NDA) is submitted for approval by the FDA. This application includes all the data on the animal testing and clinical trials. Less than 30 percent of all compounds that drug companies consider worthy of human clinical trials will have made it this far. Under usual circumstances, the FDA then has six months to review the application and to either accept or reject the new drug for commercial marketing.

By the time a new drug is FDA-approved for prescription use, it is likely that several years will have elapsed since the compound was first synthesized and considered promising enough to warrant testing. The development costs to the drug companies range from $25 million to $125 million for each drug that survives the approval process. Approximately eighty new drugs are FDA approved each year, a small fraction of the original number that have been synthesized in the laboratory.[3]

Even after release for commercial use, a new drug is still monitored for any unforeseen side effects or toxic reactions, in a stage called **Phase 4 trials.** At this point, physicians throughout the United States are instructed, through a federal program called MedWatch, to report to the FDA any instances of adverse effects resulting from the use of the new drug by their patients.

Patents and Generic Forms of Prescription Drugs

Approval by the FDA gives the drug company exclusive rights to manufacture and sell the new drug under its own brand name (beginning with a capital letter and often accompanied by a small, circled letter R just to the right of it, signifying that the name is a registered trademark). All other companies are forbidden by law to sell the compound under that brand name or any other name. These rights, called a **patent,** have a fixed duration of twenty years. The clock starts, however, at the time the original IND is submitted to the FDA, not when the drug hits the

Phase 3 trials: The third stage of clinical testing, in which an experimental drug is given to a large population of patients, through which issues of safety, effectiveness, and proper dosage levels are finalized.
Phase 4 trials: The fourth stage of clinical testing, in which possible adverse reactions to a drug, already available to the public, are monitored by physicians who have prescribed it.
patent: The exclusive right of a drug company to market a particular drug. The duration of a patent is twenty years.

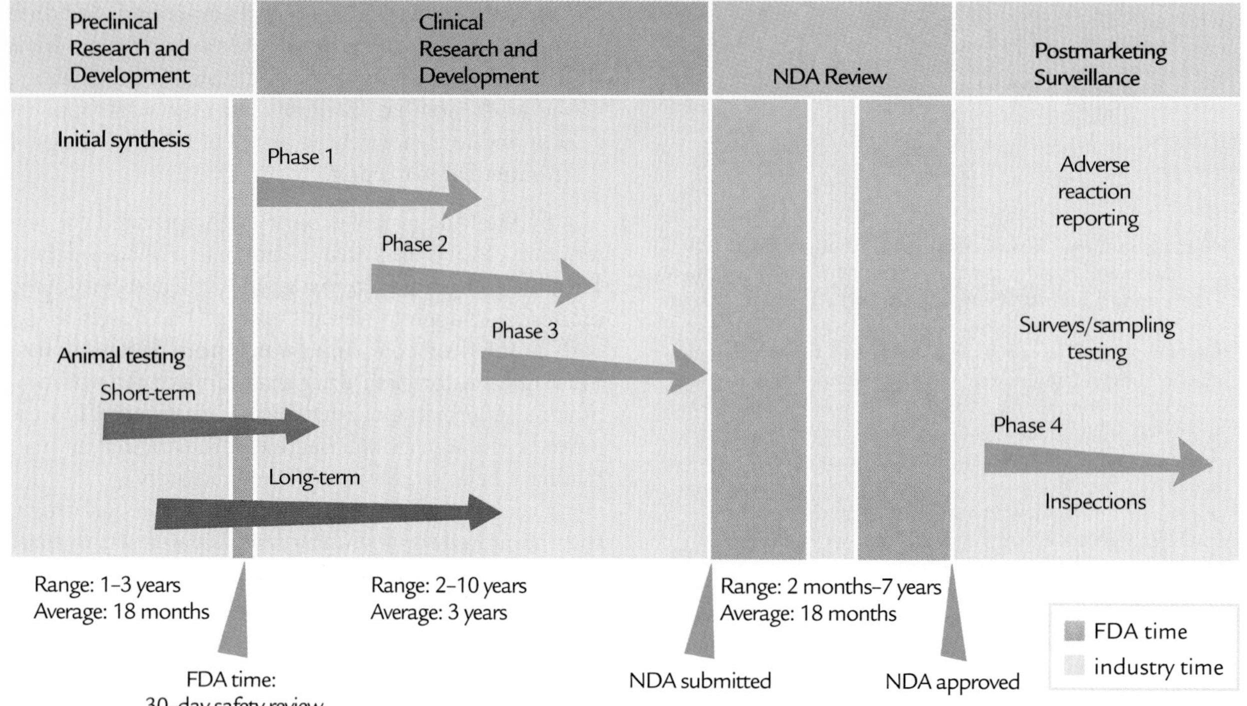

FIGURE 14.1

Development of new prescription drugs and the FDA approval process.
Source: Adapted from Young, Frank E., (1990). *The reality behind the headlines: New drug development in the United States.* Rockville MD: U.S. Food and Drug Administration, p. 3. Updated from Eichenwald, Kurt, and Kolata, Gina (1999, May 16). Drug trials hide conflicts for doctors. *New York Times,* pp. 1, 34–35.

market. Consequently, the drug company may, in reality, have patent protection for a prescription drug for only ten to twelve years. After that, the drug "goes off patent" and generic forms of it can be manufactured and sold to the public.

After the patent expires, the original drug company frequently continues to market the drug under its brand name, but now the consumer has the option of having it prescribed and purchased either as a brand drug or as a generic (and much less expensive) version. Since 1984, the FDA requires that all generic drugs demonstrate **bioequivalency** with respect to the original, brand-name drug, meaning that both versions must be shown to be chemically and pharmacologically identical.[4]

Speeding up the FDA Approval Process

Since the 1990s, not all drugs have had to travel this long and arduous road to reach the marketplace. Under special circumstances, the process can be accelerated. In 1987, the FDA authorized the use of a "treatment IND" application, specially designed for new drugs that show promise for certain seriously ill patients. Without compromising the standards for safety and effectiveness, a streamlined approval procedure now makes it possible for a novel drug treatment to reach patients who can benefit from it in a matter of months instead of years. Medical conditions for which drugs have been approved in this way include AIDS, infection associated with kidney transplants, Alzheimer's disease, Parkinson's disease, and forms of advanced cancers. One particular drug to treat AIDS and related conditions was approved in 1995 in an agency record-setting ninety-seven days.

Ultimately, the limiting factor in much of the approval process is the number of scientists and administrators assigned to examine test data from the thousands

bioequivalency: A characteristic of two drugs in which all pharmacological and physiological effects are identical.

of new drugs evaluated each year. Since 1992, the FDA has been permitted to charge drug companies user fees to support the hiring of chemists, microbiologists, and pharmacologists, as well as other professionals and support staff at the agency. In this way, larger numbers of new drugs can be evaluated more efficiently (Table 14.2).[5]

Procedures for Approving OTC Drugs

When the Kefauver-Harris Amendment took effect in 1962, with the aim of ensuring that all drugs sold in the United States were both safe and effective, the challenge with regard to prescription drugs was ambitious, but the challenge with regard to OTC drugs was even more difficult. The number of OTC drugs, as mentioned earlier, is roughly a hundred times the number of prescription drugs, and the same approximate ratio existed in 1962. Besides, most OTC drugs on the market at that time contained compounds that had been available to the public for decades or more. The FDA's solution to these difficulties was to set up two separate studies. The Drug Efficacy Study Investigation (DESI) was established to examine all existing prescription medicines, and the Over-the-Counter Review (OTC Review) was established for existing nonprescription medicines.

Whether it was in a prescription or nonprescription category, every drug was to be judged as GRAS (generally regarded as safe), GRAE (generally regarded as effective), and GRAHL (generally regarded as honestly labeled). If a drug failed to meet any one of these criteria, the drug manufacturer had six months to convince the FDA otherwise or else the drug would not be permitted to be marketed across state lines within the United States.

When the DESI was completed in 1984, twenty-two years after the enactment of the legislation, 1,092 prescription drugs out of approximately 3,000 that were reviewed were found to have failed the GRAE requirement. The OTC Review, understandably, has taken longer, especially since it took ten years after the Kefauver-Harris Amendment even to get started, and the OTC drug review process is still ongoing.

In the meantime, however, the OTC Review has produced three important changes in OTC drugs available to the consumer. First, the professional committees examining present-day OTC drugs have recommended and the FDA has approved an increase in the recommended dosage for certain OTC drugs. OTC-type antihistamines, for example, are stronger than in previous years as a result. Second, several prescription drugs have been determined to be safe enough to warrant use on an OTC basis, and consequently a growing number of prescription drugs are available for purchase on a nonprescription basis. Table 14.3 lists some of the present-day OTC drugs that had formerly been available only on a prescription basis. Third, new regulations require that OTC drugs have consumer-friendly labels so that individuals can easily determine the

TABLE 14.2

The top ten leading brands of prescription drugs

BRAND NAME (MANUFACTURER)	MEDICAL APPLICATION	SALES (in billions of dollars)*
1. Prilosec (AstraZeneca)	stomach ulcers	$4.3
2. Lipitor (Pfizer)	elevated cholesterol	3.2
3. Prevacid (TAP)	esophageal reflux and stomach ulcers	2.5
4. Prozac (Lilly)	depression	2.5
5. Zocor (Merck)	elevated cholesterol	2.3
6. Epogen (Amgen)	anemia	1.8
7. Zoloft (Pfizer)	depression	1.7
8. Celebrex (Searle)	pain	1.6
9. Paxil (GlaxoSmithKline)	depression	1.5
10. Zyprexa (Lilly)	schizophrenia	1.5

*For year ending March 31, 2000.

Source: Physicians' desk reference (54th ed.) (2000). Montvale NJ: Medical Economics Company. Stolberg, Sheryl, and Gerth, Jeff (2000, July 23). In a drug's journey to market, discovery is just the first of many steps. *New York Times,* p. 15.

TABLE 14.3

A partial list of former prescription drugs now sold over the counter

OTC BRAND NAME	GENERIC NAME	CLINICAL USE
Actifed	triprolidine	antihistamine
Aleve	naproxen	analgesic and anti-inflammatory
Benadryl	diphenhydramine	antihistamine
Dimetane, Dimetapp	brompheniramine	antihistamine
Monistat	miconazole	treatment for vaginal yeast infections
Motrin, Advil, Nuprin	ibuprofen	analgesic and anti-inflammatory
Pepcid AC	famotidine	heartburn relief
Tagamet HB	eimetidine	heartburn relief

Sources: Information courtesy of the Nonprescription Drug Manufacturers Association, Washington DC. *Physicians' desk reference* (54th ed.) (2000). Montvale NJ: Medical Economic Company. *Physicians' desk reference for nonprescription drugs* (21st ed.) (2000). Montvale NJ: Medical Economic Company.

QUICK CONCEPT  14.1

Understanding the FDA Approval Process

Check your understanding of the FDA approval process by associating each of the following scenarios with either (a) experimental studies, (b) Phase 1 trials, (c) Phase 2 trials, (d) Phase 3 trials, or (e) Phase 4 trials.

1. This phase has just ended successfully, and the drug company now prepares an application called an IND.
2. In this phase, physicians report any unusual side effects or adverse reactions to a drug that has recently been made commercially available.
3. In this phase, the subjects are healthy human volunteers.
4. During this phase, the number of patients involved is very large. If successful, the next step is the submission of an application called an NDA.
5. This phase is the first time a new compound has been tested on individuals who are actually sick.
6. In this phase, it is not a question of drug effectiveness but rather how the drug is absorbed and excreted.

Answers: 1. a 2. e 3. b 4. d 5. c 6. b

symptoms that might be relieved by the medications and the safety precautions that must be heeded in their use.[6]

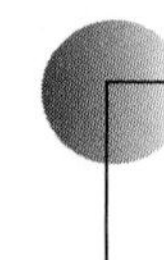

Are FDA-Approved Drugs Safe?

The answer to the safety question for FDA-approved drugs, unfortunately, is yes and no. On the one hand, the FDA approval process is designed to prevent the introduction of any new drug or the continued availability of any present drug if there is a serious question about its safety when consumed in the recommended dosage for the treatment of certain specified medical disorders. If anything, the FDA is often criticized for being overly cautious and delaying the availability of new drugs to people who need them until researchers are virtually certain there are no problems.

On the other hand, no drug is without side effects. Some of these side effects are quite minor, but others can be severe if the drug is taken by individuals with specific health problems. A quick look at the full disclosure statement that is packaged with commercial drugs will indicate to you the wide range of possible adverse effects (Health Alert). The matter is further complicated when individuals misuse the prescription or nonprescription

Health Alert 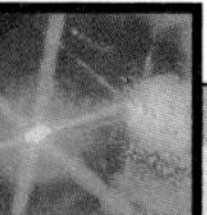

Side Effects of Common Medications

This Health Alert is a cautionary note on the side effects that may occur from the *use* of medicinal drugs at recommended dosages. Physicians often warn their patients that a stimulant drug might cause some sleep disturbance, or another might produce some gastrointestinal distress or sexual potency problems, but few of them routinely mention possible effects on the mouth, eyes, ears, or skin. Here are some common prescription and OTC drugs that can produce these types of side effects.

A Drying of the Mouth or Reduction in Saliva, as well as a Reduction in Tear Flow in the Eyes

- Lasix, Hydrodiuril, Dyrenium (diuretic drugs)
- Aldomet, Catapres, Minipress (antihypertensive drugs)
- Tofranil, Elavil (antidepressant drugs)
- Compazine, Haldol, Thorazine (antipsychotic drugs)
- Artane, Larodopa (anti-Parkinson's disease drugs)

Eye Problems

- corticosteroids, which can trigger the growth of a cataract
- digitalis (a heart stimulant), which can disrupt color vision
- sulfa drugs and diuretics, which can cause blurred vision
- antipsychotic drugs, which can cause a feeling of burning
- oral contraceptives, which can cause bleeding in the eye

Hearing and Equilibrium Problems

- aspirin, which can cause a ringing in the ears and deafness
- neomycin (antibiotic), which can cause auditory damage

Increased Skin Sensitivity to the Sun

- many antipsychotic drugs and antidepressant drugs
- tetracycline, sulfa drugs (antibiotics)
- Lasix, thiazides (diuretic drugs)
- oral contraceptives

Sources: Brody, Jane E. (1992, February 26). Personal health: Unsuspected common drugs can wreak havoc. *New York Times*, p. C13. *Physicians' desk reference: Companion guide 2000.* Montvale NJ: Medical Economics Company, pp. 1183–1448.

DRUGS . . . IN FOCUS

Redux, Fen-Phen, and Obesity

It started promisingly enough for more than 58 million Americans who are obese. In 1996, dexfenfluramine was approved by the FDA for marketing under the brand name of Redux, the first new anti-obesity drug in twenty-two years. Prior to this, a close chemical relative, fenfluramine (brand name: Pondimin) had been available for weight reduction but was relatively unpopular because it caused drowsiness. The only other alternatives were amphetamines or amphetamine-like appetite suppressants, which had their own adverse side effects (see Chapter 4).

At about the same time that Redux was introduced, another option appeared on the scene: a combination of fenfluramine and the mild amphetamine phentermine (brand names: Adipex, Fastin, Zantryl) in a "diet drug cocktail" called fen-phen. Even though each of the components had been FDA approved, their combination had not. It was an example of what is known as an "off-label" pharmaceutical, avoiding the FDA approval process but legal nonetheless, provided that it was prescribed by a licensed physician.

Redux and fen-phen were instant successes. From 1995 to 1996, sales nearly tripled from $179 million to $526 million. More than 18 million prescriptions were written in 1996 alone for either fenfluramine or phentermine. While positive effects were not universal among people taking these drugs, levels of weight reduction overall were substantial. However, it soon became apparent that major health risks existed. Information from the U.S. Centers for Disease Control and Prevention, the Mayo Clinic, and the physicians' MedWatch reporting system pinpointed two significant problems. The first was a twenty-three-fold increase among Redux users in the risk of primary pulmonary hypertension, a buildup of pressure in the tissue surrounding the lung that can interfere with lung function and eventually damage the heart. The second was an association between fen-phen and the incidence of diseased heart valves that can lead to irregular heartbeat, heart failure, or heart attack. In response to these findings, Redux and fenfluramine were officially withdrawn from the U.S. market in 1997. In 1999, the company that had marketed fen-phen agreed to pay nearly $4 billion to settle lawsuits brought by individuals who had incurred coronary problems as a result of taking the drug.

In the meantime, phentermine remains available as an appetite suppressant, and a new appetite-suppressant drug, sibutramine (brand name: Meridia), has been FDA-approved. At present, Meridia is recommended only for the individual whose physical condition carries a greater risk than the potential risks associated with the drug's side effects. Other anti-obesity approaches, under development, include chemicals that prevent the body from absorbing ingested fat.

Sources: Diet drug maker to pay $3.75B (1999, October 8). *Newsday,* p. A30. Gardin, Julius M.; Schumacher, Donald; Constantine, Ginger; Davis, Kelly D.; Leung, Cyril; and Reid, Cheryl L. (2000). Valvular abnormalities and cardiovascular status following exposure to dexfenfluramine or phentermine/fenfluramine. *Journal of the American Medical Association, 283,* 1703–1709. Kolata, Gina (1997, September 16). 2 top diet drugs are recalled amid reports of heart defects. *New York Times,* pp. A1, A2.

drug by either ignoring the manufacturer's precautionary advice or exceeding the recommended dosage levels.

The Drug Abuse Warning Network (DAWN) reports, discussed in Chapter 2, reveal the prevalence of emergency department incidences and fatalities that involve the misuse of either prescription or nonprescription drugs, as well as the abuse of illicit drugs. The incidence of medical problems associated with the misuse of nonprescription drugs (specifically analgesics) will be discussed in a later section. The misuse of prescription drugs will be the focus here.

Several prescription drugs rank prominently among the causes for serious heart emergencies. Among the drugs most frequently reported as ED (emergency department) mentions, antianxiety drugs such as alprazalom (brand name: Xanax), clonazepam (brand name: Klonopin), and diazepam (brand name: Valium) rank seventh, eighth, and eleventh, respectively. In terms of ME (medical examiner) mentions, diazepam is fifth in the rankings; the antidepressant drug amitriptyline (brand name: Elavil) is eleventh. Diphenhydramine (an antihistamine marketed in several prescription and OTC cold medications as well as OTC sleep aids) and the painkiller d-propoxyphene (brand name: Darvon) are eighth and tenth, respectively.

Three important points should be made, however, when considering these statistics. First, the rankings for these drugs are high, but their overall occurrence is low when compared to the top-ranked drugs in both ED and ME categories: cocaine, heroin and morphine, and alcohol-in-combination. Second, in 50 to 60 percent of the situations involving these prescription drugs as an ED mention, the individual had attempted suicide. Obviously, the doses ingested far exceeded recommended levels. Third, more than 70 percent of such DAWN-report incidences involve the combination of multiple drugs along with the drug in question. As an example, a diazepam overdose is unlikely to prove fatal when ingested by itself. A combination of diazepam with alcohol, however, can produce life-threatening conditions. The tendency to combine drugs with alcohol and end up with serious medical problems accounts for the "alcohol-in-combination" incident being ranked first in cases seen in hospital emergency departments and second in cases in which a patient has died.[7]

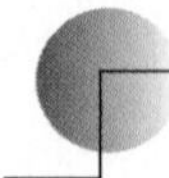

Major OTC Analgesic Drugs

Four classes of OTC drugs currently represent the $2.7 billion nonprescription analgesic market: aspirin, acetaminophen, ibuprofen, and naproxen. Of these, aspirin, ibuprofen, and naproxen are often referred to as **nonsteroidal anti-inflammatory drugs (NSAIDs).** This name identifies them as useful in reducing the swelling and pain that often results from injury or illness (anti-inflammatory) but unrelated to the cortisone-based steroids often prescribed for this purpose (nonsteroidal). Acetaminophen, as we will see, is an effective analgesic, but because it does not reduce inflammation, it is not classified as an NSAID.

Aspirin

When American pioneers traveled west in the nineteenth century, they encountered Native American tribes who were treating pain and fever by chewing willow bark, reminiscent of a remedy that had been popular in Europe from as early as 400 B.C. It turns out that willow bark contains an analgesic compound called **salicylic acid,** named from *Salix,* the botanical name for willow. The beneficial effect of pure salicylic acid on pain, however, was for a long time limited by the fact that most digestive systems could not handle it easily. In 1898, Felix Hoffman, a chemist at the Bayer Company in Germany, found that by adding an acetyl group (making the result **acetylsalicylic acid,** or **ASA**), this side effect was reduced without lessening its therapeutic power. To arrive at a name that was easier to say, company officials noted that salicylic acid also came from spirea plants: thus the name **aspirin** was born.[8]

In 1918, following World War I, Sterling Products (later Sterling Winthrop and now Bayer Corporation) bought the trademark rights to the name *aspirin.* Later, a U.S. federal judge ruled that the name was common enough to be treated generically. To this day, Bayer Corporation markets its aspirin as "Genuine Bayer Aspirin," though the ASA contained in it is identical to that in any other ASA product. In the United States, Britain, and France, aspirin is the common name for ASA, and any company marketing ASA can use the name to describe its product. In approximately seventy other countries, aspirin is a registered trademark of Bayer AG, Germany. In Canada, aspirin is a registered trademark name used exclusively to identify ASA manufactured and distributed by Bayer Corporation. In this chapter, the terms aspirin and ASA are used interchangeably.[9]

The three principal medical applications of aspirin are well known. It is an effective analgesic drug for mild to moderate pain (hence, its use in treating headaches), an **anti-inflammatory** drug in that it relieves inflammation and tenderness in joints of the body (hence, its use in treating rheumatoid arthritis), and an **antipyretic** drug in that it lowers elevated body temperature when the body is fighting infection (hence, its use in treating fever). A recommended adult dosage of 325 to 650 mg (one to two tablets or capsules), taken every four hours, is considered to be adequate for these purposes, with a recommended limit of 3,900 mg (twelve tablets or capsules) per day.[10]

Until the early 1970s, the therapeutic effects of aspirin were largely a mystery. A prominent magazine had even called aspirin "the wonder drug nobody understands."[11] The answer surfaced in a surprising way. Aspirin was found to work as an analgesic, not on a CNS level (like morphine or other opiate drugs) but rather on a peripheral level by blocking the synthesis of **prostaglandins,** a group of hormone-like chemicals normally pro-

nonsteroidal anti-inflammatory drug (NSAID): Any of a group of OTC analgesics (including aspirin, ibuprofen, and naproxen) that are unlike cortisone-based drugs and reduce the swelling caused by injury or disease.

salicylic acid (SAL-ih-SIL-ik ASS-id): A drug developed in the nineteenth century to treat mild to moderate pain, though it was extremely irritating to the stomach.

acetylsalicylic acid (ASA) (a-SEE-til-SAL-ih-SIL-ik ASS-id): A modification of salicylic acid that makes the drug less irritating to the stomach without lessening its analgesic powers.

aspirin: Any analgesic drug containing acetylsalicylic acid (ASA).

anti-inflammatory: Having an effect that reduces inflammation or soreness.

antipyretic: Having an effect that reduces body temperature and fever.

prostaglandins (PROS-tah-GLAN-dins): Hormone-like substances that are blocked by many OTC analgesic drugs.

Expanding Medical Applications for Aspirin

The anticlotting action of aspirin has led to two new applications for patients with cardiovascular disease. The first application is for the prevention of a second myocardial infarction (heart attack) among men who have previously suffered one. In addition, there is evidence that, for men over the age of fifty, a substantially lowered risk of having a heart attack in the first place could be achieved by taking a single aspirin tablet (325 mg) every other day. These benefits, by the way, do not apply to women. It is advisable to consult your doctor if you think that aspirin therapy is appropriate.

The second application is for the treatment of recurrent episodes of potentially dangerous clotting in the brain or the retina *(transient ischemic attacks, TIAs)*. These ministrokes can frequently be preliminary events to a larger stroke that causes long-lasting brain damage. The present FDA recommendation is that 1,300 mg of aspirin a day (four tablets) can be effective in reducing the chances of future TIAs or strokes in men with a history of TIAs. Once again, these benefits do not apply to women.

Though less solid evidence is available for other medical applications of aspirin, it is suspected that aspirin might be useful in preventing the severity of migraine headaches, enhancing the circulation of blood to the gums, preventing certain types of cataracts, lowering the risk of a recurrence of colorectal cancer, and lowering high blood pressure that occurs in 5 to 15 percent of all pregnancies.

Sources: Flieger, Ken (1994, January-February). Aspirin: A new look at an old drug. *FDA Consumer,* pp. 19–21. Lewis, H. D., et al. (1983). Protective effects of aspirin against acute myocardial infarction and death in men with unstable angina (Results of a Veterans Administration cooperative study). *New England Journal of Medicine, 309,* 396–403. Second chance for aspirin is also one for Bayer (1997, August 9). *New York Times,* p. 21. Steering Committee of the Physicians' Health Study Research Group (1988, January 28). Preliminary report: Findings from the aspirin component of the Ongoing Physicians' Health Study. *New England Journal of Medicine, 318* (4), 262–264.

duced by every body cell when some injury to that cell has occurred. Prostaglandins, when released following injury, also encourage inflammation in the joints. Finally, prostaglandins act on the hypothalamus of the brain to elevate body temperature, so a blocking of prostaglandins here has a fever-reducing effect. Therefore, a combination of antiprostaglandin effects, in both the central and peripheral nervous systems, explains the three therapeutic actions of aspirin.

Other physiological effects of aspirin can produce serious problems, however, and as a result three specific cautions about the use of aspirin are in order.

First, aspirin-treated patients have a higher risk of developing gastric bleeding because the drug has a direct erosive effect on the stomach wall. Anyone with a history of stomach ulcers or related stomach problems should avoid taking aspirin. Even individuals without such a history frequently suffer some degree of aspirin-related stomach discomfort. In one study, approximately 15 percent of those who took 1,000 mg of aspirin reported stomach pain, 12 percent reported heartburn, and 8 percent reported nausea or vomiting or both. The aspirin taken in these instances, however, was "uncoated." In order to reduce these symptoms, some forms of aspirin are either buffered with a coating of an antacid or "enteric-coated" so that absorption is delayed until the aspirin has moved past the stomach and into the upper intestine. These forms of aspirin alleviate the gastric problems, but they also delay the pain-reducing and other therapeutic effects.

The second caution is that aspirin increases the time it takes for blood to clot. Ordinarily, prostaglandins promote the clumping of blood platelets that is part of the normal clotting process. Therefore, when there is a reduction in the action of prostaglandins, ability of blood to clot is reduced as well. Surgical patients should not have their bleeding time increased, so they are frequently advised *not* to take aspirin a week to ten days prior to surgery. A reduction of clotting can be beneficial, however, for individuals who are susceptible to small clots that can potentially block either coronary arteries leading to a heart attack, or blood vessels in the brain, which could lead to an ischemic (blood flow–interrupting) stroke. On the other hand, aspirin increases the risk of a hemorrhagic (bleeding) stroke, since the normal clotting process is diminished. Health Line discusses the new information we have about aspirin therapy.[12]

Unfortunately, the anticlotting nature of aspirin can have serious adverse effects for women in the late stages of pregnancy, leading to prolonged labor and bleeding during delivery. In addition, a reduction in clotting can occur in their newborn babies. As a result of these significant concerns, this warning is included on the label of all aspirin products:

IT IS ESPECIALLY IMPORTANT NOT TO USE ASPIRIN DURING THE LAST 3 MONTHS OF PREGNANCY UNLESS SPECIFICALLY DIRECTED TO DO SO BY A DOCTOR BECAUSE IT MAY CAUSE PROBLEMS IN THE UNBORN CHILD OR COMPLICATIONS DURING DELIVERY.

The third caution involves children who have contracted a viral infection such as chicken pox or the flu. Aspirin has been found to be related to the development of **Reye's syndrome,** a rare but highly dangerous condition marked by lethargy, nausea and severe vomiting, disorientation, and coma. Approximately 26 percent of Reye's syndrome cases are fatal. Since 1985, a warning has been required on the labels of all aspirin products indicating that "children and teenagers should not take aspirin for chicken pox or flu symptoms before a doctor is consulted." Because it is difficult to tell if even a common cold may be the beginning of the flu, it is advisable to refrain from giving aspirin to anyone under the age of twenty. There has been a significant decrease in the incidence of Reye's syndrome in the United States since these warnings were instituted.[13]

Safety-sealed, tamper-resistant packaging became a fact of life for consumers of OTC drugs following the 1982 Tylenol poisoning crisis, when several deaths were attributed to cyanide in packages of Tylenol that had been tampered with.

Acetaminophen

Since the 1950s, **acetaminophen** (brand names: Tylenol, Datril, Anacin-3, and Panadol, among others) has been available as an OTC drug, but it is only since the 1970s that it has been a popular alternative to aspirin for analgesic and antipyretic purposes. You may notice that an anti-inflammatory purpose has been left out. Acetaminophen does not reduce inflammation and, except for reducing the associated pain, does not help in the treatment of arthritis. However, acetaminophen does not produce gastric distress nor does it interfere with the clotting process, so there are significant benefits for those individuals adversely affected by aspirin.

The fact that acetaminophen has an effect on pain equivalent to that of aspirin without some of the prominent aspirin-related side effects has made acetaminophen the leading form of OTC pain reliever in the United States. Acetaminophen products represent approximately 41 percent of the pain-relief market, with aspirin and ibuprofen accounting for 23 percent and 26 percent, respectively.[14]

This is not to say that acetaminophen is totally benign. A serious problem is its relatively high potential for causing liver damage. About 7,500 mg of acetaminophen (equivalent to fifteen 500-mg tablets of Extra-Strength Tylenol) can produce liver damage, and the combination of acetaminophen with alcohol greatly increases the risk of such a toxic reaction. In 1993, an FDA advisory panel recommended that warnings on acetaminophen labels refer to the particular risk of combining acetaminophen with alcohol. It has been recommended that individuals having more than two drinks a day restrict their intake of acetaminophen to 2 grams per day (equivalent to four extra-strength tablets or about six regular-strength tablets). The normal maximal recommended dose per day is 4 grams.

Anyone who has taken acetaminophen in this dosage range in combination with alcohol should seek medical attention immediately, prior to the appearance of symptoms related to liver disease. As an emergency medical procedure, an injection of acetylcysteine (brand name: Mucosil) can be used as an antidote for acetaminophen overdose, but this treatment is successful only if begun immediately. It may take as much as forty-eight to ninety-six hours before the symptoms of acetaminophen overdose appear, and by this time liver damage will have reached an advanced stage.[15]

Reye's syndrome (RYES SIN-drohm): A rare but highly dangerous childhood disorder that has been associated with the administration of ASA-type analgesic drugs for the treatment of certain viral infections.

acetaminophen (a-SEE-tuh-MIN-oh-fen): A type of OTC analgesic drug. A major brand name is Tylenol.

A second concern is the risk of kidney damage as a result of heavy average use or moderate cumulative use of acetaminophen. The risk of kidney failure doubles in people who have taken more than 365 acetaminophen pills over a year's time (averaging one per day) or 1,000–5,000 pills over a lifetime. Aspirin use has not been found to increase the chances of kidney damage, though, as noted earlier, aspirin has its own health risks.[16]

A third concern with acetaminophen is the risk of enhancing the effect of prescription anticlotting medications such as warfarin (brand name: Coumadin). While a reduction of clotting is often indicated for patients who suffer from clogged arteries, acetaminophen creates a situation in which the reduction of clotting is excessive, leading to hemorrhage. To this extent, acetaminophen shares the same interactive effect as aspirin and other NSAIDs.[17]

Ibuprofen

From 1968 to 1984, **ibuprofen** was available only as a prescription analgesic (brand name: Motrin), but it has since been FDA-approved as an OTC drug. Currently, ibuprofen is marketed under a variety of brand names, most prominently as Advil, Mediprin, Midol, Motrin, and Nuprin. It is effective in reducing pain, inflammation, and elevated temperature due to fever. In addition, ibuprofen has been found to be particularly effective in the treatment of menstrual cramps. As with aspirin, the mechanism behind ibuprofen's effects is to block the production of prostaglandins.

The recommended adult dosage of ibuprofen is 200 mg (one tablet) every four to six hours. Two tablets may be used but no one should exceed 1,200 mg (six tablets) in a twenty-four-hour period. There is less gastric irritation in taking ibuprofen than when taking aspirin, though some discomfort can be experienced and the warning label suggests that milk or food be consumed when taking the drug. In general, just as the mechanism behind the action of ibuprofen is similar to that of aspirin, so also ibuprofen shares the anticlotting feature associated with aspirin. An additional concern related to ibuprofen is the potential for kidney damage or kidney failure. It is not advisable for individuals who have a history of kidney disease to take ibuprofen.[18]

Recently, it has been suggested that ibuprofen might operate to prevent the developing symptoms of Alzheimer's disease, a degenerative brain disorder in which memory and cognitive abilities become impaired. More than 1,500 volunteers of all ages who had kept detailed records of their medications, including OTC analgesics, were followed over many years. Those in the study who had taken ibuprofen products for more than two years indicated a 60 percent lower risk of Alzheimer's disease relative to those who had not.[19]

Naproxen

The newest OTC analgesic drug, **naproxen,** is actually a well-known prescription drug that has been FDA-approved since 1994 for nonprescription use. When it was marketed as a prescription drug, it was known under the brand names Naprosyn and Anaprox. As an OTC drug, naproxen is available at a slightly lower dosage under the brand name Aleve.

Naproxen has analgesic, anti-inflammatory, and antipyretic effects, with a duration of action of eight to twelve hours, substantially longer than the other types of OTC analgesic drugs. The principal problem with naproxen is gastrointestinal irritation. Chronic naproxen treatment may cause gastric bleeding, ulceration, or perforation. It is important to be alert to signs of these problems while taking naproxen and to discontinue its use if any difficulties arise. It also has anticlotting effects.[20]

Analgesic Drugs and Attempted Suicide

In 1998, acetaminophen, ibuprofen, and aspirin were listed fifth, ninth, and tenth, respectively, in terms of drugs associated with ED mentions in the DAWN reports. In about 90 percent of these cases, the cause was reported as a drug overdose, and in about 80 percent of the cases the patient reported having attempted suicide. Generally speaking, the predominant demographic characteristics of an individual attempting suicide by an overdose of OTC analgesics are Caucasian, female, and between the ages of twelve and twenty-five years. Fortunately, relatively few suicide attempts involving analgesics alone (without alcohol) are successful.[21]

ibuprofen (EYE-buh-PRO-fin): A type of OTC analgesic drug. Major brand names include Advil, Motrin, and Nuprin.

naproxen (na-PROX-sin): An analgesic drug, formerly available only by prescription (brand names: Naprosyn and Anaprox). It is now available as an OTC drug under the brand name Aleve.

QUICK CONCEPT  14.2

Understanding OTC Analgesic Drugs

Check your understanding of OTC analgesic drugs by associating the following characteristics with (a) aspirin, (b) acetaminophen, (c) ibuprofen, or (d) naproxen. Some characteristics may be applicable to more than one category of OTC analgesic drug.

1. A common brand name is Tylenol.
2. Reduction of inflammation is one of the medical applications.
3. Gastric distress is most severe with this drug.
4. Combination with alcohol can lead to serious liver damage.
5. There is an anticlotting effect.
6. Blocking the production of prostaglandins is an explanation of the physiological effects of this drug.
7. It is the oldest known of the four types of analgesic drugs.

Answers: 1. b 2. a, c, and d 3. a 4. b 5. a, c, and d 6. a and c 7. a

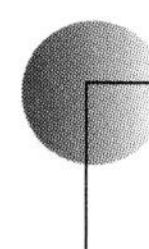

Other Major Classes of OTC Drugs

In addition to analgesic products, a number of other product categories play a major role in the overall OTC market. Three of them will be considered: weight-loss aids, sleep aids, and cough-and-cold remedies.

Weight-Loss Aids

Most of us can relate to the desire to lose weight with as little pain or inconvenience as possible. Until recently, the only FDA-approved active ingredient in OTC weight-loss aids (brand names Acutrim and Dexatrim) had been **phenylpropanolamine (PPA),** a mild CNS stimulant and nasal decongestant, which worked to suppress the appetite. In 2000, the FDA withdrew PPA from the market after it was determined that there was an increased risk of hemorrhagic (bleeding) stroke in young women. Caffeine was once included in appetite suppressant products, but the FDA has prohibited the practice. Currently available weight-loss aids contain primarily dietary supplements that are not regulated by the FDA.[22]

Sleep Aids

The only FDA-approved active ingredients in OTC sleep aids are **diphenhydramine,** an antihistamine to be taken in either a 25-mg or 50-mg dosage once a day (also available in various types of Benadryl), and **doxylamine succinate,** another antihistamine to be taken in a 25-mg dosage once a day. Brand names of such sleep aids containing diphenhydramine include Nytol QuickCaps and Sleepinal Night-time Sleep Aid; Unisom is the brand name for a sleep aid containing doxylamine succinate. Some of these products are also marketed in combination with acetaminophen as a "sleep-aid pain-relief formula" medication (Tylenol PM, for example). Individuals taking this kind of medication should be aware that they are dealing with a CNS depressant, and any combination with other depressants, such as alcohol or antihistamines contained in cough-and-cold remedies, can inadvertently enhance the overall effect.[23]

Cough-and-Cold Remedies

As we all know, a cold can be a miserable experience. It can be frustrating as well because it is a viral infection and no antibiotic drug or any other drug for that matter has yet been discovered that can prevent a cold, cure a cold, or even reduce the length of time that we have to endure a cold. All we can do is attempt to reduce its symptoms. This is where OTC remedies come into the picture. About 25 percent of all OTC drugs are marketed specifically for the control of cold symptoms, the second largest OTC category after analgesics.[24]

Choosing a cough-and-cold remedy (along with similar medications that treat allergic symptoms) depends on the symptoms that are present. Basic ingredients can in-

phenylpropanolamine (PPA) (FEN-il-pro-PAN-oh-la-meen): Formerly, the only FDA-approved active ingredient in OTC appetite-suppressants, weight-loss aids as well as cold remedies. The FDA removed PPA from the market in 2000.

diphenhydramine (DEYE-fen-HEYE-druh-meen): One of two FDA-approved active ingredients in OTC sleep-aid products, such as Nytol and Sleepinal.

doxylamine succinate (DOX-il-a-meen SUK-ih-nate): One of two FDA-approved active ingredients in OTC sleep-aid products, such as Unisom.

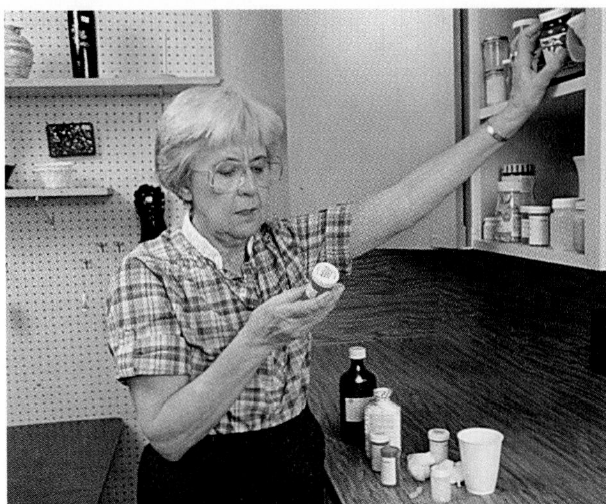

The elderly often have to contend with a multitude of medications, many of which may interact with one another.

clude an *antitussive agent,* or cough suppressant, for the control of a cough; an *expectorant* to reduce the thickness of mucus in the throat and pharynx (making it easier to cough up); a *decongestant* to widen blocked nasal passages and sinuses; an *antihistamine* to relieve the itching, sneezing, teary eyes, and runny nose; and finally an *analgesic* and *antipyretic* drug to reduce the sinus pain, headache, or fever. Most cough-and-cold medications combine these ingredients in various proportions, so it is important to read the labels carefully to identify the specific product that is best-suited for a particular combination of symptoms.

Potential problems can occur as a result of three major factors in current cough-and-cold medications. The first problem is that antihistamines are CNS depressants. Though antihistamines can sometimes act paradoxically in young children (just as stimulants can act paradoxically as depressants, see Chapter 4), they produce drowsiness and sleep in most adults. This effect might be fine for bedtime, but it is very important to refrain from driving a car, or engaging in any task that requires full attention, while taking an antihistamine product.

The second problem concerns the quantity of alcohol in several cough-and-cold remedies. With levels of alcohol sometimes reaching 25 percent, these cough-and-cold remedies can function essentially as alcoholic beverages. This factor will combine additively to the antihistamine effect and make a person even drowsier than he or she would have been with the antihistamine alone. A person should take care not to consume alcoholic beverages while being treated with an antihistamine medication.

A related issue concerns the potential abuse by young people of cough-and-cold remedies containing high levels of alcohol in order to get drunk. While this form of alcohol consumption is undoubtedly less than pleasant, some may see these products as an opportunity to bypass present restrictions on alcohol sales to underage customers. Mouthwashes also have this potential for alcohol-related abuse.

Fortunately, many cough-and-cold products include specific warnings on the labels that refer to potential difficulties that might arise if the individual is diabetic, has high blood pressure, or suffers from heart or thyroid disease. Women who are pregnant or nursing should consult their physicians or other health professionals before taking any cough-and-cold remedy (Health Alert).[25]

Health Alert

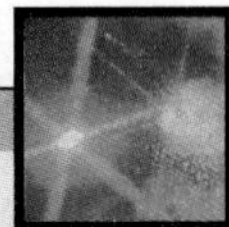

The Risks of Web Pharmacies

A 53-year-old Chicago man dies after taking Viagra, ordered over the Internet. He didn't see a doctor and was not advised that Viagra could be dangerous for individuals at risk for heart disease. This is an example of an increasing trend in the dispensing of prescription medications. Currently, there are hundreds of drug-dispensing web sites. On the one hand, they are opportunities for consumers to obtain prescription drugs more cheaply. On the other hand, consumers are vulnerable to exploitation by those who dispense these drugs without prescriptions or licenses. The National Association of Boards of Pharmacy has begun a process of certifying legitimate online pharmacies, so it is advisable to check if certification has been secured before purchasing medications in this manner. It has been proposed that the FDA be given the power to review and certify these establishments and impose heavy fines when regulations are violated. Obviously, the Internet has opened up a whole new world of e-commerce, and the prescription drug industry is not immune to these new developments.

Source: Plan: Regulate web pharmacies (1999, December 29). *Newsday,* p. A3.

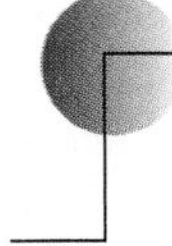

The Pharmaceutical Industry Today

About 15 years ago, I traveled to Nutley, N.J., to interview a molecular biologist at Hoffmann-La

Drugs . . . in Focus

Pushing Pills: Public Commercials for Prescription Drugs

In the last few years you might have noticed the increasing number of television, radio, and print commercials for prescription medications and wondered why you were hearing about products that would only be ordered by a physician or other health care professional. The net effect of such advertisements is that patients ask for a specific medication more frequently when they visit their doctor. Whether or not this influences the prescriptions that are issued remains an open question.

Doctors will argue that they are not susceptible to commercial messages with regard to the medications they prescribe, but undoubtedly pharmaceutical companies that invest tens of billions of dollars in promotion and advertising see a benefit in establishing a drug with "name recognition." It may not be coincidental that the best-selling prescription drugs are also the most widely advertised. Pharmaceutical companies defend their promotion campaigns as a way to alert consumers to possible treatments for medical conditions and encourage them to check with their doctors. Critics, however, see these developments as increasing the trend toward over-prescription of medications and needlessly pressuring doctors to comply with their patients' wishes. It is possible that advertisements might confuse consumers more than they educate them. As one physician has put it, "I don't think the public should be kept dumb, but what the drug companies are doing now is leapfrogging over the physicians directly to the public to create a demand for the medication."

Sources: Berkowitz, Harry, and Unger, Michael (1998, September 27). Pushing pills: Drug ads abound, but do they raise false hopes for cures? *Newsday,* pp. F8–F10. Zuger, Abigail (1999, January 11). Fever pitch: Getting doctors to prescribe is big business. *New York Times,* pp. A1, A13.

Roche. I vividly recall my host waving at an impressive little skyline of buildings worthy of a college quadrangle and proudly saying, "Valium built all this." As recently as a month ago, when I visited the gleaming research and development complex of SmithKline Beecham just outside Philadelphia, my scientific host waved at an expanse of tinted-glass buildings and explained "Tagamet paid for all of this."[26]

As this comment implies, pharmaceutical companies clearly are profitable enterprises, but like other businesses they are only as successful as the products they sell. In an extremely competitive marketplace, diversification is a key factor for continued growth. It is a little-known fact, for example, that a pharmaceutical company best known for a particular type of analgesic drug more than likely manufactures and distributes other types as well. Bayer Corporation is best identified with Bayer Aspirin, but the company also markets an acetaminophen product (Panadol), a combination of aspirin, acetaminophen, and caffeine (Vanquish), an ibuprofen product (Bayer Select Ibuprofen), and naproxen (Aleve).

In the new millennium, major pharmaceutical companies are facing increasing strains and pressures not only within their own industry but from governmental agencies and the public at large. They have been criticized for runaway prescription drug prices, excessive corporate profits, and an apparent willingness to spend nearly as much on advertising and promotion as on research and development. Spending on prescription drugs currently represents about 8 percent of the more than trillion dollars spent on health care services in the United States but has accounted for 20 percent of the increase in the cost of these services from 1997 to 1998 (see Point/Counterpoint on page 344).

The costs of prescription medications are a particular concern when viewed in terms of the economic burden placed on the elderly. They typically require a substantially greater proportion of drugs than do younger subpopulations, and, to make matters worse, they are frequently ineligible to receive reimbursements for outpatient pharmaceutical expenses. Recently, congressional legislation has been proposed to offer prescription drug coverage under Medicare. The fight to contain the high cost of prescription drugs, sometimes called "the other drug war," as well as the high cost of health care in general, is certain to continue in the years ahead.[27]

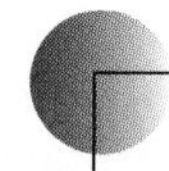

Dietary Supplements

There are well over one hundred dietary supplements currently available to the public. Of these, approximately seventy are herbal preparations, according to a recent review.[28] In Chapter 8, two supplements (androstenedione and creatine) were discussed in the context of athletic performance; in Chapter 16, one supplement

(St.-John's-wort) will be covered in the context of treating depression. In this chapter, two supplements (gingko biloba and ginseng) will be discussed in the context of improving cognitive function.

Ginkgo Biloba

Ginkgo biloba, commonly called ginkgo, is extracted from the Ginkgo tree, indigenous to Europe, Asia, and North America; its medicinal use has been recorded in Chinese texts dating back to about 3000 B.C. In its modern form, ginkgo extracts produced in Europe have been standardized to contain approximately 24 percent flavonoids and 6 percent terpenoids. These molecules are classified as antioxidants, a class of agents that inhibit platelets in the blood from sticking together. Blood circulation is improved and, presumably, the circulation of blood to the brain is enhanced. As a result, the most frequent application of ginkgo has been to improve memory or cognitive function.

Ginkgo extract has been shown to produce modest, but statistically significant, improvements in cognitive function in Alzheimer's disease patients, but whether or not it helps normal individuals remains to be determined. While ginkgo is considered relatively safe when taken in standard dosages, the anticlotting effect makes it dangerous for individuals who are taking blood-thinning medications, such as warfarin (brand name: Coumadin) or NSAIDs.[29]

Ginseng

Ginseng is extracted from the Ginseng root, grown in Asia as well as the United States. In general, Asian ginseng is considered to be of better quality than ginseng grown domestically. The active molecules in ginseng are referred to as *ginsenosides*, which function as antioxidants. While not necessarily having the same anticlotting effect as does ginkgo, ginsenosides have been reported to have caused uterine bleeding in post-menopausal women. More generally, ginseng effects can include elevations in blood pressure, nervousness, and insomnia, especially in individuals taking large dosages. The traditional application has been for improved mental alertness and concentration among the elderly, but more recently there have been claims that ginseng can benefit cognitive function in younger populations, as well as produce an enhanced sense of well-being. The research literature, however, has been difficult to evaluate, since ginsenoside amounts in ginseng products have not been standardized.[30]

gingko biloba: An herb-based dietary supplement considered to improve blood circulation and possibly increase mental alertness.
ginseng: An herb-based dietary supplement with possible applications that include an improvement in mental alertness among the elderly.

SUMMARY

- Three categories of medicinal products are available for purchase: prescription drugs (which require medical approval) and over-the-counter (OTC) drugs and dietary supplements (which are available without any restrictions).
- The U.S. Food and Drug Administration (FDA) is responsible for setting the standards of safety, effectiveness, and honesty in labeling for the first two categories.

How the Regulation of Prescription and OTC Drugs Began

- A series of federal laws, put into effect since 1906, have established the FDA as the authority for safeguarding the public health with regard to prescription and OTC drugs, as well as food products, cosmetics, and medical devices.

Procedures for Approving Prescription and OTC Drugs

- The FDA process for the approval of new prescription drugs begins with animal studies to determine their safety limits and relative toxicity. If these standards are met, clinical trials, first with healthy human volunteers and later with actual patients, are conducted to identify the optimal dosage levels and degree of effectiveness.
- Only a small proportion of new compounds developed by drug companies make it successfully through these clinical trials and are eventually approved by the FDA for marketing as new prescription drugs. The process often takes several years.
- Since 1962, all prescription and OTC drugs have been required by the FDA to be generally recognized as

safe (GRAS), effective (GRAE), and honestly labeled (GRAHL).

Are FDA-Approved Drugs Safe?

- There is considerable concern that although prescription and OTC drugs are FDA-approved for use when taken in the recommended dosages and under the recommended circumstances, misuse can result in medical emergencies and fatalities.
- The DAWN reports show that the misuse of analgesic OTC drugs, in particular, can present significant health risks.

Major OTC Analgesic Drugs

- Acetylsalicylic acid (aspirin), acetaminophen, ibuprofen, and naproxen are four types of OTC analgesic drugs available to the public.
- Because each of these types has its benefits *and* hazards, it is strongly urged that recommended dosage levels be observed and anyone with specific health problems be aware that analgesic drugs may be harmful.

Other Major Classes of OTC Drugs

- Three other classes of OTC drugs can be highlighted in terms of their use and potential for misuse. The first is the variety of weight-loss aids, which contained until 2000 the ingredient phenylpropanolamine (PPA). The second is the variety of sleep aids, with the active ingredient of either diphenhydramine or doxylamine succinate. The third is the variety of cough-and-cold remedies that generally contain some combination of antihistamine and decongestant.
- Careful use of all of these products is advised.

The Pharmaceutical Industry Today

- In the present-day pharmaceutical industry, companies have diversified their prescription and OTC products to maintain their shares of a highly competitive market.
- Pharmaceutical companies are also under pressure to reduce the prices of their products as a component of controlling overall health-care costs.

Dietary Supplements

- A large number of products, referred to as dietary supplements, are available to the public. Unlike OTC preparations, however, dietary supplements have not been evaluated by the FDA for safety and efficacy. Therefore, claims of medical benefits are often difficult to verify, and caution should be exercised.
- Of the herbal varieties of dietary supplements, gingko biloba and ginseng have been promoted as enhancing aspects of cognitive function such as mental alertness, concentration, and memory.

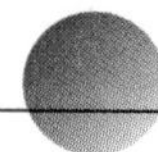

KEY TERMS

acetaminophen, p. 300
acetylsalicylic acid (ASA), p. 298
anti-inflammatory, p. 298
antipyretic, p. 298
aspirin, p. 298
bioequivalency, p. 294
diphenhydramine, p. 302
doxylamine succinate, p. 302
ginkgo biloba, p. 305
ginseng, p. 305
ibuprofen, p. 301
naproxen, p. 301
nonsteroidal anti-inflammatory drug (NSAID), p. 298
over-the-counter (OTC) drugs, p. 289
patent, p. 293
Phase 1 trials, p. 292
Phase 2 trials, p. 292
Phase 3 trials, p. 293
Phase 4 trials, p. 293
phenylpropanolamine (PPA), p. 302
prescription drugs, p. 289
prostaglandins, p. 298
Reye's syndrome, p. 300
salicylic acid, p. 298
thalidomide, p. 290

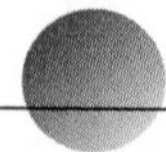

ENDNOTES

1. Patrick, William (1988). *The Food and Drug Administration.* New York: Chelsea House, pp. 29–49.
2. Burkholz, Herbert (1994). *The FDA follies.* New York: Basic Books. Patrick, *The Food and Drug Administration*, p. 40.
3. Janesh, Barbara J. (1989, January). How these little pills went to market. *Everyday Law,* pp. 40–44. Julien, Robert M. (1995). *A primer of drug action* (7th ed.). New York: Freeman, p. 47.

4. Ruling gives drug makers up to three extra years on patents (1995, May 26). *New York Times*, pp. D1, D7. Yorke, Jeffrey (1992, September). FDA ensures equivalence of generic drugs. *FDA Consumer*, pp. 11–15.
5. FDA's approval of drugs gains speed (1996, January 20). *New York Times*, p. 24. Flieger, Ken (1993, October). FDA finds new ways to speed treatments to patients. *FDA Consumer*, pp. 15–18. Henkel, John (1993, October). User fees to fund faster reviews. *FDA Consumer*, pp. 19–21.
6. Nightingale, Stuart L. (1999). From the Food and Drug Administration: New easy-to-understand labels for OTC drugs. *Journal of the American Medical Association, 281*, 1164. Segal, Marian (1991, March). Rx to OTC: The switch is on. *FDA Consumer*, pp. 9–11. Stolberg, Sheryl G. (2000, June 28). F.D.A. considers switching some prescription drugs to over-the-counter status. *New York Times*, p. A18.
7. Substance Abuse and Mental Health Services Administration (2000). *Drug Abuse Warning Network annual emergency department data 1998*. Rockville MD: Office of Applied Studies, Substance Abuse and Mental Health Services Administration, Table 2.06a. Substance Abuse and Mental Health Services Administration (2000). *Drug Abuse Warning Network annual medical examiner data 1998*. Rockville MD: Office of Applied Studies, Substance Abuse and Mental Health Services Administration, p. 39.
8. Krantz, John C. (1974). Felix Hoffman and aspirin. *Historical medical classics involving new drugs*. Baltimore: Williams and Wilkins, pp. 37–41. Levinthal, Charles F. (1988). *Messengers of paradise: Opiates and the brain*. New York: Anchor Press/Doubleday, p. 112.
9. Levinthal, *Messengers of Paradise*, p. 211. Mann, Charles C., and Plummer, Mark L. (1991). *Aspirin wars*. New York: Knopf, p. 4.
10. *Physicians' desk reference for nonprescription drugs* (21st ed.) (2000). Montvale NJ: Medical Economics Company, pp. 607–612.
11. Boehm, George A. W. (1966, September 11). Aspirin doesn't cure disease—It is the wonder drug nobody understands. *New York Times Magazine*, p. 56.
12. He, Jiang; Whelton, Paul K.; Vu, Brian; and Klag, Michael J. (1998). Aspirin and risk of hemorrhagic stroke: A meta-analysis of randomized controlled trials. *Journal of the American Medical Association, 280*, 1930–1935. *Physicians' desk reference for nonprescription drugs*, pp. 609–611.
13. Altman, Lawrence K. (1999, May 11). Tale of triumph on every aspirin bottle. *New York Times*, p. F8. *Physicians' desk reference for nonprescription drugs*, pp. 607–612. Zamula, Evelyn (1990, November). Reye syndrome: The decline of a disease. *FDA Consumer*, pp. 21–23.
14. Second chance for aspirin is also one for Bayer (1997, August 9). *New York Times*, p. 21.
15. Acetaminophen warning (1993, June 30). *New York Times*, p. C14. Morgenroth, Lynda (1989, December). High-risk pain pills. *Atlantic*, pp. 36–42. Schiødt, Frank V.; Rochling, Fedja A.; Casey, Donna L.; and Lee, William M. (1997). Acetaminophen toxicity in an urban county hospital. *New England Journal of Medicine*, 337, 1112–1117.
16. Perneger, Thomas V., Whelton, Paul K., and Klag, Michael J. (1994). Risk of kidney failure associated with the use of acetaminophen, aspirin, and nonsteroidal anti-inflammatory drugs. *New England Journal of Medicine, 331*, 1675–1679.
17. Hylek, Elaine M.; Heiman, Heather; Skates, Steven J.; Sheehan, Mary A.; and Singer, Daniel E. (1998). Acetaminophen and other risk factors for excessive warfarin anticoagulation. *Journal of the American Medical Association, 279*, 657–662.
18. Hilts, Philip J. (1996, March 27). How safe are Tylenol and Advil? Helping patients sort out risks. *New York Times*, p. C11. *Physicians' desk reference for nonprescription drugs*, pp. 661–664. U.S. Department of Health and Human Services (1984, August). *FDA Drug Bulletin*, pp. 19–20. Whelton, Andrew; Stout, Robert; Spilman, Patricia; and Klassen, David (1990). Renal effects of ibuprofen, piroxicam, and sulindac in patients with asymptomatic renal failure. *Annals of Internal Medicine, 112*, 568–576.
19. Morgan, Althea, and Clark, David (1998, April 9). CNS adverse effects of nonsteroidal anti-inflammatory drugs. *CNS Drugs*, pp. 281–290. Stewart, W. F.; Kawas, C.; Corrada, M.; and Metter, E. J. (1997). Risk of Alzheimer's disease and duration of NSAID use. *Neurology, 48* (3), 626–632.
20. *Physicians' desk reference* (54th ed.) (2000). Montvale NJ: Medical Economic Company, pp. 2631–2634.
21. Substance Abuse and Mental Health Services Administration. Annual emergency department data, Tables 2.06a, 2.11, 2.12, 2.13, 2.14. Substance Abuse and Mental Health Services Administration. Annual medical examiner data, pp. 39, 47.
22. Levy, Sandra (2000, November 20). PPA Alert: FDA moves to remove phenylpropanolamine from all decongestants and appetite suppressants. *Drug Topics*, p. 26. The new diet pills (1982, January). *Consumer Reports*, pp. 14–16.
23. *Physicians' desk reference for nonprescription drugs*, pp. 622–623.
24. *Market Share Reporter 2000* (1999). Detroit: Gale Group, p. 139.
25. *Physicians' desk reference for nonprescription drugs*, pp. 661–664. Willis, Judith L. (1991, November). Using over-the-counter medications wisely. *FDA Consumer*, pp. 35–37.
26. Quotation in Hall, Stephen S. (2000, July/August). Pharma's blockbuster habit. *Technology Review*, p. 100.
27. Barfield, Deborah (1999, November 4). Bid to curb seniors' drug costs. *Newsday*, p. A28. Gerena-Morales, Rafael (2000, January 11). Rising drug costs swell health care spending. *Newsday*, p. A37. Rosenbaum, David E. (1999, November 14). The gathering storm over prescription drugs. *New York Times*, Section 4, pp. 13, 16.
28. Karch, Steven B. (1999). *The consumer's guide to herbal medicine*. Hauppauge, NY: Advanced Research Press, pp. 25–179.

29. Karch, *The consumer's guide to herbal medicine,* pp. 13–18, 96–97. Oken, Barry S., Storzbach, Daniel M., and Kaye, Jeffrey A. (1998). The efficacy of *Ginkgo biloba* on cognitive function in Alzheimer's disease. *Archives of Neurology,* 55, 1409–1413. *Physician's desk reference for nonprescription drugs and dietary supplements* (2000). Montvale NJ: Medical Economics Company, pp. 843–845.

30. Karch, *The consumer's guide to herbal medicine,* pp. 99–101. Ochs, Ridgely (1999, November 30). Conclusion: Uncertain. Studies worldwide—from echinacea to ginseng—yield few definitive answers on risks and results. *Newsday,* pp. C8–C14. *Physician's desk reference for nonprescription drugs and dietary supplements,* pp. 845–846.

CHAPTER 15

Sedative-Hypnotics and Antianxiety Drugs

After you have completed this chapter, you will understand

- The development of barbiturates as sedative-hypnotic drugs
- The acute and chronic effects of barbiturates
- The search for the perfect nonbarbiturate sedative-hypnotic drug
- The development of benzodiazepines as antianxiety drugs
- Newly developed sedative-hypnotics and antianxiety drugs
- Present-day concerns about the recreational use of CNS depressants

Jennie never expected to be addicted to a prescription drug. After all, weren't the really dangerous drugs the ones you got from a pusher? It started with stress and anxiety, an engagement that didn't work out, trouble with the boss at work. The doctor gave her the prescription to help her fall asleep, to calm her down and get her through the day. And the drug worked, all too well. She was frightened of the thought of stopping. After several months, when she was embarrassed to ask for the fifth refill, she found another doctor who didn't ask any questions. So it went, from doctor to doctor, pharmacist to pharmacist, until she started to realize she was in trouble.

Just as cocaine, amphetamines, and other stimulants bring us up, depressants bring us down. Just as there is a desire to be stronger, faster, and more attuned to the world, there is also the desire to move apart from that world, reduce the stresses and anxieties of our lives, and fall asleep more easily. Historically, the prime psychoactive depressant drug has been alcohol. As was discussed in Chapter 9, practically every culture in the world has discovered in one way or another the effects of alcohol on the body and the mind. This chapter, however, focuses on a group of drugs called **sedative-hypnotics,** so named since they calm us down and produce sleep (from the Greek word *hypnos*, meaning "to sleep"). There are several types of depressants that promote sedation and sleep, ranging from drugs that were introduced a hundred years ago to others that have become available only recently.

This chapter also looks at drugs that provide specific relief from stress and anxiety without sedating us. These drugs have often been referred to as *tranquilizers* by virtue of their ability to make us feel peaceful or tranquil, but we will call them by their more current name, **antianxiety drugs.**

Unfortunately, sedative-hypnotics and antianxiety drugs have been subject not only to legitimate medical use but to misuse and abuse as well. Although they are available as prescription medications, many of them can be obtained from illicit sources as street drugs and are consumed for recreational purposes. The psychological problems and physical dangers associated with the misuse and abuse of these depressants are of particular concern.

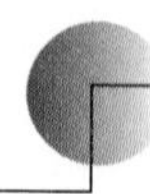

Barbiturates

In 1864, the German chemist Adolf von Baeyer combined a waste product in urine called urea and an apple extract called malonic acid to form a new chemical compound called barbituric acid. There are two often told stories about how this compound got its name. One story has it that Von Baeyer went to a local tavern to celebrate his discovery and encountered a number of artillery officers celebrating the feast day of St. Barbara, the patron saint of explosives handlers. Inspired by their celebration, the name "barbituric acid" came to mind. The other story attributes the name to a favorite barmaid whose name was Barbara.[1]

Whichever story is true (if either is), Von Baeyer's discovery of barbituric acid set the stage for the development of a class of drugs called **barbiturates.** Barbituric acid itself, however, has no behavioral effects. It is only when additional molecular groups combine with the acid to form derivatives of Von Baeyer's compound that depressant effects are observed. In 1903, the first true barbiturate, diethylbarbituric acid, was created and marketed under the name Veronal. Over the next thirty years, several major barbiturate drugs were introduced: **phenobarbital** (marketed in generic form), **amobarbital** (brand name: Amytal), **pentobarbital** (brand name: Nembutal), and **secobarbital** (brand name: Seconal).

Categories of Barbiturates

Dozens of different barbiturates have been marketed over the years, all sharing a number of common features. They are relatively tasteless and odorless, and at sufficient dosages they reliably induce sleep, although the quality of sleep is a matter that will be discussed later. Because they slow down the activity of the central nervous system, barbiturates are also useful in the treatment of epilepsy.

The principal difference among them lies in how long the depressant effects will last; a rough classification of barbiturates is based upon this factor. Barbiturates are categorized as *long-acting* (six or more hours), *intermediate-acting* (four to six hours), or *short-acting* (less than four hours). Bear in mind, however, that these groups are relative only to one another. Injectable forms of barbiturates are shorter-acting than orally administered forms of the same drug, since it takes longer for the drug to be absorbed when taken by mouth and longer for it to be eliminated from the body. Naturally, a higher dose of any drug lasts longer than a lower dose because it takes longer for all of the drug to be eliminated from the body (Table 15.1).

sedative-hypnotics: A category of depressant drugs that provide a sense of calm and sleep.
antianxiety drugs: Drugs that make the user feel more peaceful or tranquil; also called tranquilizers.
barbiturate (bar-BIT-chur-rit): A drug within a family of depressants derived from barbituric acid and used as a sedative-hypnotic and antiepileptic medication.
phenobarbital (FEEN-oh-BAR-bih-tall): A long-acting barbiturate drug, usually marketed in generic form.
amobarbital (A-moh-BAR-bih-tall): An intermediate-acting barbiturate drug. Brand name is Amytal.
pentobarbital (PEN-toh-BAR-bih-tall): A short-acting barbiturate drug. Brand name is Nembutal.
secobarbital (SEC-oh-BAR-bih-tall): A short-acting barbiturate drug. Brand name is Seconal.

TABLE 15.1

Major barbiturates

GENERIC NAME	BRAND NAME	DURATION OF ACTION	RELATIVE POTENTIAL FOR ABUSE
phenobarbital	generic*	long	low
mephobarbital	Mebaral	long	low
butalbarbital	Pheniline Forte**	intermediate	moderate
amobarbital	Amytal	intermediate	high
secobarbital and amobarbital	Tuinal	short, intermediate	high
pentobarbital	Nembutal	short	high
secobarbital	Seconal	short	high

Note: Short-acting barbiturates begin to take effect in about 15 minutes, intermediate-acting barbiturates in 30 minutes, and long-acting barbiturates in one hour.

*Phenobarbital is also available in combination with hyoscyamine, atropine, and scopolamine under the brand name Donnatal.

**Several brands combine butalbarbital with acetaminophen.

Sources: Henningfield, Jack E., and Ator, Nancy A. (1986). *Barbiturates: Sleeping potion or intoxicant?* New York: Chelsea House, p. 24. *Physicians' desk reference* (54th ed.) (2000). Montvale NJ: Medical Economics Company.

The barbiturates used in surgical anesthesia, such as thiopental (brand name: Pentothal), take effect extremely rapidly (within seconds) and last only a few minutes. For this reason, they are referred to as *ultra-short-acting barbiturates*. Because these features are undesirable to a person seeking a recreational drug, ultra-short-acting barbiturates are not commonly abused.

Acute Effects of Barbiturates

You can visualize the effects of barbiturates on the body and the mind as points along a scale ranging from mild relaxation on one end to coma and death on the other (Figure 15.1). In this sense, barbiturate effects are the same as the effects of depressants in general. The particular point that is achieved depends on the dose level that is taken.

At very low doses, the primary result of oral administrations of a barbiturate is relaxation and, paradoxically, a sense of euphoria. These effects derive chiefly from a disinhibition of the cerebral cortex, in which normal inhibitory influences from the cortex are reduced. You might recognize these symptoms as similar to the inebriating or intoxicating effects that result from low-level doses of alcohol (Drugs . . . in Focus).

As the dose level increases, lower regions of the brain become affected, specifically the reticular formation (Chapter 3). At therapeutic doses (one 100 mg capsule of secobarbital, for example), barbiturates make you feel sedated and drowsy. For this reason, patients are typically warned that barbiturates may impair the performance of driving a car or operating machinery. At higher doses, a hypnotic (sleep-inducing) effect will be achieved.

Historically, the primary use of barbiturates has been in the treatment of insomnia, and they were widely recommended for this purpose from 1903, when they were first introduced, until the development of the benzodiazepines in the 1960s. One of the reasons why barbiturates fell from favor was that the sleep induced by these drugs turned out to be far from normal. Barbiturates tend to suppress rapid eye movement (REM) sleep, a phase of everyone's sleep that comprises about 20 percent of the total sleep time each night. REM sleep is associated

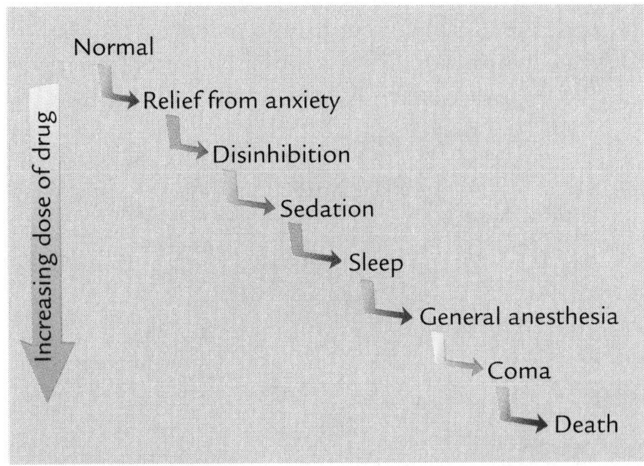

FIGURE 15.1

The downward continuum of arousal levels, as induced by depressants.

Source: Julien, Robert M. (1998). *A primer of drug action* (8th ed). Copyright © 1998 by W. H. Freeman and Company. Reprinted with permission.

Drugs . . . In Focus

Is There Any Truth Regarding "Truth Serum"?

The idea that sedative-hypnotic drugs such as amobarbital (Amytal, or "sodium amytal") may function as "truth serums" is not at all new. It has been known for centuries that depressants can produce remarkable candor and freedom from inhibition. The oldest example is simple alcohol, whose effect on loosening the tongue has led to the Latin proverb *in vino veritas* ("in wine, there is truth").

Whether or not we are guaranteed truthfulness under any of these circumstances, however, is another matter entirely. Courts have ruled that expert opinion in criminal cases based *solely* on drug-assisted testimony cannot be admitted as evidence. Controlled laboratory studies have shown that individuals under the influence of Amytal, when pressed by questioners, are as likely to give convincing renditions of fabrications (outright lies) or fantasies as they are to tell the truth.

So, perhaps, Amytal or Pentothal might be better described as "tell anything serum."

Sources: Michaelis, James I. (1966). Quaere, whether 'in vino veritas': An analysis of the truth serum cases. *Issues in Criminology, 2* (2), pp. 245–267.

Health Alert

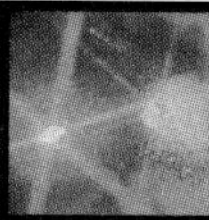

In Case of a Barbiturate Overdose Emergency . . .

What To Do

- Keep the patient awake and moving, if possible.
- If the patient cannot be kept awake, make him or her warm and elevate the feet.
- Send for emergency help immediately.

What Not To Do

- Do not give stimulants such as coffee; they may worsen convulsions later.

Likely Emergency Room Procedures

- Patient will be put on life support and artificially respirated until the barbiturates are metabolized.
- Drugs may be administered to speed up urination.
- Hemodialysis (machine-assisted filtering of the blood) may be employed to help remove the barbiturate from the bloodstream.

Source: Palfai, Tibor, and Jankiewicz, Henry (1991). *Drugs and human behavior.* Dubuque IA: W. C. Brown, p. 212.

with dreaming and general relaxation of the body. If barbiturates are consumed over many evenings and then stopped, the CNS will attempt to catch up for the lost REM sleep by producing longer REM periods on subsequent nights. This **REM-sleep rebound** effect produces vivid and upsetting nightmares, along with a barbiturate hangover the next day, during which the user feels groggy and out of sorts. In other words, barbiturates may induce sleep, but a refreshing sleep it definitely is not.[2]

Barbiturates and alcohol have frequently been combined in attempts to commit suicide.

The most serious acute risks of barbiturate use involve the possibility of a lethal overdose either from taking too high a dose level of the drug alone or from taking the drug in combination with alcohol, as when a barbiturate is taken after an evening of drinking. In these instances, sleep can all too easily slip into coma and death, since an excessive dose produces an inhibition of the respiratory centers in the medulla. The mixture of barbiturates with alcohol produces a synergistic effect (see Chapter 3), in which the combined result is greater than the sum of the effects of each drug alone (Health Alert).

REM-sleep rebound: A phenomenon associated with the withdrawal of barbiturate drugs in which the quantity of rapid eye movement (REM) sleep increases, resulting in disturbed sleep and nightmares.

Half of the lethal dose of secobarbital combined with ¼ the lethal dose of alcohol can kill in a synergistic double whammy. In another typical case of accidental overdose, a person takes a sleeping pill and awakens drugged and confused a few minutes later, annoyed at being aroused. The person then forgetfully takes another pill, or several, from the nightstand, and goes to sleep forever. This is called "drug automatism," a good reason not to keep medications within reach of the bed.[3]

During the period between 1973 and 1976, barbiturates were implicated in more than half of all drug-related deaths labeled as suicide by medical examiners. In fact, the suicide potential of barbiturates is the primary reason for their decline as a prescription drug.[4]

Chronic Effects of Barbiturates

The use of barbiturates as sleep medications often initiates a cycle of behavior that can lead to dependence. Even after brief use of barbiturates, anxiety may be temporarily increased during the day and there may be an even greater degree of insomnia than before. In addition, because a barbiturate-induced sleep typically leaves a person feeling groggy the next morning, it is tempting to take a stimulant drug during the day in order to feel completely alert. At bedtime, the person still feels the stimulant effects and is inclined to continue taking a barbiturate in order to achieve any sleep at all. To make matters worse, the brain builds up a pharmacological tolerance to barbiturates quite quickly, requiring increasingly higher doses for an equivalent effect.

Withdrawal symptoms, observed when barbiturates are discontinued, indicate a strong physical dependence on the drug. A person may experience a combination of tremors (the "shakes"), nausea and vomiting, intense perspiring, general confusion, convulsions, hallucinations, high fever, and increased heart rate. Not surprisingly, considering the parallels mentioned so far with alcohol, the barbiturate withdrawal syndrome closely resembles that of withdrawal after chronic alcohol abuse (see Chapter 10).

Professionals in the treatment of drug dependence often view the effects of barbiturate withdrawal as the most distressing as well as the most dangerous type of drug withdrawal. From a medical perspective, the withdrawal process is potentially life-threatening unless it is carried out in gradual fashion in a hospital setting. Without medical supervision, abrupt withdrawal from barbiturates carries approximately a 5 percent chance of death.[5]

Current Medical Uses of Barbiturates

Considering the problems of barbiturate use in the treatment of insomnia, it should not be surprising that a 1988 review in the *Harvard Medical School Health Letter* concluded that the clinical use of barbiturates for this problem was essentially "obsolete."[6] Nonetheless, barbiturates continue to play an important role in the treatment of epileptic seizures. Phenobarbital and mephobarbital (two long-acting barbiturates) are prescribed to prevent convulsions. Dose levels need to be monitored carefully, however, since the concentration must be high enough to control the development of seizures (despite the tendency for tolerance effects to occur over time) without being so high as to produce drowsiness.

Patterns of Barbiturate Abuse

There are clear indications that taking barbiturate drugs is positively reinforcing. Laboratory animals will eagerly press a lever to deliver intravenous injections of barbiturates, particularly for the short-acting types, at rates that are equal to those for cocaine.[7] When given the choice between pentobarbital and a nonbarbiturate depressant and given no knowledge as to the identity of the drugs, human drug abusers reliably select an oral dose of pentobarbital.[8]

Barbiturate abuse reached its peak in the 1950s and 1960s, later to be overshadowed by abuses of heroin, hallucinogens, nonbarbiturate depressants, amphetamines, and, more recently, abuses of cocaine, crack, and various stimulants and hallucinogens (Table 15.2). The principal reason was that barbiturates became less widely available as prescription drugs. Stricter controls were placed on obtaining excessive amounts of barbiturates from pharmacies, while physicians, concerned with the potential of barbiturates as ways of committing suicide, became more reluctant to prescribe them on a routine basis.

Despite their decline as major drugs of abuse, however, barbiturates are still being abused. The 2000 University of Michigan survey of high school seniors found that 9 percent of them had used some form of barbiturates during their lifetime, down from 17 percent in 1975, and 6 percent had taken them within the past year, down from 11 percent in 1975.[9]

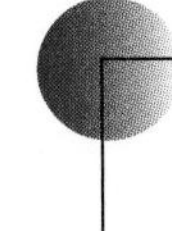

Nonbarbiturate Sedative-Hypnotics

As the hazards of barbiturate use became increasingly evident, the search was on for sedative-hypnotic

TABLE 15.2

Street names for various barbiturates

TYPE OF BARBITURATE	STREET NAME
pentobarbital (Nembutal)	abbotts, blockbusters, nebbies, nembies, nemmies, yellow bullets, yellow dolls, yellow jackets, yellows
amobarbital (Amytal)	blue angels, bluebirds, blue bullets, blue devils, blue dolls, blue heavens, blues
secobarbital (Seconal)	F-40s, Mexican reds, R.D.s, redbirds, red bullets, red devils, red dolls, reds, seccies, seggies, pinks
secobarbital and amobarbital (Tuinal)	Christmas trees, double trouble, gorilla pills, rainbows, tootsies, trees, tuies
barbiturates in general	downers, down, goofballs, G.B.s, goofers, idiot pills, King Kong pills, peanuts, pink ladies, sleepers, softballs, stumblers

Note: Like any other street drug, illicit barbiturate capsules often contain an unknown array of other substances, including strychnine, arsenic, laxatives, or milk sugars. Any yellow capsule may be "marketed" as Nembutal, any blue capsule as Amytal, or any red capsule as Seconal.

Source: Henningfield, Jack E., and Ator, Nancy A. (1986). *Barbiturates: Sleeping potion or intoxicant?* New York: Chelsea House, p. 82.

drugs that were not derivatives of barbituric acid and, it was hoped, had fewer undesirable side effects. One such drug, **chloral hydrate,** had been first synthesized as early as 1832. As a depressant for the treatment of insomnia, it has the advantage of not producing the REM-sleep rebound effect or bringing on the typical barbiturate hangover. A major disadvantage, however, is that it can severely irritate the stomach. Like other depressants, it is also highly reactive when combined with alcohol. In the nineteenth century, a few drops of chloral hydrate in a glass of whiskey became the infamous Mickey Finn, a concoction that left many an unsuspecting sailor unconscious and eventually "shanghaied" onto a boat for China.

The development of **methaqualone** (brand names: Quaalude, Sopor), first introduced in the United States in 1965, was a further attempt toward achieving the perfect sleeping pill. In 1972, methaqualone had become the sixth-best-selling drug for the treatment of insomnia. During the early 1970s, recreational use of methaqualone (popularly known as "ludes" or sopors) was rapidly spreading across the country, aided by the unfounded reputation that it had aphrodisiac properties.

The problem with methaqualone was compounded by the extensive number of prescriptions written by physicians who mistakenly saw the drug as a desirable alternative to barbiturates. On the street, quantities of methaqualone were obtained from medical prescriptions or stolen from pharmacies. Methaqualone-associated deaths started to be prominent mentions in the DAWN reports of the period (see Chapter 2). In 1984, its legal status changed to that of a Schedule I drug, the most restricted classification, which indicates a high potential for abuse and no medical benefits.[10] Though no longer manufactured by any pharmaceutical company, methaqualone is still available as an illicit drug. It is either manufactured in domestic underground laboratories or smuggled into the country from underground laboratories abroad.

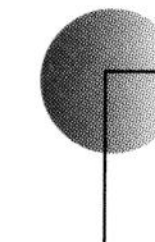

The Development of Antianxiety Drugs

If historians consider the 1950s "the age of anxiety," then it is appropriate that this period would also be marked by the development of drugs specifically intended to combat that anxiety. These drugs were originally called minor tranquilizers, to distinguish them from other drugs regarded as major tranquilizers and developed at about the same time to relieve symptoms of schizophrenia. This terminology is no longer used today, for we now know that the difference between the two drug categories is more than simply a matter of degree. Anxious people (or even people who are not bothered by anxiety) are not affected by drugs designed to treat schizophrenia. The current, and more logical, practice is to refer to drugs in terms of a specific action and purpose. The minor tranquilizers are now called *antianxiety drugs*. The major tranquilizers are now called *antipsychotic drugs*; they will be reviewed in Chapter 16.

The first antianxiety drug to be developed was **meprobamate** (brand name: Miltown), named in 1955 for a New Jersey town near the headquarters of the phar-

chloral hydrate: A depressant drug once used for the treatment of insomnia. It is highly reactive with alcohol and can severely irritate the stomach.

methaqualone (MEH-tha-QUAY-lone): A nonbarbiturate depressant drug once used as a sedative. Brand name is Quaalude.

meprobamate (MEH-pro-BAYM-ayt): A nonbarbiturate antianxiety drug and sedative. Brand name is Miltown.

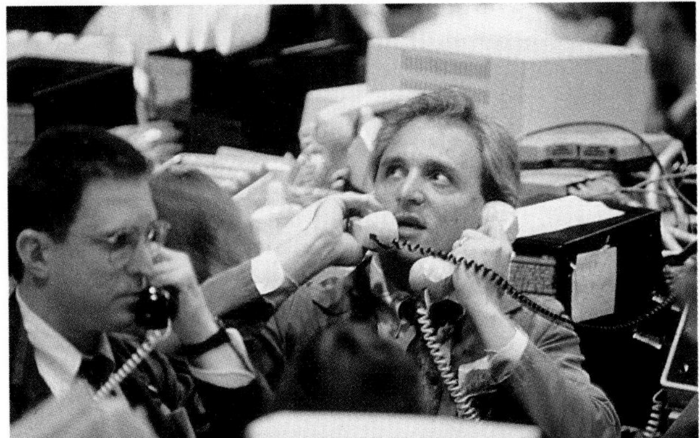

A person's job is often a source of considerable anxiety.

maceutical company that first introduced it. Miltown became an immediate hit among prescription drugs, making its name a household word and essentially a synonym for tranquilizers in general.

Even though meprobamate was the first psychoactive drug in history to be marketed as an antianxiety medication, most pharmacologists have identified the effects of this drug more in terms of sedation than of relief from anxiety.[11] Nonetheless, meprobamate is different from the other depressant drugs discussed so far in this chapter. The primary difference is in the way it works in the nervous system. Instead of inhibiting the reticular formation and the respiratory centers in the medulla as barbiturates do, meprobamate reduces the activity of acetylcholine at the nicotinic synapses where the motor nerves innervate the body's skeletal muscles (see Chapter 3). As a result, muscle contractions are weaker and general relaxation follows.

On the positive side, the toxic dose of meprobamate is relatively high, making the possibility of suicide more remote than with alcohol, barbiturates, and other depressants. In addition, judging from the reduction in autonomic responses to stressors, there are genuine signs that people on this medication are actually less anxious. On the negative side, motor reflexes are diminished, making driving more hazardous. People often complain of drowsiness, even at dose levels that should only be calming them down. Meprobamate can also produce both physical and psychological dependence, at slightly more than twice the normal recommended daily dose.[12] This is not a very wide margin for possible abuse, and as a result meprobamate is classified as a Schedule IV drug, requiring limits on the number of prescription refills. Meprobamate is still occasionally prescribed for anxiety and insomnia, but since 1960, it has been far eclipsed by a different class of antianxiety drugs called benzodiazepines.

Benzodiazepines

The introduction of a new group of drugs, called **benzodiazepines,** was a dramatic departure from all earlier attempts to treat anxiety. On the one hand, for the first time, there now were drugs that had a *selective* effect on anxiety itself, instead of producing a generalized reduction in the body's overall level of functioning. It was their tranquilizing effects, rather than their sedative effects, that made benzodiazepines so appealing to mental health professionals. On the other hand, it is important to distinguish between the well-publicized virtues of benzodiazepines when they were first introduced in the 1960s and the data that accumulated during the 1970s as millions of people experienced these new drugs. Although certainly very useful in the treatment of anxiety and other stress-related problems, benzodiazepines are no longer recognized as the miracle drugs they were promoted to be when they first entered the market.

Before taking up the specific facts about benzodiazepine drugs, it is important to understand how their discovery has given us some insight into the nature of anxiety itself. One pharmacologist has defined it this way:

> *Anxiety can be described as apprehension, tension, or uneasiness that stems from the anticipation of danger, which may be internal or external. It may be a response to stress that is associated with external stimuli, or it may be devoid of any apparent precipitating stimulus.*[13]

As Figure 15.2 shows, feelings of anxiety are considered to progress along a continuum of emotions that range in magnitude or intensity from a complete lack of concern, to moderate apprehension, justified or unjustified anxiety, finally to outright panic. You can see that some of these emotional states have a genuine adaptive purpose: We would be less able to survive in a hostile and potentially dangerous world if we were not on our guard and capable of anticipating or responding to possible hazards surrounding us. Our highly developed sympathetic autonomic nervous system (see Chapter 3) is designed to mobilize the resources of our bodies to deal with threats and challenges.

benzodiazepines (BEN-zoh-dye-AZ-eh-pins): A family of antianxiety drugs. Examples are diazepam (Valium), chlordiazepoxide (Librium), and triazolam (Halcion).

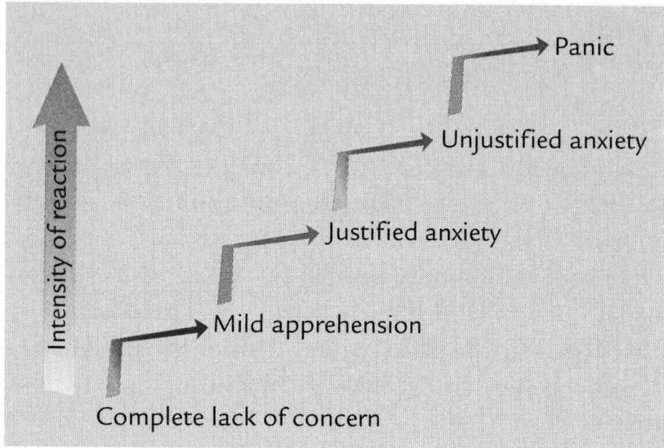

FIGURE 15.2

Levels of anxiety and stress.
Source: Julien, Robert M. (1995). *A primer of drug action* (7th ed). Copyright © 1995 by W. H. Freeman and Company.

When anxiety interferes with our daily lives or when it causes us great personal distress, however, then an adaptive emotion has become maladaptive. We refer to these conditions as **anxiety disorders.** It has been estimated that approximately 16 percent of the U.S. population (more than 40 million people) have suffered from an anxiety disorder sometime in their lifetime.[14]

Given the importance of some level of anxiety in our survival as a species, it should not be surprising that specific mechanisms in the brain have developed that concern themselves specifically with this emotion. In that sense, we can view antianxiety drugs in terms of their ability to help in the treatment of conditions in which a normal physiological process has essentially gotten out of hand.[15] The neural basis for anxiety will be examined later in this chapter.

Medical Uses of Benzodiazepines

The first marketed benzodiazepine, **chlordiazepoxide** (brand name: Librium), was introduced in 1960, followed by **diazepam** (brand name: Valium) in 1963. Table 15.3 lists twelve of the major benzodiazepine drugs currently on the market. They are all chemically related, but their potencies and time courses vary considerably. Valium, for example, is five to ten times stronger than Librium and takes effect about one hour sooner. The relatively quicker response from Valium is a principal factor in making it more popular than Librium.

The variations in benzodiazepine effects have led to different recommendations for their medical use. Oral administrations of the relatively long-acting benzodiazepines, in general, are recommended for relief from anxiety, with the effects beginning thirty minutes to four hours after ingestion. Besides Librium and Valium, other examples of this type include flurazepam (brand name: Dalmane) and clorazepate (brand name: Tranxene).

When a very quick effect is desired, an injectable form of diazepam is used either to reduce the symptoms of agitation that follow alcohol withdrawal (delirium tremens, or the DTs), as an anticonvulsant for epileptic patients, or as a preanesthetic drug to relax the patient just prior to surgery. In contrast, shorter-acting oral benzodiazepines are recommended for sleeping problems because their effects begin more quickly and wear off well

TABLE 15.3

The leading benzodiazepines on the market

TRADE NAME	GENERIC NAME	ELIMINATION HALF-LIFE (in hours)
Long-acting benzodiazepines		
Valium	diazepam	20–100
Librium	chlordiazepoxide	8–100
Limbitrol	chlordiazepoxide and amitriptyline (an antidepressant)	8–100
Dalmane	flurazepam	70–160
Tranxene	clorazepate	50–100
Intermediate-acting benzodiazepines		
Ativan	lorazepam	10–24
Klonopin	clonazepam	18–50
Restoril	temazepam	8–35
ProSom	estazolam	13–35
Short-acting benzodiazepines		
Versed	midazolam	2–5
Halcion	triazolam	2–5
Xanax	alprazolam	11–18

Sources: Julien, Robert M. (1998). *A primer of drug action* (8th ed.). New York: Freeman, p. 99. *Physicians' desk reference* (54th ed.) (2000). Montvale NJ: Medical Economics Company.

anxiety disorder: A psychological condition dominated by excessive worry, sympathetic autonomic activity, and maladaptive behavior.
chlordiazepoxide (CHLOR-dye-az-eh-POX-eyed): A major benzodiazepine drug for the treatment of anxiety. Brand name is Librium.
diazepam (dye-AZ-eh-pam): A major benzodiazepine drug for the treatment of anxiety. Brand name is Valium.

before morning. Examples of this type include triazolam (brand name: Halcion), alprazolam (brand name: Xanax), and temazepam (brand name: Restoril).

How effective are benzodiazepines for the treatment of anxiety? The best way to answer this question is to conduct a double-blind study (see Chapter 3) and compare a representative benzodiazepine such as Valium to a placebo control that looks like Valium but produces no physiological effects. In studies of this type, Valium is observed to be helpful for about 70 to 80 percent of people with an anxiety disorder. Approximately 25 to 30 percent of them, however, are helped by the placebo alone, so it is also evident that psychological factors play some role in the final outcome.[16]

Interestingly, benzodiazepines work best when the physician prescribing the medication is perceived as being warm, has a positive attitude toward use of antianxiety drugs, and believes that the patient will improve (Table 15.4).[17] The positive impact of such factors upon the outcome of treatment underscores the importance of the physician–patient relationship, along with the genuine antianxiety effects of the drug itself.

Acute Effects of Benzodiazepines

In general, benzodiazepines are absorbed relatively slowly into the bloodstream, so their relaxant effects last longer and are more gradual than those of barbiturates. The primary reason for these differences lies in the fact that benzodiazepines are absorbed from the small intestine rather than the stomach, as is the case with barbiturates. The relatively greater water-solubility, and by implication the relatively lower fat-solubility, of benzodiazepines is also a factor.

The major advantage that benzodiazepines have over barbiturates is their higher level of safety. Respiratory centers in the medulla are not affected by benzodiazepines, so it is rare that a person will die of respiratory failure from an accidental or intentional overdose. Even after taking fifty or sixty times the therapeutic dose, the person will still not stop breathing. It is almost always possible to arouse a person from the stupor that such a drug quantity would produce. In contrast, doses of barbiturates or nonbarbiturate sedatives that are ten to twenty times the therapeutic dose are lethal.[18]

Yet, we should understand that this higher level of safety assumes that *no alcohol or other depressant drugs are being taken at the same time*. If we look at the DAWN statistics, we see a major difference between the consequences of an overdose of benzodiazepines alone and an overdose of benzodiazepines in combination. For example, of the total 1998 emergency department (ED) mentions involving Valium, the patient reported in only 18 percent of these cases having ingested the drug alone. In all other cases, there was at least one other drug involved. When we look at the record of medical examiner (ME) mentions that resulted in death, the combination-drug effect is also apparent. In 1998, Valium was reported to have been involved in 8 percent of the cases (the fifth-highest-mentioned drug), but less than 3 percent of these ME mentions involved Valium alone.[19] The bottom line is that taking Valium or another benzodiazepine drug by itself is relatively safe, but taking it in combination with other drugs (particularly alcohol) is quite dangerous.

Nonetheless, despite the relatively low risk of successful suicide from Valium and other benzodiazepines, this drug family poses a number of medical risks for special populations. For elderly patients, for example, the rate of elimination of these drugs is slowed down significantly, resulting in the risk of a dangerously high buildup of benzodiazepines after several doses. In the case of a long-acting benzodiazepine such as Valium or Librium, the elimination half-life is for them as long as ten days. An elderly patient with this rate of elimination would not be totally drug free until two months had passed.

The continued accumulation of benzodiazepines in the elderly can produce a type of drug-induced dementia in which the patient suffers from confusion and loss of memory. Without understanding the patient's medication history, these symptoms can be easily mistaken for

TABLE 15.4

Factors that predict successful treatment with benzodiazepines
Physician attributes
Warmth
Liking the patient
Feeling comfortable with the patient
Believing the patient has good prospects for improvement
Patient attributes
High verbal intelligence
Compliance with the physician
Realistic treatment goals
Low verbal hostility
High level of education
High occupational status
Marital stability
Orientation and expectations prior to treatment
Realization that problems are emotional rather than physical
Expectation that drugs will be part of the treatment

Source: Rickels, Karl (1981). Benzodiazepines: Clinical use patterns. In Stephen I. Szara and Jacqueline P. Ludford (Eds.), *Benzodiazepines: A review of research results 1980* (NIDA Research Monograph 33). Rockville MD: National Institute on Drug Abuse, p. 46.

Health Line

Guidelines for Avoiding the Misuse of Benzodiazepine Drugs

- Do not think of benzodiazepines as cures. These drugs are optimally used to give temporary relief until the cause of the anxiety can be removed.
- Do not think of benzodiazepines as the main treatment. Think of them instead as a supporting treatment. Get appropriate medical, psychological, or pastoral help.
- Do not take benzodiazepines without first having a psychiatric examination to make sure that your anxiety is not due to a depression, bipolar disorder (in which mania alternates with depression), or some other treatable mental illness.
- Do not use benzodiazepines if you are a heavy drinker or suffer from alcoholism.
- Do not use benzodiazepines for insomnia for more than four nights in a row.
- Do not use benzodiazepines continuously for more than two months without a "drug holiday" (a discontinuation of the drug) lasting several weeks.
- Do not increase the dose of a benzodiazepine without consulting a physician. Do not refill your prescription without revisiting your physician.
- Do not keep more than fourteen daily doses of benzodiazepines on hand at any one time.
- Do not drive under the influence of benzodiazepines, and whatever you do, do not drive under the influence of benzodiazepines and alcohol. Be aware that psychomotor performance in general can be impaired when taking benzodiazepines and that there is a period of time after discontinuation of benzodiazepines when the drug remains active in your system. Your driving may be impaired even if you do not feel drowsy.

Sources: Lickey, Marvin E., and Gordon, Barbara (1991). *Medicine and mental illness: The use of drugs in psychiatry.* New York: Freeman, pp. 325–326. Rickels, Karl; Lucki, Irwin; Schweizer, Edward; Garcia-Espana, Felipe; and Case, W. George (1999). Psychomotor performance of long-term benzodiazepine users before, during, and after benzodiazepine discontinuation. *Journal of Clinical Psychopharmacology, 19,* 107–113. Van Laar, Margrietha W., and Volkerts, Edmund R. (1998). Driving and benzodiazepine use: Evidence that they do not mix. *CNS Drugs, 10,* 383–396.

the onset of Alzheimer's disease. A prominent pharmacologist has remarked that his 85-year-old grandmother began to experience forgetfulness and disorientation while taking Valium. "Two months after discontinuation of the drug, her dementia disappeared and she remained lucid until her death ten years later." It is for this reason that long-acting benzodiazepines are no longer recommended for this age group, and those who are currently taking these drugs are being encouraged to switch to shorter-acting forms or alternative antianxiety therapies.[20]

Chronic Effects of Benzodiazepines

The benzodiazepines were originally viewed as having few if any problems relating to a tolerance effect or an acquired dependence. We now know that the *anxiety-relieving* aspects of benzodiazepines show little or no tolerance effects when the drugs are taken at prescribed dosages, but there is a tolerance to the *sedative* effects. In other words, if the drugs are taken for the purpose of relieving anxiety, there is no problem with tolerance, but if they are taken for insomnia, more of the drug may be required in later administrations to induce sleep.[21]

We also now know that physiological symptoms appear when benzodiazepines are withdrawn. In the case of Valium and other long-acting benzodiazepines, the slow rate of elimination delays the appearance of withdrawal symptoms until between the third and sixth day following drug withdrawal. The first signs include an anxiety level that may be worse than the level for which the drug was originally prescribed. Later, there are symptoms of insomnia, restlessness, and agitation. In general, however, withdrawal symptoms are less severe than those observed after barbiturate withdrawal, occur only after long-term use, and are gone in one to four weeks (Health Line).[22]

Patterns of Benzodiazepine Misuse and Abuse

Benzodiazepines do not present the same potential for abuse that cocaine, alcohol, or the barbiturates do, for two primary reasons. First, benzodiazepines are only weak reinforcers of behavior. When trained to press a lever for an injection of Valium, for example, laboratory animals will self-administer the drug but at far less robust levels than they would show for self-administering pentobarbital or methaqualone. Studies with normal college student volunteers show that, when given the choice between a placebo and Valium and the true identity of neither choice is known, the placebo is actually preferred. For these individuals, presumably nondrug abusers and relatively anxiety free, the results show no indication of a positive Valium reaction.[23] Second, the slow onset of a benzodiazepine effect prevents the sudden "rush" feeling that is characteristic of many abused drugs such as cocaine, heroin, or amphetamines.

The foregoing is *not* to say, however, that benzodiazepines fail to be abused. It is simply that their abuse exists in the context of abusing other drugs as well, often referred to as multiple substance abuse or polydrug abuse. Alcoholics, for example, sometimes take benzodiazepines at work, in order to relax and to avoid having the smell of alcohol on their breath. Heroin abusers may take benzodiazepines to augment their euphoria and reduce their anxiety when the opiate levels in their blood begin to fall. Cocaine abusers may take the drugs to soften the crashing feeling that is experienced as the cocaine starts to wear off.[24]

Therefore, the principal social problems surrounding the taking of benzodiazepine drugs, since their introduction in the 1960s, have arisen more from their *misuse* than from their *abuse* (see Chapter 1). The greatest concern during the 1960s and 1970s was the enormous quantity of benzodiazepine prescriptions that were being written. In 1972, Valium ranked first (and Librium third) among the most frequently prescribed drugs of any type. In 1975 alone, more than 100 million such prescriptions were processed around the world, with 85 million in the United States. In Western Europe and North America, it was estimated that 10 to 20 percent of adults were taking benzodiazepines on a fairly regular basis (Portrait).[25]

More recently, the number has declined substantially, but benzodiazepines currently remain among the "top thirty" prescription medications. A major problem has been that such prescriptions were and continue to be written not by psychiatrists but by general practitioners and family doctors who respond to their patient's need for a medical answer to stress and anxiety. It is important to understand that antianxiety drugs may reduce a patient's stress and anxiety but do not really help resolve any of the social, family, and personal problems that produce that stress and anxiety. Specialists in the problems of drug misuse have phrased it this way:

> *Taking a sleeping pill may help you sleep on the nights you take one, but pills do not make one's relationship with one's spouse any better, or improve one's job situation, or change any of the stressors that may be causing the insomnia in the first place. In fact, a hidden danger occurs when the use of drugs masks these symptoms and allows the person to function under less than optimal environmental conditions.*[26]

However, one benzodiazepine, not legally available in the United States but accessible through illicit channels, *has* become subject to abuse. Health Line examines the social and personal concerns surrounding flunitrazepam (brand name: Rohypnol).

Cross-Tolerance and Cross-Dependence

If you were taking a barbiturate for an extended length of time and you developed a tolerance for its effect, you might also have developed a tolerance for another depressant drug even though you have never taken the second drug. In other words, a tolerance effect for one drug automatically induced a tolerance for another. We can see this phenomenon, called **cross-tolerance,** when we look at the physiological and psychological effects of alcohol, barbiturates, and benzodiazepines. As a result of cross-tolerance, an alcoholic will have already developed a tolerance for a barbiturate, or a barbiturate abuser will need a greater amount of an anesthetic when in surgery.

We see the interconnectedness of depressant drugs in another way. If we can relieve the withdrawal symptoms of one drug by administering another drug, then the two drugs show **cross-dependence.** In other words, if cross-dependence exists between two drugs, one drug can substitute for whatever physiological effects have been produced by a second drug that has been discontinued. The family of depressant drugs show this phenomenon. Unfortunately, cross-dependence provides a means for continuing an abused drug in the guise of a new one:

> *When drug abuse becomes obvious and embarrassing or when the preferred drug becomes unavailable, the user can switch to a cross-dependent drug to avoid the withdrawal illness. A woman who wants to conceal her drinking from the family might substitute some diazepam for her morning eye opener.*[27]

The effects of cross-tolerance and cross-dependence would not be possible if there were not a common mechanism in the brain that produced the behavioral and physiological effects. It turns out that in the case of benzodiazepines, a special receptor has been discovered that not only explains benzodiazepine effects but also

cross-tolerance: A phenomenon in which the tolerance that results from the chronic use of one drug induces a tolerance effect with regard to a second drug that has not been used before.

cross-dependence: A phenomenon in which one drug can be used to reduce the withdrawal symptoms following the discontinuance of another drug.

Portrait Barbara Gordon—A Case History of Valium Withdrawal

Jill Clayburgh (at right) in the role of Barbara Gordon in the 1982 adaptation of I'm Dancing as Fast as I Can

Barbara Gordon's 1979 autobiographical account of her experience with Valium, *I'm Dancing as Fast as I Can*, has come to represent the dark side of an era when Valium was at its peak. In the mid-1970s, 100 million prescriptions were being written for Valium each year, at dosages that were often far higher than we now know are considered safe. While Gordon's experiences are not typical, her dramatic retelling of her symptoms during an abrupt withdrawal from Valium nonetheless created a sensation. Her book and the 1982 film based on the book helped to alert the public to the potential of Valium dependence.

As a successful career woman and award-winning television producer with a satisfying personal and social life, Barbara Gordon could be considered to have had it all. But underneath the appearance of apparent success, there was significant anxiety in her life, temporarily masked by the effects of Valium. She described her experience as follows:

> *I had started taking Valium for a back problem, beginning with four milligrams a day. Now I was up to thirty and couldn't get out of the house without taking them. I was taking them* before *an anxiety attack, trying to ward it off, or to minimize the terror. And that didn't always work either.*

Gordon decided to stop taking the drug and try to get on with her life. Her psychiatrist, however, gave little support in this regard, as revealed in this conversation:

> *"I've enough pills for a while, Dr. Allen," I said. "Besides, I've come to a decision this morning. I'm not going to take Valium again—ever." . . . I waited for his response to this new-found independence of mine.*
>
> *"I've told you many times, Miss Gordon," he said with a hint of impatience, "they are nonaddictive and do a great deal to help you. Perhaps you'd like a little Stelazine [an antipsychotic medication]?" . . .*
>
> *"No, no more pills, Dr. Allen, no more pills. I'm going off Valium. What do you think of that?" And again, I waited for his response, for him to tell me how strong I was, that I was doing the right thing.*
>
> *"All right, Miss Gordon, then don't take one, not one. Do it absolutely cold. As a matter of fact, don't even have a sip of wine and I'm sure you'll do fine. Call me if you need anything or if you change your mind. But remember, don't take even one."*

The withdrawal from Valium was anything but uneventful. Once again, in her words:

> *By early afternoon, I began to feel a creeping sense of terror. It felt like little jolts of electricity, as if charged pins and needles were shooting through my body. My breathing became rapid and I began to perspire. . . . My scalp started to burn as if I had hot coals under my hair. Then I began to experience funny little twitches, spasms, a jerk of a leg, a flying arm, tiny tremors that soon turned into convulsions. I held on to the bed, trying to relax. It was impossible.*

When her relationships began to come apart and her anxiety grew, Gordon required hospitalization for several months.

It is important to understand that some of her withdrawal symptoms may have been manifestations of the underlying anxiety disorder that had been masked over the years by Valium. Fortunately, despite the "bumpy ride," Gordon eventually recovered. Her decision to publish her experiences was in part motivated by her realization that others would benefit from knowing the long-term consequences of antianxiety drugs. As she concludes:

> *They aren't just medicines. They are drugs that can be anesthetics of the emotions. And their sudden withdrawal can precipitate psychosis and, in some cases, death. Because of my strong feelings about medical mismanagement, because of the prevalence of drug abuse—and the soft-core prescription-pad variety is drug abuse all the same—I felt I had to tell my story.*

Source: Quotations from pages 50–51, 52, 311 from *I'm dancing as fast as I can* by Barbara Gordon.

explains the relationship between benzodiazepines and depressant drugs in general.

How Benzodiazepines Work in the Brain

The key factor in the action of benzodiazepines is the neurotransmitter gamma aminobutyric acid (GABA), which normally exerts an inhibitory effect on the nervous system (see Chapter 3). When benzodiazepines are in the vicinity of GABA receptors, the actions of GABA are increased. The antianxiety drugs attach themselves to their own receptors on the membrane of neurons and in doing so heighten the effect of GABA. The facilitation of GABA produces a greater inhibition and a decreased activity level in the neurons involved.[28]

The receptor described here is a large protein molecule that has multiple binding locations, arranged like docking sites for different kinds of boats. As displayed in Figure 15.3, the receptor comprises three binding sites:

Health Line

Rohypnol as a Date-Rape Drug

Flunitrazepam (brand name: Rohypnol) is a long-acting benzodiazepine, not unlike diazepam (Valium) except that it is approximately ten times stronger. Because of its extreme potency and the fact that it is highly synergistic with alcohol, Rohypnol is not legally available in the United States. It is, however, approved for medical use in Europe and South America, where it is marketed by Hoffman-La Roche Pharmaceuticals as a treatment for sleep disorders and as a surgical anesthetic. The U.S. supply of Rohypnol is smuggled into the country from Mexico and South America and sold for recreational use, frequently in its original bubble packaging.

The abuse potential of Rohypnol surfaced in the mid-1990s, when the number of pills seized by the U.S. Customs Service increased by 400 percent from 1994 to 1995 alone. Under such street names as "roofies," "rope," "wolfies," "roches," "R2," and "Mexican Valium," this drug has been promoted as an alcohol enhancer and as a strategy for getting drunk without having a blood-alcohol concentration level that would be defined as legal intoxication. Rohypnol has also been involved in numerous date-rape cases in which victims had been unknowingly slipped the drug, causing them to pass out, the ultimate vulnerable situation. The disinhibition of behavior and the subsequent memory loss of the experience is similar to an alcohol-induced blackout (see Chapter 9).

At one time, Rohypnol was odorless, colorless, and tasteless, so it could be easily combined with an alcoholic beverage without detection. Recently, in response to instances of abuse, Hoffman-La Roche has taken steps to reformulate the drug so that it turns blue when dissolved in a clear liquid. This helps to make Rohypnol somewhat more noticeable to an unsuspecting drinker, but it is important to realize that some alcoholic beverages may not show a discernible change in color, particularly under the dim illumination conditions of a typical bar.

Since 1996, U.S. federal law provides for a twenty-year sentence for the use of Rohypnol in connection with rape or other violent crime. Unfortunately, Rohypnol is an increasingly accessible illicit drug. According to one law-enforcement official in Miami, "It may be easier for teenagers to obtain flunitrazepam (Rohypnol) than alcohol." A recent study has found that a variety of benzodiazepines, all marketed by Hoffman-La Roche, are being abused and linked to sexual assaults. Because these drugs all bear the same Roche imprint on the tablets, they are collectively known as "roches."

Rohypnol is an example of a group of present-day "club drugs" that have a dangerous potential for abuse as date-rape drugs. Other examples include MDMA or Ecstasy (see Chapter 4) and GHB (to be discussed later in this chapter).

Sources: Calhoun, Sarah R.; Wesson, Donald R.; Galloway, Gantt P.; and Smith, David E. (1996). Abuse of flunitrazepam (Rohypnol) and other benzodiazepines in Austin and South Texas. *Journal of Psychoactive Drugs, 28,* 183–189. Community Epidemiology Work Group (1996). *Epidemiologic trends in drug abuse,* Volume 1: *Highlights and executive summary.* Rockville MD: National Institute on Drug Abuse, pp. 8, 64. Quotation on p. 64. Drug Enforcement Administration, U.S. Department of Justice, Washington DC, 1997.

one for sedative-hypnotics (including the barbiturates), one for benzodiazepines (and alcohol), and finally one for GABA. When GABA attaches to its binding site, there is greater inhibition if the benzodiazepine sites are also occupied at the time by a benzodiazepine drug than if they are not occupied.[29] A successful binding of a chemical at one site facilitates the binding at the others.

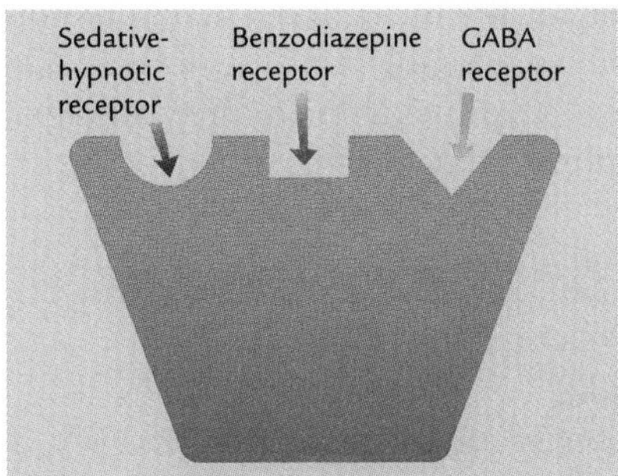

FIGURE 15.3

A simplified view of the benzodiazepine receptor.

It is not difficult, therefore, to imagine how cross-tolerance and cross-dependence among depressant drugs might occur. If two depressant drugs were to bind to the same receptor, the receptor would not be able to "tell the difference" between them. As far as the receptor is concerned, the effect is the same. Evidently, depressants share this feature: an ability to lock into a common receptor with multiple binding locations.

Where are the receptors for depressant drugs? They are understood to be localized primarily in the limbic system and the cerebral cortex. It is believed that receptors in the limbic system underlie the antianxiety action of benzodiazepines (remember that the limbic system is involved with emotionality), while receptors in the cortex underlie their sedative actions.

QUICK CONCEPT  15.1

Understanding Cross-Tolerance and Cross-Dependence

Check your understanding of cross-tolerance and cross-dependence by answering the following questions. Suppose you have two receptors in the brain, as shown here.

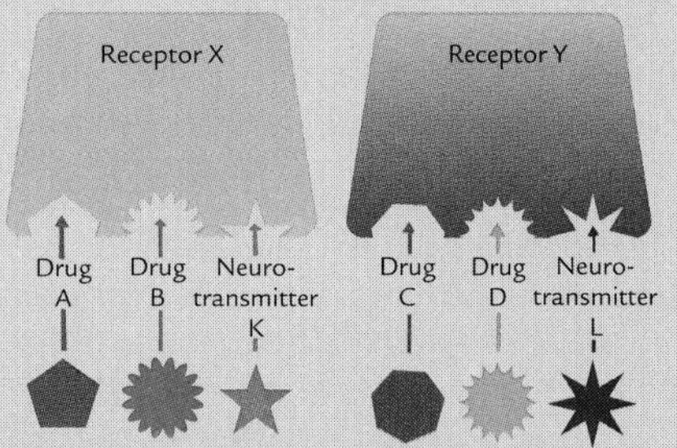

Notice that Receptor X has three binding sites, one for drug A, one for drug B, and one for neurotransmitter K. Receptor Y also has three binding sites, one for drug C, one for drug D, and one for neurotransmitter L.

Based on this information, indicate whether or not the following pairs of drugs show cross-tolerance and cross-dependence with each other.

1. drug A and drug B ❑ yes ❑ no
2. drug A and drug C ❑ yes ❑ no
3. drug B and drug C ❑ yes ❑ no
4. drug C and drug D ❑ yes ❑ no
5. drug B and drug D ❑ yes ❑ no
6. drug A and drug D ❑ yes ❑ no

Answers: 1. yes 2. no 3. no 4. yes 5. no 6. no

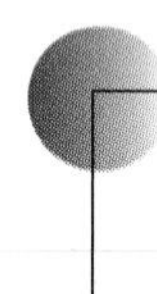

A New Generation of Sedative-Hypnotics and Antianxiety Drugs

Just as benzodiazepines represented a great advance over barbiturates, the development of new nonbenzodiazepine drugs has provided better opportunities to treat sleep disorders and anxiety. Two prominent examples of this new generation of medications are zolpidem and buspirone.

Zolpidem

Zolpidem (brand name: Ambien) is not a benzodiazepine drug, but it binds to a specific subtype of GABA receptors. This is probably the reason it produces only some of the effects usually associated with benzodiazepines, with particular usefulness in the short-term treatment of insomnia. Its strong but transient sedative effects (with a half-life of about two hours) have led to the marketing of zolpidem, since its introduction in 1993, as a sedative-hypnotic rather than an antianxiety agent. Little or no muscle relaxation is experienced.

Buspirone

Since 1986, a new type of antianxiety drug has been available called **buspirone** (brand name: BuSpar), with a number of remarkable features. It has been found to be equivalent to Valium in its ability to relieve anxiety. Yet, unlike the benzodiazepines in general, buspirone shows no cross-tolerance or cross-dependence with alcohol or other depressants and no withdrawal symptoms when discontinued after chronic use. When compared with benzodiazepines, side effects are observed less frequently and are less troublesome to the patient; 9 percent report dizziness and 7 percent report headaches. Animals do not self-administer buspirone in laboratory studies, and human volunteers indicate an absence of euphoria.

Buspirone also fails to show the impairments in motor skills that are characteristic of benzodiazepines. In other words, the relief of anxiety is attainable without the accompanying feelings and behavioral consequences of sedation. Perhaps anxiety and sedation do not necessarily have to be intertwined after all. Unlike benzodiazepines, buspirone does not affect GABA receptors in the brain but rather acts on a special subclass of serotonin receptors instead. Evidently, the influence of busiprone on serotonin produces the antianxiety effects.

Despite its virtues, however, buspirone has a distinct disadvantage: a very long delay before anxiety relief is felt. It may take weeks for the drug to become completely effective. This feature makes buspirone clearly inappropriate for relieving acute anxiety on an emergency basis, and many patients suffering from chronic anxiety may simply be too impatient to wait for the drug to take hold. Yet, on the positive side, the delay in the action of buspirone makes it highly undesirable as a drug of abuse. Do not expect to see news headlines in the future warning of an epidemic of buspirone abuse (Table 15.5).

zolpidem (ZOL-pih-dem): A nonbenzodiazepine sedative-hypnotic drug, first introduced in 1993, for the treatment of insomnia. Brand name is Ambien.
buspirone (BYOO-spir-rone): A nonbenzodiazepine antianxiety drug, first introduced in 1986. Brand name is BuSpar.

TABLE 15.5

The advantages of buspirone over other means to reduce anxiety				
FACTOR FOR POSSIBLE ABUSE	ALCOHOL	BARBITURATES	BENZODIAZEPINES	BUSPIRONE
Euphoria	++	+++	+	0
Rapid action	+++	++	+	0
Unsupervised use	++++	++	++	0
Social encouragement	++++	++	+	0
Tolerance	++	++	+	0
Physical dependence	++++	+++	++	0
Cross-tolerance	+++	+++	+++	0
Cross-dependence	+++	+++	+++	0
Total	25	20	14	0

Note: Each plus sign indicates a degree of abuse potential. The greater the total number of plus signs, the greater the overall abuse potential for each drug. A zero indicates that the drug has no value with regard to a particular factor.

Source: Modified from Lickey, Marvin E., and Gordon, Barbara (1991). *Medicine and mental illness.* New York: Freeman, p. 324.

Whether buspirone fulfills its promise as the ultimate antianxiety drug without the dangers of sedation is a question yet to be fully answered. For the long-term treatment of anxiety, however, buspirone appears to be a positive development.[30]

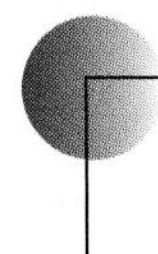

The Risks of Gamma Hydroxybutyrate (GHB)

The CNS depressant **gamma hydroxybutyrate** (shortened to **GHB**) has had a strange history. First synthesized in the 1960s, GHB was found to be produced naturally in the body in very small amounts, but no one has discovered its function. At one time, GHB was sold in health-food stores and similar establishments. It was considered to have steroid-enhancing and growth-hormone-stimulating effects, leading to interest among bodybuilders (see Chapter 8). Other promotions focused on GHB as a sedative. By 1990, however, numerous reports of GHB-related seizures and comas led the FDA to remove GHB from the legitimate market. Since then, the drug has gone underground. The manufacture of GHB is currently controlled by small clandestine laboratories, guided in many instances by formulas available on the Internet, and its sale is maintained by networks of illicit drug distributors.

Present-day GHB abuse focuses on its ability to produce euphoria, an "out-of-body" high, with an accompanying lowering of inhibitions. Frequently, a combination of GHB and alcohol can produce a lack of consciousness in about fifteen minutes and subsequent amnesia about the experience. The notoriety of GHB as a date-rape drug stems from its being colorless, odorless, and virtually tasteless. As a result, it can be easily slipped into alcoholic beverages without the knowledge of the drinker (Health Alert).[31]

QUICK CONCEPT 

15.2

Understanding the Abuse Potential in Drugs

Each of the following statements describes a particular attribute of a new drug. Based on material in this chapter, judge whether each description, when taken by itself, either increases or decreases the abuse potential of the drug.

1. Drug fails to produce euphoria at any dose levels.
2. Drug acts very quickly.
3. Drug is cross-tolerant to barbiturates and alcohol.
4. Drug is not available to the public.
5. There are tolerance effects when taking this drug.
6. The drug can be used without the need for medical supervision of dose or dosage schedule.

Answers: 1. decreases 2. increases 3. increases 4. decreases 5. increases 6. increases

gamma hydroxybutyrate (GHB) (GAM-ma heye-DROX-ee-BYOO-tih-rate): A powerful CNS depressant, often abused to induce euphoria and sedation. When slipped in an alcoholic beverage without the knowledge of the drinker, GHB has been employed as a date-rape drug.

Health Alert

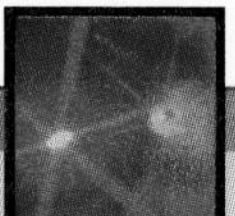

GHB and Date-Rape: Ways to Avoid Trouble

Be aware of various slang terms for gamma hydroxybutyrate (GHB):

Cherry Meth	G-rrifick
Easy Lay	Liquid E, Liquid X
Fantasy	Salty Water
Gamma 10	Scoop
Georgia Home Boy	Somatomac
Grievous Bodily Harm	

Protective strategies for women:

- Watch the person who pours you a drink, even if it's a friend or a bartender. Even better, don't drink what you can't open or pour yourself. Avoid punch bowls and shared containers. Never accept a drink offered to you by a stranger.
- Don't leave a drink alone, not while you are dancing, using the restroom, or making a phone call. If you have left it alone, it is better to toss it.
- Appoint a designated "sober" friend to check up on you at parties, bars, clubs, etc.
- If a friend seems extremely drunk or sick after a drink and has trouble breathing, call 911 immediately.
- If you have been slipped GHB, the drug will take effect within 10 to 30 minutes. Initially, you will feel dizzy or nauseous or develop a severe headache. You can be incapacitated rapidly. This is the time when having a nondrinking friend nearby is crucial. A GHB rapist may wait for his victim to show visible signs that the drug is active, then offer "help" by escorting her out of the club or bar.
- If you wake up in a strange place and believe you have been sexually assaulted while under the influence of GHB, do not urinate until you have been admitted to a hospital. There is an approximately 12-hour window of opportunity to detect GHB through urinanalysis.

A final note:

Be aware that CNS depressants of various types, including Rohypnol (see Health Line on page 321), as well as CNS stimulants and hallucinogens, can be combined with alcohol and used as date-rape drugs. But the original date-rape drug is simply alcohol.

Sources: Cannon, Angie (1999, May 24). Sex, drugs, and sudden death. *U.S. News and World Report,* p. 73. Office of National Drug Control Policy (1998, October). ONDCP Drug Policy Information Clearinghouse Fact Sheet: Gamma hydroxybutyrate (GHB). Washington DC: Executive Office of the President.

SUMMARY

Barbiturates

- Introduced in 1903 and in use until approximately 1960, the primary sedative-hypnotics, drugs that produce sedation and sleep, belonged to the barbiturate family of drugs.
- Barbiturates are typically classified by virtue of how long their depressant effects are felt, from long-acting (example: phenobarbital) to intermediate-acting (examples: butalbarbital and amobarbital) to short-acting (examples: pentobarbital and secobarbital).
- A major disadvantage of barbiturates is the potential of a lethal overdose, particularly when combined with other depressants such as alcohol. In addition, barbiturate withdrawal symptoms are very severe and require careful medical attention.

Nonbarbiturate Sedative-Hypnotics

- Methaqualone (Quaalude) was introduced in the 1960s as an alternate to barbiturates for sedation and sleep. Unfortunately, this drug produced undesirable side effects and became subject to widespread abuse. It is no longer available as a licit drug.

The Development of Antianxiety Drugs

- Beginning in the 1950s, a major effort was made by the pharmaceutical industry to develop a drug that would relieve anxiety (tranquilize) rather than merely depress the CNS (sedate).
- Meprobamate (Miltown) was introduced in 1955 for this purpose, though it is now understood that the

effects of this drug result more from its sedative properties than its ability to relieve anxiety.

Benzodiazepines

- The introduction of benzodiazepines, specifically diazepam (Valium) and chlordiazepoxide (Librium), in the early 1960s, was a significant breakthrough in the development of antianxiety drugs. These drugs selectively affect specific receptors in the brain instead of acting as general depressants of the nervous system.
- In general, benzodiazepines are safer drugs than barbiturates, when taken alone. When taken in combination with alcohol, however, dangerous synergistic effects are observed.
- Social problems concerning the taking of benzodiazepine drugs during the 1970s centered around the widespread misuse of the drug. Prescriptions were written too frequently and for excessive dosages.
- Benzodiazepines produce their effects by binding onto receptors in the limbic system and cerebral cortex in the brain that are sensitive to the inhibitory neurotransmitter gamma aminobutyric acid (GABA).

A New Generation of Sedative-Hypnotics and Antianxiety Drugs

- Recently developed nonbenzodiazepines have provided better opportunities to treat sleep disorders and anxiety. Two examples are zolpidem and buspirone.
- Zolpidem (brand name: Ambien) has been useful as a sedative-hypnotic in the treatment of insomnia. It has strong but transient sedative effects and produces little or no muscle relaxation.
- Buspirone (brand name: BuSpar) has been useful as an antianxiety medication that does not cause sedation. There are a number of advantages of buspirone over traditional benzodiazepines, but a significant disadvantage is the considerable delay in its antianxiety action.

The Risks of Gamma Hydroxybutyrate (GHB)

- Gamma hydroxybutyrate (GHB) is a CNS depressant, first used by bodybuilders because of the possibility that it had growth-hormone-stimulating effects. Today, GHB is an underground drug, available only through clandestine channels.
- As with Rohypnol, the depressant effects of GHB have made it attractive as a club drug. Its involvement as a potential date-rape drug has raised very serious concerns.

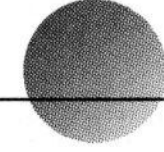

KEY TERMS

amobarbital, p. 310
antianxiety drugs, p. 310
anxiety disorder, p. 316
barbiturate, p. 310
benzodiazepines, p. 315
buspirone, p. 322
chloral hydrate, p. 314
chlordiazepoxide, p. 316
cross-dependence, p. 319
cross-tolerance, p. 319
diazepam, p. 316
gamma hydroxybutyrate (GHB), p. 323
meprobamate, p. 314
methaqualone, p. 314
pentobarbital, p. 310
phenobarbital, p. 310
REM-sleep rebound, p. 312
secobarbital, p. 310
sedative-hypnotics, p. 310
zolpidem, p. 322

ENDNOTES

1. Palfai, Tibor, and Jankiewicz, Henry (1991). *Drugs and human behavior.* Dubuque IA: W. C. Brown, p. 203.
2. Jacobs, Michael R., and Fehr, Kevin O'B. (1987). *Drugs and drug abuse: A reference text* (2nd ed.). Toronto: Addiction Research Foundation, pp. 183–194.
3. Palfai and Jankiewicz, *Drugs and human behavior,* p. 213.
4. Jacobs and Fehr, *Drugs and drug abuse,* p. 189.
5. Kauffman, Janice F., Shaffer, Howard, and Burglass, Milton E. (1985). The biological basics: Drugs and their effects. In Thomas E. Bratter and Gary G. Forrest (Eds.), *Alcoholism and substance abuse: Strategies for clinical intervention.* New York: Free Press, pp. 107–136.

6. Sleeping pills and antianxiety drugs (1988). *The Harvard Medical School Mental Health Letter, 5* (6), 1–4.
7. Griffiths, Roland R.; Lukas, Scott E.; Bradford, L. D.; Brady, Joseph V.; and Snell, Jack D. (1981). Self-injection of barbiturates and benzodiazepines in baboons. *Psychopharmacology, 75*, 101–109.
8. Griffiths, Roland R., Bigelow, George, and Liebson, Ira (1979). Human drug self-administration: Double-blind comparison of pentobarbital, diazepam, chlorpromazine, and placebo. *Journal of Pharmacology and Experimental Therapeutics, 210*, 301–310.
9. Johnston, Lloyd D. (2000, December 14). "Ecstasy" use rises sharply among teens in 2000; use of many other drugs stays steady, but significant declines are reported for some. News release from the University of Michigan, Ann Arbor, Tables 1 and 2.
10. Carroll, Marilyn, and Gallo, Gary (1985). *Quaaludes: The quest for oblivion*. New York: Chelsea House.
11. Julien, Robert M. (2001). *A primer of drug action* (9th ed.). New York: Worth, p. 54.
12. Berger, Philip A., and Tinklenberg, Jared R. (1977). Treatment of abusers of alcohol and other addictive drugs. In Jack D. Barchas, Philip A. Berger, Roland D. Caranello, and Glen R. Elliott (Eds.), *Psychopharmacology: From theory to practice*. New York: Oxford University Press, pp. 355–385.
13. Julien, Robert M. (1998). *A primer of drug action* (8th ed.). New York: Freeman, p. 93.
14. Robins, Lee N.; Helzer, John E.; Weissman, Myrna M.; Orvaschel, Helen; Gruenberg, Ernest; Burke, Jack D., Jr.; and Regier, Darrel A. (1984). Lifetime prevalence of specific psychiatric disorders in three sites. *Archives of General Psychiatry, 41*, 949–958.
15. Julien, *A primer of drug action* (9th ed.), p. 561.
16. Leavitt, Fred (1982). *Drugs and behavior* (2nd ed.). New York: Wiley.
17. Rickels, Karl (1981). Benzodiazepines: Clinical use patterns. In Stephen I. Szara and Jacqueline P. Ludford (Eds.), *Benzodiazepines: A review of research results 1980* (NIDA Research Monograph 33). Rockville MD: National Institute on Drug Abuse, pp. 43–60.
18. Lickey, Marvin E., and Gordon, Barbara (1991). *Medicine and mental illness*. New York: Freeman, p. 280.
19. Substance Abuse and Mental Health Services Administration (2000). Annual emergency department data 1998. Data from the Drug Abuse Warning Network (DAWN). Rockville MD: Substance Abuse and Mental Health Services Administration, Office of Applied Studies, Tables 2.06a, 2.19. Substance Abuse and Mental Health Services Administration (2000). Annual medical examiner data 1998. Data from the Drug Abuse Warning Network (DAWN). Rockville MD: Substance Abuse and Mental Health Services Administration, Office of Applied Studies, pp. 39, 54.
20. Julien, *A primer of drug action* (9th ed.), p. 161. Salzman, Carl (1999). An 87-year-old woman taking a benzodiazepine. *Journal of the American Medical Association, 281*, 1121–1125.
21. Rickels, Karl; Case, W. George; Downing, Robert W.; and Winokur, Andrew (1983). Long-term diazepam therapy and clinical outcome. *Journal of the American Medical Association, 250*, 767–771.
22. Julien, *A primer of drug action* (9th ed.), pp. 153–163.
23. Griffiths, Roland R., and Ator, Nancy A. (1981). Benzodiazepine self-administration in animals and humans: A comprehensive literature review. In Stephen I. Szara and Jacqueline P. Ludford (Eds.), *Benzodiazepines: A review of research results, 1980* (NIDA Research Monograph 33). Rockville MD: National Institute on Drug Abuse, pp. 22–36.
24. Julien, *A primer of drug action* (8th ed.), pp. 106–107.
25. Lickey and Gordon, *Medicine and mental illness*, p. 278.
26. Maistro, Stephen A., Galizio, Mark, and Connors, Gerard J. (1995). *Drug use and abuse* (2nd ed.). Fort Worth TX: Harcourt Press, p. 256.
27. Lickey and Gordon, *Medicine and mental illness*, p. 323.
28. Mohler, H., and Okada, T. (1977). Benzodiazepine receptors in rat brain: Demonstration in the central nervous system. *Science, 198*, 849–851. Squires, Richard F., and Braestrup, Claus (1977). Benzodiazepine receptors in rat brain. *Nature, 266*, 732–734.
29. Lickey and Gordon, *Medicine and mental illness*, p. 291. Nelson, John, and Chouinard, Guy (1996). Benzodiazepines: Mechanisms of action and clinical indications. In Andrius Baskys and Gary Remington (Eds.). *Brain mechanisms and psychotropic drugs*. Boca Raton FL: CRC Press, pp. 213–238.
30. Julien, *a primer of drug action* (9th ed.), pp. 169–171.
31. Cannon, Angie (1999, May 24). Sex, drugs, and sudden death. *U.S. News and World Report*, p. 73. Dyer, J. E. (2000). Evolving abuse of GHB in California: Bodybuilding drug to date-rape drug. *Journal of Toxicology: Clinical Toxicology*, 38, 184. Sanguineti, Vincenzo R., Angelo, Anita, and Frank, Marion R. (1997). GHB: A home brew. *American Journal of Drug and Alcohol Abuse*, 23, 637–642.

CHAPTER 16

Drugs for Treating Schizophrenia and Mood Disorders

After you have completed this chapter, you will understand

- The development of antipsychotic drugs
- How antipsychotic drugs work in the brain
- Types of antidepressant medication
- How antidepressants work in the brain
- Treatment for panic attacks, mania, bipolar disorder, and obsessive-compulsive disorder
- Social policies regarding psychiatric drug treatment

I was extremely nervous. That's why my thoughts were completely paralyzed. Dr. Thompson's great-great-grandmother last month told me herself that I better be on my guard about those paralyzing thoughts. Now lately, I suppose the medicine has killed off that stuff. That old woman's voice doesn't visit me anymore. I'm a lot calmer now. My brain works better. That's how it seems to me. I reckon the medicine just took those bad thoughts away. Don't ask me how it did it, 'cause I don't know. But it did.

—A schizophrenic patient under Thorazine

Many drugs have the potential to liberate the mind from symptoms of mental illness, either moderate or severe in degree. Chapter 15 dealt, in part, with the use of antianxiety drugs in the treatment of generalized stress and anxiety. This chapter will look at a special class of psychoactive drugs that can relieve severe emotional distress, reduce intense personal suffering, and enable deeply troubled people to lead relatively normal lives. The primary focus will be on medications used for the treatment of two major forms of mental illness: schizophrenia and mood disorders such as depression or mania. All drugs used in treating mental illness are often referred to as **psychiatric drugs,** because they are prescribed and supervised by psychiatrists. An alternative term, **psychotropic medication,** refers to the fact that their pharmacological effects move the patient closer to a normal state of mind (*trop*, meaning "to turn toward").

These drugs are something of a two-edged sword. On the one hand, the development of psychiatric drugs has brought about nothing short of a revolution in the quality of mental-health care, as well as a major insight into the biochemical nature of mental illness. Millions of schizophrenic and depressed people have benefited from psychiatric drugs. On the other hand, these medications have significant side effects, and whether they should be used as extensively as they are is a matter of controversy among many mental-health professionals.

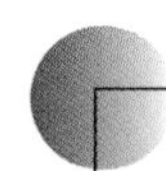

The Biomedical Model

Using the term *mental illness* to describe the symptoms of disorders such as schizophrenia, depression, or mania implies that we are viewing abnormal psychological and behavioral symptoms as being no different from symptoms arising from a physical disease such as pneumonia or a stroke. This viewpoint, commonly referred to as the **biomedical model,** holds that abnormal thoughts and behaviors are results of biochemical processes in the brain. According to this model, the effectiveness of psychiatric drugs in changing such symptoms is a function of altering these biochemical processes toward a more normal state.

Not everyone believes wholeheartedly in the biomedical model, and some mental-health professionals have considered alternative points of view. It is possible that adverse sociological factors, psychodynamic factors, or behavioral and cognitive factors also play a role in producing abnormal thoughts and behaviors. The fact remains, however, that for many patients the administration of psychiatric drugs is an effective means for treating schizophrenia and mood disorders. Because these drugs are affecting the brain, the inference is inescapable that the improvements observed in such patients are directly related to the biochemical changes that the drugs produce. In other words, from the perspective of developing therapeutic approaches toward these patients, the biomedical model seems to work.

We can also look at the genetic evidence in favor of the biomedical model, particularly in the case of patterns of schizophrenia. For example, the concordance rate for schizophrenia in pairs of identical twins (corresponding to the probability of one twin becoming schizophrenic if the other twin already is) has been estimated to be 46 percent, compared to a concordance rate of 15 percent in pairs of fraternal twins. Given the highly similar environmental influences on identical and fraternal twins, the difference in the two concordance rates indicates a strong genetic component. In addition, the incidence of schizophrenia shows a remarkable stability throughout the world, across such widely separated cultures and societies as those of Swedes, Eskimos, and West African tribal peoples. If a common biological factor were not operating, it is unlikely that we would be seeing such a consistent pattern. Indeed, recent evidence indicates that there are specific chromosomal genes that predispose individuals to the development of schizophrenia.[1]

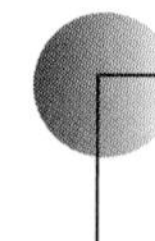

Antipsychotic Drugs and Schizophrenia

Drugs specifically intended to treat schizophrenia are traditionally referred to as **antipsychotic drugs.** Before considering these drugs in detail, however, it is helpful first to take a careful look at the often misunderstood symptoms of schizophrenia itself.

psychiatric drugs: Medications used to treat forms of mental illness.

psychotropic medication: An alternative term for psychiatric drugs.

biomedical model: A theoretical position that mental disorders are caused by abnormal biochemical processes in the brain.

antipsychotic drugs: Medications used to treat symptoms of schizophrenia.

schizophrenia: A major mental illness, characterized by being "cut off" from a sense of reality. Symptoms of schizophrenia may include hallucinations and delusional thinking.

The Symptoms of Schizophrenia

The name **schizophrenia** literally means "split-mind," a term that unfortunately has led to a widespread misconception about how schizophrenic patients typically think and behave. Schizophrenic patients do not have a split or multiple personality. Such psychiatric conditions exist, but they are referred to as *dissociative disorders*. The accurate way of viewing a schizophrenic is in terms of an individual being "split off" or "broken off" from a firm sense of reality. The presence of **delusions** (beliefs not rooted in reality) leading to feelings of persecution or paranoia and the presence of auditory hallucinations commonly in the form of "voices," often torment the patient on a daily basis.

Not all schizophrenics, however, have delusions or hallucinations. Some may display a significant "split" in the connections that normally exist among the processes of thinking, emotion, and action. The expression of emotion may be dulled or altogether absent; verbal expressions or mannerisms may be entirely inappropriate to a given situation; odd postures may be assumed for long periods of time (a condition called **catatonia**). Given the wide diversity in schizophrenic behaviors, it is possible that we may be dealing with a cluster of disorders collectively known as schizophrenia rather than simply one singular psychiatric condition.

Overall, the prevalence of schizophrenia is approximately 1 percent of the general U.S. population, representing a total of more than 2.5 million people. Schizophrenic patients, however, constitute between 40 and 50 percent of all patients in U.S. psychiatric hospitals.[2]

A catatonic schizophrenic woman displays the classic symptoms of immobility and unusual body posture.

The Early Days of Antipsychotic Drug Treatment

To appreciate the difference antipsychotic drugs have made in the treatment of schizophrenia, we have to go back to the mid-1950s. Prior to that time, the principal methods of dealing with schizophrenic patients included the heavy administration of barbiturates and neurosurgical interventions such as prefrontal lobotomies. These treatments produced severely apathetic and sedated patients. By 1955, the total population of hospitalized psychiatric patients in the United States (of which schizophrenics represented the majority) had risen to about 560,000, roughly 50 percent of all those hospitalized for *any* reason. The demand for facilities to house psychiatric patients was quickly reaching crisis proportions.[3]

With the introduction of antipsychotic drugs around 1955, the tide turned. For the first time, symptoms of a major mental disorder such as schizophrenia were genuinely alleviated. Many schizophrenic patients could now be treated on an outpatient basis:

> *While virtually all symptoms decreased with use of antipsychotics, the decrease in symptoms of confusion and disorganization was the greatest. For example, incoherent speech became coherent. Personal hygiene improved, patients dressed themselves, washed, combed their hair, and used the toilet. Patients who had not spoken or responded to others became responsive to questions and requests. . . . Antipsychotics do not always eliminate delusions and hallucinations, but the drugs usually permit the patient to recognize hallucinations and delusions as such and to know that they are symptoms of disease.*[4]

Over the next thirty years, the resident population in U.S. mental hospitals decreased by 80 percent, a result of

---

delusions: Ideas that have no foundation in reality.
catatonia (CAT-ah-TONE-yah): A symptom displayed by some schizophrenic patients, characterized by a rigid, prolonged body posture.

---

two principal factors. The first was the beneficial effect of antipsychotic medications on approximately half the schizophrenic population, allowing them to lead relatively normal lives outside a mental hospital. The second was a policy of deinstitutionalization, in which psychiatric patients of all types were admitted to mental hospitals only for limited periods of time. The social consequences of deinstitutionalization will be considered later in this chapter.[5]

The Nature of Antipsychotic Drug Treatment

For most schizophrenic patients, antipsychotic drugs are administered orally in daily doses. In a few cases, i.v. or i.m. injections are given when a highly agitated patient has to be subdued quickly. When administered orally, the benefits appear slowly over a period of a few weeks. During the initial days of treatment, patients usually feel sedated, but the degree of sedation generally declines as the antipsychotic effects begin to appear. In general, activity levels tend to become normal, with agitated patients becoming more relaxed and withdrawn patients becoming more sociable. When receiving the proper dosage, patients remain reasonably alert. Because they do not produce euphoria, tolerance, or psychological dependence, antipsychotic drugs have a low potential for misuse or abuse. They also are quite safe from the risks of accidental overdose because even massive doses do not impair breathing.[6] This chapter's Portrait offers a look at the personal experiences of a patient in recovery through antipsychotic drug therapy.

In order to minimize side effects, the customary practice is to administer gradually increasing doses of antipsychotic medication until symptoms appear to moderate. Once the patient is responding well to a particular level of the drug, it is then customary to lower the dose to determine the least amount of drug required to achieve a beneficial effect. Until recently, schizophrenic patients were eventually placed on a maintenance drug dose indefinitely. Today, many psychiatrists no longer keep their patients on antipsychotic medications for long periods of time. Instead, the drugs are administered only when severe symptoms arise and are withdrawn completely when the symptoms are eliminated. This practice is called **target dosing.**[7]

Among the medications currently on the market for the treatment of schizophrenia (Table 16.1), most are highly similar in terms of both benefits and side effects. These drugs are referred to as **typical antipsychotic drugs;** they include chlorpromazine (brand name: Thorazine), haloperidol (brand name: Haldol), thiothixene (brand name: Navane), and thioridizine (brand name: Mellaril). Four major exceptions are clozapine (brand name: Clozaril), risperidone (brand name: Risperdal), olanzapine (brand name: Zyprexa), and ziprasidone (brand name: Zeldox). Clozaril, Risperdal, Zyprexa, and Zeldox are

TABLE 16.1

Currently available antipsychotic medications

GENERIC NAME	BRAND NAME	DAILY RECOMMENDED ORAL DOSAGE IN MILLIGRAMS
Phenothiazines		
chlorpromazine	Thorazine	100–500*
fluphenazine	Prolixin	5–20*
mesoridazine	Serentil	100–300*
perphenazine	Trilafon, Etrafon**	12–24*
pimozide	Orap	1–2
prochlorperazine	Compazine	50–150*
thioridazine	Mellaril	150–600
trifluoperazine	Stelazine	10–30*
Butyrophenones		
haloperidol	Haldol	1–12*
Thioxanthenes		
thiothixene	Navane	10–30*
Dibenzoxazepines		
clozapine	Clozaril	300–900
loxapine	Loxitane	20–60*
quetiapine	Seroquel	50–400
Dihydroindolones		
molindone	Moban	100–225
Benzisoxasoles		
risperidone	Risperdal	1–3
olanzapine	Zyprexa	10
ziprasidone	Zeldox	80–160

*Also available in injectable forms.
**Etrafon is a combination of perphenazine and amitriptyline (an antidepressant).

Sources: Updated from Julien, Robert M. (2001). *A primer of drug action* (9th ed.). New York: Worth. *Physicians' desk reference* (54th ed.). (2000). Montvale NJ: Medical Economics Data.

target dosing: A strategy of drug treatment in which only minimal dosage levels are administered to control symptoms and drug treatment is withdrawn when symptoms subside.

typical antipsychotic drugs: A majority of available antipsychotic medications, all of which are associated with the possibility of Parkinson's-like side effects.

Portrait Mark Vonnegut—Thorazine and Recovery

In his eloquent autobiography *Eden Express*, Mark Vonnegut writes of his battle with the demons of schizophrenia, his love-hate feelings about Thorazine, and his growing recognition that the biochemistry of his brain was responsible for his deeply troubled life. A child of the sixties, follower of the counterculture movement of that era, and son of the famous writer Kurt Vonnegut, Mark Vonnegut began to experience hallucinations and feel his personality coming undone. In his words,

> *By this time the voices had gotten very clear. At first I'd had to strain to hear or understand them. They were soft and working with some pretty tricky codes. Snap-crackle-pops, the sound of the wind with blinking lights and horns for punctuation. I broke the code and somehow was able to internalize it to the point where it was just like hearing words. . . . The voices weren't much fun in the beginning. Part of it was simply my being uncomfortable about hearing voices no matter what they had to say, but . . . later the voices could be very pleasant.*

For years of his life, Vonnegut was a hospitalized schizophrenic. His treatment with ordinary psychotherapy was fruitless. When he was administered Thorazine and the drug took hold, he would become ambivalent about its effects:

> *On Thorazine everything's a bore. Not a bore, exactly. Boredom implies impatience. You can read comic books and Reader's Digest forever. You can tolerate talking to jerks forever. . . . The weather is dull, the flowers are dull, nothing's very impressive. . . . When I did manage to get excited about some things, impatient with some things, interested in some things, it still didn't have the old zing to it.*

Nonetheless, he knew that Thorazine was helping him. When he first entered a hospital, he was totally disoriented. With Thorazine, things started to clear:

> *It took a while before I was able to pay much attention to the fact [that I was in a hospital]. . . . Little by little, with the help of massive doses of Thorazine in the ass and in my milkshakes (which was all they could get me to eat), little by little it started mattering to me where I was and what was going on.*

Eventually, Vonnegut could look back on those years. He recognized the treatment he had undergone would be only a primitive first step toward understanding the process of schizophrenia:

> *While I very likely owe my life to Thorazine, I doubt if I will ever develop much affection for it. . . .There are great insights to be gained from schizophrenia, but remember that they won't do you or anyone else much good unless you recover.*

Note: Since Vonnegut's book appeared, many health professionals have concluded that he was probably suffering more from bipolar disorder (formerly known as manic-depression) than schizophrenia. Thorazine, it turns out, has a beneficial effect on both disorders. Today, Vonnegut would more likely have been treated with a therapeutic drug specifically developed to improve symptoms of bipolar disorder, such as lithium carbonate or Depakote.

Source: Vonnegut, Mark (1975). *Eden express*. New York: Praeger, quotations pp. 106, 195–196, 197, 210–211, 213, and 214.

considered **atypical antipsychotic drugs,** with pharmacological profiles that are quite different from earlier medications.

Typical Antipsychotic Drugs: Side Effects and Risks

The side effects of typical antipsychotic drugs range from relatively minor inconveniences to severe neurological difficulties. Patients may develop a dry mouth, blurred vision, dizziness, or weight gain. The skin can become oversensitized to the sun so that burning occurs even after a minimum of exposure. More significant reactions, however, include a severe disturbance in movement-control systems in the brain (see Chapter 3). Patients may develop a stiff, shuffling walk, a lack of spontaneity, restlessness, a fixed facial expression, and loss of coordinated movements such as the free swinging of the arms during walking. These problems are called **Parkinson's-like symptoms** because they resemble many of the features of Parkinson's disease. In fact, some types of anti-Parkinson's medication, such as trihexyphenidyl (brand name: Artane), benztropine (brand name: Cogentin), and procyclidine

atypical antipsychotic drugs: Relatively new antipsychotic medications that, unlike earlier medications used for treating schizophrenia, do not produce Parkinson's-like side effects. Clozaril, Risperdal, Zyprexa, and Zeldox are examples.

Parkinson's-like symptoms: Side effects of typical antipsychotic drugs, involving a fixed facial expression and difficulty walking.

(brand name: Kemadrin), are frequently given along with antipsychotic drugs to reduce the incidence of these particular side effects. Strangely, administration of the original drug developed to relieve Parkinson's disease symptoms, L-Dopa, makes matters worse rather than better.[8]

The side effects listed here that are associated with typical antipsychotic drugs disappear when the medication is either reduced in dosage or withdrawn, with one exception. Some patients develop **tardive dyskinesia,** a neurological syndrome that may appear after two or more years of continual drug treatment. Tardive dyskinesia, which literally means "a movement disorder arriving late," consists of jerky, tic-like movements of the lips, tongue, jaw, and face. Patients may smack their lips or flick their tongues in and out as frequently as twenty times in thirty seconds; their walking may become progressively unsteady, or they may rock back and forth while seated. It has been estimated that the likelihood of developing tardive dyskinesia as a result of long-term treatment with typical antipsychotic drugs is about 15 to 20 percent. Women and elderly patients show a higher incidence than men and younger patients in general.[9]

Although it is true that many patients who acquire tardive dyskinesia display only mild symptoms, the fact that it may occur at all is a source of great concern both among psychiatrists and the families of schizophrenic patients who have to confront the possibility of an irreversible side effect as socially debilitating as schizophrenia itself. Withdrawal from drug treatment frequently has little impact on the symptoms of tardive dyskinesia. Increasing the dose can block tardive dyskinesia but also increases the potential for more severe reactions if and when the dosage levels are reduced. Unfortunately, the prospect of this Catch-22 situation has led many nonhospitalized patients to forgo their medication and risk a relapse into schizophrenia. Fortunately, as we will see, the recent development of new antipsychotic drugs has greatly reduced the incidence of tardive dyskinesia and related motor side-effects.[10]

Atypical Antipsychotic Drugs

A new generation of atypical antipsychotic drugs has been developed since the late 1980s that allows more complete treatment of schizophrenic patients, without the potential for undesirable motor side-effects. For example, Clozaril is quite unlike typical antipsychotic medications in that Parkinson's-like symptoms and tardive dyskinesia are rare. In addition, Clozaril is effective in reducing a wide range of schizophrenic symptoms in many patients who have not been helped by chlorpromazine or other medications in the typical antipsychotic drug category. This medication obviously offers significant advantages over typical antipsychotic drugs. However, a unique feature of Clozaril is the 1–2 percent chance of developing a potentially lethal blood disease called **agranulocytosis,** a condition involving the loss of white blood cells and a decline in the immune system as a result. If early signs of agranulocytosis are detected, Clozaril can be withdrawn and the patient will recover. Therefore, as a safeguard, Clozaril-treated patients must undergo weekly blood tests for the entire time they are under treatment. The need for regular blood testing has made Clozaril treatment far more expensive than traditional treatment with typical antipsychotic drugs.

Three other atypical drugs currently are available for the treatment of schizophrenia: Risperdal, Zyprexa, and Zeldox. Like Clozaril, each is highly effective in reducing schizophrenic symptoms while maintaining a very low incidence of Parkinson's-like side effects and tardive dyskinesia. Unlike Clozaril, however, none of these drugs is linked to agranulocytosis. Therefore, there is no need for blood testing to identify this potential problem.[11]

Effects of Antipsychotic Drugs on the Brain

When the first antipsychotic drugs were introduced in the 1950s, the question of how they work at a neuronal level in the brain was a total mystery. In those days, drugs were "discovered" quite accidentally. Chlorpromazine, for example, was first administered as a treatment for severe vomiting (which remains one of its applications today) and a sedative for presurgical patients. Only later was it recognized as having beneficial effects on schizophrenia.

As haphazard as the development of psychiatric drugs was at that time, however, a common thread frequently connected them, suggesting that a common mechanism might be responsible for their actions. In the case of antipsychotic drugs, there was an unmistakable connection between the improvement in schizophrenic

tardive dyskinesia (TAR-div DIS-keh-NEEZ-ee-ah): A serious side effect affecting approximately 15 percent of schizophrenic patients who have undergone chronic treatment with typical antipsychotic drugs.
agranulocytosis (A-GRAN-yoo-loh-seye-TOH-sis): A potentially lethal blood disorder associated with the antipsychotic drug clozapine.

Hallucinations, Schizophrenia, Drugs, and the Brain

A 57-year-old man with a brain abscess (a mass of dead neurons and related cells) caused by bacterial meningitis began to hear faint sounds of choral music reminiscent of German folk songs he had once heard in his youth, even though there was no chorus and no music. This "concert in the mind" continued for five weeks, then disappeared. A French patient heard popular French songs while another heard Mozart; a Canadian heard Glenn Miller tunes. These experiences have been called musical hallucinations and, under different circumstances, might have been indicative of schizophrenia. In these cases, however, these individuals were alert to their surroundings, coherent in their beliefs about the world, and aware that they were only imagining the music. The continual stream of sound was regarded as annoying but not frightening. Evidently, specific brain lesions, whether caused by meningitis, stroke, tumors, or encephalitis, have the potential for disrupting the normal communication pathways between sensory areas of the cerebral cortex and regions in the hindbrain. The result appears to be a release of musical memories.

Could biochemical abnormalities produce similar forms of auditory hallucinations in schizophrenia? There is evidence that schizophrenic patients, during an experience of hearing hallucinatory "voices," show increased neural activity precisely in those regions of the cerebral cortex that would normally be excited during the experience of normal hearing. After antipsychotic drugs are administered and hallucinatory behavior diminishes, so does the increased neural activity during times of silence. A reasonable hypothesis is that there are complex interacting relationships between the cerebral cortex and underlying brain tissue that produce both normal experiences as well as, in some cases, abnormal experiences characteristic of mental illness.

These remarkable findings underscore a central point: psychological phenomena are connected to biochemical events in the brain. The potential of psychotropic medication in helping individuals who are anxious, depressed, manic, schizophrenic, or suffering from a host of other psychological problems is a testament to the understanding we now have about the relationship between brain functioning and mental life. At the same time, we need to recognize that the progress we have made represents only a point on a long road toward a full and comprehensive picture. The gaps that currently exist in that picture are humbling reminders of how far we have yet to go.

Sources: Dierks, Thomas; Linden, David E.; Jandi, Martin; Formisano, Elia; Goebel, Rainer; Lanfermann, Heinrich; and Singer, Wolf (1999). Activation of Heschl's gyrus during auditory hallucinations. *Neuron, 22,* 615–621. Schielke, Eva, Reuter, Uwe, and Hoffmann, Olaf. (2000). Musical hallucinations with dorsal pontine lesions. *Neurology, 55,* 454–455.

symptoms and the often observed signs of Parkinson's-like motor problems. Could this connection provide a clue as to the underlying biochemistry of schizophrenia?

Fortunately, by 1963, the biochemical nature of Parkinson's disease was beginning to be understood. Essentially, its symptoms were found to be a result of a deficiency in dopamine-releasing neurons in an area of the midbrain called the substantia nigra (see Chapter 3).[12] One result was the development of new treatment drugs that helped Parkinson's patients by boosting the activity of dopamine systems in the brain.

The second result was an insight into the mechanism behind antipsychotic drugs. The reasoning was that if Parkinson's-like symptoms were appearing when patients' schizophrenic symptoms were improving and if Parkinson's disease was due to a dopamine deficiency, then perhaps the antipsychotic drugs were actually reducing the activity level of dopamine in the brain. By implication, schizophrenia would be tied to an excessively high level of dopamine activity, and treating it would be a matter of bringing that level down (Heath Line).

Evidence for a dopamine involvement in schizophrenia comes from a variety of sources. You would predict that an overdose of L-Dopa, an anti-Parkinson's drug that elevates the activity of dopamine systems in the brain, would produce schizophrenic-like behavior, and it does. Parkinson's patients need to be careful about the dose levels of their medication to avoid displaying signs of disorientation, disturbed thinking, paranoia, or catatonia. Another prediction is that the mechanism behind the action of antipsychotic drugs would be specifically associated with a decline in dopamine activity. It turns out that all the typical antipsychotic drugs block the stimulation of dopamine-sensitive receptor sites. In fact, the drugs that are most effective in blocking dopamine are the very same drugs that are most effective in treating schizophrenia. Likewise, drugs that are relatively weak blockers of dopamine are relatively ineffective in treatment.

Other evidence, however, points to the possibility that the dopamine connection might be only a first step toward understanding schizophrenia. Researchers know that dopamine-sensitive receptors in the brain can be broken down into subtypes. At least six subtypes have been identified so far. Typical antipsychotic drugs block a particular receptor subtype called D_2 receptors. Atypical antipsychotic drugs, however, operate in a somewhat different way. For example, clozapine appears to block a subtype called D_4 receptors, and the others appear to block D_2 and S_2 (a subtype sensitive to serotonin) receptors simultaneously. The absence of Parkinson's-like side effects during Clozaril, Risperdal, Zyprexa, and Zeldox treatment appears to be related to a particular set of receptor subtypes that is affected. The development of future antipsychotic drugs will depend on a more thorough understanding of the complexity of receptor subtypes in the brain.[13]

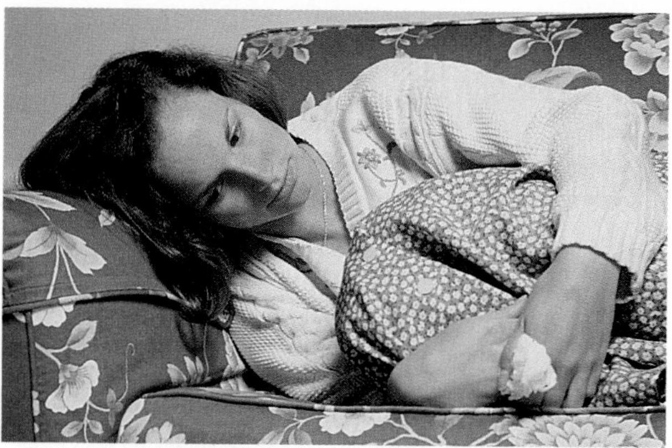

Antidepressant medications have been of great benefit to those showing extreme symptoms of major depression.

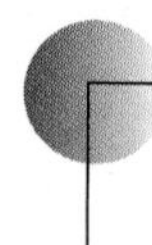

Drugs Used to Treat Mood Disorders

Severe and debilitating depression, usually referred to as major depression, is the most common form of mood disorder. It has been estimated that about 5 percent of the U.S. population will have suffered an episode of major depression at some time in life. A large number of famous men and women in history—from the Roman emperor Tiberius and Queen Victoria to Tchaikovsky, Dostoevski, Abraham Lincoln, and Sigmund Freud—were depressed during prolonged periods of their lives.

Major depression is an emotional state far beyond ordinary feelings of sadness, grief, or remorse. Many depressed individuals have turned to alcohol for relief. As we know, however, the depressant action of alcohol on the nervous system not only makes matters worse but also sets the stage for alcohol dependence and alcoholism (see Chapter 10). A more immediate concern, obviously, is the risk of suicide. Although not all people who either attempt or actually commit suicide are depressed, the inclination toward depression increases the risk substantially. On the one hand, only about 15 percent of depressed people are suicidal; on the other, however, most suicide-prone people are or have been depressed. Ironically, the likelihood of a suicide attempt is highest in the initial phase of an upswing in mood after a deep period of depression. When the depression is at its most intense, the depressed individual has little energy to carry out suicidal feelings and thoughts.[14]

Drugs used to treat major depression are referred to as **antidepressants.** Such drugs fall into three general categories: MAO inhibitors, tricyclic types, and the recently introduced atypical antidepressants.

MAO Inhibitors

Like the earliest antipsychotic medications, the earliest antidepressants were discovered accidentally, with their applications frequently having little to do with psychological disorders. One early antidepressant was originally intended for the treatment of tuberculosis. It was soon recognized that the improvement in the patient's spirits was not merely a matter of reduced symptoms of this disease. When depressed but otherwise healthy individuals were given the drug, a significant improvement in mood was observed. Eventually, it was discovered that other chemically similar drugs were also effective antidepressants. The key factor connecting them all was their ability to inhibit the enzyme **monoamine oxidase (MAO),** hence their classification as **MAO inhibitors.** Two MAO inhibitors are currently marketed for the treatment of depression: phenelzine (brand name: Nardil) and tranylcypromine (brand name: Parnate).

Despite their benefits in the treatment of depression, MAO inhibitors are safely administered only to patients whose dietary habits can be carefully supervised or who can be relied on to observe certain specific dietary restrictions. The problem is that MAO inhibitors inhibit

antidepressants: Drugs prescribed and used for the treatment of depression.

monoamine oxidase (MAO) (MON-oh-AY-meen OX-ih-dace): An enzyme that breaks down dopamine, norepinephrine, or serotonin at their respective synapses in the brain.

MAO inhibitors: Antidepressants that reduce the effects of monoamine oxidase (MAO) in the brain.

MAO not only in the brain but elsewhere in the body as well. In the liver, MAO serves a useful function in breaking down a chemical called *tyramine*. Too high a level of tyramine produces a highly toxic reaction by elevating the blood pressure and increasing the chances of a stroke. Therefore, although MAO inhibitors are useful at the level of the brain, they also remove the individual's natural safety barrier against the harmful effects of excessive tyramine. Ordinarily, this action would not be a problem, except for the fact that tyramine is contained in many foods and drinks.

Because any food product or drink that involves fermentation or aging in its processing contains high levels of tyramine, combining one with an MAO inhibitor can be highly dangerous. Therefore, any such food or drink must be avoided by patients on MAO-inhibitor antidepressants. MAO inhibitors continue to be an option in the treatment of depression, but the difficulty in maintaining this kind of restricted diet for long periods of time has made other drug approaches more desirable. One of the alternative options is the administration of tricyclic antidepressant drugs.

Tricyclic Antidepressants

Tricyclic antidepressants all have a three-ring portion in their molecular structure, hence their name. Of the dozen or so tricyclic drugs on the market, four of the most prominent are amitriptyline (brand name: Elavil) nortriptyline (brand name: Parmelor), desipramine (brand name: Norpramin), and imipramine (brand name: Tofranil). Because tricyclic drugs do not operate specifically on MAO, the problems inherent in a potentially high level of tyramine are not an issue and dietary restrictions are unnecessary. As a result, depressed patients being treated on an outpatient basis can be given these types of antidepressants more safely. Those patients with cardiovascular problems, however, need to be monitored regularly because high doses of tricyclic drugs can produce an irregular or elevated heart rate. Some patients with cardiovascular disease cannot be treated with tricyclic drugs at all.

Atypical Antidepressants

Certain newer forms of antidepressant drugs bear no chemical similarity to either MAO inhibitors or tricyclic types. Hence, for lack of a better label, they are collectively referred to as **atypical antidepressants.** Some of these, such as venlafaxine (brand name: Effexor) and nefazodone (brand name: Serzone), have effects on serotonin and norepinephrine in the brain, in a similar manner as earlier formulations. But among the atypical antidepressants, a special subcategory of drugs has effects on serotonin alone. These drugs are referred to as **selective serotonin reuptake inhibitors (SSRI)** and include fluoxetine (brand name: Prozac), paroxetine (brand name: Paxil), sertraline (brand name: Zoloft), and citalopram (brand name: Celexa). Undoubtedly, Prozac is the best known and has attracted the most attention as well as the most controversy.

By all accounts, Prozac (along with other atypical antidepressants) has been viewed as a genuine breakthrough in the treatment of major depression. Introduced in 1987, it has quickly become the number one antidepressant medication on the strength of its effectiveness in reducing depressive symptoms with comparatively few side effects. In particular, Prozac is safe for cardiovascular patients who would have difficulty with tricyclic medications, and many patients whose feelings of depression have not been reduced by other antidepressants respond well to Prozac. Also, unlike tricyclic antidepressants, Prozac carries only an extremely remote risk of overdose.

Personal testimonials to the benefits of Prozac treatment abound. One pharmacist has offered this observation on his Prozac customers:

> *Most of these people used to come in here and complain.... Now they're saying, "I never felt better." ... I can't tell when someone's on medication but I sure can tell when they're off.*[15]

Are there significant drawbacks to Prozac treatment? The answer, unfortunately, is yes. Some patients report agitation and feelings of nausea, sexual problems, and in a few cases, an increase in suicidal thoughts after taking Prozac. There is an increased risk of seizures, though this side effect can be controlled either by lowering the dose or combining the drug with antiseizure medication. Another source of concern is the tendency for such a

tricyclic antidepressants: A class of antidepressant drugs. Brand names include Elavil, Norpramin, and Tofranil.
atypical antidepressants: Relatively new antidepressant drugs that bear no chemical similarity to either MAO inhibitors or tricyclic drugs. Atypical antidepressants include selective serotonin reuptake inhibitors (SSRIs).
selective serotonin reuptake inhibitors (SSRIs): A group of atypical antidepressants that slow down the reuptake of serotonin at synapses in the brain. Prozac is a prominent example.

Health Line

Is There a Dark Side to Prozac?

Few psychiatric medications, with the exception of Valium, have met with more controversy than Prozac. Despite its enormous popularity as an antidepressant, Prozac has also been a subject of scorn and fear. In 1990, one psychiatrist reported that his Prozac-treated patients developed intense, violent suicidal thoughts, a phenomenon that has since been estimated to occur anywhere from 3 to 15 percent of the time. Yet a careful examination of patients affected this way has shown that such instances have also been observed in severely depressed patients.

It is not clear whether thoughts of suicide are tied to the specific effects of the drug or to the emotional aspects of the disorder itself. In a 1991 review of this issue, the FDA concluded that Prozac was still safe to use as directed, though physicians are warned that "the possibility of a suicide attempt is inherent in depression and may persist until significant remission occurs. Close supervision of high risk patients should accompany initial drug therapy."

Accusations that Prozac can induce violent behavior, including homicide, form the basis of several pending lawsuits. Some defense attorneys have adopted the "Prozac defense," claiming that their clients were not responsible for a homicidal act while under Prozac treatment. So far, however, the results in the courts have been mixed. There have been no instances of acquittal based on this line of reasoning, though in a few cases the terms of sentences have been reduced. In the meantime, the FDA has officially ruled that no evidence exists for violent behavior as a direct result of taking Prozac.

Sources: Glenmullen, Joseph (2000). *Prozac backlash: Overcoming the dangers of Prozac, Zoloft, Paxil, and other antidepressants with safe, effective alternatives.* New York: Simon and Schuster. Hamilton, David P. (1991). Antidepressants—Suicide link to get another look. *Science, 253,* 1083. Kramer, Peter D. (1993). *Listening to Prozac.* New York: Viking Press. *Physicians' desk reference* (54th ed.) (2000). Montvale NJ: Medical Economics Company, pp. 859–863. Rosenbaum, Jerrold F. (1994). Clinical trial by media: The Prozac story. In Harold I. Schwartz (Ed.), *Psychiatric practice under fire: The influence of government, the media, and special interests on somatic therapies.* Washington DC: American Psychiatric Press, pp. 3–28.

popular drug as Prozac to be overprescribed (more than 20 million prescriptions were filled in 1996 alone), not only as a treatment for major depression but also for milder episodes of depression and related ailments that might have been better treated by traditional psychotherapy or counseling.

Long-term effects of taking Prozac are unknown. A potential problem is that Prozac may simply be too good; patients may be reluctant to withdraw from it because they fear the return of depressive feelings. The potential for this form of psychological dependence remains an important concern with Prozac as well as other psychiatric drugs. There is, however, no evidence for tolerance or physical withdrawal symptoms with Prozac.

The bottom line to the Prozac story, given our experience with the introduction of new psychoactive drugs over more than a century, should by now be familiar. New drugs, even those like Prozac that are recognized as having great promise, should always be administered with caution (Health Line). Prozac may certainly be an advance in the treatment of depression, but it is far from a "wonder drug." In the meantime, several other atypical antidepressants have established themselves on the market, in competition with Prozac and claiming pharmacological profiles that may be superior to it.[16]

Effects of Antidepressant Drugs on the Brain

When MAO inhibitors were discovered to be effective in reducing symptoms of depression, theories concerning the mechanism behind the action of these drugs turned to the properties of MAO itself. As enzymes, MAO molecules were known to inactivate dopamine, norepinephrine, and serotonin (collectively referred to as monoamines) at the synapses where these neurotransmitters operate. We can think of a drug as producing a double-negative effect on these neurotransmitters. By inhibiting MAO, we are inhibiting an inhibitor, and the net result will be a rise in the activity level of dopamine, norepinephrine, or serotonin. If so, then it would be logical to theorize that depression is associated with a lower-than-normal level of any one of these neurotransmitters or some combination of the three.

With the discovery of tricyclic antidepressants, it has been possible to focus on a more specific biochemical theory. Unlike MAO inhibitors, tricyclic drugs do not act on enzymes in the synapse. Instead, they slow down the reuptake of norepinephrine and serotonin at their respective synapses. Since the reuptake process allows neurotransmitter molecules to be reabsorbed from the

QUICK CONCEPT  16.1

Understanding the Biochemistry of Mental Illness

Check your understanding of the current biochemical theories of schizophrenia and mood disorders by associating each of the following psychiatric drug actions with the most likely clinical outcomes.

Psychiatric Drug Actions

1. Drug W reduces the level of dopamine in the brain.
2. Drug X increases the level of serotonin in the brain.
3. Drug Y increases the level of norepinephrine and serotonin in the brain.
4. Drug Z increases the level of dopamine in the brain.
5. Drug Q increases the activity of monoamine oxidase (MAO).

Predicted Clinical Outcomes

a. Schizophrenic symptoms will improve.
b. Schizophrenic symptoms will get worse.
c. Depressive symptoms will improve.
d. Depressive symptoms will get worse.

Answers: 1. a 2. c 3. c 4. b 5. d

receptor sites back to the neuron that released them in the first place (see Chapter 3), a slowing down means that these neurotransmitter molecules now remain in the receptor site for a longer period of time. When the neurotransmitter stays in the receptors longer, the receptors are stimulated more intensely. In other words, the effect of tricyclic drugs is to increase the activity level of norepinephrine and serotonin. Following the line of reasoning presented earlier, depression would be associated with a lower-than-normal level of activity with respect to these neurotransmitters.

Prozac was unique in that it was not "discovered" as much as it was designed with a specific purpose in mind. The intent was to identify a chemical that slowed down the reuptake of serotonin alone, hence its eventual designation as a selective serotonin reuptake inhibitor (SSRI). Since its introduction, Prozac has been joined by other SSRIs that share this pharmacological feature.

On a theoretical level, the successful development of Prozac and other SSRIs as effective antidepressants has provided strong evidence for the involvement of serotonin in providing the optimal level of mood in a person's life. This fact does not necessarily mean, however, that serotonin is the exclusive neurotransmitter system in the regulation of mood. As noted earlier, a sizable proportion of depressive patients benefit from the administration of tricyclic drugs and certain non-SSRI atypical antidepressants (such as Effexor and Serzone), implying that a norepinephrine system is involved as well. It may well be that there are two different forms of depression with similar enough behavioral symptoms to be clinically indistinguishable—one related to an abnormal serotonin system and one related to an abnormal norepinephrine system in the brain.[17]

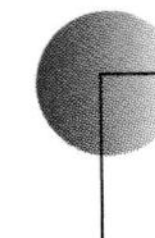

Drugs for Other Types of Mental Illness

In addition to drugs designated for the treatment of schizophrenia and depression, there exists a range of psychotropic drugs that are useful in dealing with other mental disorders. Here are three prominent examples.

Panic Attacks

A panic attack is a sudden feeling of extreme anxiety that may be associated with a particular environmental situation (crossing a bridge, being out in an open area) or with nothing at all. The unpredictable nature of its onset can be a great hardship in maintaining a normal quality of life. It is not surprising that some of the benzodiazepines reviewed in Chapter 15, such as Klonopin and Xanax, have been FDA-approved for the treatment of panic disorders. However, two antidepressants, Paxil and Zoloft, have been recommended for this purpose as well.

Mania and Bipolar Disorder

A mood disorder can encompass forms other than simple depression. Some individuals may display symptoms of **mania** that are as disruptive to themselves and their families as depression. Symptoms of mania include sleeplessness, impulsiveness (a manic patient with a credit card is a dangerous combination), irritability, and feelings of grandeur. Others may display mood swings back and forth between depression and mania (a condition

mania: A mood disorder characterized by agitation, bursts of energy, and impulsiveness.

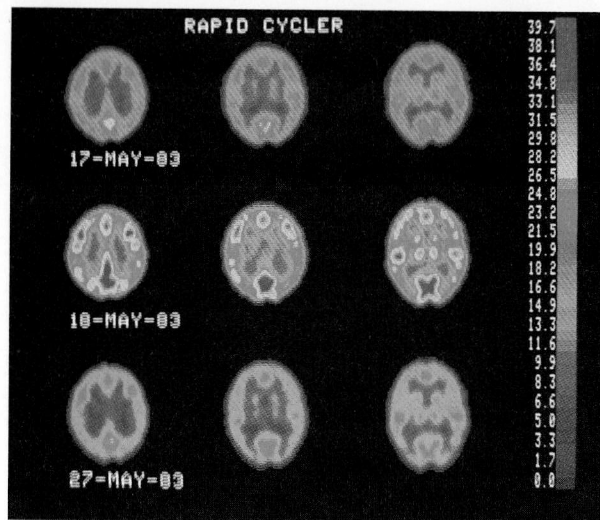

These brain scans show significant differences in the neural activity (yellow and red areas being the highest) of a bipolar disorder patient during times of alternating depression (top and bottom rows) and hypomania, a mild form of mania (middle row). Similar scans have identified differences in neural activity between normal and schizophrenic individuals.

referred to as **bipolar disorder,** formerly known as manic-depression). Until recently, the primary psychiatric drug for the treatment of either mania or bipolar disorder has been **lithium carbonate.** Unfortunately, lithium carbonate is effective for only 50 percent of patients showing these symptoms, and those who respond well to it must undergo periodic blood testing to avoid potential toxic effects to the thyroid gland and kidneys.[18]

The drug valproate (brand name: Depakote) has now been found to help patients suffering from either mania or bipolar disorder, as an alternative to lithium carbonate. Recently, it has been found to be useful in conjunction with antipsychotic medication when psychotic symptoms are accompanied by an instability of mood. Valproate was originally introduced for the treatment of epilepsy, for which it continues to be prescribed. The mechanism by which it influences levels of mood is unclear. Drawing from the understanding we have about depression, however, a good possibility is that the beneficial effects of valproate will be found to be linked to an alteration in the activity level of either serotonin or norepinephrine.[19]

Obsessive-Compulsive Disorder (OCD)

A small percentage of people, estimated at 2–4 percent of the U.S. population, suffer from a series of persistent, uncontrollable, and unwanted thoughts (obsessions) and urges to carry out, in repeated ritual-like fashion, seemingly senseless behaviors (compulsions). This condition is referred to as **obsessive-compulsive disorder (OCD).** A useful drug in OCD treatment has been clomipramine (brand name: Anafranil). Technically, clomipramine is a tricyclic drug, as are several other antidepressants, but because it slows down serotonin reuptake exclusively, it is frequently included in the category of SSRIs. Not surprisingly, other SSRIs have been found to be effective OCD therapies, including fluvoxamine (brand name: Luvox), which has been specifically FDA-approved for treating OCD.[20]

Off-Label Usage of Psychotropic Medications

Increasingly, psychotropic medications have been used for purposes other than those specified by the FDA when they were first approved. This practice is referred to as **off-label usage.** By law, physicians are given considerable latitude to prescribe drugs for their patients that they consider appropriate for a specific set of symptoms, even if there is no official sanction for that particular application. There is a growing recognition, for example, that some antidepressants may be useful in the treatment of anxiety and some antianxiety medications may be useful in the treatment of depression. In some instances, official changes are made by the FDA to widen the possible applications from those originally designated when the drug was introduced. In general, this kind of "cross-over" pharmacotherapy is on the rise and is part of the challenge we face in our attempt to understand biochemical bases for normal as well as abnormal behavior.[21]

---

bipolar disorder: A mood disorder in which the patient swings back and forth between feelings of depression and mania.

lithium (LITH-ee-um) carbonate: A psychiatric drug used in the treatment of mania or bipolar disorder.

obsessive-compulsive disorder (OCD): A mental illness in which individuals have persistent and unwanted thoughts (obsessions) and continuing urges to engage in specific behaviors (compulsions).

off-label usage: The practice of prescribing the use of a particular medication, even if the drug in question has not been FDA-approved for that purpose.

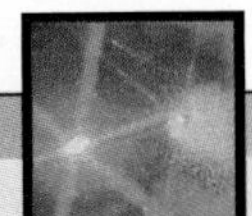

The Risks of Interactions between St.-John's-wort and Prescription Drugs

While the direct side effects of St.-John's-wort are relatively mild, there is increasing concern about its interacting effects with certain prescription drugs. The herbal antidepressant reduces blood levels of indinavir (brand name: Crixivan), a major drug used in HIV treatment. Other evidence indicates that St.-John's-wort reduces levels of digoxin (brand name: Lanoxin), used for treating congestive heart failure; bronchodilator drugs for treating asthma; carbamazepine (brand name: Tegretol), used for treating epilepsy; and warfarin (brand name: Coumadin), used as a blood-thinner. These herbal supplement/drug interactions are potentially dangerous, since the benefits of major life-saving drugs may be reduced as a result. You may recall that another herbal supplement, gingko biloba, has the opposite effect on blood-thinning medications, increasing their effects rather than decreasing them. The additive interaction on blood-thinning medications is also shared by some OTC analgesic products (see Chapter 14).

Unfortunately, many people do not think taking an herbal supplement is important information they should tell their physician when being prescribed medication. Recently, the FDA has disallowed dietary supplements from being promoted for common pregnancy-related conditions like morning sickness and leg swelling, pending new studies regarding their safety. In addition, there is concern over the increase in dietary supplements being taken by the elderly. Two specific supplements, gingko biloba and St.-John's-wort, are currently marketed as aids in reducing memory loss and depression, respectively. The elderly are particularly drawn to these products as possible remedies, in part as a convenience to them and as a response to the increasing costs of prescription medication. Since this population typically takes a sizable number of medicines for their particular medical conditions, the probability of an adverse interaction is increased.

Sources: Henney, Jane E. (2000). Risk of drug interactions with St.-John's-wort. *Journal of the American Medical Association, 283,* 1679. Lantz, Melinda S., Buchalter, Eric, and Giambanco, Vincent (1999). St.-John's-wort and antidepressant drug interactions in the elderly. *Journal of Geriatric Psychiatry and Neurology, 12,* 7–10. Stolberg, Sheryl G. (2000, February 10). FDA bars marketing of supplements to pregnant women. *New York Times,* p. A28.

St.-John's-wort: An Herbal Alternative for Treating Depression

It is believed that ancient Greeks used an extract from a yellow-flowered plant, now known as **St.-John's-wort** (*Hypericum perforматum*), to drive away evil spirits and banish sadness. Today, it is increasingly clear that the herb has the potential for treating depression. Since the early 1980s, St.-John's-wort has been a popular remedy in Europe for depression. In Germany, more prescriptions are currently written each year for *Hypericum* extract than for Prozac or other SSRI medications, and for good reason. A 1994 study tracking the herb's effect in more than three thousand depressed patients found that 80 percent either reported feeling less depressed than before or completely recovered. In an extensive series of controlled studies reported in 1996, St.-John's-wort was found to be three times more effective than a placebo for reducing mild to moderately severe depressive symptoms. In addition, *Hypericum* extract is now known to inhibit serotonin and norepinephrine uptake, consistent with its antidepressant action.

Though the definitive word awaits results from clinical trials of St.-John's-wort in the United States, the results so far are encouraging. It will be important to compare its ability to relieve depressive symptoms against the standard SSRI antidepressants available today. We already know that the direct side effects of St.-John's-wort are relatively mild. Mild gastrointestinal symptoms, fatigue, and sensitivity to light appear to be the major adverse reactions when taking this herb.

Since it is derived from a natural herb, St.-John's-wort is available commercially in the United States, without restriction, as a dietary supplement. Even so, experts in the field of herbal medicine caution that depressed patients should consult their physician before switching to St.-John's-wort or self-supplementing their present antidepressant medication (Health Alert).[22]

St.-John's-wort: A dietary supplement, derived from an herbal extract, that has potential as a treatment for depressive symptoms.

DRUGS . . . IN FOCUS

Psychiatric Drugs and the Civil Liberties Debate

Let's imagine that you are a hospitalized psychiatric patient, either voluntarily or involuntarily committed to a mental-health facility on the basis of a diagnosis of schizophrenia. You are handed your daily medication that has been prescribed by a staff psychiatrist. There has been a careful diagnosis of your mental illness and a determination that the medication is appropriate and effective in reducing your symptoms. Can you refuse to take it? Do you even have to give a reason for your refusal? If you are asked to participate in a study in which a new experimental drug is being tested against a placebo, should you be required to do so? If you signed an informed consent, are you mentally competent to know what you are agreeing to do? If you state that you are mentally competent but have been diagnosed as a schizophrenic, would your self-assessment be considered valid?

These are a few of the difficult questions currently being faced in mental-health treatment facilities and in the development of new therapeutic drugs. Few of them have been totally resolved. In the late 1960s in Minnesota and New York, physicians were successfully sued for *not* medicating committed, drug-refusing patients. However, in 1975 in Massachusetts, physicians were successfully sued *for* medicating drug-refusing patients. Court decisions since 1979 regarding a patient's right to refuse medication have generally been in the patient's favor, though the decision as to the mental competence of an individual patient is frequently left to a judge's ruling.

Another controversy has arisen surrounding the rights of patients in the development of new drugs, particularly with regard to the treatment of schizophrenia. Should these patients participate in clinical testing trials for experimental antipsychotic medications? On the one hand, as a research psychiatrist has put it, "We must figure out this disease. . . . Unfortunately, there are no animal models for hallucinations and thought disorders. There is no substitute for studying humans." On the other hand, as a civil rights attorney has said, "Persons with severe psychiatric disabilities cannot be made guinea pigs for the greater good of humanity."

What do you think?

Sources: Amarasingham, Lorna R. (1980). Social and cultural perspectives on medication refusal. *American Journal of Psychiatry, 137,* 353–358. Gutheil, Thomas G. (1980). In search of true freedom: Drug refusal, involuntary medication, and "Rotting with your rights on." *American Journal of Psychiatry, 137,* 327–328.

Psychiatric Drugs, Social Policy, and Deinstitutionalization

Prior to the 1960s, the dominant approach to treating severely impaired psychiatric patients was institutionalization in large state-supported mental hospitals. In such places, the treatment of choice, medication, could be controlled by psychiatrists and hospital staff. During the 1960s, the policy toward treating the mentally ill started to change. Responsibility for treatment shifted from centralized institutions to decentralized community mental-health clinics. Proponents argued that these smaller centers could provide a more humane setting for psychiatric patients, closer to their homes and families.

Where has this policy left psychiatric patients? With more and more court cases upholding the illegality of involuntary commitment (requiring a patient to be hospitalized against his or her will) unless there is a clear danger to society, many patients have ended up drifting in and out of mental-health facilities, no longer supervised carefully enough to take their medication regularly or attend to their personal needs. As a result, many have become rootless, without homes or sources of social support. Recent studies indicate that approximately one-third

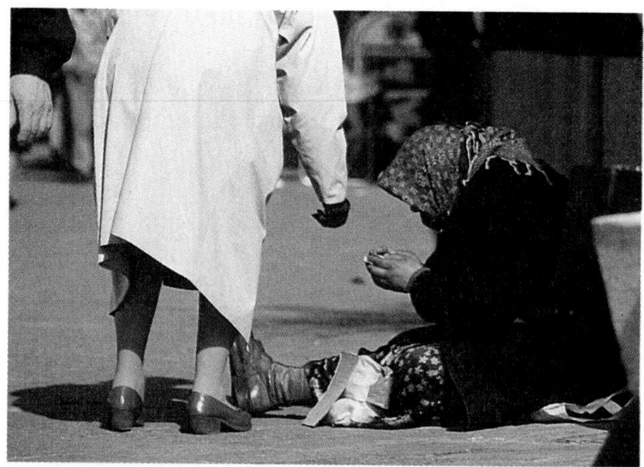

The plight of the homeless is sometimes the plight of deeply troubled individuals adrift from the protection and aid of mental-health professionals.

of all homeless people suffer from schizophrenia or mood disorders, with another one-third contending with severe alcohol- and other drug-abuse problems. Ten to twenty percent are burdened with a dual diagnosis of severe mental illness and substance abuse. The problems of such individuals continue to present a major challenge to our society (Drugs . . . in Focus). In the words of one psychologist, "Deinstitutionalization has apparently moved some disordered people from the back wards of our mental hospitals to the back alleys of our slums."[23]

SUMMARY

- The development of psychiatric drugs to treat major mental illnesses such as schizophrenia and mood disorders has both revolutionized the field of mental health and provided insights into the biochemical basis for mental illness.
- As effective as psychiatric drugs might be for the mentally ill, none is without side effects. The perfect drug has yet to appear on the scene.

The Biomedical Model

- The biomedical model, a prevalent viewpoint among mental-health professions, asserts that abnormal thoughts and behaviors are results of biochemical processes in the brain.

Antipsychotic Drugs and Schizophrenia

- Antipsychotic drugs for schizophrenic patients fall into two broad categories: typical and atypical.
- The typical antipsychotic drugs are effective in reducing symptoms for many patients, but they also carry with them the potential for the development of severe movement-related motor problems.
- A newer class of drugs, called atypical antipsychotic medications, does not produce this particular side effect.
- In general, antipsychotic medications are believed to be clinically effective on the basis of their action on dopamine-releasing neurons in the brain.

Drugs Used to Treat Mood Disorders

- Antidepressant drugs can be classified in three groups: MAO inhibitors, tricyclic antidepressants, and atypical antidepressants.
- The MAO inhibitors were the first group to be developed for the treatment of depression. Although they are effective, patients need to be on a restricted diet to avoid serious adverse side effects.
- Tricyclic antidepressants do not require dietary restrictions, but their effects on the cardiovascular system make them undesirable for certain patients.
- The newest group, atypical antidepressants, includes the well-known and widely used drug fluoxetine (brand name: Prozac). Despite the advantages of Prozac as an antidepressant, concerns have been raised as to its overuse.
- The effectiveness of antidepressants has been linked to an alteration in either serotonin or norepinephrine systems in the brain.

Drugs for Other Types of Mental Illness

- Feelings of extreme anxiety (panic) have been treated successfully with either specific benzodiazepines or SSRI-type antidepressants.
- Mania and extreme mood swings (bipolar disorder) are two mood disorders that have been treated successfully with lithium carbonate or valproate (brand name: Depakote).
- Specific antidepressants have been used to relieve symptoms of intrusive, repetitive thoughts or behaviors that are characteristic of obsessive-compulsive disorder (OCD).

St.-John's-wort

- Increasing attention has focused on the application of Saint-John's-wort in the treatment of depressive symptoms. Widely used in Europe, clinical trials of this herbal extract in the United States remain to be completed.

Psychiatric Drugs, Social Policy, and Deinstitutionalization

- Since the 1960s, a growing number of psychiatric patients are treated outside a centralized hospital or institution and are placed in treatment-care clinics in the community.

- The question of psychiatric patients' rights is a present-day issue of great concern.

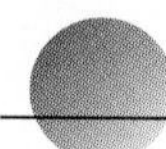

KEY TERMS

agranulocytosis, p. 332
antidepressants, p. 334
antipsychotic drugs, p. 328
atypical antidepressants, p. 335
atypical antipsychotic drugs, p. 331
biomedical model, p. 328
bipolar disorder, p. 338
catatonia, p. 329
delusions, p. 329
lithium carbonate, p. 338
mania, p. 337
MAO inhibitors, p. 334
monoamine oxidase (MAO), p. 334
obsessive-compulsive disorder (OCD), p. 338
off-label usage, p. 338
Parkinson's-like symptoms, p. 331
psychiatric drugs, p. 328
psychotropic medication, p. 328
St.-John's-wort, p. 339
schizophrenia, p. 328
selective serotonin reuptake inhibitors (SSRIs), p. 335
tardive dyskinesia, p. 332
target dosing, p. 330
tricyclic antidepressants, p. 335
typical antipsychotic drugs, p. 330

ENDNOTES

1. Blouin, Jean-Louis et al. (1998). Schizophrenia susceptibility loci on chromosomes 13q32 and 8p21. *Nature Genetics, 20,* 70–73. Murphy, Jane M. (1976). Psychiatric labeling in cross-cultural perspective. *Science, 191,* 1019–1028. Nicol, Susan E., and Gottesman, Irving I. (1983). Clues to the genetics and neurobiology of schizophrenia. *American Scientist, 71,* 398–404.
2. American Psychiatric Association (1994). *Diagnostic and statistical manual* (4th ed.). Washington DC: American Psychiatric Association, pp. 278–290. Benjamin, Ludy T., Hopkins, J. Roy, and Nation, Jack R. (1994). *Psychology* (3rd ed.). New York: Macmillan, p. 660.
3. Levinthal, Charles F. (1988). *Messengers of paradise: Opiates and the brain.* New York: Anchor Press/Doubleday, pp. 60–61. Snyder, Solomon H. (1974). *Madness and the brain.* New York: McGraw-Hill, pp. 19–21.
4. Lickey, Marvin E., and Gordon, Barbara (1991). *Medicine and mental illness: The use of drugs in psychiatry.* New York: Freeman, p. 92.
5. Hollister, Leo E. (1983). *Clinical pharmacology of psychotherapeutic drugs* (2nd ed.). New York: Churchill Livingston, pp. 110–171.
6. Davis, John M. (1980). Antipsychotic drugs. In Harold I. Kaplan, Arnold M. Freedman, and Benjamin J. Saddock (Eds.), *Comprehensive textbook of psychiatry.* Vol. 3. Baltimore: Williams and Wilkins, pp. 2257–2289.
7. Baron, Robert A. (1992). *Psychology* (2nd ed.). Boston: Allyn and Bacon, p. 593. Meltzer, Herbert Y. (1993). New drugs for treatment of schizophrenia. *Psychiatric Clinics of North America, 16,* 365–385.
8. Honigfeld, Gilbert, and Howard, Alfreda (1973). *Psychiatric drugs: A desk reference.* New York: Academic Press, p. 37. Silverstone, Trevor, and Turner, Paul (1978). *Drug treatment in psychiatry* (2nd ed.). London: Routledge and Kegan Paul, pp. 106–108.
9. Lickey and Gordon, *Medicine and mental illness,* pp.132–133.
10. Palfai, Tibor, and Jankiewicz, Henry (1991). *Drugs and human behavior.* Dubuque IA: W. C. Brown, p. 259.
11. Chou, James C.-Y., and Serper, Mark R. (1998). Ziprasidone—A new highly atypical antipsychotic. *Essentials of Psychopharmacology, 2,* 463–485. Green, Ben (1999). Focus on olanzapine. *Current Medical Research and Opinion, 15,* 79–85. Julien, Robert M. (2001). *A primer of drug action* (9th ed.). New York: Worth, pp. 509–522. Reid, William H. (1999). New vs. old antipsychotics: The Texas experience. *Journal of Clinical Psychiatry, 60* (suppl. 1), 23–25. Swartz, J. Randolph; Ananth, Jambur; Smith, Michael W.; Burgoyne, Karl S.; Gadasally, Rangaswamy; and Arai, Yoshi (1999). Olanzapine treatment after clozapine-induced granulocytopenia in 3 patients. *Journal of Clinical Psychiatry, 60,* 119–121.
12. Duvoisin, Roger C. (1991). *Parkinson's disease: A guide for patient and family* (3rd ed.). New York: Raven Press. Hornykiewicz, Oleh (1974). The mechanisms of L-dopamine in Parkinson's disease. *Life Sciences, 15,* 1249–1259.
13. Butcher, James (2000). News: Dopamine hypothesis gains more support. *Lancet, 356,* 140. Healy, D. (1991). D_1 and D_2 and D_3. *British Journal of Psychiatry, 159,* 319–324. Remington, Gary (1996). Neuroleptics. In Andrius Baskys and Gary Remington (Eds.), *Brain mechanisms and psychotropic drugs.* Boca Raton FL: CRC Press, pp. 193–211.
14. Lefton, Lester A. (1994). *Psychology* (5th ed.). Boston: Allyn and Bacon, p. 481.
15. Quotation in Geoffrey Cowley (1990, March 26), The promise of Prozac. *Newsweek,* p. 39.

16. Cramer, Peter D. (1993). *Listening to Prozac.* New York: Viking. Glenmullen, Joseph (2000). *Prozac backlash: Overcoming the dangers of Prozac, Zoloft, Paxil, and other antidepressants with safe, effective alternatives.* New York: Simon and Schuster. Goode, Erica (1999, July 27). Some still despair in a Prozac nation. *New York Times*, pp. F1, F7. Morrow, David J. (1998, October 11). Lusting after Prozac. *New York Times*, Section 3, pp. 1, 8.
17. Kamil, Rifaat (1996). Antidepressants. In Andrius Baskys and Gary Remington (Eds.), *Brain mechanisms and psychotropic drugs.* Boca Raton FL: CRC Press, pp. 153–180. Levinthal, Charles F. (1990). *Introduction to physiological psychology* (3rd ed.). Englewood Cliffs NJ: Prentice-Hall, pp. 174–177. Maas, James W. (1975). Biogenic amines of depression. *Archives of General Psychiatry*, 32, 1357–1361.
18. Bower, Bruce (1991). Manic depression: Success story dims. *Science News*, *139*, 324–325.
19. Joffee, Russell T., and Young, L. Trevor (1996). Mood-stabilizing agents. In Andrius Baskys and Gary Remington (Eds.), *Brain mechanisms and psychotropic drugs.* Boca Raton FL: CRC Press, pp. 181–192. Johnson, F. Neil (1984). *The history of lithium therapy.* New York: Macmillan. Shelton, Richard C. (1999). Mood-stabilizing drugs in depression. *Journal of Clinical Psychiatry*, *60* (Suppl. 5), 37–40. Waring, E. W.; Dewan, V. K.; Cohen, D.; and Grewal, R. (1999). Risperidone as an adjunct to valproic acid. *Canadian Journal of Psychiatry*, *44*, 189–190.
20. Julien, *A primer of drug action*, pp. 461–481. Weiten, Wayne (1995). *Psychology: Themes and variations* (3rd ed.). Pacific Grove CA: Brooks/Cole, p. 569.
21. Barlow, David H.; Gorman, Jack M.; Shear, M. Katherine; and Woods, Scott W. (2000). Cognitive-behavioral therapy, imipramine, or their combination for panic disorder. *Journal of the American Medical Association*, 283, 2529–2536. Brady, Kathleen; Pearlstein, Teri; Asnis, Gregory M.; Baker, Dewleen; Rothbaum, Barbara; Sikes, Carolyn R.; and Farfel, Gail M. (2000). Efficacy and safety of sertraline treatment of posttraumatic stress disorder. *Journal of the American Medical Association*, 283, 1837–1844. Gelenberg, Alan J.; Lydiard, R. Bruce; Rudolph, Richard L.; Aguiar, Loren; Haskins, J. Thomas; and Salinas, Eliseo (2000). Efficacy of venlafaxine extended-release capsules in nondepressed outpatients with generalized anxiety disorder: A 6-month randomized controlled trial. *Journal of the American Medical Association*, 283, 3082–3088.
22. Cott, Jerry M., and Fugh-Berman, Adriane (1998). Is St.-John's-wort (*Hypericum performatum*) an effective antidepressant? *Journal of Nervous and Mental Disease, 186*, 500–501. Neary, Joseph T., and Bu, Yurong (1999). *Hypericum* LI 160 inhibits uptake of serotonin and norepinephrine in astrocytes. *Brain Research, 816*, 358–363. Salzman, Carl (1998). St.-John's-wort. *Harvard Review of Psychiatry*, 5, 333–335. Wheatley, David (1998). *Hypericum* extract: Potential in the treatment of depression. *CNS Drugs*, 6, 431–440.
23. Drake, Robert E., Osher, Fred C., and Wallace, Michael A. (1991). Homelessness and dual diagnosis. *American Psychologist, 46*, 1149–1158. Fischer, Pamela J., and Breakey, William R. (1991). The epidemiology of alcohol, drug, and mental disorders among homeless persons. *American Psychologist, 46*, 1115–1128. Quotation in Weiten, *Psychology: Themes and variations*, p. 630.

Point Counterpoint

How Do We Get Orphan Drugs Adopted?

The following discussion of viewpoints represents the opinions of people on both sides of the controversial issue of adopting orphan drugs. Read them with an open mind. Don't think you have to come up with the final answer, nor should you necessarily agree with the argument you read last. Many of the ideas in this feature come from sources listed.

POINT

The issue should be pretty clear. We have people out there who are very sick; some are dying. But according to the pharmaceutical industry they don't count because there are too few of them to service and still make a profit. We need more effort on the part of drug companies to help these people, the true "orphans" in the world of pharmaceutical treatment.

COUNTERPOINT

Now hold on. Before you start painting the drug industry as a bunch of Simon Legrees, let's look at the facts, not the rhetoric. Since 1983, we have the Orphan Drug Act, which has been responsible for providing dozens of new drugs for patients with AIDS, rare blood and metabolic disorders, and unusual forms of cancer. These are disorders for which there are fewer than 200,000 patients in the United States. As a result of the act, new products that would not have been developed before are now being marketed to these people, and as a result lives are being saved. If it hadn't been for the Orphan Drug Act, for example, today we probably would not have drugs such as AZT, which prolongs the lives of AIDS patients, or pentamidine isethionate, which treats the pneumonia that strikes many people with AIDS.

POINT

True, up to a point. Let's review exactly what this Orphan Drug Act has been doing. First of all, the government has given the drug companies a tax credit of 50 percent of all costs incurred in conducting human clinical trials for these orphan drugs in any given year, and the remaining 50 percent of the costs can be a tax-deductible business expense. You're talking about a total reduction of 73 percent in taxes that might have been paid. Not a bad deal at all. It's not as if the drug companies are doing the public a favor.

COUNTERPOINT

These tax concessions have been necessary. Otherwise, drug companies could not have afforded the enormous expenses incurred in developing a new drug when the market for that drug is so small. Like it or not, it's a matter of economic reality.

POINT

Let's talk a little economic reality. There's a drug called Ceradase that is marketed by Genzyme Corporation, a biotechnology company. For severe cases of Gaucher's disease, an inherited enzyme disorder, it costs as much as $300,000 a year to treat the disease with Ceradase. This drug is considered the world's most expensive drug. Is it necessary to charge such a high price when the development was subsidized in part by the taxpayer?

COUNTERPOINT

Genzyme says that the cost of Ceradase treatment is soon to come down. Besides, the company has been losing money for at least the first ten years of its history, despite its success with Ceradase. Given the costs of research into drugs that never reach the market (the "dry holes"), the rewards of a successful drug are justified.

POINT

We are still faced with a situation in which companies are reaping huge annual sales from orphan drugs, in some cases two to three times the research costs that were incurred in developing them. And they are enjoying a seven-year exclusive monopoly on their sales, all thanks to the Orphan Drug Act.

COUNTERPOINT

The seven-year patent is necessary to recoup the expenses of other orphan drugs that don't make the headlines like Ceradase.

POINT

What about having a ceiling of $200 million in sales from an orphan drug, after which the company relinquishes its monopoly? At least, this limit would encourage competition for those blockbuster drugs that more than likely would have been developed without the act. Besides, "true" orphan drugs would never reach this sales trigger level anyway.

COUNTERPOINT

Any change in the law would essentially kill orphan-drug research. It would eliminate any incentive to get these drugs out to the people who need them. The law is working for now. Let's not tamper with it.

Critical Thinking Questions for Further Debate

1. Do you think the Orphan Drug Act favors the pharmaceutical companies or the American public?
2. Should governmental tax credits be tied to the annual profits of major pharmaceutical companies?

Sources: Asbury, Carolyn H. (1985). *Orphan drugs: Medical versus market value.* Lexington MA: Lexington Books. Cushman, John R. (1992, January 22). Incentives for research on drugs are debated. *New York Times*, p. A13. Hamilton, Robert A. (1990, November). Rare disease treatments: "Orphans" saving lives. *FDA Consumer*, pp. 7–10.

PART 5 TREATMENT, PREVENTION, AND EDUCATION

CHAPTER 17

Prevention and Treatment: Strategies for Change

After you have completed this chapter, you will understand

- Three major types of intervention in drug-abuse prevention
- The biopsychosocial approach to drug-abuse treatment
- Prison-alternative and prison-based treatment programs
- Efforts to create a drug-free workplace in the United States
- Issues related to the personal decision to seek treatment
- The importance of family dynamics in drug abuse and treatment
- Considerations when deciding on a particular treatment program

I would lie about everything, and I lied to everybody. I was so good at it because it was so easy to do. My parents were in major denial, and I played off of that. What is all that drug stuff in my room? Oh, I'm just holding it for a friend. It would get me so angry that the lies worked so well with them. They would never call me on anything. It became a way of life. But after a while I got sick and tired of all the lying. And I started to think about the possibility that I might be dead at an early age. Half of my friends are now dead; the other half are in jail. That's why I'm here to get help. I had to change somehow. It really just came down to that.

—A seventeen-year-old recovering drug abuser; explaining why he came to Daytop Village

Consider for a moment the goal of preventing the misuse and abuse of psychoactive drugs in our society. Everyone is obviously in favor of prevention; no one questions that the personal damage and social havoc wrought by the sale, distribution, and consumption of illicit drugs are devastating. As political leaders continually remind us, we have to "do something" if this monster is to be slain. At the same time, we are appalled by the magnitude of preventable disease and death associated with licit drugs such as alcohol and nicotine. It is imperative that we reduce the risks to our health and the health of our families and friends.

Yet, as unanimous as we may be in the necessity for some prevention strategy, the issues are terribly complex and the answers have been elusive. So far, we have enjoyed only partial success in this area. Health professionals have found it difficult to devise a program that guarantees a significant and long-lasting impact on an individual's inclination to use drugs. In these final two chapters, we turn to an examination of drug-abuse prevention in our society.

QUICK CONCEPT CHECK 17.1

Understanding Drug-Abuse Prevention Programs

Check your understanding of the three basic types of intervention in drug-abuse prevention by matching the following five scenarios with (a) primary, (b) secondary, or (c) tertiary prevention.

1. Midnight basketball sessions keep teenagers from drinking on weekends out of boredom.
2. Young children receive lessons on how to refuse the offer of drugs from a friend or acquaintance.
3. A child learns about "good drugs" and "bad drugs" in the first grade.
4. A man learns how to live without cocaine following a successful cocaine treatment program.
5. College students organize a "responsible drinking" program on campus.

Answers: 1. b 2. a 3. a 4. c 5. b

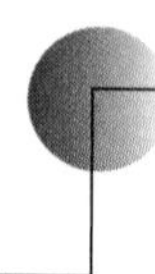

Ways to Approach Drug-Abuse Prevention

Traditionally, efforts to prevent the abuse of drugs have been divided into three types of intervention: primary, secondary, and tertiary. Each has its own target population and goals.

In **primary prevention,** efforts are directed to those who have not had any experience with drugs or those who have been only minimally exposed. The objective is to prevent drug abuse from starting in the first place, "nipping the problem in the bud" so to speak. Targets in primary prevention programs are most frequently elementary school or middle school youths, and intervention usually occurs within a school-based curriculum or specific educational program. For example, a primary prevention program would include teaching peer-refusal skills that students can use when they are offered marijuana, alcohol, or cigarettes (that is, ways to say no).

In **secondary prevention,** the target population has already had some experience with drugs. The objective is to limit the extent of drug abuse (reducing it, if possible), prevent the spread of drug abuse to substances beyond the drugs already encountered, and teach strategies for the responsible use of licit drugs such as alcohol. Ordinarily, those receiving secondary-prevention efforts are older than those involved in primary-prevention programs. High school students who are identified as alcohol or other drug users may participate in a program that emphasizes social alternatives to drug-taking behavior. College students may focus on the skills necessary to restrict their behavior to the moderate use of alcohol, the dangers of combining drinking and driving, and the signs of chronic alcohol abuse.

In **tertiary prevention,** the objective is to ensure that an individual who has entered treatment for some form of drug abuse problem stays drug-free, without reverting to former patterns of drug-taking behavior. Successful prevention of relapse is the ultimate indication that the treatment has taken hold.[1]

This chapter concentrates on tertiary-prevention efforts, specifically those treatment interventions intended to rescue an individual from a life of drug abuse. Chapter 18 will focus on primary- and secondary-prevention

primary prevention: A type of intervention in which the goal is to forestall the onset of drug use by an individual who has had little or no previous exposure to drugs.
secondary prevention: A type of intervention in which the goal is to reduce the extent of drug use in individuals who have already had some exposure to drugs.
tertiary (TER-shee-eh-ree) prevention: A type of intervention in which the goal is to prevent the relapse in an individual following recovery in a drug treatment program.

Acupuncture as a Potential Treatment for Cocaine Abuse

Recent research indicates that a sizable number of cocaine abusers can be successfully treated for their cocaine dependence through acupuncture, the insertion of small needles into specific locations of the skin. A study reported on in 2000 randomly assigned men and women to three groups, all of whom were receiving methadone maintenance treatment for heroin abuse but were still using cocaine on a regular basis. One group had needles inserted at four acupuncture sites in the ear five times a week for eight weeks. A second group had needles inserted for the same amount of time at sites along the rim of the ear that are not commonly used in acupuncture therapy (the equivalent of a placebo control), while a third group listened to a relaxation tape for that period. Approximately 54 percent of the first group tested negative for cocaine in urinanalysis tests conducted at the end of the study. The percentage of individuals in the first group achieving a cocaine-free condition was more than twice that of the second group and six times when compared to the third group.

These promising findings are the latest in a series of experiments showing the advantage of acupuncture in drug-abuse treatment. In this study, however, the addition of the second group for comparison purposes was a critical element allowing the researchers to maintain that success was not just a matter of the insertion of needles per se or the attention given to individuals in the study. It should be noted that the success rate for acupuncture treatment was not very high, just a bit more than one-half of the individuals in the first group. Nonetheless, it was still impressive, given the difficulty in treating cocaine abusers in general. The benefits of acupuncture treatment are the low costs involved and the lack of side effects. In addition, it is possible to treat pregnant women who are abusing cocaine, without being concerned with the pharmaceutical effects on the developing fetus.

While there is no clear understanding, at this point, of how acupuncture might work, the fact that acupuncture is known to stimulate the release of morphine-like endorphins (Chapter 5) may provide a link to explaining its success in cocaine-abuse treatment. It is possible that endorphin release alters the functioning of the nucleus accumbens in the brain and reduces the feelings of craving for cocaine. You can be sure that future research studies will be forthcoming.

Sources: Avants, S. K.; Margolin, A.; Holford, T. R.; and Kosten, T. R. (2000). A randomized controlled trial of auricular acupuncture for cocaine dependence. *Archives of Internal Medicine, 160,* 2305–2312. Howell, Embry M., Heiser, Nancy, and Harrington, Mary (1999). A review of recent findings on substance abuse treatment for pregnant women. *Journal of Substance Abuse Treatment, 16,* 195–219.

efforts, primarily the array of school- and community-based educational programs available at the present time.

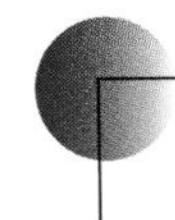

A Biopsychosocial Strategy for Treatment

Treatment programs for abusers of specific drugs have been reviewed in earlier chapters. In some cases, a treatment program is uniquely tailored for individuals seeking help in dealing with a certain form of drug abuse. A methadone or LAAM maintenance program (see Chapter 5), for example, is not appropriate for a cocaine abuser or an alcoholic, since the intent is to substitute an illicit, unpredictable opiate (heroin) with an opiate that can be medically supervised (methadone or LAAM). The use of disulfiram (Antabuse) is restricted to the treatment of alcoholism (see Chapter 10) because it is a specific inhibitor of enzymes involved in the breakdown of alcohol and its effects are not felt if alcohol is not in the system (Health Line).

However, a treatment approach can cut across different forms of drug abuse. We have seen how so-called twelve-step programs have been useful not only for alcohol abusers in the traditional Alcoholics Anonymous format but also for individuals seeking help with heroin abuse (Narcotics Anonymous) or cocaine abuse (Cocaine Anonymous). You may recall that one particular location in the brain, the nucleus accumbens, seems to be stimulated by a variety of dependence-producing drugs (opiates, cocaine, alcohol, and nicotine). The recent use of naltrexone, an opiate antagonist, in the treatment of alcoholism (see Chapter 10) as well as heroin abuse (see Chapter 5) is a good example of the cross-over value of current drug treatment strategies. Given the evidence for a common neural and neurochemical basis for drug dependence in general, it makes sense that a common approach might work in its treatment.[2]

The consideration of a common treatment approach is dictated also by a fact of life regarding drugs in our society today. The reality is that not one but several types of drugs, either licit or illicit, are often involved in

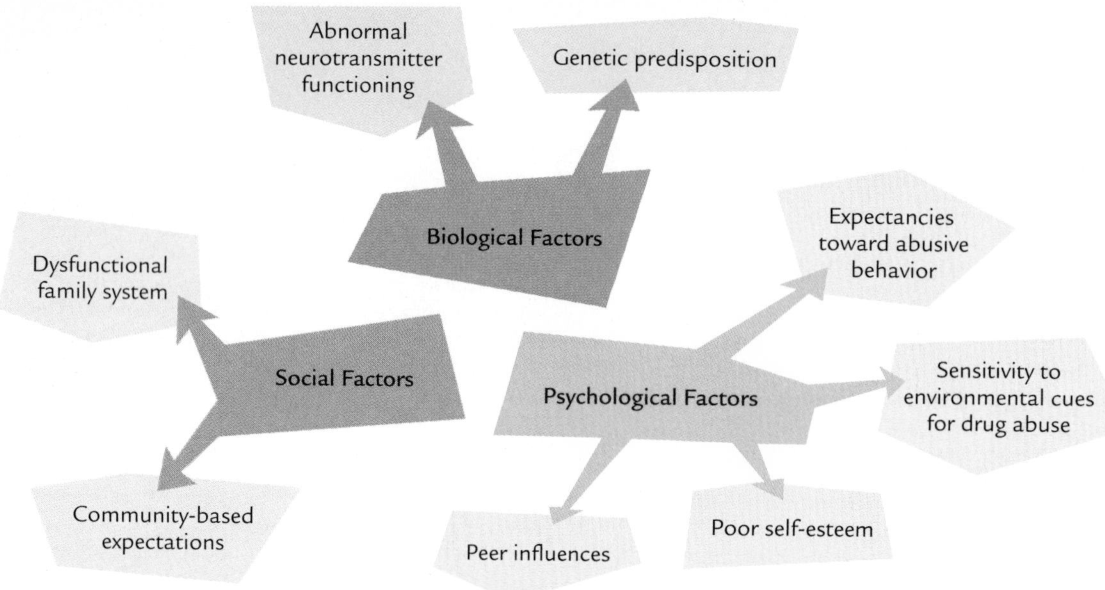

FIGURE 17.1

The biopsychosocial model asserts that there are multiple pathways to drug abuse.

Source: Modified from Margolis, Robert D., and Zweben, Joan E. (1998). *Treating patients with alcohol and other drug problems: An integrated approach.* Washington DC: American Psychological Association, pp. 76–87.

an individual's "dependence profile." It is an uncommon individual who abuses only a single drug. An abuser of heroin will also frequently smoke marijuana and tobacco, drink alcohol, or dabble in any of a variety of available street drugs. These individuals, referred to as *polydrug abusers*, benefit most from a treatment program that acknowledges the fact that more than one form of drug dependence exists at the same time. In such cases, the most effective program is one that addresses a host of *multiple substance abuse* problems. For these reasons, as we review approaches toward tertiary prevention in this chapter, keep in mind that the term *drug abuse* is meant to include the possible abuse of a wide range of substances.

Inevitably, success in drug-abuse treatment rests upon the recognition that there are multiple pathways to drug abuse and dependence. For each individual, there is a specific combination of biological, psychological, and social factors that has played a role in getting that person to the point at which treatment is necessary. This integrated approach to treatment has often been called the **biopsychosocial model** (Figure 17.1). Unfortunately, in the history of drug-abuse treatment in the United States over the years, there has too often been a tendency to view the problems of drug abuse, particularly illicit drug abuse, through a limited perspective. The next section reviews the issues related to law enforcement and punishment.

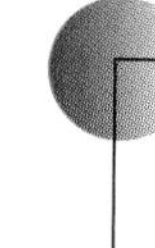

Incarceration and Other Punitive Measures in the United States

A natural response to the presence of an individual whose behavior poses a significant threat to society is to remove that individual from society and provide some form of containment or **incarceration** in a prison, jail, or other secure environment. Besides protecting society at large, incarceration is intended to be preventive in the long run by (1) reducing the likelihood that the individual will behave in a similar way in the future, after

biopsychosocial model: A perspective on drug-abuse treatment that recognizes the biological, psychological, and social factors underlying drug-taking behavior and encourages an integrated approach, based upon these factors, in designing an individual's treatment program.
incarceration: Imprisonment for a fixed length of time.

the sentence is completed, and (2) conveying the message to others who might contemplate engaging in similar behavior that a comparable punishment would apply to them as well. The first goal is referred to as **rehabilitation**; the second goal is referred to as **deterrence.**

Prevention through Law Enforcement

Drug-control laws in general have been formulated over the years according to the philosophy that punitive measures such as incarceration or financial penalties (fines) lead to rehabilitation on a personal level and deterrence on a societal level. The five categories or schedules of controlled substances, adopted by the Comprehensive Drug Abuse Prevention and Control Act of 1970, were designed not only to set up limitations in public access to different types of drugs but also to establish different levels of criminal penalties for unauthorized behavior related to these drugs, based on their potential for abuse.

Specifically, the law defined **drug trafficking** as the unauthorized manufacture, distribution by sale or gift, or possession with intent to distribute any controlled substance (Table 17.1). The severity of the penalties that were established by federal laws enacted in 1970, and revised in 1986 and 1988, has varied according to the schedule of the controlled substance involved, with Schedule I violations being the most severely punished and Schedule V violations being the least. As a result of the Anti–Drug-Abuse Acts of 1986 and 1988, a number of special circumstances also are considered in arriving at the penalty imposed:

- Penalties are doubled for first-offense trafficking of Schedule I or II controlled substances if death or bodily injury results from the use of such substances.
- Penalties for the sale of drugs by a person over twenty-one years old to someone under the age of eighteen are increased to up to double those imposed for sale to an adult.
- Penalties for the sale of drugs within 1,000 feet of an elementary or secondary school are increased to up to double those imposed when the sale is made elsewhere.
- Fines for companies or business associations are generally 2½ times greater than for individuals. In either case, penalties include the forfeiture of cars, boats, or planes that have been used in the illegal conveyance of controlled substances.
- If a family is living in public housing, the entire family can be evicted if a family member is convicted of criminal activity, including drug trafficking, on or near the public-housing premises.

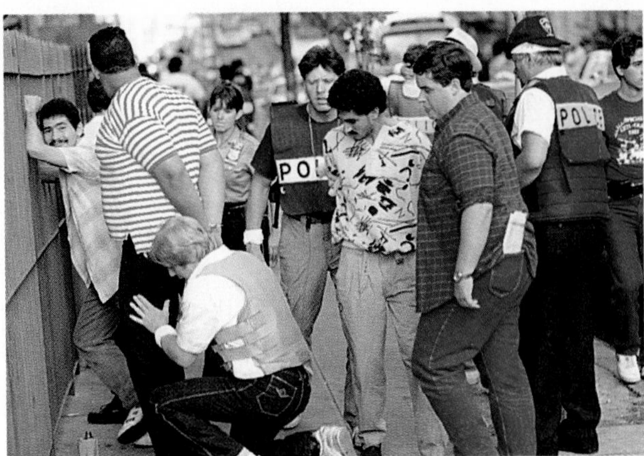

Police officers arrest drug offenders in a drug bust.

Federal penalties for **simple possession,** defined as having on one's person any illegal or nonprescribed controlled substance in *any* of the five schedules for one's own use, are much simpler. First-offense violators face a maximum of one year imprisonment and a fine of between $1,000 and $5,000. Second-offense violators face a minimum of fifteen days up to a maximum of two years and a fine of up to $10,000.[3] Notice that, in terms of federal penalties for simple possession, an unprescribed Valium tablet (a Schedule IV drug) is considered equivalent to a vial of crack cocaine (a Schedule I drug) (Drugs . . . in Focus).

Federal penalties set the standard for the punishment of drug offenses in the United States, but most drug-related offenses are prosecuted at the state rather than the federal level, and state regulations for simple possession and drug trafficking can vary widely. In cases of simple possession of small amounts of marijuana, some U.S. states might be more lenient (see Chapter 7), whereas in cases of heroin possession some states might be more

rehabilitation: A process of change through which there is a reduced likelihood that a pattern of problematic behavior will recur.
deterrence: The reduced likelihood that a person might engage in a pattern of problematic behavior in the future.
drug trafficking: The unauthorized manufacture, distribution by sale or gift, or possession with intent to distribute any controlled substance.
simple possession: Having on one's person any illegal or nonprescribed controlled substance for one's own use.

TABLE 17.1

Current federal penalties for drug trafficking, according to each of five controlled substance schedules (CSS)

CSS	2ND OFFENSE PENALTY	1ST OFFENSE PENALTY	QUANTITY	DRUG	QUANTITY	1ST OFFENSE PENALTY	2ND OFFENSE PENALTY
I and II	Not less than 10 years. Not more than life. If death or serious injury, not less than life. Fine of not more than $4 million individual, $10 million other than individual.	Not less than 5 years. Not more than 40 years. If death or serious injury, not less than 20 years. Not more than life. Fine of not more than $2 million individual, $5 million other than individual.	10–99 gm or 100–999 gm mixture	METHAMPHETAMINE	100 gm or more or 1 kg[a] or more mixture	Not less than 10 years. Not more than life. If death or serious injury, not less than 20 years. Not more than life. Fine of not more than $4 million individual, $10 million other than individual.	Not less than 20 years. Not more than life. If death or serious injury, not less than life. Fine of not more than $8 million individual, $20 million other than individual.
			100–999 gm mixture	HEROIN	1 kg or more mixture		
			500–4,999 gm mixture	COCAINE	5 kg or more mixture		
			5–49 gm mixture	COCAINE BASE	50 gm or more mixture		
			10–99 gm or 100–999 gm mixture	PCP	100 gm or more or 1 kg or more mixture		
			1–10 gm mixture	LSD	10 gm or more mixture		
			40–399 gm mixture	FENTANYL	400 gm or more mixture		
			10–99 gm mixture	FENTANYL ANALOGUE	100 gm or more mixture		

CSS	DRUG	QUANTITY	1ST OFFENSE PENALTY	2ND OFFENSE PENALTY
	Others[b]	Any	Not more than 20 years. If death or serious injury, not less than 20 years, not more than life. Fine $1 million individual, $5 million not individual.	Not more than 30 years. If death or serious injury, life. Fine $2 million individual, $10 million not individual.
III	All	Any	Not more than 5 years. Fine not more than $250,000 individual, $1 million not individual.	Not more than 10 years. Fine not more than $500,000 individual, $2 million not individual.
IV	All	Any	Not more than 3 years. Fine not more than $250,000 individual, $1 million not individual.	Not more than 6 years. Fine not more than $500,000 individual, $2 million not individual.
V	All	Any	Not more than 1 year. Fine not more than $100,000 individual, $250,000 not individual.	Not more than 2 years. Fine not more than $200,000 individual, $500,000 not individual.

[a]Law as originally enacted states 100 gm. Congress requested technical correction to 1 kg.

[b]Does not include marijuana, hashish, or hash oil.

Note: Trafficking penalties distinguish between Schedule I drugs excluding marijuana (above) and marijuana itself (page 351).

(Continued)

TABLE 17.1 *(Continued)*

Current federal penalties for drug trafficking, according to each of five controlled substance schedules (CSS)

QUANTITY	DESCRIPTION	1ST OFFENSE	2ND OFFENSE
1,000 kg or more; or 1,000 or more plants	Marijuana Mixture containing detectable quantity[c]	Not less than 10 years, not more than life. If death or serious injury, not less than 20 years, not more than life. Fine not more than $4 million individual, $10 million other than individual.	Not less than 20 years, not more than life. If death or serious injury, not less than life. Fine not more than $8 million individual, $20 million other than individual.
100 kg to 1,000 kg; or 100–999 plants	Marijuana Mixture containing detectable quantity[c]	Not less than 5 years, not more than 40 years. If death or serious injury, not less than 20 years, not more than life. Fine not more than $2 million individual, $5 million other than individual.	Not less than 10 years, not more than life. If death or serious injury, not less than life. Fine not more than $4 million individual, $10 million other than individual.
50 to 100 kg	Marijuana	Not more than 20 years. If death or serious injury, not less than 20 years, not more than life. Fine $1 million individual, $5 million other than individual.	Not more than 30 years. If death or serious injury, life. Fine $2 million individual, $10 million other than individual.
10 to 100 kg	Hashish		
1 to 100 kg	Hashish Oil		
50–99 plants	Marijuana	Not more than 5 years. Fine not more than $250,000, $1 million other than individual.	Not more than 10 years. Fine $500,000 individual, $2 million other than individual.
Less than 50 kg	Marijuana		
Less than 10 kg	Hashish		
Less than 1 kg	Hashish Oil		

[c]Includes hashish and hashish oil.

Source: Drug Enforcement Administration, U.S. Department of Justice.

stringent. Certain aspects of drug-taking behavior, such as the day-to-day regulation of alcohol sales and distribution, are regulated primarily by state and local municipalities, unless interstate commerce is involved. States and local municipalities have also taken on regulatory authority with regard to **drug paraphernalia,** products whose predominant use is to administer, prepare, package, or store illicit drugs (Table 17.2). Nearly all U.S. states have statutes making it unlawful to sell these items to minors, unless they are accompanied by a parent or legal guardian. In addition, the importation, exportation, and advertising of drug paraphernalia are prohibited.[4]

A look at the inmate population at federal and state levels gives us an idea of how drug enforcement responsibilities in the United States have been distributed. Drug-related offenses represent the reason for the incarceration of approximately 60 percent of all inmates in federal prisons. In fact, about three-fourths of the total growth in the federal prison population since 1980 can be accounted for by the increase in the number of drug offenders sentenced under the anti–drug-abuse laws.

Yet it is more likely that a drug offender is serving his or her time in a state prison because state inmates in general outnumber federal inmates by more than ten to one. Drug offenses represent no more than 20 percent of the sentences among inmates in state prisons, but the larger state inmate population as a whole more than compensates for the lower percentage. The bottom line is this: Of every five drug offenders presently incarcerated, four are in a state prison and one is in a federal prison.[5]

What happens to these people who are arrested and convicted of drug-law violations? Does the criminal justice

drug paraphernalia: Products that are considered to be used to administer, prepare, package, or store illicit drugs.

DRUGS . . . IN FOCUS

Penalties for Crack versus Penalties for Cocaine: A Racial Disparity?

You may have noticed in Table 17.1 the distinction between penalties for cocaine itself (the powdered form) and those for cocaine base (crack) under the 1986 Anti-Drug-Abuse Act. Though the effects of both drugs are very similar, a mandatory minimum prison sentence of five years is imposed upon conviction of possessing more than 500 grams of powder forms of cocaine, whereas the possession of as little as 5 grams of crack can result in the same penalty. In 1988, federal penalties for possession of more than 5 grams of cocaine powder was set at a minimum of one year in prison; the penalty for possessing an equivalent amount of crack was set at a minimum of five years.

This disparity, according to critics of this policy, has resulted in far more African Americans in prison for five years or more than white drug offenders. Why? Statistics show that whites are more likely to snort or inject cocaine, whereas African Americans are more likely to smoke cocaine in its cheaper crack form. The differential effects of drug law enforcement for the two forms of cocaine are reflected in a drug-offense inmate population that is currently divided along racial lines. On the one hand, 90 percent of crack cocaine convictions involve African Americans; on the other, nearly two-thirds of powder cocaine abusers in the United States are white. Moreover, it is more common for offenses relating to the possession of powder cocaine to be prosecuted under state regulations, under which mandatory minimum sentences frequently do not apply.

Recently, federal officials have recommended a smaller gap between the two circumstances. One proposal is to raise the five-year sentence threshold in crack cases from 5 grams to somewhere between 25 and 75 grams and lower the threshold for powder cocaine cases from 500 grams down to somewhere between 125 and 375 grams. The gap would still remain, but the disparity would be far less than is presently in force.

Sources: Hatsukami, Dorothy K., and Fischman, Marian W. (1996). Crack cocaine and cocaine hydrochloride: Are the differences myth or reality? *Journal of the American Medical Association, 276,* 1580–1588. Wren, Christopher S. (1997, July 22). Reno and top drug official urge smaller gap in cocaine sentences. *New York Times,* pp. A1, A12.

---

system provide a deterrent against drug abuse by others in society? We will defer an examination of this question to the discussion of primary and secondary prevention in Chapter 18. A more immediate question at this point is whether the criminal justice system offers any opportunities for rehabilitation.

TABLE 17.2

A partial list of items classified as drug paraphernalia
roach clips
pipe/bowl screens
smoking papers
rolling machines
bongs and water pipes
bowl loaders
stash cleaners and containers
snorters
drying devices
conversion/purification kits
crack kits
free-basing kits
diluents and adulterants designed for "cutting" controlled substances
miniature spoons and straws

Source: Healey, Kerry (1988). *State and local experience with drug paraphernalia.* Washington DC: U.S. Government Printing Office.

Prison-Alternative and Prison-Based Treatment Programs

A large number of drug offenders who could potentially be incarcerated are instead offered treatment as an alternative to imprisonment or other punitive measures. Approximately 50 percent of all individuals who enter a publicly funded drug treatment program have done so because of direct or indirect legal pressure. Since the late 1980s, it has been common for arrestees demonstrating drug dependence to be "steered" toward drug treatment as a condition for having prosecution postponed, a prison sentence reduced or avoided, or some form of probationary status approved.

If a person chooses the treatment option, he or she is expected to be accountable for entering and remaining in the treatment program. A probationary officer or other authority acts as a supervisor, and typically a series of negative (clean) urinalysis tests for drugs (Chapter 8) is used to track a person's compliance. In many cases, a therapeutic community (TC) approach, such as Daytop Village, Samaritan Village, or a similar organization (Portrait), is chosen

Portrait Monsignor William O'Brien—Founder of Daytop Village

In 1957, Monsignor William O'Brien was a simple parish priest in Tuckahoe, New York, a quiet suburban town north of New York City. He was quite unprepared for the gritty facts of life on urban streets when he was assigned to serve at St. Patrick's Cathedral in the center of Manhattan. For the first time, he came face to face with the desperate and the despondent victims of drug abuse. Both crushed and touched, he wanted to help them as a priest and counselor, but he soon discovered how difficult such cases can be. In his own words,

> *I reached out for two years to help drug addicts and I was the biggest disaster in New York. Because it's just the thing you can't do with alcoholics and drug addicts. They'd go in the parish house bathroom and shoot up behind your back. . . . I discovered a hard discovery. I first had to deal with the human before I could go to the divine. Otherwise, I was building a house on sand.*

In 1963, Monsignor O'Brien helped establish a small center in New York, based on a then-unique concept of drug treatment intervention: an intensive, therapeutic community where drug-dependent people could relearn how to live their lives, could move toward a drug-free way of thinking. The center was called Daytop (short for Drug Addicts Yielding to Persuasion) Village, and it was the beginning of what is today the oldest and largest drug-free, therapeutic community program for AOD (alcohol and other drugs) dependence in the United States. Since the 1980s, Daytop Village has expanded beyond its twenty-nine centers in this country to more than sixty-six international locations around the world.

Monsignor William O'Brien

More than 93,000 individuals have participated in Daytop, and the overwhelming majority of them have reclaimed their lives as a result of its programs. As a reflection of the growing levels of drug use among young people in the 1990s, it is not surprising that teenagers, once comprising scarcely 25 percent of the Daytop client population, now represent half the total. Referrals to Daytop increase steadily and an extensive waiting list for new entrants has no end. Monsignor O'Brien continues to direct Daytop Village through its expansion. He also continues, in the face of budgetary cutbacks at the federal and state levels, to be an eloquent spokesman for therapeutic communities, and AOD treatment in general, as a strategic weapon in our society's ongoing war on drugs.

Sources: Marriot, Michel (1989, November 13). A pioneer in residential drug treatment reaches out. *New York Times*, p. B2. Nieves, Evelyn (1996, August 25). Wresting a life from the grip of addiction. *New York Times*, p. 41. O'Brien, William B., and Henican, Ellis (1993). *You can't do it alone*. New York: Simon and Schuster. Daytop Village, Inc., New York, New York, 1997.

as an option to prison. TC programs for heroin abuse were described in Chapter 5, but their usefulness has been demonstrated for drug abuse in general.[6]

It may not be surprising that a person entering a treatment program as a result of legal pressure is as likely to succeed, and sometimes is more likely to succeed, than a person entering on a volunteer basis. A volunteer always has the freedom to drop out. Indeed, drug researchers claim that one of the greatest obstacles to rehabilitation is the temptation to quit the program. Obviously, when the alternative is prison or continued prosecution for drug violations, the incentive to complete the treatment is quite powerful. As one counselor has observed, "Those who have a lot to lose are on the whole better candidates for treatment success."[7]

For those who *are* sentenced to prison, a previous history of drug abuse or dependence continues to present difficulties that do not go away just because the inmate is now behind bars. A substantial percentage of male arrestees test positive for one or more illicit drugs at the time of arrest, regardless of the reason for their arrest. It has been estimated that, of the approximately 1.1 million inmates in U.S. federal and state prisons, one-half have been regular users of controlled substances.

Since the mid-1980s, the Stay'n Out program has become a model for the application of therapeutic community principles (similar to those of Daytop Village or Samaritan Village) to a correctional setting. Established as a separate unit within the prison, Stay'n Out makes use of group and individual counseling sessions that help inmates explore issues of personal development. It is a demanding experience, and many inmates choose to return to traditional prison cells after only a few weeks. Nonetheless, for those individuals spending nine to twelve months in the program, fewer than 23 percent have been found to have violated parole or returned to prison in the three years after release. This figure should be compared to more than 50 percent who would have done so if no treatment had been provided or if standard counseling had been offered.

Other treatment programs modeled after Stay'n Out have shown a comparable level of effectiveness. Unfortunately, however, it has been estimated that less than

20 percent of prisoners with drug abuse problems in the United States receive any kind of treatment program while incarcerated. The potential for prison-based rehabilitation is there, but the resources available for effective interventions are currently far from adequate.[8]

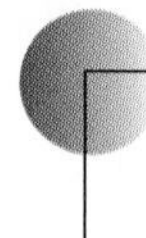

Prevention and Treatment in the Workplace

The workplace has been recognized as an important focus for drug prevention and treatment. The 1988 Drug-free Workplace Act requires that all companies and businesses receiving any U.S. federal contracts or grants provide a drug-free workplace. Specifically, organizations must initiate a comprehensive and continuing program of drug education and awareness. Employees must also be notified that the distribution, possession, or unauthorized use of controlled substances is prohibited in that workplace and that actions will be taken against any employee violating these rules. Supervisors are advised to be especially alert to changes in a worker that might signal early or progressive stages in the abuse of alcohol and or other drugs. These signals include chronic absenteeism, a sudden change in physical appearance or behavior, spasmodic work pace, unexpectedly lower quantity or quality of work, partial or unexplained absences, a pattern of excuse-making or lying, the avoidance of supervisors or coworkers, and on-the-job accidents or lost time from such accidents.[9]

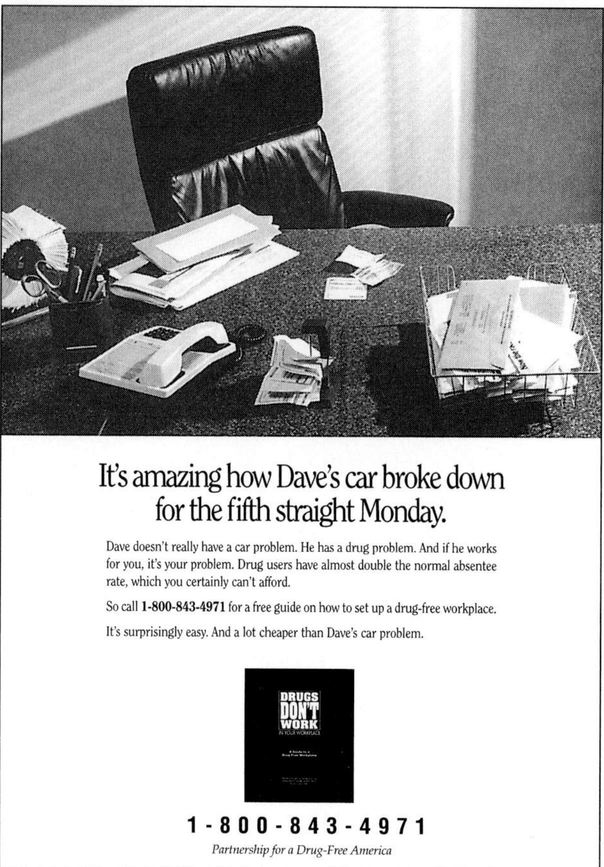

Drug problems are major sources of worker absenteeism and decreased productivity.

Employee Assistance Programs

By executive order of President Reagan in 1986, all U.S. federal agencies were directed to establish an employee assistance program (EAP) for governmental employees. Nongovernmental organizations have since been encouraged (but not required) by the 1988 Act to establish EAP services as well, so as to identify and counsel employees with personal problems that are connected to drug abuse or dependence and to provide referrals to community agencies where these individuals can get further help. Though not technically required to do so, steadily increasing numbers of American businesses have set up EAPs and are becoming committed to prevention and treatment. By the mid-1990s, approximately half of all private nonagricultural worksites with fifty or more full-time employees had ongoing EAP services. Traditionally, the emphasis in EAPs has been on problems resulting from alcohol abuse, understandable given that this category represents such a large proportion of drug abuse in general (Chapter 10). This emphasis remains, but there is a growing awareness that the range of drug abuse problems is wider than alcoholism.[10]

Drug Testing in the Workplace

The 1986 Executive Order also mandated preemployment drug screening of all federal employees as well as periodic, random schedules of drug testing afterward. Assuming the most commonly available EMIT urinalysis were used (see Chapter 8), drug testing refers to a screening for opiates, amphetamines, cocaine, benzodiazepines, and marijuana. (It is not known whether the president at the time or subsequent presidents since 1986 have been included in this requirement.)

As with the policy regarding EAPs under the 1988 Drug-free Workplace Act, statutes do not require drug testing for employees other than those working for the federal government. Nonetheless, as of 1996, according to a survey conducted by the American Management Association, seven out of every eight American companies, whether they are covered by the 1988 act or not, have established policies for drug testing procedures either as part of the job application process or as a way of monitoring drug use among employees on a periodic basis.[11]

While it is easy to understand the rationale for drug testing in the workplace in the overall scheme of drug prevention, the procedure has raised a number of important issues regarding individual rights. Is the taking of a urine sample a violation of a person's freedom from "unreasonable search and seizure" as guaranteed by the Fourth Amendment to the U.S. Constitution? It turns out that if the government requires it, the decision rests on the question of whether there is reasonable or unreasonable cause for the drug testing to occur. In cases in which a threat to public safety is involved, the cause has been ruled as reasonable. However, if a private business requires it, the legal rights of employees are somewhat murky. An employee typically accepts his or her job offer with the assumption and agreement that periodic monitoring of drug use will take place, but whether this understanding is a form of implied coercion is an open question.

If you lose your job as a result of testing positive in a drug test, has there been a violation of your right to "due process" as guaranteed by the Fifth Amendment? The courts have ruled that this right would be violated only if the method of drug screening were unreliable, if the analysis and reporting were carried out in an unreliable manner, or if it could not be shown that the presence of any one of the screened substances had a relationship to job impairment. In general, screening methods are not perfectly reliable, the handling of drug tests is not perfectly controlled, and the relationship between drug use and a decline in job performance is not perfectly clear, but drug tests have nonetheless been judged to have met reasonable standards and the practice is allowed. The bottom line is that drug testing, despite its obvious infringements on individual privacy, has become a fact of life in corporate America.[12]

Nonetheless, despite the increasing acceptance of drug testing as a tool for drug-abuse prevention in the workplace, there will always be questions about the impact on workers themselves. For example, the possibility of false positives (when an individual tests positive but has not been using a particular drug) or false negatives (when an individual who, on the basis of prior drug use, should test positive for a particular drug, does not do so) during drug testing can present unfortunate consequences. Consider this possible preemployment screening scenario:

> *Suppose that the EMIT test were 100 percent effective in spotting drug users (it is not) and that it has a false-positive rate of 3 percent (which is not unreasonable). In a group of 100 prospective employees, one person has recently taken an illegal drug. Since the test is 100 percent effective, that person will be caught, but three other people (the 3 percent false-positive rate) will also. Therefore, 75 percent of those who fail the test are innocent parties.*[13]

Another problem is that companies are not required to follow up a positive EMIT test result with another more sensitive method, such as one using the GC/MS procedure (Chapter 8). Some companies allow for retesting in general, but most do not. In the American Management Association survey mentioned earlier, 22 percent of the companies reported that workers who tested positive were immediately dismissed from their positions.[14]

The Prevalence and Economic Costs of Alcohol and Other Drug Abuse in the Workplace

When considering the scope of drug-abuse problems in the workplace, it is all too easy to look at high-profile instances of on-the-job accidents involving the effects of either illicit drugs or alcohol. In 1991, a New York subway operator crashed his train near a station in lower Manhattan, resulting in five deaths and 215 injuries. The operator admitted that he had been drinking prior to the crash, and his BAC level was measured at 0.21 percent, more than twice the legal limit of 0.10 percent in New York. In 1987, a Conrail train brakeman and an engineer were found to be responsible for a collision that resulted in sixteen deaths and 170 injuries. Drug testing revealed traces of marijuana in their systems, though it was not clear if they were intoxicated at the time of the accident.

These conspicuous examples do not accurately reflect the impact of alcohol and other drug abuse in the workplace for a number of reasons. First, the likelihood of an adverse effect is not adequately reflected in news reports, any more than the impact of drug toxicity on our society can be assessed by reading the news stories of public figures and celebrities who have died of drug overdoses (Chapter 2). Second, in many cases, we are limited in determining the extent to which we can connect drug use with the tragic consequences of an accident because some drugs leave metabolites in the system long after they have stopped producing behavioral effects. In the case of the Conrail incident, the continued presence of marijuana metabolites for weeks after marijuana use can make the positive test results irrelevant. Nonetheless, we are greatly influenced in our thinking by the media coverage of such events.

Obviously, we must turn to estimates gathered from other sources of information. Unfortunately, these estimates are "soft," having large margins of error. Even so, they leave little doubt that the abuse of alcohol and other drugs has a major impact on workplace productivity. On the basis of its own studies, the federal Center for Substance Abuse Prevention (CSAP) estimates that, relative to nonabusers, abusers of alcohol and other drugs

- are 5 times more likely to file a workers' compensation claim
- are 2.5 times more likely to be absent from work for eight days or more
- are 3.6 times more likely to be involved in an accident on the job
- are 5 times more likely to be personally injured on the job
- are 3 times more likely to be late for work
- are 2.2 times more likely to request early dismissal from work or time off
- use 16 times more sick leave

Overall, the estimated costs of the loss in productivity as a result of such behavior amount to $60–$100 billion each year.[15]

The Impact of Drug-Free Workplace Policies

Given the adverse effects of drug abuse on productivity, we should expect to see substantial economic and personal benefits when drug-free workplace policies are in place. In one well-documented case, a program developed by the Southern Pacific Railroad Company in the 1980s, extensive drug testing was required for all employees who had been involved in a company accident or rule violation. As a result, the annual number of accidents decreased from 911 to 168 in three years and the financial losses from such accidents decreased from $6.4 million to $1.2 million. During the first few months of the new testing program, it was found that 22–24 percent of employees who had had some human-factor-related accident tested positive for alcohol or other drugs, a figure that fell to 3 percent three years later.[16]

It makes sense that drug-abuse prevention programs would have the greatest impact in companies within the transportation industry, owing to the close relationship between drug-induced impairments in performance and the incidence of industrial accidents. Beyond this application, however, it is widely recognized that a similar impact, if not one as dramatic in magnitude, can be demonstrated in any business setting. The reasons relate to the basic goals of prevention, as discussed earlier: deterrence and rehabilitation. The practice of testing for illicit drug use in the workplace functions as an effective deterrent among workers because the likelihood is strong that illicit drug use will be detected. In addition, EAP services can function as an effective rehabilitative tool because those workers who might otherwise not receive help with drug-abuse problems of all kinds now will be referred to appropriate agencies for treatment services.[17]

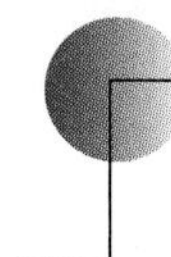

The Personal Journey to Treatment and Recovery

Individuals who seek help in a treatment program have typically been "jolted" by some external force in their lives. They may have no other option except imprisonment for drug offenses; they may be at risk of losing their job because their supervisor has identified an unproductive pattern of behavior; a spouse may have threatened to leave if something is not done; a friend may have died from a drug overdose or a drug-related accident. Any of these crises or others similar to them can force the question and the decision to seek treatment.[18]

The prospect of entering a treatment program is typically the most frightening experience the abuser has ever had in his or her life. Treatment counselors frequently hear the questions, "Couldn't I just cut down?" or "Couldn't I just give up drugs temporarily?" or "How will I be able to take the pain of withdrawal?" or "How will I be able to stand the humiliation?" Far from stalling tactics, these questions represent real obstacles to taking that crucial first step.[19]

Rehabilitation and the Stages of Change

Rehabilitation from drug abuse and dependence has three major goals. First, the long decline in physical and psychological functioning that has accumulated over the years must be reversed. Drugs take a heavy toll on the user's medical condition and his or her personal relationships. Second, the use of all psychoactive substances must stop, not simply the one or two that are causing the immediate problem and not merely for a limited period of time. Thus the motivation to stop using alcohol and other drugs and to remain abstinent on a permanent basis must be strong, and stay strong. Third, a life-style free of alcohol and other drugs must be rebuilt, from scratch if necessary. This frequently means giving up the old friends and the old places where drugs

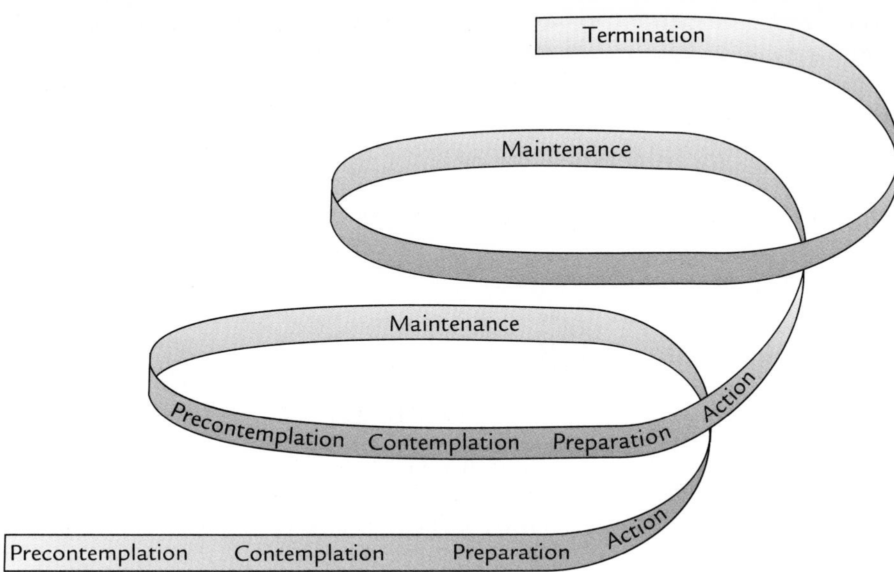

FIGURE 17.2

A spiral model of the stages of change in the recovery from drug abuse and dependence.
Source: Prochaska, James O., DiClemente, Carlo C., and Norcross, John C. (1992). In search of how people change: Applications to addictive behaviors. *American Psychologist, 47,* p. 1104. Copyright © 1992 by the American Psychological Association. Adapted with permission.

were part of an abuser's life, and finding new friends and places that reinforce a drug-free existence. A determination to stay clean and sober requires avoiding high-risk situations, defined as those that increase the possibility of relapse.[20]

We can understand the journey toward rehabilitation by examining five separate stages through which the recovering individual must pass.[21] These stages are (1) precontemplation, (2) contemplation, (3) preparation, (4) action, and (5) maintenance. Rather than thinking of these stages as a linear progression, however, it is more accurate to think of them as points along a spiral (Figure 17.2); more than likely, a person will recycle through the stages multiple times before he or she is totally rehabilitated. Unfortunately, relapse is the rule rather than the exception in the process of recovery. The following is an examination of each stage in detail.

- *Precontemplation.* Individuals who are in the **precontemplation stage** may *wish* to change but lack the serious intention to undergo change in the foreseeable future or may be unaware of how significant their problems have become. They may be entering treatment at this time only because they perceive that a crisis is at hand. They may even demonstrate a change in behavior while the pressure is on, but once the pressure is off, they revert to their former ways. It is often difficult for a counselor to deal with a drug abuser during the precontemplation stage because the abuser still feels committed to positive aspects of drug use. A principal goal at this point is to induce inconsistencies in the abuser's perception of drugs in general.
- *Contemplation.* In the **contemplation stage,** individuals are aware that a problem exists and are thinking about overcoming it but have not yet made a commitment to take action. At this point, drug abusers may struggle with the prospect of the tremendous amount of effort and energy needed to overcome the problem. Counselors can help them by highlighting the negative aspects of drug use, making reasonable assurances about the recovery process, and building the self-confidence necessary to change.
- *Preparation.* Individuals in the **preparation stage** are defined as those who are seriously considering taking action in the next thirty days and have unsuccessfully taken action over the past twelve months. Alcohol abusers or tobacco smokers may at this point set a "quit

precontemplation stage: A stage of change in which the individual may wish to change but either lacks the serious intention to undergo change in the foreseeable future or is unaware of how significant his or her problem has become.
contemplation stage: A stage of change in which the individual is aware that a problem exists and is thinking about overcoming it but has not yet made a commitment to take action.
preparation stage: A stage of change in which the individual seriously considers taking action to overcome a problem in the next thirty days and has unsuccessfully taken action over the past twelve months.

date," or a heroin abuser may make a firm date to enter a therapeutic community within the next month. Because drug abusers are fully capable of stating a clear commitment to change at the preparation stage, counselors can begin to discuss the specific steps in the recovery process, strategies for avoiding problems or postponements, and ways to involve friends and family members.

- *Action.* The **action stage** is the point at which individuals actually modify their behavior, their experiences, and their environment in order to overcome their problem. Drug use has now stopped. This is the most fragile stage; abusers are at a high risk for giving in to drug cravings and experiencing mixed feelings about the psychological costs of staying clean. If they successfully resist these urges to return to drug use, the counselor should strongly reinforce their restraint. If they slip back to drug use temporarily then return to abstinence, the counselor should praise their efforts to turn their life around. An important message to be conveyed at this stage is that a fundamental change in life-style and a strong support system of friends and family will reduce the chances of relapse.
- *Maintenance stage.* Individuals in the **maintenance stage** have been drug free for a minimum of six months. They have developed new skills and strategies to avoid backsliding and are consolidating a life-style free of drugs. Here, the counselor must simultaneously acknowledge the success that has been achieved and emphasize that the struggle will never be totally over. The maintenance stage is ultimately open-ended, in that it continues for the rest of the ex-user's life. Therefore, it may be necessary to have booster sessions from time to time, so that the maintenance stage is itself maintained.

QUICK CONCEPT  17.2

Understanding the Stages of Change

Check your understanding of the stages of change by matching each quotation, on the left, with the appropriate stage in treatment, on the right. Quotations are assumed to be statements made by a drug abuser at a particular point in the process of treatment and recovery.

1. "Yeah, I know I drink too much but I'm not ready to do something about it yet."
2. "I may need a boost right now to help me hold on to the changes I've made. It's been nearly two years since I used drugs."
3. "I don't have any big problems. I have a right to do whatever I want."
4. "Although I like snorting coke, it might be time to quit."
5. "It's New Year's Eve and I've set two weeks from now as the day I'm quitting. I want everyone to know that."
6. "It's been six weeks since I smoked a joint, and I can tell already how different things seem to be."

a. precontemplation stage
b. contemplation stage
c. preparation stage
d. action stage
e. maintenance stage

Answers: 1. b 2. e 3. a 4. b 5. c 6. d

Stages of Change and Other Problems in Life

If these stages of change seem vaguely familiar to you, with or without a drug-related problem, it is no accident. Problems may take many different forms, but the difficulties that we face when we confront these problems have a great deal in common. We may wish to lose weight, get more exercise, stop smoking, end an unhappy relationship, seek out a physician to help a medical condition, or any of a number of actions that might lead toward a healthier and more productive life. We only have to witness the popularity of New Year's Eve resolutions to appreciate the fact that our desire to take steps to change is part of simply being human. And yet, we often feel frustrated when our intentions do not prevail, and those resolutions are left unfulfilled. You may find it helpful to look at your own personal journey toward resolving a problem in your life in terms of the five stages of change.[22]

action stage: A stage of change in which the individual actually modifies his or her behavior and environment in order to overcome a problem.

maintenance stage: A stage of change in which the individual has become drug free for a minimum of six months and has developed new skills and strategies that reduce the probability of relapse.

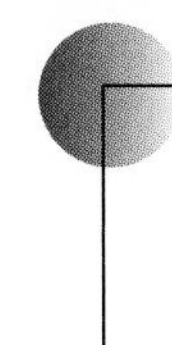

The Importance of Family Systems in Prevention and Treatment

Family members of a drug abuser can be highly resistant to becoming involved in the treatment process, often abdicating any responsibility for the problems that abuse has produced. Their embarrassment, shame, and personal feelings of inadequacy in the face of the abuser's drug-dominated life-style are overwhelming. Resistance to change may also come from a family's assumption that they must assume the responsibility when the drug abuser has not. This second scenario results in a pattern of enabling behavior.

Family Dynamics in Drug Abuse

Learning how the family has coped with having a drug abuser as a family member is crucial not only in understanding the origins of the abuse but also in maximizing the chances of successful treatment (Health Alert). A prominent therapist and author has put it this way:

> *The individuals in this (family) system are all compensating in different yet similar ways. It's as if they were walking around with a heavy weight on one's shoulder; they either have to lean to one side to walk properly or use all their energy to try to compensate and look like they are walking upright. Both positions require a great deal of energy.*[23]

The pattern of family reactions to the conditions of drug abuse in many ways resembles the stages people go through when grieving the loss of a loved one.

- *Denial.* Feelings of denial help family members avoid feelings of humiliation and shame, not to mention their own sense of responsibility. They might rationalize that their family is no different from most others. If they talk with people outside the family system, it is typically done to reinforce their denial. They want assurance that their denial of problems is not a delusion.
- *Anger.* Expressed verbally or physically, anger is a strategy for avoiding feelings of shame by blaming others in the family for the problem. Causing a fight at home is sometimes a way for the abuser to get out of the house and to escape to a place where the abuse of alcohol or other drugs is more easily tolerated. Needless to say, the pattern of family interaction is confused and unpredictable.

Health Alert

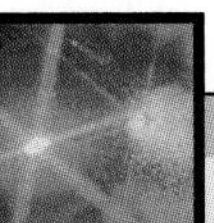

Coping with a Child's Abuse of Alcohol or Other Drugs: What Parents Should and Should Not Do

The negative impact of enabling behaviors on anyone's path to recovery is particularly evident in the interactions between a parent and a child. Beyond simply recognizing the process of enabling, parents (and other family members as well) should learn the skills necessary to "disenable" or disengage from the ongoing abuse. It is a critical step to take in order to establish a family climate in which treatment and rehabilitation can advance. Here are some guidelines:

You Should Avoid

feeling hurt or guilty when your child turns his or her anger on you

nagging your child about the destructive effects of drug abuse; it will only provoke your child to continue the abusive behavior in a more surreptitious way

hiding your child's abuse from other family members or friends or making excuses to them about your child's behavior

making threats you neither mean nor can effectively enforce

You Should Never

confront your child when you are angry

use physical or verbal abuse toward your child

be the janitor for your child's messes by paying fines, repairing property damage, and so on

You Should

remember that your responsibility lies in helping your son or daughter recover from a sickness

Source: Schaefer, Dick (1987). *Choices and consequences: What to do when a teenager uses alcohol/drugs.* Minneapolis MN: Johnson Institute Books, pp. 82–84.

Treatment for drug-related problems is optimized when there is positive involvement from the family.

- *Bargaining.* When a major crisis ensues, family members can no longer deny the problem or react in anger. Implicit agreements are made that if a pattern of drug abuse will stop, the family will respond in a positive way. Conversely, a bargain might be struck that if the family tolerates the continuation of drug abuse, then the abuser will continue to support the family financially.
- *Feeling.* Earlier reactions, now exhausted, are replaced by a pervasive anxiety and obsessiveness toward the entire situation. Family members may cry at the slightest provocation or find themselves immobilized in carrying out their daily lives.
- *Acceptance.* Denial, anger, and bargaining have failed, and feelings have become too disruptive. The family is forced to seek help; they realize that they have a problem, and they are ready to do whatever is necessary to overcome or resolve it. It is at this point that the contemplation and preparation stages of change begin.[24]

Enabling Behaviors as Obstacles to Rehabilitation

The adverse impact of enabling on the life of an alcoholic was discussed in Chapter 10, but it should be evident that applications hold for all forms of drug abuse. In general, enablers take on themselves the responsibility that has been rejected by someone else. In effect, they try to cushion the consequences that inevitably occur as a result of that other person's irresponsibility. This pattern of behavior can take several forms.[25]

- *Avoiding and shielding.* Enablers make up excuses to avoid social situations where drug abuse is going on and keep up appearances when among friends or neighbors. They may stay away from home as much as they can in order to avoid dealing with the family situation.
- *Attempting to control.* Enablers might buy gifts in an attempt to divert the abuser from dealing with his or her problems. They might threaten to injure themselves in an attempt to get the family member to stop.
- *Taking over responsibilities.* Enablers might assume the responsibility of waking the abuser of alcohol or other drugs in time for work in the morning. They might take second jobs to cover the bills that have piled up because money has been squandered on alcohol and other drugs.
- *Rationalizing and accepting.* Enablers might communicate the belief that the episodes of drug abuse were only isolated and sporadic, that family members were not *really* endangered, or that there was a positive side to the drug-taking behavior, such as the relief of depression or anxiety.
- *Cooperation and collaborating.* At an extreme level, enablers might facilitate the process of drug abuse by helping to clean and purify drugs, drinking along with an alcoholic, or loaning money to purchase street drugs or alcohol so that stealing money is not necessary.

Survival Roles and Coping Mechanisms

The problems of growing up in a dysfunctional family system were examined in Chapter 10 in the case of children of alcoholic parents. Not surprisingly, the interpersonal problems within the family unit are similar for any situation in which drug abuse or dependence is involved. Sharon Wegscheider-Cruse has been an influential theorist in pointing out specific ways of coping with this difficult circumstance. In her view, there are five basic roles that a family member may assume. While each of these roles eventually works to the detriment of the individual, understanding them helps the family during the process of counseling and facilitates the eventual reconstruction of family relationships.[26]

- *Chief Enabler.* In this role, the chief enabler takes on the principal responsibility for the family member involved in alcohol or other drug abuse. These responsibilities include shielding and denying the extent of dysfunctionality in the family, controlling the abuser's life, and rationalizing the negative effects on others in the family.

- *Family Hero.* As a compensation for the failures of the family, the family hero will strive to be the model child, escaping the dysfunctional system through personal achievement. This individual will be outwardly successful but feel like an overachiever and a fraud, undeserving of success and happiness.
- *Family Scapegoat.* This is an effort to divert attention away from real problems within the family through antisocial behavior. The family scapegoat role often results in delinquency in school and elsewhere.
- *The Lost Child.* This is a role that is intended to reduce the pain and suffering within the family, by isolating oneself from family dynamics and denying one's own feelings and needs. Often, the lost child "fades into the woodwork," becoming disconnected emotionally and physically from the family.
- *Family Mascot.* Through humor and self-disparaging behavior, the family mascot strives to divert attention away from the dysfunctionality of the family. As a result, however, the price paid for calm and emotional relief is a lack of maturity and a diminished sense of personal self-esteem.

Resistance at the Beginning, Support along the Way

Given the variety of possible dysfunctional interactions within the family, it is not surprising that it is difficult to get a person to seek help in a meaningful way. Abusers might feel protective of their families, not wishing to add more pain and anguish to what they have already suffered. For their part, families might reinforce these protective feelings by being appreciative that the abuser is thinking of them. Abusers might feel that involving the family in treatment may uncover their own communication of inaccurate or distorted information to the counselor. There is also the fear that if counselors criticize family members for sharing the responsibility for drug abuse, family members might later retaliate by making domestic life even worse than it is.[27]

Whatever the difficulties in family dynamics at the onset of treatment, there is no doubt that family support is crucial as treatment progresses. Counselors frequently emphasize that family members and friends should not feel the burden of responsibility for the problem itself, nor are they responsible for the abuser's decision to enter (or reject) treatment. Instead, their responsibility is to support the abuser along the way to recovery by changing as well. In the case of alcoholism, the establishment of sobriety does not always ensure a smooth, placid relationship within the family. As a therapist has expressed it, the entire family needs to "reestablish communication, work through old resentments, develop trust, and strive to produce a comfortable and rewarding relationship."[28] A drug-free family is more than a family without drugs in their lives; it is a family that is completely different from what it has been before.

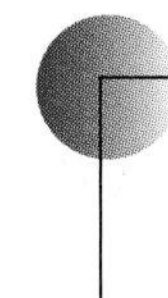

Finding the Right Drug-Abuse Treatment and Prevention Program

Seeking treatment in general may be difficult enough, but there are also the decisions that must be made regarding the type of program that is best suited for a given individual. Health professionals recommend a comprehensive drug-abuse treatment, based upon a combination of therapies and other services that have been tailored to specific needs (Figure 17.3).

Certain general guidelines can help in this process. First, outpatient treatment should be given preference over inpatient; among the advanges, an outpatient approach is less costly and concentrates on the adjustment to a drug-free life in the context of functioning in the "real world." Consider inpatient treatment (1) when outpatient treatment has failed, (2) when medical or psychiatric problems require hospitalization, (3) when outpatient treatment facilities are a great distance from home, or (4) when problems are so severe so as to warrant a removal from the current environment for a length of time. If inpatient treatment is chosen, the program should be kept as short as possible, usually two to four weeks, as longer inpatient care has not been demonstrated to be any more effective. Second, a pharmacological approach (such as methadone maintenance or naltrexone treatment) should be combined with psychotherapy or behavioral counseling whenever possible. A multipronged approach is usually the most effective one. Third, self-help groups such as Alcoholics Anonymous (AA) and similar organizations should be considered; they cost nothing and are helpful not only in the action stage of change but in the maintenance stage that follows. Fourth, contact should be continued with the treatment facility for at least six to twelve months. This ongoing connection minimizes the possibility of dropping out of the program or relapse during maintenance. Fifth, drug abusers with few sources of social support should consider a half-way or recovery house for three to six months.[29]

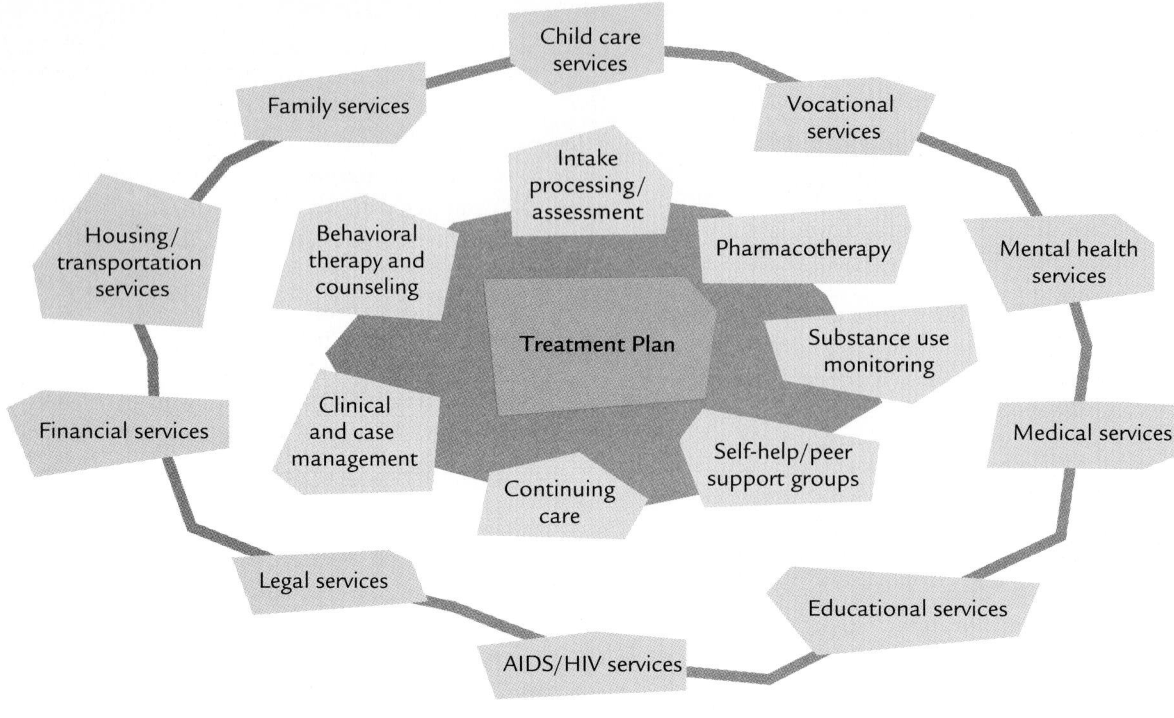

FIGURE 17.3

Components of a comprehensive treatment program for drug abuse.

Modified from National Institute on Drug Abuse (1999), *Principles of drug addiction treatment: A research-based guide.* Rockville MD: National Institute on Drug Abuse, p. 14.

Judging the Quality of the Treatment Facility

Claims that sound "too good to be true" are never made by a high-quality drug-abuse treatment facility, and advertisements give only a superficial impression of what the program might really entail. A good idea is to interview key people at the facility in person. The principal characteristics to look for are the following:

- The facility employs professionals familiar with the specific type of drug abuse problem for which help is being sought.
- The facility employs medical personnel or has a working association with medical personnel who can assess the medical status of clients and provide medical treatment if necessary, particularly when pharmacological treatment is an element in the program.
- The facility encourages family therapy for clients who have intact families.
- The facility provides both group and individual counseling.
- The facility integrates their program into self-help support groups (such as AA) and encourages clients to continue to participate in support groups after treatment ends. It should also maintain after-care and relapse-prevention programs on its own.
- The physical structure of the facility is clean and attractive, regardless of its age. The staff is competent, with a capacity to be both tough and compassionate. They should be cordial to you and willing to answer all your questions, including those that involve costs. Services are typically covered by some form of medical insurance.
- The facility is accredited by the Joint Commission for the Accreditation of Healthcare Organizations (JCAHO) and is licensed by the state in which it operates.[30]

Information Resources

Information about treatment options in your community can be found in newspapers and classified sections (yellow pages) of telephone directories, under Alcoholism or Drug Abuse and Addiction Treatment. Web sites on the Internet are also very helpful. A national information and referral service is available through www.drughelp.org.

SUMMARY

Ways to Approach Drug-Abuse Prevention

- Drug-abuse prevention efforts fall into three basic categories of intervention: primary, secondary, and tertiary.
- Primary prevention focuses on populations that have had only minimal exposure to drugs or none at all. Secondary prevention focuses on populations whose drug experience has not yet been associated with serious long-term problems. Tertiary prevention focuses on populations who have entered drug treatment; the goal is to prevent relapse.

A Biopsychosocial Strategy for Treatment

- Because many individuals experience problems stemming from polydrug abuse, treatment programs must consider common difficulties associated with a range of alcohol and other drugs.
- Chances of success in drug-abuse treatment can be increased by looking at the combination of biological, psychological, and social factors leading to drug abuse. This is referred to as the biopsychosocial model.

Incarceration and Other Punitive Measures in the United States

- Federal laws since 1970 have established a hierarchy of criminal penalties for drug trafficking, depending on the schedule of the controlled substance, amounts that are involved, and special circumstances under which violations have been committed.
- In some cases, abusers of illicit drugs who are arrested for violating drug control laws are given the option of a treatment program rather than prosecution and imprisonment. For those who are sentenced to a prison term, a limited number of opportunities for drug treatment exist within the prison system.

Prevention and Treatment in the Workplace

- Since the mid-1980s, a growing number of companies and other businesses have adopted measures to encourage a drug-free workplace. This involves, in part, the establishment of educational programs that increase workers' awareness of alcohol abuse, the abuse of illicit drugs, and the impact of these behaviors on productivity and the quality of the workers' lives.
- One element of most drug-free workplace programs is an employee assistance program (EAP), serving to help workers with abuse problems. Another element is a policy of drug testing, serving to reduce illicit drug use among workers and employment applicants.
- Although employee assistance programs and drug testing have been readily accepted among U.S. businesses, questions about the extent to which drug testing violates personal privacy and individual rights still remain.

The Personal Journey to Treatment and Recovery

- The road to recovery can be understood in terms of five stages of change: precontemplation, contemplation, preparation, action, and maintenance. It is possible to recycle through these stages multiple times in a kind of spiraling pattern before long-term recovery is attained.
- The five stages of change are applicable to the resolution of any life problems, not just those associated with drug abuse.

The Importance of the Family System in Prevention and Treatment

- It is critical to examine the family dynamics surrounding a drug abuser not only to understand the situational problems that have developed but also to anticipate and deal with the obstacles that might derail treatment. Family units typically pass through the stages of denial, anger, bargaining, feeling, and finally acceptance as treatment is at first rejected then sought.
- One major way that family systems can jeopardize successful treatment is through enabling behavior, in which family members assume many of the responsibilities that are rejected by the drug abuser. Enabling can take several forms.
- Family support is crucial for a treatment program to be successful and for relapse to be avoided, though the responsibility always remains with the abuser.

Finding the Right Drug-Abuse Treatment and Prevention Program

- It is important to consider the goals and objectives of a treatment program to find the one best suited to the person seeking help. Decisions must be made regarding the inpatient/outpatient format for treatment or whether a pharmacological intervention is indicated.

- It is also important to inspect the treatment facility in person. An open relationship with the treatment staff, their willingness to answer all questions about the treatment program, a judgment that the staff will be both tough and compassionate, and the licensure and/or accreditation status of the facility are among the major criteria to be weighed.

KEY TERMS

action stage, p. 358
biopsychosocial model, p. 348
contemplation stage, p. 357
deterrence, p. 349
drug paraphernalia, p. 351
drug trafficking, p. 349
incarceration, p. 348
maintenance stage, p. 358
precontemplation stage, p. 357
preparation stage, p. 357
primary prevention, p. 346
rehabilitation, p. 349
secondary prevention, p. 346
simple possession, p. 349
tertiary prevention, p. 346

ENDNOTES

1. Swisher, John D. (1979). Prevention issues. In R. L. DuPont, A. Goldstein, and J. O'Donnell (Eds.). *Handbook on drug abuse.* Washington DC: National Institute on Drug Abuse, pp. 423–435.
2. Julien, Robert M. (2001). *A primer of drug action* (9th ed.). New York: Worth, pp. 371–377.
3. Drug Enforcement Agency, U.S. Department of Justice. Statutes of the Controlled Substances Act of 1970, as amended and revised in 1986 and 1988.
4. Healey, Kerry (1988). *State and local experience with drug paraphernalia laws.* Washington DC: U.S. Government Printing Office, pp. 69–73.
5. Bureau of Justice Statistics (1999, January). Special report: Substance abuse and treatment, state and federal prisoners, 1997. Washington DC: U.S. Department of Justice. *The 1997 National Drug Control Strategy* (1997). Washington DC: Office of National Drug Control Policy.
6. Meeks, Linda, Heit, Philip, and Page, Randy (1994). *Drugs, alcohol, and tobacco.* Blacklick OH: Meeks-Heit Publishing, pp. 220–221. Wexler, Harry K. (1994). Progress in prison substance abuse treatment: A five year report. *Journal of Drug Issues, 24,* 349–360.
7. Meeks, Heit, and Page, *Drugs,* p. 221.
8. Center for Substance Abuse Treatment (1997). *50 strategies for substance abuse treatment.* Rockville MD: Substance Abuse and Mental Health Services Administration. Inciardi, James A.; Martin, Steven S.; Butzin, Clifford A.; Hooper, Robert M.; and Harrison, Lana D. (1997). An effective model of prison-based treatment for drug-involved offenders. *Journal of Drug Issues, 27,* 261–278. Lipton, Douglas S. (1994). The correctional opportunity: Pathways to drug treatment for offenders. *Journal of Drug Issues, 24,* 331–348. National Center on Addiction and Substance Abuse at Columbia University (1998, January). Behind bars: Substance abuse and America's prison population. Bureau of Justice Statistics, Special Report.
9. Adapted from McNeece, C. Aaron, and DiNitto, Diana M. (1994). *Chemical dependency: A systems approach.* Englewood Cliffs NJ: Prentice Hall, p. 153.
10. French, Michael T., Zarkin, Gary A., and Bray, Jeremy W. (1995). A methodology for evaluating the costs and benefits of employee assistance programs. *Journal of Drug Issues, 25,* 451–470.
11. Drug testing in the workplace (July/August 1996). *Prevention Pipeline,* p. 3. Meeks, Heit, and Page, *Drugs,* p. 215. U.S. Department of Labor (1990). *An employer's guide to dealing with substance abuse.* Washington DC: U.S. Department of Labor.
12. Comerford, Anthony W. (1999). Work dysfunction and addiction. *Journal of Substance Abuse Treatment, 16,* 247–253. Engelhart, Paul F., Robinson, Holly, and Kates, Hannah (1997). The workplace. In Joyce H. Lowinson, Pedro Ruiz, Robert B. Millman, and John G. Langrod (Eds.), *Substance abuse: A comprehensive textbook.* Baltimore: Williams and Wilkins, pp. 874–884. Normand, J., Lempert, R., and O'Brien, C. (Eds.) (1994). *Under the influence? Drugs and the American work force.* Washington DC: National Academy Press.
13. Avis, Harry (1996). *Drugs and life* (3rd ed.). Dubuque IA: Brown and Benchmark, p. 256.
14. Avis, *Drugs and Life.* Fishbein, Diana H., and Pease, Susan E. (1996). *The dynamics of drug abuse.* Needham Heights MA: Allyn and Bacon. *Prevention Pipeline,* p. 3.
15. Center for Substance Abuse Prevention (1994). *Making the link: Alcohol, tobacco, and other drugs in the workplace.* Rockville MD: Center for Substance Abuse Prevention. Substance abuse in the workplace (1996, July/August). *Prevention Pipeline,* p. 2.

16. National Transportation Safety Board (1988). *Alcohol/drug use and its impact on railroad safety: Safety study.* Washington DC: U.S. Department of Transportation.
17. Blum, Terry C., and Roman, Paul M. (1995). *Cost-effectiveness and preventive implications of employee assistance programs.* Rockville MD: Substance Abuse and Mental Health Services Administration. Meeks, Heit, and Page, *Drugs,* p. 214.
18. Meeks, Heit, and Page, *Drugs,* p. 219.
19. Schuckit, Marc A. (1995). *Educating yourself about alcohol and drugs: A people's primer.* New York: Plenum Press, pp. 131–153.
20. Ibid., pp. 189–216.
21. Dijkstra, Arie, Roijackers, Jolanda, and DeVries, Hein (1998). Smokers in four stages of readiness to change. *Addictive Behaviors,* 23, 339–350. Prochaska, James O., DiClemente, Carlo C., and Norcross, John C. (1992). In search of how people change. *American Psychologist,* 47, 1102–1114.
22. Norman, Gregory J.; Velicer, Wayne F.; Fava, Joseph L.; and Prochaska, James O. (1998). Dynamic typology clustering within the stages of change for smoking cessation. *Addictive Behaviors,* 23, 139–153. Prochaska, James O. (1994). *Changing for good.* New York: William Morrow. Velicer, Wayne F.; Norman, Gregory J.; Fava, Joseph L.; and Prochaska, James O. (1999). Testing 40 predictions from the transtheoretical model. *Addictive Behaviors,* 24, 455–469.
23. Fields, Richard (1998). *Drugs in perspective* (3rd ed.). Dubuque IA: WCB McGraw-Hill, p. 136.
24. Ibid., pp. 173–178.
25. Ibid., pp. 172–173. Margolis, Robert D., and Zweben, Joan E. (1998). *Treating patients with alcohol and other drug problems: An integrated approach.* Washington DC: American Psychological Association. Nelson, Charles (1988). The style of enabling behavior. In David E. Smith, and Donald Wesson (Eds.), *Treating cocaine dependence.* Center City MN: Hazelden Foundation.
26. Wegscheider-Cruse, Sharon (1981). *Another chance: Hope and health for the alcoholic family.* Palo Alto CA: Science and Behavior Books.
27. Fields, *Drugs and alcohol,* pp. 190–194.
28. Schuckit, *Educating yourself,* pp. 229–230.
29. Schuckit, Marc A. (1995). *Drug and alcohol abuse: A clinical guide to diagnosis and treatment* (4th ed.). New York: Plenum Press, pp. 306–308.
30. Adapted from Donatelle, Rebecca J., and Davis, Lorraine G. (2000). *Access to health* (6th ed.). Needham Heights MA: Allyn and Bacon, p. 219.

CHAPTER

18 Prevention and Education: Schools, Community, and Family

After you have completed this chapter, you will understand

- The National Drug Control Policy and Healthy People 2000 and 2010 strategies and goals for alcohol, tobacco, and other drug prevention
- Approaches to prevention and education that have failed in the past
- Successful school-based prevention and education programs
- Risk factors, protective factors, and resiliency theory
- Community-based prevention and the impact of mass media
- The importance of family systems in prevention and education
- Multicultural issues in prevention and education

Your daughter is pretty and popular. She's the homecoming queen and the editor of the school paper. So you think you're safe. You're not. Your son is on the swimming team, a star athlete. He's talking about going to medical school. So you think you're safe. You're not. That's what brings me here: I'm just like you. I thought I was safe too. What a kid needs today is self-esteem, right? Something to make him feel good about himself. A stable home life. And you'll get by. Wrong.

Drugs in America.

Not a ghetto problem. Not a suburban problem. Not a problem of divorced parents. Not a working parent's problem. Drugs are everywhere and they're everybody's problem. They're in big cities and in small rural communities. They strike troubled families and families whose children are seeming achievers, good students, athletes, prom queens.

—*Beth Polson,* Not my kid: A parent's guide to kids and drugs

The ruinous impact of illicit drugs on young people in the United States is one of the most emotion-laden social issues of our day. Perhaps the most disturbing aspect of recent reports regarding the incidence of drug use is that the increases have been particularly evident in the youngest age category studied, eighth graders who are thirteen or fourteen years old. The need for effective prevention and education programs to stem this tide is a deeply personal issue, and we ask ourselves: What can be done?

This final chapter focuses on the efforts we are making in the area of primary and secondary prevention. In the case of primary prevention, we are assuming that the target population for these interventions may have been exposed to drug-taking behavior in other people but have not had drug experiences of their own. We recognize that the potential for young people to engage in drug use themselves is substantial, and only through an effective primary prevention can we keep that potential from turning into reality. It is increasingly clear that the age of onset for drug-taking behavior of any kind is a key factor in determining problems later in life. For example, a young person who begins drinking before the age of fifteen is twice as likely to develop a pattern of alcohol abuse and four times as likely to develop alcohol dependence than an individual who begins drinking at the age of twenty-one. In general, if the age of onset can be delayed significantly, there is the possibility of reducing the incidence of drug-taking abuse or dependence.[1]

In the case of secondary prevention, we are concentrating on the life-style of a somewhat older population, and our goal is to minimize the problems associated with drug-taking behavior, assuming that some level of that behavior already exists. As mentioned in Chapter 17, emphasis is placed on social alternatives to behaviors involving alcohol and other drugs among high school students. At the college level, the moderate use of alcohol, and particularly the avoidance of alcohol binging, as well as education about the personal risks of some of the newer club drugs, are all elements in a program of secondary prevention.

Whether we are addressing issues of primary or secondary prevention, however, we must remain fully aware that the entire range of drug-taking behaviors needs to be considered. This range encompasses not only illicit drug use but also the drinking of alcohol, the inappropriate use of medications, and the consumption of tobacco products. As a consequence, it will be useful in this chapter to adopt a somewhat awkward but necessary phrase *alcohol, tobacco, and other drug (ATOD) prevention* to describe our society's response in this regard. As we will see, a conspicuous target behavior within the overall mission of prevention and education in recent years has been tobacco use among young people.

ATOD Prevention: Strategies, Goals, and Objectives

The federal Center for Substance Abuse Prevention (CSAP) defines ATOD prevention in terms of two major components. The first is the promotion of constructive life-styles and norms that discourage ATOD use. The second is the development of social and physical environments that facilitate these ATOD-free life-styles. You may recall from Chapter 1 that two groups of factors play a major role in predicting the extent of ATOD use in a particular individual—risk factors that increase the likelihood of ATOD use and protective factors that decrease it. You can think of the two components of prevention in those terms. On one hand, it is a matter of minimizing the impact of risk factors in an individual's life. On the other hand, it is a matter of maximizing the impact of protective factors that provide the basis for resiliency toward the temptations of ATOD use. The number of "developmental assets" (see Chapter 1) increases the chances that ATOD prevention and education efforts will be successful.

Strategies for ATOD Prevention

The CSAP has identified seven basic strategies for achieving ATOD prevention in our society. They form the foundation for many ATOD prevention programs currently in place.[2]

- Raising awareness of the dangers of ATOD use and the benefits of constructive behavior
- Promoting good parenting skills and strengthening family relationships
- Building academic/vocational skills to allow individuals the potential of developing into contributing members of society
- Providing mentoring and positive role-modeling for youth
- Building social skills to enable the development of a strong self-image that leads to positive life-decisions
- Mobilizing communities to establish environments enhancing positive personal development
- Strengthening and supporting policies that promote healthy life-styles and change community norms

Strategic Goals for ATOD Prevention

As in any good game plan, however, the strategies are aimless without goals. A set of five strategic goals that provide focus and direction for our efforts in ATOD prevention has been established by the U.S. Office of National Drug Control Policy.

- *Goal 1: Educate and enable America's youth to reject illegal drugs as well as alcohol and tobacco.* Educators include parents or other caregivers, teachers, coaches, clergy, health professionals, and business and community leaders. These players should develop community coalitions and partnerships with the media, entertainment industry, and professional sports organizations to promote prevention programs and reduce the glamorization of illegal drugs and the use of alcohol and tobacco by youth.
- *Goal 2: Increase the safety of America's citizens by substantially reducing drug-related crime and violence.* Effective rehabilitation at all stages of the criminal justice system, as described in Chapter 17, should be developed and implemented. Law enforcement task forces at federal, state, and local levels must be strengthened to combat drug-related violence and drug trafficking in general.
- *Goal 3: Reduce the health and social costs to the public of illegal drug abuse.* Effective treatment for ATOD problems should be supported and promoted. Drug-free workplace programs are a key component of the overall prevention effort. Education and training of professionals who work with ATOD abusers should be supported, as well as research relating to the development of new medications and treatments for ATOD abuse and dependence.
- *Goal 4: Shield America's air, land, and sea frontiers from the drug threat.* It is necessary to improve the coordination and effectiveness of operations that detect, disrupt, deter, and seize illegal drugs coming into the United States through its borders. An important element in this goal is the improvement of bilateral and regional cooperation with Mexico as well as other countries involved in the trafficking of cocaine, heroin, marijuana, and other illegal drugs, in order to reduce the flow of illegal drugs into this country.
- *Goal 5: Break foreign and domestic drug sources of supply.* There should be a net reduction in the worldwide cultivation of coca, opium, and marijuana as well as the production of illegal drugs such as methamphetamine. Major international drug trafficking cartel organizations must be disrupted and dismantled by the prosecution and incarceration of their leaders, as well as the promotion of international laws that prevent money laundering.[3]

The Public Health Model of ATOD Prevention

It is important to recognize that an ATOD-free life constitutes a major element in a healthy life and, in turn, a healthy society. Figure 18.1 shows dramatically how ATOD-taking behaviors impact upon the nation's health in general. As you can see, one-half of all preventable deaths in the United States are accounted for by the abuse of either alcohol products (9 percent), tobacco products

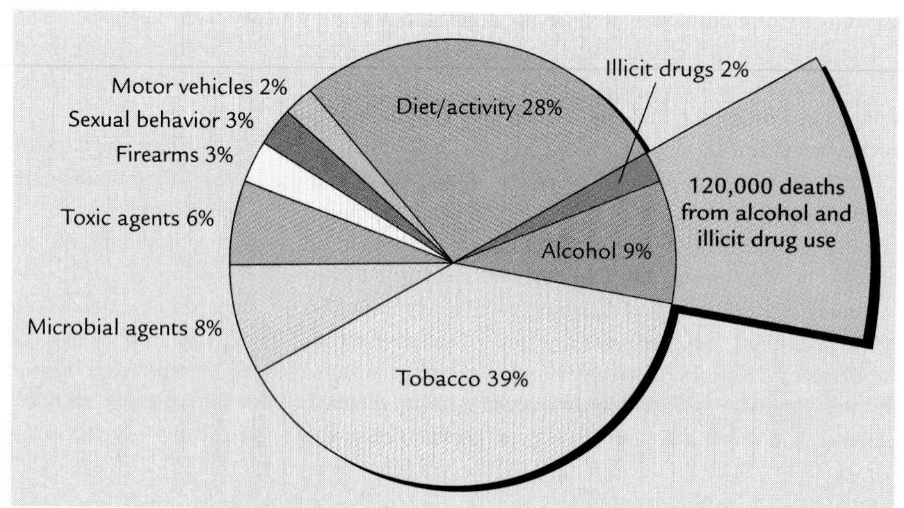

FIGURE 18.1

The relative incidence of deaths associated with ATOD use annually in the United States.
Source: Center for Substance Abuse Prevention, Substance Abuse and Mental Health Services Administration.

The Public Health Model and the Analogy of Infectious Disease

The idea that reducing the negative consequences of drug-taking behavior is a desirable goal for the enhancement of the overall health of society is often referred to as the Public Health Model. As Avram Goldstein, a prominent drug-abuse researcher and policy analyst, has pointed out, the problems of reducing drug-taking behavior have many similarities to wresting control over an infectious disease. A virus, for example, infects some people who are relatively more susceptible than others (in other words, there are risk factors), while some people will be relatively immune (in other words, there are protective factors). Public-health measures can be established to reduce or eradicate the virus (as we attempt to reduce the supply of illicit drugs from reaching the consumer); specific vaccinations can be discovered to increase a person's resistance to the virus, just as we search for primary prevention programs in drug abuse.

We can carry the analogy further. Medical treatment for an infectious disease is considered uncontroversial and necessary for two reasons. First, we are alleviating the suffering of the infected individual; second, we are reducing the pool of infection to limit the spread to others. Analogously, drug-abuse treatment is desirable in order to relieve the negative consequences of drug abuse, as well as reduce the social influence of drug abusers on nondrug abusers in our society.

Goldstein asks a provocative question:

> There are individuals who contribute to the AIDS epidemic by having promiscuous sexual contacts without taking elementary precautions. Are those behaviors, which contribute to the spread of infectious disease, really different in principle from that of pack-a-day cigarette smokers who will not try to quit, despite all the evidence of physical harm to themselves and their families?

There is certainly no consensus on how the problem of drug abuse should be conceptualized. Some have objected to the implications of the Public Health Model, arguing that it ignores the moral and ethical choices that are made in establishing a pattern of drug-taking behavior. You may recognize a similar controversy, discussed in Chapter 10, regarding the question of whether alcoholism should be considered a disease.

Sources: Goldstein, Avram (1994). *Addiction: From biology to drug policy.* New York: Freeman. Quotation on p. 10. Jonas, Steven (1997). Public health approaches. In Joyce H. Lowinson, Pedro Ruiz, Robert B. Millman, and John G. Langrod (Eds.), *Substance abuse: A comprehensive textbook,* pp. 775–785.

(39 percent), or illicit drugs (2 percent). Each year, more than 500,000 deaths are attributed to these three circumstances (Health Line).[4]

It is not surprising that, in 1992, when the U.S. Public Health Service established its long-range health-promoting goals in a program called Healthy People 2000, a major component was devoted to ATOD use among young people aged between twelve and twenty-five years.[5] According to their projections, by the year 2000, using baseline figures from the period 1987–1991, the United States should have achieved the following goals:

- Increased by at least one year the average age of first use of alcohol, tobacco, and marijuana.
- Reduced alcohol, marijuana, and cocaine use, measured by past thirty-day use, by 50 percent and tobacco use among young people by 53 percent.
- Increased the percentage of young people who perceive social disapproval in the heavy use of alcohol, occasional use of marijuana, trying cocaine once or twice, or smoking one or more packs of cigarettes per day to 70, 85, 95, and 95 percent, respectively.
- Reduced the percentage who have engaged in recent heavy alcohol drinking by 15 percent among high school seniors and 23 percent among college students.
- Increased the percentage of high school seniors who associate a risk of physical or psychological harm with heavy use of alcohol, trying cocaine once or twice, or regular use of marijuana, or smoking one or more packs of cigarettes per day to 70, 80, 90, and 95 percent, respectively.
- Reduced the percentage of male high school seniors who use anabolic steroids to 3 percent.
- Reduced alcohol-related motor vehicle deaths by 44 percent, cirrhosis-related deaths by 35 percent, and drug-abuse–related hospital emergency room visits by 20 percent.

Unfortunately, by 2000, most of these goals were not met. In fact, in the areas of teenage ATOD prevalence rates, we had actually lost ground. Nonetheless, a new program called Healthy People 2010 has been recently enacted, with a new set of target goals.[6] Whether we will be more successful in this new endeavor by that time remains to be seen.

Lessons from the Past: Prevention Approaches That Have Failed

When deciding how to solve a problem, it always helps to look at what has *not* worked in the past. That way, we can avoid wasting time, effort, and money on nonsolutions. In the general opinion of health professionals and researchers, the following efforts have been largely unsuccessful with regard to primary prevention, when positioned as the major thrust of a particular program. Nonetheless, some of these approaches have been incorporated successfully as one of several components within an overall effective package.

Reducing the Availability of Drugs

It is reasonable to expect that the problems of illicit drug abuse would diminish if the availability of these drugs were reduced or eliminated altogether. This is essentially the "supply/availability" argument in drug prevention, and you will recall that the last two of the five major goals in the National Drug Control Strategy concerned the reduction of the manufacture and distribution of illicit drugs into and within the United States. As noted in Chapter 2, a huge amount of governmental resources is spent on reducing the supply or availability of these substances.

According to the economic principle of supply and demand, however, a decline in supply or availability works to produce an increase in value and an increase in demand. If one accepts the first viewpoint, then reductions in supply or availability should help prevent drug-taking behavior; if one accepts the second viewpoint, then such reductions should exacerbate the situation. Which theoretical viewpoint is operating with respect to illicit drugs (or with respect to alcohol, tobacco, and other licit drugs) is a point of controversy among health professionals both inside and outside the government.

Given the fact that the United States has adopted the policy of reducing the supply or availability of illicit drugs as part of an overall national strategy, how successful have we been? Have we been able, for example, to reduce the production of illicit drugs around the world and their influx into the United States? Unfortunately, drug cultivation (such as the harvesting of opium, coca leaves, and marijuana) and the exportation of processed illicit drugs from their points of origin are so deeply entrenched in many regions of the world and the resourcefulness of drug producers is so great that our global efforts have been frustratingly inadequate. As was pointed out in Chapter 2, a production crackdown in one region only serves to create a marketing vacuum that another region quickly fills. Moreover, efforts to control international drug smuggling have been embarrassingly unsuccessful, despite well-publicized drug busts, arrests, and seizures. It is estimated that only a tiny fraction of illicit drugs are interdicted at U.S. borders.[7]

With respect to alcohol, a strategy of reduced availability has been implemented on a nationwide basis since 1984 for a specific age group, by prohibiting alcohol to young people under the age of twenty-one (see Chapter 9). Prior to this time, some states had adopted this policy while neighboring states had not, allowing for comparisons in alcohol consumption rates and the incidence of alcohol-related automobile accidents. In one study, the percentage of teenage, nighttime, single-vehicle accident fatalities in Massachusetts was found to have declined in 1979 (the year the legal drinking age in that state was raised to twenty-one) to a significantly greater degree than in New York, which at that time still had a minimum drinking age of eighteen. That was the good news.

The bad news was that levels of alcohol consumption in this age range stayed the same. Therefore, although one particular consequence of immoderate alcohol use (drunk driving) was reduced as a secondary prevention intervention, the prevalence of alcohol use itself as a primary prevention intervention was unaffected. As we are all aware, underage drinking still is widespread; minors still find opportunities to drink and to drink in excess. The fact that minimum-age requirements have only a limited effect on drinking among minors reinforces the complexity of dealing with primary prevention, whether we are considering licit or illicit drugs.[8]

Punitive Measures

In the last chapter, the question of deterrence was raised with respect to the preventive role of law-enforcement and judicial policies toward drug offenders. The expectation from such policies is that an individual would be less inclined to use and abuse illicit drugs for fear of being arrested, prosecuted, convicted, and incarcerated. The available statistics show that this deterrent factor has failed to take hold. The enticements of many psychoactive drugs are extremely powerful, and the imposition of harsh penalties has frequently been delayed or inconsistent. Mandatory minimum-sentencing laws (see Chapter 17) have resulted in a clogged judicial system and vastly overcrowded prisons, without any noticeable dent in the trafficking in or consumption of illicit drugs. Although the enforcement of these penalties may be defended in terms of an overall social policy toward illicit drugs, it has evidently failed as a means for either primary or secondary prevention.[9]

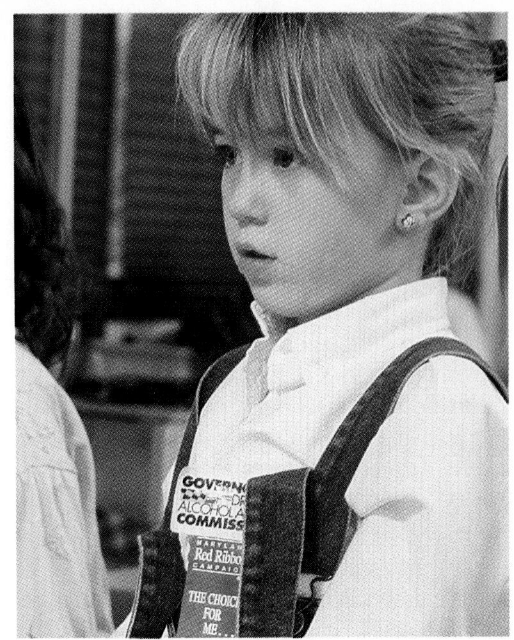

Designations of drug-free school zones are prominent features of many school-based drug prevention programs.

Scare Tactics and Negative Education

In the late 1960s, the suddenly widespread use of marijuana, amphetamines, barbiturates, LSD, and other hallucinogens, first among students on college campuses and later among youth at large, spawned a number of hastily designed programs based on the arousal of fear and exaggerated or blatantly inaccurate information about the risks involved. They were the products of panic rather than careful thought.

As might be imagined, such efforts turned young people off precisely at the time when they were turning themselves on to an array of exotic and seemingly innocuous drug-taking experiences. Professionals have called it the "reefer madness approach," an allusion to the government-sponsored movie of the 1930s that attempted to scare people away from experimenting with marijuana (see Chapter 7). These programs accomplished little, except to erode even further the credibility of the adult presenters in the eyes of youths who often knew (or thought they knew) a great deal more about drugs and their effects.[10]

Objective Information Approaches

At the opposite end of the emotional spectrum are programs designed to present information about drugs and their potential dangers in a straightforward, nonjudgmental way. Unfortunately, evaluations of this "just the facts, ma'am" approach have found that youths exposed to such primary prevention programs are no less likely to use drugs later in their lives and sometimes are *more* likely to use them. These programs tend to increase their curiosity about drugs in general, obviously something the program planners want to avoid.[11]

Despite these failures, however, it would be a mistake to dismiss the informational aspect of any ATOD prevention program completely out of hand, particularly when the information is presented in a low-fear atmosphere.[12] The overall value of an informational approach appears to depend on whether the target population consists of high-risk or low-risk children:

> *Providing information to low-risk youth on the health and legal implications of using illegal drugs often is enough incentive for them to avoid using drugs. When low-risk young people really understand the dangers of drugs, they choose to remain drug-free. High-risk youth may not be so easily dissuaded from using drugs, and for them additional intervention is necessary.*[13]

Magic Bullets and Promotional Campaigns

A variety of antidrug promotional materials such as T-shirts, caps, rings, buttons, bumper stickers, posters, rap songs, school assembly productions, books, and brochures is available and frequently seen as "magic bullets" that can clinch success in an ATOD prevention program. Their appeal lies in their high visibility; these items give a clear signal to the public at large that something is being done. Yet, although they may be helpful in deglamorizing ATOD use and providing a forum for young people to express their feelings about drugs, promotional items are inadequate by themselves to reduce ATOD abuse overall. They do, however, remain viable components of more comprehensive programs that will be examined later in the chapter.[14]

Self-Esteem Enhancement and Affective Education

In the early 1970s, several ATOD prevention programs were developed that emphasized the affective or emotional component of drug-taking behavior rather than specific information about drugs. In the wake of research that showed a relationship between drug abuse and psychological variables such as low self-esteem, poor decision-making skills, and poor interpersonal communication skills, programs were instituted that incorporated role-playing exercises with other assignments designed to help young people get in touch with their own emotions and feel better about themselves. This effort, called **affective education,** was an attempt to deal with underlying emotional and attitudinal factors rather than specific behaviors related to ATOD use (in fact, alcohol, tobacco, and other drugs were seldom mentioned at all). Affective education was based on the observation that ATOD users had difficulty identifying and expressing emotions such as anger and love. In a related set of programs called **values clarification,** moral values were actively taught to children, on the assumption that ATOD users frequently have a poorly developed sense of where their life is going and lack the moral "compass" to guide their behavior.

Difficulties arose, however, when parents, community leaders, and frequently educators themselves argued that the emphasis of affective education was inappropriate for public schools. In regard to values clarification, there was concern that a system of morality was being imposed on students without respecting their individual backgrounds and cultures. This kind of instruction, it was felt, was more suited for religious education settings.[15]

Beyond these considerations, the bottom line was that neither affective education nor values clarification was effective in preventing ATOD use. Some researchers have recently questioned the basic premise that self-esteem is a major factor at all. As a result, affective issues are no longer viewed as central considerations in primary or secondary prevention. Nonetheless, they can be found as components in more comprehensive prevention programs, discussed later, that have been more successful.[16]

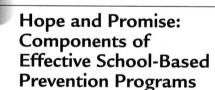

Hope and Promise: Components of Effective School-Based Prevention Programs

One of the major lessons to be learned from evaluations of previous ATOD prevention efforts is that there is a far greater chance for success when the programs are multifaceted than when they focus on only a single aspect of drug-taking behavior. We need to remember that success can be measured in various ways. A school-based ATOD program, for example, might be considered successful if it enjoys support from parents, administrators, and teachers. It might be considered successful if there is evidence of a change in a child's view toward ATOD use or in the child's stated inclination to engage in ATOD use in the future.

However gratifying these effects may be to the community, they do not impact on the core issue: Is the prevalence of ATOD use reduced? *The goals of any prevention program aimed at young people is to lower the numbers of new ATOD users or to delay the first use of alcohol and tobacco toward an age at which they are considered adults.* In order to be considered "research-based," prevention programs must be evaluated against a control group that did not receive the intervention; otherwise it is impossible to determine whether the effect of the program itself was greater than doing nothing at all.

Evaluations of ATOD prevention programs frequently have looked only at the "exit results" in the form of short-term effects, such as changes in how young people feel after the program has ended or how they think they will act in the future, rather than long-term effects such as actual ATOD use over an extended period of time. Obviously, we are far more interested in the latter. With these considerations in mind, it is useful to examine the components of programs that have been judged effective. The following are elements of a school-based, ATOD prevention curriculum that has been shown to work.

Peer-Refusal Skills

A number of school-based programs, developed during the 1980s, have included the teaching of personal and social skills as well as techniques for resisting various forms of social pressure to smoke, drink, or use other drugs (often referred to as **peer-refusal skills**). The emphasis is directed toward an individual's relationships among his or her peers and the surrounding social climate. Rather than simply prodding adolescents to "just say no," these pro-

affective education: An approach in ATOD prevention programs that emphasizes the building of self-esteem and an improved self-image.

values clarification: An approach in ATOD prevention programs that teaches positive social values and attitudes.

peer-refusal skills: Techniques by which an individual can resist peer pressure to use alcohol, tobacco, or other drugs.

Health Line

Peer-Refusal Skills: Ten Ways to Make It Easier to Say No

- Make it simple. There is no need for explanations. Keep your refusal direct and to the point.
- Know the facts. If you know something is bad for you, it is easier to make it part of your refusal.
- Have something else to do. You can suggest some alternative activity.
- Walk away. If the pressure begins to feel threatening to you, just leave.
- Avoid the situation. Stay away from places where you might be pressured. If there is a party where you might be pressured, simply don't go.
- Change the subject. Surprisingly, this works.
- Hang out with friends who aren't ATOD users. Pressure won't be there.
- Be a broken record. You can be firm without sounding angry or irritated. A little repetition may be needed.
- Use the "fogging" technique of passive resistance. If they criticize you for refusing, simply agree and let it pass over you. Don't let their reactions get to you.
- Refuse to continue discussing it. Tell them you made up your mind and you are not going to talk about it anymore.

Source: Center for Substance Abuse Prevention, Substance Abuse and Mental Health Services Administration.

grams teach them *how* to do so when placed in often uncomfortable social circumstances. Health Line lists some specific techniques that have been taught to help deflect peer pressure regarding ATOD use.

Primary prevention programs using peer-refusal skill training have been shown to reduce the rate of tobacco smoking, as well as alcohol drinking and marijuana smoking, by 35–45 percent. With respect to tobacco smoking, this approach has been even more effective for young people identified as being in a high-risk category (in that their friends or family smoked) than for other students.[17]

Anxiety and Stress Reduction

Adolescence can be an enormously stressful time, and ATOD use is frequently an option chosen to reduce feelings of anxiety, particularly when an individual has inadequate coping skills to deal with that anxiety. It is therefore useful to learn techniques of self-relaxation and stress management and to practice the application of these techniques to everyday situations.

Social Skills and Personal Decision Making

Peer-refusal skills are but one example of a range of assertiveness skills that allow young people to express their feelings, needs, preferences, and opinions directly and honestly, without fearing that they will jeopardize their friendships or lose the respect of others. Learning assertiveness skills not only helps advance the goals of primary prevention but also fosters positive interpersonal relationships throughout life. Tasks in social skills training have included the ability to initiate social interactions (introducing oneself to a stranger), offer a compliment to others, engage in conversation, and express feelings and opinions. Lessons generally involve a combination of instruction, demonstration, feedback, reinforcement, behavioral rehearsal, and extended practice through behavioral homework assignments.

A related skill is the ability to make decisions in a thoughtful and careful way. Emphasis is placed on the identification of problem situations, the formulation of goals, the generation of alternative solutions, and the consideration of the likely consequences of each. Lessons also focus on identifying persuasive advertising appeals and exploring counterarguments that can defuse them. Primary prevention programs using a social skills training approach have been shown to reduce the likelihood that a young person will try smoking by 42–75 percent and the likelihood that a nonsmoker will be a regular smoker in a one-year follow-up by 56–67 percent.[18]

A Model School-Based Prevention Program: Life Skills Training

One of the most well-researched efforts in school-based ATOD prevention is the Life Skills Training (LST) program, developed by Gilbert Botvin at the Cornell University Medical College in New York City. It is directed toward seventh-grade students in a fifteen-session curriculum, with ten additional booster sessions in the eighth grade and five in the ninth grade.[19] Not surprisingly, the effective components of primary prevention discussed so far have been incorporated in this program. The major elements include the following:

- A *cognitive component* designed to provide information concerning the short-term consequences of alcohol, tobacco, and other drugs. Unlike traditional prevention approaches, LST includes only minimal information concerning the long-term health consequences of ATOD use. Evidently, it is not useful to tell young people about what might happen when they are "old." Instead, information is provided concerning immediate negative effects, the decreasing social acceptability of ATOD use, and actual prevalence rates among adults and adolescents. This last element of the lesson is to counter the myth that ATOD use is the norm in their age group, that "everyone's doing it."

- A *decision-making component* designed to facilitate critical thinking and independent decision making. Students learn to evaluate the role of the media in behavior as well as to formulate counterarguments and other cognitive strategies to resist advertising pressures.
- A *stress-reduction component* designed to help students develop ways to lessen anxiety. Students learn relaxation techniques and cognitive techniques to manage stress.
- A *social skills component* designed to teach social assertiveness and specific techniques for resisting peer pressure to engage in ATOD use.
- A *self-directed behavior-change component* designed to facilitate self-improvement and encourage a sense of personal control and self-esteem. Students are assigned to identify a skill or behavior that they would like to change or improve and to develop a long-term goal over an eight-week period and short-term objectives that can be met week by week.

Originally designed as a smoking-prevention program, LST presently focuses on issues related to the use of alcohol and marijuana as well as tobacco. During the program, students engage in peer interactions, demonstrations, exercises, and extended homework assignments (Figure 18.2). A series of studies have consistently shown its effectiveness in reducing tobacco, alcohol, and marijuana use, even in a long-range follow-up over a six-year period. In addition, reductions have been seen among inner-city minority students as well as white middle-class youths, an encouraging sign that primary prevention strategies can influence adolescents regardless of their social backgrounds.[20] As Botvin has expressed it, these studies will ultimately "give us an intervention that we can use in cities and towns and villages across the United States without having to develop separate intervention approaches for each and every different population."[21]

Drug Abuse Resistance Education (DARE)

The Drug Abuse Resistance Education program, commonly known as DARE, is undoubtedly the best-known school-based ATOD prevention program in the United States and perhaps the world. It was developed in 1983 as a collaborative effort by the Los Angeles Police Department and the Los Angeles United School District to bring uniformed police officers into kindergarten and elementary grade classrooms to teach basic drug information, peer-refusal skills, self-management techniques, and alternatives to drug use.

Quite rapidly, the DARE program expanded until today it has been established in all fifty U.S. states, in all Native American schools administered by the Bureau of Indian Affairs, the U.S. Department of Defense schools worldwide, and in school systems in many foreign countries. There are also teacher-orientation sessions, officer–student interactions at playgrounds and cafeterias, and parent-education evenings.[22]

Responses to Project DARE from teachers, principals, students, and police officers are typically enthusiastic, and it is clear that the program has struck a responsive chord for a public that has pushed for active prevention programs in the schools. Part of this enthusiasm can be seen as coming from the image of police departments shifting their emphasis from exclusively "supply reduction" to a larger social role in "demand reduction."

Yet, despite its success in the area of public relations, the evidence supporting the effectiveness of DARE in achieving genuine reductions in ATOD use is weak. In general, children who participated in the DARE program have a more negative attitude toward drugs one year later than children who did not, as well as a greater capability to resist peer pressure and a lower estimate of how many of their peers smoked cigarettes. However, there were no significant differences between DARE and non-DARE groups in the level of ATOD use itself. Recent studies show few differences in drug use, drug attitudes, or self-esteem when young people are measured ten years after the administration of the DARE program.[23]

Why DARE remains popular when its effectiveness has been consistently challenged is an interesting question. Some health professionals in this field theorize that the popularity of DARE is, in part, a result of the perception among parents and DARE supporters that it *appears* to work, through a process of informally comparing children who go through DARE against an image of those children who do not:

> *The adults rightly perceive that most children who go through DARE do not engage in problematic drug use. Unfortunately, these individuals may not realize that the vast majority of children, even without any intervention, do not engage in problematic drug use. . . . That is, adults may believe that drug use among adolescents is much more frequent than it actually is. When the children who go through DARE*

FIGURE 18.2

A sample homework assignment for the Life Skills Training program for ATOD prevention.
Source: Mathias, Robert (1997, March/April). From the 'burbs to the 'hood . . . This program reduces student's risk of drug use. *NIDA Notes,* pp. 1, 5–6. Reprinted with permission.

Whose Opinion Counts?
(Influences on Your Decisions)

1. Write a list of who or what you think about when you make a decision.

___

___

___

2. For each of the following decisions, check off all of the things that influence your choice. For example, when you decide what to wear, do you think about your own opinions, your friends' opinions, your mother's opinions, etc.? You can check more than one influence for each decision.

Influences

Decisions I Make

This → Influences This ↓	My Opinion	My Friends' Opinion	My Parents' Opinion	My Past Experiences, Successes, and Failures	What I See on TV	What I Read About	What It Costs (in Time, Money, Convenience)
What to Wear							
How to Cut My Hair							
What to Eat							
What Music to Listen to							
What Movies to See							
What I Like to Do							

Look at all of your answers. Where do you have the most checks? Your friends, parents, media? Sometimes you don't realize how much we worry about what other people think. Are you really making decisions that are right for you?

are compared to this "normative" group of drug-using teens, DARE appears effective.[24]

Resiliency and Primary Prevention Efforts

Successful school-based prevention programs are built around the central idea that an individual is less inclined to engage in ATOD use if the protective factors in his or her life are enhanced and the risk factors are diminished. Only then can a young person be resilient enough to overcome the temptations of alcohol, tobacco, and other drugs. **Resiliency,** defined as the inclination to resist the effect of risk factors through the action of protective

resiliency: The inclination to resist the negative impact of risk factors in a person's life through the positive impact of protective factors.

QUICK CONCEPT  18.1

Understanding ATOD Prevention and Education

Check your understanding of ATOD prevention and education strategies by deciding whether the following approaches would or would not be effective (in and of themselves) in reducing ATOD use or delaying its onset, based on the available research.

	WOULD BE EFFECTIVE	WOULD NOT BE EFFECTIVE
1. Scare tactics	❑	❑
2. Life skills training	❑	❑
3. Peer-refusal skills training	❑	❑
4. Values clarification	❑	❑
5. Objective information	❑	❑
6. Anxiety reduction and stress management	❑	❑
7. Assertiveness training	❑	❑
8. Training in problem solving and goal setting	❑	❑

Answers 1. would not 2. would 3. would 4. would not 5. would not 6. would 7. would 8. would

factors, can be a make-or-break element in his or her social development. Social and personal skills, as well as other aspects of successful primary prevention efforts, enhance protective factors with respect to ATOD use and other forms of deviant behavior. In order to be more effective, however, it is necessary to incorporate aspects of a person's environment beyond the school itself in the fight against ATOD use. In the next section, we turn to primary prevention efforts that involve the community at large.[25]

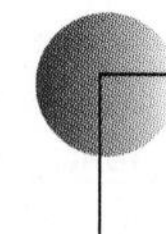

Community-Based Prevention Programs

Community-based prevention programs offer several obvious advantages over those restricted to schools. The first is the greater opportunity to involve parents and other family members, religious institutions, and the media as collaborative agents for change. The most important factor here is the comprehensive nature of such programs. They draw on multiple social institutions that have been demonstrated to represent protective factors in an individual's life, such as the family, religious groups, and community organizations. In addition, corporations and businesses can be contributing partners, in both a financial and nonfinancial sense. Undoubtedly, we are in a better position to tackle the complexities of ATOD use through the use of multiple strategies rather than a single approach.

Components of an Effective Community-Based Program

Typically, many of the prevention components that have been incorporated in the schools are also components in community-based programs, such as the dissemination of information, stress management, and life skills training. Other approaches can be handled better in a community setting. For example, although schools can promote the possibility of alternative student activities that provide positive and constructive means for addressing feelings of boredom, frustration, and powerlessness (activities such as Midnight Basketball and Boys and Girls Clubs), the community is in a better position than the schools to provide these activities.

There is also a greater opportunity in the community to elicit the involvement of significant individuals to act as positive role models, referred to as **impactors,** and to enlist the help of the mass media to promote antidrug messages in the press and on television. In addition, community-based programs can be more influential in promoting changes in public policy that foster opportunities for education, employment, and self-development.[26]

Alternative-Behavior Programming

It should not be surprising that it is easier to say no to drugs when you can say yes to something else. In community-based prevention programs, a major effort is made to provide the activities and outlets that steer people away from the high-risk situations associated with ATOD use. Owing to the fact that adolescents spend a majority of their time outside school, and it is outside school that the preponderance of ATOD use occurs, community pro-

impactors: Individuals in the community who function as positive role models to children and adolescents in ATOD prevention programs.

TABLE 18.1

Alternative behaviors to drug use: Needs and motives

LEVEL OF EXPERIENCE	NEEDS AND MOTIVES	ALTERNATIVES
Physical	Physical satisfaction, more energy	Athletics, dance/exercise, hiking, carpentry, or outdoor work
Sensory	Stimulation of sensory experience	Sensory awareness training, sky diving, experiencing
Emotional	Relief from anxiety, mood elevation, emotional relaxation	Individual counseling, group therapy
Interpersonal	Peer acceptance, defiance of authority figures	Confidence training, sensitivity groups, helping others in distress
Social/environmental	Promotion of social change or identification with a subculture	Social service; community action; helping the poor, aged, handicapped; environmental activism
Intellectual	Escape from boredom, curiosity, or inclination to explore one's own awareness	Reading, creative games, memory training, discussion groups
Creative/aesthetic	Increase in one's creativity or enjoyment of images and thoughts	Nongraded instruction in visual arts, music, drama, crafts, cooking, gardening, writing, singing
Philosophical	Discovery of the meaning of life, organization of a belief system	Discussions, study of ethics or other philosophical literature
Spiritual/mystical	Transcendence of organized religion, spiritual insight or enlightenment	Study of world religions, meditation, yoga
Miscellaneous	Adventure, risk taking, "kicks"	Outward Bound survival training, meaningful employment

Source: Adapted from Cohen, Allan Y. (1972). The journey beyond trips: Alternatives to drugs. In David E. Smith and George R. Gay (Eds.), *It's so good, don't even try it once: Heroin in perspective.* Englewood Cliffs NJ: Prentice Hall, pp. 191–192.

grams have the best chance of providing the necessary interventions. In fact, adolescents at highest risk of engaging in ATOD use are the least likely even to be attending school on the days that prevention efforts are delivered.[27]

Table 18.1 gives a sampling of alternative behaviors corresponding to a particular individual's interests and needs. One way of thinking about alternative-behavior programming is that a person is trading a negative dependence (on alcohol, tobacco, or other drugs) that causes harm on a physical or psychological level for a positive dependence that causes no harm and taps into pleasures from within.

How effective is alternative-behavior programming with regard to ATOD prevention? An extensive analysis was reported in 1981 in a review of 127 studies involving different types of prevention programs. Of these, only twelve studies involved alternative behaviors, and seven out of the twelve reported no significant impact on program participants. The other five studies, however, had positive outcomes, which resulted in alternative-behavior programming being ranked second in position among ten other approaches to ATOD prevention. In a later 1986 review, alternative-behavior programming was identified as being highly successful for at-risk adolescents such as ATOD users, juvenile delinquents, and students having problems in school. On the basis of these evaluations, the general view is that alternative-behavior programming can work and deserves to have a place in comprehensive prevention programs.[28]

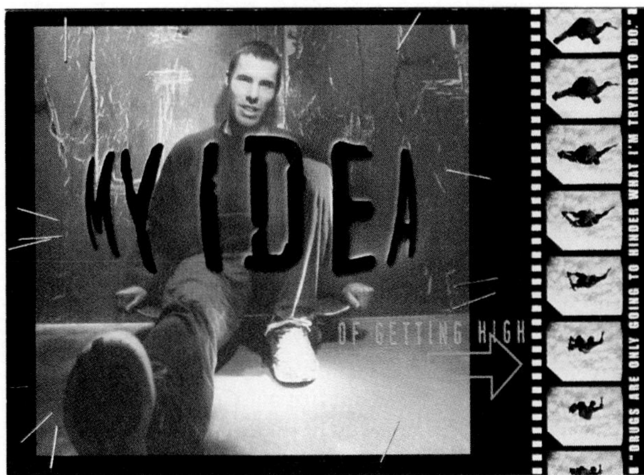

Skateboarding champion Andy Macdonald explains his way of getting high, in this media message from the Partnership for a Drug-Free America.

Scene segments from an antidrug media message on television. (Courtesy of the Partnership for a Drug-Free America, New York.)

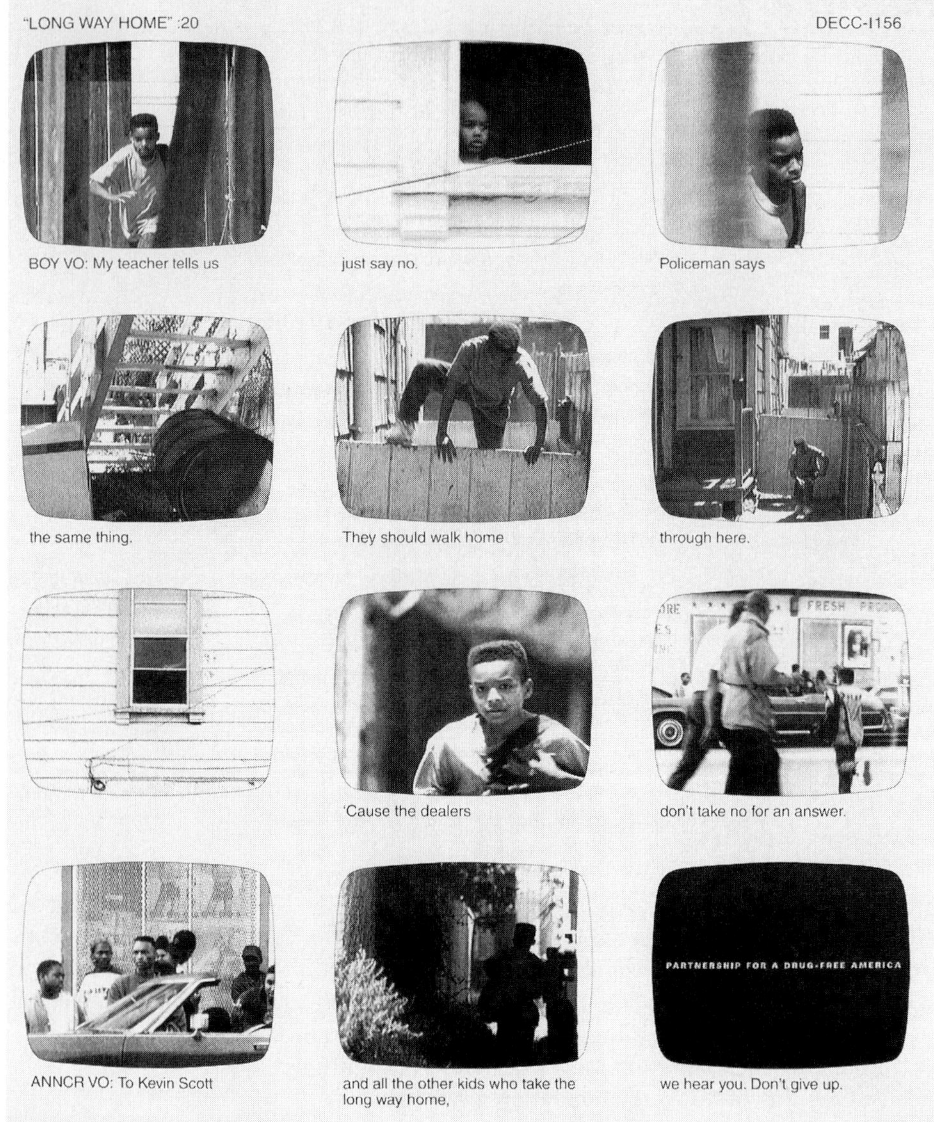

"LONG WAY HOME" :20
DECC-I156
BOY VO: My teacher tells us
just say no.
Policeman says
the same thing.
They should walk home
through here.
'Cause the dealers
don't take no for an answer.
ANNCR VO: To Kevin Scott
and all the other kids who take the long way home,
we hear you. Don't give up.
PARTNERSHIP FOR A DRUG-FREE AMERICA

The Influence of Mass Media

Adolescents spend a lot of time watching TV; in fact, by the time he or she graduates from high school, the average teenager has watched over the years an estimated 22,000 hours of TV.[29] It makes sense that the medium of TV should have a major role in ATOD prevention. Antidrug messages, however, have been largely confined to public-service announcements, brief commercials, and limited program series. Even so, the impact can be substantial. A prominent example is a series of memorable and persuasive antidrug advertisements on TV, on the radio, and in print. These ads, beginning in 1987, are sponsored by the Partnership for a Drug-Free America (PDFA), a nonprofit coalition of professionals from the communications industry, whose mission is to reduce demand for drugs in America. Since the early 1990s, a number of PDFA spots have targeted inner-city children living in high-risk drug-use environments. A 1994 study of the responses of more than fifteen thousand New York City school children has shown indications of an increasingly strong antidrug position, particularly among African American respondents and children attending schools in below-poverty-line areas.[30] This trend is in contrast to statistics showing increased overall ATOD use and a softening of antidrug attitudes across the nation as a whole since 1992 (see Chapter 1).

In 1998, the PDFA entered into a "public-private partnership" with the Office of National Drug Control Policy to coordinate antidrug media messages. Since that time, media time has been purchased by the federal government rather than donated by network television or radio stations and other media outlets. Production costs incurred by advertising agencies are now reimbursed by public funds, but their creative expenditures are still offered free as a public service.

Unfortunately, despite the intensified efforts to publicize antidrug information in the media, there are factors that have the potential to undermine these efforts. For example, media interest in drug-abuse issues in general has declined since 1990. The number of drug-related stories on network news broadcasts dropped by 87 percent from 1989 to 1994. News coverage has increased somewhat since 1994, due principally to a recognition of an increase in the rates of illicit drug use among young people, but it is still below levels seen in the 1980s. In addition, there are a rapidly growing number of Internet web sites devoted to information about marijuana cultivation, illicit drug use in general, and drug paraphernalia. These pro-drug outlets have proliferated since the advent of online services.[31]

A Model Community-Based Prevention Program: Project STAR

An ambitious, comprehensive program called Project STAR (Students Taught Awareness and Resistance), developed by Mary Anne Pentz at the University of Southern California, has been utilized since the mid-1980s in more than a dozen communities in the greater Kansas City metropolitan area. Three main components are employed:

- A *school-based component,* stressing drug-resistance skills, similar to the LST program in New York City, that are taught to middle school and junior high school students.
- A *parent program component,* in which parents work with their children on Project STAR homework, learn family communication skills, and become involved in community action.
- A *health policy change component,* by which community organizations develop and implement policies that affect ATOD-related laws. One example is the establishing and monitoring of drug-free sites in the community. For all components, mass media are used to promote and reinforce the activities of the project.

Evaluation reports of Project STAR indicate that rates of alcohol drinking, tobacco smoking, and marijuana use among junior high school students in the program are significantly lower than students in a control group. Both short-term and long-term reductions have been observed.[32]

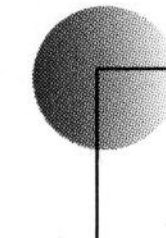

Family Systems in Primary and Secondary Prevention

It can be argued that family influences form the cornerstone of any successful ATOD prevention program, just as we have seen the impact of the family on alcohol and drug abuse treatment (see Chapter 17). In effect, the family is the first line of defense against alcohol, tobacco, and other drugs (Figure 18.3). Reaching the parents or guardians of youths at greatest risk, however, is a difficult task. Too often, ATOD prevention programs are attended by those parents or guardians who do not really need the information; those who need the information the most—parents who are either in denial, too embarrassed, or too out of control themselves—are notably absent. Other parents or guardians may need and genuinely want to participate, but they may have difficulty attending because of lack of child care, lack of transportation, scheduling conflicts with their employment, or language differences. Several of the factors that prevent their attendance are the

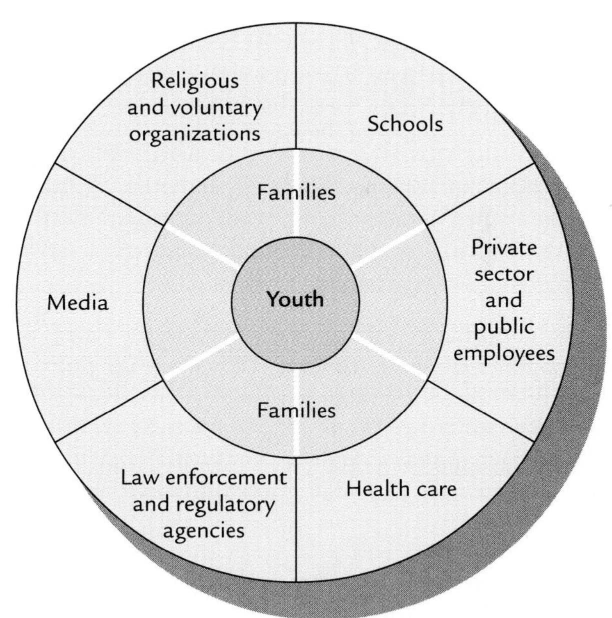

FIGURE 18.3

A schematic of various factors that impact upon families, and youth in turn, in ATOD prevention.
Source: Adapted from Fields, Richard (1998). *Drugs in perspective* (3rd ed.). Dubuque IA: WCB McGraw-Hill, p. 309. Reprinted with permission of The McGraw-Hill Companies.

same factors that increase the risk of ATOD use among their children.[33]

The power of a Grandpa.
Children have a very special relationship with Grandma and Grandpa. That's why grandparents can be such powerful allies in helping keep a kid off drugs.
Grandparents are cool. Relaxed. They're not on the firing line every day. Some days a kid hates his folks. He never hates his grandparents. Grandparents ask direct, point-blank, embarrassing questions you're too nervous to ask:
"Who's the girl?"
"How come you're doing poorly in history?"
"Why are your eyes always red?"
"Did you go to the doctor? What did he say?"
The same kid who cons his parents is ashamed to lie to Grandpa. Without betraying their trust, a loving, understanding grandparent can discuss the danger of drugs openly with the child he adores. And should.
• The average age of first-time drug use among teens is 13. Some kids start at 9.
• 1 out of 4 American kids between 9 and 12 is offered illegal drugs. 22% of these kids receive the offer from a friend. And 10% named a family member as their source.
• Illegal drugs are linked to increased violence in many communities, to AIDS, to birth defects, drug-related crime, and homelessness.
As a grandparent, you hold a special place in the hearts and minds of your grandchildren. Share your knowledge, your love, your faith in them. Use your power as an influencer to steer your grandchildren away from drugs.
If you don't have the words, we do. We'll send you information on how to talk to your grandkids about drugs. Just ask for your free copy of *Keeping Youth Drug-Free*. Call 1-800-788-2800 or visit our websites, www.projectknow.com or www.drugfreeamerica.org.
Grandma, Grandpa. Talk to your grandkids. You don't realize the power you have to save them.
Office of National Drug Control Policy
Partnership for a Drug-Free America

Communication between grandparents and grandchildren can be an important tool in ATOD prevention.

Special Roles in ATOD Prevention

Although obstacles exist, comprehensive ATOD prevention programs strive to incorporate parents or guardians, as well as other family members, into the overall effort. The reason lies in the variety of special roles they play in influencing children with regard to ATOD use:

- As role models, parents or guardians may drink alcoholic beverages, smoke, or drink excessive amounts of caffeinated coffee, not thinking of these habits as ATOD use. They can avoid sending their children signals about ATOD abstinence that are inconsistent at best, hypocritical at worst.
- As educators or resources for information, they can help by conveying verbal messages about health risks that are accurate and sincere.
- As family policymakers and rule setters, they can convey a clear understanding of the consequence of ATOD use. If a parent or guardian cannot or will not back up family rules with logical and consistent consequences, the risk increases that rules will be broken.
- As stimulators of enjoyable family activities, parents or guardians can provide alternative-behavior programming necessary to steer youth away from high-risk situations.
- As consultants against peer pressure, parents or guardians can help reinforce the peer-refusal skills of their children. Children and adolescents frequently report that a strongly negative reaction at home was the single most important reason for their refusing alcohol, tobacco, and other drugs from their peers.

Dysfunctional Communication within the Family

One further aspect of parenting deserves special mention as it pertains to ATOD prevention: the tendency to engage in enabling behaviors. As was noted in Chapter 17, enabling behaviors on the part of a spouse, family member, or friend can inadvertently aggravate problems associated with alcohol and other drug abuse, and serve as a major obstacle to recovery. In the context of primary and secondary prevention, enabling behaviors on the part of a parent or guardian can have an equally detrimental influence. Enabling behaviors give children the message that it is all right to engage in ATOD use. They also make it easier for children to engage in these behaviors by protecting them from the negative consequences of ATOD use.

The need for better lines of communication between parents and teenagers is illustrated in a 1998 PDFA survey. When asked whether they talked to their teenagers

sociocultural filters: A set of considerations specific to a particular culture or community that can influence the reception and acceptance of public information.

DRUGS . . . IN FOCUS

A Test Kit for Drugs in the Home: Whom Can You Trust?

In 1995, a drug detection company introduced a commercial kit capable of testing for illicit drugs in the home. Marketed for parents who wish to check for possible drug abuse among their children, the kit consists of a 3-inch premoistened pad that can be wiped across desk tops, telephones, books, clothing, or other items. The pad is mailed to the company, where an analysis for the presence of cocaine, crack cocaine, heroin, methamphetamine, LSD, marijuana, and PCP is performed. The testing destroys the sample so it cannot be used later in any court proceedings. The results of the analysis are then mailed to the parents.

The fact that the test kit is designed to be used by parents with or without their children's knowledge has raised a number of controversial issues. On the one hand, the kit is promoted as a potent new weapon in the battle against the increased levels of drug abuse among young people. From this point of view, parents are now able to get early help for their children before drug abuse problems become too great. On the other hand, the kit can also be viewed as a new weapon in the battle of the generations. Detractors argue that it sets up an atmosphere of distrust between parents and their children.

What do you think? If you were a parent, would you consider this new testing kit as a step forward or a step backward in the effort to prevent drug abuse in your family?

Sources: Kit to test for drugs at home (1995, March 29). *Newsday,* p. A8. Winslow, Olivia, and Lam, Chau (1995, March 30). Test fuels drugs debate. *Newsday,* pp. A6, A51.

about drugs at least once, 98 percent of parents reported that they had done so, but only 65 percent of teenagers recalled such a conversation. Barely 27 percent of teenagers reported learning at lot at home about the risks of drug use, even though virtually all of their parents said they had discussed the topic. Justifiably, antidrug media campaigns have focused on parent-child communication skills, specifically on the difficulty many parents have in talking to their children about sensitive subjects like drugs. There are recent indications that effective communication is on the rise.[34] Drugs . . . in Focus, however, examines an option that may be necessary when family communication breaks down.

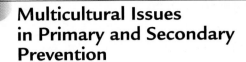

Multicultural Issues in Primary and Secondary Prevention

In the case of ATOD prevention efforts, it is important to remember that information intended to reach individuals of a specific culture must pass through a series of **sociocultural filters.** Understanding this filtering process is essential in order to maximize the reception and acceptance of ATOD prevention information.

Prevention Approaches among Latino Groups

A good example of the need to recognize sociocultural filters is the set of special concerns associated with communicating ATOD information to Latinos, a diverse group of approximately 32 million people living throughout the United States.[35] The following insights concerning elements of the Latino community have a strong bearing on an ATOD prevention program's chances of succeeding.

- Because of the importance Latinos confer on the family and religious institutions, prevention and treatment efforts should be targeted to include the entire family and, if possible, its religious leaders. Prevention efforts will be most effective when counselors reinforce family units and value them as a whole.
- Prevention programs are needed to help Latino fathers recognize how important their role or example is to their sons' and daughters' self-image regarding alcohol and other drugs. Because being a good father is part of *machismo,* it is important that the men become full partners in parenting. Mothers should be encouraged to learn strategies for including their husbands in family interactions at home.
- Because a Latina woman with alcohol or other drug problems is strongly associated with a violation of womanly ideals of purity, discipline, and self-sacrifice, educational efforts should concentrate on reducing the shame associated with her reaching out for help.

Prevention Approaches among African American Groups

Another set of special concerns exist with regard to communicating ATOD information in African American communities.[36] Some basic generalizations have proven

INHALANTS...
(Sprays / Aerosols / Glues)

EVIL SPIRITS THAT BREAK THE BONDS BETWEEN OURSELVES AND OUR ELDERS, DISRUPT THE CIRCLE OF OUR FAMILY SYSTEM, DESTROY THE HARMONY BETWEEN US AND ALL CREATION.

FOR OUR OWN SURVIVAL, THE SURVIVAL OF OUR FAMILY, OUR TRIBE AND THE INDIAN NATION, WE MUST RESIST THESE SPIRITS OF DEATH.

This ATOD prevention message focuses on inhalant abuse among Native American children, adolescents, and young adults through the sociocultural filter of their community.

helpful in optimizing the design of ATOD prevention programs for these groups of people.

- African American youths tend to use drugs other than alcohol after they form the attitudes and adopt behaviors associated with delinquency. The most common examples of delinquency include drug dealing, shoplifting, and petty theft. With regard to the designing of media campaigns, it is the deglamorization of the drug dealer that appears to be most helpful in primary prevention efforts among African American youths.
- Drug use and social problems are likely to be interrelated in African American neighborhoods. The effects of alcohol and other drug use are intensified when other factors exist, such as high unemployment, poverty, poor health care, and poor nutrition.
- Several research studies have shown that most African American youths, even those in low-income areas, do manage to escape from the pressures to use alcohol and other drugs. The protective factors of staying in school, solid family bonds, strong religious beliefs, high self-esteem, adequate coping strategies, social skills, and steady employment all build on one another to provide resiliency on the part of high-risk children and adolescents. As noted before, prevention programs developed with protective factors in mind have the greatest chance for success.

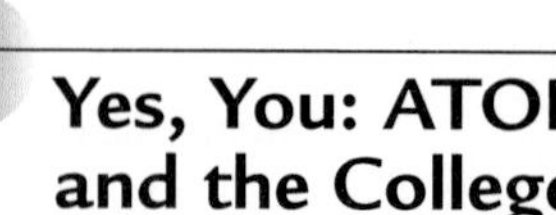

Yes, You: ATOD Prevention and the College Student

In turning to the subject of prevention among college students, we first need to recognize that we are hardly speaking of a homogeneous population. U.S. college students comprise all racial, ethnic, and socioeconomic groups and are likely to come from all parts of the world. They include undergraduates and graduates, full-time and part-time students, residential students and commuters, students of traditional college age and students who are considerably older.

In particular, there are marked differences in the objectives of a prevention program between those under twenty-one and those who are older. In the former group, the goal may be "no use of" (or abstinence from) alcohol, tobacco, and other drugs, whereas in the latter group the goal may be the low-risk (that is, responsible) consumption of alcohol and no use of tobacco and other drugs. The term "low-risk consumption" refers to a level of use restricted by considerations of physical health, family background, pregnancy risk, the law, safety, and other personal concerns.

As an example of how these considerations might apply, guidelines might stipulate that pregnant women, recovering alcoholics or those with a family history of alcoholism, people driving cars or heavy machinery, people on medications, or those under the age of twenty-one should not drink alcohol at all. Although the distinction between under–twenty-one and over–twenty-one preventive goals is applicable in many community-oriented programs, it is an especially difficult challenge for prevention efforts when the target population on a college campus contains both subgroups so closely intermingled.[37]

A second challenge comes from the widely held expectation that heavy alcoholic drinking, as well as some illicit drug use, during the college years represents something of a rite of passage. College alumni (and potential benefactors) frequently impede the implementation of drug and alcohol crackdowns, arguing that "we did it when we were in school."[38] Moreover, national surveys in 2000 indicate that by the end of high school about 80 percent of all students have consumed alcoholic beverages, 62 percent have been drunk at least once, and 49 percent have smoked marijuana. Therefore, we cannot say that use of these drugs is a new experience for many college students.[39] Given this base of prior exposure, it is not surprising that further experimentation and more extensive patterns of ATOD use will occur.

The emphasis on most campuses is on the prevention and control of alcohol; however, it is less common for college administrations to focus on the problems associated with drugs other than alcohol. Although programs for alcohol education are virtually certain to be present on college campuses, attention directed toward comparable activities related specifically to drugs other than alcohol lags behind.

A third challenge relates to the discussion earlier in this chapter on alternative-behavior programming. Students frequently complain of a lack of recreational and social activities and facilities available on campuses during periods of time when classes are not in session.

Prevention Approaches on College Campuses

On the positive side, college campuses have the potential for being ideal environments for comprehensive ATOD prevention programs because they combine features of school and community settings. Here are some strategies for prevention on the college campus:

- Develop a multifaceted prevention program of assessment, education, policy, and enforcement. Involve students, faculty, and administrators together to determine the degree of availability and demand for alcohol and other drugs on campus and in the surrounding community and initiate public information and education efforts.
- Incorporate alcohol and other drug education into the curriculum. Faculty members can use drug-related situations as teachable moments, include drug topics in their course syllabi, and develop courses or course projects on issues relating to alcohol and other drugs.
- Ensure that hypocrisy is not the rule of the day. ATOD prevention is not a goal for college students only but is a larger issue that affects all members of the academic community, including faculty and administration.
- Encourage environments that lessen the pressures to engage in ATOD use. Foster more places where social and recreational activities can take place spontaneously and at hours when the most enticing alternative may be the consumption of alcohol and other drugs. A recent promising sign is the growing popularity of drug-free dormitories on many college campuses, where student residents specifically choose to refrain from alcohol, tobacco, and other drugs.[40]

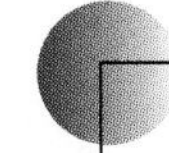

Where You Can Go for Help

From everything that has been reviewed in this introduction to drug-taking behavior in today's society, it is clear that as decision-makers we need all the help we can get. Fortunately, information or guidance is all around us (Portrait). For local referral sources, check out the yellow pages of your telephone book under Alcoholism Information or Drug Abuse and Addiction Information. There are also numerous web sites on the Internet that are specifically designed to provide assistance with any problem associated with alcohol, tobacco, and other drug abuse. Good luck.

Portrait Meredith Poulten—A Counselor on the Front Lines

Since 1987, in the high school in Medway, Massachusetts, a quiet suburban town outside Boston, young people have had a place to go for help, for a referral, for a sympathetic ear, or just to sit and relax for a few minutes from the pressures of school, parents, and peers. It is called a Walk-in Center, with entrances both within the school and directly from the outside, and Meredith Poulten, its director and counselor, has been its driving force since its inception. The center deals with contemporary issues of teen suicide, depression, family conflicts, sexuality, alcohol and other drugs, self-esteem, physical health, and personal hygiene—not from a distance but as the daily reality of today's adolescents.

Out of an average of 150 student contacts per week in this center, more than half concern alcohol or other drug involvement at some level. Before the center was established, such students were essentially on their own, "self-medicating" their problems, in the words of Poulten, rather than learning to handle the stresses of their lives. The school guidance department was oriented toward academic needs rather than day-to-day student problems, and many students have said that there was too great a stigma attached to talking to the school psychologist. As one student has expressed it, "I talk to Mrs. P. every day. She's more of a friend than a counselor. I can talk to her about anything." Another student admitted that were it not for the center, he would have been dead in less than a month.

Meredith Poulten

The functioning of Poulten's Walk-in Center illustrates that the problems of today's youth do not fit into neat categories. They live in a world where drugs and sex are readily available and the pressure to indulge in both is high. At the same time, society equates success with being first and being second-best with failure. For many students, communication with parents is next to impossible. Even when parents are open-minded about their child's circumstances, "You don't want to talk to your parents about your problems," says a student, "because you always want to please them."

Sources: Graham, Fiona (1989, October 11). A place to call their own. *The Country Gazette* (Medway MA), pp. 1, 14. Hudson, Ted (1991, February 20). Letter to the Editor: Medway High Walk-in Center must be spared. *The Country Gazette* (Medway MA), p. 3. Meredith Poulten, personal communication, 2001.

SUMMARY

ATOD Prevention: Strategies, Goals, and Objectives

- The overall strategy for alcohol, tobacco, and other drug (ATOD) prevention and education is to minimize the risk factors in a person's life with respect to ATOD use and maximize the protective factors.
- Five goals have been set by the Office of National Drug Control Policy: Educating and enabling young people to reject ATOD use; increasing public safety by reducing drug-related crime and violence; reducing the health and social costs of illicit drugs; reducing the influx of illicit drugs from abroad; and reducing foreign and domestic sources of illicit drugs.
- In 1992, the federal program, Healthy People 2000, set specific objectives to be reached by 2000 regarding aspects of personal health, including those that pertain to ATOD use. More recently, a new program, Healthy People 2010, was begun to work on achieving objectives that have not yet been met.

Lessons from the Past: Prevention Approaches That Have Failed

- Several strategies have been largely unsuccessful in meeting the goals of ATOD prevention. They include the reliance on supply/availability reduction, punitive judicial policies, scare tactics, objective information, and affective education.

Hope and Promise: Components of Effective School-Based Prevention Programs

- Effective school-based programs have incorporated a combination of peer-refusal skills training, relaxation and stress management, and training in social skills and personal decision making.
- The Life Skills Training program in New York City is a model for programs incorporating components for effective ATOD prevention.

Community-Based Prevention Programs

- Community-based programs make use of a broader range of resources, including community leaders and public figures as positive role models, opportunities for alternative-behavior programming, and the mass media.
- Recent efforts by the media have had a major impact on the image of ATOD use in both high-risk populations and others in the community.
- Project STAR in Kansas City is a model for programs incorporating community-wide components of ATOD prevention.

Family Systems in Primary and Secondary Prevention

- Community-based prevention programs are increasingly mindful of the importance of the family, particularly parents, as the first line of defense in ATOD prevention efforts.

Multicultural Issues in Primary and Secondary Prevention

- Special cultural considerations need to be made when communicating with specific subgroups such as Latino and African American individuals.

Yes, You: ATOD Prevention and the College Student

- On college campuses, ATOD prevention programs are incorporating features of both school-based and community-based approaches.
- ATOD prevention programs should involve faculty and administrators, as well as students, in an overall comprehensive strategy.

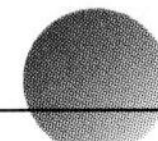

KEY TERMS

affective education, p. 372
impactors, p. 376
peer-refusal skills, p. 372
resiliency, p. 375
sociocultural filters, p. 380
values clarification, p. 372

ENDNOTES

1. Grant, Bridget F., and Dawson, Deborah A. (1997). Age at onset of alcohol use and its association with DSM-IV alcohol abuse and dependence: Results from the National Longitudinal Alcohol Epidemiological Survey. *Journal of Substance Abuse*, 9, 103–110. Grant, Bridget F., and Dawson, Deborah A. (1998). Age of onset of drug use and its association with DSM-IV drug abuse and dependence: Results from the National Longitudinal Alcohol Epidemiological Survey. *Journal of Substance Abuse, 10*, 163–173.
2. Adapted from the Center for Substance Abuse Prevention, Substance Abuse and Mental Health Services Administration, 1995.
3. Office of National Drug Control Policy (2001). *The national drug control strategy: 2001 annual report.* Washington DC: Office of National Drug Control Policy, Executive Office of the President.
4. McGinnis, J. Michael, and Foege, William H. (1993, November 10). Actual causes of death in the United States. *Journal of the American Medical Association*, 270, 2207–2212.
5. Public Health Service (1992). *Healthy people 2000: National health promotion and disease prevention objectives—Summary report.* Boston: Jones and Bartlett.
6. Marwick, Charles (2000). Healthy People 2010 initiative launched. *Journal of the American Medical Association*, 283, 989–990. Public Health Service (2000). *Healthy People 2010: National health promotion and disease prevention objectives: Conference edition.* Bethesda MD: Public Health Service.
7. Goode, Erich (1999). *Drugs in American society* (5th ed.). New York: McGraw-Hill College, pp. 385–387.
8. Hingson, Ralph W.; Scotch, Norman; Mangione, Thomas; Meyers, Allan; Glantz, Leonard; Heeren, Timothy; Lin, Nan; Mucatel, March; and Pierce, Glenn (1983). Impact of legislation raising the legal drinking age in Massachusetts from 18 to 21. *American Journal of Public Health*, 73, 163–170.
9. Goode, *Drugs in American society*, pp. 381–418. Steinberg, Neil (1994, May 5). The law of unintended consequences. *Rolling Stone*, pp. 33–34.

10. Funkhouser, Judith E., and Denniston, Robert W. (1992). Historical perspective. In Mary A. Jansen (Ed.), *A promising future: Alcohol and other drug problem prevention services improvement* (OSAP Prevention Monograph 10). Rockville MD: Office of Substance Abuse Prevention, pp. 5–15.
11. Flay, Brian R., and Sobel, Judith L. (1983). The role of mass media in preventing adolescent substance abuse. In Thomas J. Glynn, Carl G. Leukenfeld, and Jacqueline P. Ludford (Eds.), *Preventive adolescent drug abuse.* Rockville MD: National Institute on Drug Abuse, pp. 5–35. Swisher, John D.; Crawford, J.; Goldstein, R.; and Yura, M. (1971). Drug education: Pushing or preventing. *Peabody Journal of Education, 49,* 68–75.
12. Williams, R., Ward, D., and Gray, L. (1985). The persistence of experimentally induced cognitive change: A neglected dimension in the assessment of drug prevention programs. *Journal of Drug Education, 15,* 33–42.
13. Meeks, Linda, Heit, Philip, and Page, Randy (1994). *Drugs, alcohol, and tobacco.* Blacklick OH: Meeks Heit Publishing, p. 201.
14. Ibid., p. 202.
15. McBride, Duane C., Mutch, Patricia B., and Chitwood, Dale D. (1996). Religious belief and the initiation and prevention of drug use among youth. In Clyde B. McCoy, Lisa R. Metsch, and James A. Inciardi (Eds.), *Intervening with drug-involved youth.* Thousand Oaks CA: Sage Publications, pp. 110–130.
16. Schroeder, Debra S., Laflin, Molly T., and Weis, David L. (1993). Is there a relationship between self-esteem and drug use? Methodological and statistical limitations of the research. *Journal of Drug Issues, 22,* 645–665. Yuen, Francis K. O., and Pardeck, John T. (1998). Effective strategies for preventing substance abuse among children and adolescents. *Early Child Development and Care, 145,* 119–131.
17. Best, J. Allan; Flay, Brian R.; Towson, Shelagh M. J.; Ryan, Katherine B.; Perry, Cheryl L.; Brown, K. Stephen; Kersell, Mary W.; and d'Avernas, Josie R. (1984). Smoking prevention and the concept of risk. *Journal of Applied Social Psychology, 14,* 257–273.
18. Botvin, Gilbert J., and Botvin, Elizabeth M. (1992). School-based and community-based prevention approaches. In J. H. Lewisohn, P. Ruiz, and R. B. Millman (Eds.), *Substance abuse: A comprehensive textbook* (2nd ed.). Baltimore: Williams and Wilkins, pp. 910–927. Orlandi, Mario A. (1986). Prevention technologies for drug-involved youth. In Clyde B. McCoy, Lisa R. Metsch, and James A. Inciardi (Eds.), *Intervening with drug-involved youth.* Thousand Oaks CA: Sage Publications, pp. 81–100. Schinke, Steven P., and Gilchrist, Lewayne D. (1983). Primary prevention of tobacco smoking. *Journal of School Health, 53,* 416–419.
19. Botvin, Gilbert J., and Tortu, Stephanie (1988). Preventing adolescent substance abuse through life skills training. In Richard M. Price, Emory L. Cowen, Raymond P. Lorion, and Julia Ramos-McKay (Eds.), *Fourteen ounces of prevention: A casebook for practitioners.* Washington DC: American Psychological Association, pp. 98–110.
20. Botvin, Gilbert J.; Baker, Eli; Dusenbury, Linda; Botvin, Elizabeth M.; and Diaz, Tracy (1995). Long-term follow-up results of a randomized drug abuse prevention trial in a white middle-class population. *Journal of the American Medical Association, 273,* 1106–1112. Botvin, Gilbert J.; Epstein Jennifer A.; Baker, Eli; Diaz, Tracy; and Ifill-Williams, Michelle (1997). School-based drug abuse prevention with inner-city minority youth. *Journal of Child and Adolescent Substance Abuse, 6,* 5–19.
21. Mathias, Robert (1997, March/April). From the 'burbs to the 'hood . . . This program reduces student's risk of drug use. *NIDA Notes,* pp. 1, 5–6. Quotation on p. 6.
22. Cavazos, Lauro F. (1989). *What works: Schools without drugs.* Washington DC: U.S. Department of Education, p. 38.
23. Clayton, Richard R., Cattarello, Anne M., and Johnstone, Bryan M. (1996). The effectiveness of Drug Abuse Resistance Education (Project DARE): 5-year follow-up results. *Preventive Medicine, 25,* 307–318. Lynam, Donald R.; Milich, Richard; Zimmerman, Rick; Novak, Scott P.; Logan, T. K.; Martin, Catherine; Leukefeld, Carl; and Clayton, Richard (1999). Project DARE: No effects at 10-year follow-up. *Journal of Consulting and Clinical Psychology, 67,* 590–593.
24. Lynam, Project DARE, p. 593.
25. Brook, Judith S., and Brook, David W. (1996). Risk and protective factors for drug use. In Clyde B. McCoy, Lisa R. Metsch, and James A. Inciardi (Eds.), *Intervening with drug-involved youth.* Thousand Oaks CA: Sage Publications, pp. 23–44. Catalano, Richard F.; Kosterman, Rick; Hawkins, J. David; Newcomb, Michael D.; and Abbott, Robert D. (1996). Modeling the etiology of adolescent substance use: A test of the social development model. *Journal of Drug Issues, 23,* 429–455.
26. Benard, Bonnie (1990). An overview of community-based prevention. In Ketty H. Rey, Christopher L. Faegre, and Patti Lowery (Eds.), *Prevention research findings: 1988* (OSAP Prevention Monograph 3). Rockville MD: Office of Substance Abuse Prevention, pp. 126–147. Winick, Charles, and Larson, Mary Jo (1997). Community action programs. In Joyce H. Lowinson, Pedro Ruiz, Robert B. Millman, and John G. Langrod (Eds.), *Substance abuse: A comprehensive textbook.* Baltimore: Williams and Wilkins, pp. 755–764.
27. Rhodes, Jean E., and Jason, Leonard A. (1991). The social stress model of alcohol and other drug abuse: A basis for comprehensive, community-based prevention. In Ketty H. Rey, Christopher L. Faegre, and Patti Lowery (Eds.), *Prevention resarch findings: 1988* (OSAP Prevention Monograph 3). Rockville MD: Office of Substance Abuse Prevention, pp. 155–171.
28. Tobler, Nancy S. (1986). Meta-analysis of 143 adolescent drug prevention programs: Quantitative outcome results of

program participants compared to a control group. *Journal of Drug Issues, 16,* 537–567.

29. Zeuschner, Raymond (1997). *Communicating today* (2nd ed.). Boston: Allyn and Bacon, p. 372.
30. Partnership for a Drug-Free America (1994, July 12). New study shows children in NYC becoming more anti-drug, bucking national trends (Press release). Partnership for a Drug-Free America, New York.
31. Center for Media and Public Affairs. Cited in Sussman, Steve; Stacy, Alan W.; Dent, Clyde W.; Simon, Thomas R.; and Johnson, C. Anderson (1996). Marijuana use: Current issues and new research directions. *Journal of Drug Issues, 26,* p. 714. Partnership for a Drug-Free America, New York. Wren, Christopher S. (1997, June 20). A seductive drug culture flourishes on the Internet. *New York Times,* pp. A1, A22.
32. National Institute on Drug Abuse (1997). *Preventing drug use among children and adolescents: A research-based guide.* Rockville MD: National Institute on Drug Abuse. Orlandi, Prevention technologies for drug-involved youth. Pentz, Mary Anne (1995). The school-community interface in comprehensive school health education. In S. Stansfield (Ed.), *1996 Institute of Medicine Annual Report, Committee on Comprehensive School Health Programs.* Washington DC: National Academy Press, 1995. Pentz, Mary Anne, and Valente, T. (1993). Project STAR: A substance abuse prevention campaign in Kansas City. In T. E. Backer, E. Rogers, M. Rogers, and R. Denniston (Eds.), *Impact of organizations on mass media behavior campaigns.* Newbury Park CA: Sage, pp. 37–66.
33. Fields, Richard (1998). *Drugs in perspective* (3rd ed.). Boston: WCB McGraw-Hill, pp. 291–314. Kumpfer, Karol L. (1991). How to get hard-to-reach parents involved in parenting programs. *Parent training is prevention: Preventing alcohol and other drug problems among youth in the family.* Rockville MD: Office of Substance Abuse Prevention, pp. 87–95. National Center on Addiction and Substance Abuse at Columbia University (1999). No safe haven: Children of substance-abusing parents. New York: National Center on Addiction and Substance Abuse.
34. Partnership for a Drug-Free America (1998). Partnership attitude tracking survey: Parents say they're talking, but only 27% of teens—1 in 4—are learning a lot at home about the risk of drugs. Partnership for a Drug-Free America (1999). Partnership attitude tracking survey: More parents talking with kids about drugs more often, and appear to be having an impact. Information courtesy of Partnership for a Drug-Free America, New York.
35. Hernandez, Lawrence P., and Lucero, Ed (1996). La Familia community drug and alcohol prevention program: Family-centered model for working with inner-city Hispanic families. *Journal of Primary Prevention, 16,* 255–272. Office of Substance Abuse Prevention (1990). *The fact is . . . reaching Hispanic/Latino audiences requires cultural sensitivity.* Rockville MD: National Clearinghouse for Alcohol and Drug Information, National Institute on Drug Abuse.
36. Hahn, Ellen J., and Rado, Mary (1996). African-American Head Start parent involvement in drug prevention. *American Journal of Health Behavior, 20,* 41–51. Office of Substance Abuse Prevention (1990). *The fact is . . . alcohol and other drug use is a special concern for African American families and communities.* Rockville MD: National Clearinghouse for Drug and Alcohol Information, National Institute on Drug Abuse.
37. Office of Substance Abuse Prevention (1991). *Faculty members' handbook: Strategies for preventing alcohol and other drug problems.* Rockville MD: National Clearinghouse for Alcohol and Drug Information, National Institute on Drug Abuse, p. 4.
38. Hersh, Richard H. (1994, September 26). The culture of neglect: Our colleges have to lead, not follow. *Newsweek,* pp. 12–13.
39. Johnston, Lloyd D. (2000, December 14). "Ecstasy" use rises sharply among teens in 2000; use of many other drugs stays steady, but significant declines are reported for some. News release from the University of Michigan, Ann Arbor, Table 1.
40. Office of Educational Research and Improvement (1990). *A guide for college presidents and governing bodies: Strategies for eliminating alcohol and other drug abuse on campuses.* Washington DC: U.S. Department of Education. Office of Substance Abuse Prevention. *Faculty members' handbook,* pp. 21–25.

Point Counterpoint

Do We DARE or Don't We?

The following discussion of viewpoints presents the opinions of people on both sides of the controversial issues regarding the Project DARE prevention program. Don't think you have to come up with the final answer, nor should you necessarily agree with the argument you read last. Many of the ideas in this feature come from sources listed.

POINT

No program in recent years has had the success of Project DARE in reaching millions of schoolchildren with an ATOD prevention message. DARE is now the primary educational program in our war on drugs in America. Every year, in school district after school district, police officers from the community serve to administer DARE sessions, and all of them have received eighty hours of training for the job, at no cost to the educational districts that receive this service.

COUNTERPOINT

No one questions the success of DARE, but how effective is it in reducing ATOD use among the children it serves? At least fifteen evaluation studies of the long-term effects of DARE have been conducted by reputable researchers or research centers since the early 1990s, and the results are remarkably consistent. When DARE programs are compared with control groups, the studies show little or no differences in the level of ATOD use or onset of use among adolescents.

POINT

That position continues on and on. It's quite possible the researchers don't know how to measure things. There is more at stake here than good statistics. If those researchers could just see the kids' faces during the DARE sessions, they'd know how much good it's doing. Besides, a DARE police officer in the classroom is a symbol that the community at large is involved in ATOD prevention, that law enforcement is on the side of the kids, that it is not just a matter of reducing the supply of drugs but reducing the demand for them at the grass-roots level.

COUNTERPOINT

But don't you think there would be some indication of effectiveness among all these studies? It's true that students, teachers, administrators, parents, police, and political leaders feel good about DARE because it means something is being done about substance abuse, but we are talking about a program budget of approximately $750 million a year with $600 million coming from federal, state, and local sources. A publicly funded program like DARE, therefore, ought to be accountable for what it achieves. How can DARE maintain this standard of accountability?

POINT

First of all, there were positive effects in the studies you referred to. There was a significant increase in the level of self-esteem among children in the DARE program. Second, those evaluation studies were working with the DARE program before it was substantially revised. DARE sessions are now much more interactive than they had been in the past. In other words, the whole curriculum has been redesigned.

COUNTERPOINT

To coin a phrase, show me the data. The latest studies in 1999 show no advantages gained from the DARE program after a six-year and ten-year follow-up. The results simply aren't there. In the meantime, given the situation as it stands now, why should DARE remain the dominant ATOD prevention program in the United States?

Critical Thinking Questions for Further Debate

1. DARE seems like such a good idea. Why do you think it fails to reduce drug use?
2. Suppose you are a sixteen-year-old teenager using illicit drugs as well as smoking cigarettes. What program back in the fifth or sixth grade, do you think, would have prevented this from happening? Suppose you are a sixteen-year-old teenager not engaging in this behavior. Did DARE make a difference in your life?

Sources: Lynam, Donald R.; Milich, Richard; Zimmerman, Rick; Novak, Scott P.; Logan, T. K.; Martin, Catherine; Leukefeld, Carl; and Clayton, Richard (1999). Project DARE: No effects at 10-year follow-up. *Journal of Consulting and Clinical Psychology, 67,* 590–593. Wysong, Earl, and Wright, David W. (1995). A decade of DARE: Efficacy, politics, and drug education. *Sociological Focus, 28,* 283–311.

Photo Credits

Page 2, Spencer Grant/Stock, Boston; page 7, Victor Englebert/Photo Researchers, Inc.; page 8, Corbis-Bettmann; page 10 top, Dennis Stock/Magnum Photos; page 10 bottom, Henry Diltz; page 17, Grapes-Michaud/Photo Researchers, Inc.; page 19, AP/Wide World Photos; page 21, Courtesy of Karen Schlendorf; page 32, Chuck Nacke/Woodfin Camp & Associates; page 35, Eugene Richards/Magnum Photos; page 40, Robert McElroy/Woodfin Camp & Associates; page 45, UPI/Corbis-Bettmann; page 48, Chris E. Brown/Stock, Boston; page 53, Will Hart; page 55, Robert Harbison; page 62, Bruce Ayres/Stone; page 70, Katherine Lambert © 1991 Discover Magazine; page 72, Mitch Wojnarowicz/The Image Works; page 79, Corbis-Bettmann; page 82, Photofest; page 85, Spencer Grant/ Index Stock Imagery; page 88, AP/Wide World Photos; page 92, Dan McCoy/Rainbow; page 102, AP/Wide World Photos; page 104, Corbis-Bettmann; page 107, Corbis-Bettmann; page 109, Alexis Duclos/Liaison Agency; page 119, Roswell Angier/Stock, Boston; page 129, Frank Capri/SAGA/Woodfin Camp & Associates; page 130 top, Gene Anthony/Black Star; page 130 bottom, David Hoffman; page 148, Gene Anthony/ Black Star; page 151, Topham/The Image Works; page 161, Stacy Rosenstock/Impact Visuals; page 163, Kenneth Hayden/Black Star; pages 170, 171, AP/Wide World Photos; page 172, Catherine Karnow/Woodfin Camp & Associates; page 175, NYT Graphics/NYT Pictures; page 180, Blair Seitz/Photo Researchers, Inc.; page 188, Courtesy of The Lewis Walpole Library, Yale University; page 189, George Steinmetz; page 190, Bob Daemmrich/The Image Works; page 199, Larry Kolvoord/The Image Works; page 200, NYT Graphics/ NYT Pictures; page 201, Courtesy of Candace Lightner; page 209, National Clearinghouse for Alcohol & Drug Information; page 213, Corbis-Bettmann; page 215 top, Martin M. Rotker/Photo Researchers, Inc.; page 215 bottom, Biophoto Associates/Science Source/Photo Researchers, Inc.; page 218, George Steinmetz; page 224, Hank Morgan/Science Source/ Photo Researchers, Inc.; page 226, Compliments of the Wilson House, East Dorset, VT; page 234, Corbis-Bettmann; page 237, John Coletti/Index Stock Imagery; page 239, Reuters/Corbis-Bettmann; page 248, Richard Hutchings/Photo Researchers, Inc.; page 249, AP/Wide World Photos; page 250, National Library of Medicine; page 252, Courtesy of California Department of Health Services; page 260, Sam Abell/National Geographic Image Collection; page 262, Corbis-Bettmann; page 265, Used with permission of Hershey Corporation; page 268, Blair Seitz/Photo Researchers, Inc.; page 271, Stock, Boston; page 276, North Wind Picture Archives; page 280, Reuters/Corbis-Bettmann; page 281, Barry C. Allen/The Palm Beach Post; page 282, Courtesy of the National Inhalant Prevention Coalition, Austin, Texas, 800-269-4237; page 289, Spencer Grant/Stock, Boston; page 291, UPI/Corbis-Bettman; page 300, Steve Leonard/Black Star; page 303, Bob Daemmrich/Stock, Boston; page 312, Will McIntyre/Photo Researchers, Inc.; page 315, Jonathan Kirn/Liaison Agency; page 320, Photofest; pages 329, 334, Will Hart; page 338, Courtesy of Dr. Lewis Baxter and Dr. Michael Phelps, UCLA School of Medicine; page 340, Robert Harbison; page 349, Eli Reed/ Magnum Photos; page 353, Courtesy of DAYTOP Village, Inc.; page 354, Courtesy of Partnership for a Drug-Free America; page 360, Shackman/Monkmeyer; page 371, Jim Pickerell; pages 377, 378, 380, Courtesy of Partnership for a Drug-Free America; page 382, Native American Posters. Artwork courtesy of Blas E. Lopez; page 384, Courtesy of Meredith Poulton/The Milford Daily News.

Index

Note: **Boldface** indicates key terms and the pages where they are defined.